ETHICS

AND

PUBLIC POLICY

edited by

TOM L. BEAUCHAMP

Georgetown University

PRENTICE-HALL, INC., Englewood Cliffs, New Jersey

Library of Congress Cataloging in Publication Data

BEAUCHAMP, TOM L   comp.
  Ethics and public policy.

  Includes bibliographies.
    1. Social ethics—Addresses, essays, lectures.
  2. Social problems—Addresses, essays, lectures.
  I. Title.
  HM216.B25   170   74-23772
  ISBN 0-13-290601-5
  ISBN 0-13-290593-0   pbk.

170
B 372e
1975

© 1975 by
PRENTICE-HALL, INC.
Englewood Cliffs, New Jersey

Printed in the United States of America.

10 9 8 7 6 5 4 3 2 1

PRENTICE-HALL INTERNATIONAL, INC., London
PRENTICE-HALL OF AUSTRALIA, PTY., LTD., Sydney
PRENTICE-HALL OF CANADA, LTD., Toronto
PRENTICE-HALL OF INDIA PRIVATE LIMITED, New Delhi
PRENTICE-HALL OF JAPAN, INC., Tokyo

CONTENTS

94703

PREFACE

The authors of the essays reprinted here share the conviction that many social issues are in fundamental respects ethical problems. Each author attempts to show the importance of critical analysis and ethical theory for the resolution of actual controversies. I have specifically arranged the articles, wherever possible, in an order which reflects a controversy among them. Even when there is no direct debate, I have selected philosophers who represent widely divergent viewpoints. No attempt has been made, however, either to provide a definitive arrangement of schools of thought or to include all important articles on the subjects treated.

This book has been produced, in part, to dispel the warped but widespread notion that contemporary moral philosophy is little more than definitional concept-chopping, dignified by the title "meta-ethics." Modern ethics stands accused by students, and even by professional philosophers, of being utterly remote from practical problems. Its so-called "analytical" style and its frequent failure to discuss actual social issues have given it a reputation of being barren and boring. These complaints are not without substantial foundation; ethics has often been so taught and written. But the accusation of its general irrelevance is seriously misguided, as I hope the reader of this collection of essays will agree.

Many people have contributed to the improvement of this book. My greatest debts are to Elizabeth and Monroe Beardsley, Martin Benjamin, Dan Brock, Baruch Brody, and John Troyer, each of whom, at various stages, read the whole manuscript and made numerous valuable suggestions. For useful corrections and proposals I also thank Judy Thomson, Marvin Kohl, and many present and former students. For three special acts of generosity—far more helpful than these individuals could know—

I am indebted to Joel Feinberg, Leon Kass, and John Rawls. Finally, I wish to acknowledge the invaluable aid of two nonphilosophers: Ms. Teru Uyeyama, my production-editor, who demonstrated to perfection how her profession is properly practiced, and my wife Martha, the legalite, to whom I owe the sting of a constant insistence that philosophical writing be jargon free.

Tom L. Beauchamp

Chapter 1

RACIAL AND SEXUAL
DISCRIMINATION

INTRODUCTION

A recent pamphlet on women's liberation begins on the following bitter note:

> After years of lethargy and submission to the status quo, more and more American women have aroused themselves and are joining rebellious blacks and student radicals in contesting the capitalist establishment. . . .
>
> Just as Afro-Americans are striving to find out why they were thrust into servitude and how they can speedily free themselves, so do these newly awakened women want to know how and why they have become subjugated to male rule and what can be done [in this struggle for equality].*

Whether or not one finds this rhetoric needlessly harsh, there can be no doubt that in recent years many blacks and women have come to believe that they, along with North American Indians and other minority groups,

---

* Evelyn Reed, *Problems of Women's Liberation* (New York: Pathfinder Press, 1971), p. 7.

have been unequally treated and subjected to continuous degradation by a white male power structure. As a matter of economics, they note that women and nonwhites jointly share only 4 percent of those jobs in the United States paying a salary of more than $15,000, 96 percent are held by white males. As a matter of social status, women resent treatment as mere sex objects; blacks, the subtle expectation that they will be the white man's servant. In this chapter problems of racial and sexual discrimination are subjected to ethical scrutiny. We will study primarily three issues: (1) the ideal of equality for all people, regardless of race, creed, or sex; (2) the nature and justice of compensatory programs for those who have been discriminated against; and (3) whether compensatory justice in racial and sexual matters results in some form of unwarranted reverse discrimination.

The Ideal of Equality

If we say that all people should be treated equally, what ideal of equality are we espousing? We clearly are not in *all* respects equal. We must, then, determine the *relevant* respects in terms of which everyone should be treated equally. Aristotle argued that as long as men are equal in all the respects relevant to the type of treatment under consideration, they should be treated equally; when they are unequal, they should, in proportion, be treated as unequals. For example, if someone is being hired as a teacher, that person should receive equal consideration along with everyone else on the merits of teaching ability. Only if one is demonstrably less or more capable than others as a teacher should one be treated unequally. Here race and sex, no less than a factor such as weight, are irrelevant characteristics. This Aristotelian view is an intelligent thesis about equality, one that almost everyone would agree states a necessary condition of equality. But is it also a sufficient condition? Here there is far less agreement. At least three widely held views now exist on the nature of equality (understood as an ideal), all of which appear in the readings in this chapter. It will be helpful to examine all three before proceeding further.

1. *Equality as a Procedural Principle.* This first view of equality does not move far beyond Aristotle, if it moves beyond him at all. According to its proponents, there is no single specifiable respect or set of respects in terms of which all people should be equally considered. Rather, there is only a procedural principle of impartiality by which we ought to abide in all circumstances: "No person should be treated unequally, despite all differences with other persons, until such time as it has been shown that there is a difference between them relevant to the treatment at stake." The point of the principle is that he who seeks to treat someone

unequally must prove that the person deserves unequal treatment by showing a relevant difference between that person and others. Special favoritism and prejudice are supposedly eliminated in this way. The supporters of this view argue that particular contexts normally provide *rules* to determine differences, but where there are no rules then anyone who wishes to discriminate must provide an argument against equal treatment. This view of equality is sometimes called "formal" equality because it does not specify which *particular* differences should allow us to discriminate between people. Instead it simply treats like cases alike, where "like cases" are analyzed in terms of a given set of rules. It should be noticed that the procedural principle does not rule out hiring blacks *because* they are blacks or women *because* they are women, so long as they are equal with white or male candidates in the relevant respects (for example, teaching ability). Indeed, the principle *permits* this practice, assuming one has a good reason for hiring a woman or a black.

Does this view provide a sufficient condition of equality? Many think it does not. By not distinguishing specific relevant differences, it seems not only to be an empty theory but also to allow the institutionalization of various forms of inequality, including inequalities in the very rules determining "equal treatment." Any criteria of relevance deemed acceptable, argue opponents, seem in this view to be in moral fairness acceptable. For example, if it is judged a good reason for not interviewing women for jobs that they make male interviewers nervous, then this introduces a relevant difference. This implication of the theory, if I have drawn it correctly here, seems to render it useless as a tool for criticizing even blatant injustice. After all, the theory so construed is perfectly compatible with tyrannical rule and with caste systems; it allows through the back door the institutional favoritisms it appears to eliminate.

2. *Equality as a Set of Fundamental Rights.* Moral rights have various origins. If I swear to you that I will tell the whole truth and nothing but the truth, you acquire a right to be told the truth. Still other rights are transmitted by family ties. But do all rights rest on such contingent relations? Many philosophers have maintained that we have fundamental rights, irrespective of merit, just because we are human. This view gives rise to a second view of equality, one closely tied to the classically rooted idea that humanity is a quality possessed by all people. This humanity is said to confer rights to impartial treatment in matters of justice, freedom, equality of opportunity, and so on. Members of minority groups often complain about treatment that destroys their human dignity and self-respect. One interpretation of these complaints is to say that their fundamental human rights are being violated; stronger language has it that their very *humanity* is being violated. According to this idea of equality, these human rights are so fundamental that they take precedence over

all other considerations. Or if they do not always take precedence, then anyone who challenges this equality of rights begins with an extraordinarily strong presumption against his case that must be overcome by careful impartial reasoning. If inequalities themselves are validly institutionalized, it is argued, this can only be for the purpose of ensuring the greater freedom, justice, and well-being of the individuals in society. Disagreements should be resolved not, for example, by weighing conflicting *interests*, but rather by weighing conflicting *rights*, for it is only by reference to rights that institutional structures can properly be measured.

Again, however, many philosophers have not found this an attractive alternative. What are we to do when basic rights conflict? If persons who come into conflict appeal to the right of free pursuit, how are we to arbitrate their different interests? And, perhaps most important, it is not clear that this second and supposedly stronger view of equality overcomes the main problem of the procedural principle view, for it seems entirely compatible with the institutionalization of radical inequalities. Rights are notoriously *nonspecific*. After all, haven't most people long thought that women in Western societies, for example, live in a society that provides equality of freedom and opportunity? Formally, the early feminist movement achieved all its goals: Women were admitted to universities and professions, given the right to vote, and so on. Yet the proportion of women to men in professional life has been decreasing ever since. Have women been treated equally by the mere acquisition of these "rights?" And, more specifically, is it not the case that for years segregation in schools was judged consistent with, if not in fact an instance of, *equality?* Otherwise, why was the expression "separate but equal" used?

3. *Equality as Balanced Distribution.* A third view of the ideal of equality tries to connect equality with the idea of a balanced distribution of benefits and hardships. Its adherents argue that because the meritocratic conception of "equal opportunity *if* equally qualified" magnifies differences between individuals by upgrading the superior, it is ineffectual in combating natural and systematic inequalities. They argue instead both that the inequalities produced by nature or by systematic underprivilege should be minimized or overcome and that we should alter those features in individuals' circumstances which prevent them from realizing their natural abilities. For example, it seems that men are presently better employed than women because of *systems* of employment. Perhaps we should have social policies that expressly attempt to compensate for such a disadvantage (for example, by giving preferential treatment in recruitment and screening processes). Similarly, it can be argued that people with great natural physical or mental talent have too much of an advantage until we balance the circumstances. The point can be stated more

generally: Those who work hard in society should not be penalized because others who work only *equally* hard are different (merely) by virtue of being born with desirable natural abilities. This is not a call for total uniformity in society (and hence for mediocrity, as some maintain), but rather is an appeal to the idea that a society will remain one of unequals so long as radical disparities in benefits, burdens, opportunities, and education are allowed to exist. The ideal of equality, then, is properly a matter of equalizing the distribution of these items.

Numerous objections have also been advanced against this treatment of equality. First, it is said that the theory misses what rightly should be its own target. "Equality," as we use the term, say opponents, is not so much a matter of overcoming inequalities as it is of meeting fundamental needs. When the state compensates citizens with special education programs, preferential hiring, and health benefits, it is in order to meet fundamental needs required for human welfare. But the meeting of basic needs is perfectly compatible with even great inequalities in income and other benefits. Second, it is often objected that there is nothing unreasonable about distributing according to merit, or need, or both merit and need. In fact, it is often argued that the incentives resulting from distribution according to merit (desert) and the handicaps overcome by distribution according to need together produce a more progressive set of economic benefits than would the economic uniformities of a welfare state. Third, it has of late frequently been maintained that to equalize by removing inequalities is to create a threat to the quality of certain institutions fundamental to the welfare and advancement of society. To equalize the number of positions for blacks and women in the business and university communities is to dilute the quality by cutting down on the total pool of available talent (white males).

Compensatory Justice

When a person or group of persons seeks to initiate or to change a system of social benefits, they frequently appeal to others' sympathy and benevolence. Charity drives, for example, make such an appeal. Other requests, however, are far more forcible: they invoke ideals such as equality and justice in order to support claims that people have certain rights—perhaps legal and perhaps moral—for which they do not have to be in the debt of others' generosity. Denial of these rights is thought to be in itself grounds for complaint and redress. We do not allow violations of the Bill of Rights or of moral rights, for example, because such violations deprive people of what we believe to be entitlements and perhaps necessities, not mere luxuries. This is all part of our conception of social justice, which itself we think a necessity and not a luxury for civilized society.

Using this conception, we may come to think that a severe injustice has been done to a certain group. Naturally we wish to restore the balance of justice by compensating them for their loss. The principle of compensatory justice says that whenever an injustice has been committed, just compensation or reparation is owed the injured parties. It is now a widespread view that minority groups discriminated against in the past, including women, blacks, North American Indians, and French Canadians, should be recompensed for these injustices by compensatory policies such as the Affirmative Action or Equal Opportunity programs. It is not difficult to understand the attractions of this view. For years, opportunities for blacks and women to participate in some of society's most desirable institutions have been limited by deliberate barriers or quotas. In addition, even when barriers were formally or legally dropped, matters often did not improve.

Because of this history of discrimination and its persistence, there are those who believe we could restore the balance of justice by making it easier for women and blacks to obtain admission to educational institutions and job interviews. Special programs also presumably avoid the problem of token approval of more equal distribution. This system seems clearly, however, to involve a network of preferential treatments, and it raises the following question: If quotas or social policies require that, for example, a woman or a black be given preference over a white man otherwise better qualified (that is, if the circumstances had been anonymous the white man would have been selected), is this an acceptable instance of compensatory justice or is it a pure and simple case of treating the white man unjustly? It has been variously argued in answer that such practices are (a) just, (b) unjust, (c) not unjust, but also not required by our concepts of justice and equality.

Those who claim that such compensatory measures are just, or perhaps required by justice, argue that the past lives in the present: The victims of past discrimination against blacks are still handicapped or discriminated against, while the families of slave owners are still being unduly enriched by inheritance laws. Those who have inherited wealth accumulated by iniquitous practices do not have as much right to the wealth, it is argued, as do the children of slaves, who at least have a right of compensation. In the case of women in Western societies, it is argued that their culture fosters a lack of self-confidence, prejudicially excludes them from much of the work force, and treats them as a low-paid auxiliary labor unit. Hence only extraordinarily independent women can be expected to compete even psychologically with men.

Those who claim that compensatory measures are unjust argue variously that no criteria exist for measuring compensation, that the extent of discrimination is now minor (insufficiently broad to justify preferential treatment), that none of those actually harmed in previous eras is here to be compensated, and that many of the problems are biological (probably genetic) rather than social in origin. Instead of providing compensation, they argue, we should continue to provide justice by strict equality and merit while attacking the roots of discrimination. In addition, some now successful but once underprivileged minority groups (Italians, for example) argue that their long struggle for equality is jeopardized by programs favoring blacks and women. Their view is that they will suffer unfairly, having already suffered enough, or that they will not suffer only because they too will be compensated for past oppressions. But is it not absurd, they say, to suggest that *all* groups oppressed in the past—blacks and women being only two among a great many—should receive compensatory reparations? Are we not compounding initial injustices with a vastly complicated system of further injustices? A final major argument against compensatory measures is that equality of opportunity in society is destroyed by an enforced system of *reverse discrimination,* a topic we shall take up below.

Those who claim that compensatory measures which benefit racial or sexual groups are not unjust but also are not required by concepts of justice and equality maintain, as Thomas Nagel puts it, that "the system from which [preferential policies] depart is already unjust for reasons having nothing to do with racial or sexual discrimination." The arguments for this striking conclusion are discussed in detail in the Nagel selection at the end of this chapter.

Reverse Discrimination

Suppose we take the principle of compensatory justice quite seriously, and suppose we also agree that there has been and still is significant racial and sexual discrimination. We will naturally be tempted to institute policies of compensatory justice. These policies might include making access to desirable positions easier and possibly direct financial reparations. By balancing inequalities in this way, however, we seem to create reverse inequalities. We make white males, for example, less than equal in competition with those in whose favor we are now discriminating. The justice of this discrimination has become an important issue because it seems that we are employing irrelevant characteristics, such as being black or female, as relevant moral criteria.

The major question takes the following form: Certain groups have been discriminated against because their members possess a morally irrelevant characteristic (color, sex). This characteristic, however, has been *treated* as morally relevant and has produced injustices. Is it now morally permissible to use that same characteristic as a relevant criterion to morally justify preferential consideration? The use of such a characteristic would seem simply to continue the original wrongdoing by discriminating in reverse. No one really denies that discrimination does occur as a result of preferential treatment, the issue turns on the justice or injustice of the discrimination *if* it is based on morally irrelevant characteristics. Those who believe the practice to be just face an apparent contradiction: If the members of a racial or sexual group have been discriminated against on the basis of a morally irrelevant characteristic, is it not contradictory to argue that this same characteristic is now morally relevant as a basis for compensation to members of that group?

Whether this reverse discrimination is just or unjust is obviously a matter of immediate social importance. The following four positions, though they do not exhaust the possibilities, are the most prominent current arguments:

1. *The characteristics are morally irrelevant, therefore reverse discrimination is justified.* Here the argument is made that one must be consistent in ethics and that reverse discrimination involves a blatant inconsistency. Compensation is just, but discrimination violates equality and so is never just, no matter which individuals or groups are discriminated against.

2. *The characteristics are morally irrelevant but the special treatment of groups is not based on these characteristics, and therefore reverse discrimination is not justified.* Here the argument is that preferential treatments are based not on being black or on being a woman but rather have their basis in unfair treatment, which just happens to have been unfair because persons were discriminated against on the basis of a morally irrelevant characteristic (blackness, femaleness).

3. *The characteristics are morally irrelevant but the special treatment of groups is still based on these characteristics, and therefore reverse discrimination in favor of groups is not justified.* This argument is not identical with the first. Here it is not claimed that compensation to individuals for past harms is wrong, but only that it is wrong as applied to *groups.* Harms are always relevant in matters of compensatory justice, but membership in a group is irrelevant precisely because it is based on a morally irrelevant characteristic.

4. *The characteristics should be irrelevant but historically have been made morally relevant, and therefore reverse discrimination is justified.* Here the argument is that those who discriminated against racial and sexual groups made race and sex morally relevant with respect to the principle of compensatory justice. It is morally required, then, that reverse discrimination be directed toward benefits for these groups *as groups.* Otherwise the target of the discrimination is missed.

Arguments in the Selections

John Stuart Mill presents a classic and eloquent appeal for complete sexual equality. He traces the origin of sexually discriminatory beliefs to the fact that society was organized with individual women in bondage to individual men. He argues that this was and is a form of unjustified slavery and that no historical reasons for discrimination constitute worthy ethical reasons. Mill, however, seems more disturbed about the denial of legal rights to women than about the actual treatment most women received, though he has often been misunderstood on this point. His deeper point seems to be that even if the vast majority of women are not mistreated, we nonetheless ought (for utilitarian reasons) to remove social institutions that can and do foster despotism—much as a society ought to protect itself against the possibility of dictatorship even though it presently has no dictator. Accordingly, it is the possible even more than the actual abuse of male power that concerns Mill. Of particular importance is a distinction he draws between human *nature* and human *circumstance*. He contends that what his countrymen refer to as "the nature of women" is merely an artificial and prejudicial characterization— the result of circumstantial repression and "unnatural stimulation." He asks rhetorically, "But was there ever any domination which did not appear natural to those who possessed it?" In a more positive vein, Mill argues that queens have ruled with as much character and ability as kings, that women are generally more successful in practical affairs than men, and that most of the alleged inferior characteristics of women can be explained purely by reference to the strong social demands that women be meek, submissive, and sexually attractive.

Virginia Held takes up questions of how long it is reasonable to expect the victims of gross social inequality to wait for the redress of their grievances and what would count as reasonable progress toward equality without requiring a loss of self-respect. Her article is an attempt to set forth grounds on which individual women and nonwhites who are discriminated against could evaluate a given rate of progress as satisfactory or as unsatisfactory, especially in the area of equal occupational opportunity. She contends that present policies based on efficient economic allocations (Pareto criteria), in which no one now holding a privileged position will be asked to relinquish anything, are unacceptable, for even if they result in gradual improvement, this improvement is a token gesture inconsistent with self-respect. Yet she also finds that the *immediate* realization of equality would lead to a self-defeating institutional breakdown. Faced with this dilemma, she suggests a compromise—a calculated though "plodding" rate of reform whereby those occupying positions of unjustified privilege would have to accept some immediate loss of privilege.

Graham Hughes is concerned with the justifiability of demands for reparations to black Americans on the basis of a debt owed to them, especially in the light of precedents set by reparations to American Indians. He considers some sacrifice by the more affluent white majority necessary in order to eliminate both disrespectful attitudes and, more important, economic inequality. He entertains the possibility of tax concessions and other economic aid, and in an important conclusion, maintains that "We must acknowledge that the large institutional changes which will be necessary in order to achieve rectification of major social injustices can only be accomplished at the cost of some individual injustice. The cost must of course be minimized and nobody should be asked to bear too heavy a burden of sacrifice." This burden will involve, he thinks, a form of reverse discrimination, but he finds this discrimination not unjustified since one intended consequence of its implementation is the removal of all need to have programs requiring reverse discrimination. Hughes also warns that moral demands for black separatism will become increasingly justified if major injustices to disadvantaged minorities are not removed in a reasonable period of time.

Thomas Nagel, in the final selection, considers the question of whether preferential and quota policies for blacks and women are unjust when instituted to remove systematic inequalities. He argues that "although preferential policies are not required by justice, they are not seriously unjust either—because the system from which they depart is already unjust for reasons having nothing to do with racial or sexual discrimination." Nagel is referring here to the system of social rewards, which he believes broadly discriminatory on the basis of differences in talents, gifts, and effort expended. Whatever the merit of superior talent, Nagel does not think it sufficient to justify the very wide differences in reward presently operative in our society. For this reason he argues that the most serious present injustice is neither a racial nor a sexual one but rather is an economic injustice rooted in the perspective that smart people *deserve* far more than do dumb people. By employing this general approach to social injustice, Nagel is able to conclude that compensatory treatment in favor of blacks and women need not be seriously unjust and may be warranted by considerations of social utility, even if reverse discrimination is required as part of the treatment.

On the Subjection of Women *

John Stuart Mill

The object of this Essay is to explain as clearly as I am able, the grounds of an opinion which I have held from the very earliest period when I had formed any opinions at all on social or political matters, and which, instead of being weakened or modified, has been constantly growing stronger by the progress of reflection and the experience of life. That the priniciple which regulates the existing social relations between the two sexes—the legal subordination of one sex to the other—is wrong in itself, and now one of the chief hindrances to human improvement; and that it ought to be replaced by a principle of perfect equality, admitting no power or privilege on the one side, nor disability on the other.

The very words necessary to express the task I have undertaken, show how arduous it is. But it would be a mistake to suppose that the difficulty of the case must lie in the insufficiency or obscurity of the grounds of reason on which my conviction rests. The difficulty is that which exists in all cases in which there is a mass of feeling to be contended against. So long as an opinion is strongly rooted in the feelings, it gains rather than loses in stability by having a preponderating weight of argument against it. For if it were accepted as a result of argument, the refutation of the argument might shake the solidity of the conviction; but when it rests solely on feeling, the worse it fares in argumentative contest, the more persuaded its adherents are that their feeling must have some deeper ground, which the arguments do not reach; and while the feeling remains, it is always throwing up fresh intrenchments of argument to repair any breach made in the old. And there are so many causes tending to make the feelings connected with this subject the most intense and most deeply-rooted of all those which gather round and protect old institutions and customs, that we need not wonder to find them as yet less undermined and loosened than any of the rest by the progress of the great modern spiritual and social transition; nor suppose that the barbarisms to which men cling longest must be less barbarisms than those which they earlier shake off. . . .

---

* From the original edition published by Longmans, Green, Reades, and Dyer (London, 1869).

The generality of a practice is in some cases a strong presumption that it is, or at all events once was, conducive to laudable ends. This is the case, when the practice was first adopted, or afterwards kept up, as a means to such ends, and was grounded on experience of the mode in which they could be most effectually attained. If the authority of men over women, when first established, had been the result of a conscientious comparison between different modes of constituting the government of society; if, after trying various other modes of social organisation—the government of women over men, equality between the two, and such mixed and divided modes of government as might be invented—it had been decided, on the testimony of experience, that the mode in which women are wholly under the rule of men, having no share at all in public concerns, and each in private being under the legal obligation of obedience to the man with whom she has associated her destiny, was the arrangement most conducive to the happiness and well-being of both; its general adoption might then be fairly thought to be some evidence that, at the time when it was adopted, it was the best: though even then the considerations which recommended it may, like so many other primeval social facts of the greatest importance, have subsequently, in the course of ages, ceased to exist. But the state of the case is in every respect the reverse of this. In the first place, the opinion in favour of the present system, which entirely subordinates the weaker sex to the stronger, rests upon theory only; for there never has been trial made of any other: so that experience, in the sense in which it is vulgarly opposed to theory, cannot be pretended to have pronounced any verdict. And in the second place, the adoption of this system of inequality never was the result of deliberation, or forethought, or any social ideas, or any notion whatever of what conduced to the benefit of humanity or the good order of society. It arose simply from the fact that from the very earliest twilight of human society, every woman (owing to the value attached to her by men, combined with her inferiority in muscular strength) was found in a state of bondage to some man. Laws and systems of polity always begin by recognising the relations they find already existing between individuals. They convert what was a mere physical fact into a legal right, give it the sanction of society, and principally aim at the substitution of public and organised means of asserting and protecting these rights, instead of the irregular and lawless conflict of physical strength. Those who had already been compelled to obedience became in this manner legally bound to it. Slavery, from being a mere affair of force between the master and the slave, became regularised and a matter of compact among the masters, who, binding themselves to one another for common protection, guaranteed by their collective strength the private possessions of each, including his slaves. In early times, the great majority of the male sex were slaves, as well as the whole of the female. And many ages elapsed, some of them ages of high cultivation, before any thinker was bold enough to question the rightfulness, and the absolute social necessity, either of the one slavery or of the other. By degrees such thinkers did arise; and (the general progress of society assisting) the slavery of the male sex has, in all the countries of Christian Europe at least (though, in one of them, only within the last few years) been at length abolished, and that of the female sex has been gradually changed into a milder form of dependence. But this dependence, as it exists at present, is not an original institution, taking a fresh start from considerations of justice and social expediency—it is the primitive state of slavery lasting on, through successive mitigations and modifications occasioned by the same causes which have softened the general manners, and brought all human relations more under the control of justice and the influence of humanity. It has not lost the taint of its brutal origin. No presumption in its favour, therefore, can be drawn from the fact of its existence. . . .

In struggles for political emancipation, everybody knows how often its champions are bought off by bribes, or daunted by terrors. In the case of women, each individual of the subject-class is in a chronic state of bribery and intimidation combined. In setting up the standard of resistance, a large number of the leaders, and still more of the followers, must make an almost complete sacrifice of the pleasures or the alleviations of their own individual lot. If ever any system of privilege and enforced subjection had its yoke tightly riveted on the necks of those who are kept down by it, this has. I have not yet shown that it is a wrong system: but everyone who is capable of thinking on the subject must see that even if it is, it was certain to outlast all other forms of unjust authority. And when some of the grossest of the other forms still exist in many civilised countries, and have only recently been got rid of in others, it would be strange if that which is so much the deepest rooted had yet been perceptibly shaken anywhere. There is more reason to wonder that the protests and testimonies against it should have been so numerous and so weighty as they are.

Some will object, that a comparison cannot fairly be made between the government of the male sex and the forms of unjust power which I have adduced in illustration of it, since these are arbitrary, and the effect of mere usurpation, while it on the contrary is natural. But was there ever any domination which did not appear natural to those who possessed it? There was a time when the division of mankind into two classes, a small one of masters and a numerous one of slaves, appeared, even to the most cultivated minds, to be natural, and the only natural, condition of the human race. No less an intellect, and one which contributed no less to the progress of human thought, than Aristotle, held this opinion without doubt or misgiving; and rested it on the same premises on which the same assertion in regard to the dominion of men over women is usually based, namely that there are different natures among mankind, free natures, and slave natures; that the Greeks were of a free nature, the barbarian races of Thracians and Asiatics of a slave nature. But why need I go back to Aristotle? Did not the slave-owners of the Southern United States maintain the same doctrine, with all the fanaticism with which men cling to the theories that justify their passions and legitimate their personal interests? Did they not call heaven and earth to witness that the dominion of the white man over the black is natural, that the black race is by nature incapable of freedom, and marked out for slavery? some even going so far as to say that freedom of manual labourers is an unnatural order of things anywhere. . . .

The subjection of women to men being a universal custom, any departure from it quite naturally appears unnatural. But how entirely, even in this case, the feeling is dependent on custom, appears by ample experience. Nothing so much astonishes the people of distant parts of the world, when they first learn anything about England, as to be told that it is under a queen; the thing seems to them so unnatural as to be almost incredible. To Englishmen this does not seem in the least degree unnatural, because they are used to it; but they do feel it unnatural that women should be soldiers or Members of Parliament. In the feudal ages, on the contrary, war and politics were not thought unnatural to women, because not unusual; it seemed natural that women of the privileged classes should be of manly character, inferior in nothing but bodily strength to their husbands and fathers. The independence of women seemed rather less unnatural to the Greeks than to other ancients, on account of the fabulous Amazons (whom they believed to be historical), and the partial example afforded by the Spartan women; who, though no less subordinate by law than in other Greek states, were more free in fact, and being trained to bodily exercises in the same manner with men, gave ample proof that they were not naturally disqualified for them. There can be little doubt that Spartan experience suggested to Plato, among many other of his doctrines, that of the social and political equality of the two sexes.

But, it will be said, the rule of men over women differs from all these others in not being a rule of force: it is accepted voluntarily; women make no complaint, and are consenting parties to it. In the first place, a great number of women do not accept it. Ever since there have been women able to make their sentiments known by their writings (the only mode of publicity which society permits to them), an increasing number of them have recorded protests against their present social condition: and recently many thousands of them, headed by the most eminent women known to the public, have petitioned Parliament for their admission to the Parliamentary Suffrage. The claim of women to be educated as solidly, and in the same branches of knowledge, as men, is urged with growing intensity, and with a great prospect of success; while the demand for their admission into professions and occupations hitherto closed against them, becomes every year more urgent. Though there are not in this country, as there are in the United States, periodical conventions and an organised party to agitate for the Rights of Women, there is a numerous and active society organised and managed by women, for the more limited object of obtaining the political franchise. . . . There is never any want of women who complain of ill-usage by their husbands. There would be infinitely more, if complaint were not the greatest of all provocatives to a repetition and increase of the ill-usage. It is this which frustrates all attempts to maintain the power but protect the woman against its abuses. In no other case (except that of a child) is the person who has been proved judicially to have suffered an injury, replaced under the physical power of the culprit who inflicted it. Accordingly wives, even in the most extreme and protracted cases of bodily ill-usage, hardly ever dare avail themselves of the laws made for their protection: and if, in a moment of irrepressible indignation, or by the interference of neighbours, they are induced to do so, their whole effort afterwards is to disclose as little as they can, and to beg off their tyrant from his merited chastisement.

All causes, social and natural, combine to make it unlikely that women should be collectively rebellious to the power of men. They are so far in a position different from all other subject classes, that their masters require something more from them than actual service. Men do not want solely the obedience of women, they want their sentiments. All men, except the most brutish, desire to have, in the woman most nearly connected with them, not a forced slave but a willing one, not a slave merely, but a favourite. They have therefore put everything in practice to enslave their minds. The masters of all other slaves rely, for maintaining obedience, on fear; either fear of themselves, or religious fears. The masters of women wanted more than simple obedience, and they turned the whole force of education to effect their purpose. All women are brought up from the very earliest years in the belief that their ideal of character is the very opposite to that of men; not self-will, and government by self-control, but submission, and yielding to the control of others. All the moralities tell them that it is the duty of women, and all the current sentimentalities that it is their nature, to live for others; to make complete abnegation of themselves, and to have no life but in their affections. And by their affections are meant the only ones they are allowed to have—those to the men with whom they are connected, or to the children who constitute an additional and indefeasible tie between them and a man. When we put together three things—first, the natural attraction between opposite sexes; secondly, the wife's entire dependence on the husband, every privilege or pleasure she has being either his gift, or depending entirely on his will; and lastly, that the principal object of human pursuit, consideration, and all objects of social ambition, can in general be sought or obtained by her only through him, it would be a miracle if the object of being attractive to men had not become the polar star of feminine education and formation of character. And, this great means of influence over the minds of women having been acquired, an instinct of selfishness made men avail themselves of it to the utmost as a means of holding women in subjection, by representing to them meekness, submissiveness, and resignation of all individual will into the hands of a man, as an essential part of sexual attractiveness. Can it be doubted that any of the other yokes which mankind have succeeded in breaking, would have subsisted till now if the same means had existed, and had been so sedulously used, to bow down their minds to it?. . .

The preceding considerations are amply sufficient to show that custom, however universal it may be, affords in this case no presumption, and ought not to create any prejudice, in favour of the arrangements which place women in social and political subjection to men. But I may go farther, and maintain that the course of history, and the tendencies of progressive human society, afford not only no presumption in favour of this system of inequality of rights, but a strong one against it; and that, so far as the whole course of human improvement up to the time, the whole stream of modern tendencies, warrants any inference on the subject, it is, that this relic of the past is discordant with the future, and must necessarily disappear. . . .

The least that can be demanded is, that the question should not be considered as prejudged by existing fact and existing opinion, but open to discussion on its merits, as a question of justice and expediency: the decision on this, as on any of the other social arrangements of mankind, depending on what an enlightened estimate of tendencies and consequences may show to be most advantageous to humanity in general, without distinction of sex. And the discussion must be a real discussion, descending to foundations, and not resting satisfied with vague and general assertions. It will not do, for instance, to assert in general terms, that the experience of mankind has pronounced in favour of the existing system. Experience cannot possibly have decided between two courses, so long as there has only been experience of one. If it be said that the doctrine of the equality of the sexes rests only on theory, it must be remembered that the contrary doctrine also has only theory to rest upon. All that is proved in its favour by direct experience, is that mankind have been able to exist under it, and to attain the degree of improvement and prosperity which we now see; but whether that prosperity has been attained sooner, or is now greater, than it would have been under the other system, experience does not say. On the other hand, experience does say, that every step in improvement has been so invariably accompanied by a step made in raising the social position of women, that historians and philosophers have been led to adopt their elevation or debasement as on the whole the surest test and most correct measure of the civilisation of a people or an age. Through all the progressive period of human history, the condition of women has been approaching nearer to equality with men. This does not of itself prove that the assimilation must go on to complete equality; but it assuredly affords some presumption that such is the case.

Neither does it avail anything to say that the *nature* of the two sexes adapts them to their present functions and position, and renders these appropriate to them. Standing on the ground of common sense and the constitution of the human mind, I deny that anyone knows, or can know, the nature of the two sexes, as long as they have only been seen in their present relation to one another. If men had ever been found in society without women, or women without men, or if there had been a society of men and women in which the women were not under the control of the men, something might have been positively known about the mental and moral differences which may be inherent in the nature of each. What is now called the nature of women is an eminently artificial thing—the result of forced repression in some directions, unnatural stimulation in others. It may be asserted without scruple, that no other class of dependents have had their character so entirely distorted from its natural proportions by their relation with their masters; for, if conquered and slave races have been, in some respects, more forcibly repressed, whatever in them has not been crushed down by an iron heel has generally been let alone, and if left with any liberty of development, it has developed itself according to its own laws; but in the case of women, a hot-house and stove cultivation has always been carried on of some of the capabilities of their nature, for the benefit and pleasure of their masters. Then, because certain products of the general vital force sprout luxuriantly and reach a great development in this heated atmosphere and under this active nurture and watering, while other shoots from the same root, which are left outside in the wintry air, with ice purposely heaped all round them, have stunted growth, and some are burnt off with fire and disappear; men, with that inability to recognise their own work which distinguishes the unanalytic mind, indolently believe that the tree grows of itself in the way they have made it grow, and that it would die if one half of it were not kept in a vapour bath and the other half in the snow.

Of all difficulties which impede the progress of thought, and the formation of well-grounded opinions on life and social arrangements, the greatest is now the unspeakable ignorance and inattention of mankind in respect to the influences which form human character. Whatever any portion of the human species now are, or seem to be, such, it is supposed, they have a natural tendency to be: even when the most elementary knowledge of the circumstances in which they have been placed, clearly points out the causes that made them what they are. Because a cottier deeply in arrears to his landlord is not industrious, there are people who think that the Irish are naturally idle. Because constitutions can be overthrown when the authorities appointed to execute them turn their arms against them, there are people who think the French incapable of free government. Because the Greeks cheated the Turks, and the Turks only plundered the Greeks, there are persons who think that the Turks are naturally more sincere: and because women, as is often said, care nothing about politics except their personalities, it is supposed that the general good is naturally less interesting to women than to men. History, which is now so much better understood than formerly, teaches another lesson: if only by showing the extraordinary susceptibility of human nature to external influences, and the extreme variableness of those of its manifestations which are supposed to be most universal and uniform. But in history, as in travelling, men usually see only what they already had in their own minds; and few learn much from history, who do not bring much with them to its study.

Hence, in regard to that most difficult question, what are the natural differences between the two sexes—a subject on which it is impossible in the present state of society to obtain complete and correct knowledge —while almost everybody dogmatises upon it, almost all neglect and make light of the only means by which any partial insight can be obtained into it. This is, an analytic study of the most important department of psychology, the laws of the influence of circumstances on character. For, however great and apparently ineradicable the moral and intellectual differences between men and women might be, the evidence of there being natural differences could only be negative. Those only could be inferred to be natural which could not possibly be artificial —the residuum, after deducting every characteristic of either sex which can admit of being explained from education or external circumstances. The profoundest knowledge of the laws of the formation of character is indispensable to entitle anyone to affirm even that there is any difference, much more what the difference is, between the two sexes considered as moral and rational beings; and since no one, as yet, has that knowledge (for there is hardly any subject which, in proportion to its importance, has been so little studied), no one is thus far entitled to any positive opinion on the subject. Conjectures are all that can at present be made; conjectures more or less probable, according as more or less authorised by such knowledge as we yet have of the laws of psychology, as applied to the formation of character. . . .

The general opinion of men is supposed to be, that the natural vocation of a woman is that of a wife and mother. I say, is supposed to be, because, judging from acts—from the whole of the present constitution of society—one might infer that their opinion was the direct contrary. They might be supposed to think that the alleged natural vocation of women was of all things the most repugnant to their nature; insomuch that if they are free to do anything else—if any other means of living or occupation of their time and faculties, is open, which has any chance of appearing desirable to them—there will not be enough of them who will be willing to accept the condition said to be natural to them. If this is the real opinion of men in general, it would be well that it should be spoken out. I should like to hear somebody openly enunciating the doctrine (it is already implied in much that is written on the subject)—"It is necessary to society that women should marry and produce children. They will not do so unless they are compelled. Therefore it is necessary to compel them." The merits of the case would then be clearly defined. It would be exactly that of the slave-holders of South Carolina and Louisiana. "It is necessary that cotton and sugar should be grown. White men cannot produce them. Negroes will not, for any wages which we choose to give. *Ergo* they must be compelled." An illustration still closer to the point is that of impressment. Sailors must absolutely be had to defend the country. It often happens that they will not voluntarily enlist. Therefore there must be the power of forcing them. How often has this logic been used! and, but for one flaw in it, without doubt it would have been successful up to this day. But it is open to the retort—First pay the sailors the honest value of the labour. When you have made it as well worth their while to serve you, as to work for other employers, you will have no more difficulty than others have in obtaining their services. To this there is no logical answer except "I will not": and as people are now not only ashamed, but are not desirous, to rob the labourer of his hire, impressment is no longer advocated. Those who attempt to force women into marriage by closing all other doors against them, lay themselves open to a similar retort. If they mean what they say, their opinion must evidently be, that men do not render the married condition so desirable to women, as to induce them to accept it for its own recommendations. It is not a sign of one's thinking the boon one offers very attractive, when one allows only Hobson's choice, "that or none." And here, I believe, is the clue to the feelings of those men, who have a real antipathy to the equal freedom of women. I believe they are afraid, not lest women should be unwilling to marry, for I do not think that anyone in reality has that apprehension; but lest they should insist that marriage should be on equal conditions; lest all women of spirit and capacity should prefer doing almost anything else, not in their own eyes degrading, rather than marry, when marrying is giving themselves a master, and a master too of all their earthly possessions. And truly, if this consequence were necessarily incident to marriage, I think that the apprehension would be very well founded. I agree in thinking it probable that few women, capable of anything else, would, unless under an irresistible *entraînement*, rendering them for the time insensible to anything but itself, choose such a lot, when any other means were open to them of filling a conventionally honourable place in life: and if men are determined that the law of marriage shall be a law of despotism, they are quite right, in point of mere policy, in leaving to women only Hobson's choice. But, in that case, all that has been done in the modern world to relax the chain on the minds of women has been a mistake. They never should have been allowed to receive a literary education. Women who read, much more women who write, are, in the existing constitution of things, a contradiction and a disturbing element: and it was wrong to bring women up with any acquirements but those of an odalisque, or of a domestic servant.

Reparations for Blacks? *

Graham Hughes

The poor have always been with us but the disadvantaged have arrived more recently on the scene. "Poor" is a good, plain descriptive word, but "disadvantaged" and its fashionable interchangeable adjective "underprivileged" are more subtle as well as euphemistic. They seem to hint at some assumption of guilt by the presumably advantaged or privileged majority; they suggest a moral duty to act in some way to rectify a situation of social injustice. But the nature of the moral duty

* From *The New York University Law Review* 43 (1968). Footnotes included. Reprinted by permission of the author and publisher.

involved, the weight of the burden of guilt that one ought properly to shoulder and what measures of rectification might be appropriate are very much in dispute.

It is not easy for government to make a public confession that one section of the community has been treated unjustly and has a good claim to reparation. But American legislative history does have a recent precedent of this kind. A federal statute of 1946 [1] set up an Indian Claims Commission with jurisdiction to hear and resolve claims arising from the seizure of Indian property and breaches by the United States of its treaties with the Indian nations and tribes. In subsequent proceedings it was held that the Government of the United States was liable to pay compensation for, among other places, the whole of Kansas. If we are willing to applaud this tardy effort at reparation, we might ask whether there are not good arguments for its extension. If a proper sense of shame at our forerunners' dealings with the Indians prompted the Act of 1946, can we feel any less sense of shame at their dealings with the black population of America? There is not very much to choose between the sporadic outbursts of genocidal rage that were displayed towards the Indians and the settled, institutional policy of slavery that was applied to the Negro. So if a public confession can be made in statutory form of the just claims of American Indians for compensation (a phenomenon uncomfortably close in time and nature to post-war Germany's reparation payments to Jews) why should we not initiate similar schemes for reparation to black Americans?

There are of course differences. There was no seizure of land owned by black people (though there was surely an unjust seizure of labor) nor was there a breach of treaties. Thus, with black Americans it is not as easy in a legalistic sense to identify the proper plaintiffs. With American Indians we can single out the members of tribal groups as the proper recipients of compensation for lands seized from their tribe or from the breach of treaties with their tribe, but with black Americans the inheritors of the complaints are more numerous and diffuse. For these reasons it is not possible to set up a viable argument for compensation payments to Negroes within the confines of existing legal theory, but there remains the question of the strength of the moral case for instituting both public and private schemes of a compensatory nature.

It would certainly be easy to list some practical or utilitarian considerations which would seem to favor such policies. The still half-submerged position of black people causes discontent amongst them and leads to social unrest with the prospect of episodic violent disturbances. Any society which contains a substantial minority who harbor deep

---

[1] Act of Aug. 13, 1946, ch. 959, § 1, 60 Stat. 1049.

resentment because they feel themselves excluded from full participation in the benefits of that society carries within it seeds of schism and disorder. Ordinary political wisdom dictates the adoption of a program to alleviate and ultimately remove the resentment by demonstrating to the minority groups that the fullest benefits of life in that society are fairly open to them. Again, if it is true, as we are often told, that poverty and other social ills which cluster around poverty are great causes of crimes, then we might also expect that any remedial program designed to eliminate or greatly reduce the incidence of poverty would at the same time greatly reduce the crime rate and so bring very obvious benefits to society. Then it is immediately apparent that the general level of prosperity would be elevated by the removal from the welfare rolls of millions of people and their transformation into members of productive, income-producing families. Indeed, all these objectives are now the common-places of one stream of political rhetoric in the United States and, in some fashion, they represent official Govenment policy and claim to be translated into action in such ways as the manifold activities of the Office of Economic Opportunity.

But the purely utilitarian arguments here are not all on one side. Measures which have an air of singling out minority groups for favored treatment may have the perverse effect of arousing resentment in other groups and so may lead to further social unrest. In purely economic terms, it might be more efficient to invest in expanding productive activities which can draw on an existing supply of skilled white labor and technicians rather than to engage in the slow and costly task of, for example, job-training programs for unskilled and ill-educated black people. And, again, if we encourage the employment of minority group members in positions where managerial or technical skill is called for, it may be, in view of the inferior level of education that often obtains among such groups, that we shall employ less efficient people than we otherwise might. The utilitarian arguments thus are mixed. What must be emphasized is that, even if they were conclusively ranked against large-scale remedial intervention, utilitarian considerations would have to yield here to the demands of justice.

Let us suppose that 80 per cent of the population of the United States enjoy a standard of living which does not fall below X units of well-being, but that the remaining 20 per cent live at a standard which moves on a scale between X − 1 and X − 20 units of well-being. A continuation of present social institutions and practices might ensure the further upward movement of the standard of living of the comfortable 80 per cent but might even further depress the standard of living of the remaining 20 per cent, or at least indefinitely postpone the narrowing of the gap between them and the more affluent. But a change in social institutions and practices is conceivable by which the living standards of the depressed groups would move more swiftly towards the X point; such a change, however, would entail some lowering of the standard of living of the 80 per cent majority and might lead to some of them falling below the X point. Let us assume that this is a democratic society so that general decisions about fundamental matters of policy are from time to time presented to the electorate. The comparatively affluent 80 per cent would thus be in a position to determine whether to adhere to present social patterns which would ensure a continuation of their progressive affluence or, on the other hand, to assume a measure of sacrifice in order to elevate the position of those who were less happily placed.

Whether that is the actual situation in the United States or not, the model is a useful one to suggest an argument that needs to be developed, that the moral claims of justice can be such that sacrifices can be properly demanded in some situations. Utility may not dictate a sacrifice where justice may. Let us also observe here initially that we are not speaking of sacrificial acts that spring from love or compassion. Parents make sacrifices for their children out of love, and outside the family there are no doubt countless instances of persons who out of love or compassion willingly curtail their own material interests in order to help others. But this is not (except in a religious context) a demand that we can make on people; and it is not the way that minority groups would, I think, want to present their demands. Black people in America are not saying to white people, "You ought to help us because you ought to love us and make sacrifices for us out of charity and compassion." They are saying, rather, "You owe us something. Please pay your debt." This is in the nature of a claim and, like all claims, it needs to be scrutinized.

Recent writing on the theme of social justice provides a basis for advancing such a claim. Professor John Rawls of Harvard has offered an analysis of the concept of justice which is essentially based on the notion of fairness rather than on the notion of utility. Rawls asks us to imagine a contractual model in which persons who wish to embark on the enterprise of living together socially meet to formulate basic principles which will govern their relations with each other. At this point they do not know what positions will be assigned to them in the contemplated social order, whether they will be manual workers or executives, whether they will be more or less affluent, what talents or skills they may or may not possess that will be valued in that society. They will thus wish to arrive at principles which will ensure that whatever positions they occupy in the society they will not have cause to complain. Rawls suggests that the principles they will arrive at might be expressed as follows:

[F]irst, each person participating in a practice, or affected by it, has an equal right to the most extensive liberty compatible with a like liberty for all; and second, inequalities are arbitrary unless it is reasonable to expect that they will work out for everyone's advantage, and provided the positions and offices to which they attach, or from which they may be gained, are open to all. These principles express justice as a complex of three ideas: liberty, equality, and reward for services contributing to the common good.[2]

An English writer, W. G. Runciman, has taken up Rawls' principles and extended them in a context very relevant to the present discussion:

The parties to the contract are, after all, required to envisage a society whose general level of well-being is such that not only is nobody starving but a good many people are earning sums very much more than adequate for the current average level of wants. Many of those at or near the bottom of the income distribution may be in possession of consumer goods which would seem to the members of other or earlier societies to be beyond the dreams of avarice. But they may be conscious of being, for example, much less well housed than the majority of their society; and at the same time, they may be aware that a good many of their fellow citizens have a great deal more than the average income. They accordingly put forward a claim that those earning much above the average should be sufficiently taxed to bring them some way closer to the general level, the money so raised to be set aside in a fund to be used for raising the standard of housing among those whose incomes are least adequate to enable them to approach the average standard. There is no question of doing away with the rights of the greater contributors to earn more than others in accordance with the criteria agreed in advance. The claim is only that where marked inequalities exist in terms of whatever standard is current then justice requires that some priority should be given to needs (in this sense) over and above the other two criteria.[3]

This contractual model provides a firm foundation for a partial redistribution of wealth when gross inequalities exist. It is an argument which might have a particular appeal to lawyers since it has as its theme the notion of evaluating human institutions by the criterion of what terms in a hypothetical agreement would be equitable. At the same time it is a way of presenting a judgment of injustice that should have an immediate appeal to the ordinary man for it entails a question to which we can all respond without sophisticated argument: "Would you be willing to enter a lottery in which you had a random chance of being a black person in the United States?" We may guess that the majority

---

[2] Rawls, "Justice as Fairness," 67 *Philosophical Review* (1968), pp. 164, 165.
[3] W. Runciman, *Relative Deprivation and Social Justice* (1966), pp. 265–66.

reply is going to be negative. It would also be negative, of course, if the chance in the lottery were to be healthy or sick, assuming that the person we invite to enter the lottery is presently healthy. But the point is that being sick is for the most part a natural accident while the miseries that surround the business of being black in America are the product of past and present institutions and social practices. If these institutions and practices have resulted in a position where a person would not be willing to take a fair chance of being black then they must be condemned as unjust and a corresponding duty to rectify arises.

The application of the Rawls-Runciman approach to the position of the racial minorities in the United States does, however, present some difficulties. The approach presumes a group who are identified by their common economic depression. Now it is evidently true that there is a tremendously significant overlap in the United States between economic depression and belonging to a racial minority, but the circles are not exactly coterminous. There are many economically depressed whites and there are some prosperous black people, Puerto Ricans, Mexican-Americans, and American Indians. It is also true that the complaints of racial minorities in the United States are by no means confined to pointing to inequalities in their economic status. They complain, and again with justice, of a lack of respect paid to them by the community as a whole. Here, again, a useful distinction has been made by Mr. Runciman between the concepts of "praise" and "respect." Praise is that which we accord to a man because of his demonstrated talent or virtue; there is no injustice in praising a great writer or lawyer more than a mediocre one. Indeed it is quite proper to praise a class as a whole if we believe that most members of the class are members of it because they possess admirable skills and talents. So to praise writers or lawyers in general is unexceptionable. Praise may become an offense to principles of justice, however, when it is predicated simply on membership in a group without any evaluation of the individual's performance as a member of the group. This would be to accord respect to status irrespective of the merit of the individual. Now to denigrate one's fellow man, irrespective of his personal merit in performance or virtue, on the ground alone of his membership in a racial group or an economic class, is clearly to step out of the permissible field of praise and to move into illegitimate respect for status. There may be inequalities of praise but there must be equality of respect. Runciman writes:

> If we suppose the parties to the contract to be envisaging the possibility that different status may be accorded to them in their eventual society depending on the colour of their skin, it is obvious that they will rule out such a system on principle. If I do not know whether I shall have a black skin or a white one, I shall surely be unwilling to

agree to any principle whereby either the one or the other will secure
for me unequal treatment in the hierarchies of class, status or power.
But suppose someone wishes to defend discrimination of this kind as
no violation of social justice. It would be absurd for him to try to
describe colour prejudice in terms of differential praise. Afrikaaners
in South Africa, or white Southerners in the United States, can hardly
be described as *praising* each other for the colour of their skins. What
they accord to each other, and what the parties to the contract would
stipulate against, is differential respect.[4]

Following this kind of analysis, we might then say that some racial
minority groups, including blacks in the United States, have a well-
grounded double complaint of injustice, based partly on their grossly
unequal economic status and partly on disrespect shown to them on
the irrational basis of their race or color. Though the two claims can
be separated analytically, it is evident that they are empirically much
connected. Disrespect shown to people because of their color makes it
difficult for them to advance economically and continued economic depression makes it more difficult to eradicate irrational disrespect. But the
resolutions of the injustices are not necessarily interdependent. Economic
inequality might be eradicated without an accompanying elimination
of unjust demonstrations of disrespect, though we can surely expect the
removal of the one to have a substantial impact on the other.

There is a need, though, to distinguish between acknowledging
that black people have well-grounded complaints of injustice and
making accusations against individual members of the white majority
or against whites in general. There are probably not more than a few
black people today who were ever formally slaves, and there are
probably even fewer white slave owners surviving. Whether a white
person is guilty of injustice must depend on a careful examination of his
personal behavior, for the recognition of a victim of social injustice does
not automatically identify a doer of injustice. There is, in some black
polemics, an unfortunate tendency to talk about the guilt of the white
man as almost some inverted version of the white man's burden. This
is fashionably expressed in such obscure accusatory phrases as "unconscious racism."

One could, I suppose, be an unconscious racist. This I think would
have to mean either (1) that in spite of impeccable behavior one
harbored irrational fears or fantasies about racial distinctions or (2)
(in the stronger sense) that, while professing egalitarian attitudes one
was impelled into more or less subtle acts of racial discrimination by
the presence of such unconscious fears and fantasies. Undoubtedly there

---

4 *Id.* at 275–76.

are white and black people who suffer from this second type of personality defect. As used in certain black polemics, however, the term "unconscious racism" has lost this sensible and limited connotation and has become simply a scourge to be applied to white people in general. As such it is tinged with the element of injustice to which I referred earlier; it shows disrespect to a person because of his status, in this case the white color of his skin, without making any effort to examine his personal performance and merits.

The term "unconscious racism" may have a third meaning. It may refer to white people who, while they behave impeccably in the sense that they never commit an overt act that might be tinged with racism, are felt to be guilty of inertia or indolence or indifference in that they are doing little or nothing in an affirmative way to improve the position of black people in the United States. This charge, if it should be brought, has legitimate aspects to it, but I think it is most inappropriately put are doing little or nothing in an affirmative way to improve the position of the human race that in their personal lives they are slow and lazy about righting social wrongs and miseries. Black people are, I believe, just as guilty of this as white people, for their common humanity makes this inevitable. If white people are not active enough in doing something about the social injustice suffered by black people, neither are black people active enough in helping the American Indian or the mentally ill or the starving Biafrans. We are most of us indolent most of the time, and it is very proper that we should be reminded that this is a failing, but it is also proper to point out that it is not equivalent to the offense of racism.

But even if the charge of racism is perhaps unfairly made against many white people, the sins of omission of which most are guilty are grievous enough in this context. For the injustices, economic and social, under which blacks in America labor are the product of institutions and practices which for the most part were and are operated by whites for white advantage. The white majority thus cannot escape the affirmative duty to take positive steps of rectification.

Any translation into action of an acknowledgment of injustice of this sort must involve traumatic readjustments. In the first place it may necessitate a confession that, no matter how great the wealth of the United States, we cannot afford the costs of an adventurist and aggressive foreign policy while huge expenditures are needed to mount an attack on social injustices at home. Secondly, there may be a need to increase levels of taxation in the United States to something approaching the rates that apply in Britain. However painful this step, it must be faced as the most elementary necessity in paying an equitable debt. The surplus wealth accumulated might in part be directly redistributed as suggested by negative income tax proposals; enormous sums must be invested in housing, education, health services and job training. Both at a governmental level and with private institutions it will probably also be necessary in the short run to institute a policy of discrimination in reverse in favor of disadvantaged groups. The Republic of Ireland and other nations accept a policy of tax exemption and other inducements for industrialists who will set up factories in their territory. The Government of the United States has encouraged the aircraft industry and the oil industry with generous tax concessions. If the general interests of the economy can be taken as a justification for concessions to certain industries, concessions which must inevitably increase the private wealth of those who are financially concerned in these industries, then why should the social policy of correcting injustices not be a justification for similar steps? Why can we not offer tax concessions and other economic aid to business enterprises which can satisfy certain criteria relating to the contribution they make to the disadvantaged groups and the participation of members of disadvantaged groups in their financial and managerial aspects? Small movements in this direction are already visible through some operations of the Office of Economic Opportunity, grants made by the Small Business Administration, and especially through the efforts of some private foundations, but a much larger channeling of public funds into this effort is surely a matter of urgency.

Already some private institutions are in some degree pursuing a program of discrimination in reverse in favor of minority groups. These practices are probably at the moment mostly confined to educational institutions who officially or unofficially admit black and other minority group students who have less than normal admission qualifications. They certainly raise the most sensitive and difficult issues that surround the demands of social justice in this area, for they involve making decisions and choices which are bound to give rise to counterclaims of injustice. What if a white student has to be refused admission to a college so that a place can be found for a black student of lower qualifications? The white student will almost certainly feel aggrieved and might reasonably raise a complaint of injustice. There is no perfectly satisfactory solution for this dilemma. We must acknowledge that the large institutional changes which will be necessary in order to achieve rectification of major social injustices can only be accomplished at the cost of some individual injustice. The cost must of course be minimized and nobody should be asked to bear too heavy a burden of sacrifice. If our white student were to be denied a college education at all, the sacrifice would be too great reasonably to be imposed. If the sacrifice requires that he attend a somewhat less desirable college, it is one that in the short run we may have to demand if there is to be any acceleration of the social advance of underprivileged groups.

With admission to educational institutions one of the most vexing questions is the precise identification of a disadvantaged applicant. We might simply and bluntly say that we mean Negroes, Puerto Ricans, Mexican-Americans, and American Indians and leave it at that. But then what if the black applicant comes from a rich family and went to an excellent school before applying to the present institution? Should he receive the preferential treatment which would not be accorded to the son of an unemployed white West Virginia coal miner? The proper answer here must be in the nature of a compromise. In the first place it would be wrong to make race or color the sole criterion of disadvantage, particularly for admission to universities and the granting of scholarship assistance. Disadvantage is admittedly an impossibly elusive concept to capture in any set of rules. A young person's early educational preparation may be deficient through no fault of his own for a wide variety of reasons, ranging through bad schools to emotional stress in the family. But while we cannot hope to be subtle enough in our valuations to assess nicely the amount of compensation called for in such cases, we can certainly establish criteria which have to do fairly broadly with economic disadvantage and which are not confined to questions of race. While this would enable us to extend the preferential treatment to the son of the unemployed white West Virginia coal miner, should it lead us to deny the preference to the black applicant who comes from a rich family and went to an excellent school? I think not, because black people are disadvantaged as a group and what is therefore most necessary is that large numbers of them should be assisted along the paths of economic and educational advancement. This need is so pressing that in the short run at least the mere fact of a person's being black in the United States is a sufficient reason for providing compensatory techniques even though that person may in some ways appear fortunate in his personal background. As a member of the black minority he has almost certainly in any case suffered from disrespect shown by some in the majority group; but, even if he may have been personally lucky enough to escape this, the question of social justice is here a question of group advancement and we may legitimately use him for the benefit of his group. It is, as I have already suggested, impermissible to impose too great a sacrifice on an individual to further the ends of social justice, but it could hardly be argued that conferring a medium-sized benefit on an individual is not a legitimate way of pursuing objectives for a group.

It should be emphasized that techniques of discrimination in reverse ought to be regarded as a short-term measure for meeting a crisis of thundering urgency. Such techniques are ones that we should use reluctantly for the moral reason that they do sometimes involve imposing sacrifices on other individuals and for the utilitarian reason that they have a tendency to arouse resentment in other groups. The ideal to which we must work is of course the provision of a basic primary educational system which will be of such uniformly good quality on a national level that, combined with the elimination of gross economic inequality, it will remove the necessity for compensatory expedients. But this end will not be achieved in a year or two and, in the meantime, justice requires that we cannot stand by and ignore the hopelessly uncompetitive position into which the inequities of our social system have forced many people. And at the same time a short-term program of discrimination in reverse can be justified by the argument that it is itself a powerful technique for advancing the crusade against group inequalities and therefore, if successful, will remove the reason for its own existence.

I have suggested earlier that the claim of injustice put up by black people in the United States is compounded of gross economic inequality and lack of respect and that advancement in one of these directions will not inevitably bring comparable advancement in the other. The claim to respect is certainly not a demand for love and black people often point out perfectly reasonably that they are not very bothered whether white people love them or not. Manifestations of disrespect, however, are a social and not a private emotional phenomenon and they can scarcely fail to make a minority uncomfortable when practiced by a large majority. It is to be hoped that in the United States the now well-established and on the whole vigorous legal campaign to enforce the civil rights of black people, coupled with the only incipient program to improve their economic opportunities, will in a reasonable space of time diminish to manageable proportions the injustice of disrespect.

But if, in the passage of a reasonable time which need not be specified, there is a showing of fundamental failure either in the economic elevation of the black community or in the respect it receives in the community at large, black Americans will then have cause for a fundamental reappraisal of their attitude to the United States as a political society. They would be in a position to advance a strong moral case for political separatism, which might either take the form of partition and a black republic or a demand for black autonomous enclaves within the federal framework. This is not a comment on the prospects of political success that would attend such demands but only an assertion that such claims would then be morally well grounded. Demands of this nature are already voiced by some elements of black leadership. If the white majority in the United States is seriously interested in avoiding a situation in which these demands could be presented with justification, then it will have to commit itself with determination and urgency to a policy of reparation that can eradicate the deep stains of social injustice from American society.

Reasonable Progress and Self-Respect *

Virginia Held †

How long is it reasonable to expect the victims of gross social inequity to wait for the redress of their grievances? Clearly, if *no* aspect of a gradual improvement is going to benefit a given individual in that individual's lifetime, it is not in the interest of that individual to wait for the fruits of that improvement. On the other hand, if equality can be achieved quickly only at the price of much pain and destruction, should an individual accept progressive rather than immediate solutions?

I shall try to consider in this paper some aspects of what might be thought of as "reasonable progress" toward equality, progress that would be so gradual as to require the violation of a person's self-respect. I shall try to suggest, at least at an abstract level, some grounds on which an aggrieved individual might, with self-respect, reasonably accept a given rate of progress as satisfactory, or reject it as unsatisfactory.

This discussion will have to do entirely with what John Rawls calls "partial compliance theory," which considers principles appropriate for dealing with injustice. Rawls is not himself primarily concerned with such questions in his theory of justice; he asserts that "ideal theory . . . provides . . . the only basis for the systematic grasp of these more pressing problems." [1] From a different vantage point, however, these priorities of theory may be questioned. If the existence of a particular injustice confronts one inescapably, it would seem that questions of dealing with it may well be raised before a satisfactory settlement of the problems of ideal theory can be reached.

* Reprinted from *The Monist*, Vol. 57, No. 1 (1973), La Salle, Illinois, with the permission of the author and publisher.
† I wish to thank Sidney Morgenbesser and Mary Mothersill for their very helpful, patient—and conflicting—comments on this paper.

[1] John Rawls, *A Theory of Justice* (Cambridge, Mass.: The Belknap Press of Harvard University Press, 1971), pp. 8–9.

Equality, Justice, and Occupational Opportunities

It is possible that some suggestions made here may be applicable to a wider range of issues than those I shall consider, to a delineation, perhaps, of criteria on which a reasonable person faced with large-scale existing injustices in many arrangements of a given society might choose between policies of "reform" and policies of "revolution." But I shall limit my discussion to a particular aspect of what I take to be existing injustice. I shall assume that on any plausible account of the meanings or principles of justice and equality, and of the connection between them,[2] one aspect of injustice in an advanced society is the large-scale failure to provide what I shall call "an equal opportunity for occupational attainment." For any individual faced with such failure, the question will arise: what should be done to deal with this injustice, and are there principles which should guide a reasonable person in deciding? I will take for granted that it is eminently reasonable for any member of an advanced and economically, politically and legally substantial social system, to expect equal occupational opportunities. And I will take for granted that a society failing to provide such opportunities is, in that respect, unjust. To have an equal chance, whether one is male or female, white or nonwhite, for the unequal attainments of our various occupations is one requirement of justice. Justice is here at issue not because the concepts of justice and equality are interchangeable, but because one respect in which all persons deserve to be treated as equals is in the provisions by a society of equal opportunities for occupational attainments.

Recent figures show that 96 percent of the jobs in the United States providing an income of more than $15,000 a year are held by white males. Women and nonwhites share the remaining 4 percent about equally.[3] A separate recent study of 5000 women aged thirty to forty-four who had worked full time every year since leaving school, acquiring as much job experience as men in the same age group, shows that women consistently earn far less than men of the same age, with the same education, in the same sorts of occupations.[4] Comparable conclusions have often been drawn concerning the higher earnings of white as compared to nonwhites. As one gazes about at the leading institutions—political, economic, aca-

---

[2] Among the more important recent discussions, in addition to Rawls's, are Alan Gewirth, "The Justification of Egalitarian Justice," *American Philosophical Quarterly,* 8, No. 4 (October, 1971), 331–41; Stanley I. Benn, "Egalitarianism and the Equal Consideration of Interests," and Hugo A. Bedau, "Radical Egalitarianism," both in *Justice and Equality,* ed. by Hugo A. Bedau (Englewood Cliffs, N.J.: Prentice-Hall, Inc., 1971).

[3] John Kenneth Galbraith, Edwin Kuh, and Lester C. Thurow, "The Galbraith Plan to Promote the Minorities," *New York Times Magazine,* August 22, 1971.

[4] *New York Times,* March 26, 1972, IV, p. 6.

demic—of the society around us, the virtual exclusion of women and nonwhites from their leading positions is too clearly visible to require comment.

Women and nonwhites do not now have anything remotely resembling equal occupational attainments, with all that such attainments provide in the way of independence, self-development, well-being, and the capacity to affect one's society. Nor do women and nonwhites now have equal opportunities to enter into various occupations and to advance within them, although the extent of this inequality is somewhat more difficult to ascertain. It cannot be known in advance whether genuinely equal opportunities would produce equal occupational attainments, between persons, groups, sexes, races. But this truism should not be used, as it has been, as a ground for claiming that current disparities of attainment indicate nothing about disparities of opportunity.

A lack of "equal opportunity for occupational attainment" involves more than overt discrimination at the point of hiring or promotion, although evidence of even this is widespread and well known. Background conditions, such as unequal treatment relating to occupational preparation and expectations, in the course of childhood upbringing and education, ego development, psychological counseling, technical and higher education, etc., which would make it more difficult for women and nonwhites as a group than for white males as a group to succeed occupationally, are factors contributing to the denial of equal opportunities for occupational attainment. Expectations that other obligations, such as those of caring for children, automatically fall more heavily on mothers as a group than they do on fathers as a group, or on society at large, contribute to the denial of equal opportunities because they make attainment of even the lower occupational levels, and to a greater extent the levels above the lower ones, more difficult for women as a group than for men as a group. Of course there will be difficulties in determining which background conditions are significant and relevant and which are unavoidable or trivial.[5] Still, where the discussion concerns the lack of

---

[5] In "Equality of Opportunity," *Ethics*, 81, No. 3 (April, 1971), Charles Frankel presents the following example: "Suppose it were the case . . . that I really could have competed successfully with Mickey Mantle, but that, being a city boy, I was discouraged from a very early age from doing so. My parents put other goals before me; there was not enough open space to play; my companions were an improperly motivated group who never offered me competition sufficient to challenge me, and who, in fact, often preferred to read books. . . . If all this were the case, why could I not complain that I never had equality of opportunity with Mickey Mantle?" But as long as gross inequalities of opportunity exist for vast numbers of persons because of such very fundamental attributes as sex and race, it is relatively unnecessary for us to be concerned with whether such minor additional factors as those here described should also be considered.

occupational equality for a group defined by such completely basic characteristics as sex and race, avoidable background conditions which can be judged to make occupational attainments for members of such groups more difficult merely by their possession of these characteristics can be taken to be factors contributing to a lack of equal opportunities for occupational attainments.

Certainly, equality of opportunity is not enough. Even if everyone in a given group had an equal opportunity for, say, economic reward, we should still be repelled by an outcome such that some groan in hunger while others drown in superfluity. A society that provided equal opportunities for occupational attainment might be highly and unjustifiably inegalitarian if the gap between the satisfactions of and powers attached to these occupations were unduly wide, or if the total number of positions available—of all kinds or of any given kind—were unjustifiably limited. Here, however, I shall concentrate on equality of opportunity for participation in a given total of occupational activity,[6] however unjustifiably limited, or unjustifiably rewarded or structured. Admittedly, this is one small part only of the wider question of just occupational arrangements.[7]

Privileges and Pareto Criteria

It seems reasonable to assert that many of those persons now occupying favored positions within existing organizations owe their advantages to some preferential treatment: they are members of a group of persons who have been privileged in hiring and promotion in accordance with normal practices of long standing, persons who have been offered better educational preparation than others of the same basic talents, persons whose egos have been strengthened more than members of other groups, and so forth. Some such organizations now intend to discontinue

---

[6] This would not preclude splitting one position into two or more, rearranging the rewards and powers attached to given positions, or taxing those in given positions in order to provide other positions. But the grounds for doing so with which I shall be concerned will be the provision of equal occupational opportunities, not other aspects of justice or equality.

[7] In his "Critique of the Gotha Program," Marx commented that "it was in general a mistake to make a fuss about so-called *distribution* and put the principal stress on it. Any distribution whatever of the means of consumption is only a consequence of the distribution of the conditions of production themselves. . . . Vulgar socialism (and from it in turn a section of the democracy) has taken over from the bourgeois economists the consideration and treatment of distribution as independent of the mode of production. . . ." (Marx and Engels, *Basic Writings on Politics and Philosophy*, ed. by Lewis S. Feuer [New York: Doubleday & Co., Anchor Books, 1959], p. 120). Analogously, to discuss only a more just division of opportunities for current occupational activities and to be unaware of the unjustifiability of current occupational structures would approach vulgarity, and yet such discussion is worth attention as one aspect of alternative possibilities.

policies that embody preferential treatment for members of this favored group, and some are under legal pressure to begin to do so.

The terms in which new policies offering equal opportunities are usually considered are those of new policies for new jobs. When a job becomes available or a new vacancy in an existing position occurs, those who would have been privileged under previous arrangements will now be asked to face competition from others on a basis of equality in hiring and promotion. But those persons already safely occupying secure positions are not asked to yield any of their privileges,[8] either the privileges of occupancy or of enjoying the present rewards and powers attached to such occupancy. If voluntarily resigning one position is going to require the formerly privileged to suffer the exposure of equal competition, persons in secure positions are not likely to leave one position unless they have another secured that is as satisfactory; this is to exchange one privileged position for another, not to yield privilege.

What such schemes of new policies for new jobs do is to import into the area of providing occupational opportunity recommendations derived from the concept of a "Pareto optimum," or efficient economic allocation. A Pareto optimal configuration is one in which no one can be better off without someone being worse off. The criterion based on this notion provides that a distribution of goods or means of production is to be considered efficient when there is no way for one individual affected to gain without some other individual affected having to lose.[9] A change

---

[8] Professor Sidney Hook has charged that for the Department of Health, Education and Welfare to require from universities actual evidence of intentions to begin to equalize employment opportunities for minorities and women threatens to undermine the quality of our universities (Sidney Hook, "Discrimination Against the Qualified?" New York Times, Op-Ed page, November 5, 1971.) In answering this charge, J. Stanley Pottinger of HEW has explained that "attempting to awaken universities to these problems and lead them to take their own corrective action does not mean that white males on campus must now consider their days numbered" (J. Stanley Pottinger, "Come Now, Professor Hook," New York Times, Op-Ed page, December 16, 1971). And if white males in safe positions on campus are unaffected by new policies for new jobs, white males in safe positions in business corporations and the professions are affected still less by the kinds of equal opportunity policies that have been under consideration, although the attempt to require the privileged to choose their successors on a basis of equal opportunity has produced a considerable outcry. As this article goes to press, it is uncertain whether even the modest efforts of recent years to promote new policies for new jobs will be continued.

[9] I have chosen to use a formulation of the Pareto criterion in terms of individuals being "better off" or "worse off," rather than a formulation in terms of individuals having subjective preferences for one social situation or another. Of course the considerations of either approach can be read into the other, and there are problems either way, but the more objective formulation seems to me more helpful. Hence, the more psychological dissatisfaction that one individual may feel when another individual becomes "better off" will not be considered part of what makes the first individual "worse off." And, on the other side of this range of concepts, justice will not depend upon whether persons in fact do or do not at any given

such that some will gain as long as no others lose, is, by this criterion, always recommended, and a change requiring anyone to lose anything is always recommended against. Thus, in the provision of jobs, if an existing organization having no women or nonwhites above a given level creates a new position above this level or finds itself with a new vacancy here, and now, if in fairly applying the requirements for this position, a woman or nonwhite is chosen to fill it, the result is that one person gains a new position, no one else loses occupational standing already attained,[10] and Pareto criteria are satisfied.

Many persons now favoring progress toward equal opportunity imagine such policies to be adequate. But is it reasonable to expect the victims of embedded injustices to accept such terms for improvement?

Let us try to consider some aspects and implications of these issues by abstracting the following model from some situations now faced by those who are denied equal opportunities for occupational attainments:

Imagine an organization in which there are one hundred positions paying more than $15,000 a year. Many of these pay considerably more than this, and involve greater influence, and there are an indefinite number of positions in this organization which pay less than this. Following current averages, ninety-six of the one hundred positions in question are occupied by white males, two by women, two by nonwhites. I shall take becoming a member of the class of those with such positions as equivalent in this model to having an opportunity to go further in one's occupational attainments in this organization over a future period of some length. Some of those entering this class will drop out of it, some will remain at the level of entry, some will attain higher levels, some far higher ones. If we

---

point in time feel unjustly treated, but on whether there are or are not good reasons for their so feeling. On the Pareto criterion, see D. M. Winch, *Analytical Welfare Economics* (Baltimore: Penguin Books, 1971), esp. Chap. 4; Rawls, *Theory of Justice*, pp. 66–72; and A. K. Sen, *Collective Choice and Social Welfare* (San Francisco: Holden-Day, 1970), Chaps. 2 and 2*.

[10] Of course candidates who would have been unjustly favored in the past, and are no longer so favored, have in one sense "lost" an advantage they previously would have had. But since the situation considered is one where a new job or new chance for promotion is added to those already in existence, even these candidates have lost nothing relative to the situation before there was this new opening, although it is even this supposed "loss" that so angers Paul Seabury (Paul Seabury, "HEW and the Universities," *Commentary*, 53, No. 2 [February, 1972]). One could well argue that if women and nonwhites are not only treated equally for the new position but favored for them, this is just in hastening the end of injustices which they, as a group, have suffered in the past. However, that only *new* positions are available for such a purpose is unjust, in that it puts the entire burden of ending past injustices towards women and nonwhites on the other candidates for new positions and none at all on those in entrenched positions of privilege. But this is to argue, once again, the deficiences of Pareto criteria in dealing with situations of injustice.

assume that disparity would be the result of lack of equal opportunity and its causes rather than because of a disparity in wholly free choices not to seek occupational attainments, then equal opportunity between groups for further attainments in this organization would require equal representation among those becoming members of this class.

Suppose that under normal conditions of growth, turnover, and retirement, one new position paying more than $15,000 a year (in constant dollars) is created by this organization each year, and four positions are vacated by turnover, retirement, etc. Let us say, then, that the five positions open each year are filled on a basis of equality. To simplify the problem I shall calculate the expectations for women only although comparable calculations could be made for nonwhites. Due to past inequalities at lower and wider levels, the supply of candidates for these positions would be, let us say, averaged over the span of time involved, four male to one female. Given the fair application of criteria requiring equality in filling these positions, let us say that one additional woman per year would succeed in entering the class of those with positions earning more than $15,000, while there would be no loss in the number of women already holding such positions.

At this rate, it would take some ninety-four years for women to achieve equal occupational opportunities to go further in this organization. If we revise the four to one figure, given the changes that might occur over so long a period, we might assume it to be as nearly equal as three male to two female, with two women per year entering the class of those able to continue to progress. It would still take some forty-seven years for women to achieve equal opportunities for occupational attainments in this organization, never mind what persons with equal opportunities would be able to do in advancing further, once they had entered the class in question.

Obviously, no one can have any plausible interest in waiting ninety-four years for equality. Nor can anyone have a serious interest in waiting forty-seven years, since those embarking upon an occupation even at as early an age as twenty will have passed the normal point of retirement before attaining it.

A scheme in which no one now holding a privileged position will be asked to relinquish anything, and only such vacancies as occur through death, retirement, and the creation of new positions will be filled on a basis of equal opportunity, is hardly in the interests of all those who will gain nothing from such a change. Can an individual person justifiably accept such a policy, which will very slightly increase the possibilities of equal opportunity for occupational attainment for any given victim of past injustice, but which will leave the vast majority of victims now seeking equal opportunities no better off than they were before? If we label progress of this kind "gradual improvement"—the application of Pareto criteria to the issue of equality of opportunity for occupational attainments—the victims of inequality have good reason to find it thoroughly unacceptable.

Pareto criteria are questionable even when one can presume a satisfactory base line, because they ignore relative positions between persons, and it might well be the case that if one person of a pair were to gain a substantial increase in power, say, this would upset a satisfactory relation between them even though the second person were to lose no power himself.[11] However, Pareto criteria are not merely questionable but highly inadequate in dealing with situations of injustice and inequality.[12] As A. K. Sen has expressed it, "a society or an economy can be Pareto-optimal and still be perfectly disgusting,"[13] and among the ways in which it can be disgusting is in its injustice.

At worst, Pareto criteria contribute to a deepening of injustice, judging it a good thing that someone with excessive wealth or power gain even more of them, as long as no one else loses the pathetic, meagre amount he or she already has. At best, Pareto criteria simply fail to contribute anything towards correcting injustice, since they do not provide a basis for favoring the gain of the exploited over the gain of the exploiters. In any case, Pareto criteria are simply beside the point where the issue is not an addition to the existing amount of goods, services, jobs or opportunities, but a problem of dividing more equally, or fairly distributing, the existing amounts, whatever they are. To apply Pareto criteria to current patterns of gross inequality of opportunities for occupational attainments is to make less than a token gesture toward equality. And as growth becomes less and less the automatic goal of advanced economies and organizations, Pareto criteria become less and less suitable for dealing with their distributions of employment opportunities. But what alternatives should the victims strive for?

---

11 What is meant is not merely that the second person in fact does not feel resentment before the change, but that the relation is satisfactory in some more objective sense.

12 And this is the case even when one leaves out entirely any consideration of justice in the retributive sense, or even in a sense justifying rehabilitation. The latter might require that if one set of persons had for thousands of years been the victims of gross inequality, the beneficiaries of such victimization should themselves, for some comparable time span, experience some comparable or appropriate inequality. But in spite of longstanding injustices benefiting white males at the expense of women and nonwhites, no victims or critics seriously advocate a society in which white males would be relegated to the occupational opportunities now available to women and nonwhites, even for a short period, to broaden their experience and sharpen their perceptions, much less on grounds of retribution.

13 Collective Choice and Social Welfare, p. 22.

Rights, Interests and Self-respect

If we abandon Pareto criteria, and the illusion that equality can be attained with no loss to anyone, we may ask who should be asked to lose how much, and what interests must be taken into account. Justice does not depend on such calculations of interest; justice confers rights. It is clear that women and nonwhites have rights to equal opportunities for occupational attainments based on the concepts of justice and equality I have assumed. But the issue here involves their interests in alternative approaches to achieving these rights in practice, rights the realization of which they are at present being denied in avoidable ways.[14] In considering this question, we are dealing with the justifiability of alternative courses of action. And we might seem, in this transitional period, to have to consider the interests of one group in preventing this realization. Such a conflict ought not to arise; where it does it ought to be settled on grounds of rights, not interests. And yet it is not being so settled, and those whose rights are being thwarted must choose, if they can, justifiable courses of action to take in such circumstances. On what grounds can such a choice be made? In considering this question, it may be helpful to try to delineate the requirements of self-respect.

When rights conflict, it may happen that some rights are unavoidably denied to some persons. If we consider not a right to compete on equal terms for a given job, but, say, a right to a job, we may say that where persons have the positions they do as a result of the fair application of justifiable procedures, there may be a conflict between the rights of these persons to their jobs, and the rights of other persons to comparable jobs. The solution might then be to increase the total number of jobs, and by an adequate effort of the society to redistribute resources towards the provision of employment and away from other things, to provide for the realization of both sets of rights.

But where persons have acquired their positions as a result of unjustifiable procedures, we can conclude that although they may have interests in maintaining these positions, they do not have rights to do so. And if their maintaining these positions prevents the realization of the rights of others, we can conclude that the rights of these others are being avoidably denied.

Avoidably to deny to persons their rights is an affront to their self-respect. For persons to acquiesce in the avoidable denial of their own rights is to lack self-respect. As between forms of nonacquiescence, it is

---

[14] I have intentionally not distinguished here between moral and legal rights, since the discussion is, I think, independent of the kind of rights being asserted, although of course for other contexts this would have to be clarified.

reasonable for persons whose rights are being avoidably denied to act fully in accordance with their interests, without regard to the interests of others in denying them such rights; then, for them voluntarily to yield their own interests in securing their rights to the interests of others in thwarting them is incompatible with their self-respect.

To act without regard for the interests of those with superior power is to court disaster and to risk various aspects of destruction on both sides. But if anything less is incompatible with self-respect, could any alternative be acceptable? Are there moral obligations, perhaps, which supersede self-respect? Perhaps the victims of injustice have an obligation to future generations to temper the pursuit of their interests in realizing their rights and to avoid the risks of destruction and institutional breakdown, so that although they themselves will gain nothing from a slow improvement, their children will enjoy its benefits. But this consideration seems balanced or outweighed by the wrongness of allowing the present beneficiaries of unjust privileges to continue their victimization undisturbed.

The Risks of Immediate Equality

Let us return to our previous model in which we can view some relevant choices at an abstract level. Let us consider an alternative under which all positions based on privilege in this organization would be suddenly vacated and let us label it "immediate equality." Of course in reality not all white males are in the same situation: some may themselves have suffered from an inequality of occupational opportunity, some may occupy their positions by right rather than privilege. But if in our model we suppose that all the occupied positions in this organization are reopened and refilled through selection procedures providing equality of opportunity, this should not disturb those who rightfully hold their positions, since they will regain them.

Assuming that such a transformation could be brought about somehow (a huge assumption, of course, but not one to be dealt with here) either by organized boycotts, by strikes, by disruptions, by political pressure leading to legislation, or by judicial decision, it would require a kind of destruction of the organizational supports of the class of persons holding positions of power in this organization, and might seem plausibly, in this context, an overthrow of an existing arrangement. It would not result in immediate equality of opportunity as defined in this model, because the supply of candidates would remain artificially unequal for at least a short period of time, but it would result in a dramatically rapid rate of progress: on the first candidate ratio assumed above, already highly optimistic for this context, if the privileged positions would be reopened annually, equal opportunity could be achieved in little more than three years.

If one could suppose that the organization, and the occupational positions being sought, would remain virtually intact, and that the only change would be for the privileged class of persons now to face competition for their positions on a basis of equality, every victim of past injustice would have an overwhelming interest in "immediate equality." In justifiably pursuing his or her own interests in realizing his or her rights, the only problem would be to weigh huge gains immediately against the same gains in the far distant future, and the solution would be obvious.

But we would have little basis for such a supposition. Some of those actually occupying established positions are rightfully there, and most seem to have an entrenched belief, which they would not be willing to test, that they belong to this group. Privileged classes can probably not be expected to yield to even the most just demands without resistance. Hence, a more plausible assumption for this model would be that many of the privileged would resist the sudden overthrow of the organizational supports of their positions even to the point of the destruction of the organization and the occupational activities within it, and that many others would be willing to accept the risks of such resistance.

So we might have to suppose that the immediate realization of equal opportunities for occupational attainments in this organization would lead to the breakdown of the organization and its positions. In that case, opportunities for the formerly privileged and the formerly victimized would be equal only because they were, in this organization, nil for both. And in that case the former victims would gain nothing from "immediate equality" as they would gain nothing from "gradual improvement," and the history of victimization would continue in either case.

Neither course of action would be in the interests of those seeking the realization of their rights. And yet, there is a difference between the two forms of defeat as here outlined. If the victims of inequality choose "immediate equality" in this context, they *risk* defeat; if they choose "gradual improvement" in this context, they accept defeat as certain. *Given such a choice, the former seems compatible with self-respect in a way in which the latter does not.*

Of course the supposition that there might be collective action on the part of the victims to bring about change is open to question. The more likely prospect might remain individual defiance of the organization denying equality of opportunity, and defeat of the defiant individual by the organization's privileged members. But even at the individual level, to risk defeat in attaining equality is compatible with self-respect in a way in which acquiescing in certain defeat is not. And recognition of this might plausibly bring the argument back to a consideration of the collective policy which would be justifiable, and which would, if anything could, reduce the likelihood of defeat.

Alternatives to Defeat

Other alternatives than these two forms of defeat should of course be considered. Instead of supposing certain defeat through "gradual improvement" and a risk of defeat through "immediate equality," predictions of our actual situation might be such as to indicate certain defeat through "immediate equality," and only probable defeat through "gradual improvement." This is the picture which established organizations have an interest in promoting: they suggest that if those who have suffered injustices will be patient, attitudes will change, and the rate of improvement will increase. But for this assertion to be plausible, there would have to be evidence of an increase in the rate of equalization, and as long as Pareto criteria continue to be applied, there is no reason to suppose any such increase to be likely. Clarity about the actual yields to be produced by given rates of progress can do much to dispel illusions on these matters.

From what has been said before, we can conclude that for a person to accept the certain defeat of his or her interests in realizing a right is incompatible with that person's self-respect. For a person to risk the probable defeat of these interests may be compatible with self-respect, when these are the only choices, but it may be personally as well as socially destructive. We can add that for an organization to try to buy off selected individuals by offering them a personal increase in the probabilities of their own opportunities for occupational attainments only at the expense of a decrease in the probabilities for other victims, is to make an unjust and probably coercive offer [15] incompatible with the self-respect of all the victims.

But if Pareto criteria produce a rate of progress in equalization incompatible with the self-respect of the victims of injustice, and if the immediate realization of equality would lead to self-defeating institutional breakdown, what alternative could be recommended? The situation as outlined is highly volatile. Persons facing almost certain defeat no matter which course they choose are desperate persons, for whom slight possibilities of escape from these alternatives loom disproportionately acceptable. Any risk, no matter how little it promises, is better than certain defeat. Those who have nothing to lose have everything to gain, and

---

[15] For a discussion, see Virginia Held, "Coercion and Coercive Offers," in *Coercion*, NOMOS XIV, ed. by J. Ronald Pennock and John W. Chapman (Chicago: Aldine-Atherton, 1972).

since a willingness to take risks tends to vary inversely with the magnitude of the loss being risked, those for whom desperate measures are an only hope will not be lacking in such willingness.

It is hard to see any plausible grounds on which to recommend a given rate of progress in achieving equal opportunity as acceptable. Yet it may perhaps be worth considering, as an alternative to "gradual improvement" and "immediate equality" as outlined in the above model, a midpoint of some sort. While there is nothing at all conclusive about a majority vote, or a better than .5 probability, or about compromise as such, in the absence of reasons not to accept such midpoints, they do in other spheres of human activity provide at least *a* reason in favor of acceptance, although never a conclusive one. Among a given group of people, when we have no reason to reject a majority vote, that a majority favors a given position may provide one reason to accept it. For a given uncertain outcome, that its probability is greater than even gives us one reason, though not a strong one, to except [accept] it. And as between two irreconcilable positions, we have a reason to begin the process of resolution at a point midway between them.

If such suggestions could be adapted to the problem at hand, we might consider their relevance to accepting or rejecting a given rate of progress. If we take as given a person's expectable span of years of working life, could we then say that a rate of progress providing equal opportunities for occupational attainments by its midpoint should be acknowledged as having *a* ground, however inconclusive, for acceptance? Thus, to take our previous example, if a person at age twenty might realistically expect equal opportunities by the age of forty-two, this would provide almost half of this person's expected working years without equality, and a shade more than half with equality. For the victims of injustice as discussed here, torn between prospects of defeat, such terms for ending that injustice might not seem incompatible with their self-respect, although waiting any longer might be.

Yet to provide progress at even such a plodding rate would require efforts to bring about equalization considerably beyond those currently receiving even token discussion. Such efforts would of course require those occupying positions of unjustified privilege to accept some loss of their privileges, though quite possibly indirectly, through some form of taxation for the provision of other positions, and through the rearrangement of occupational activities, and the conditions for them.

It is, certainly, painful to lose privileges. But it is not incompatible with one's self-respect. On the contrary, to continue to benefit willingly from injustice, particularly after one is aware that one is doing so, would seem to be incompatible with the respect a reasonable person should accord himself as a moral being.

Equal Treatment and Compensatory Discrimination *

Thomas Nagel

It is currently easier, or widely thought to be easier, to get certain jobs or to gain admission to certain educational institutions if one is black or a woman than if one is a white man. Whether or not this is true, many people think it should be true, and many others think it should not. The question is: If a black person or a woman is admitted to a law school or medical school, or appointed to a certain academic or administrative post, in preference to a white man who is in other respects better qualified,[1] and if this is done in pursuit of a preferential policy or to fill a quota, is it unjust? Can the white man complain that he has been unjustly treated? It is important to investigate the justice of such practices, because if they are unjust, it is much more difficult to defend them on grounds of social utility. I shall argue that although preferential policies are not required by justice, they are not seriously unjust either—because the system from which they depart is already unjust for reasons having nothing to do with racial or sexual discrimination.

I

In the United States, the following steps seem to have led us to a situation in which these questions arise. First, and not very long ago, it came to be widely accepted that deliberate barriers against the admission

---

* "Equal Treatment and Compensatory Discrimination," by Thomas Nagel, *Philosophy and Public Affairs*, Vol. II, No. 4. Copyright © 1973 by Princeton University Press, pp. 348–63. Reprinted by permission of Princeton University Press.

[1] By saying that the white man is "in other respects better qualified" I mean that if, e.g., a black candidate with similar qualifications had been available for the position, he would have been selected in preference to the black candidate who was in fact selected; or, if the choice had been between two white male candidates of corresponding qualifications, this one would have been selected. Ditto for two white or two black women. (I realize that it may not always be easy to determine similarity of qualifications, and that in some cases similarity of credentials may give evidence of a difference in qualifications—because, e.g., one person had to overcome more severe obstacles to acquire those credentials.)

of blacks and women to desirable positions should be abolished. Their abolition is by no means complete, and certain educational institutions, for example, may be able to maintain limiting quotas on the admission of women for some time. But deliberate discrimination is widely condemned.

Secondly, it was recognized that even without explicit barriers there could be discrimination, either consciously or unconsciously motivated, and this gave support to self-conscious efforts at impartiality, careful consideration of candidates belonging to the class discriminated against, and attention to the proportions of blacks and women in desirable positions, as evidence that otherwise undetectable bias might be influencing the selections. (Another, related consideration is that criteria which were good predictors of performance for one group might turn out to be poor predictors of performance for another group, so that the continued employment of those criteria might introduce a concealed inequity.)

The third step came with the realization that a social system may continue to deny different races or sexes equal opportunity or equal access to desirable positions even after the discriminatory barriers to those positions have been lifted. Socially-caused inequality in the capacity to make use of available opportunities or to compete for available positions may persist, because the society systematically provides to one group more than to another certain educational, social, or economic advantages. Such advantages improve one's competitive position in seeking access to jobs or places in professional schools. Where there has recently been widespread deliberate discrimination in many areas, it will not be surprising if the formerly excluded group experiences relative difficulty in gaining access to newly opened positions, and it is plausible to explain the difficulty at least partly in terms of disadvantages produced by past discrimination. This leads to the adoption of compensatory measures, in the form of special training programs, or financial support, or day-care centers, or apprenticeships, or tutoring. Such measures are designed to qualify those whose reduced qualifications are due to racial or sexual discrimination, either because they have been the direct victims of such discrimination, or because they are deprived as a result of membership in a group or community many of whose other members have been discriminated against. The second of these types of influence covers a great deal, and the importance of the social contribution is not always easy to establish. Nevertheless its effects typically include the loss of such goods as self-esteem, self-confidence, motivation, and ambition—all of which contribute to competitive success and none of which is easily restored by special training programs. Even if social injustice has produced such effects, it may be difficult for society to eradicate them.

This type of justification for compensatory programs raises another question. If it depends on the claim that the disadvantages being compensated for are the product of social injustice, then it becomes important how great the contribution of social injustice actually is, and to what extent the situation is due to social causes not involving injustice, or to causes that are not social, but biological. If one believes that society's responsibility for compensatory measures extends only to those disadvantages due to social injustice, one will assign political importance to the degree, if any, to which racial differences in average I.Q. are genetically influenced, or the innate contribution, if any, to the statistical differences, if any, in emotional or intellectual characteristics between men and women. Also, if one believes that among socially-produced inequalities, there is a crucial distinction for the requirement of compensation between those which are produced unjustly and those which are merely the incidental results of just social arrangements, then it will be very important to decide exactly where that line falls: whether, for example, certain intentions must be referred to in arguing that a disadvantage has been unjustly imposed. But let me put those issues aside for the moment.

The fourth stage comes when it is acknowledged that some unjustly caused disadvantages, which create difficulties of access to positions formally open to all, cannot be overcome by special programs of preparatory or remedial training. One is then faced with the alternative of either allowing the effects of social injustice to confer a disadvantage in the access to desirable positions that are filled simply on the basis of qualifications relevant to performance in those positions, or else instituting a system of compensatory discrimination in the selection process to increase access for those whose qualifications are lower at least partly as a result of unjust discrimination in other situations and at other times (and possibly against other persons). This is a difficult choice, and it would certainly be preferable to find a more direct method of rectification, than to balance inequality in one part of the social system by introducing a reverse inequality at a different point. If the society as a whole contains serious injustices with complex effects, there is probably, in any case, no way for a single institution within that society to adjust its criteria for competitive admission or employment so that the effects of injustice are nullified as far as that institution is concerned. There is consequently considerable appeal to the position that places should be filled solely by reference to the criteria relevant to performance, and if this tends to amplify or extend the effects of inequitable treatment elsewhere, the remedy must be found in a more direct attack on those differences in qualifications, rather than in the introduction of irrelevant criteria of appointment or admission which will also sacrifice efficiency, productivity, or effectiveness of the institution in its specific tasks.

At this fourth stage we therefore find a broad division of opinion.

There are those who believe that nothing further can legitimately be done in the short run, once the *remediable* unjust inequalities of opportunity between individuals have been dealt with: the irremediable ones are unjust, but any further steps to counterbalance them by reverse discrimination would also be unjust, because they must employ irrelevant criteria. On the other hand, there are those who find it unacceptable in such circumstances to stay with the restricted criteria usually related to successful performance, and who believe that differential admission or hiring standards for worse-off groups are justified because they roughly, though only approximately, compensate for the inequalities of opportunity produced by past injustice.

But at this point there is some temptation to resolve the dilemma and strengthen the argument for preferential standards by proceeding to a fifth stage. One may reflect that if the criteria relevant to the prediction of performance are not inviolable it may not matter whether one violates them to compensate for disadvantages caused by injustice or disadvantages caused in other ways. The fundamental issue is what grounds to use in assigning or admitting people to desirable positions. To settle that issue, one does not have to settle the question of the degree to which racial or sexual discrepancies are socially produced, because the differentials in reward ordinarily correlated with differences in qualifications are not the result of natural justice, but simply the effect of a competitive system trying to fill positions and perform tasks efficiently. Certain abilities may be relevant to filling a job from the point of view of efficiency, but they are not relevant from the point of view of justice, because they provide no indication that one deserves the rewards that go with holding that job. The qualities, experience, and attainments that make success in a certain position likely do not in themselves merit the rewards that happen to attach to occupancy of that position in a competitive economy.

Consequently it might be concluded that if women or black people are less qualified, for *whatever* reason, in the respects that lead to success in the professions that our society rewards most highly, then it would be just to compensate for this disadvantage, within the limits permitted by efficiency, by having suitably different standards for these groups, and thus bringing their access to desirable positions more into line with that of others. Compensatory discrimination would not, on this view, have to be tailored to deal only with the effects of past injustice.

But it is clear that this is not a stable position. For if one abandons the condition that to qualify for compensation an inequity must be socially caused, then there is no reason to restrict the compensatory measures to well-defined racial or sexual groups. Compensatory selection procedures would have to be applied on an individual basis, within as well as between such groups—each person, regardless of race, sex, or qualifications, being granted equal access to the desirable positions, within limits set by efficiency. This might require randomization of law and medical school admissions, for example, from among all the candidates who were above some minimum standard enabling them to do the work. If we were to act on the principle that different abilities do not merit different rewards, it would result in much more equality than is demanded by proponents of compensatory discrimination.

There is no likelihood that such a radical course will be adopted in the United States, but the fact that it seems to follow naturally from a certain view about how to deal with racial or sexual injustice reveals something important. When we try to deal with the inequality in advantages that results from a disparity in qualifications (however produced) between races or sexes, we are up against a pervasive and fundamental feature of the system, which at every turn exacts costs and presents obstacles in response to attempts to reduce the inequalities. We must face the possibility that the primary injustice with which we have to contend lies in this feature itself, and that some of the worst aspects of what we now perceive as racial or sexual injustice are merely conspicuous manifestations of the great social injustice of differential reward.

II

If differences in the capacity to succeed in the tasks that any society rewards well are visibly correlated, for whatever reason, with other characteristics such as race or religion or social origin, then a system of liberal equality of opportunity will give the appearance of supporting racial or religious or class injustice. Where there is no such correlation, there can be the appearance of justice through equal opportunity. But in reality, there is similar injustice in both cases, and it lies in the schedule of rewards.

The liberal idea of equal treatment demands that people receive equal opportunities if they are equally qualified by talent or education to utilize those opportunities. In requiring the relativization of equal treatment to characteristics in which people are very unequal, it guarantees that the social order will reflect and probably magnify the initial distinctions produced by nature and the past. Liberalism has therefore come under increasing attack in recent years, on the ground that the familiar principle of equal treatment, with its meritocratic conception of relevant differences, seems too weak to combat the inequalities dispensed by nature and the ordinary workings of the social system.

This criticism of the view that people deserve the rewards that accrue to them as a result of their natural talents is not based on the idea that no one can be said to deserve anything.[2] For if no one deserves anything, then no inequalities are contrary to desert, and desert provides no argument for equality. Rather, I am suggesting that for many benefits and disadvantages, certain characteristics of the recipient *are* relevant to what he deserves. If people are equal in the relevant respects, that by itself constitutes a reason to distribute the benefit to them equally.[3]

The relevant features will vary with the benefit or disadvantage, and so will the weight of the resulting considerations of desert. Desert may sometimes, in fact, be a rather unimportant consideration in determining what ought to be done. But I do wish to claim, with reference to a central case, that differential abilities are not usually among the characteristics that determine whether people *deserve* economic and social benefits (though of course they determine whether people *get* such benefits). In fact, I believe that nearly all characteristics are irrelevant to what people deserve in this dimension, and that most people therefore deserve to be treated equally.[4] Perhaps voluntary differences in effort or moral differences in conduct have some bearing on economic and social desert. I do not have a precise view about what features are relevant. I contend only that they are features in which most people do not differ enough to justify very wide differences in reward.[5] (While I realize that these claims are controversial, I shall not try to defend them here, nor to defend the legitimacy of the notion of desert itself. If these things make no sense, neither does the rest of my argument.)

A decision that people are equally or unequally deserving in some respect is not the end of the story. First of all, desert can sometimes be

---

[2] Rawls appears to regard this as the basis of his own view. He believes it makes sense to speak of positive desert only in the context of distributions by a just system, and not as a pre-institutional conception that can be used to measure the justice of the system. John Rawls, *A Theory of Justice* (Cambridge, Mass., 1971), pp. 310–13.

[3] Essentially this view is put forward by Bernard Williams in "The Idea of Equality," in *Philosophy, Politics, and Society* (Second Series), ed. P. Laslett and W. G. Runciman (Oxford, 1964), pp. 110–31.

[4] This is distinct from a case in which nothing is relevant because there is no desert in the matter. In that case the fact that people differed in no relevant characteristics would not create a presumption that they be treated equally. It would leave the determination of their treatment entirely to other considerations.

[5] It is *not* my view that we cannot be said to deserve the *results* of anything which we do not deserve. It is true that a person does not deserve his intelligence, and I have maintained that he does not deserve the rewards that superior intelligence can provide. But neither does he deserve his bad moral character or his above-average willingness to work, yet I believe that he probably does deserve the punishments or rewards that flow from those qualities. For an illuminating discussion of these matters, see Robert Nozick, *Anarchy, State, and Utopia* (New York, Basic Books: forthcoming), Chap. 7.

overridden, for example by liberty or even by efficiency. In some cases the presumption of equality is rather weak, and not much is required to depart from it. This will be so if the interest in question is minor or temporally circumscribed, and does not represent an important value in the subject's life.

Secondly, it may be that although an inequality is contrary to desert, no one can benefit from its removal: all that can be done is to worsen the position of those who benefit undeservedly from its presence. Even if one believes that desert is a very important factor in determining just distributions, one need not object to inequalities that are to no one's disadvantage. In other words, it is possible to accept something like Rawls's Difference Principle from the standpoint of an egalitarian view of desert.[6] (I say it is possible. It may not be required. Some may reject the Difference Principle because they regard equality of treatment as a more stringent requirement.)

Thirdly (and most significantly for the present discussion), a determination of relative desert in the distribution of a particular advantage does not even settle the question of *desert* in every case, for there may be other advantages and disadvantages whose distribution is tied to that of the first, and the characteristics relevant to the determination of desert are not necessarily the same from one advantage to another. This bears on the case under consideration in the following way. I have said that people with different talents do not thereby deserve different economic and social rewards. They may, however, deserve different opportunities to exercise and develop those talents.[7] Whenever the distribution of two different types of benefit is connected in this way, through social or economic mechanisms or through natural human reactions, it may be impossible to avoid a distribution contrary to the conditions of desert in respect of at least one of the benefits. Therefore it is likely that a dilemma will arise in which it appears that injustice cannot be entirely avoided. It may then be necessary to decide that justice in the distribution of one advantage has priority over justice in the distribution of another that automatically goes with it.

In the case under discussion, there appears to be a conflict between justice in the distribution of educational and professional opportunities and justice in the distribution of economic and social rewards. I do not deny that there is a presumption, based on something more than efficiency,

---

6 Rawls, *op. cit.*, pp. 75–80.

7 Either because differences of ability are relevant to degree of desert in these respects or because people are equally deserving of opportunities proportional to their talents. More likely the latter.

in favor of giving equal opportunities to those equally likely to succeed. But if the presumption in favor of economic equality is considerably stronger, the justification for departing from it must be stronger too. If this is so, then when "educational" justice and economic justice come into conflict, it will sometimes be necessary to sacrifice the former to the latter.

III

In thinking about racial and sexual discrimination, the view that economic justice has priority may tempt one to proceed to what I have called the fifth stage. One may be inclined to adopt admission quotas, for example, proportional to the representation of a given group in the population, because one senses the injustice of differential rewards per se. Whatever explains the small number of women or blacks in the professions, it has the result that they have less of the financial and social benefits that accrue to members of the professions, and what accounts for those differences cannot justify them. So justice requires that more women and blacks be admitted to the professions.

The trouble with this solution is that it does not locate the injustice accurately, but merely tries to correct the racially or sexually skewed economic distribution which is one of its more conspicuous symptoms. We are enabled to perceive the situation as unjust because we see it, e.g., through its racial manifestations, and race is a subject by now associated in our minds with injustice. However, little is gained by merely transferring the same system of differential rewards, suitably adjusted to achieve comparable proportions, to the class of blacks or the class of women. If it is unjust to reward people differentially for what certain characteristics enable them to do, it is equally unjust whether the distinction is made between a white man and a black man or between two black men, or two white women, or two black women. There is no way of attacking the unjust reward schedules (if indeed they are unjust) of a meritocratic system by attacking their racial or sexual manifestations directly.

In most societies reward is a function of demand, and many of the human characteristics most in demand result largely from *gifts* or *talents*. The greatest injustice in this society, I believe, is neither racial nor sexual but intellectual. I do not mean that it is unjust that some people are more intelligent than others. Nor do I mean that society rewards people differentially simply on the basis of their intelligence: usually it does not. Nevertheless it provides on the average much larger rewards for tasks that require superior intelligence than for those that do not. This is simply the way things work out in a technologically ad-

vanced society with a market economy. It does not reflect a social judgment that smart people *deserve* the opportunity to make more money
than dumb people. They may deserve richer educational opportunity,
but they do not therefore deserve the material wealth that goes with it.
Similar things could be said about society's differential reward of achievements facilitated by other talents or gifts, like beauty, athletic ability,
musicality, etc. But intelligence and its development by education provide
a particularly significant and pervasive example.

However, a general reform of the current schedule of rewards, even
if they are unjust, is beyond the power of individual educational or
business institutions, working through their admissions or appointments
policies. A competitive economy is bound to reward those with certain
training and abilities, and a refusal to do so will put any business enterprise in a poor competitive position. Similarly, those who succeed in
medical school or law school will tend to earn more than those who do
not—whatever criteria of admission the schools adopt. It is not the
procedures of appointment or admission, based on criteria that predict
success, that are unjust, but rather what happens as a result of success.

No doubt a completely just solution is not ready to hand. If, as I
have claimed, different factors are relevant to what is deserved in the
distribution of different benefits and disadvantages, and if the distribution
of several distinct advantages is sometimes connected even though the
relevant factors are not, then inevitably there will be injustice in some
respect, and it may be practically impossible to substitute a principle of
distribution which avoids it completely.

Justice may require that we try to reduce the automatic connections
between material advantages, cultural opportunity, and institutional
authority. But such changes can be brought about, if at all, only by
large alterations in the social system, the system of taxation, and the
salary structure. They will not be achieved by modifying the admissions
or hiring policies of colleges and universities, or even banks, law firms,
and businesses.

Compensatory measures in admissions or appointment can be defended on grounds of justice only to the extent that they compensate
for specific disadvantages which have themselves been unjustly caused,
by factors distinct from the general meritocratic character of the system
of distribution of advantageous positions. Such contributions are difficult
to verify or estimate; they probably vary among individuals in the
oppressed group. Moreover, it is not obvious that where a justification for
preferential treatment exists, it is strong enough to create an obligation,
since it is doubtful that one element of a pluralistic society is obliged to
adopt discriminatory measures to counteract injustice due to another
element, or even to the society as a whole.

IV

These considerations suggest that an argument on grounds of justice for the imposition of racial or sexual quotas would be difficult to construct without the aid of premises about the source of unequal qualifications between members of different groups. The more speculative the premises, the weaker the argument. But the question with which I began was not whether compensatory discrimination is *required* by justice, but whether it is *compatible* with justice. To that question I think we can give a different answer. If the reflections about differential reward to which we have been led are correct, then compensatory discrimination need not be seriously unjust, and it may be warranted not by justice but by considerations of social utility. I say not *seriously* unjust, to acknowledge that a departure from the standards relevant to distribution of intellectual opportunities *per se* is itself a kind of injustice. But its seriousness is lessened because the factors relevant to the distribution of intellectual opportunity are irrelevant to the distribution of those material benefits that go with it. This weakens the claim of someone who argues that by virtue of those qualities that make him likely to succeed in a certain position, he deserves to be selected for that position in preference to someone whose qualifications make it likely that he will succeed less well. He cannot claim that justice requires the allocation of positions on the basis of ability, because the result of such allocation, in the present system, is serious injustice of a different kind.

My contention, then, is that where the allocation of one benefit on relevant grounds carries with it the allocation of other, more significant benefits to which those grounds are irrelevant, the departure from those grounds need not be a serious offense against justice. This may be so for two reasons. First, the presumption of equal treatment of relevantly equal persons in respect of the first benefit may not be very strong to begin with. Second, the fairness of abiding by that presumption may be overshadowed by the unfairness of the other distribution correlated with it. Consequently, it may be acceptable to depart from the "relevant" grounds for undramatic reasons of social utility, that would not justify more flagrant and undiluted examples of unfairness. Naturally a deviation from the usual method will appear unjust to those who are accustomed to regarding ability to succeed as the correct criterion, but this appearance may be an illusion. That depends on how much injustice is involved in the usual method, and whether the reasons for departing from it are good enough, even though they do not correct the injustice.

The problem, of course, is to say what a good reason is. I do not want to produce an argument that will justify not only compensatory discrimination on social grounds, but also ordinary racial or sexual discrimination designed to preserve internal harmony in a business, for instance. Even someone who thought that the system of differential economic rewards for different abilities was unjust would presumably regard it as an *additional* injustice if standard racial, religious, or sexual discrimination were a factor in the assignment of individuals to highly rewarded positions.

I can offer only a partial account of what makes systematic racial or sexual discrimination so exceptionally unjust. It has no social advantages, and it attaches a sense of reduced worth to a feature with which people are born.[8] A psychological consequence of the systematic attachment of social disadvantages to a certain inborn feature is that both the possessors of the feature and others begin to regard it as an essential and important characteristic, and one which reduces the esteem in which its possessor can be held.[9] Concomitantly, those who do not possess the characteristic gain a certain amount of free esteem by comparison, and the arrangement thus constitutes a gross sacrifice of the most basic personal interests of some for the interests of others, with those sacrificed being on the bottom. (It is because similar things can be said about the social and economic disadvantages that attach to low intelligence that I am inclined to regard that, too, as a major injustice.)

Reverse discrimination need not have these consequences, and it can have social advantages. Suppose, for example, that there is need for a great increase in the number of black doctors, because the health needs of the black community are unlikely to be met otherwise. And suppose that at the present average level of premedical qualifications among black applicants, it would require a huge expansion of total medical school enrollment to supply the desirable absolute number of black doctors without adopting differential admission standards. Such an expansion may be unacceptable either because of its cost or because it would produce a total supply of doctors, black and white, much greater than the society requires. This is a strong argument for accepting reverse discrimination, not on grounds of justice but on grounds of social utility. (In addition, there is the salutary effect on the aspirations and

---

[8] For a detailed and penetrating treatment of this and a number of other matters discussed here, see Owen M. Fiss, "A Theory of Fair Employment Laws," *University of Chicago Law Review* 38 (Winter 1971), 235–314.

[9] This effect would not be produced by an idiosyncratic discriminatory practice limited to a few eccentrics. If some people decided they would have nothing to do with anyone left-handed, everyone else, including the left-handed, would regard it as a silly objection to an inessential feature. But if everyone shunned the left-handed, left-handedness would become a strong component of their self-image, and those discriminated against would feel they were being despised for their essence. What people regard as their essence is not independent of what they get admired and despised for.

expectations of other blacks, from the visibility of exemplars in formerly inaccessible positions.)

The argument in the other direction, from the point of view of the qualified white applicants who are turned away, is not nearly as strong as the argument against standard racial discrimination. The self-esteem of whites as a group is not endangered by such a practice, since the situation arises only because of their general social dominance, and the aim of the practice is only to benefit blacks, and not to exclude whites. Moreover, although the interests of some are being sacrificed to further the interests of others, it is the better placed who are being sacrificed and the worst placed who are being helped.[10] It is an important feature of the case that the discriminatory measure is designed to favor a group whose social position is exceptionally depressed, with destructive consequences both for the self-esteem of members of the group and for the health and cohesion of the society.[11]

If, therefore, a discriminatory admissions or appointments policy is adopted to mitigate a grave social evil, and it favors a group in a particularly unfortunate social position, and if for these reasons it diverges from a meritocratic system for the assignment of positions which is not itself required by justice, then the discriminatory practice is probably not unjust.[12]

It is not without its costs, however. Not only does it inevitably produce resentment in the better qualified who are passed over because of the policy, but it also allows those in the discriminated-against group who would in fact have failed to gain a desired position in any case on the basis of their qualifications to feel that they may have lost out to someone less qualified because of the discriminatory policy. Similarly, such a practice cannot do much for the self-esteem of those who know they have benefited from it, and it may threaten the self-esteem of those in the favored group who would in fact have gained their positions even in the absence of the discriminatory policy, but who cannot be sure that they are not among its beneficiaries. This is what leads institutions to lie about their policies in this regard, or to hide them behind clouds of obscurantist rhetoric about the discriminatory character of stan-

---

[10] This is a preferable direction of sacrifice if one accepts Rawls's egalitarian assumptions about distributive justice. Rawls, *op. cit.*, pp. 100–103.

[11] It is therefore not, as some have feared, the first step toward an imposition of minimal or maximal quotas for all racial, religious, and ethnic subgroups of the society.

[12] Adam Morton has suggested an interesting alternative, which I shall not try to develop: namely, that the practice is justified not by social utility, but because it will contribute to a more just situation in the future. The practice considered in itself may be unjust, but it is warranted by its greater contribution to justice over the long term, through eradication of a self-perpetuating pattern.

dard admissions criteria. Such concealment is possible and even justified up to a point, but the costs cannot be entirely evaded, and discriminatory practices of this sort will be tolerable only so long as they are clearly contributing to the eradication of great social evils.

V

When racial and sexual injustice have been reduced, we shall still be left with the great injustice of the smart and the dumb, who are so differently rewarded for comparable effort. This would be an injustice even if the system of differential economic and social rewards had no systematic sexual or racial reflection. On the other hand, if the social esteem and economic advantages attaching to different occupations and educational achievements were much more uniform, there would be little cause for concern about racial, ethnic, or sexual patterns in education or work. But of course we do not at present have a method of divorcing professional status from social esteem and economic reward, at least not without a gigantic increase in total social control, on the Chinese model. Perhaps someone will discover a way in which the socially produced inequalities (especially the economic ones) between the intelligent and the unintelligent, the talented and the untalented, or even the beautiful and the ugly, can be reduced without limiting the availabiliy of opportunities, products and services, and without resort to increased coercion or decreased liberty in the choice of work or style of life. In the absence of such a utopian solution, however, the familiar task of balancing liberty against equality will remain with us.[13]

SELECTED SUPPLEMENTARY READING

ACTON, H. B., J. PLAMENATZ, and W. D. LAMONT, "Symposium, Rights," *Proceedings of the Aristotelian Society*, 24 (1950, Supplementary Volume).

ALTHAM, J. E. J., "Rawls' Difference Principle," *Philosophy*, 48 (1973).

BAYLES, MICHAEL D., "Reparations to Wronged Groups," *Analysis*, 33 (1973).

BEDAU, HUGO, ed., *Justice and Equality*. Englewood Cliffs, N.J.: Prentice-Hall, Inc., 1971.

BEDAU, HUGO A., "Compensatory Injustice and the Black Manifesto," *The Monist*, 56 (1972).

---

[13] I have presented an earlier version of this paper to the New York Group of the Society for Philosophy and Public Affairs, the Princeton Undergraduate Philosophy Club, and the Society for Ethical and Legal Philosophy, and I thank those audiences for their suggestions.

BENN, STANLEY I., "Egalitarianism and the Equal Consideration of Interests," in Bedau, ed., *Justice and Equality*.

BLACKSTONE, W. T., "On the Meaning and Justification of the Equality Principle," *Ethics*, 77 (1967).

BRANDT, RICHARD, ed. *Social Justice*. Englewood Cliffs, N.J.: Prentice-Hall, Inc., 1962.

BROWN, STUART M., JR., "Inalienable Rights," *Philosophical Review*, 64 (1955).

CARE, NORMAN S., "Runciman on Social Equality," *Philosophical Quarterly*, 18 (1968).

COWAN, J. L., "Inverse Discrimination," *Analysis*, 32 (1972).

CRANSTON, MAURICE W., *What Are Human Rights?* New York: Taplinger Publishing Co., 1963.

FRANKEL, CHARLES, "Equality of Opportunity," *Ethics*, 81 (1970–1971).

GORDON, SCOTT, "John Rawls's Difference Principle, Utilitarianism, and the Optimum Degree of Inequality," *Journal of Philosophy*, 70 (1973).

HAACK, SUSAN, "On the Moral Relevance of Sex," *Philosophy*, 49 (1974).

HUGHES, GRAHAM, "The Right to Special Treatment," in *The Rights of Americans*, ed. Norman Dorsen. New York: Pantheon Books, 1971.

"Human Rights," *Monist*, 52 (1968).

JAGGAR, ALISON, "On Sexual Equality," *Ethics*, 84 (1974).

KAUFMAN, ARNOLD S., and MICHAEL HARRINGTON, "Black Reparations—Two Views," *Dissent*, 16 (1969).

LICHTMAN, J., "The Ethics of Compensatory Justice," *Law in Transition Quarterly*, 1 (1964).

LUCAS, J. R., "Because You Are a Woman," *Philosophy*, 48 (1973).

———, "Justice," *Philosophy*, 47 (1972).

MARGOLIS, JOSEPH, "That All Men Are Created Equal," *Journal of Philosophy*, 52 (1955).

MARGOLIS, JOSEPH, and CLORINDA MARGOLIS, "Black and White Politics," *Social Theory and Practice*, 1 (1970–1971).

NEWTON, LISA H., "Reverse Discrimination as Unjustified," *Ethics*, 83 (1973).

NICKEL, J. W., "Discrimination and Morally Relevant Characteristics," *Analysis*, 32 (1972).

PLAMENATZ, JOHN, "Equality of Opportunity," in Bryson et al., *Aspects of Human Equality*. New York: Harper, 1957.

RAWLS, JOHN, *A Theory of Justice*. Cambridge, Mass.: Harvard University Press, 1971.

RUNCIMAN, W. G., *Relative Deprivation and Social Justice*. London: Routledge and Kegan Paul, 1966.

———, "Social Equality," *Philosophical Quarterly*, 17 (1967).

SHINER, ROGER A., "Individuals, Groups and Inverse Discrimination," *Analysis*, 33 (1973).

SILVESTRI, PHILIP, "The Justification of Inverse Discrimination," *Analysis*, 33 (1973).

SPIEGELBERG, HERBERT, "A Defence of Human Equality," *Philosophical Review*, 53 (1944).

TAYLOR, PAUL W., "Reverse Discrimination and Compensatory Justice," *Analysis*, 33 (1973).

THOMSON, JUDITH, "Preferential Hiring," *Philosophy and Public Affairs*, 2 (1973).

WARD, ANDREW, "The Idea of Equality Reconsidered," *Philosophy*, 48 (1973).

WILLIAMS, B. A. O., "The Idea of Equality," in *Philosophy, Politics, and Society*, eds. P. Laslett and W. G. Runciman. New York: Barnes and Noble, Inc., 1962.

"Women's Liberation: Ethical, Social, and Political Issues," *Monist*, 57 (1973).

WOOZLEY, A. D., "Injustice," *American Philosophical Quarterly*, Monograph, 7 (1973).

Chapter 2

CRIMINAL PUNISHMENT AND THE DEATH PENALTY

INTRODUCTION

Recent prison riots have occasioned a crisis of conscience by bringing into the open what penologists have long known: Prisons are institutions in which severe punishment and inhuman conditions breed hardened criminals rather than reformed citizens. Public discussion in the aftermath of the riots has also made it clear that we have no very systematic reasons to justify the manner in which we treat convicted criminals. This state of affairs is not simply a contemporary phenomenon produced by the modern world of impersonal, decaying, and pressure-packed cities, for the nineteenth-century philosopher Jeremy Bentham found these same problems in his native England. Bentham diligently campaigned in an effort to show that both the *practical system* of criminal punishment and the *theoretical justification* for it were in need of major reform. He found the practice of punishment brutal, overly expensive, and its court procedure vague. He regarded the prevailing theoretical justifications as deficient because they were retributive in character; that is, punishment was thought to be justified because a criminal offender's pernicious act deserved repayment. Bentham thought that punishment could be just only

if it were reformatory and deterrent in character. Since his time philosophers and legal thinkers have vigorously debated these issues, with the
ethical controversies chiefly settling on questions of theoretical justification. Since it is (prima facie) morally wrong to inflict intended suffering
and since punishment consists in such infliction, ethicists are concerned
to say why we are sometimes justified in doing so. In this chapter we shall
explore recent central lines of argument on the question of justification.

The Justification of Criminal Punishment

In its most general form the problem of justifying criminal punishment centers on the following question: "Under what *conditions* is
criminal punishment justified?" The major philosophical theories that
have been devised to answer the demand that punishment be justified
are customarily split into two opposed camps—retributivist and utilitarian. Some philosophers, however, are more accurately described as
holding some combination of these positions, and thus fall into a third
category.

Retributivists characteristically emphasize the moral and legal guilt
of the offender, the deserved character of a penalty, and the principle
that society reciprocally has a right to punish criminal offenders. They
generally deny that the consequences of sentencing are relevant to the
problem of justifying punishment and stress instead that the crime itself
justifies punishment. Their position here is influenced by those trends
in moral philosophy that emphasize the fulfillment of obligations and the
avoidance of injustices. Retributivists derive their views about punishment from an evaluation of the criminal act when placed in a context of
social obligations. Society, they argue, is an integrated, law-governed
system of both mutual benefits and indebtednesses. To act against this
system in a criminal manner is to receive undeserved benefits. The criminal then owes society a debt for what he has taken. He deserves the
punishment, which is effectively a discharging of his obligation. The
punishment of criminals is justified, then, in much the same way the
collecting of a debt is justified.

Utilitarians, on the other hand, typically maintain that although all
suffering involved in punishment is evil, it is justified if its threat or
enforcement produces positive individual and social consequences, such as
deterrence of crime, reformation of character, and rehabilitation of skills.
This position is dictated in large measure by a wider utilitarian philosophy, with its stress on the production of good consequences and the
avoidance of suffering. Utilitarians, like retributivists, look at the criminal
act in a social context. They agree with retributivists that society is a
system of mutual benefits but ask whether the social benefits of punish-

ment outweigh the suffering involved. If benefits such as deterrence and reformation do outweigh the suffering, this fact is said to *justify* punishment. On the other hand, if the suffering outweighs the benefits (so that more evil than good results), then punishment is not justified, even if a person in some respects deserves to be punished. The punishment would serve no worthwhile social function. This is clearly a consequentialist argument: One should always perform the action that produces the greatest possible balance of good over evil, whether in matters of punishment or in other moral matters.

An increasingly popular thesis recently advanced is that although each of these staple theories is individually insufficient to justify punishment, some combination of elements taken from both is sufficient. Those who espouse this reconciling view might be called *utilitarian retributivists*. They emphasize the necessity of both positive social benefits and the avoidance of excessive injustice. To cite one example of this approach, it has been maintained that punishment is justified both because it is deserved and because it has a deterrent effect, but is not justified if only one of the two criteria has been satisfied. This view aims at the result of not punishing those who do not deserve it and of not punishing at all unless the penalty serves either as an individual or as a social deterrent. Presumably this alternative escapes the central criticisms of both utilitarianism (it allows punishment of the innocent) and retributivism (it allows punishment with no worthwhile result).

In order to evaluate these attempts to justify punishment, it is useful to distinguish between the justification of punishment as an *institution* and the justification of punishment in *individual cases*—especially if one is inclined toward a reconciling position. (John Rawls has referred to a more general form of this distinction as that between "justifying a practice and justifying a particular action falling under it.") To some philosophers utilitarianism has appeared far more plausible as a theory justifying a system of punishment in general—the whole institution of punishment procedures and standards—than as a theory justifying individual cases of punishment. It seems unsatisfactory in the latter cases, because utilitarianism appears to justify the punishment of innocent persons whenever such punishment produces less social harm than their nonpunishment would produce. But utilitarianism is not subject to this objection, and is intuitively appealing, if it is understood to justify the institution of punishment in general.

Retributivism is in the reverse situation. It seems less acceptable as a general justification of the institution because it denies the significance of evaluating the advantages and disadvantages of social institutions; yet this evaluation is normally the way we justify their existence. Nonetheless, retributivism is plausible when construed (more legalistically) as justifying individual cases of punishment, for it is a well-entrenched social belief that intentional violations of the law *deserve* penalties correlative to the offense, and similarly, that punishment seems undeserved unless there has been such an offense. Looked at from these two perspectives, then, it may be possible to reconcile the utilitarian and retributivist positions. Utilitarianism is seen as taking an *external* view of the institution in order to justify it as a body of rules, while retributivism is seen as taking an *internal* view of the institution and its rules in order to justify particular instances of punishment.

The Death Penalty

In England the following kind of death penalty was being imposed as late as 1812:

> That you and each of you, be taken to the place from whence you came, and from thence be drawn on a hurdle to the place of execution, where you shall be hanged by the neck, not till you are dead; that you be severally taken down, while yet alive, and your bowels be taken out and burnt before your faces—that your heads be then cut off, and your bodies cut into four quarters, to be at the King's disposal. And God have mercy on your souls.*

There can be little reasonable doubt that this particular death sentence prescribes unjustifiably cruel and unusual punishment. Since this period in English history there have been modifications in both the methods of execution and in the number of crimes thought to deserve capital punishment. Movements to abolish the death penalty completely have gained strong footholds.

Several times in American history the death penalty has been abolished by individual states, only to be promptly restored. In 1972, on a five to four vote, the United States Supreme Court abolished the death penalty in all states. Collectively, the nine separate opinions of the justices clearly reflect all sides of the controversy over judicial homicide. The debate, however, is by no means restricted to the United States; whether a society can justifiably punish any severe crimes by death and, if so, which ones is now a near universal question.

The seven major considerations traditionally used to oppose the death penalty are the following: (1) Capital punishment is a primitive retributive idea based on revenge; (2) judicial mistakes lead to the death of innocent persons; (3) the sentence is often imposed unfairly against underprivileged groups; (4) the dignity and sanctity of human life are threatened by this form of punishment; (5) no evidence shows capital punishment to have a deterrent effect; (6) judges and juries opposed to

---

* As quoted by Hugo Bedau in *The Death Penalty in America*, p. 3.

the death penalty often let criminals go free without any punishment; and (7) the right to life cannot be legitimately taken away from any person. In contrast, the five major considerations traditionally used in favor of the death penalty are the following: (1) At least some forms of crime are deterred by the threat of death; (2) society has a right to punish capital offenses with similar sentences; (3) some crimes deserve the death penalty; (4) capital punishment protects society by completely preventing recidivism in capital offenses; and (5) persons sentenced to life imprisonment should at least be able to choose death. It is plausible to suppose that those who think capital punishment can or cannot be justified divide along retributivist and utilitarian lines. This hypothesis is misleading, however. Capital punishment laws have usually been framed with the *dual* intent that they be both retributive and preventive. Moreover, although there are typical retributivist *forms* of justification that do differ discernibly from utilitarian forms, members of both camps have argued in some cases *for* and in some cases *against* capital punishment.

In their arguments utilitarians emphasize that the justification of the death penalty should focus on its deterrent effect. Those who oppose the death penalty usually argue that there is no reliable statistical evidence to indicate that the death penalty deters anyone except the person executed. (They need not argue this thesis for all criminal sanctions, of course.) Since the evidence is unreliable and since imprisonment is less cruel than death, they suggest that there is a strong presumption against killing anyone, at least until better evidence is available. They also argue that one effect of a system of execution is to diminish the value and dignity traditionally attributed to human life. Just as a lowering of ethical standards anywhere (for example, in the world of business) leads to lesser expectations by those who must conform to the standards, so, they argue, the lowering of standards pertaining to the preservation and rehabilitation of human life leads to its general devaluation. Utilitarians of this persuasion also argue that there is a paradox in making crimes such as skyjacking, rape, and kidnapping capital offenses *along with* murder. In this case the criminal has been given an incentive to kill the best witness against him rather than a reason to abstain from a capital offense.

Other utilitarians who support the death penalty argue that although statistics do not prove either deterrence or nondeterrence, specifiable conditions indicate deterrence to any man of common sense. Consider, for example, an inmate serving a life sentence in a country with no death penalty. Why should he not wantonly kill guards during escape attempts? He cannot suffer greater punishment. No punishment could be a deterrent in this case except death. Also, far from lowering ethical standards, argue these utilitarians, the death sentence raises these standards by indicating to people the seriousness with which we value life itself. What means could possibly teach respect for life, freedom, and dignity better, they reason, than the death penalty? If the threat of death has the effect of averting any murders at all, especially of innocent men, then is not capital punishment justified for that reason alone?

Retributivists reject the utilitarian emphasis on deterrence because they think punishing individuals as a *means* to the deterrence of others is either wrong or deficient in its theoretical grasp of the justification of punishment. They emphasize in their arguments, as we would expect, the right society has to exact retribution from offenders by meting out a penalty commensurate with the offense. Those retributivists who support the death penalty argue that homicide is always malicious except where retributively justified. In the case of a criminal who intentionally and with forethought takes the life of another, the principle of reciprocity seems at least to justify, if not to demand, the taking of the criminal's life. Should not penalties be graded, they say, precisely in accordance with the severity of the crime?

Other retributivists, however, argue that the taking of any human life is never deserved as a penalty because it is morally wrong to take a human life under any conditions. Their point is that no penalty itself morally wrong (absolutely, not merely prima facie) can possibly be a morally right sentence. Since the right to life is an inalienable right, they maintain, it is always wrong to take a life. They also maintain that death sentences are often unjustified ways of oppressing minority groups and the poor, and that many people deserving no penalty at all, because they were innocent, have lost their lives through systems allowing the death penalty. This terminal penalty is obviously irrevocable in a way other punishment is not. If we are to have a system that fairly hands out what is deserved, argue these retributivists, we should hesitate to sanction the death penalty, since it robs us of the possibility of rewarding the innocent when they have, only after death, been determined to be innocent.

It is reasonably clear that these arguments often hinge on larger considerations such as whether there are inalienable human rights, whether death serves as a serious deterrent, and most important, whether retributivist criteria or utilitarian criteria, or both, rightly should serve as criteria for the justification of *capital* punishment. Although some of these considerations are straightforwardly factual—for example, whether the threat of death in fact is a serious deterrent—others are distinctly ethical.

Arguments in the Selections

Richard B. Brandt introduces the debate between utilitarians and retributivists by analyzing the differences between them and by evaluating the most prominent objections often advanced against each. Brandt cautiously defends a form of "rule-utilitarianism," which he understands as the theory that "our actions, whether legislative or otherwise, should be guided by a set of prescriptions, the conscientious following of which by all would have maximum net expectable utility." Brandt argues that no major retributivist critique of utilitarianism succeeds against this form of the theory, though he finds some of the better known versions of utilitarianism deficient and does concede that even his utilitarian theory does not in all cases square with ordinary convictions concerning appropriate punishment. Brandt concludes his article with a criticism of what he takes to be the least objectionable forms of retributivism. He argues that they can be assimilated, through a slight extension, within the framework of utilitarianism.

H. L. A. Hart defends a sophisticated reconciling theory—a form of utilitarian retributivism—that attempts to move beyond the more traditional questions considered by Brandt. Hart argues that we must distinguish superficially similar questions without supposing that some one set of moral principles will suffice to answer each inquiry about punishment. To this end he discusses questions of the definition of punishment, the nature of a criminal offense, the general justifying aim of criminal punishment, who may be punished (including the punishment-of-innocents problem), and to what extent criminals may be punished. He argues that many confusions result from not keeping both the issues and the principles separate.

One confusion is that between a community's *aim* in setting up laws regulating criminal punishment (an aim that might be immoral) and the *justification* of punishment. Another confusion is that between retribution as a general justifying aim and retribution as the thesis that only those who have broken the law may be punished. Hart thinks utilitarians and retributivists are often only "shadow-fighting" because they fail to acknowledge such distinctions. He contends that many of these confusions may be avoided if it is "recognized that it is perfectly consistent to assert *both* that the General Justifying Aim of the practice of punishment is its beneficial consequences *and* that the pursuit of this General Aim should be qualified or restricted out of deference to principles of Distribution which require that punishment should be only of an offender for an offence." From this perspective Hart is able to defend retributivism as a theory justifying the manner in which punishment is *distributed* (to whom punishment may be applied) without being forced to criticize utilitarianism as a theory about the general justifying aim of punishment.

Ernest van den Haag and **Hugo Bedau**, in the two concluding articles in this chapter, debate the merits of two major positions on the death penalty. Van den Haag argues that any case for the death penalty must be built on its deterrent effect. He even argues that principles of justice are weighty in this case only because they implicitly depend on deterrence arguments. He further maintains that the sociological uncertainty that confronts us over the actual deterrent effect produced by executions favors the death penalty so long as future victims of murder might be saved by having the institution. Van den Haag thinks the added severity of death penalties may add to the deterrent effect, but in any case the burden of proof is on those who would abolish the penalty. He argues to the conclusion that "we have no right to risk additional future victims of murder for the sake of sparing convicted murderers; on the contrary, our moral obligation is to risk the possible ineffectiveness of executions."

Bedau contends, however, that van den Haag's arguments involve serious confusions and evasions. Bedau first argues that evidence for the deterrent effect is far less conclusive than van den Haag admits and then argues against the view that the added severity of the death penalty adds to its deterrent effect. Bedau thinks the latter claim is unempirical—on the order of a hunch. By way of positive argument, Bedau points out that advocacy of the death penalty is tantamount to advocacy of state power to take human life deliberately. All conditions being equal, he argues, one would hope supporters of this view would be able to provide considerable evidence for its efficacy. He finds no such evidence in van den Haag's article—or elsewhere, for that matter.

Retributive Justice and Criminal Law *

Richard B. Brandt

There are two distinct ways in which there can be injustice in the treatment of criminals. First, criminals are *punished* whereas noncriminals are not. Punishment, however, is *unequal* treatment, in a matter that involves distribution of things good or bad. Therefore, if punishment is to be just, it must be shown that the unequal treatment is required by moral principles of weight. Thus, one thing that must be done in order to show that the practice of punishing criminals is not unjust, is to show that there are moral principles that require it. But second, the *procedures of applying* the principles directing unequal treatment for criminals may themselves operate unequally. One man gets a "fair" trial and another does not. There can be inequality in the chances given people to escape the application of legal sanctions in their case. Part of treating people "justly," then, is providing legal devices so that everyone has an equal hearing: scrupulous adherence to the rules of evidence, opportunity for appeal to higher courts for remedy of deviation from standard rules in the lower courts, and so on. We shall not here consider details about how legal institutions should be devised in order to secure equal application of the law; that is a specialized inquiry that departs too far from the main problems of ethical principle. It is a part of "justice," however. Indeed, we may view "criminal justice" as having two main aspects: just laws for the punishment of offenders and procedures insuring just application of these laws by the courts and other judicial machinery.

The existence of just laws directing certain punishments for certain offenses, then, is not the whole of justice for the criminal, but we shall concentrate on identifying such laws.

Another question that may be raised is whether it is not artificial to confine our problem, as we have been doing so far, to the treatment of criminals by the legal system. Are there not other punishments, and will not the principles that justify one also justify them all? Many people believe that there is and ought to be divine punishment for the wicked in an afterlife. Children are punished by their parents for going swimming in disobedience to orders or for refusing to eat an egg for breakfast. A sergeant may punish a private with K.P. duty, if he appears for inspection with his shoes inadequately cleaned. The teacher may punish a pupil by making him stay after school, for having thrown chalk around the classroom. Do not all these cases of punishment raise the same fundamental issues?

Yes, they do. An adequate theory of punishment for improper conduct will explain or justify all these various kinds of punishment, insofar as they can be justified. It is misleading to confine ourselves to the complex case of legal systems. Indeed, if we look at primitive societies, we see that there is no sharp break between less formal systems of punishment and the elaborate systems of criminal justice used in the more advanced societies today. In their case, we may wish to speak of a "system" of criminal justice, although these societies have neither formal courts of law nor judges, and only a minimum in the way of prescribed rules of procedure against wrongdoers. So, we must consider what moral principles justify the "unequal treatment" of punishment [1] gen-

---

[1] Webster defines "punishment" as "any pain, suffering, or loss inflicted on or suffered by a person because of a crime or evildoing."

erally. Nevertheless, it is proper to give emphasis to the special problems of the legal institution of criminal justice, on account of its importance. . . .

The Utilitarian Theory of Criminal Justice

Historically there has been a cleavage of opinion about the kind of general ethical principles required for coherence with our concrete justified beliefs about criminal justice (those concrete beliefs that are compatible with our "qualified" attitudes)—a cleavage already found in the parallel problem of economic justice. Many writers have thought that a utilitarian principle is adequate. Others have thought that some non-utilitarian principle, or more than one, is necessary. Most of the latter writers (formalists) have espoused some form of *retributive* principle— that is, a principle roughly to the effect that a wrongdoer should be punished approximately in correspondence with either the moral reprehensibility of his offense or with the magnitude of his breach or of the public harm he commits. However, as we shall see, there are other types of formalist theory.

It is convenient to begin with the utilitarian theory. Since we have [elsewhere] tentatively concluded that an "extended" rule-utilitarianism is the most tenable form of theory, we shall have this particular type of theory in mind. For present purposes, however, it would make no difference, except at two or three points where we shall make note of the fact, if we confined our attention to a straight rule-utilitarian principle. There is no harm in thinking of the matter in this way. We can ignore the distinction between hedonistic and pluralistic forms for the present topic.

The essence of the rule-utilitarian theory, we recall, is that our actions, whether legislative or otherwise, should be guided by a set of prescriptions, the conscientious following of which by all would have maximum net expectable utility. As a result, the utilitarian is not, just as such, committed to any particular view about how anti-social behavior should be treated by society—or even to the view that society should do anything at all about immoral conduct. It is only the utilitarian principle *combined* with statements about the kind of laws and practices which will maximize expectable utility that has such consequences. Therefore, utilitarians are free to differ from one another about the character of an ideal system of criminal justice; some utilitarians think that the system prevalent in Great Britain and the United States essentially corresponds to the ideal, but others think that the only system that can be justified is markedly different from the actual systems in these Western countries. We shall concentrate our discussion, however, on the more traditional line of utilitarian thought which holds that roughly the actual system of criminal law, say in the United States, is morally justifiable, and we shall follow roughly the classic exposition of the reasoning given by Jeremy Bentham [2]—but modifying this freely when we feel amendment is called for. At the end of the chapter we shall look briefly at a different view.

Traditional utilitarian thinking about criminal justice has found the rationale of the practice, in the United States, for example, in three main facts. (Those who disagree think the first two of these "facts" happen not to be the case.) (1) People who are tempted to misbehave, to trample on the rights of others, to sacrifice public welfare for personal gain, can usually be deterred from misconduct by fear of punishment, such as death, imprisonment, or fine. (2) Imprisonment or fine will teach malefactors a lesson; their characters may be improved, and at any rate a personal experience of punishment will make them less likely to misbehave again. (3) Imprisonment will certainly have the result of physically preventing past malefactors from misbehaving, during the period of their incarceration.

In view of these suppositions, traditional utilitarian thinking has concluded that having laws forbidding certain kinds of behavior on pain of punishment, and having machinery for the fair enforcement of these laws, is justified by the fact that it maximizes expectable utility. Misconduct is not to be punished just for its own sake; malefactors must be punished for their past acts, according to law, as a way of maximizing expectable utility.

The utilitarian principle, of course, has implications for decisions about the severity of punishment to be administered. Punishment is itself an evil, and hence should be avoided where this is consistent with the public good. Punishment should have precisely such a degree of severity (not more or less) that the probable disutility of greater severity just balances the probable gain in utility (less crime because of the more serious threat). The cost, in other words, should be counted along with the value of what is bought; and we should buy protection up to the point where the cost is greater than the protection is worth. How severe will such punishment be? Jeremy Bentham had many sensible things to say about this. Punishment, he said, must be severe enough so that it is to no one's advantage to commit an offense even if he receives the punishment; a fine of $10 for bank robbery would give no security at all. Further, since many criminals will be undetected, we must make the penalty heavy enough in comparison with the prospective gain from crime, that a prospective criminal will consider the risk hardly worth

---

[2] In *Principles of Morals and Legislation.*

it, even considering that it is not certain he will be punished at all. Again, the more serious offenses should carry the heavier penalties, not only because the greater disutility justifies the use of heavier penalties in order to prevent them, but also because criminals should be motivated to commit a less serious rather than a more serious offense. Bentham thought the prescribed penalties should allow for some variation at the discretion of the judge, so that the actual suffering caused should roughly be the same in all cases; thus, a heavier fine will be imposed on a rich man than on a poor man.

Bentham also argued that the goal of maximum utility requires that certain facts should *excuse* from culpability, for the reason that punishment in such cases "must be inefficacious." He listed as such (1) the fact that the relevant law was passed only after the act of the accused, (2) that the law had not been made public, (3) that the criminal was an infant, insane, or was intoxicated, (4) that the crime was done under physical compulsion, (5) that the agent was ignorant of the probable consequences of his act or was acting on the basis of an innocent misapprehension of the facts, such that the act the agent thought he was performing was a lawful one, and (6) that the motivation to commit the offense was so strong that no threat of law could prevent the crime. Bentham also thought that punishment should be remitted if the crime was a collective one and the number of the guilty so large that great suffering would be caused by its imposition, or if the offender held an important post and his services were important for the public, or if the public or foreign powers would be offended by the punishment; but we shall ignore this part of his view.

Bentham's account of the logic of legal "defenses" needs amendment. What he should have argued is that *not* punishing in certain types of cases (cases where such defenses as those just indicated can be offered) reduces the amount of suffering imposed by law and the insecurity of everybody, and that failure to impose punishment in these types of case will cause only a negligible increase in the incidence of crime.

How satisfactory is this theory of criminal justice? Does it have any implications that are far from being acceptable when compared with concrete justified convictions about what practices are morally right? [3]

---

[3] Act-utilitarians face some special problems. For instance, if I am an act-utilitarian and serve on a jury, I shall work to get a verdict that will do the most good, irrespective of the charges of the judge, and of any oath I may have taken to give a reasonable answer to certain questions on the basis of the evidence presented—unless I think my doing so will have indirect effects on the institution of the jury, public confidence in it, and so on. This is certainly not what we think a juror should do. Of course, neither a juror nor a judge can escape his prima facie obligation to do what good he can; this obligation is present in some form in every theory. The act-utilitarian, however, makes this the whole of one's responsibility.

Many criminologists, as we shall see at the end of this chapter, would argue that Bentham was mistaken in his facts: The deterrence value of threat of punishment, they say, is much less than he imagined, and criminals are seldom reformed by spending time in prison. If these contentions are correct, then the ideal rules for society's treatment of malefactors are very different from what Bentham thought, and from what actual practice is today in the United States. To say all this, however, is not to show that the utilitarian *principle* is incorrect, for in view of these facts presumably the attitudes of a "qualified" person would not be favorable to criminal justice as practiced today. Utilitarian theory might still be correct, but its implications would be different from what Bentham thought—and they might coincide with justified ethical judgments. We shall return to this.

The whole utilitarian approach, however, has been criticized on the ground that it ought not in consistency to approve of *any* excuses from criminal liability.[4] Or at least, it should do so only after careful empirical inquiries. It is not obvious, it is argued, that we increase net expectable utility by permitting such defenses. At the least, the utilitarian is committed to defend the concept of "strict liability." Why? Because we could get a more strongly deterrent effect if everyone knew that *all behavior* of a certain sort would be punished, irrespective of mistaken supposals of fact, compulsion, and so on. The critics admit that knowledge that all behavior of a certain sort will be punished will hardly deter from crime the insane, persons acting under compulsion, persons acting under erroneous beliefs about facts, and others, but, as Professor Hart points out, it does not follow from this that general knowledge that certain acts will always be punished will not be salutary.

The utilitarian, however, has a solid defense against charges of this sort. We must bear in mind (as the critics do not) that the utilitarian principle, *taken by itself, implies nothing whatever* about whether a system of law should excuse persons on the basis of certain defenses. What the utilitarian does say is that, when we *combine* the principle of utilitarianism with *true* propositions about a certain thing or situation, then we shall come out with true statements about obligations. The utilitarian is certainly not committed to saying that one will derive true propositions about obligations if one starts with *false* propositions about fact or about what will maximize welfare, or with *no* such propositions at all. Therefore the criticism sometimes made (for example, by Hart),

---

4 See H. L. A. Hart, "Legal Responsibility and Excuses," in Sidney Hook (ed.), *Determinism and Freedom* (New York: New York University Press, 1958), pp. 81–104; and David Braybrooke, "Professor Stevenson, Voltaire, and the Case of Admiral Byng," *Journal of Philosophy*, LIII (1956), 787–96.

that utilitarian theory does not render it "obviously" or "necessarily" the case that the recognized excuses from criminal liability should be accepted as excusing from punishment, is beside the point. Morever, in fact the utilitarian can properly claim that we do have excellent reason for believing that the general public would be no better motivated to avoid criminal offenses than it now is, if the insane and others were also punished along with intentional wrongdoers. Indeed, he may reasonably claim that the example of punishment of these individuals could only have a hardening effect—like public executions. Furthermore, the utilitarian can point out that abolition of the standard exculpating excuses would lead to serious insecurity. Imagine the pleasure of driving an automobile if one knew one could be executed for running down a child whom it was absolutely impossible to avoid striking! One certainly does not maximize expectable utility by eliminating the traditional excuses. In general, then, the utilitarian theory is not threatened by its implica-ions about exculpating excuses.

It might also be objected against utilitarianism that it cannot recognize the validity of *mitigating* excuses (which presumably have the support of "qualified" attitudes). Would not consequences be better if the distinction between premeditated and impulsive acts were abolished? The utilitarian can reply that people who commit impulsive crimes, in the heat of anger, do not give thought to legal penalties; they would not be deterred by a stricter law. Moreover, such a person is unlikely to repeat his crime, so that a mild sentence saves an essentially good man for society.[5] Something can also be said in support of the practice of judges in giving a milder sentence when a person's temptation is severe: at least the *extended* rule-utilitarian can say, in defense of the practice of punishing less severely the crime of a man who has had few opportunities in life, that a judge ought to do what he can to repair inequalities in life, and that a mild sentence to a man who has had few opportunities is one way of doing this. There are, then, utilitarian supports for recognizing the mitigating excuses.

Sometimes it is objected to utilitarianism that it must view imprisonment for crime as morally no different from quarantine. This, it is said, shows that the utilitarian theory must be mistaken, since actually there is a vast moral difference between being quarantined and being imprisoned for crime. *Why* is it supposed utilitarian theory must view imprisonment as a kind of quarantine? The answer is that utilitarianism

---

[5] The utilitarian must admit that the same thing is true for many deliberate murders; and probably he should also admit that some people who commit a crime in the heat of anger would have found time to think had they known that a grave penalty awaited them.

looks to the future; the treatment it prescribes for individuals is treatment with an eye to maximizing net expectable utility. The leper is quarantined because otherwise he will expose others to disease. The criminal is imprisoned because otherwise he, or others who are not deterred by the threat of punishment, will expose the public to crime. Both the convicted criminal and the leper are making contributions to the public good. So, quarantine and imprisonment are essentially personal sacrifices for the public welfare, if we think of punishment as the utilitarian does. But in fact, the argument goes on, we feel there is a vast difference. The public is obligated to do what is possible to make the leper comfortable, to make his necessary sacrifice as easy for him and his family as possible. But we feel no obligation to make imprisonment as comfortable as possible.

Again the utilitarian has a reply. He can say that people cannot help contracting leprosy, but they can avoid committing crimes—and the very discomforts and harshness of prison life are deterring factors. If prison life were made attractive, there might be more criminals—not to mention the indolent who would commit a crime in order to enjoy the benefits of public support. Furthermore, the utilitarian can say, why should we feel that we "ought to make it up to" a quarantined leper? At least partly because it is useful to encourage willingness to make such sacrifices. But we do not at all wish to encourage the criminal to make his "sacrifice"; rather, we wish him not to commit his crimes. There is all the difference between the kind of treatment justified on utilitarian grounds for a person who may have to make a sacrifice for the public welfare through no fault of his own, and for a person who is required to make a sacrifice because he has selfishly and deliberately trampled on the rights of others, in clear view of the fact that if he is apprehended society must make an example of him. There are all sorts of utilitarian reasons for being kindly to persons of the former type, and stern with people of the latter type.

Another popular objection to the utilitarian theory is that the utilitarian must approve of prosecutors or judges occasionally withholding evidence known to them, for the sake of convicting an innocent man, if the public welfare really is served by so doing. Critics of the theory would not deny that there *can* be circumstances where the dangers are so severe that such action is called for; they only say that utilitarianism calls for it all too frequently. Is this criticism justified? Clearly, the utilitarian is not committed to advocating that a provision should be written into the *law* so as to permit punishment of persons for crimes they did not commit if to do so would serve the public good. Any such provision would be a shattering blow to public confidence and security. The question is only whether there should be an informal moral rule to the same effect, for the guidance of judges and prosecutors. Will the rule-utilitarian necessarily be committed to far too sweeping a moral rule on this point? We must recall that he is not in the position of the act-utilitarian, who must say that an innocent man must be punished if in *his particular case* the public welfare would be served by his punishment. The rule-utilitarian rather asserts only that an innocent man should be punished if he falls within a class of cases such that net expectable utility is maximized if *all* members of the class are punished, taking into account the possible disastrous effects on public confidence if it is generally known that judges and prosecutors are guided by such a rule. Moreover, the "extended" rule-utilitarian has a further reason for not punishing an innocent man unless he has had more than his equal share of the good things of life already; namely, that there is an obligation to promote equality of welfare, whereas severe punishment is heaping "illfare" on one individual person. When we take these considerations into account, it is *not* obvious that the rule-utilitarian (or the "extended" rule-utilitarian) is committed to action that we are jusifiably convinced is immoral.[6]

In recent years, some philosophers have sought to rescue the utilitarian from his supposed difficulty of being committed to advocate the punishment of innocent men, by a verbal point. Their argument is that it is *logically* guaranteed that only a guilty man may be *punished*. "Punishment," it is said, like "reward" and "forgive," has a backward reference; we properly speak of "punishing *for . . . ,*" and if we inflict suffering on someone for the sake of utility and irrespective of guilt for some offense, it is a misuse of the word "punishment" to speak of such a person as being punished.[7] It is not clear, however, that anything is accomplished by this verbal move. If these writers are correct, then it is self-contradictory to say "innocent men may be punished for the sake of the public good," and no one can say that utilitarian theory commits one to uttering such a self-contradiction. But it may still be that utilitarian theory commits one to advocating that prosecutors suppress evidence on certain occasions, that judges aid in conducting unfair trials and pronounce sentences out of line with custom for a particular type of case in times of public danger, and, in short, that innocent men be *locked up* or *executed*—only not *"punished"*—for the sake of the public

---

6 In any case, a tenable theory of punishment must approve of punishing persons who are *morally* blameless. Suppose someone commits treason for moral reasons. We may have to say that his deed is not reprehensible at all, and might even (considering the risk he took for his principles) be morally admirable. Yet we think such persons must be punished no matter what their motives; people cannot be permitted to take the law into their own hands.

7 For some discussion of the grammar of "punish," see A. M. Quinton, "On Punishment," *Analysis*, XIV (1954), 133–42; and K. Baier, "Is Punishment Retributive?" *Analysis*, XVI (1955), 25–32.

welfare. So, if there is a difficulty here at all for the utilitarian theory, the verbal maneuver of these philosophers seems not to remove it.

Everything considered, the utilitarian theory seems to be in much less dire distress, in respect of its implications for criminal justice, than has sometimes been supposed. It does not seem possible to show that in any important way its implications are clearly in conflict with our valid convictions about what is right. The worst that can be said is that utilitarian theory does not in a clear-cut way definitely require us to espouse some practices we are inclined to espouse. But to this the utilitarian may make two replies. First, that there is reason to think our ordinary convictions about punishment for crime ought to be thoroughly re-examined in important respects. We shall briefly examine later some proposals currently receiving the strong support of criminologists. Second, the utilitarian may reply that if we consider our convictions about punishments we should administer *as a parent*—and this is the point where our moral opinions are least likely to be affected by the sheer weight of tradition—we shall find that we think according to the principles of rule-utilitarianism. Parents do regard their punishment of their children as justified only in view of the future good of the child, and in order to make life in the home tolerable and in order to distribute jobs and sacrifices equally.

The Retributive Theory of Criminal Justice

If utilitarian ethical principles are regarded as not enough, then the basic system of "axioms" may be enlarged or modified by further principles of a nonutilitarian sort. A formalist system of principles of course may, like Ross' system, contain utilitarian elements, for example, a principle asserting that there is a prima facie obligation to do what good we can.

Any system of basic principles that contains nonutilitarian principles relevant to the treatment of criminals may be called a "retributive" theory of criminal justice. However, it seems better to reserve the term "retributive theory" for a theory that asserts that it is a basic principle of ethics roughly that pain or loss should be caused to persons who have done wrong, with a severity corresponding with the moral gravity of their deed —and of course the "gravity" of the deed not being defined to accord exactly with the utilitarian theory about how severely wrongdoers should be made to suffer.[8] In saying that such a principle is a "basic" principle

---

[8] Notice that we do not need to use the word "punish" at all in stating the retributive theory. This is fatal to the contention of some recent writers that the "retributive" theory—which they interpret as asserting, "Only the guilty should be punished"—is true by definition. See the explanation of this proposal on p. 74. In fact, the traditional retributive theory has far more to it than merely the claim that only the guilty should be punished.

of ethics, proponents of the retributive theory deny the possibility of deriving this principle from any principle directing to do good, that is, from any kind of utilitarian principle.

Let us now examine some formalist theories, beginning with what may be viewed as the traditional retributive theory. In order to get a concrete account before us, let us look at a statement by Immanual Kant. He writes:

> Juridical punishment . . . can be inflicted on a criminal, never *just* as instrumental to the achievement of some other good for the criminal himself or for the civil society, but *only* because he has committed a crime; for a man may never be used just as a means to the ends of another person or mixed up with the objects of Real Right—against which his innate personality protects him, even if he is condemned to lose his civil personality. He must first be found culpable, before there is any thought of turning his punishment to advantage either for himself or society. Penal law is a *categorical* imperative, and woe to him who crawls through the serpentine maze of utilitarian theory in order to find an excuse, in some advantage to someone, for releasing the criminal from punishment or any degree of it, in line with the pharasaical proverb "It is better that one man die than that a whole people perish"; for if justice perishes, there is no more value in man living on the earth. . . . What mode and degree of punishment, then, is the principle and standard of public justice? Nothing but the *principle of equality*. . . . Thus, whatever undeserved evil you inflict on another person, you inflict on yourself. If you insult another, you insult yourself; if you steal from another, you steal from yourself; if you strike another, you strike yourself; if you kill another, you kill yourself. Only the rule of retribution *(lex talionis)*—only, of course, before the bar of justice, not in your own private judgment— can determine the quality and quantity of punishment. . . . Now it appears that differences of rank and class do not permit the exact retribution of like with like; but even if retribution is not possible according to the exact letter, it is still always valid in respect of effect, taking into account the feelings of the superior party. . . . So, for example, a fine for slander has little proportion to the insult, since any one who is well off can then permit himself the luxury of such behavior at his own pleasure; yet the violation of the honor of one person can be the equivalent of damage to the pride of another party, if the court condemns the offender not only to retract and apologize, but to submit to some meaner ordeal such as kissing the hand of the injured person. . . . [But] if a person has committed murder, he must die. There is no likeness or proportion between life, however painful, and death; and therefore there is no equality between the crime of murder and the retaliation of it but what is judicially accomplished by the execution of the criminal. . . . Even if a civil society decided, with the agreement of all, to dissolve (for instance, if an

island society decided to break up and scatter into all parts of the world), the last murderer in the prison must first be brought to justice, in order that everyone be meted out desert for his deeds, and in order that the guilt of blood may not taint people who have failed to carry through the punishment—because such a people would have to be regarded as parties to a public violation of justice. . . . The equalization of punishment with offense is possible only through the rule of retribution . . . as is manifest from the fact that only then is sentence pronounced proportionate to internal wickedness. . . .[9]

The essence of Kant's point is that the utilitarian theory of punishment makes the false claim that man or society has the right to use another man as a means to the welfare of others, as if he were a physical thing. (The reverse of this is the equally false claim, he thinks, that a man need not be punished if that suits the needs of society, irrespective of the quality of his wrongdoing.) A man may be punished *only* if he has done something wrong (and hence it is immoral to punish an innocent man); and if he has done something wrong he *must* be punished. Kant does not hold merely that there is a prima facie obligation on society to punish one who has infringed the rights of others; it is an absolute over-all obligation—punishment must absolutely be meted out or society itself is guilty of wrong. Moreover, a person should be punished to the extent of his injury of his victim. Kant suggests in the last sentence that this amount of punishment corresponds with the moral turpitude of the criminal in that offense (presumably because, at least in the ordinary case, a man may be supposed to have intended to do what he does, so that what he does reflects the state of his character.)[10]

More recent writers have stated much the same theory in a somewhat sharper form. Mr. C. W. K. Mundle, for instance, has stated it as follows:

The theory to be discussed involves three elements, two ethical claims and a verbal recommendation:
    Claim 1, that the fact that a person has committed a moral offense provides a sufficient reason for his being made to suffer;
    Claim 2 (or "the principle of proportion"), that if (or when) people are made to suffer for their offences, the suffering imposed ought to be proportionate to the moral gravity of their offences;
    and *the verbal recommendation* that "punishment" should be ap-

---

[9] *Gesammelte Werke* (Cassirer edition, Berlin, 1922), VII, 138–40; see translation by W. Hastie of I. Kant, *The Philosophy of Law* (Edinburgh: T. and T. Clark, 1887), pp. 194 ff.

[10] A survey of historical opinions on the *lex talionis* is to be found in S. Pufendorf, *De Jure Naturae et Gentium* (Oxford: Clarendon Press, 1934), Bk. 8, chap. 3, pp. 1214 ff.

plied only to cases in which a person is made to suffer because (for the reason that) he deserves it on account of a moral offence.[11]

The traditional retributive principle is perhaps best stated today in a way suggested by Ross' formalist system, somewhat as follows: "It is prima facie obligatory for society to cause pain or loss to every person who commits a morally objectionable act to an extent corresponding with the moral gravity of his offense." [12] We can assume that other considerations, such as the obligation to avoid general insecurity, will require that punishment be imposed only for infractions of properly publicized laws, by specially authorized persons, and after a trial according to procedures selected in order to guarantee a fair application of the law.

The foregoing principle remains ambiguous, however, until we decide how to interpret the terms "morally objectionable" and "moral gravity of his offense." Two possible interpretations are more convincing than any others. (1) The terms may be taken to refer to moral reprehensibility in the sense of the preceding chapter, to an act's showing defect of character, and unfavorable attitudes toward the agent being justified on account of it. (2) Or they may be taken to refer to deliberate failure to conform conduct to *subjective* obligation—"moral gravity" being construed as the degree of subjective obligation, everything considered, not to do what the agent did. Let us call (1) the "moral reprehensibility" version, and (2) the *lex talionis* version. Kant's theory is closer to the *lex talionis* version, but is different from it, since the degree of subjective obligation not to perform an act is not necessarily a matter simply of the amount of harm done to other persons. The two versions are not so very different, but they do have different implications.[13]

---

[11] "Punishment and Desert," *Philosophical Quarterly*, IV (1954), 216–28. Mundle himself, however, thinks it possible to justify punishment satisfactorily on utilitarian lines (p. 228). A similar theory is advocated by Professor Jerome Hall, *General Principles of Criminal Law* (Indianapolis: Bobbs-Merrill Co., Inc., 1947), under the name of "the just theory" of punishment. He writes (p. 132): "A major postulate of the theory of just punishment is that punishment should be rationally related to moral culpability. In the greatest part of the criminal law, the gravity of the harm committed is a valid measure of moral culpability inasmuch as the harm intended is substantially the same as the harm committed." We should notice that this theory is a theory explaining why laws threatening punishment for offenses should be passed and enforced, not merely a theory why the state should carry out its threat to punish once the law has been adopted.

[12] In order to avoid saying that society as such has a "moral obligation," this statement must be understood as a statement about the obligations of the individuals constituting society, of the type suggested for the parallel formulation of the prima facie obligation corresponding to a prima facie right in R. B. Brandt, *Ethical Theory*, p. 438.

[13] A "*lex talionis*" theory might be so defined that no distinction ought to be made between manslaughter and murder, since the damage to another person is the same in either case. This is perhaps Kant's view. What a person guilty of manslaughter does deliberately, however, is simply *risk* another person's life. The *lex talionis* principle as stated allows for this, since the subjective obligation not to take a risk of this sort is presumably less than the obligation not to do what will certainly cause death.

Whichever way we take it, the principle as stated differs in two further respects from the principle apparently supported by Kant. First, it only asserts that there is a prima facie obligation to punish, whereas Kant supposed there is an absolute obligation. As such, the principle does not tell us that we ought ever really to punish, in the total circumstances. In a developed formalist theory, there would be rules giving more information on this point. Second, the principle as stated agrees with Kant in proposing that the more serious offense should be punished *more* severely, but it does not tell us *how* severely any action should be punished.

The content of such a retributive principle—whichever interpretation we adopt—could be incorporated within the framework of an "extended" rule-utilitarianism, by making a further "extension." That is, one could assert that it is *intrinsically desirable* that people be punished for their morally objectionable deeds, to a degree proportionate to the gravity of the deed. Punishment, then, would be an impersonal intrinsic good, along with equality of welfare. A theory approximately of this sort, but within the framework of act-utilitarianism (strictly, universal impersonal pluralism), was asserted by G. E. Moore, who wrote:

> It is in this way that the theory of vindictive punishment may be vindicated. The infliction of pain on a person whose state of mind is bad may, if the pain be not too intense, create a state of things that is better *on the whole* than if the evil state of mind had existed un-punished.[14]

Should we accept the retributive principle as a basic "axiom" about moral obligation (or else the assertion that it is intrinsically better for offenders to be punished than to go unpunished)? Various considerations suggest that we should answer this question *negatively*.

1. Our ethical theory is *simpler* without this principle, and therefore it should be rejected unless it enables us to deduce, as theorems (when we combine it with true factual premises), ethical principles which are valid, and which cannot be deduced without it. But since our discussion of the rule-utilitarian theory of punishment has not disclosed any major objection to that theory—any concrete judgments coherent with our "qualified" attitudes which are inconsistent with the rule-utilitarian theory, or which do not follow from this theory (with the "extension" involving the intrinsic worth of equality of welfare)—there is no reason to complicate our theory by adding a retributive principle.

2. We shall see that some people today question the whole practice of assigning "penalties to fit the crime." They think treatment of the criminal should be criminal-centered, not crime-centered. If their point is well-taken, the retributive principle is not true.

---

[14] *Principia Ethica* (Cambridge, Eng.: Cambridge University Press, 1904), p. 214.

3. The retributive principle, in whichever form we take it, asserts in effect that a principal aim of the law is to punish either moral guilt or intentional deviation from subjective obligation. But if so, then it ought to punish merely *attempted* crimes as severely as successful crimes. Moral reprehensibility, as we have seen, is equal in the two cases; and since an attempt is a case of setting oneself to commit a crime, it is as much a deliberate deviation from subjective obligation as the successful commission of a crime. Assuming that this implication is incorrect, clearly the retributive principle alone will not do as a principle guiding legislative practice.

4. The "moral reprehensibility" form of the theory is open to serious objection. According to it, laws should be so framed that no one will be punished, no matter what he does, if he is morally blameless. This is objectionable. It is of great importance that the law be able to set up standards of conduct, and require all to conform, whether or not they are convinced of the desirability of the standards. The law must be in a position to demand certain conduct from individuals, say in the Defense Department, whose conscientious deliberations might lead them to betray secrets essential to the national defense. Again, the law must be in a position to ban some practice like polygamy, irrespective of the value judgments of any persons. Therefore we must again say that the retributive principle cannot be the only principle guiding the framing of law and judicial practice.

5. The *lex talionis* version of the theory has its special difficulties. For instance, it is inconsistent with recognition of a difference between first degree murder, second degree murder, and manslaughter on account of provocation, since the degree of subjective obligation is equal in all these cases. Furthermore, the theory is inconsistent with holding that various circumstances are good reasons for imposing a relatively mild penalty, which in practice are regarded as good reasons and which we must agree morally are valid reasons. Thus we must conclude, again, that the retributive principle cannot be the only principle behind justified legal procedures, and one must question ever more forcibly what good reason there can be for saying that a retributive principle must be included in any satisfactory ethical theory.

A Second Formalist Theory

An interesting nonutilitarian alternative to the traditional retributive theory has been proposed by W. D. Ross. The essential idea of his theory is stated thus:

> Rights of any human being are correlative to duties incumbent on the owner of rights, or, to put it otherwise, to rights owned by those

against whom he has rights; and the main element in any one's right to life or liberty or property is extinguished by his failure to respect the corresponding rights in others. There is thus a distinction in kind which we all in fact recognize, but which utilitarianism cannot admit, between the punishment of a person who has invaded the rights of others and the infliction of pain or restraint on one who has not. The state ought, in its effort to maintain the rights of innocent persons, to take what steps are necessary to prevent violations of these rights; and the offender, by violating the life or liberty or property of another has lost his own right to have his life, liberty, or property respected, so that the state has no *prima facie* duty to spare him, as it has a *prima facie* duty to spare the innocent. It is morally at liberty to injure him as he has injured others . . . exactly as consideration both of the good of the community and of his own good requires.[15]

Ross' view differs from the retributive principle, as stated, in several ways. (What he says is not quite consistent; that side of his view is here emphasized which permits his theory to be classified as an interesting and novel one.) First, the commission of a moral offense does not establish a prima facie obligation to punish to a degree corresponding with the gravity of the offense, but a *permission* to punish up to a limit corresponding with the gravity of the offense. Second, the extent to which society should avail itself of its right to punish is determined solely by considerations of promoting the public good, of protecting rights. Third, the state's right to punish the malefactor arises from the fact that the malefactor's rights *not* to be injured in respect of life, liberty, or property go only as far as he respects the rights of others. The culprit, Ross says, "has lost his *prima facie* rights of life, liberty, or property, only in so far as these rested on an explicit or implicit undertaking to respect the corresponding rights in others, and in so far as he has failed to respect those rights."[16]

Ross himself appears to think (like Kant) of the "moral gravity" of an offense as fixed by the actual injury done someone. His theory is made more plausible, however, if we think of it as construing "moral gravity" either in the moral reprehensibility, or in the *lex talionis* sense, as these have already been defined.

Ross' theory is closer to utilitarianism than is the retributive theory,

---

15 *The Right and the Good* (Oxford: Clarendon Press, 1930), pp. 60–61.

16 *Ibid.*, p. 62. Ross also thinks it is intrinsically desirable for happiness to be distributed in accord with moral goodness, and that we have an obligation to produce this good like other goods; but he thinks that punishment of crimes by the state is not a likely way to achieve it. It is impracticable and outside the legitimate business of the state for it to concern itself with achieving this good. Moral goodness, Ross thinks, is in any case a function of character as a whole, and not of particular actions.

on account of its second point: the proposal that considerations of public welfare are the sole determinant of how far society should avail itself (by passing laws to that effect) of its right to punish malefactors. But it is not a utilitarian theory because the right to punish is not established by appeal to utility.

Is this "permissive" type of retributive theory subject to the same objections as the standard retributive theory described above? First, if there are no objections to a straight form of extended rule-utilitarianism, we still do not *need* the theory; it is a cumbersome complication. Second, if we interpret it in the "moral reprehensibility" form, the fourth objection to the standard theory is a decisive objection to it. Where there is no moral blame, this theory implies (in this form) that there is no right to punish. Third, Ross' theory is at least *less* open to the second and third objections we raised to the traditional theory, since on his view the moral gravity of an offense only determines a right to punish. Everything considered, Ross' theory, especially in the *lex talionis* form, seems slightly superior to the traditional retributive theory as we have stated it (and much superior to Kant's formulation); but there is no reason for adopting it in preference to the simpler rule-utilitarian theory (with the "extension" already argued for).

There are still other theories about why punishment by the state is justified. Perhaps the most important of these is the proposal that criminals have in some sense *consented* to the operation of a system of criminal justice, and therefore have consented to the application of this system to them. This theory is dubious on several counts. First, it may be questioned whether they have consented, explicitly or in any other manner. Second, even if they have, it does not follow that what is done to them is right. People often consent to things, for example, contracts, when the arrangement consented to is unfair to them. The theory might be amended to say, not that they *have* consented, but that they *would* consent if they were rational and knew what they really wanted. But in this form the theory is open to a third objection, for it may be asked: *Why* must they consent if they are rational? Because the system is right and fair? If the system's being right and fair is to be the reason for their rational assent, then it seems that in order to show that they will consent if they are rational, we must first show that the system is right and fair. We cannot first prove that the system is right and fair by showing that they will assent if they are rational. If so, then the main question whether the system *is* right and fair is still to be answered. Alternatively, it may be replied that the reason why they must consent is that a criminal must see that his *own self-interest* is best served by a system of law and order, that he would not wish to live outside such a system. Hence, if he is reasonable, he must consent to his own punishment as implied by the system of law and order which is a fundamental precondition of his own personal welfare. But is it convincing to argue that a criminal must recognize that his own personal welfare is best served by a particular system of law and order which requires that he himself be destroyed? This is highly dubious.[17]

Utilitarianism and Reform

Some thinkers today believe that criminal justice in Great Britain and the United States is in need of substantial revision. If we agree with their proposals, we have even less reason for favoring the retributive principle; but we must also question the traditional utilitarian emphasis on deterrence as the primary function of the institution of criminal justice.

Their proposal, roughly, is that we should extend, to all criminal justice, the practices of juvenile courts and institutions for the reform of juvenile offenders. Here, retributive concepts have been largely discarded at least in theory, and psychiatric treatment and programs for the prevention of crime by means of slum clearance, the organization of boys' clubs, and so forth, have replaced even deterrence as guiding ideas for social action.

The extension of these practices to criminal justice as a whole would work somewhat as follows: First, the present court procedure would be used to determine whether an offense has actually been committed. Such procedure would necessarily include ordinary rules about the admission of evidence, trial by jury, and the exculpating justifications and excuses for offenses (such as wrong suppositions about the facts). Second, if an accused were adjudged guilty, decisions about his treatment would then be in the hands of the experts, who would determine what treatment was called for and when the individual was ready for return to normal social living. The trial court might, of course, set some maximum period during which such experts would have a right to control the treatment of the criminal. What the experts would do would be decided by the criminal's condition; it would be criminal-centered treatment, not crime-centered treatment.

One might object to this proposal that it overlooks the necessity of disagreeable penalties for crime, in order to deter prospective criminals

---

[17] See T. H. Green, *Lectures on Political Obligation* (London: Longmans, Green & Co., 1950), pp. 186–87; G. W. F. Hegel, *The Philosophy of Right* (Oxford: Clarendon Press, 1942), pp. 69–71; Bernard Bosanquet, *The Philosophical Theory of the State* (London: Macmillan & Co., Ltd., 1930); S. Pufendorf, *op. cit.*, II, p. 1168.

effectively. But it is doubtful whether threats of punishment have as much deterrent value as is often supposed. Threats of punishment will have little effect on morons, or on persons to whom normal living offers few prospects of an interesting existence.[18] Moreover, persons from better economic or social circumstances will be deterred sufficiently by the prospect of conviction in a public trial and being at the disposal of a board for a period of years.

Such proposals have their difficulties. For instance, would the police be as safe as they are, if criminals knew that killing a policeman would be no more serious in its consequences than the crime for which the policeman was trying to arrest them? However, there is much factual evidence for answering such questions, since systems of criminal justice along such lines are already in operation in some parts of the world, in particular among the Scandinavian countries. In fact, in some states the actual practice is closer to the projected system than one might expect from books on legal theory.

Another objection that many would raise is that psychiatry and criminology have not yet advanced far enough for such weighty decisions about the treatment of criminals to be placed in their hands. The treatment of criminals might vary drastically depending on the particular theoretical predilections of a given theorist, or on his personal likes and dislikes. One can probably say as much, or more, however, about the differences between judges, in their policies for picking a particular sentence within the range permitted by law.

An institution of criminal justice operating on such basic principles would come closer to our views about how parents should treat their children, or teachers their students, than the more traditional practices of criminal justice today.

We should repeat that this view about the ideal form for an institution of criminal justice is not in conflict with utilitarianism; in fact it is utilitarian in outlook. The motivation behind advocating it is the thought that such a system would do more good. It differs from the kind of institution traditionally advocated by utilitarians like Bentham only in making different factual assumptions, primarily about the deterrence value of threat of imprisonment, and the actual effect of imprisonment on the attitudes of the criminal.

---

[18] It is said that picking pockets was once a capital offense in England, and hangings were public, in order to get the maximum deterrent effect. But hangings in public had to be abolished, because such crimes as picking pockets were so frequent during the spectacle! See N. F. Cantor, *Crime, Criminals, and Criminal Justice* (New York: Henry Holt & Company, Inc., 1932).

Prolegomenon to the Principles of Punishment *

H. L. A. Hart

1. Introductory

The main object of this paper is to provide a framework for the discussion of the mounting perplexities which now surround the institution of criminal punishment, and to show that any morally tolerable account of this institution must exhibit it as a compromise between distinct and partly conflicting principles.

General interest in the topic of punishment has never been greater than it is at present and I doubt if the public discussion of it has ever been more confused. The interest and the confusion are both in part due to relatively modern scepticism about two elements which have figured as essential parts of the traditionally opposed 'theories' of punishment. On the one hand, the old Benthamite confidence in fear of the penalties threatened by the law as a powerful deterrent, has waned with the growing realization that the part played by calculation of any sort in anti-social behaviour has been exaggerated. On the other hand a cloud of doubt has settled over the keystone of 'retributive' theory. Its advocates can no longer speak with the old confidence that statements of the form 'This man who has broken the law could have kept it' had a univocal or agreed meaning; or where scepticism does not attach to the *meaning* of this form of statement, it has shaken the confidence that we are generally able to distinguish the cases where a statement of this form is true from those where it is not.[1]

Yet quite apart from the uncertainty engendered by these funda-

---

* From *Punishment and Responsibility* by H. L. A. Hart. © Oxford University Press, and by permission of The Clarendon Press, Oxford. This chapter was originally written as the Presidential Address to the Aristotelian Society on 19 October 1959.

[1] See Barbara Wootton, *Social Science and Social Pathology* (1959), for a comprehensive modern statement of these doubts.

mental doubts, which seem to call in question the accounts given of the efficacy, and the morality of punishment by all the old competing theories, the public utterances of those who conceive themselves to be expounding, as plain men for other plain men, orthodox or common-sense principles (untouched by modern psychological doubts) are uneasy. Their words often sound as if the authors had not fully grasped their meaning or did not intend the words to be taken quite literally. A glance at the parliamentary debates or the *Report of the Royal Commission on Capital Punishment* [2] shows that many are now troubled by the suspicion that the view that there is just one supreme value or objective (e.g. Deterrence, Retribution or Reform) in terms of which *all* questions about the justification of punishment are to be answered, is somehow wrong; yet, from what is said on such occasions no clear account of what the different values or objectives are, or how they fit together in the justification of punishment, can be extracted.[3]

No one expects judges or statesmen occupied in the business of sending people to the gallows or prison, or in making (or unmaking) laws which enable this to be done, to have much time for philosophical discussion of the principles which make it morally tolerable to do these things. A judicial bench is not and should not be a professorial chair. Yet what is said in public debates about punishment by those specially concerned with it as judges or legislators is important. Few are likely to be more circumspect, and if what they say seems, as it often does, unclear, one-sided and easily refutable by pointing to some aspect of things which they have overlooked, it is likely that in our inherited ways of talking or thinking about punishment there is some persistent drive towards an over-simplification of multiple issues which require separate consideration. To counter this drive what is most needed is *not* the simple admission that instead of a single value or aim (Deterrence, Retribution, Reform or any other) a plurality of different values and aims should be given as a conjunctive answer to some *single* question concerning the justification of punishment. What is needed is the realization that different principles (each of which may in a sense be called a 'justification') are relevant at different points in any morally acceptable account of pun-

---

[2] (1953) Cmd. 8932.

[3] In the Lords' debate in July 1956 the Lord Chancellor agreed with Lord Denning that 'the ultimate justification of any punishment is not that it is a deterrent but that it is the emphatic denunciation by the community of a crime' yet also said that 'the real crux' of the question at issue is whether capital punishment is a uniquely effective deterrent. See 198 *H. L. Deb* (5th July) 576, 577, 596 (1956). In his article, 'An Approach to the Problems of Punishment'; *Philosophy* (1958), Mr. S. I. Benn rightly observes of Lord Denning's view that denunciation does not imply the deliberate imposition of suffering which is the feature needing justification (p. 328, n. 1).

ishment. What we should look for are answers to a number of different questions such as: What justifies the general practice of punishment? To whom may punishment be applied? How severely may we punish? In dealing with these and other questions concerning punishment we should bear in mind that in this, as in most other social institutions, the pursuit of one aim may be qualified by or provide an opportunity, not to be missed, for the pursuit of others. Till we have developed this sense of the complexity of punishment (and this prolegomenon aims only to do this) we shall be in no fit state to assess the extent to which the whole institution has been eroded by, or needs to be adapted to, new beliefs about the human mind.

2. Justifying Aims and Principles of Distribution

There is, I think, an analogy worth considering between the concept of punishment and that of property. In both cases we have to do with a social institution of which the centrally important form is a structure of *legal* rules, even if it would be dogmatic to deny the names of punishment or property to the similar though more rudimentary rule-regulated practices within groups such as a family, or a school, or in customary societies whose customs may lack some of the standard or salient features of law (e.g. legislation, organized sanctions, courts). In both cases we are confronted by a complex institution presenting different inter-related features calling for separate explanation; or, if the morality of the institution is challenged, for separate justification. In both cases failure to distinguish separate questions or attempting to answer them all by reference to a single principle ends in confusion. Thus in the case of property we should distinguish between the question of the *definition* of property, the question why and in what circumstance it is a *good* institution to maintain, and the questions in what ways individuals may become *entitled* to acquire property and *how much* they should be allowed to acquire. These we may call questions of *Definition, General Justifying Aim,* and *Distribution* with the last subdivided into questions of *Title* and *Amount.* It is salutary to take some classical exposition of the idea of property, say Locke's chapter 'Of Property' in the *Second Treatise,*[4] and to observe how much darkness is spread by the use of a single notion (in this case 'the labour of (a man's) body and the work of his hands') to answer all these different questions which press upon us when we reflect on the institution of property. In the case of punishment the beginning of wisdom (though by no means its end) is to distinguish similar questions and confront them separately.

---

[4] Chapter 5.

a. Definition

Here I shall simply draw upon the recent admirable work scattered through English philosophical[5] journals and add to it only an admonition of my own against the abuse of definition in the philosophical discussion of punishment. So with Mr. Benn and Professor Flew I shall define the standard or central case of 'punishment' in terms of five elements:

i.   It must involve pain or other consequences normally considered unpleasant.
ii.   It must be for an offence against legal rules.
iii. It must be of an actual or supposed offender for his offence.
iv.   It must be intentionally administered by human beings other than the offender.
v.   It must be imposed and administered by an authority constituted by a legal system against which the offence is committed.

In calling this the standard or central case of punishment I shall relegate to the position of sub-standard or secondary cases the following among many other possibilities:

a.   Punishments for breaches of legal rules imposed or administered otherwise than by officials (decentralised sanctions).
b.   Punishments for breaches of non-legal rules or orders (punishments in a family or school).
c.   Vicarious or collective punishment of some member of a social group for actions done by others without the former's authorization, encouragement, control or permission.
d.   Punishment of persons (otherwise than under (c)) who neither are in fact nor supposed to be offenders.

The chief importance of listing these sub-standard cases is to prevent the use of what I shall call the 'definitional stop' in discussions of punishment. This is an abuse of definition especially tempting when use is made of conditions (ii) and (iii) of the standard case in arguing against the utilitarian claim that the practice of punishment is justified by the beneficial consequences resulting from the observance of the laws which it secures. Here the stock 'retributive' argument [6] is: If *this* is the justification of punishment, why not apply it, when it pays to do so, to those innocent of any crime, chosen at random, or to the wife and children of the of-

---

[5] K. Baier, 'Is Punishment Retributive?', *Analysis* (1955), p. 25. A. Flew, 'The Justification of Punishment,' *Philosophy* (1954), p. 291. S. I. Benn, *op cit.*, pp. 325–26.
[6] A. C. Ewing, *The Morality of Punishment*, D. J. B. Hawkins, *Punishment and Moral Responsibility* (The King's Good Servant, p. 92), J. D. Mabbott, 'Punishment', *Mind* (1939), p. 152.

fender? And here the wrong reply is: *That*, by definition, would not be 'punishment' and it is the justification of punishment which is in issue.[7] Not only will this definitional stop fail to satisfy the advocate of 'Retribution', it would prevent us from investigating the very thing which modern scepticism most calls in question: namely the rational and moral status of our preference for a system of punishment under which measures painful to individuals are to be taken against them only when they have committed an offence. Why do we prefer this to other forms of social hygiene which we might employ to prevent anti-social behavior and which we do employ in special circumstances, sometimes with reluctance? No account of punishment can afford to dismiss this question with a definition.

b. The Nature of an Offence

Before we reach any question of justification we must identify a preliminary question to which the answer is so simple that the question may not appear worth asking; yet it is clear that some curious 'theories' of punishment gain their only plausibility from ignoring it, and others from confusing it with other questions. This question is: Why are certain kinds of action forbidden by law and so made crimes or offences? The answer is: To announce to society that these actions are not to be done and to secure that fewer of them are done. These are the common immediate aims of making any conduct a criminal offence and until we have laws made with these primary aims we shall lack the notion of a 'crime' and so of a 'criminal'. Without recourse to the simple idea that the criminal law sets up, in its rules, standards of behaviour to encourage certain types of conduct and discourage others we cannot distinguish a punishment in the form of a fine from a tax on a course of conduct.[8] This indeed is one grave objection to those theories of law which in the interests of simplicity or uniformity obscure the distinction between primary laws setting standards for behaviour and secondary laws specifying what officials must or may do when they are broken. Such theories insist that all legal rules are 'really' directions to officials to exact 'sanctions' under certain conditions,

---

[7] Mr. Benn seemed to succumb at times to the temptation to give 'The short answer to the critics of utilitarian theories of punishment—that they are theories of *punishment* not of any sort of technique involving suffering' (*op cit.*, p. 332). He has since told me that he does not now rely on the definitional stop.

[8] This generally clear distinction may be blurred. Taxes may be imposed to discourage the activities taxed though the law does not announce this as it does when it makes them criminal. Conversely fines payable for some criminal offences because of a depreciation of currrency become so small that they are cheerfully paid and offences are frequent. They are then felt to be mere taxes because the sense is lost that the rule is meant to be taken seriously as a standard of behaviour.

e.g. if people kill.[9] Yet only if we keep alive the distinction (which such theories thus obscure) between the primary objective of the law in encouraging or discouraging certain kinds of behaviour, and its merely ancillary sanction or remedial steps, can we give sense to the notion of a crime or offence.

It is important however to stress the fact that in thus identifying the immediate aims of the criminal law we have not reached the stage of justification. There are indeed many forms of undesirable behaviour which it would be foolish (because ineffective or too costly) to attempt to inhibit by use of the law and some of these may be better left to educators, trades unions, churches, marriage guidance councils or other non-legal agencies. Conversely there are some forms of conduct which we believe cannot be effectively inhibited without use of the law. But it is only too plain that in fact the law may make activities criminal which it is morally important to promote and the suppression of these may be quite unjustifiable. Yet confusion between the simple immediate aim of any criminal legislation and the justification of punishment seems to be the most charitable explanation of the claim that punishment is *justified* as an 'emphatic denunciation by the community of a crime'. Lord Denning's dictum that this is the ultimate justification of punishment [10] can be saved from Mr. Benn's criticism, noted above, only if it is treated as a blurred statement of the truth that the aim not of punishment, but of criminal legislation is indeed to denounce certain types of conduct as something not to be practised. Conversely the immediate aim of criminal legislation cannot be any of the things which are usually mentioned as justifying punishment: for until it is settled what conduct is to be legally denounced and discouraged we have not settled from what we are to *deter* people, or who are to be considered *criminals* from whom we are to exact *retribution,* or on whom we are to wreak *vengeance,* or whom we are to *reform.*

Even those who look upon human law as a mere instrument for enforcing 'morality as such' (itself conceived as the law of God or Nature) and who at the stage of justifying punishment wish to appeal not to socially beneficial consequences but simply to the intrinsic value of inflicting suffering on wrongdoers who have disturbed by their offence the moral order, would not deny that the aim of criminal legislation is to set up types of behaviour (in this case conformity with a pre-existing moral law) as legal standards of behaviour and to secure conformity with them. No doubt in all communities certain moral offences, e.g. killing, will always be selected for suppression as crimes and it is conceivable that this

---

9 Cf. Kelsen, *General Theory of Law and State* (1945), pp. 30–33, 33–34, 143–44. 'Law is the primary norm, which stipulates the sanction. . . .' (*ibid,* 61).

10 In evidence to the Royal Commission on Capital Punishment, Cmd. 8932. para. 53 (1953). *Supra,* p. 2, n. 3.

may be done not to protect human beings from being killed but to save the potential murderer from sin; but it would be paradoxical to look upon the law as designed not to discourage murder at all (even conceived as sin rather than harm) but simply to extract the penalty from the murderer.

c. General Justifying Aim

I shall not here criticize the intelligibility or consistency or adequacy of those theories that are united in denying that the practice of a system of punishment is justified by its beneficial consequences and claim instead that the main justification of the practice lies in the fact that when breach of the law involves moral guilt the application to the offender of the pain of punishment is itself a thing of value. A great variety of claims of this character, designating 'Retribution' or 'Expiation' or 'Reprobation' as the justifying aim, fall in spite of differences under this rough general description. Though in fact I agree with Mr. Benn [11] in thinking that these all either avoid the question of justification altogether or are in spite of their protestations disguised forms of Utilitarianism, I shall assume that Retribution, defined simply as the application of the pains of punishment to an offender who is morally guilty, may figure among the conceivable justifying aims of a system of punishment. Here I shall merely insist that it is one thing to use the word Retribution *at this point* in an account of the principle of punishment in order to designate the General Justifying Aim of the system, and quite another to use it to secure that to the question 'To whom may punishment be applied?' (the question of Distribution), the answer given is 'Only to an offender for an offence'. Failure to distinguish Retribution as a General Justifying Aim from retribution as the simple insistence that only those who have broken the law—and voluntarily broken it—may be punished, may be traced in many writers: even perhaps in Mr. J. D. Mabbott's [12] otherwise most illuminating essay. We shall distinguish the latter from Retribution in General Aim as 'retribution in Distribution'. Much confusing shadow-fighting between utilitarians and their opponents may be avoided if it is recognized that it is perfectly consistent to assert *both* that the General Justifying Aim of the practice of punishment is its beneficial consequences *and* that the pursuit of this General Aim should be qualified or restricted out of deference to principles of Distribution which require that punishment should be only of an offender for an offence. Conversely it does not in the least follow from the admission of the latter principle of retribution in Distribution that the General Justifying Aim of punishment is Retribution though of

---

[11] *Op cit.*, pp. 326–35.
[12] *Op cit. supra* n. 6. It is not always quite clear what he considers a 'retributive' theory to be.

course Retribution in General Aim entails retribution in Distribution.

We shall consider later the principles of justice lying at the root of retribution in Distribution. Meanwhile it is worth observing that both the old fashioned Retributionist (in General Aim) and the most modern sceptic often make the same (and, I think, wholly mistaken) assumption that sense can only be made of the restrictive principle that punishment be applied only to an offender for an offence if the General Justifying Aim of the practice of punishment is Retribution. The sceptic consequently imputes to all systems of punishment (when they are restricted by the principle of retribution in Distribution) all the irrationality he finds in the idea of Retribution as a General Justifying Aim; conversely the advocates of the latter think the admission of retribution in Distribution is a refutation of the utilitarian claim that the social consequences of punishment are its Justifying Aim.

The most general lesson to be learnt from this extends beyond the topic of punishment. It is, that in relation to any social institution, after stating what general aim or value its maintenance fosters we should enquire whether there are any and if so what principles limiting the unqualified pursuit of that aim or value. Just because the pursuit of any single social aim always has its restrictive qualifier, our main social institutions always possess a plurality of features which can only be understood as a compromise between partly discrepant principles. This is true even of relatively minor legal institutions like that of a contract. In general this is designed to enable individuals to give effect to their wishes to create structures of legal rights and duties, and so to change, in certain ways, their legal position. Yet at the same time there is need to protect those who, in good faith, understand a verbal offer made to them to mean what it would ordinarily mean, accept it, and then act on the footing that a valid contract has been concluded. As against them, it would be unfair to allow the other party to say that the words he used in his verbal offer or the interpretation put on them did not express his real wishes or intention. Hence principles of 'estoppel' or doctrines of the 'objective sense' of a contract are introduced to prevent this and to qualify the principle that the law enforces contracts in order to give effect to the joint wishes of the contracting parties.

d. Distribution

This as in the case of property has two aspects (i) Liability (Who may be punished?) and (ii) Amount. In this section I shall chiefly be concerned with the first of these.[13]

---

[13] Amount is considered below in Section III (in connexion with Mitigation) and Section V.

From the foregoing discussions two things emerge. First, though we may be clear as to what value the practice of punishment is to promote, we have still to answer as a question of Distribution 'Who may be punished?' Secondly, if in answer to this question we say 'only an offender for an offence' this admission of retribution in Distribution is not a principle from which anything follows as to the severity or amount of punishment; in particular it neither licenses nor requires, as Retribution in General Aim does, more severe punishments than deterrence or other utilitarian criteria would require.

The root question to be considered is, however, why we attach the moral importance which we do to retribution in Distribution. Here I shall consider the efforts made to show that restriction of punishment to offenders is a simple consequence of whatever principles (Retributive or Utilitarian) constitute the Justifying Aim of punishment.

The standard example used by philosophers to bring out the importance of retribution in Distribution is that of a wholly innocent person who has not even unintentionally done anything which the law punishes if done intentionally. It is supposed that in order to avert some social catastrophe officials of the system fabricate evidence on which he is charged, tried, convicted and sent to prison or death. Or it is supposed that without resort to any fraud more persons may be deterred from crime if wives and children of offenders were punished vicariously for their crimes. In some forms this kind of thing may be ruled out by a consistent sufficiently comprehensive utilitarianism.[14] Certainly expedients involving fraud or faked charges might be very difficult to justify on utilitarian grounds. We can of course imagine that a negro might be sent to prison or executed on a false charge of rape in order to avoid widespread lynching of many others; but a *system* which openly empowered authorities to do this kind of thing, even if it succeeded in averting specific evils like lynching, would awaken such apprehension and insecurity that any gain from the exercise of these powers would by any utilitarian calculation be offset by the misery caused by their existence. But official resort to this kind of fraud on a particular occasion in breach of the rules and the subsequent indemnification of the officials responsible might save many lives and so be thought to yield a clear surplus of value. Certainly vicarious punishment of an offender's family might do so and legal systems have occasionally though exceptionally resorted to this. An example of it is the Roman *Lex Quisquis* providing for the punishment of the children of those guilty of *majestas*.[15] In extreme cases many might still think it right to resort to these expedients but we should do so with the sense of sacri-

---

[14] See J. Rawls, 'Two Concepts of Rules,' *Philosophical Review* (1955), pp. 4–13.

[15] Constitution of emperors Arcadius and Honorius (A.D. 397).

ficing an important principle. We should be conscious of choosing the lesser of two evils, and this would be inexplicable if the principle sacrificed to utility were itself only a requirement of utility.

Similarly the moral importance of the restriction of punishment to the offender cannot be explained as merely a consequence of the principle that the General Justifying Aim is Retribution for immorality involved in breaking the law. Retribution in the Distribution of punishment has a value quite independent of Retribution as Justifying Aim. This is shown by the fact that we attach importance to the restrictive principle that only offenders may be punished, even where breach of this law might not be thought immoral. Indeed even where the laws themselves are hideously immoral as in Nazi Germany, e.g. forbidding activities (helping the sick or destitute of some racial group) which might be thought morally obligatory, the absence of the principle restricting punishment to the offender would be a further *special* iniquity; whereas admission of this principle would represent some residual respect for justice shown in the administration of morally bad laws.

On Deterrence and the Death Penalty *

Ernest van den Haag

I

If rehabilitation and the protection of society from unrehabilitated offenders were the only purposes of legal punishment the death penalty could be abolished: it cannot attain the first end, and is not needed for the second. No case for the death penalty can be made unless "doing justice," or "deterring others," are among our penal aims.[1] Each of these purposes can justify capital punishment by itself; opponents, therefore, must show that neither actually does, while proponents can rest their case on either.

---

* "On Deterrence and the Death Penalty," by Ernest van den Haag. Reprinted by special permission of the *Journal of Criminal Law, Criminology and Police Science*, Copyright © 1969 by Northwestern University School of Law, Vol. 60, No. 2 (1969).

[1] Social solidarity of "community feeling" (here to be ignored) might be dealt with as a form of deterrence.

Although the argument from justice is intellectually more interesting, and, in my view, decisive enough, utilitarian arguments have more appeal: the claim that capital punishment is useless because it does not deter others, is most persuasive. I shall, therefore, focus on this claim. Lest the argument be thought to be unduly narrow, I shall show, nonetheless, that some claims of injustice rest on premises which the claimants reject when arguments for capital punishment are derived therefrom; while other claims of injustice have no independent standing: their weight depends on the weight given to deterrence.

II

Capital punishment is regarded as unjust because it may lead to the execution of innocents, or because the guilty poor (or disadvantaged) are more likely to be executed than the guilty rich.

Regardless of merit, these claims are relevant only if "doing justice" is one purpose of punishment. Unless one regards it as good, or, at least, better, that the guilty be punished rather than the innocent, and that the equally guilty be punished equally,[2] unless, that is, one wants penalties to be just, one cannot object to them because they are not. However, if one does include justice among the purposes of punishment, it becomes possible to justify any one punishment—even death—on grounds of justice. Yet, those who object to the death penalty because of its alleged injustice, usually deny not only the merits, or the sufficiency, of specific arguments based on justice, but the propriety of justice as an argument: they exclude "doing justice" as a purpose of legal punishment. If justice is not a purpose of penalties, injustice cannot be an objection to the death penalty, or to any other; if it is, justice cannot be ruled out as an argument for any penalty.

Consider the claim of injustice on its merits now. A convicted man may be found to have been innocent; if he was executed, the penalty cannot be reversed. Except for fines, penalties never can be reversed. Time spent in prison cannot be returned. However a prison sentence may be remitted once the prisoner serving it is found innocent; and he can be compensated for the time served (although compensation ordinarily cannot repair the harm). Thus, though (nearly) all penalties are irreversible, the death penalty, unlike others, is irrevocable as well.

Despite all precautions, errors will occur in judicial proceedings: the innocent may be found guilty;[3] or the guilty rich may more easily escape conviction, or receive lesser penalties than the guilty poor. However,

---

[2] Certainly a major meaning of *suum cuique tribue.*

[3] I am not concerned here with the converse injustice, *which I regard as no less grave.*

these injustices do not reside in the penalties inflicted but in their mal-distribution. It is not the penalty—whether death or prison—which is un-just when inflicted on the innocent, but its imposition on the innocent. Inequity between poor and rich also involves distribution, not the penalty distributed.[4] Thus injustice is not an objection to the death penalty but to the distributive process—the trial. Trials are more likely to be fair when life is at stake—the death penalty is probably less often unjustly inflicted than others. It requires special consideration not because it is more, or more often, unjust than other penalties, but because it is always irre-vocable.

Can any amount of deterrence justify the possibility of irrevocable injustice? Surely injustice is unjustifiable in each actual individual case; it must be objected to whenever it occurs. But we are concerned here with the process that may produce injustice, and with the penalty that would make it irrevocable—not with the actual individual cases produced, but with the general rules which may produce them. To consider objections to a general rule (the provision of any penalties by law) we must com-pare the likely net result of alternative rules and select the rule (or penalty) likely to produce the least injustice. For however one defines justice, to support it cannot mean less than to favor the least injustice. If the death of innocents because of judicial error is unjust, so is the death of innocents by murder. If some murders could be avoided by a penalty conceivably more deterrent than others—such as the death penalty—then the question becomes: which penalty will minimize the number of inno-cents killed (by crime and by punishment)? It follows that the irre-vocable injustice sometimes inflicted by the death penalty would not significantly militate against it, if capital punishment deters enough murders to reduce the total number of innocents killed so that fewer are lost than would be lost without it.

In general, the possibility of injustice argues against penalization of any kind only if the expected usefulness of penalization is less important than the probable harm (particularly to innocents) and the probable inequities. The possibility of injustice argues against the death penalty only inasmuch as the added usefulness (deterrence) expected from irrevocability is thought less important than the added harm. (Were my argument specifically concerned with justice, I could compare the injustice inflicted by the courts with the injustice—outside the courts—avoided by the judicial process. I.e., "important" here may be used to include everything to which importance is attached.)

---

[4] Such inequity, though likely, has not been demonstrated. Note that, since there are more poor than rich, there are likely to be more guilty poor; and, if poverty contributes to crime, the proportion of the poor who are criminals also should be higher than that of the rich.

We must briefly examine now the general use and effectiveness of deterrence to decide whether the death penalty could add enough deterrence to be warranted.

III

Does any punishment "deter others" at all? Doubts have been thrown on this effect because it is thought to depend on the incorrect rationalistic psychology of some of its 18th and 19th century proponents. Actually deterrence does not depend on rational calculation, on rationality or even on capacity for it; nor do arguments for it depend on rationalistic psychology. Deterrence depends on the likelihood and on the regularity—not on the rationality—of human responses to danger; and further on the possibility of reinforcing internal controls by vicarious external experiences.

Responsiveness to danger is generally found in human behavior; the danger can, but need not, come from the law or from society; nor need it be explicitly verbalized. Unless intent on suicide, people do not jump from high mountain cliffs, however tempted to fly through the air; and they take precautions against falling. The mere risk of injury often restrains us from doing what is otherwise attractive; we refrain even when we have no direct experience, and usually without explicit computation of probabilities, let alone conscious weighing of expected pleasure against possible pain. One abstains from dangerous acts because of vague, inchoate, habitual and, above all, preconscious fears. Risks and rewards are more often felt than calculated; one abstains without accounting to oneself, because "it isn't done," or because one literally does not conceive of the action one refrains from. Animals as well refrain from painful or injurious experiences presumably without calculation; and the threat of punishment can be used to regulate their conduct.

Unlike natural dangers, legal threats are constructed deliberately by legislators to restrain actions which may impair the social order. Thus legislation transforms social into individual dangers. Most people further transform external into internal danger: they acquire a sense of moral obligation, a conscience, which threatens them, should they do what is wrong. Arising originally from the external authority of rulers and rules, conscience is internalized and becomes independent of external forces. However, conscience is constantly reinforced in those whom it controls by the coercive imposition of external authority on recalcitrants and on those who have not acquired it. Most people refrain from offenses because they feel an obligation to behave lawfully. But this obligation would scarcely be felt if those who do not feel or follow it were not to suffer punishment.

Although the legislators may calculate their threats and the responses to be produced, the effectiveness of the threats neither requires nor depends on calculations by those responding. The predictor (or producer) of effects must calculate; those whose responses are predicted (or produced) need not. Hence, although legislation (and legislators) should be rational, subjects, to be deterred as intended, need not be: they need only be responsive.

Punishments deter those who have not violated the law for the same reasons—and in the same degrees (apart from internalization: moral obligation) as do natural dangers. Often natural dangers—all dangers not deliberately created by legislation (e.g., injury of the criminal inflicted by the crime victim) are insufficient. Thus, the fear of injury (natural danger) does not suffice to control city traffic; it must be reinforced by the legal punishment meted out to those who violate the rules. These punishments keep most people observing the regulations. However, where (in the absence of natural danger) the threatened punishment is so light that the advantage of violating rules tends to exceed the disadvantage of being punished (divided by the risk), the rule is violated (i.e., parking fines are too light). In this case the feeling of obligation tends to vanish as well. Elsewhere punishment deters.

To be sure, not everybody responds to threatened punishment. Nonresponsibe persons may be (a) self-destructive or (b) incapable of responding to threats, or even of grasping them. Increases in the size, or certainty, of penalties would not affect these two groups. A third group (c) might respond to more certain or more severe penalties.[5] If the punishment threatened for burglary, robbery, or rape were a $5 fine in North Carolina, and 5 years in prison in South Carolina, I have no doubt that the North Carolina treasury would become quite opulent until vigilante justice would provide the deterrence not provided by law. Whether to increase penalties (or improve enforcement) depends on the importance of the rule to society, the size and likely reaction of the group that did not respond before, and the acceptance of the added punishment and enforcement required to deter it. Observation would have to locate the points—likely to differ in different times and places—at which diminishing, zero, and negative returns set in. There is no reason to believe that all present and future offenders belong to the a priori non-responsive

---

[5] I neglect those motivated by civil disobedience or, generally, moral or political passion. Deterring them depends less on penalties than on the moral support they receive, though penalties play a role. I also neglect those who may belong to all three groups listed, some successively, some even simultaneously, such as drug addicts. Finally, I must altogether omit the far from negligible role problems of apprehension and conviction play in deterrence—beyond saying that by reducing the government's ability to apprehend and convict, courts are able to reduce the risks of offenders.

groups, or that all penalties have reached the point of diminishing, let alone zero returns.

IV

Even though its effectiveness seems obvious, punishment as a deterrent has fallen into disrepute. Some ideas which help explain this progressive heedlessness were uttered by Lester Pearson, then Prime Minister of Canada, when, in opposing the death penalty, he proposed that instead "the state seek to eradicate the causes of crime—slums, ghettos and personality disorders." [6]

"Slum, ghettos and personality disorders" have not been shown, singly or collectively, to be "the causes" of crime.

1. The crime rate in the slums is indeed higher than elsewhere; but so is the death rate in hospitals. Slums are no more "causes" of crime, than hospitals are of death; they are locations of crime, as hospitals are of death. Slums and hospitals attract people selectively; neither is the "cause" of the condition (disease in hospitals, poverty in slums) that leads to the selective attraction.

As for poverty which draws people into slums, and, sometimes, into crime, any relative disadvantage may lead to ambition, frustration, resentment and, if insufficiently restrained, to crime. Not all relative disadvantages can be eliminated; indeed very few can be, and their elimination increases the resentment generated by the remaining ones; not even relative poverty can be removed altogether. (Absolute poverty—whatever that may be—hardly affects crime.) However, though contributory, relative disadvantages are not a necessary or sufficient cause of crime: most poor people do not commit crimes, and some rich people do. Hence, "eradication of poverty" would, at most, remove one (doubtful) cause of crime.

In the United States, the decline of poverty has not been associated with a reduction of crime. Poverty measured in dollars of constant purchasing power, according to present government standards and statistics, was the condition of $\frac{1}{2}$ of all our families in 1920; of $\frac{1}{5}$th in 1962; and of less than $\frac{1}{6}$ in 1966. In 1967, 5.3 million families out of 49.8 million were poor—$\frac{1}{9}$ of all families in the United States. If crime has been reduced in a similar manner, it is a well kept secret.

Those who regard poverty as a cause of crime often draw a wrong inference from a true proposition: the rich will not commit certain crimes—

---

[6] *N.Y. Times*, Nov. 24, 1967, at 22. The actual psychological and other factors which bear on the disrepute—as distinguished from the rationalizations—cannot be examined here.

Rockefeller never riots; nor does he steal. (He mugs, but only on T.V.) Yet while wealth may be the cause of not committing (certain) crimes, it does not follow that poverty (absence of wealth) is the cause of committing them. Water extinguishes or prevents fire; but its absence is not the cause of fire. Thus, if poverty could be abolished, if everybody had all "necessities" (I don't pretend to know what this would mean), crime would remain, for, in the words of Aristoteles "the greatest crimes are committed not for the sake of basic necessities but for the sake of superfluities." Superfluities cannot be provided by the government; they would be what the government does not provide.

2. Negro ghettos have a high, Chinese ghettos have a low crime rate. Ethnic separation, voluntary or forced, obviously has little to do with crime; I can think of no reason why it should.[7]

3. I cannot see how the state could "eradicate" personality disorders even if all causes and cures were known and available. (They are not.) Further, the known incidence of personality disorders within the prison population does not exceed the known incidence outside—though our knowledge of both is tenuous. Nor are personality disorders necessary, or sufficient causes for criminal offenses, unless these be identified by means of (moral, not clinical) definition with personality disorders. In this case, Mr. Pearson would have proposed to "eradicate" crime by eradicating crime—certainly a sound, but not a helpful idea.

Mr. Pearson's views are part as well of the mental furniture of the former U.S. Attorney General, Ramsey Clark, who told a congressional committee that ". . . only the elimination of the causes of crime can make a significant and lasting difference in the incidence of crime." Uncharitably interpreted, Mr. Clark revealed that only the elimination of causes eliminates effects—a sleazy cliche and wrong to boot. Given the benefit of the doubt, Mr. Clark probably meant that the causes of crime are social; and that therefore crime can be reduced "only" by non-penal (social) measures.

This view suggests a fireman who declines fire-fighting apparatus by pointing out that "in the long run only the elimination of the causes" of fire "can make a significant and lasting difference in the incidence" of fire, and that fire-fighting equipment does not eliminate "the causes"—except that such a fireman would probably not rise to fire chief. Actually, whether fires are checked depends on equipment and on the efforts of the firemen using it no less than on the presence of "the causes": inflammable ma-

---

[7] Mixed areas, incidentally, have higher crime rates than segregated ones. See, e.g., Ross & van den Haag, *The Fabric of Society*, 102–4 (1957). Because slums are bad (morally) and crime is, many people seem to reason that "slums spawn crime"—which confuses some sort of moral with a causal relation.

terials. So with crimes. Laws, courts and police actions are no less important in restraining them, than "the causes" are in impelling them. If firemen (or attorneys general) pass the buck and refuse to use the means available, we may all be burned while waiting for "the long run" and "the elimination of the causes."

Whether any activity—be it lawful or unlawful—takes place depends on whether the desire for it, or for whatever is to be secured by it, is stronger than the desire to avoid the costs involved. Accordingly people work, attend college, commit crimes, go to the movies—or refrain from any of these activities. Attendance at a theatre may be high because the show is entertaining and because the price of admission is low. Obviously the attendance depends on both—on the combination of expected gratification and cost. The wish, motive or impulse for doing anything—the experienced, or expected, gratification—is the cause of doing it; the wish to avoid the cost is the cause of not doing it. One is no more and no less "cause" than the other. (Common speech supports this use of "cause" no less than logic: "Why did you go to Jamaica?" "*Because* it is such a beautiful place." "Why didn't you go to Jamaica?" "*Because* it is too expensive."—"Why do you buy this?" "*Because* it is so cheap." "Why don't you buy that?" "*Because* it is too expensive.") Penalties (costs) are causes of lawfulness, or (if too low or uncertain) of unlawfulness, of crime. People do commit crimes because, given their conditions, the desire for the satisfaction sought prevails. They refrain if the desire to avoid the cost prevails. Given the desire, low cost (penalty) causes the action, and high cost restraint. Given the cost, desire becomes the causal variable. Neither is intrinsically more causal than the other. The crime rate increases if the cost is reduced or the desire raised. It can be decreased by raising the cost or by reducing the desire.

The cost of crime is more easily and swiftly changed than the conditions producing the inclination to it. Further, the costs are very largely within the power of the government to change, whereas the conditions producing propensity to crime are often only indirectly affected by government action, and some are altogether beyond the control of the government. Our unilateral emphasis on these conditions and our undue neglect of costs may contribute to an unnecessarily high crime rate.

V

The foregoing suggests the question posed by the death penalty: is the deterrence added (return) sufficiently above zero to warrant irrevocability (or other, less clear, disadvantages)? The question is not only whether the penalty deters, but whether it deters more than alternatives and whether the difference exceeds the cost of irrevocability. (I shall assume that the alternative is actual life imprisonment so as to exclude the complication produced by the release of the unrehabilitated.)

In some fairly infrequent but important circumstances the death penalty is the only possible deterrent. Thus, in case of acute *coups d'état,* or of acute substantial attempts to overthrow the government, prospective rebels would altogether discount the threat of any prison sentence. They would not be deterred because they believe the swift victory of the revolution will invalidate a prison sentence and turn it into an advantage. Execution would be the only deterrent because, unlike prison sentences, it cannot be revoked by victorious rebels. The same reasoning applies to deterring spies or traitors in wartime. Finally, men who, by virtue of past acts, are already serving, or are threatened, by a life sentence, could be deterred from further offenses only by the threat of the death penalty.[8]

What about criminals who do not fall into any of these (often ignored) classes? Prof. Thorsten Sellin has made a careful study of the available statistics: he concluded that they do not yield evidence for the deterring effect of the death penalty.[9] Somewhat surprisingly, Prof. Sellin seems to think that this lack of evidence for deterrence is evidence for the lack of deterrence. It is not. It means that deterrence has not been demonstrated statistically—not that non-deterrence has been.

It is entirely possible, indeed likely (as Prof. Sellin appears willing to concede), that the statistics used, though the best available, are nonetheless too slender a reed to rest conclusions on. They indicate that the homicide rate does not vary greatly between similar areas with or without the death penalty, and in the same area before and after abolition. However, the similar areas are not similar enough; the periods are not long enough; many social differences and changes, other than the abolition of the death penalty, may account for the variation (or lack of) in homicide rates with and without, before and after abolition; some of these social differences and changes are likely to have affected homicide rates. I am unaware of any statistical analysis which adjusts for such changes and differences. And logically, it is quite consistent with the postulated deterrent effect of capital punishment that there be less homicide after abolition: with retention there might have been still less.

Homicide rates do not depend exclusively on penalties any more than do other crime rates. A number of conditions which influence the pro-

---

[8] Cautious revolutionaries, uncertain of final victory, might be impressed by prison sentences—but not in the acute stage, when faith in victory is high. And one can increase even the severity of a life sentence in prison. Finally, harsh punishment of rebels can intensify rebellious impulses. These points, though they qualify it, hardly impair the force of the argument.

[9] Prof. Sellin considered mainly homicide statistics. His work may be found in his *Capital Punishment* (1967), or, most conveniently, in Bedau, *The Death Penalty in America* (1964), which also offers other material, mainly against the death penalty.

pensity to crime, demographic, economic or generally social, changes or differences—even such matters as changes of the divorce laws or of the cotton price—may influence the homicide rate. Therefore variation or constancy cannot be attributed to variations or constancy of the penalties, unless we know that no other factor influencing the homicide rate has changed. Usually we don't. To believe the death penalty deterrent does not require one to believe that the death penalty, or any other, is the only, or the decisive causal variable; this would be as absurd as the converse mistake that "social causes" are the only, or always the decisive factor. To favor capital punishment, the efficacy of neither variable need be denied. It is enough to affirm that the severity of the penalty may influence some potential criminals, and that the added severity of the death penalty adds to deterrence, or may do so. It is quite possible that such a deterrent effect may be offset (or intensified) by non-penal factors which affect propensity; its presence or absence therefore may be hard, and perhaps impossible to demonstrate.

Contrary to what Prof. Sellin *et al.* seem to presume, I doubt that offenders are aware of the absence of presence of the death penalty state by state or period by period. Such unawareness argues against the assumption of a calculating murderer. However, unawareness does not argue against the death penalty if by deterrence we mean a preconscious, general response to a severe, but not necessarily specifically and explicitly apprehended, or calculated threat. A constant homicide rate, despite abolition, may occur because of unawareness and not because of lack of deterrence: people remain deterred for a lengthy interval by the severity of the penalty in the past, or by the severity of penalties used in similar circumstances nearby.

I do not argue for a version of deterrence which would require me to believe that an individual shuns murder while in North Dakota, because of the death penalty, and merrily goes to it in South Dakota since it has been abolished there; or that he will start the murderous career from which he had hitherto refrained, after abolition. I hold that the generalized threat of the death penalty may be a deterrent, and the more so, the more generally applied. Deterrence will not cease in the particular areas of abolition or at the particular times of abolition. Rather, general deterrence will be somewhat weakened, through local (partial) abolition. Even such weakening will be hard to detect owing to changes in many offsetting, or reinforcing, factors.

For all of these reasons, I doubt that the presence or absence of a deterrent effect of the death penalty is likely to be demonstrable by statistical means. The statistics presented by Prof. Sellin *et al.*, show only that there is no statistical proof for the deterrent effect of the death penalty. But they do not show that there is no deterrent effect. Not to demonstrate presence of the effect is not the same as to demonstrate its absence; certainly not when there are plausible explanations for the non-demonstrability of the effect.

It is on our uncertainty that the case for deterrence must rest.[10]

VI

If we do not know whether the death penalty will deter others, we are confronted with two uncertainties. If we impose the death penalty, and achieve no deterrent effect thereby, the life of a convicted murderer has been expended in vain (from a deterrent viewpoint). There is a net loss. If we impose the death sentence and thereby deter some future murderers, we spared the lives of some future victims (the prospective murderers gain too; they are spared punishment because they were deterred). In this case, the death penalty has led to a net gain, unless the life of a convicted murderer is valued more highly than that of the unknown victim, or victims (and the non-imprisonment of the deterred non-murderer).

The calculation can be turned around, of course. The absence of the death penalty may harm no one and therefore produce a gain—the life of the convicted murderer. Or it may kill future victims of murderers who could have been deterred, and thus produce a loss—their life.

To be sure, we must risk something certain—the death (or life) of the convicted man, for something uncertain—the death (or life) of the victims of murderers who may be deterred. This is in the nature of uncertainty—when we invest, or gamble, we risk the money we have for an uncertain gain. Many human actions, most commitments—including marriage and crime—share this characteristic with the deterrent purpose of any penalization, and with its rehabilitative purpose (and even with the protective).

More proof is demanded for the deterrent effect of the death penalty than is demanded for the deterrent effect of other penalties. This is not justified by the absence of other utilitarian purposes such as protection and rehabilitation; they involve no less uncertainty than deterrence.[11]

Irrevocability may support a demand for some reason to expect more

---

[10] In view of the strong emotions aroused (itself an indication of effectiveness to me: might murderers not be as upset over the death penalty as those who wish to spare them?) and because I believe penalties must reflect community feeling to be effective, I oppose mandatory death sentences and favor optional recommendations by juries after their finding of guilt. The opposite course risks the non-conviction of guilty defendents by juries who do not want to see them executed.

[11] Rehabilitation or protection are of minor importance in our actual penal system (though not in our theory). We confine many people who do not need rehabilitation and against whom we do not need protection (e.g., the exasperated husband who killed his wife); we release many unrehabilitated offenders against whom protection is needed. Certainly rehabilitation and protection are not, and deterrence is, the main actual function of legal punishment, if we disregard non-utilitarian purposes.

deterrence than revocable penalties might produce, but not a demand for more proof of deterrence, as has been pointed out above. The reason for expecting more deterrence lies in the greater severity, the terrifying effect inherent in finality. Since it seems more important to spare victims than to spare murderers, the burden of proving that the greater severity inherent in irrevocability adds nothing to deterrence lies on those who oppose capital punishment. Proponents of the death penalty need show only that there is no more uncertainty about it than about greater severity in general.

The demand that the death penalty be proved more deterrent than alternatives can not be satisfied any more than the demand that six years in prison be proved to be more deterrent than three. But the uncertainty which confronts us favors the death penalty as long as by imposing it we might save future victims of murder. This effect is as plausible as the general idea that penalties have deterrent effects which increase with their severity. Though we have no proof of the positive deterrence of the penalty, we also have no proof of zero, or negative effectiveness. I believe we have no right to risk additional future victims of murder for the sake of sparing convicted murderers; on the contrary, our moral obligation is to risk the possible ineffectiveness of executions. However rationalized, the opposite view appears to be motivated by the simple fact that executions are more subjected to social control than murder. However, this applies to all penalties and does not argue for the abolition of any.

Deterrence and the Death Penalty:

A Reconsideration *

Hugo Adam Bedau

Professor Van den Haag's recent article, "On Deterrence and the Death Penalty," [1] raises a number of points of that mixed (i.e., empirical-

---

* "Deterrence and the Death Penalty: a Reconsideration" by Hugo Adam Bedau. Reprinted by special permission of the *Journal of Criminal Law, Criminology and Police Science*, Copyright © 1971 by Northwestern University School of Law, Vol. 61, No. 4 (1971)

[1] Van den Haag, "On Deterrence and the Death Penalty," 60 *J. Crim. L. C. & P.S.* 141 (1969). This is a "revised version" under the same title of an article which first appeared in 78 *Ethics* 280 (1968). The author is grateful to Professor Van den Haag for the provision of a reprint of each version of the article.

and-conceptual-and-normative) character which typifies most actual reasoning in social and political controversy but which (except when its purely formal aspects are in question) tends to be ignored by philosophers. This discussion will pass by any number of tempting points in his critique in order to focus in detail only on those which affect his asserted major topic—the issue of deterrence as it bears on the retention or abolition of the death penalty.

Van den Haag's main contentions appear to be the following:

1. Abolitionists of a utilitarian persuasion "claim that capital punishment is useless because it does not deter others. . . ." [2]

2. There are some classes of criminals and some circumstances for which "the death penalty is the only possible deterrent." [3]

3. As things currently stand, "deterrence [of criminal homicide by the death penalty] has not been demonstrated statistically"; but it is erroneous to assume that "non-deterrence" has been demonstrated statistically. [4]

4. The death penalty is to be favored over imprisonment because "the added severity of the death penalty adds to deterrence, or may do so." [5]

5. "Since it seems more important to spare victims than to spare murderers, the burden of proving that the greater severity inherent in irrevocability adds nothing to deterrence lies on those who oppose capital punishment." [6]

The refutation of the foregoing assertions will constitute the task of this article. The rebuttal arguments may be succinctly summarized as follows: regarding (1), utilitarian abolitionists do not argue as Van den Haag claims, and they would be in error if they did; his assertion in (2), that situations exist in which the death penalty is the only possible deterrent, is misleading and, in the interesting cases, is empirically insignificant; concerning (3), the heart of the dispute, Van den Haag is correct in affirming that deterrence has not been determined statistically, but he is incorrect in denying that non-deterrence has been demonstrated statistically; his suggestion, (4), that the added severity of the death penalty contributes to its deterrent function, is unempirical and one-sided as well;

---

[2] 60 *J. Crim. L. C. & P.S.* 141 (1969).
[3] *Id.* at 145.
[4] *Id.*
[5] *Id.* at 146.
[6] *Id.* at 147.

finally, his contention regarding the burden of proof, (5), which he would impose entirely upon abolitionists, is a dodge and is based on a muddled analysis.

The reason for pursuing in some detail what at first might appear to be mere polemical controversy is not that Professor Van den Haag's essay is so persuasive nor that it is likely to be of unusual influence. The reason is that the issues he raises, even though they are familiar, have not been adequately discussed, despite a dozen state, congressional, and foreign government investigations into capital punishment in recent years. In Massachusetts, for example, several persons under sentence of death have been granted stays of execution pending the final report of a special legislative commission to investigate the death penalty. The exclusive mandate of this commission is to study the question of deterrence.[7] Its provisional conclusions, published late in 1968, though not in line with Professor Van den Haag's views, are open to the kind of criticism he makes. This suggests that his reasoning may be representative of many who have tried to understand the arguments and research studies brought forward by those who would abolish the death penalty, and therefore that his errors are worth exposure and correction.

I

The claim Van den Haag professes to find "most persuasive"—"capital punishment is useless because it does not deter others"—is strange, and it is strange that he finds it so persuasive. Anyone who would make this claim must assume that only deterrent efficacy is relevant to assessing the utility of a punishment. In a footnote, Van den Haag implicitly concedes that deterrence may not be the only utilitarian consideration, when he asserts that whatever our penal "theory" may tell us, "deterrence is . . . the *main actual* function of legal punishment if we disregard nonutilitarian ones." [8] But he does not pursue this qualification. It may be conceded that if "the main actual function" means the main intended or professed function of a punishment for those responsible for instituting it, deter-

---

[7] See ch. 150, Mass. Acts & Resolves 929 (1969); *Mass. Legislative Report, Interim Report of the Special Commission Established to Make an Investigation and Study Relative to the Effectiveness of Capital Punishment as a Deterrent to Crime* (1968) (unpublished).

[8] Van den Haag, *supra* note 1, at 147 n. 11 (emphasis added).

rence is probably the main function of punishment. His definition of deterrence, however, remains vulnerable. According to Van den Haag, it is "a preconscious, general response to a severe but not necessarily specifically and explicitly apprehended or calculated threat." [9]

This definition of deterrence has two merits and at least one fatal defect. First, it preserves the idea that "a law can have no deterrent effect upon a potential criminal if he is unaware of its existence." [10] Surely, this is a truism necessary to the establishment of a definition of "deterrence." Second, by emphasizing threats, it avoids the errors in defining deterrence as "the preventative effect which actual or theoretical punishment of offenders has upon potential offenders." [11] On such a definition, one could not distinguish between the *deterrent* effect of the death penalty and its more inclusive *preventive* effects. Obviously, an executed criminal is prevented from further crimes, but not by having been deterred from them.[12]

Only rarely will the preventive and the deterrent effects of a given punishment be equivalent. Van den Haag's definition, however, falls before a similar objection upon consideration of the general, though by no means universal, desire of persons to avoid capture and punishment for the crimes they commit. Some criminologists have thought this desire to be the primary outcome of severe punishments. If so, then the outcome can result whether or not the deterrent function succeeds. Yet such a desire to avoid punishment is embraced by Van den Haag's rubric of "general response" and therefore could count as evidence for the deterrent efficacy of a punishment! Since Van den Haag's conception of deterrence does not discriminate between such fundamentally different types of "general response" to the threat of punishment, it is too ill-formulated as a definition to be of any serious use.

Among the ideas to be incorporated into any definition of deterrence are a pair of truisms: if someone has been deterred then he doesn't commit the crime, and conversely if someone does commit a crime then he hasn't been deterred. Likewise, the key notion in deterrence is prevention

---

[9] *Id.* at 146.

[10] Ball, "The Deterrence Concept in Criminology and Law," 46 *P. Crim. L., C & P.S.* 347, 351 (1955).

[11] Id. at 347.

[12] Ball writes that "Capital punishment can be totally effective as a deterrent. . . . The executed murderer is no longer a threat to society. He has been permanently deterred." *Id.* at 353. This is an erroneous conclusion to reach, and when Ball goes on to use it to argue in favor of the deterrent efficacy of the death penalty, it reveals the menace which lies hidden in a faulty definition.

by threat of punishment. Therefore, assume (Definition 1) that a given punishment (P) is a *deterrent* for a given person (A) with respect to a given crime (C) at a given time (*t*) if and only if A does not commit C at *t* because he believes he runs some risk of P if he commits C and A prefers, *ceteris paribus*, not to suffer P for committing C. This definition does not presuppose that P really is the punishment for C (a person could be deterred through a mistaken belief); it does not presuppose that A runs a high risk of incurring P (the degree of risk could be zero); or that A consciously thinks of P prior to *t* (the theory needed to account for the operation of A's beliefs and preferences on his conduct is left open). Nor does it presuppose that anyone ever suffers P (P could be a "perfect" deterrent), nor that only P could have deterred A from C (some sanction less severe than P might have worked as well). Finally, it does not presuppose that because P deters A at *t* from C, therefore P would deter A at any other time or anyone else at *t*. The definition insures that we cannot argue erroneously from the fact that A does not commit C to the conclusion that P has succeeded as a deterrent: the definition contains conditions which prevent this. Further, the definition prevents the commission of the more subtle converse error of arguing from the fact that A has not been deterred by P to the conclusion that A will (or must have) commit(ted) C. Both these errors arise from supposing that "the educative, moralizing and habituative effects of punishment," [13] which serve to prevent the bulk of the public from committing crime, are euphemisms for "deterrence" or operate by the same mechanisms that deterrence does.

Definition 1 suggests a general functional analogue appropriate to express scientific measurements of *differential deterrent efficacy* of a given punishment for a given crime with respect to a given population (Definition 2). Let us say that a given punishment P deters a given population H from a crime C to the degree D that the members of H do not commit C because they believe that they run some risk of P if they commit C and, *ceteris paribus*, they prefer not to suffer P for committing C. If D = 0, then P has completely failed as a deterrent, whereas if D = 1, P has proved to be a perfect deterrent. Given this definition and the appropriate empirical results for various values of P, C, and H, it should be possible to establish on inductive grounds the relative effectiveness of a given punishment (the value of D) as a deterrent.

Definition 2 in turn suggests the following corollary for assertions of

[13] Zimring and Hawkins, *Deterrence and Marginal Groups*, 5 *Journal of Research in Crime and Delinquency* 100 (1968).

relative superior deterrent efficacy of one punishment over another: a given punishment P_1 is a superior deterrent to another punishment P_2 with respect to some crime C and some population H if and only if: the members of H believe that they are liable to P_1 upon committing C, then they commit C to the degree d_1; whereas if the members of H believe that they are liable to P_2 upon committing C, then they commit C to the degree d_2; and $d_1 < d_2$. This formulation plainly allows the P_1 may be a more effective deterrent than P_2 for C_1 and yet less effective as a deterrent than P_2 for a different crime C_2 (with H constant), and so forth for other possibilities. When speaking about deterrence in the sections which follow, these definitions and this corollary are presupposed.

Even if Van den Haag's notion of deterrence did not need to be reformulated to incorporate the above improvements, there would still be a decisive objection to his claim. Neither classic nor contemporary utilitarians have argued for or against the death penalty *solely* on the ground of deterrence, nor would their ethical theory entitle them to do so. One measure of the non-deterrent utility of the death penalty derives from its elimination (through death of a known criminal) of future possible crimes from that source; another arises from the elimination of the criminal's probable adverse influence upon others to emulate his ways; another lies in the generally lower budgetary outlays of tax monies needed to finance a system of capital punishment as opposed to long-term imprisonment. There are still further consequences apart from deterrence which the scrupulous utilitarian must weigh, along with the three previously mentioned. Therefore, it is incorrect to assume that a demonstrated failure of the deterrent effect of the death penalty would generate an inference, on utilitarian assumptions, that "the death penalty is useless" and therefore ought to be abolished. The problem for the utilitarian is to make commensurable such diverse social utilities as those measured by deterrent efficacy, administrative costs, etc., and then to determine which penal policy in fact maximizes utility. Finally, inspection of sample arguments actually used by abolitionists [14] will show that Van den Haag has attacked a straw man: there are few if any contemporary abolitionists (and Van den Haag names none) who argue solely from professedly utilitarian assumptions, and there is none among the non-utilitarians who would abolish the death penalty solely on grounds of its deterrent inefficacy.

---

[14] See the several essays reprinted in H. Bedau, *The Death Penalty in America* 166–70 (Rev. ed. 1967).

II

Governments faced by incipient rebellion or threatened by a *coup d'état* may well conclude, as Van den Haag insists they should, that rebels (as well as traitors and spies) can be deterred, if at all, by the threat of death, since "swift victory" of the revolution "will invalidate [the deterrent efficacy] of a prison sentence." [15] But this does not reveal the importance of providing such deterrence, any more than the fact that a threat of expulsion is the severest deterrent available to university authorities reveals whether they should insist on expelling campus rebels. Also, since severe penalties might have the effect of creating martyrs for the cause, they could provoke attempts to overthrow the government to secure a kind of political sainthood. This possibility Van den Haag recognizes but claims in a footnote that it "hardly impairs the force of the argument." [16] From a logical point of view it impairs the argument considerably; from an empirical point of view, since one is wholly without any reliable facts or hypotheses on politics in such extreme situations, the entire controversy remains quite speculative.

The one important class of criminals deterrable, if at all, by the death penalty consists, according to Van den Haag, of those already under "life" sentence or guilty of a crime punishable by "life." In a trivial sense, he is correct; a person already suffering a given punishment, P, for a given crime, C_1, could not be expected to be deterred by anticipating the re-infliction of P were he to commit C_2. For if the dread of P did not deter him from committing C_1, how could the dread of P deter him from committing C_2 given that he is already experiencing P? This generalization seems to apply whenever P = "life" imprisonment. Actually, the truth is a bit more complex, because in practice (as Van den Haag concedes, again in a footnote) so-called "life" imprisonment always has its aggravations (e.g., solitary confinement) and its mitigations (parole eligibility). These make it logically possible to deter a person already convicted of criminal homicide and serving "life" imprisonment from committing another such crime. The aggravations available are not, in practice, likely to provide much added deterrent effect; but exactly how likely or unlikely this effect is remains a matter for empirical investigation, not idle guess-

---

[15] Van den Haag, *supra* note 1, at 145. The same argument has been advanced earlier in Hook, 7 *The New York Law Forum* 278–83 (1961). For the revised version of this argument, see H. Bedau, *supra* note 14, at 150–51.

[16] Van den Haag, *supra* note 1, at 145 n. 8.

work. Van den Haag's seeming truism, therefore, relies for its plausibility on the false assumption that "life" imprisonment is a uniform punishment not open to further deterrence-relevant aggravations and mitigations.

Empirically, the objection to his point is that persons already serving a "life" sentence do not in general constitute a source of genuine alarm to custodial personnel. Being already incarcerated and integrated into the reward structure of prison life, they do not seem to need the deterrent controls allegedly necessary for other prisoners and the general public.[17] There are convicts who are exceptions to this generalization, but there is no known way of identifying them in advance, and their number has proved to be small. It would be irrational, therefore, to design a penal policy which invokes the death penalty for the apparent purpose of deterring such convicted offenders from further criminal homicide.[18] Van den Haag cites no evidence that such policies accomplish their alleged purpose, and a review of authorities reveals none. The real question which Van den Haag's argument raises is: Is there any class of actual or potential criminals for which the death penalty exerts a marginally superior deterrent effect over every less severe alternative? With reference to this question there is no evidence at all, one way or the other. Until a determination is made as to whether there is a "marginal group" for whom the death penalty serves as a superior deterrent, there is no reason to indulge Van den Haag in his speculations.[19]

III

It is not clear why Van den Haag is so anxious to discuss whether there is evidence that the death penalty is a deterrent, or whether, as he thinks, there is no evidence that it is not a deterrent. For the issue over abolishing the death penalty, as all serious students of the subject have known for decades, is not whether (1) *the death penalty is a deterrent,* but whether (2) *the death penalty is a superior deterrent to "life" imprisonment,* and consequently the evidential dispute is also not over (1) but only over (2). As this author has argued elsewhere,[20] abolitionists have reason to contest (1) only if they are against *all* punitive alternatives to the death

---

[17] See, e.g., Sellin, "Prison Homicides," in *Capital Punishment* 154–160 (T. Sellin ed. 1967).

[18] Rhode Island (1852), North Dakota (1915), New York (1965), Vermont (1965), and New Mexico (1969), have all qualified their abolition of the death penalty by enacting such a policy. See H. Bedau, *supra* note 14, at 12.

[19] Zimring and Hawkins, *supra* note 13, at 104–5, explain that by a marginal group they mean "the entire class of persons who are objectively on the margin of a particular form of criminal behavior, or, in other words, the class of persons 'next most likely' to engage in criminal behavior in question."

[20] H. Bedau, *supra* note 14, at 260–61.

penalty. Since few abolitionists (and none cited by Van den Haag) take this extreme view, and since most are, in fact, reconciled to a punitive alternative of "life" imprisonment, we may concentrate on (2) here. It should be noticed in passing, however, that if (1) could be demonstrated to be false, there would be no need for abolitionists to marshall evidence against (2). Since the truth of (1) is a presupposition of (2), the falsity of (1) would obviate (2) entirely. While it is true that some abolitionists may be faulted for writing as if the falsity of (1) followed from the falsity of (2), this is not a complaint Van den Haag makes nor is it an error of inference upon which the argument against the death penalty depends. Similar considerations inveigh against certain pro-death penalty arguments. Proponents must do more than establish (1), they must also provide evidence in favor of (2); and they cannot infer from evidence which establishes (1) that (2) is true or even probable (unless, of course, that evidence would establish (2) independently). These considerations show us how important it is to distinguish (1) and (2) and the questions of evidence which each raises. Van den Haag never directly discusses (2); he only observes in passing that "the question is not only whether the death penalty deters but whether it deters more than alternatives. . . ." [21] Since he explicitly argues over the evidential status of (1), it is unclear whether he chose to ignore (2) or whether he thinks that his arguments regarding the evidence for (1) also have consequences for (2). Perhaps Van den Haag thinks that if there is no evidence disconfirming (1), then there can be no evidence disconfirming (2); or perhaps he thinks that none of the evidence disconfirming (2) also disconfirms (1). (If he thinks either, he is wrong.) Or perhaps he is careless, conceding on the one hand that (2) is important to the issue of abolition of the death penalty, only to slide back into a discussion exclusively about (1).

Van den Haag writes as if his chief contentions were these two: first, we must not confuse (a) the assertion that there is no evidence that (1), with (b) the assertion that there is evidence that not-(1), i.e, evidence that (1) is false; and second, abolitionists have asserted (b) whereas all they are entitled to assert is (a).[22] I grant, as anyone must, that the dis-

---

21 Van den Haag, *supra* note 1, at 145.

22 Van den Haag accuses Professor Thornsten Sellin, a criminologist "who has made a careful study of the available statistics," of appearing to "think that this lack of evidence for deterrence is evidence for the lack of deterrence." *Id.* That is, Van den Haag claims Sellin thinks that (a) is (b)! Sellin's writings, see, e.g., note 17 *supra*, do not support the contention that he "thinks" the one "is" the other. A review of his writings, which span the years from 1953–1967, will reveal a certain vacillation between the two manners of stating his conclusion. His most recent statement is unqualified in the (b) form. See Sellin, *supra* note 17, at 138. Since Van den Haag also cited this author's, *The Death Penalty in America, supra* note 14, though not in this connection, it should be added that the distinction between (a)

tinction between (a) and (b) is legitimate and important. But since, as I have argued, (1) need not be at issue in the death penalty controversy, neither are (a) and (b). What is at issue, even though Van den Haag's discussion obscures the point, is whether abolitionists must content themselves with asserting that there is no evidence against (2), or whether they may go further and assert that there is evidence that not-(2) (evidence that (2) is false). Whereas Van den Haag would presumably confine abolitionists to the former, weaker assertion, it shall be argued that they may make the stronger, latter, assertion.

In order to see the issue fairly it is necessary to see how (2) has so far been submitted to empirical test. First of all, the issue has been confined to the death penalty for criminal homicide; consequently, it is not (2) but a subsidiary proposition which critics of the death penalty have tested—(2a) *the death penalty is a superior deterrent to "life" imprisonment for the crime of criminal homicide.* The falsification of (2a) does not entail the falsity of (2); the death penalty could still be a superior deterrent to "life" imprisonment for the crime of burglary, etc. However, the disconfirmation of (2a) would be obviously a significant partial disconfirmation of (2). Secondly, (2a) has not been tested directly but only indirectly. No one has devised a way to count or estimate directly the number of persons in a given population who have been deterred from criminal homicide by the fear of the penalty. The difficulties in doing so are plain enough. For instance, it would be possible to infer from the countable numbers who have not been deterred (because they did commit a given crime) that everyone else in the population was deterred, but only on the assumption that the only reason why a person did not commit a given crime is because he was deterred. Unfortunately for this argument (though happily enough otherwise) this assumption is almost certainly false, as we have noted above in section I. Other methods which might be devised to test (2a) directly have proved equally unfeasible. Yet it would be absurd to insist that there can be no *evidence* for

---

and (b) was there made; but it was not insisted, as it is here, that the argument entitles abolitionists to assert (b). See *id.* at 264–65. For the views of writers, all criminologists, who have recently stated the same or a stronger conclusion, see, e.g., Chambliss, "Types of Deviance and the Effectiveness of Legal Sanctions," 1967 *Wis. L. Rev.* 703, 706 (1967) ("Capital punishment does not act as an effective deterrent to murder"); Morris & Zimring, "Deterrence and Correction," 381 *The Annals* 137, 143 (1969) ("The capital punishment controversy has produced the most reliable information on the general deterrent effect of a criminal sanction. It now seems established and accepted that . . . the death penalty makes no difference to the homicide rate . . . ."); Reckless, "The Use of the Death Penalty," 15 *Crime & Delinq.* 43, 52 (1969) ("[T]he evidence indicates that [the death penalty for murder] has no discernible effects in the United States. . . ."); Doleschal, "The Deterrent Effect of Legal Punishment," 1 *Information Rev. on Crime and Delinq.* 1, 7 (1969) ("Capital punishment is ineffective in deterring murder").

or against (2a) unless it is *direct* evidence for or against it. Because Van den Haag nowhere indicated what he thinks would count as evidence, direct or indirect, for or against (1), much less (2), his insistence upon the distinction between (a) and (b) and his rebuke to abolitionists is in danger of implicitly relying upon just this absurdity.

How, then, has the indirect argument for (2a) proceeded? During the past generation, at least six different hypotheses have been formulated, as corollaries of (2a), as follows: [23]

    i.   Death penalty jurisdictions should have a lower annual rate of criminal homicide than abolition jurisdictions;

    ii.   Jurisdictions which abolished the death penalty should show an increased annual rate of criminal homicide after abolition;

    iii.   Jurisdictions which reintroduced the death penalty should show a decreased annual rate of criminal homicide after reintroduction;

    iv.   Given two contiguous jurisdictions differing chiefly in that one has the death penalty and the other does not, the latter should show a higher annual rate of criminal homicide;

    v.   Police officers on duty should suffer a higher annual rate of criminal assault and homicide in abolition jurisdictions than in death penalty jurisdictions;

    vi.   Prisoners and prison personnel should suffer a higher annual rate of criminal assault and homicide from life-term prisoners in abolition jurisdictions than in death penalty jurisdictions.

It could be objected to these six hypotheses that they are, as a set, insufficient to settle the question posed by (2a) no matter what the evidence for them may be—that the falsity of (i)–(vi) does not entail the falsity of (2a). Or it could be objected that each of (i)–(vi) has been too

---

[23] The relevant research, regarding each of the six hypotheses in the text, is as follows:

(i) Schuessler, "The Deterrent Influence of the Death Penalty," 284 *The Annals* 54, 57 (1952); Reckless, "The Use of the Death Penalty—A Factual Statement," 15 *Crime and Delinq.* 43, 52 (1969) (Table No. 9).

(ii) Thorsten Sellin, *The Death Penalty*, reprinted in H. Bedau, *supra* note 17, at 135–38.

(iii) Sellin, *supra* note 17, at 34–38; reprinted in H. Bedau, *supra* note 14, at 339–43.

(iv) See works cited in (iii).

(v) *Canada, Minutes and Proceedings of Evidence, Joint Committee of the Senate and House of Commons of Capital Punishment and Corporeal Punishment and Lotteries* and *The State Police and the Death Penalty*, app. F pt. I, at 718–35 (1955); "The Death Penalty and Police Safety," in H. Bedau, *supra* note 14, at 284–301, and in *Capital Punishment, supra* note 17, at 138–54.

(vi) *Massachusetts, Report and Recommendations of the Special Commission [on] the Death Penalty*, 1958, in H. Bedau, *supra* note 14, at 400; Sellin, "Prison Homicides," in *Capital Punishment, supra* note 17, at 154–60.

inadequately tested or insufficiently disconfirmed to establish any dis-confirmation of (2a), even though it is conceded that if (i)–(vi) were highly disconfirmed they would disconfirm (2a). Van den Haag's line of attack is not entirely clear as between these two alternatives. It appears that he should take the former line of criticism in its most extreme version. How else could he argue his chief point, that the research used by abolitionists has so far failed to produce *any* evidence against (1)—we may take him to mean (2) or (2a)? Only if (i)–(vi) were *irrelevant* to (2a) could it be fairly concluded from the evidential disconfirmation of (i)–(vi) that there is still no disconfirmation of (2a). And this is Van den Haag's central contention. The other ways to construe Van den Haag's reasoning are too implausible to be considered: he cannot think that the evidence is indifferent to or *confirms* (i)–(vi); nor can he think that there has been no *attempt* at all to disconfirm (2a); nor can he think that the evidence which disconfirms (i)–(vi) is not therewith also evidence which confirms the negations of (i)–(vi). If any of these three were true it would be a good reason for saying that there is "no evidence" against (2a); but each is patently false. If one inspects (i)–(vi) and (2a), it is difficult to see how one could argue that disconfirmation of the former does not constitute disconfirmation of the latter, even if it might be argued that verification of the former does not constitute verification of the latter. Therefore, there is nothing to be gained by further pursuit of this first line of attack.

Elsewhere, Van den Haag seems to adopt the alternative criticism, albeit rather crudely, as when he argues (against (iv), seemingly, since he nowhere formulated (i)–(vi)) that "the similar areas are not similar enough." [24] He fails to explain why the rates of criminal homicide in Michigan and in Illinois from 1920 to 1960 are not relevant, but simply alleges that the states aren't "similar enough." His criticism, does, however, tacitly concede that if the jurisdictions *were* "similar enough," then it would be logically possible to argue from the evidence against (iv) to the disconfirmation of (2a). And this seems to be in keeping with the nature of the case. Thus it is this second line of attack which needs closer examination.

Van den Haag's own position and objections apart, what is likely to strike the neutral observer who studies the ways in which (i)–(vi) have been tested and declared disconfirmed is that their disconfirmation, and *a fortiori*, the disconfirmation of (2a), is imperfect for two related reasons. First, all the tests rely upon *unproved empirical assumptions;* second, it is not known whether there is any *statistical significance* to the results of the tests. It is important to make these concessions, and aboli-

---

[24] Van den Haag, *supra* note 1, at 146.

tionists and other disbelievers in the deterrent efficacy of the death penalty have not always done so.

It is not possible here to review all the evidence and reach a judgment on the empirical status of (i)–(vi). But it is possible and desirable to illustrate how the two qualifications cited above must be understood, and then to assess their effect on the empirical status of (2a). The absence of statistical significance may be illustrated by reference to hypothesis (v). According to the published studies, the annual rate of assaults upon on-duty policemen in abolition jurisdictions is lower than in death penalty jurisdictions.[25] But the studies do not answer whether the difference is statistically significant because the data were not submitted to tests of statistical significance. Nor is there any known method by which the data could be subjected to any such tests. This is, of course, no reason to suppose that the evidence is really not evidence after all, or that though it is evidence against (i) it is not evidence against (2a). Statistical significance is, after all, only a measure of the strength of evidence, not a *sine qua non* of evidential status.

The qualification concerning unproved assumptions is more important, and is worth examining somewhat more fully (though, again, only illustratively). Consider hypothesis (i). Is one entitled to infer that (i) is disconfirmed because in fact a study of the annual homicide rates (as measured by vital statistics showing cause of death) unquestionably indicates that the rate in all abolition states is consistently lower than in all death penalty states? To make this inference one must assume that (A_1) homicides as measured by vital statistics are in a generally constant ratio to criminal homicides, (A_2) the years for which the evidence has been gathered are representative and not atypical, (A_3) however much fluctuations in the homicide rate owe to other factors, there is a non-negligible proportion which is a function of the severity of the penalty, and (A_4) the deterrent effect of a penalty is not significantly weakened by its infrequent imposition. There are, of course, other assumptions, but these are central and sufficiently representative here. Assumption A_1 is effectively unmeasurable because the concept of a criminal homicide is the concept of a homicide which *deserves* to be criminally prosecuted. Nevertheless, A_1 has been accepted by criminologists for over a generation.[26] A_2 is confirmable, on the other hand, and bit by bit, a year at a time, seems to be being confirmed. Assumption A_3 is rather more interesting. To the degree to which it is admitted or insisted that other factors than the severity of the penalty affect the rate of homicide, to that degree

---

[25] A rate of 1.2 attacks per 100,000 population in abolition jurisdictions as opposed to 1.3 per 100,000 population in death penalty jurisdictions.

[26] For a discussion surrounding this point, see H. Bedau, *supra* note 14, at 56–74.

A_3 becomes increasingly dubious; but at the same time testing (2a) by (i) becomes increasingly unimportant. The urgency of testing (2a) rests upon the assumption that it is the deterrent efficacy of penalties which is the chief factor in the rate of crimes, and it is absurd to hold that assumption and at the same time doubt A_3. On the other hand, A_4 is almost certainly false (and has been believed so by Bentham and other social theorists for nearly two hundred years). The falsity of A_4, however, is not of fatal harm to the disconfirmation of (i) because it is not known how infrequently a severe penalty such as death or life imprisonment may be imposed without decreasing its deterrent efficacy. The available information on this point leads one to doubt that for the general population the frequency with which the death sentence is imposed makes any significant difference to the volume of criminal homicide.[27]

These four assumptions and the way in which they bear upon interpretation and evaluation of the evidence against (i), and therefore the disconfirmation of (2a), are typical of what one finds as one examines the work of criminologists as it relates to the rest of these corollaries of (2a). Is it reasonable, in the light of these considerations, to infer that there is no evidence against (i)–(vi), or that although there may be evidence against (i)–(vi), there is none against (2a)? Probably not. Short of unidentified and probably unobtainable "crucial experiments," it is impossible to marshall evidence for (2a) or for (i)–(vi) except by means of certain additional assumptions such as A_1–A_4. To reason otherwise is to rely on nothing more than the fact that it is logically possible to grant the evidence against (i)–(vi) and yet deny that (2a) is false; or it is to insist that the assumptions which the inference relies upon are not plausible assumptions at all (or though plausible are themselves not confirmed) and that no other assumptions can be brought forward which will both be immune to objections and still preserve the linkage between the evidence, (i)–(vi), and (2a). The danger now is that one will repudiate assumptions such as A_1–A_4 so as to guarantee the failure of efforts to disconfirm (2a) via disconfirmation of (i)–(vi); or else that one will place the standards of evidence too high before one accepts the disconfirmation. In either case one has begun to engage in the familiar but discreditable practice of "protecting the hypothesis" by making it in effect immune to any kind of disconfirmation.

In sum, then, the abolitionist's argument regarding deterrence has the following structure: an empirical proposition not directly testable, (2),

[27] See R. Dann, The Deterrent Effect of Capital Punishment (1935); Savitz, "A Study in Capital Punishment," 49 J. Crim. L. C. & P. S. 338, 338–41 (1958) (reprinted in H. Bedau, supra note 14, at 315–32); Graves, "A Doctor Looks at Capital Punishment," 10 Med. Arts & Sciences 137, 137–41 (1956) (reprinted in H. Bedau, supra note 14, at 322–32).

has a significant corollary, (2a), which in turn suggests a number of corollaries, (i)–(vi), each of which is testable with varying degrees of indirectness. Each of (i)–(vi) has been tested. To accept the results as evidence disconfirming (i)–(vi) and as therefore disconfirming (2a), it is necessary to make certain assumptions, of which A_1–A_4 are typical. These assumptions in turn are not all testable much less directly confirmed; some of them, in their most plausible formulation, may even be false (but not in that formulation necessary to the inference, however). Since this structure of indirect testing, corollary hypotheses, unproved assumptions, is typical of the circumstances which face us when we wish to consider the evidence for or against any complex empirical hypothesis such as (2), I conclude that while (2) has by no means been disproved (whatever that might mean), it is equally clear that (2) has been disconfirmed, rather than confirmed or left untouched, by the inductive arguments surveyed.

An attempt has been made to review and appraise the chief "statistical" arguments, as Van den Haag calls them, marshalled during the past fifteen years or so in this country by those critical of the death penalty. But in order to assess these arguments more adequately, it is helpful to keep in mind two other considerations. First, most of the criminologists sceptical of (1) are led to this attitude not by the route we have examined —the argument against (2)—but by a general theory of the causation of crimes of personal violence. Given their confidence in that theory, and the evidence for it, they tend not to credit seriously the idea that the death penalty deters (very much), much less the idea that it is a superior deterrent to a severe alternative such as "life" imprisonment (which may not deter very much, either).[28] The interested reader should consult in particular Professor Marvin Wolfgang's monograph on this subject.[29] Second, very little of the empirical research purporting to establish the presence or absence of deterrent efficacy of a given punishment is entirely reliable, because almost no effort has been made to isolate the relevant variables. Surely, it is platitudinously true that *some* persons in *some* situations considering *some* crimes can be deterred from committing them by *some* penalties. To go beyond this, however, and supplant these variables with a series of well-confirmed functional hypotheses about the deterrent effect of current legal sanctions is not possible today.[30]

---

28 See, for an excellent critique of a recent study in deterrence, Zimring and Hawkins, *supra* note 13, at 111–14.

29 M. Wolfgang, *Patterns of Criminal Homicide* (1958).

30 For a general review, see Doleschal, "The Deterrent Effect of Legal Punishment: A Review of the Literature, 1 *Information Review on Crime and Delinq.* 1, 1–17 (1969), and the many research studies cited therein, especially the survey by Morris and Zimring, *supra* note 22, at 137–46.

Even if one cannot argue, as Van den Haag does, that there is no evidence against the claim that the death penalty is a better deterrent than life imprisonment, this does not yet settle the reliability of the evidence. Van den Haag could, after all, give up his extreme initial position and retreat to the concession that although there is evidence against the superior deterrent efficacy of the death penalty, still, the evidence is not very good, indeed, not good enough to make reasonable the policy of abolishing the death penalty. The reply, so far as there is one, short of further empirical studies (which undoubtedly are desirable), is twofold: the evidence against (i)−(vi) is uniformly confirmatory; and this evidence is in turn made intelligible by the chief current sociological theory of the causation of crimes of personal violence. Finally, there do not seem to be any good empirical reasons in favor of keeping the death penalty, as a deterrent or for any other reason, a point to be amplified in the next section.

IV

Van den Haag rests considerable weight on the claims that "the added severity of the death penalty adds to deterrence, or may do so"; and that "the generalized threat of the death penalty may be a deterrent, and the more so, the more generally applied." These claims are open to criticism on at least three grounds.

First, as the modal auxiliaries signal, Van den Haag has not really committed himself to any affirmative empirical claim, but only to a truism. It is always logically possible, no matter what the evidence, that a given penalty which is *ex hypothesi* more severe than an alternative, may be a better deterrent under some conditions not often realized and be proven so by evidence not ever detectable. For this reason, there is no possible way to prove that Van den Haag's claims are false, no possible preponderance of evidence against his conclusions which must, logically, force him to give them up. One would have hoped those who believe in the deterrent superiority of the death penalty could, at this late date, offer their critics something more persuasive than logical possibilities. As it is, Van den Haag's appeal to possible evidence comes perilously close to an argument from ignorance: the possible evidence one might gather is used to offset the actual evidence that has been gathered.

Second, Van den Haag rightly regards his conclusion above as merely an instance of the general principle that, *ceteris paribus,* The Greater the Severity the Greater the Deterrence, a "plausible" idea, as he says. Yet the advantage on behalf of the death penalty produced by this principle is a function entirely of the evidence for the principle itself. But no evidence at all is offered to make this plausible principle into a confirmed hypothesis of contemporary criminological theory of special relevance to crimes of personal violence. Until evidence concerning specific crimes, specific penalties, and specific criminal populations is brought forward to show that in general The Greater the Severity the Greater the Deterrence, the risk of being stupified by the merely plausible is run. Besides, without any evidence for this principle there will be a complete standoff with the abolitionist (who, of course, can play the same game), because he has his own equally plausible first principle: The Greater the Severity of Punishment the Greater the Brutality Provoked Throughout Society. When at last, exhausted and frustrated by mere plausibilities, one once again turns to study the evidence, he will find that the current literature on deterrence in criminology does not encourage a belief in Van den Haag's principle.[31]

Third, Van den Haag has not given any reason why, in the quest for deterrent efficacy, one should fasten, as he does, on the severity of the punishments in question, rather than, as Bentham long ago counselled, on all the relevant factors, notably the ease, speed, and reliability with which the punishment can be inflicted. Van den Haag cannot hope to convince anyone who has studied the matter that the death penalty and "life" imprisonment differ only in their severity and that in all other respects affecting deterrent efficacy they are equivalent; and if he believes this himself it would be interesting to have seen his evidence for it. The only thing to be said in favor of fastening exclusively upon the question of severity in the appraisal of punishments for their relative deterrent efficacy is this: to augment the severity of a punishment usually imposes little if any added direct cost to operate the penal system; it even may be cheaper. This is bound to please the harried taxpayer, and at the same time gratify the demand on government to "do something" about crime. Beyond that, emphasizing the severity of punishments as the main, or indeed the sole, variable relevant to deterrent efficacy is unbelievably superficial.

V

Van den Haag's final point concerning where the burden of proof lies is based, he admits, on playing off a certainty (the death of the persons executed) against a risk (that innocent persons, otherwise the would-be victims of those deterrable only by the death penalty, would be killed).[32] This is not analogous, as he seems to think it is, with the general nature of gambling, investment, and other risk-taking enterprises.

---

[31] See authorities cited notes 22 and 30 *supra*.

[32] The same objection has been previously raised in Feinberg, "Review of the Death Penalty in America," 76 *Ethics* 63 (1965).

In none of them is death deliberately inflicted, as it is, for instance, when carrot seedlings are weeded out to enable those remaining to grow larger (a eugenic analogy, by the way, which might be more useful to Van den Haag's purpose). In none, is it necessary to *sacrifice* a present loss in the hope of securing a future net gain; there is only the risk of a loss in that hope. Moreover, in gambling ventures one recoups what he risked if he wins, whereas in executions society must lose something (the lives of persons executed) no matter if it loses or wins (the lives of innocents protected). Van den Haag's attempt to locate the burden of proof by appeal to principles of gambling is a failure.

Far more significantly, Van den Haag frames the issue in such a way that the abolitionist has no chance of discharging the burden of proof once he accepts it. For what evidence could be marshalled to prove what Van den Haag wants proved, that "the greater severity inherent in irrevocability [of the death penalty] . . . adds nothing to deterrence"? The evidence alluded to at the end of section IV does tend to show that this generalization (the negation of Van den Haag's own principle) is indeed true, but it does not prove its unqualified validity. It must be concluded therefore, that either Van den Haag is wrong in his argument which shows the locus of burden of proof to lie on the abolitionist, or one must accept less than proof in order to discharge this burden (in which case, the very argument Van den Haag advances shows that the burden of proof now lies on those who would retain the death penalty).

"Burden of proof" in areas outside judicial precincts, where evidentiary questions are at stake, tends to be a rhetorical phrase and nothing more. Anyone interested in the truth of a matter will not defer gathering evidence pending a determination of where the burden of proof lies. For those who do think there is a question of burden of proof, as Van den Haag does, they should consider this: Advocacy of the death penalty is advocacy of a rule of penal law which empowers the state to deliberately take human life and in general to threaten the public with the taking of life. *Ceteris paribus,* one would think anyone favoring such a rule would be ready to offer considerable evidence for its necessity and efficacy. Surely, some showing of necessity, some evidentiary proof, is to be expected to satisfy the sceptical. Exactly when and in what circumstances have the apologists for capital punishment offered evidence to support their contentions? Where is that evidence recorded for us to inspect, comparable to the evidence cited in section III against the superior deterrent efficacy of the death penalty? Van den Haag conspicuously cited no such evidence, and so it is with all other proponents of the death penalty. The insistence that the burden of proof lies on abolitionists, therefore, is nothing but the rhetorical demand of every defender of the status quo who insists upon evidence from those who would effect change, while reserving throughout the right to dictate criteria and standards of proof and refusing to offer evidence for his own view.

The death penalty is a sufficiently momentous matter and of sufficient controversy that the admittedly imperfect evidence assembled over the past generation by those friendly to abolition should by now be countered by evidence tending to support the opposite, retentionist, position. It remains a somewhat sad curiosity that nothing of the sort has happened; no one has ever published research tending to show, however inconclusively, that the death penalty after all is a deterrent and a superior deterrent to "life" imprisonment. Among scholars at least, if not among legislators and other politicians, the perennial appeal to burden of proof really ought to give way to offering of proof by those interested enough to argue the issue.

SELECTED SUPPLEMENTARY READING

Acton, H. B., ed., *The Philosophy of Punishment*. London: Macmillan, 1969.

Armstrong, K. G., "The Retributivist Hits Back," *Mind*, 70 (1961).

Baier, Kurt, "Is Punishment Retributive?" *Analysis*, 16 (1955).

Bedau, Hugo, "The Courts, the Constitution and Capital Punishment." *Utah Law Review* (1968).

———, ed., *The Death Penalty in America* (rev. ed.). Garden City, N.Y.: Doubleday, 1967.

———, "The Death Penalty as a Deterrent" and "A Concluding Note on Deterrence and the Death Penalty," *Ethics*, 80, 81 (1970).

———, *The Right to Life and Other Essays on the Death Penalty*. New York: Pegasus, 1969.

———, "A Social Philosopher Looks at the Death Penalty," *American Journal of Psychiatry*, 123 (1967).

Benn, S. I., "An Approach to the Problems of Punishment," *Philosophy*, 33 (1958).

———, "Punishment," in *The Encyclopedia of Philosophy*, ed. P. Edwards. New York: Macmillan, 1967.

Darrow, Clarence, "Why Capital Punishment?" *The Story of My Life*. New York, N.Y.: Charles Scribner's Sons, 1932, Chap. 10.

Doyle, James F., "Justice and Legal Punishment," *Philosophy*, 42 (1967).

Ewing, A. C., *The Morality of Punishment*. London: Routledge and Kegan Paul, 1929.

Ezorsky, Gertrude, ed., *Philosophical Perspectives on Punishment*. Albany, N.Y.: State University of New York Press, 1972.

Feinberg, Joel, "Crime, Clutchability, and Individual Treatment," in *Doing and Deserving*. Princeton, N.J.: Princeton University Press, 1970.

———, "On Justifying Legal Punishment," in *Responsibility*, ed. C. Friedrich. New York: Liberal Arts Press, 1960.

FITZGERALD, P., *Criminal Law and Punishment*. Oxford: Clarendon Press, 1962.

FLEW, ANTONY, "The Justification of Punishment," *Philosophy*, 29 (1954).

GENDIN, S., "A Plausible Theory of Retribution," *Journal of Value Inquiry*, 6 (1972).

GOLDINGER, MILTON, ed., *Punishment and Human Rights*. Cambridge, Mass.: Schenkman Publishing Company, 1974.

HART, H. L. A., *Law, Liberty and Morality*. New York: Random House, 1963.

——, "Murder and the Principles of Punishment: England and the United States," *Northwestern Law Review*, 52 (1958).

——, *Punishment and Responsibility*. Oxford: Clarendon Press, 1968.

HOCHKAMMER, WILLIAM O., "The Capital Punishment Controversy," *The Journal of Criminal Law, Criminology, and Police Science*, 60 (1969).

HONDERICH, T., ed., *Punishment: The Supposed Justifications*. New York: Harcourt, Brace and World, 1970.

HOOK, SIDNEY, "The Death Sentence," in *The Death Penalty in America*, ed. Bedau.

KALVEN, HARRY, JR., and HANS LEISEL, "The American Jury and the Death Penalty," *University of Chicago Law Review*, 33 (1966).

KAUFMAN, A., "Anthony Quinton on Punishment," *Analysis*, 20 (1959).

——, "The Reform Theory of Punishment," *Ethics*, 71 (1960).

LONG, THOMAS A., "Capital Punishment—'Cruel and Unusual'?" *Ethics*, 83 (1973).

LUCAS, J. R., "Or Else," *Proceedings of the Aristotelian Society* (1968–69).

MADDEN, E. H., ROLLO HANDY, AND MARVIN FARBER, eds., *Philosophical Perspectives on Punishment*. Springfield, Ill.: Charles C Thomas, 1968.

MARGOLIS, JOSEPH, "Punishment and Prisons," *Social Theory and Practice*, 2 (1973).

MORRIS, HERBERT, "Persons and Punishment," *The Monist*, 52 (October 1968).

——, "Punishment for Thoughts," *The Monist*, 49 (1965).

MUNDLE, C., "Punishment and Desert," *Philosophical Quarterly*, 4 (1954).

PLAMENATZ, J., "Responsibility, Blame and Punishment," in *Philosophy, Politics and Society* (3rd Series), eds. P. Laslett and W. G. Runciman. Oxford: Basil Blackwell, 1967.

RAWLS, J., "Two Concepts of Rules," *Philosophical Review*, 64 (1955).

VAN DEN HAAG, E., "On Deterrence and the Death Penalty," and "Deterrence and the Death Penalty: A Rejoinder." *Ethics*, 78, 81, (1968, 1970).

Chapter **3**

CIVIL DISOBEDIENCE

INTRODUCTION

In a now classic scene, Socrates was convicted both of corrupting the youth of Athens and of atheism. The aura of a witchhunt surrounded the trial, and Socrates was sentenced, quite unjustly, to death. While awaiting the end, he was visited in prison by his friend Crito, who informed him that an escape could be arranged and offered a number of reasons to justify that escape: He was innocent, he could continue his valuable work in philosophy; his friends would otherwise appear disloyal for not helping him escape; he would not have to abandon his sons. Socrates, however, regarded such reasons as emotionally tinged and as insufficient to warrant his escape. He countered with his own reasons why he should stay: Since he had always taught respect for the law, it would now be unprincipled and hypocritical of him to disobey it. Moreover, if he disobeyed a law he did not like, such disobedience would seem to sanction general disobedience of the law. The law, he thought, could not survive such wanton disregard. Socrates further argued that one's tacit agreement to abide by the law was a binding obligation, even if the law could on occasion be turned against those who had made the agreement. For these reasons Socrates contended that what we now call an act of civil disobedience against the law is itself an expression of ingratitude and is a violation of the principles of justice.

On the other hand, Socrates also gave expression to a second and somewhat conflicting view about one's obligations to the state. He maintained at his trial that if the court were to find him guilty and were to stipulate as his punishment that he could no longer philosophize (which in his accusers' eyes meant practicing the corruption of youth), he would openly disobey such a sentence. Apparently Socrates thought that some legal decisions could not be supported because they are *too* unjust. They would therefore have to be disobeyed, though openly and without attempting to escape punishment for one's acts. In the end he left his followers with a nagging ethical puzzle: How does one determine when obedience to the state is required and when it is not?

Situations such as the one in which Socrates and his followers found themselves force us to ponder the question, "Under what conditions, if any, would it be right to escape legally proper punishment or to disobey a presumably legitimate order by the authorities who govern one's country?" Virtually everyone is willing to concede that there have been some moments in history such that, had one been a citizen of a particular country, one would have been justified in ignoring the dictates of authorities. The period of Nazi rule in Germany is the most frequently cited example, but there are numerous others. On the other hand, almost everyone would also be willing to grant that there are some conditions under which one would not be justified in ignoring the commands of authorities. Even the anarchist generally concedes that one ought to do what is morally right and so one ought to act in accordance with the orders of the state when they are morally right. Philosophers are interested in establishing criteria for justified and unjustified disobedience and for justified and unjustified obedience. More specifically, they are concerned with the following major issues:

1. Under what conditions, if any, is civil disobedience justified?
2. Is violent, as distinguished from passive, disobedience warranted under any circumstances?
3. Are selective acts of disobedience, such as selective conscientious objection, ethically defensible?
4. Are disobedient acts ever justified in a functioning democratic state?

Before we consider the major attempts to justify civil disobedience, some conceptual issues implicit in questions (1), (2), and (4) must be resolved.

The Concept of Civil Disobedience

The problem of civil disobedience within a democratic state is regarded as especially serious, because such actions are usually conceived as *by definition* ones that violate a law, often a law that has been upheld by a nation's highest court. It has sometimes been argued that civil disobedience may be justified only on the grounds that a "higher law" of the land provides legal support for the actions of the civil disobedient. But this claim and many similar ones raise fundamental issues concerning the proper analysis of the very concept of *civil* disobedience. The word "civil" has several distinct meanings, but if constitutional laws actually sanction one's "disobedient" actions, it is hard to see in what ways they are civilly disobedient rather than being legally justified.

For these reasons, among others, most writers on civil disobedience agree that, by definition, an act is civilly disobedient only if it breaks a law regarded as invalid by a disobedient who appeals to justifying reasons that are nonlegal. These are logically or conceptually necessary conditions of civil disobedience, though they may not be sufficient conditions. The civil disobedient may also be distinguished from both the *criminal* and the *revolutionary* by his different objectives. A civil disobedient generally supports the state's legal system and disobeys only individual laws or judicial decisions that he regards as unjust. One reason Socrates' case is interesting is that he would have disobeyed a judicial decision without objecting to the laws on which the decision was ostensibly based. The revolutionary, in contrast, regards the entire system as corrupt and advocates complete overthrow of the package of laws. The nonrevolutionary criminal disobedient is not inclined in either direction. He is interested exclusively in personal gain or avoidance of loss, not in justice for citizens in general. Of course, the civil disobedient does violate laws and in that respect is often regarded by the state as criminal, but most (not all) writers on civil disobedience have felt that the differences in motivation and in danger to society are sufficient to warrant the distinction between criminal and civil disobedience.

The Appeal to Conscience

The general problem of a sound justification of disobedience (question 1 above) can now be considered. The problem is associated in many nonphilosophical writings with that of one's "duty to one's conscience." Yet it has almost always been thought by ethical philosophers that an appeal to conscience alone is insufficient. After all, consciences vary radically, are often altered by circumstance and training, seem subject to impulse and whim, and are rather more acute when, for instance, a policeman is sighted than when there are no enforcers. The reliability of conscience seems, then, not to be self-certifying; support is needed from an external source. This is further corroborated by the fact that many appeals to the rightness of an action on the grounds that "my conscience was my guide" seem to external observers to be rationalizations for an immoral act. Also, the adoption of Thoreau's principle that "the only obligation which I have a right to assume is to do at any time what I think right" seems to lead to a moral relativism of personal feelings. Of course relativism and even anarchism are serious philosophical positions, but most people have not thought that the problem of justification must terminate here. When they have pondered the matter they have found themselves with the problem of working out a philosophically adequate account of justified disobedience and its proper relationship to the undeniably important principle of *conscientious* action.

The problem may be presented in the form of a dilemma. On the one hand, we tend to think that if one conscientiously considers a course of action and comes to think it right, then one ought to pursue it. On the other hand, it seems obvious that merely thinking something right is not sufficient to make it right. We thus return to the problem of rationally justifying such decisions. In this century we have witnessed a number of agonizing appraisals of this sort by such people as Gandhi in India and those in the European Underground, and more recently in America by Martin Luther King, Jr., and a number of enlisted men who determined that they were willing to risk a court-martial rather than continue the bombing missions to which they were assigned in Vietnam. Ethicists have been very much interested in the principles that render these actions either justified or unjustified.

The Conflict Between Legal and Moral Obligations

We must now consider what has almost certainly proved to be the central problem in the history of attempts to justify civil disobedience. The problem originates with the question, implicitly raised above, whether proper justification can be provided for violations of laws that have been upheld by a nation's highest courts. As we have seen, it seems unlikely that an appeal to individual conscience or to the existence of higher statutory laws would be of great value. But now another dilemma presents itself. On the one hand, we think we have a (prima facie) moral obligation to obey the law and to support generally the rule of law. On the other hand we think this moral obligation is not so strong that it outweighs all other (prima facie) moral obligations, and yet we find it exceedingly difficult to determine in most controversial cases which moral obligation outweighs which. Clearly one has to weigh the importance of a particular issue against the degree of harm that would result from disobedience, but how does one weigh the worth of competing justifying reasons?

Philosophers have held widely divergent positions on these questions of justification. Although many fundamental issues are responsible for their differences, the nature of one's obligations to the state has been the major issue. The various positions can be roughly divided into the following types (though each position could itself be divided into several subtypes):

1. No-justification theories
2. Legal justification theories
3. Moral justification theories
4. Individual justification theories

Those who hold *no-justification theories* maintain that there is no justification for acts of civil disobedience in an orderly society. One has an absolute obligation to obey authoritatively enacted law and all violations are either intrinsically immoral or subversions of social and governmental processes requisite for the very existence of social order and the institution of morality. No valid distinction between types of violations can be drawn that would justify one set of disobedient acts and leave another set unjustified. This view has long been popular with governmental authorities who regard all questions of justification as resolvable only by reference to the law itself.

Those who espouse *legal justification theories* agree that citizens have a strong duty to obey the law, but they add that one has a right to violate a law if in one's informed judgment the law is itself either unconstitutional or invalid. The disobedient action must have a legally sound basis in a "higher law" of the state and must not be undertaken merely for purposes that the disobedient regards as ethically important. Former United States Supreme Court Justice Abe Fortas thought this legal basis—and not a purely moral basis—was the proper justification for violation of segregation laws prior to their being judged unconstitutional by the Supreme Court.

The defenders of *moral justification theories* regard such legal views as significant but insufficient. Although they almost always agree that a citizen has a primary duty to obey just laws, they hold that a citizen also has a right to break the law when it seriously violates fundamental moral principles. If a state by law (higher or otherwise) creates situations of discrimination, violation of liberties, and/or other injustices, one has a moral right, and possibly a duty, to violate such laws. The actual moral basis differs from ethicist to ethicist, but all agree that since the laws themselves are in question and in need of justification, there are situations in which no adequate justification of an act of civil disobedience can be made merely by citing actual laws; it must be accomplished by reference to some independent moral standard. The several discussions of conscience found in the selections in this chapter primarily concern whether or not conscience is such an independent moral standard, especially when there is moral disagreement. But there are almost as many forms of moral disobedience theories as there are theories of the foundations of morality.

Finally, proponents of *individual justification theories* maintain that principled moral decisions and not the authority of the state should ultimately determine one's obligations. Hence, if individuals have good moral grounds for an action that is contrary to laws of the state, the moral grounds take precedence. According to this theory, even if one should act in accordance with laws, one should do so only because one independently regards such actions as one's duty; one should not act because the laws tell one to so act. In short, one has no obligation to the laws simply because they are the laws. This view has been popular with some supporters of conscience theories and with supporters of anarchism and of some revolutionary political theories. Many parts of Thoreau's classic treatise on civil disobedience seem to take this approach to the justification of disobedience.

Arguments in the Selections

John Rawls, in the opening essay in this chapter, discusses several fundamental issues in the attempt to justify civil disobedience. Rawls finds the grounds for one's moral obligation to obey the law in an extended form of the social contract theory, according to which citizens have an obligation to obey the law if they knowingly accept the benefits of society. Rawls even argues that citizens are bound to comply with *unjust* laws enacted by the majority. Having established this basis for obligation to law, Rawls then contends that the burden of moral justification for disobedience rests heavily on the disobedient. Nonetheless, he is aware that severe injustices may be perpetrated and so allows that one does have a right to engage in civil disobedience in such a state if one is subjected to an extended and deliberate injustice which violates the liberties of equal citizenship and if the results of disobedience would be generally positive. Rawls stipulates, however, that such acts must be entirely peaceful, that they must address the sense of justice of the majority, that they must be disobedient to law only "within the limits of fidelity to law," and that the actors must be willing to accept legal punishment for their actions.

Marshall Cohen relates the role of civil disobedience to the structure of functioning constitutional democracies, where he thinks the problem is an especially acute one. Cohen contends that civil disobedience must be carefully distinguished from mere conscientious refusal and from both criminal and revolutionary activity. He first examines the reasons for which civil disobedients accept punishment and suffering and construes these reasons to be strategic, but not justifying: The disobedient's willingness to accept punishment establishes his seriousness, weakens the will of the opposition, and emphasizes a general commitment to law even though a law is being violated. Cohen then considers Rawls's views when violence against persons is involved, but finds Rawls's position less convincing when violence against property is at stake, and not at all convincing when violence against the self is in question. Cohen's article ends with an examination of some constitutional problems as they bear on civil disobedience. Of special significance are the following conclusions: (1) One's normal moral obligations to obey the law cease at the point when one solemnly believes that a law or set of laws constitute violations of those basic constitutional arrangements that implement principles of freedom and justice. (2) "If the argument for civil disobedience is strengthened when there is reason to believe that the courts are in error it is strengthened still more when there is reason to believe that the courts will refuse to adjudicate the issues at all." Indirect disobedience (the breaking of laws to protest still other laws) is both "justifiable and necessary."

Graham Hughes and *Kai Nielsen* offer brief responses to Cohen. Hughes is particularly concerned with the concept of fidelity to law. He agrees with Cohen that this concept is rendered far too simplistic if construed as referring to an obligation not to question court decisions. Quite the contrary, Hughes contends that fidelity to law requires a constant reexamination of court decisions in terms of moral and legal principles, rather than "a slavish genuflexion to the court's latest pronouncement." Hughes's leading criticism of Cohen centers on the problem of who rightly has the prerogative to determine that a legal duty has been breached. In opposition to Cohen, Hughes thinks it wrong-headed to suppose the President and the Congress have this prerogative as well as the courts. He argues that the very concept of *illegality* requires reference to "an authoritative tribunal which, under the law, *ought to rule* on the question."

Nielsen is concerned with still other problems. He maintains that there is a crucial ambiguity in Cohen's treatment of the concept of civil disobedience, but that on the most likely interpretation Cohen makes "paying the penalty" a defining characteristic of what could count as legitimate civil disobedience. Nielsen thinks that cases can be adduced to show that this condition is too strong. In addition, Nielsen believes there are several means other than willingness to accept punishment by which the civil disobedient may show his seriousness and depth of commitment to the law. In a concluding section he builds on these contentions with arguments intended to show that even though both Rawls and Cohen are right in contending that civil disobedience is by definition nonviolent in intent, there nonetheless are circumstances in which violence is justified. He argues for the view that even though violence is an *intrinsic evil,* it nonetheless is sometimes a moral and political necessity which can be justified as an *instrumental good.*

The Justification
of Civil Disobedience *

John Rawls

I. Introduction

I should like to discuss briefly, and in an informal way, the grounds of civil disobedience in a constitutional democracy. Thus, I shall limit my remarks to the conditions under which we may, by civil disobedience, properly oppose legally established democratic authority; I am not concerned with the situation under other kinds of government nor, except incidentally, with other forms of resistance. My thought is that in a reasonably just (though of course not perfectly just) democratic regime, civil disobedience, when it is justified, is normally to be understood as a political action which addresses the sense of justice of the majority in order to urge reconsideration of the measures protested and to warn that in the firm opinion of the dissenters the conditions of social cooperation are not being honored. This characterization of civil disobedience is intended to apply to dissent on fundamental questions of internal policy, a limitation which I shall follow to simplify our question.

---

* Originally presented at the meetings of the American Political Science Association, September 1966. Some revisions have been made and two paragraphs have been added to the last section. Copyright © 1968 by John Rawls.

II. The Social Contract Doctrine

It is obvious that the justification of civil disobedience depends upon the theory of political obligation in general, and so we may appropriately begin with a few comments on this question. The two chief virtues of social institutions are justice and efficiency, where by the efficiency of institutions I understand their effectiveness for certain social conditions and ends the fulfillment of which is to everyone's advantage. We should comply with and do our part in just and efficient social arrangements for at least two reasons: first of all, we have a natural duty not to oppose the establishment of just and efficient institutions (when they do not yet exist) and to uphold and comply with them (when they do exist); and second, assuming that we have knowingly accepted the benefits of these institutions and plan to continue to do so, and that we have encouraged and expect others to do their part, we also have an obligation to do our share when, as the arrangement requires, it comes our turn. Thus, we often have both a natural duty as well as an obligation to support just and efficient institutions, the obligation arising from our voluntary acts while the duty does not.

Now all this is perhaps obvious enough, but it does not take us very far. Any more particular conclusions depend upon the conception of justice which is the basis of a theory of political obligation. I believe that the appropriate conception, at least for an account of political obligation in a constitutional democracy, is that of the social contract theory from which so much of our political thought derives. If we are careful to interpret it in a suitably general way, I hold that this doctrine provides a satisfactory basis for political theory, indeed even for ethical theory itself, but this is beyond our present concern.[1] The interpretation I suggest is the following: that the principles to which social arrangements must conform, and in particular the principles of justice, are those which free and rational men would agree to in an original position of equal liberty; and similarly, the principles which govern men's relations to institutions and define their natural duties and obligations are the principles to which they would consent when so situated. It should be noted straightway that in this interpretation of the contract

---

[1] By the social contract theory I have in mind the doctrine found in Locke, Rousseau, and Kant. I have attempted to give an interpretation of this view in "Justice as Fairness," *Philosophical Review* (April, 1958); "Justice and Constitutional Liberty," *Nomos, VI* (1963); "The Sense of Justice," *Philosophical Review* (July, 1963). [Ed. note. See also "Distributive Justice," in Peter Laslett and W. G. Runciman, eds., *Philosophy, Politics and Society* (1967), and *A Theory of Justice* (Cambridge, Mass.: The Belknap Press of Harvard University Press, 1971).]

theory the principles of justice are understood as the outcome of a hypothetical agreement. They are principles which would be agreed to if the situation of the original position were to arise. There is no mention of an actual agreement nor need such an agreement ever be made. Social arrangements are just or unjust according to whether they accord with the principles for assigning and securing fundamental rights and liberties which would be chosen in the original position. This position is, to be sure, the analytic analogue of the traditional notion of the state of nature, but it must not be mistaken for a historical occasion. Rather it is a hypothetical situation which embodies the basic ideas of the contract doctrine; the description of this situation enables us to work out which principles would be adopted. I must now say something about these matters.

The contract doctrine has always supposed that the persons in the original position have equal powers and rights, that is, that they are symmetrically situated with respect to any arrangements for reaching agreement, and that coalitions and the like are excluded. But it is an essential element (which has not been sufficiently observed although it is implicit in Kant's version of the theory) that there are very strong restrictions on what the contracting parties are presumed to know. In particular, I interpret the theory to hold that the parties do not know their positions in society, past, present, or future; nor do they know which institutions exist. Again, they do not know their own place in the distribution of natural talents and abilities, whether they are intelligent or strong, man or woman, and so on. Finally, they do not know their own particular interests and preferences or the system of ends which they wish to advance: they do not know their conception of the good. In all these respects the parties are confronted with a veil of ignorance which prevents any one from being able to take advantage of his good fortune or particular interests or from being disadvantaged by them. What the parties do know (or assume) is that Hume's circumstances of justice obtain: namely, that the bounty of nature is not so generous as to render cooperative schemes superfluous nor so harsh as to make them impossible. Moreover, they assume that the extent of their altruism is limited and that, in general, they do not take an interest in one another's interests. Thus, given the special features of the original position, each man tries to do the best he can for himself by insisting on principles calculated to protect and advance his system of ends whatever it turns out to be.

I believe that as a consequence of the peculiar nature of the original position there would be an agreement on the following two principles for assigning rights and duties and for regulating distributive shares as these are determined by the fundamental institutions of society: first, each person is to have an equal right to the most extensive liberty compatible with a like liberty for all; second, social and economic inequalities (as defined by the institutional structure or fostered by it) are to be arranged so that they are both to everyone's advantage and attached to positions and offices open to all. In view of the content of these two principles and their application to the main institutions of society, and therefore to the social system as a whole, we may regard them as the two principles of justice. Basic social arrangements are just insofar as they conform to these principles, and we can, if we like, discuss questions of justice directly by reference to them. But a deeper understanding of the justification of civil disobedience requires, I think, an account of the derivation of these principles provided by the doctrine of the social contract. Part of our task is to show why this is so.

III. The Grounds of Compliance with an Unjust Law

If we assume that in the original position men would agree both to the principle of doing their part when they have accepted and plan to continue to accept the benefits of just institutions (the principle of fairness), and also to the principle of not preventing the establishment of just institutions and of upholding and complying with them when they do exist, then the contract doctrine easily accounts for our having to conform to just institutions. But how does it account for the fact that we are normally required to comply with unjust laws as well? The injustice of a law is not a sufficient ground for not complying with it any more than the legal validity of legislation is always sufficient to require obedience to it. Sometimes one hears these extremes asserted, but I think that we need not take them seriously.

An answer to our question can be given by elaborating the social contract theory in the following way. I interpret it to hold that one is to envisage a series of agreements as follows: first, men are to agree upon the principles of justice in the original position. Then they are to move to a constitutional convention in which they choose a constitution that satisfies the principles of justice already chosen. Finally they assume the role of a legislative body and guided by the principles of justice enact laws subject to the constraints and procedures of the just constitution. The decisions reached in any stage are binding in all subsequent stages. Now whereas in the original position the contracting parties have no knowledge of their society or of their own position in it, in both a constitutional convention and a legislature, they do know certain general facts about their institutions, for example, the statistics regarding employment and output required for fiscal and economic policy. But no one knows particular facts about his own social class or his place in the distribution of natural assets. On each occasion the contracting parties have the knowledge required to make their agreement rational from the appropriate point of view, but not so much as to make them prejudiced. They are unable to tailor principles and legislation to take advantage of their social or natural position; a veil of ignorance prevents their knowing what this position is. With this series of agreements in mind, we can characterize just laws and policies as those which would be enacted were this whole process correctly carried out.

In choosing a constitution the aim is to find among the just constitutions the one which is most likely, given the general facts about the society in question, to lead to just and effective legislation. The principles of justice provide a criterion for the laws desired; the problem is to find a set of political procedures that will give this outcome. I shall assume that, at least under the normal conditions of a modern state, the best constitution is some form of democratic regime affirming equal political liberty and using some sort of majority (or other plurality) rule. Thus it follows that on the contract theory a constitutional democracy of some sort is required by the principles of justice. At the same time it is essential to observe that the constitutional process is always a case of what we may call imperfect procedural justice: that is, there is no feasible political procedure which guarantees that the enacted legislation is just even though we have (let us suppose) a standard for just legislation. In simple cases, such as games of fair division, there are procedures which always lead to the right outcome (assume that equal shares is fair and let the man who cuts the cake take the last piece). These situations are those of perfect procedural justice. In other cases it does not matter what the outcome is as long as the fair procedure is followed: fairness of the process is transferred to the result (fair gambling is an instance of this). These situations are those of pure procedural justice. The constitutional process, like a criminal trial, resembles neither of these; the result matters and we have a standard for it. The difficulty is that we cannot frame a procedure which guarantees that only just and effective legislation is enacted. Thus even under a just constitution unjust laws may be passed and unjust policies enforced. Some form of the majority principle is necessary but the majority may be mistaken, more or less willfully, in what it legislates. In agreeing to a democratic constitution (as an instance of imperfect procedural justice) one accepts at the same time the principle of majority rule. Assuming that the constitution is just and that we have accepted and plan to continue to accept its benefits, we then have both an obligation and a natural duty (and in any case the duty) to comply with what the majority enacts even though it may be unjust. In this way we become bound to follow unjust laws, not always, of course, but provided the injustice does not exceed certain limits. We recognize that we must run the risk of suffering from the defects of one another's sense of justice; this burden we are prepared to carry as long as it is more or less evenly distributed or does not weigh too heavily. Justice binds us to a just constitution and to the unjust laws which may be enacted under it in precisely the same way that it binds us to any other social arrangement. Once we take the sequence of stages into account, there is nothing unusual in our being required to comply with unjust laws.

It should be observed that the majority principle has a secondary place as a rule of procedure which is perhaps the most efficient one under usual circumstances for working a democratic constitution. The basis for it rests essentially upon the principles of justice and therefore we may, when conditions allow, appeal to these principles against unjust legislation. The justice of the constitution does not insure the justice of laws enacted under it; and while we often have both an obligation and a duty to comply with what the majority legislates (as long as it does not exceed certain limits), there is, of course, no corresponding obligation or duty to regard what the majority enacts as itself just. The right to make law does not guarantee that the decision is rightly made; and while the citizen submits in his conduct to the judgment of democratic authority, he does not submit his judgment to it.[2] And if in his judgment the enactments of the majority exceed certain bounds of injustice, the citizen may consider civil disobedience. For we are not required to accept the majority's acts unconditionally and to acquiesce in the denial of our and others' liberties; rather we submit our conduct to democratic authority to the extent necessary to share the burden of working a constitutional regime, distorted as it must inevitably be by men's lack of wisdom and the defects of their sense of justice.

IV. The Place of Civil Disobedience in a Constitutional Democracy

We are now in a position to say a few things about civil disobedience. I shall understand it to be a public, nonviolent, and conscientious act contrary to law usually done with the intent to bring about a change in the policies or laws of the government.[3] Civil disobedience is a political act in the sense that it is an act justified by moral principles which define a conception of civil society and the public good. It rests, then, on political conviction as opposed to a search for self or group interest; and in the case of a constitutional democracy, we may assume that this con-

---

[2] On this point see A. E. Murphy's review of Yves Simon's *The Philosophy of Democratic Government* (1951) in the *Philosophical Review* (April, 1952).

[3] Here I follow H. A. Bedau's definition of civil disobedience. See his "On Civil Disobedience," *Journal of Philosophy* (October, 1961).

viction involves the conception of justice (say that expressed by the contract doctrine) which underlies the constitution itself. That is, in a viable democratic regime there is a common conception of justice by reference to which its citizens regulate their political affairs and interpret the constitution. Civil disobedience is a public act which the dissenter believes to be justified by this conception of justice and for this reason it may be understood as addressing the sense of justice of the majority in order to urge reconsideration of the measures protested and to warn that, in the sincere opinion of the dissenters, the conditions of social cooperation are not being honored. For the principles of justice express precisely such conditions, and their persistent and deliberate violation in regard to basic liberties over any extended period of time cuts the ties of community and invites either submission or forceful resistance. By engaging in civil disobedience a minority leads the majority to consider whether it wants to have its acts taken in this way, or whether, in view of the common sense of justice, it wishes to acknowledge the claims of the minority.

Civil disobedience is also civil in another sense. Not only is it the outcome of a sincere conviction based on principles which regulate civic life, but it is public and nonviolent, that is, it is done in a situation where arrest and punishment are expected and accepted without resistance. In this way it manifests a respect for legal procedures. Civil disobedience expresses disobedience to law within the limits of fidelity to law, and this feature of it helps to establish in the eyes of the majority that it is indeed conscientious and sincere, that it really is meant to address their sense of justice.[4] Being completely open about one's acts and being willing to accept the legal consequences of one's conduct is a bond given to make good one's sincerity, for that one's deeds are conscientious is not easy to demonstrate to another or even before oneself. No doubt it is possible to imagine a legal system in which conscientious belief that the law is unjust is accepted as a defense for noncompliance, and men of great honesty who are confident in one another might make such a system work. But as things are such a scheme would be unstable; we must pay a price in order to establish that we believe our actions have a moral basis in the convictions of the community.

The nonviolent nature of civil disobedience refers to the fact that it is intended to address the sense of justice of the majority and as such it is a form of speech, an expression of conviction. To engage in violent acts likely to injure and to hurt is incompatible with civil disobedience as a mode of address. Indeed, an interference with the basic rights of others tends to obscure the civilly disobedient quality of one's act. Civil

---

[4] For a fuller discussion of this point to which I am indebted, see Charles Fried, "Moral Causation," *Harvard Law Review* (1964).

disobedience is nonviolent in the further sense that the legal penalty for one's action is accepted and that resistance is not (at least for the moment) contemplated. Nonviolence in this sense is to be distinguished from nonviolence as a religious or pacifist principle. While those engaging in civil disobedience have often held some such principle, there is no necessary connection between it and civil disobedience. For on the interpretation suggested, civil disobedience in a democratic society is best understood as an appeal to the principles of justice, the fundamental conditions of willing social cooperation among free men, which in the view of the community as a whole are expressed in the constitution and guide its interpretation. Being an appeal to the moral basis of public life, civil disobedience is a political and not primarily a religious act. It addresses itself to the common principles of justice which men can require one another to follow and not to the aspirations of love which they cannot. Moreover by taking part in civilly disobedient acts one does not foreswear indefinitely the idea of forceful resistance; for if the appeal against injustice is repeatedly denied, then the majority has declared its intention to invite submission or resistance and the latter may conceivably be justified even in a democratic regime. We are not required to acquiesce in the crushing of fundamental liberties by democratic majorities which have shown themselves blind to the principles of justice upon which justification of the constitution depends.

V. The Justification of Civil Disobedience

So far we have said nothing about the justification of civil disobedience, that is, the conditions under which civil disobedience may be engaged in consistent with the principles of justice that support a democratic regime. Our task is to see how the characterization of civil disobedience as addressed to the sense of justice of the majority (or to the citizens as a body) determines when such action is justified.

First of all, we may suppose that the normal political appeals to the majority have already been made in good faith and have been rejected, and that the standard means of redress have been tried. Thus, for example, existing political parties are indifferent to the claims of the minority and attempts to repeal the laws protested have been met with further repression since legal institutions are in the control of the majority. While civil disobedience should be recognized, I think, as a form of political action within the limits of fidelity to the rule of law, at the same time it is a rather desperate act just within these limits, and therefore it should, in general, be undertaken as a last resort when standard democratic processes have failed. In this sense it is not a normal political action. When it is justified there has been a serious breakdown; not only is there grave injustice in the law but a refusal more or less deliberate to correct it.

Second, since civil disobedience is a political act addressed to the sense of justice of the majority, it should usually be limited to substantial and clear violations of justice and preferably to those which, if rectified, will establish a basis for doing away with remaining injustices. For this reason there is a presumption in favor of restricting civil disobedience to violations of the first principle of justice, the principle of equal liberty, and to barriers which contravene the second principle, the principle of open offices which protects equality of opportunity. It is not, of course, always easy to tell whether these principles are satisfied. But if we think of them as guaranteeing the fundamental equal political and civil liberties (including freedom of conscience and liberty of thought) and equality of opportunity, then it is often relatively clear whether their principles are being honored. After all, the equal liberties are defined by the visible structure of social institutions; they are to be incorporated into the recognized practice, if not the letter, of social arrangements. When minorities are denied the right to vote or to hold certain political offices, when certain religious groups are repressed and others denied equality of opportunity in the economy, this is often obvious and there is no doubt that justice is not being given. However, the first part of the second principle which requires that inequalities be to everyone's advantage is a much more imprecise and controversial matter. Not only is there a problem of assigning it a determinate and precise sense, but even if we do so and agree on what it should be, there is often a wide variety of reasonable opinion as to whether the principle is satisfied. The reason for this is that the principle applies primarily to fundamental economic and social policies. The choice of these depends upon theoretical and speculative beliefs as well as upon a wealth of concrete information, and all of this mixed with judgment and plain hunch, not to mention in actual cases prejudice and self-interest. Thus unless the laws of taxation are clearly designed to attack a basic equal liberty, they should not be protested by civil disobedience; the appeal to justice is not sufficiently clear and its resolution is best left to the political process. But violations of the equal liberties that define the common status of citizenship are another matter. The deliberate denial of these more or less over any extended period of time in the face of normal political protest is, in general, an appropriate object of civil disobedience. We may think of the social system as divided roughly into two parts, one which incorporates the fundamental equal liberties (including equality of opportunity) and another which embodies social and economic policies properly aimed at promoting the advantage of everyone. As a rule civil disobedience is best limited to the former where the appeal to justice is not only more definite and precise, but where, if it is effective, it tends to correct the injustices in the latter.

Third, civil disobedience should be restricted to those cases where the dissenter is willing to affirm that everyone else similarly subjected to the same degree of injustice has the right to protest in a similar way. That is, we must be prepared to authorize others to dissent in similar situations and in the same way, and to accept the consequences of their doing so. Thus, we may hold, for example, that the widespread disposition to disobey civilly clear violations of fundamental liberties more or less deliberate over an extended period of time would raise the degree of justice throughout society and would insure men's self-esteem as well as their respect for one another. Indeed, I believe this to be true, though certainly it is partly a matter of conjecture. As the contract doctrine emphasizes, since the principles of justice are principles which we would agree to in an original position of equality when we do not know our social position and the like, the refusal to grant justice is either the denial of the other as an equal (as one in regard to whom we are prepared to constrain our actions by principles which we would consent to) or the manifestation of a willingness to take advantage of natural contingencies and social fortune at his expense. In either case, injustice invites submission or resistance; but submission arouses the contempt of the oppressor and confirms him in his intention. If straightway, after a decent period of time to make reasonable political appeals in the normal way, men were in general to dissent by civil disobedience from infractions of the fundamental equal liberties, these liberties would, I believe, be more rather than less secure. Legitimate civil disobedience properly exercised is a stabilizing device in a constitutional regime, tending to make it more firmly just.

Sometimes, however, there may be a complication in connection with this third condition. It is possible, although perhaps unlikely, that there are so many persons or groups with a sound case for resorting to civil disobedience (as judged by the foregoing criteria) that disorder would follow if they all did so. There might be serious injury to the just constitution. Or again, a group might be so large that some extra precaution is necessary in the extent to which its members organize and engage in civil disobedience. Theoretically the case is one in which a number of persons or groups are equally entitled to and all want to resort to civil disobedience, yet if they all do this, grave consequences for everyone may result. The question, then, is who among them may exercise their right, and it falls under the general problem of fairness. I cannot discuss the complexities of the matter here. Often a lottery or a rationing system can be set up to handle the case; but unfortunately the circumstances of civil disobedience rule out this solution. It suffices to note that a problem of fairness may arise and that those who contemplate civil disobedience should take it into account. They may have to reach an understanding as to who can exercise their right in the immediate situation and to recognize the need for special constraint.

The final condition, of a different nature, is the following. We have been considering when one has a right to engage in civil disobedience, and our conclusion is that one has this right should three conditions hold: when one is subject to injustice more or less deliberate over an extended period of time in the face of normal political protests; where the injustice is a clear violation of the liberties of equal citizenship; and provided that the general disposition to protest similarly in similar cases would have acceptable consequences. These conditions are not, I think, exhaustive but they seem to cover the more obvious points; yet even when they are satisfied and one has the right to engage in civil disobedience, there is still the different question of whether one should exercise this right, that is, whether by doing so one is likely to further one's ends. Having established one's right to protest one is then free to consider these tactical questions. We may be acting within our rights but still foolishly if our action only serves to provoke the harsh retaliation of the majority; and it is likely to do so if the majority lacks a sense of justice, or if the action is poorly timed or not well designed to make the appeal to the sense of justice effective. It is easy to think of instances of this sort, and in each case these practical questions have to be faced. From the standpoint of the theory of political obligation we can only say that the exercise of the right should be rational and reasonably designed to advance the protester's aims, and that weighing tactical questions presupposes that one has already established one's right, since tactical advantages in themselves do not support it.

VI. Conclusion: Several Objections Considered

In a reasonably affluent democratic society justice becomes the first virtue of institutions. Social arrangements irrespective of their efficiency must be reformed if they are significantly unjust. No increase in efficiency in the form of greater advantages for many justifies the loss of liberty of a few. That we believe this is shown by the fact that in a democracy the fundamental liberties of citizenship are not understood as the outcome of political bargaining nor are they subject to the calculus of social interests. Rather these liberties are fixed points which serve to limit political transactions and which determine the scope of calculations of social advantage. It is this fundamental place of the equal liberties which makes their systematic violation over any extended period of time a proper object of civil disobedience. For to deny men these rights is to infringe the conditions of social cooperation among free and rational persons, a fact which is evident to the citizens of a constitutional regime since it follows from the principles of justice which underlie their institutions. The justification of civil disobedience rests on the priority of justice and the equal liberties which it guarantees.

It is natural to object to this view of civil disobedience that it relies too heavily upon the existence of a sense of justice. Some may hold that the feeling for justice is not a vital political force, and that what moves men are various other interests, the desire for wealth, power, prestige, and so on. Now this is a large question the answer to which is highly conjectural and each tends to have his own opinion. But there are two remarks which may clarify what I have said: first, I have assumed that there is in a constitutional regime a common sense of justice the principles of which are recognized to support the constitution and to guide its interpretation. In any given situation particular men may be tempted to violate these principles, but the collective force in their behalf is usually effective since they are seen as the necessary terms of cooperation among free men; and presumably the citizens of a democracy (or sufficiently many of them) want to see justice done. Where these assumptions fail, the justifying conditions for civil disobedience (the first three) are not affected, but the rationality of engaging in it certainly is. In this case, unless the costs of repressing civil dissent injures the economic self-interest (or whatever) of the majority, protest may simply make the position of the minority worse. No doubt as a tactical matter civil disobedience is more effective when its appeal coincides with other interests, but a constitutional regime is not viable in the long run without an attachment to the principles of justice of the sort which we have assumed.

Then, further, there may be a misapprehension about the manner in which a sense of justice manifests itself. There is a tendency to think that it is shown by professions of the relevant principles together with actions of an altruistic nature requiring a considerable degree of self-sacrifice. But these conditions are obviously too strong, for the majority's sense of justice may show itself simply in its being unable to undertake the measures required to suppress the minority and to punish as the law requires the various acts of civil disobedience. The sense of justice undermines the will to uphold unjust institutions, and so a majority despite its superior power may give way. It is unprepared to force the minority to be subject to injustice. Thus, although the majority's action is reluctant and grudging, the role of the sense of justice is nevertheless essential, for without it the majority would have been willing to enforce the law and to defend its position. Once we see the sense of justice as working in this negative way to make established injustices indefensible, then it is recognized as a central element of democratic politics.

Finally, it may be objected against this account that it does not settle the question of who is to say when the situation is such as to justify civil disobedience. And because it does not answer this question, it invites anarchy by encouraging every man to decide the matter for himself. Now the reply to this is that each man must indeed settle this question for himself, although he may, of course, decide wrongly. This is true on any theory of political duty and obligation, at least on any theory compatible with the principles of a democratic constitution. The citizen is responsible for what he does. If we usually think that we should comply with the law, this is because our political principles normally lead to this conclusion. There is a presumption in favor of compliance in the absence of good reasons to the contrary. But because each man is responsible and must decide for himself as best he can whether the circumstances justify civil disobedience, it does not follow that he may decide as he pleases. It is not by looking to our personal interests or to political allegiances narrowly construed, that we should make up our mind. The citizen must decide on the basis of the principles of justice that underlie and guide the interpretation of the constitution and in the light of his sincere conviction as to how these principles should be applied in the circumstances. If he concludes that conditions obtain which justify civil disobedience and conducts himself accordingly, he has acted conscientiously and perhaps mistakenly, but not in any case at his convenience.

In a democratic society each man must act as he thinks the principles of political right require him to. We are to follow our understanding of these principles, and we cannot do otherwise. There can be no morally binding legal interpretation of these principles, not even by a supreme court or legislature. Nor is there any infallible procedure for determining what or who is right. In our system the Supreme Court, Congress, and the President often put forward rival interpretations of the Constitution. Although the Court has the final say in settling any particular case, it is not immune from powerful political influence that may change its reading of the law of the land. The Court presents its point of view by reason and argument; its conception of the Constitution must, if it is to endure, persuade men of its soundness.[5] The final court of appeal is not the Court, or Congress, or the President, but the electorate as a whole. The civilly disobedient appeal in effect to this body. There is no danger of anarchy as long as there is a sufficient working agreement in men's conceptions of

---

[5] For a presentation of this view to which I am indebted, see A. M. Bickel, *The Least Dangerous Branch* (Indianapolis, 1962), especially Chaps. 5 and 6.

political justice and what it requires. That men can achieve such an understanding when the essential political liberties are maintained is the
assumption implicit in democratic institutions. There is no way to avoid
entirely the risk of divisive strife. But if legitimate civil disobedience
seems to threaten civil peace, the responsibility falls not so much on those
who protest as upon those whose abuse of authority and power justifies
such opposition.

Civil Disobedience in a Constitutional Democracy *

Marshall Cohen

In traditional democratic theory revolution provides the only alternative to normal politics. If conditions do not justify overthrowing the
government a dissenter must confine himself to protesting against them.
He may protest by speaking against the government, or by voting against
it, but this meager list exhausts the possibilities. Due to the very great
originality of Gandhi we can now envisage, and many people have in fact
begun to practice, a third type of protest—civil disobedience. If it does
not qualify as normal politics it is not a kind of revolutionary activity,
either.

Unfortunately, the term "civil disobedience," which always suffered
from a certain ambiguity, has now been utterly debased in the vulgar
national debate on "law and order." It has been used to describe everything from bringing a test-case in the federal courts to taking aim at a
federal official. Indeed, for Vice-President Agnew it has become a code-
word describing the activities of muggers, arsonists, draft evaders, campaign hecklers, campus militants, anti-war demonstrators, juvenile delin-
quents and political assassins. Anyone who wishes to defend the practice
of civil disobedience must therefore explain just what it is that he wishes
to defend. And in doing so I shall not hesitate to free Gandhi's conception
from its religious bias and from those political emphases peculiarly appro-

---

* From *Philosophic Exchange* (1970 Edition). An earlier version of this essay
appeared in *The Massachusetts Review*, Vol. X (Spring, 1969), No. 2, pp.
211–26. Reprinted by permission of the author and publishers.

priate to the fundamentally undemocratic circumstances in which he worked. Only then will it be possible to reject Ambassador Kennan's confident assertion that civil disobedience "has no place" in a democratic society, or Justice Fortas' apparently more liberal view that "indirect" disobedience at least has no such place.

The civil disobedient is often described as a man who defies the law out of conscience or moral belief. But this description is imprecise, and it fails to distinguish him from the moral innovator on the one hand, or the conscientious refuser on the other. Unlike the moral innovator, the civil disobedient does not invoke the standards of a higher morality or of a special religious dispensation. He is no Zarathustra proposing a transvaluation of all values, and he does not ask the public to act on principles that it plainly rejects. If he acts out of conscience it is important to remember that he appeals to it as well, and the principles he invokes are principles that he takes to be generally acknowledged. It is to protest the fact that the majority has violated these principles that the disobedient undertakes his disobedience, and it is this element of protest that distinguishes his actions from those of the conscientious refuser. For the doctor who performs a clandestine abortion, or the youth who surreptitiously evades the draft, may be acting out of moral motives—the doctor to fulfill his obligations to a patient, the youth to avoid complicity in an evil undertaking— but they are not defying the law in order to protest the course of public conduct. They can achieve their purposes in private, and their defiance of the law need never come to light. The civil disobedient's actions are political by their very nature, however, and it is essential that they be performed in public, or called to the public's attention.

It is for this reason that the civil disobedient characteristically notifies government officials of the time and place of his actions and attempts to make clear the point of his protest. Obviously, one of the problems of a modern democracy is that many immoral actions taken in the people's name are only dimly known to them, if they are known at all. In such cases, the main difficulty in touching the public's conscience may well be the difficulty in making the public conscious. The civil disobedient may therefore find that in addition to making his actions public it is necessary to gain for them a wide publicity as well. Indeed, Bertrand Russell has suggested that making propaganda, and bringing the facts of political life to the attention of an ignorant, and often bemused, electorate constitutes the main function of disobedience at the present time. It is certainly true that nothing attracts the attention of the masses, and of the mass media, like flamboyant violations of the law, and it would be unrealistic of those who have political grievances not to exploit this fact. But it is important—especially in this connection—to recall Gandhi's warning that the technique of law violation ought to be used sparingly—like the surgeon's knife. For, in the end, the public will lose its will, and indeed its ability, to distinguish between those who employ these techniques whenever they wish to advertise their political opinions and those, the true dissenters, who use them only to protest deep violations of political principle. The techniques will then be of little use to anybody.

After openly breaking the law, the traditional disobedient willingly pays the penalty. This is one of the characteristics that serve to distinguish him from the typical criminal (his appeal to conscience is another) and it helps to establish the seriousness of his views and the depth of his commitment as well. Unfortunately, paying the penalty will not always demonstrate that his actions are in fact disinterested. For the youth protesting the draft, or the welfare recipient protesting poverty, has an obvious and substantial interest in the success of his cause. If the majority suspects that these interests color the disobedient's perception of the issues involved, its suspicions may prove fatal to his ultimate success. This is one reason why the practice of civil disobedience should not be limited to those who are directly injured by the government's immoral or lawless course (as Judge Wyzanski and others have suggested). A show of support by those who have no substantial interest in the matter may carry special weight with a confused, and even with an active sceptical, majority. The majority simply cannot dismiss those over thirty-five as draft-dodgers or those who earn over $35,000 a year as boondogglers. It may therefore consider the issues at stake, and this is the first objective of the civil disobedient.

It is in misinterpreting the role of punishment in the theory of civil disobedience that Ambassador Kennan makes one of his most conspicuous errors. For the theory of civil disobedience does not suggest (although such exponents as James Farmer and Harris Wofford have sometimes argued) that the disobedient's actions are justified by his willingness to pay the penalty that the law prescribes. The idea that paying the penalty justifies breaking the law derives, not from Gandhi and the tradition of civil disobedience, but Oliver Wendell Holmes and the tradition of legal realism. According to Holmes and the legal realists the law characteristically presents us with an option—either to obey, or to suffer the consequences that attach to disobedience. This doctrine is indefensible even in the area of contract law where it arose, and where it has a fragile plausibility, but it is plainly absurd to suppose that the citizen has such an option in the area of criminal law. Criminal punishments are not a simple tax on criminal misconduct, and the citizen is not given the option of engaging in such conduct on the condition that he pay the tax. It is mindless to suppose that murder, rape, or arson would be justified if only one were willing to pay the penalty, and the civil disobedient is committed to no such mindlessness. Holmes was looking at the law from the point of view of a bad man for whom paying the penalty is always an option and often a source of advantage. Gandhi considered it from the point of view of a good man for whom paying the penalty is often a necessity and always a source of pain. Accepting punishment does not justify the act of civil disobedience, but it helps to establish the disobedient's seriousness and his fidelity to law in the eyes of the majority whose actions have, in his opinion, justified it.

The disobedient's willingness to suffer punishment has another purpose as well. It is meant to weaken the will of the transgressors and to dissuade them from a course of action that the dissenters consider immoral. For, if the transgressors do not draw back, they may be forced to punish some of the most scrupulous and dedicated members of the community. The fact that this is so will often persuade those who heedlessly supported the original measures, not to mention those who supported them with a dim sense of their injustice, to withdraw their support or even to join the opposition. Forcing others to suffer for their moral beliefs is a high price to pay for pursuing a questionable course of conduct and many will prefer not to pay it.

The disobedient's willingness to face suffering and punishment may be seen, then, as a useful way of reinforcing the effects of his protest and appeal. It constitutes a use of pressure, to be sure, but this pressure does not amount to coercion. If the majority remains unconvinced, it will consider itself free to act as it wishes and to impose legal sanctions if these should be required. On occasion, however, the dissenters may actually attempt to coerce the majority. They may attempt to create a situation in which the majority cannot pursue its purposes unless it acts in ways that it believes to be morally impermissible. The actions of the captain and the crew of The Golden Rule provide a case in point. For, when they sailed into the government's nuclear testing grounds in the Central Pacific these men were not simply registering a protest against its testing program and hoping that their arrest would give the public painful second thoughts. Rather, they were telling the government that it would have to incinerate them if it wished to proceed as planned and this, they hoped, the government would find it impossible to do. In cases like this the dissenters cross the line that separates civil disobedience from those forms of political action that actually attempt to paralyze the majority's will or the government's operations. As such, they may be compared to public strikes and acts of sabotage (although such acts normally employ quite different methods) and they constitute a form of incipient rebellion. Certainly, they issue a more radical challenge to governmental authority than the civil disobedient wishes to pose.

The disobedient's interest in establishing that his actions are neither rebellious nor revolutionary provides him with a final reason for accepting punishment. For, by accepting the punishment prescribed by law the disobedient is able to emphasize his commitment to law, and it is especially important for him to do so in a democratic society. The values that the disobedient wishes to defend are, after all, precisely the values that are best served by a democracy under law, if only these laws remain within bounds. Should it come to a choice, the disobedient's ultimate commitment is certainly to justice, and not to the will of the majority. But his present purpose is to persuade the majority not to force this choice upon him and his present intention is to make the established system viable. It must not be supposed, incidentally, that the civil disobedient's position implies that he will never submit to the requirements of an unjust law. In fact, the citizen in a democracy often has a moral obligation to do just that. But there are limits to the injustice he will endure as there are limits to the injustice he will perpetuate. It is the civil disobedient's conviction that these limits have been reached.

Of course, it does not follow from the fact that the disobedient is willing to pay the penalty that the government ought to exact it. The disobedient has been placed in an acute moral dilemma and he may have acted with good will toward the community. Certainly, his punishment may cause profound ruptures in the community. All these facts, and others, ought to be considered by the government in deciding whether to prosecute, and by the judiciary in deciding the terms of sentence. It will often be in the government's and, indeed, in the community's best interests to act with flexibility and discretion in these matters and it is a particularly barbarous fallacy to suppose that the government owes the disobedient his just portion of punishment. That it may owe him a day in court when he wishes to raise constitutional issues, perhaps even a day free from the threat of punishment, is another, insufficiently canvassed question, that cannot be pursued here.

The dissenter may commit illegal action, but in the view of Gandhi and of Martin Luther King such actions ought to be non-violent in nature. Gandhi and King were of course, committed to non-violence quite generally and as a matter of religious principle. Their views in this matter are therefore unconvincing to those who are willing to contemplate the use of violence in certain circumstances. Thoreau, for one, was not opposed to its occasional use. In the famous essay that gave currency to the very term "civil disobedience" he remarked that when conscience is wounded a little blood is shed, and the suggestion that on occasion a little blood ought to be shed in return was not far to seek. In later life Thoreau did, in fact, endorse the violence of John Brown and his associates without scruple. It is possible to share Thoreau's general attitudes rather than Gandhi's or King's, and to hold, nevertheless, that violence, or at least certain forms of it, are incompatible with the distinctive purposes of civil disobedience. Thus, John Rawls, to whom these remarks are very much indebted, argues that violent actions are incompatible with the nature of civil disobedience because they will be understood as threats, not as appeals. And it is possible to add that the fear of violence (or of sudden death) puts men beyond the reach of rational and moral persuasion. There is a time for violence in human affairs, but, when it arrives, civil disobedience is no longer an appropriate form of political activity.

Rawls' suggestion is persuasive and especially so when it restricts the prohibition on violence against other persons. It is less convincing when violence against property is in question. For the violation of symbolically important public property may be a dramatic, and not very dangerous, way of lodging effective protests, and the razing of the slums has been understood as a cry of despair as often as it has been perceived as a declaration of war. The argument against violence is at its weakest in the case of violence against the self. A sacrifice like Norman Morrison's, far from frustrating the purposes of civil disobedience, realized them in a peculiarly impressive and moving way. If it inspired fear it was not the fear of sudden death but the fear of eternal wrath, and that is a fear that often brings men to their moral senses.

Civil disobedience is, then, an appeal to the public to alter certain laws or policies that the minority takes to be incompatible with the fundamental principles of morality, principles to which it believes the majority is committed. If the minority is mistaken and the majority is not in fact committed to them civil disobedience will undoubtedly prove a pointless form of political activity, but it will not, for that reason, be an unjustifiable one. The moral duty to obey particular laws derives from the moral duty to support constitutional arrangements on which others have relied, so long as it is reasonable to believe that these arrangements are intended to implement, and are capable of implementing, the principles of freedom and justice. But one's moral obligation to obey particular laws lapses when one solemnly believes that such laws constitute deep violations of those arrangements, or of the principles on which they rest. (It goes without saying that discharging one's moral duty is not the only legitimate ground for obeying the law.) These principles of political morality normally find expression in the public morality of the state and, given the circumstances of the modern democracies, they guarantee to citizens the basic freedoms (including freedom to participate in the political life) and also a minimum of justice (by which I understand not only the disinterested administration of justice, but also a fair share of the benefits of the common life). In addition, they prohibit inflicting pain and suffering on innocent persons and they require fidelity to the idea of justice between nations. These principles are adumbrated, and often find remarkably full expression, in the constitutions of modern states, although the constitution, especially the constitution as interpreted by the courts, may be an imperfect expression of them. Thus, our own public morality, as articulated in the Constitution, makes very broad guarantees of freedom and justice in the First, the Fifth, and the Fourteenth Amendments, and Article VI makes treaties part of the supreme law of the land. The treaties to which we are in fact a party define the rights of foreign peoples in considerable detail and they enumerate the legitimate grounds, and acceptable methods, of war.

I have little doubt that, at the present time, the government of the United States is violating these principles of political morality and providing dissenters with legitimate grounds for civil disobedience. It is important to recall, however, that the public morality of our society, especially as it is articulated in the federal constitution, gives voice to these very principles, and we must now examine the consequences of this fact for the traditional theory of civil disobedience. For, on the traditional view a man who commits civil disobedience believes that he is, in fact, violating a legally valid (if morally unsupportable) law or order. But in a constitutional democracy like our own those who are asked to conform to laws that they think immoral will typically be in a position to claim, and if they are legally well-advised they will claim, that the laws in question are unconstitutional nullities, not laws at all.[1]

The altered position I have described was, of course, the position of Martin Luther King and his disciples in the civil rights movement. As one would expect, they rarely, if ever, pleaded guilty to violating the laws under which they were charged. Rather, they argued that the laws were themselves in violation of the federal constitution and that they were, in consequence, invalid and without legal effect. In a remarkable number of cases (when federal legislation had not already rendered the issues moot) the courts agreed with them.

Despite the fact that they did not believe themselves to be violating the law, Martin Luther King and his followers continued to refer to themselves as civil disobedients. Justice Fortas has fallen in with their usage and this fact has, I believe, contributed to his wholly undeserved reputation for having a liberal, and even a concessive position on the issue of civil disobedience. For it is one thing to endorse "civil disobedience" of the type practiced by King and quite another thing to endorse civil

---

[1] Irving Kristol is, therefore either being obtuse or supercilious when he writes that "those who are morally committed to civil disobedience can properly claim that the law which arrests them, or the law that punishes them is so perverse as to be without authority. What they may not do in good conscience is to practice civil disobedience and then hire a clever lawyer to argue that it wasn't a violation of the law at all, but rather the exercise of a right."

disobedience in the stricter, traditional and more serious sense. Certainly, Justice Fortas has not endorsed civil disobedience in this more traditional sense. In fact, his liberalism comes to nothing more than this: the dissenter is granted a moral right to test, or to try to test, the validity of a law that he considers immoral and believes to be unconstitutional. It finds its consummation in a proposition that Vice-President Agnew would hardly contest: if the courts agree that the law is invalid, the dissenter was within his legal rights in refusing to obey it.

The fact that Justice Fortas has not endorsed anything like the classical conception of civil disobedience becomes apparent when we consider his attitude toward the "disobedient" who does not win, but who loses in the courts. For on Justice Fortas' view the man who loses in court is under a moral, as well as a legal, obligation to refrain from any further disobedience (he has had his day in court) and he is morally, as well as legally, obliged to suffer the punishment prescribed by law (that is the way we play the game). Surely, this is a rigid and untenable view; indeed, Justice Fortas implies on occasion that even he does not really accept it. If Congress passed a law requiring Negroes to observe a discriminatory curfew, to confine themselves to certain restricted geographical areas (as Ambassador Kennan has now hinted might be a good idea) and go naked through the streets if they wished to apply for welfare few would suppose that they had a moral obligation to do so. The fact that the courts ultimately sustained such a law would not alter the situation in any serious way. But it is hardly necessary to seek examples that may seem fantastic or purely theoretical. After all, the Court on which Judge Fortas sat once decided the Dred Scott case and it is hard to believe that Justice Fortas, or anyone else, is going to say (at least at this late date) that in the period following the Fugitive Slave Law and the Dred Scott decision abolitionists had a moral obligation to return slaves to their owners or that slaves had an obligation to return of their own free will.

Even if we were to assume that the Court's interpretation of the Constitution in the Dred Scott case was a defensible one it would not follow that one had a moral obligation to acquiesce in its decision. For the Constitution itself would then have been in violation of the fundamental principles of political morality and one simply does not have a moral obligation to abide by such a constitution. Of course, there is very good reason to doubt that the constitution did in fact mean what the Court said it meant and it is important, now to challenge the view that the constitution, or that the law, is inevitably what the courts say it is. For the doctrine gives a false view of the nature of law and of what it means to obey it.

The English school of Hobbes and Austin held that the law is to be identified with the command of the sovereign and, insofar as he delegates authority to them, with the decisions and orders of his courts. The American legal realists have associated the law and the courts even more closely. For Holmes the law is "nothing more pretentious" than a prophecy of what the courts will do; for Fortas "the rule of law" requires nothing more ignoble than acquiescing in whatever they may have commanded. The objections to such views are powerful indeed, and a far more persuasive and commonsense tradition holds that the law is to be identified, not with the holdings of courts, but with the authorized rules and principles that the courts interpret and apply. Of course, the interpretations and holdings of courts must be considered in determining the state of the law (the doctrine of precedent has an important place in our jurisprudence), but these interpretations and decisions must not be identified with the law. For one thing, the courts can misinterpret the law, and their decisions are often mistaken. When this is so it would be foolish and harmful to identify these dubious interpretations and questionable decisions with the law itself. Certainly the courts do not do so. It may have taken the Union Armies to "reverse" the Dred Scott case, but the courts often admit that they have been in error and agree to reverse themselves. Indeed, the Supreme Court has reversed itself in such momentous cases as *Erie R.R. v. Tomkins, Brown v. Board of Education,* and *West Virginia State Board of Education v. Barnette.*

This fact is of importance to the dissenter for a number of reasons. In the first place, it may strengthen the case for disobedience on purely moral grounds. For, as Ronald Dworkin has observed,[2] it is one thing for a man to sacrifice his principles (or to violate his conscience) when it is plain that the law requires him to do so. But it is quite another thing for him to do so when the law, or the court's view of it, is of questionable validity. In addition to making a moral difference the fact that the courts may be wrong makes a practical difference as well. One of the disobedient's aims is to change the existing law and the most effective way of doing so in a constitutional democracy will often be to persuade the courts that the obnoxious legislation is unconstitutional. Continued defiance of the law may be the only practical way for the dissenter to obtain a rehearing of the questions at issue and even when other methods are available the disobedient's willingness to face criminal punishment in defense of his beliefs may help the court to see that it had misjudged the strength, and perhaps even the nature, of his interests in the first place.

For this reason it is possible to agree with Dworkin's claim that the Jehovah's Witnesses behaved properly in refusing to observe Justice Fortas' canons of correct behavior after the Court found against them in the first "flag-salute" case. As they saw it, the law denied them a basic religious freedom and they were being asked to violate their fundamental

---

[2] *The New York Review of Books,* Vol. X, No. 11, June 6, 1968, pp. 14–21.

religious convictions on the basis of dubious constitutional doctrine. Continued defiance did not require them to injure the interests, or abridge the rights, of others in any serious way and, in the end, it probably helped to convince the Court that its original decision had been mistaken. In any event, the Court did reverse itself in the well-known case of *West Virginia State Board of Education v. Barnette* only a few years later. As it now viewed the matter the intransigent Witnesses had only been exercising their constitutional rights all along. The moral is plain. It is often those who insist on their legal rights, rather than those who acquiesce in the fallible (and occasionally supine and even corrupt) opinions of courts, who strengthen the "rule of law" that Justice Fortas is so anxious to defend.

If the argument for civil disobedience is strengthened when there is reason to believe that the courts are in error it is strengthened still more when there is reason to believe that the courts will refuse to adjudicate the issues at all. This is, of course, precisely what they have refused to do in the crucial cases arising out of the war in Vietnam. In the "Spock" case the trial court invoked the "political question" doctrine and denied its jurisdiction to hear any issues concerning the legality of the war or of its conduct. And in the cases of David Mitchell (who refused to report for induction) and of the "Fort Hood" three (who refused to report for service in Vietnam) the Supreme Court simply denied *certiorari*. It has been suggested that when the courts invoke the "political question" doctrine and refuse to adjudicate the issues the disobedient wishes to raise, their action is tantamount to finding that the executive is legally free to perform these very actions.[3] But it is far more plausible to argue that when they invoke this doctrine they assume a wholly agnostic position on the issues involved and simply enforce as law the determinations of the "political" branches. In the case of the "Fort Hood" three this agnostic attitude is assumed toward questions that Justice Stewart and Justice Douglas consider, and that plainly are, "of great magnitude." In his dissent to the Court's decision denying *certiorari* in the case of the "Fort Hood" three Justice Stewart indicates that these questions include, among others, these:

1. Is the present United States military activity in Vietnam a "war" within the meaning of Article I, Section 8, Clause 11 of the Constitution?

11. If so, may the Executive constitutionally order the petitioners to participate in that military activity, when no war has been declared by the Congress?

---

[3] Graham Hughes, "Civil Disobedience and The Political Question Doctrine," *New York University Law Review*, Vol. 43, March 1968, No. 1 pp. 15–16.

III.   Of what relevance to Question II are the present treaty obligations of the United States?

IV.   Of what relevance to Question II is the joint Congressional ("Tonkin Bay") Resolution of August 10, 1964?

    (a)   Do present United States military operations fall within the terms of the Joint Resolution?

    (b)   If the Joint Resolution purports to give the Chief Executive authority to commit United States forces to armed conflict limited in scope only by his own absolute discretion, is the Resolution a constitutionally impermissible delegation of all or part of Congress' power to declare war?

"These are," he continues, "large and deeply troubling questions. Whether the Court would ultimately reach them depends, of course, upon the resolution of serious preliminary issues of justiciability. We cannot make these problems go away simply by refusing to hear the case of three obscure Army privates. I intimate not even tentative views upon any of these matters, but I think the Court should squarely face them by granting certiorari and setting this case for oral argument."

In turn, I do not wish to intimate any views on the "political question" doctrine or on the Court's unwillingness to review the actions of the executive and legislative branches in these sensitive areas. But it is important to recognize that the Court's refusal to consider these matters can only increase the weight that the three obscure Army privates, and others like them, must give to their own appraisal of the issues.[4] Certainly, a very formidable body of opinion supports the view that the government's behavior is in many particulars both illegal and unconstitutional. And there is little doubt, I believe, that it has frequently violated the principles of international law and morality. The case for disobedience in these circumstances is very strong.

The discussion has focussed, so far, on what Gandhi called "defensive," and others have called "direct," disobedience. In cases of this type the law the dissenter violates is the very law that he regards as immoral. It will be worth commenting, briefly and in conclusion, on what Gandhi called "offensive," and others have called "indirect," disobedience. For in this type of disobedience the dissenter violates laws (usually traffic laws or the laws of trespass) that he finds unobjectionable in themselves in order to protest still other laws, policies or orders that he thinks immoral and even wicked. While Justice Fortas displays some sympathy for those who engage in "direct" disobedience (the courts may, after all, vindicate them) his hostility to those who practice indirect disobedience is unremit-

---

[4] Professor Michael Katz has objected to this contention as it was formulated in the *Massachusetts Review* version of this essay and I have replied to his objection in that journal, Vol. XI, No. 1, Winter 1970, pp. 172–75.

ting (there is no doubt that they are disobedients in the strict sense). In his view their behavior is unnecessary and unjustifiable; it is, in fact, nothing less than a form of "warfare" against society.

I would argue, to the contrary, that "indirect" disobedience is both justifiable and necessary. It is justified, as all civil disobedience is justified, as a solemn protest at a comparable level of depth. In particular, it must not be supposed that whenever the government violates the principles of political morality it does so by enacting a positively wicked law that the dissenters can protest "directly." For instance, the object of protest may well be the government's failure to pass a law, or to enforce one. Thus, Ralph Abernathy's violation of the law of trespass was meant to protest the government's failure to enact an adequate poverty program, and the obstruction of segregated construction sites is a familiar technique for protesting the government's failure to enforce fair employment practices statutes that have long been part of the law.[5] Then, too, the object of protest may be a governmental policy or order, rather than a law, strictly speaking. It makes no sense to speak of violating the government's policy or intervening in the affairs of foreign states and the ordinary citizen is in no position to defy orders issued to military personnel. It is for this reason that such "indirect" methods of protest as sit-ins at draft boards and demonstrations at the Pentagon have been employed to protest the government's violent intervention in Vietnam, and this is why men have even endured self-immolation to protest the military's use of fire-bombs against a defenseless civilian population. It is unfortunate that these are the acts of "warfare" that Justice Fortas finds it most important to protest. In fact, the government's various failures and transgressions constitute a far greater threat to "the rule of law" that he is so concerned to defend. It is one of the great merits of those who practice civil disobedience to have seen this and to have acted on their painful knowledge.

---

[5] It is worth noting the view of the present Solicitor General (and former Dean of the Harvard Law School) on a related point. Mr. Griswold writes that he "cannot distinguish in principle the legal quality of the determination . . . to block a workman from entering a segregated job site from the determination to fire shots into a civil rights leader's home to protest integration." If all Mr. Griswold means by his fine periphrastic phrase ("cannot distinguish in principle the legal quality") is that both actions are illegal few will dispute his point. If he means anything else—perhaps that they are equally serious violations of the law—it is to his credit that he couldn't quite bring himself to say so.

Response to Professor Marshall Cohen *

Graham Hughes

Professor Cohen has given us a clear, sensible and subtle essay on civil disobedience and there is only one aspect of his analysis with which I shall want to take issue. I would also wish to make some comments from the standpoint of a lawyer and perhaps particularly from the perspective of a criminal and constitutional lawyer.

First I want to agree emphatically with Professor Cohen (and with Ronald Dworkin who has also made this point)[1] that the concept of fidelity to law would be vulgarized and made distortingly simple if we understood it as referring to an obligation not to question the decision of a court, even the Supreme Court. Such a position would involve the error of failing to distinguish between the concept of a legal system and the concept of authority within the system. The court is certainly established by the norms of the system as the proper authoritative organ to make decisions which legally bind the parties but to acknowledge this is very different from saying that the court is an infallible, oracular spokesman for correct or best statements of the law. To assert this would, indeed, be contrary to the traditions and practices of lawyers who are constantly arguing in the courts and in the classrooms that the Supreme Court was wrong when it came to one decision or another. The position which Professor Cohen properly attacks is perhaps a confused legacy of the realist movement in American jurisprudence. The realists were in the habit of talking about the law more in terms of what judges do in deciding cases than in terms of rules and principles. But even the realists would have said that the law on a particular point is a prediction of what a court will decide tomorrow rather than a record of what it decided yesterday. Once we look upon the law more illuminatingly as a body of rules and principles, as a process of reasoning and argument, the correct position is even more apparent. Fidelity to law requires a constant reexamination of de-

---

* From *Philosophic Exchange* (1970 Edition). Reprinted by permission of the author and publisher.

[1] Dworkin, "Civil Disobedience, The Case Against Prosecution." *New York Review of Books*, Vol. X, No. 11, June 6, 1968.

cisions in terms of rules and principles rather than a slavish genuflexion to the court's latest pronouncement.

There is of course an important difference between arguing that the court's decision was wrong in law and asserting the reservation of a privilege to refuse to comply. Professor Dworkin has argued (and I understand Professor Cohen to be agreeing with him) that the authoritative nature of the court within the system is an important reason which should incline the citizen in the direction of compliance even if he should believe the court to be wrong. But both these writers would go on to assert that it is not always a decisive reason. A strong moral position against the implications of the decision may be a reason for disobedience and this would be relevantly and significantly supported by the added contention that the court's decision was wrong in law. This is a position which I do not think is inconsistent with a lawyer's inclination to support the rule of law. The rule of law cannot live with the proposition that anyone may have a privilege to disobey when even compliance would be inconvenient or whenever he disagrees with the policy judgment implicit in the law. But it is able to survive alongside the position that there is a moral justfication for disobedience when it is in terms of an appeal to conscience.[2]

If civil disobedience can sometimes, perhaps often in the United States, be grounded in a position which partakes both of moral claims and legal claims, what practical lesson is there for law enforcement officers and judges? At the least, as Ronald Dworkin has argued,[3] we may suggest that the motivation, the moral positions and arguments that underlie the disobedience, are perfectly proper matters to be considered by enforcement officials in exercising the discretionary function of deciding whether to prosecute or not and by judges in determining what sentence to hand down if a conviction ensues. I would go further and suggest, as I have done elsewhere,[4] that it is conceivably proper, though attended with some difficulties, for the courts to hold that a defendant's reasonable belief in the unconstitutionality of a statute under which he is prosecuted might in some cases be recognized as a defense leading to an acquittal. The question of whether the statute is constitutional is not, after all, the same question as whether the defendant is a guilty person deserving of punishment. Guilt in criminal law has always included elements which go beyond the doing of a prohibited act. The prosecution must show *mens rea* or guilty mind in the accused and *mens rea* is dis-

---

[2] See Wasserstrom, "The Obligation to Obey the Law," 10 *U.C.L.A. Law Review*, 780 (1963).

[3] Dworkin, *op cit., Supra* n. 1.

[4] Hughes, "Civil Disobedience and the Political Question Doctrine" 43 *N.Y.U. Law Rev.*, 1 (1968).

RESPONSE TO PROFESSOR MARSHALL COHEN   159

placed by a variety of possible justifying circumstances. The belief that the statute which he apparently violated was unconstitutional might be regarded as a justifying circumstance without any strain on classical principles of criminal law. The limits of such a doctrine would certainly be narrow and would embrace only a small number of civil disobedience cases and perhaps only those which Professor Cohen has suggested should not be thought of as typical instances of civil disobedience at all. Cases of "indirect" disobedience would not be touched at all. And even where the defense was prima facie appropriate, as where the defendant asserted that he believed the statute which he violated to be unconstitutional, there would be a question as to whether a court could continue to regard the belief as reasonable once it ran contrary to an explicit decision of the Supreme Court on the point at issue.

Professor Cohen has suggested that it is perfectly consistent with the practice of civil disobedience for the defendant in such a case to claim in his defense when prosecuted that the law under which he is charged is unconstitutional. I agree completely but there is a more difficult question here which ought to be considered. The defendant's attorney may wish to raise matters which do not go to the constitutionality of the law in question but are rather "technical" arguments—e.g. that certain testimony is inadmissible under the laws of evidence or that a judge was in error in ruling against the defendant's motion to discover part of the prosecution's case. Is it consistent with a posture of civil disobedience to raise such points? Does the civil disobedient have an obligation to renounce all defenses and arguments of a legal nature other than an attack on the constitutionality of the law under which he is indicted? This question was raised by some in connection with the trial of Dr. Spock where issues of constitutionality were raised by the defense alongside a number of other "technical" defenses.

It certainly is consistent with fidelity to law in the broad sense to raise defenses which are generally proper in a trial. But the question here of course is whether it is consistent with the appeal to conscience which the disobedient is asserting. Perhaps here we must distinguish between a whole range of possibilities. At the one extreme it would clearly eradicate all elements of appeal to conscience if the defendant at his trial were to exercise his right to stand mute and put the prosecution to its burden of proof and then argue that they had simply failed to adduce sufficient evidence for a conviction. The notion of an appeal to conscience would seem to include of necessity at least the absence of a denial that the act was done by the accused and some positive proclamation of the reasons for doing it. If a proclamation of the reasons for doing the act is to be included then this would seem to entail an admission that the accused did the act. The necessity for such an admission does not mandate a formal guilty plea, for the procedural context of a guilty plea may deprive the defendant of a forum for making his appeal to conscience, but it is certainly inconsistent with any defense or objection which avoids the opportunity to justify the conduct in question.

The necessity of not denying the act does not however entail the abandonment of all technical objections. A defendant who is a civil disobedient may surely assert, consistently with his posture of appeal to conscience, that the prosecution should present its case in a lawful and proper manner. For, if he is willing to be convicted, this is only provided that the conviction be according to law. Part of what he insists upon in his appeal to conscience is that the state should behave in a lawful and constitutional manner. There is of course the risk (if that is the right word) that the successful raising of an objection to the prosecution's procedures may be sufficiently decisive to result in an acquittal. Here indeed there may be a choice to be made, for the defendant may take the view that the value to be preserved by holding the prosecution to full legal propriety in its presentation of the case against him is outweighed by the added strength that his appeal to conscience will gain from conviction and submission to punishment. But the contrary choice, though it may have the practical outcome of diluting the strength of the appeal to conscience, is not irreconcilable with the initial posture of civil disobedience.

Professor Cohen has expressly taken issue with what I have written on an earlier occasion and here I continue to some extent to disagree with him. In his text, with elaboration in a footnote, Professor Cohen writes:

"It has been suggested that when the courts invoke the 'political question' doctrine and refuse to adjudicate the issues the disobedient wishes to raise, their action is tantamount to finding that the executive is legally free to perform these very actions. But it is far more plausible to argue that when they invoke this doctrine they assume a wholly agnostic position on the issues involved and simply enforce as law the determinations of the political branches." [5] The weakness of Professor Cohen's position here seems to be revealed in the curious paradox involved in the last sentence quoted. I do not see how the courts can be said to "enforce as law the determinations of the political branches" and at the same time be said to take "a wholly agnostic position." The ruling that the action of the executive cannot be challenged in a legal forum with its implicit corollary that the mechanisms of law enforcement may be properly used to enforce the executive determination is too much charged with positive consequences to be dismissed in this way.

---

[5] *Supra.*

The point is that a decision of the Supreme Court that an issue is not justiciable because it involves a political question is itself a decision of a point of law about the jurisdiction of the Court. As such it amounts to a ruling that no tribunal exists which has the legal power in the instant case to declare the act of the executive unlawful. This certainly has a less affirmative impact than a procedure by which the court took jurisdiction of the case and interpreted the substantive provision of the constitution in the executive's favor. But it does at the least mean that in the instant case the executive has a legal privilege to act as it has done in the bare sense that no institution has the legal capacity to declare its action unlawful.

I must be careful to insist here that I am not falling into the error of arguing that a legal duty cannot exist in the absence of enforceability. Lawyers are very familiar with situations where a duty is not directly enforceable against the one who was in breach but yet remains significant for practical purposes of attaching liability vicariously to others. But in the political question area the issue is not one of enforceability but rather of justiciability. A less rarified example from another field may serve to make the point. If X who is domiciled in New Jersey is run over in Newark by an automobile driven by Y, also domiciled in New Jersey, there is no way at all in which X can maintain an action against Y in the courts of New York State. Does this mean that under the law of New York Y did not commit a breach of legal duty when he ran down X? For a lawyer the only sensible answer to this question must be in the affirmative. An application of the political question doctrine, though on a much more exotic plane, has the same juridical significance. It is a holding to the effect that no adjudicative tribunal has the power to interpret the limits of executive power in a given area, carrying with it the implication that challenges to such power can only be made in the political arena.

Professor Cohen seeks to avoid this conclusion by arguing that the judgment that a legal duty has been breached "is by no means the exclusive prerogative of the courts." He suggests that "the President, the Congress and even the public may, and often must, make such judgments." [6] It is perhaps here that the heart of the disagreement between Professor Cohen and myself emerges. As a lawyer I am uncomfortable with a usage which can refer to a judgment as legal in the absence of any norm which can be taken to characterize the judgment as authoritative. It is of course true that individuals can make legal judgments which are not in themselves authoritative but the notion of legal judgment here is a derivative one which takes color from the existence of *some* institution which is empowered to make an authoritative judgment on the issue. So I may

---

[6] *Supra.*

make a legal judgment that the Supreme Court has been wrong in some of its decisions which invoke the political question doctrine. I would then simply be disagreeing with the Court's interpretation of the law of the political question doctrine. But it would not make sense for me to contend that while I do not question the application of the political question doctrine by the Court I still want to argue that the action of the executive is in some sense illegal. Another way of putting this is to say that any argument I may wish to make asserting the illegality of the executive's action is essentially dependent on a prior argument that the court was mistaken in its application of the political question doctrine, and is, therefore, a concession that the concept of illegality is dependent on locating an authoritative tribunal which, under the law, ought to rule on the question. If Professor Cohen could concede this much, then perhaps we are not after all in disagreement.

Remarks on Violence and Paying the Penalty *

Kai Nielsen

I

I labor under the misfortune of almost entirely agreeing with what Profesor Cohen has to say about civil disobedience in a constitutional democracy. To add to my discomfiture, the one place where I seriously question his argument, I accept and take to be of crucial importance the underlying point behind his argument.

What I shall do in this circumstance is first to bring out my one important disagreement with Professor Cohen and then very briefly discuss violence as a political tactic. The latter is relevant to our deliberations here, for it is now felt by many that over such major issues as the oppression of the blacks, the draft and the Indo-Chinese war the time for civil disobedience is past, that things have been escalated to such an extent and the perfidy and moral sloth of the American government is so great, that continued civil disobedience is of no avail. We are left, as we face Babylon, with the stark alternatives of submission (perhaps ac-

---

* From *Philosophic Exchange* (1970 Edition). Footnotes included. Reprinted by permission of the author and publisher.

companied by what the Germans call *innere Emigration*), literal immigration or a resistance going beyond civil disobedience which may involve some forms of violence. It is terribly important and terribly difficult to try to ascertain whether this is our situation and whether over such large issues acts of civil disobedience are useless. These are also embarrassing questions for a philosopher for they are not questions which can be resolved simply by using the tools of his trade, i.e. conceptual analysis, though conceptual analysis is relevant to their resolution. But they are weighty human and political issues, so let us see if we can make some headway with them.

II

I shall commence with the point where I have a disagreement with Marshall Cohen. Cohen remarks that "After openly breaking the law, the traditional disobedient willingly pays the penalty." This might be taken in two ways. It might be taken simply as a description of what people who regard themselves as engaging in civil disobedience do. But then it is surely not the case that all people who engage in what they believe to be civil disobedience are willing to pay the penalty. Their public defiance of a law they regard as so immoral that it requires disobedience is sometimes followed by forms of legal evasion. I think Cohen would reply that in such a circumstance their acts are not properly characterizable, as "civil disobedience." And if this would be his reply, then his "After openly breaking the law, the traditional disobedient willingly pays the penalty" would take my second reading, namely it would be a statement about the defining characteristics of what could count as "legitimate civil disobedience." That is to say, an act would not be a legitimate act of civil disobedience unless the obedient were willing to pay the penalty if the courts find against him.

Cohen's claim—taken now in this second way—is too strong. What is a standard way, no doubt the most important way, of showing the disobedient's fidelity to the law is not the only way. Moreover, there are cases, as I shall show below, that cannot be handled by Cohen's condition.

First consider a situation in which what the disobedient finds particularly objectionable about a law is the penalty for its violation. Suppose the penalty for possessing marijuana was twenty years imprisonment. A disobedient might deliberately and openly violate the law, making a political, moral point with his violation, and yet be quite unwilling to accept such a penalty. He could quite consistently with being a civil disobedient fight that penalty. His fighting such a penalty need not evidence any betrayal of the community—though he would need some alternative means to show his fidelity to the law. But surely he could do this by willingly submitting to control of the courts rather than attempting to become a fugitive. He need not endure the very penalty he regards as thoroughly unjust.[1]

Moreover, there are situations in which the civil disobedient need not knuckle in to the law where the law's control of his behavior in a certain determinate way flows from his act of civil disobedience. For this dark saying to become clear, consider this example. Suppose—say around 1950—a doctor in a small town in the United States with a predominantly Catholic population announces that when it is medically feasible he will perform free abortions to people seeking them. Let us further suppose that he actually does this and that the Catholic Church makes a great outcry against him. As a result of this outcry, he is barred from the two hospitals in town, his practice falls off and the like. But suppose he persists in performing abortions, until finally legal action is taken against him. If he then flees the country to evade imprisonment, after losing his fight in the courts, it is surely not the case that he has shown that he was insincere, that his acts contributed toward eroding the moral foundations of civil disobedience, betrayed the community or exhibited contempt for the law. He surely in his behavior was showing high moral integrity. It was without a profit motive and could very well have been without any exhibitionistic intent. He had a moral point to make and he made it through his words and deeds and he had much to lose personally by persisting in this behavior. Even in evading the law by fleeing the country, he has not shown contempt for the law or a lack of fidelity to the law if his evasions meet two conditions. First of all, they are all derivative from his attempting to evade imprisonment for his deliberate act of disobedience, which—but for the question of his evading punishment—would have *clearly* counted as a civilly disobedient act. Second of all, they must be acts which do not violate anyone's rights in a serious way or cause greater misery or injustice all around, than would his submitting to punishment.

More generally there are alternative ways for the civil disobedient to show his seriousness and the depth of his commitment than by being willing to accept the punishment. Accepting the punishment is only one test among many for the disobedient's actually having acted out of conscience in order to remind the public that in his judgment grave injustices are occurring and that conditions essential for humane social cooperation are not being honored. Being willing to pay the penalty is no doubt the most common test of the disobedient's intent but it is not the only one.

---

[1] For the first example and some of the conceptual points I am indebted to an unpublished essay by Sidney Gendin.

It is not a necessary condition for an act's being a genuine act of civil disobedience.

Cohen's essay is admittedly indebted at several points to Ronald Dworkin's brilliant essay "Civil Disobedience: The Case Against Prosecution." [2] Yet just at the very point we are presently discussing Cohen misses, I believe, an important insight in Dworkin's essay. When people challenge the draft laws, for example, and refuse to obey them in the public, principled and deliberate fashion of a civil disobedient, they are persuaded that the laws are often unconstitutional and in such a situation, Dworkin argues, their case about constitutionality is a strong one. But then they do not regard themselves as having broken a law, for they believe on reasonable grounds that the law they are disobeying is invalid, e.g. unconstitutional, and believing this they have no obligation at all in terms of fair play or anything else to accept the punishment.

What Cohen fails to give sufficient attention to in *this context,* though he generally does, is that there are cases and cases and situations and situations and that civil disobedience will not come to the same thing in all circumstances. He is perfectly correct in maintaining that it is "especially important" for a civil disobedient in a democratic society to accept the punishment for his civil disobedience, for "by accepting the punishment prescribed by the law the disobedient is able to emphasize commitment to law." He reinforces his claim about the gravity and the urgency of the plea he makes to his government and fellow citizens by his willingness to suffer for his beliefs. Clearly this is an important matter. I have only been concerned to show that this is not the only way to exhibit a commitment to the rule of law or a determination to civilly fight corruption in the palace of justice.

III

I would now like to turn to the topic of violence and authority. An act of civil disobedience must be nonviolent at least in intent. Gandhi and King argued for such limitations on religious grounds, but Rawls and Cohen give grounds for such a limitation which are independent of any religious commitment.[3] In engaging in civil disobedience, we are in the very nature of the case making appeals to the conscience of our fellow citizens and—in the typical case—to the men who run the government. We are trying to persuade intellectually and morally; we are not—and

---

[2] Ronald Dworkin, "Civil Disobedience: The Case Against Prosecution," in *Social Justice,* Howard Kiefer & Milton Munitz (eds.) (New York: 1970).

[3] John Rawls "The Justification of Civil Disobedience" in *Civil Disobedience: Theory and Practice,* Hugo Adam Bedau (ed.) (New York: 1969), pp. 241–55 [reprinted in this text].

indeed cannot—since we are making a moral and politically educational appeal, seeking to change behavior and laws non-rationally through threats and by fear. Cohen's conclusion then seems to be the appropriate one: "There is a time for violence in human affairs, but when it arrives, civil disobedience is no longer an appropriate form of political activity." The question then becomes, when is the appropriate time for violence in human affairs? In what contexts is it justifiable, what ends may it legitimately serve, what forms may it take and what limits must it observe for it to be justified violence? A lover of violence, a man indifferent to human suffering or injury, is scarcely human. Violence is indeed something which is in normal circumstances morally outrageous. It is infantile and immoral to romanticize it, but under certain circumstances it may be a grim moral and political necessity. What might those circumstances be?

What I want to say about this is quite simple. It has been said thousands of times before and it will be said thousands of times again. My excuse for repeating it is that it continually gets neglected in much of the current rather hysterical and/or romantic talk about violence.

Consider first what violence is. To do violence to someone is to injure him. Violence is the infliction of injury or damage on some person(s) or property and it is *in itself* always bad. But it is sometimes *instrumentally* valuable, i.e. worth doing, when, everything considered, the pain, suffering and injustice we overcome by engaging in violence outweighs the pain, suffering and injustice that results from allowing the conditions to remain which the violent action, and the violent action alone, could effectively overcome.

There is, of course, great difficulty in ascertaining when these conditions obtain. Many, who would accept this as an abstract principle, feel that it is of very little practical value, for we have no way on such a vast scale of determining the relative amounts of suffering and injustice. At best we can act confidently with hindsight. Surely such "a calculus of historical possibilities" could never be anything like exact; the best we could reasonably hope for is some not implausible estimate of the likely consequences. But some doubt that we can even attain that.

No one in his right mind would deny that there is a problem here, but I think that it is an exaggeration to maintain that we can never make anything resembling plausible estimates here. As horrible as the French revolution and to a lesser degree the long English revolution were, they did bring about an improvement of conditions which would not otherwise have obtained. No good case has ever been made for the claim that the improved conditions would have, with less suffering and misery, come about without the revolution. This may well have been true of the American revolution, but it is hardly true for such major transformations of the social order as are represented by French and English revolutions.

To the objection that this is knowledge we can only gain with hind-sight, from the long perspective of history, but could not have been known or reasonably believed at the time these revolutions were impend-ing or occurring, the answer should be that there are recent revolutions, i.e. the Chinese, the Cuban or the Yugoslavian revolutions, of which it is far from clear that the violence necessary to make them and sustain them was not justified. They are, of course, engulfed in controversy and there is much to be said on all sides of this question, but we have some sense of the criteria to be used in making such a judgment and—to take an outstanding example—it is far from clear, American propaganda to the contrary notwithstanding, that the Cuban revolution was not justified and an advance, hardly otherwise obtainable, in freedom and social justice for the Cuban people.

In asking whether in a given situation revolutionary violence is justi-fied, we should consider whether it would bring about the kind of im-provement in the quality of life characterized above to a degree which is not otherwise obtainable, and with what is on balance the avoidance of greater evil and/or the achievement of a greater good than would otherwise have obtained. In speaking of "a greater good" here we are talking about the extension of freedom, the achievement of greater equal-ity and justice and an increase in human happiness.

What must be reiterated is that violence is intrinsically evil and can only be justified as something which is sometimes an instrumental good. (After all something can be intrinsically good and instrumentally bad, instrumentally good and intrinsically bad and the like, e.g. the stabbing pain one feels when one touches a hot object.) No more violence is justi-fied than the violence necessary to secure the revolution under the con-ditions characterized above or, where the violence is not revolutionary violence, to secure the desired social change where it, everything con-sidered, would result in less misery and more happiness and justice all around, than would obtain if the employment of violence is rejected.

It is often said that violence is never justified in a democracy. But it seems to me that exactly the same considerations apply here as apply generally. We only have to add, as another important consideration, the instrumental value of sticking with democratic procedures. This would make us ask tough questions about how well these procedures are func-tioning or are likely to function in the future without resort to violence.

We must also, of course, ask to what extent resort to violence will even further undermine them and what alternatives are at hand. But surely there is nothing *intrinsically* desirable about democracy such that we could reasonably make the general claim that violence is never justi-fied in a democracy. It depends on the democracy and the conditions there, including whether it is only a democracy in name or whether it is a functioning democracy. We must go case by case. Revolutionary violence in Sweden or Canada would be quite unjustified. Conditions exist there which make possible a peaceful and orderly transition to socialism. Rhodesia and the United States are something else again. Concerning these latter countries, besides the moral considerations discussed above, there are all kinds of hard practical questions to be asked. In the United States, for example, morality aside, the recent bombings and window breaking during demonstrations are plainly unjustified. There is no revolutionary base at present in the United States from which to launch a revolution or a basic social transformation. This base must be built around working class people who have the potential power, numbers and organization to make such a transformation. But while there is a revolutionary *potential* among working class people—half of the blue collar workers make less than ninety dollars a week—the workers have for the most part not attained class consciousness. A central role of students and other intelligentsia in such an activity is to develop—difficult as that indeed is—solidarity with workers and to help awaken class consciousness in them and a recognition that a socialist transformation of society is in their own interests and in their own power.[4] Questions of the legitimacy of violence must always be seen against this background.

Talk of violence along with "Law and Order," in the United States at least, is for the most part ideological talk. Powerful established interests and their Yes Men—their paid hirelings—among the intelligentsia decry violence instead of considering the circumstances in which it is not in order. Utilizing the emotive force of "violence" they by ideological legerdemain play on people's fears and moral sentiments—after all violence is intrinsically evil—and thus help make them antagonistic to the Left. Irrational resort to violence by the neanderthal Left plays into the hands of such defenders of the *status quo* and produces in reactionary forces much greater and even less justified forms of violence. Such political behavior should not drive a reasonable man into some absolute acceptance of the principles of non-violence, but should make him wary of ill-considered uses of violence and should drive him to a general consideration of the conditions under which violence is justified. I have tried to contribute something toward the answer to that central question. What I have said is perhaps overly simple, but it seems to me at least a base from which we should start, and it very much needs to be shown, amidst all the loose talk pro and con about violence, how it is overly simple and where it needs to be modified, if it indeed is overly simple or needs to be modified.

---

[4] Hilary Putnam has some interesting and level-headed things to say about this. Hilary Putnam "From 'Resistance' to Student-Worker Alliance" in *The New Left: A Collection of Essays*, Priscilla Long (ed.) (Boston: 1969), pp. 318–34.

SELECTED SUPPLEMENTARY READING

ARENDT, HANNAH, "Civil Disobedience," in *Crises of the Republic*. New York: Harcourt, Brace and World, 1972.

BAY, CHRISTIAN, "Civil Disobedience," *International Encyclopedia of the Social Sciences*. New York: Macmillan, 1968.

BEDAU, H. A., "On Civil Disobedience," *The Journal of Philosophy*, 58 (1961).

——, ed., *Civil Disobedience: Theory and Practice*. New York: Pegasus, 1969.

BLACK, CHARLES L., JR., "The Problem of the Compatibility of Civil Disobedience with American Institutions of Government," *Texas Law Review*, 43 (1965).

BLACK, VIRGINIA, "The Two Faces of Civil Disobedience," *Social Theory and Practice*, 1 (1970–71).

BLACKSTONE, W. T., "Civil Disobedience: Is It Justified?" *Georgia Law Review*, 3 (1969).

BROWN, STUART M., JR., "Civil Disobedience," *The Journal of Philosophy*, 58 (1961).

CHOMSKY, NOAM, WILLIAM EARLE, and JOHN R. SILBER, "Philosophers and Public Policy: A Symposium," *Ethics* (October 1968).

COHEN, CARL, *Civil Disobedience*. New York: Columbia University Press, 1971.

——, "Civil Disobedience and the Law," *Rutgers Law Review*, 21 (1966).

COHEN, MARSHALL, "Civil Disobedience in a Constitutional Democracy," *The Massachusetts Review*, 10 (1969).

COX, ARCHIBALD, et al., *Civil Rights, the Constitution, and the Courts*. Cambridge, Mass.: Harvard University Press, 1967.

DWORKIN, RONALD, "A Theory of Civil Disobedience," in *Ethics and Social Justice*, eds. Howard E. Kiefer and Milton K. Munitz. New York: New York University Press, 1968.

FORTAS, ABE, *Concerning Dissent and Civil Disobedience*. New York: Signet (NAL), 1968.

HALL, ROBERT T., "Legal Toleration of Civil Disobedience," *Ethics*, 81 (January 1971).

——, *The Morality of Civil Disobedience*. New York: Harper Torchbooks, 1971.

HELD, V., K. NIELSEN, and C. PARSONS, eds., *Philosophy and Political Action*. Oxford: Oxford University Press, 1972, Part Two.

HOOK, SIDNEY, ed., *Law and Philosophy*. New York: New York University Press, 1964.

——, "Social Protest and Civil Disobedience," in *Moral Problems in Contemporary Society*, ed. Paul Kurtz. Englewood Cliffs, N.J.: Prentice-Hall, Inc., 1968.

HUGHES, GRAHAM, "Civil Disobedience and the Political-Question Doctrine," *New York University Law Review*, 43 (1968).

KEETON, MORRIS, "The Morality of Civil Disobedience," *Texas Law Review*, 43 (1965).

KING, MARTIN LUTHER, JR., "Letter from Birmingham City Jail," *Liberation* (June 1963).

LEWIS, H. D., "Obedience to Conscience," *Mind*, 54 (1945).

MACCALLUM, GERALD C., JR., "Some Truths and Untruths about Civil Disobedience," in *Nomos*, XII. New York: Atherton Press, 1970.

MARTIN, REX, "Civil Disobedience," *Ethics* (January 1970).

RUSSELL, BERTRAND, "Civil Disobedience," *The New Statesman* (February 17, 1961).

·SIBLEY, MULFORD Q., *The Obligation to Disobey*. New York: Council on Religion and International Affairs, 1970.

——, "On Political Obligation and Civil Disobedience," *Journal of the Minnesota Academy of Science* (1965).

SINGER, PETER, *Democracy and Disobedience*. Oxford: Clarendon Press, 1973.

THALBERG, IRVING, "Philosophical Problems of Civil Disobedience," *Scientia*, 101 (1966).

VAN DEN HAAG, ERNEST, "Government, Conscience, and Disobedience," in *Sidney Hook and the Contemporary World*, ed. Paul Kurtz. New York: John Day Company, 1968.

WALZER, MICHAEL, "The Obligation to Disobey," *Ethics* (April 1967). Also in *Political Theory and Social Change*, ed. David Spitz. New York: Atherton Press, 1967.

——, *Obligations: Essays on Disobedience, War, and Citizenship*. Cambridge, Mass.: Harvard University Press, 1970.

WASSERSTROM, RICHARD A., "Disobeying the Law," *Journal of Philosophy*, 58 (October 1961).

——, "The Obligation to Obey the Law," *U.C.L.A. Law Review*, 10 (1963).

WEINGARTNER, RUDOLF H., "Justifying Civil Disobedience," *Columbia Forum*, 9 (1966).

WOOZLEY, A. D., "Socrates on Disobeying the Law," in *Socrates*, ed. Gregory Vlastos. Garden City, N.Y.: Doubleday, 1971.

ZINN, HOWARD, *Disobedience and Democracy: Nine Fallacies on Law and Order*. New York: Random House, 1968.

Chapter 4

WAR

INTRODUCTION

In August 1939, having staged a fabricated "Polish" border attack on Germany, Adolf Hitler addressed the German nation as follows:

> The Germans in Poland are being persecuted by bloody terror and driven from their homes. Several acts of frontier violation, which cannot be tolerated by a great power, show that Poland is no longer prepared to respect the Reich's frontiers. To put an end to these mad acts, I can see no other way but from now onwards to meet force with force.[*]

Though an instance of exceptional deceit, Hitler's justification for entry into war was a classic one: self-defense against unjust aggression. The sorry aftermath of Germany's participation in World War II needs no retelling here. But that piece of history does raise, in a particularly poignant way, a number of stubborn *ethical* questions raised by virtually all wars.

---

[*] As quoted in Whitney R. Harris, *Tyranny on Trial: The Evidence at Nuremberg* (Dallas, 1954), p. 126.

If Germany's actions during World War II were not justified, as most everyone now agrees, then what sorts of war activities, if any, are justifiable? This question implicitly raises all the important issues to be discussed in this chapter. (1) Can criteria be provided to distinguish a *just* war from an *unjust* war? (2) Should one be a pacifist or perhaps a selective conscientious objector? (3) Even if one concedes that at least some war efforts are justified—such as the Allied retaliation against Germany—would one without serious qualification concede that every sort of behavior whatever is justified as a *means* to victory? If some conduct by warring nations should be prohibited, on what ethical basis is the prohibition grounded? And how, on that basis, does one properly determine what the so-called laws of war should be?

In this chapter we shall consider all three issues—the just war, pacifism, and laws of war.

The Just War

What conditions would have to be met in order for a war to be just? As we shall see, in most sophisticated theories several conditions have been proposed. But first a word of caution about the question itself is needed. Whenever one encounters a set of conditions specified by a philosopher one should be careful to determine whether it is to be understood as a set of (1) necessary conditions, (2) sufficient conditions, or (3) both necessary and sufficient conditions. If the set is merely taken to be necessary, then even if all the conditions are satisfied, the war may still not be just (because the set is not sufficient). For example, aggression by an enemy may be a necessary condition, but is it sufficient? If the set is merely taken to be sufficient, then although the presence of all the conditions warrants our calling a war just, there may be other conditions (specifiable by an alternative theory) that would *also* be sufficient for a just war. For example, being forced into self-defense may be a sufficient condition, but might not some other condition(s) also be sufficient? Most philosophers, naturally, would like to provide a set of both necessary and sufficient conditions, and no doubt most theories of the just war have intended to provide them, but there has been a great deal of ambiguity surrounding precisely how sweeping the justifications were intended to be. With this brief warning, we may proceed to the major conditions cited as justifications for war.

The following conditions (1–7) have played a crucial role in the history of thought about just wars. Each was probably originally conceived as at least a necessary condition to be met for a war to be just, and the set as a whole or some combination of its members has also been regarded by some thinkers as conjointly sufficient conditions. It is also important to distinguish conditions 1 to 4 from 5 to 7. The first four conditions are meant to morally justify *entry* into wars, whereas the last three are meant to morally justify *strategic means* once the war has been entered.

1. *The enemy must be an aggressor forcing one or more nations into a posture of self-defense.* Since about 1919 it has more and more been thought that initiation of an aggressive war should be a crime under international law, and today aggression is probably the chief criterion of unjust behavior in the realm of international law. Indeed, since World War I the language of "just war" and "unjust war" has largely been replaced in legal circles by the expressions "defensive war" and "aggressive war." Nonetheless, it is often objected that both "self-defense" and "aggression" are hopelessly vague terms. The United States, for example, has traditionally maintained that the Monroe Doctrine allows self-defense to cover any attack of a friendly nation in the Americas and that the United States has the *right* so to define self-defense in this case.

"Aggression" is similarly troublesome. At the conferences to draft the London Charter the Russian representative declared a definition impossible. The United States, when justifying entry into Vietnam, argued that under the United Nations Charter (Article 51) North Vietnam was an aggressor against South Vietnam and that this fact justified American entry as a matter of "collective defense." Even in 1915, before much thought had been given to self-defense justifications at the level of international law, Bertrand Russell strongly objected to the criterion on grounds that it can be used, very conveniently, to justify virtually anything.

2. *The objective of the war must be some good (certainly including peace) that is in the general interest of those who fight it and not against the general interest of mankind.* Like the first criterion, this one is frequently attacked as so lacking in specific restraint that it can be conveniently used to justify even acts of territorial conquest and religious conversion. How, after all, does one finally arbitrate conflicting claims among rational people who maintain that their nations are respectively struggling for "the cause of mankind"?

3. *The war must be declared by an authority with legal standing.* Thomas Aquinas stated the reason for this condition in the thirteenth century: "Since the care of the State is confided to Princes . . . it is to them that it *belongs* to bear the sword in combats for the defense of the State against external enemies." The main objection to this criterion is its general irrelevance. If two leaders in opposing states declare war, the war would be equally just for both states (other things being equal).

The "proper channels" criterion has seemed to many to be a criterion of a *legal* war, but not of a *just* war. Cannot men in power be even more irresponsible and inflict even more damage than those without?

4. *All reasonable means of peaceful negotiation must be attempted before war is declared.* This criterion is generally found acceptable but only as a necessary condition of a just war, not as a sufficient one.

5. *Damage done to the enemy must not intentionally surpass (a) that necessary to win the war and (b) that appropriate and required after the war as punishment.* Although this criterion has historically enjoyed the status of being eminently reasonable in the minds of many, it is now often found objectionable because of the nature of modern wars, which involve obliteration and atomic bombings, free fire zones, and horrendous refugee camps, as well as demands for total surrender. In the face of such practices the criterion seems to some utterly anachronistic. It is also notoriously difficult to *measure* the damage done when such practices are employed, as the use of the atomic bomb at Hiroshima and Nagasaki well illustrated.

6. *War activities must not violate recognized laws of war.* No doubt this would be a good criterion if we possessed adequate laws of war or even an adequate understanding of the status of international law. Unfortunately, as we shall see below, adequacy is almost as difficult to achieve here as in the case of the just war.

7. *Every attempt must be made to avoid killing the innocent.* Although war conditions make it extremely difficult to distinguish the innocent from the noninnocent, this criterion too would generally be accepted as a necessary condition of just wars.

Pacifism

Perhaps no set of conditions whatever is sufficient to justify war. This is the pacifist position, or at least one form of it. Throughout its long history its adherents have presented a variety of justifications for their position. It has been argued, for example, that war is in effect murder under the guise of nationalism, that passive resistance is psychologically efficacious in reorienting the attitude of the enemy, and that if pacifism were a universal value the leaders of sovereign states would be forced by their subjects to negotiate rather than to resort to armed violence. In addition to these general reasons, somewhat more personal reasons in favor of pacifism have also been expressed—for example, that conscience demands it and that a sense of reverence for life requires it.

These reasons, however, have not played a central role in pacifist thinking. If there is anything approximating a generally or widely held view among pacifists, it would perhaps be the following argument: War is, in no instance, the only effective means either to the prevention or reduction of serious wrongs or to the promotion of important but un-afforded freedoms. Quite the contrary; we can achieve our desired social objectives better by entirely peaceful means. Certainly the most im-portant of human values are sometimes threatened by invasions and other acts of aggression, but equally warlike responses only compound the difficulty by bringing greater measures of evil into the world. The existence of any military organization at all inevitably leads to atrocities. In short, war is counterproductive. It is anything but effective in the recovery of a nonviolent society based on principles of justice and equality; those who resort to war to settle disputes undermine the very possibility of such a society.

In opposition to pacifism it has been argued that pacifist protests in wartime have almost always been totally ineffective in stopping war machines and that no powerful aggressive force has ever been or is likely to be stopped by pacifism. Those who support this line of thought argue that even if most wars are not just, some wars (those satisfying acceptable criteria of just wars) are the only effective means to the elimination of terrible evils. In an imperfect world in which power-mad rulers sometimes prevail over moral principles, the preservation of funda-mental human freedoms may well depend on such a counterforce. This argument is a difficult one for pacifists to counter because it in effect maintains that pacifistic attitudes are to be encouraged up to the point at which noble ends *cannot* (given a "realistic" estimate of the enemy's intent and power) be achieved by pacifist means. That such means are inadequate is just what the pacifist denies.

Laws of War

Suppose we assume both that pacifism is untenable and that there are conditions which justify war. It is still problematic both which *ends* it is morally justifiable to pursue and what *means* are morally acceptable in the pursuit of just ends. The problem of proper ends is the least thorny. Occasionally a country is at war but mixes just ends, such as the defeat of an aggressor, with unjust ends, such as territorial expansion. Are the war acts of a country with such a *dual* purpose morally justifiable? One can usually circumvent this problem by carefully detailing the criteria of just wars so that it becomes a necessary condition of any just war that no unjust ends are pursued.

The problem of proper *means*, assuming just ends and so a just war, is more difficult. War is largely constituted by acts that would be both immoral and criminal if performed in time of peace: killing, stealing property, intentionally wounding, and so on. But in war such activity is not considered criminal because somehow the conditions of war protect participants from most criminal charges. Still, the range of immunity is not without limits, for we do have needless cruelties called "war crimes," such as the now notorious events at My Lai. We group unconscionable offenses (for example, murdering prisoners rather than confining them) under the label of atrocities, a clear indication that they are not justified even in war. Such acts, we may think, remain outside the range of immunity from prosecution afforded to most war activities. A perpetual hope has been that these moral limits could be agreed upon and codified into international laws acceptable to all nations. The problem of how to justify such a set of moral restraints—whether they be written or unwritten—is called the problem of laws of war.

In discussions of the laws of war *immoral* acts deserving condemnation must be distinguished from *criminal* acts punishable by law. However immoral, no wartime offense is criminal unless some sort of statute is violated. Nor is the charge of immorality likely to carry much weight of censure unless the threat of penalties is reinforced by codified law. (In fact, common expressions such as "war crime" and "crime against humanity" have had and will continue to have little concrete meaning until international laws are developed to govern their scope. As with the expression "laws of war" itself, these expressions developed from so-called customary laws—those not created by statutes formally enacted by legislative bodies. These laws are historically the legal foundation of treaties such as The Hague and Geneva Conventions.) On the other hand, the development of international laws depends upon a principled specification of immoral actions that exceed the limits of immunity afforded "basic" war activities. The *ethical* problem involved in discussions of the laws of war, then, is this: What is the ethical basis for prohibiting certain behavior and how, on that basis, does one properly determine what the laws should be?

Several problems are involved in any attempt to give a comprehensive answer to this question. First, given war's general environment of immoral activity, can one reasonably expect to use *ethical* standards to formulate laws that govern conduct in an obviously *immoral* context? Second, is there either moral worth or social benefit in having such laws? After all, the laws permit as well as prohibit conduct. What are the ultimate social consequences of formally permitting killing and destruction that otherwise is both immoral and criminal? Third, it seems that we have to "lower" our ethical standards in order to condemn behavior in war. But what sense, if any, does it make to speak of a *lower* morality or *lowered* moral standards? Fourth, should laws of war even attempt to prohibit activities directly connected with the war (for example, types of weapons used) or should they govern only those activities indirectly connected (for example, stealing food from private citizens)? Fifth, and perhaps most serious, is it not hopeless to try to differentiate just war conditions from unjust ones? As Telford Taylor, United States Chief Counsel at Nuremberg, has pointed out:

> Is there any significant difference between killing a babe-in-arms by a bomb dropped from a high-flying aircraft, or by an infantry-man's point-blank gunfire? . . . the distinction is seldom articulated other than by describing the aviator's act as more "impersonal" than the ground soldier's.
>
> This may be psychologically valid, but surely is not morally satisfactory.*

Sixth, suppose some activity such as torture is not permitted under the laws of war. Suppose further that hundreds of lives can be saved by torturing one man. Ought one to refrain from torture under such conditions? And can one be held responsible for immoral behavior in such cases, given that one's intention is to save lives, not to torture for the sake of torturing? Finally, is the moral justification for such laws that they have good consequences (utilitarianism), or that they specify moral duties independently of judgments of consequences (deontology), or both, or neither?

These are the kinds of problems with which ethicists interested in the laws of war have occupied themselves. Quite obviously, an equal number of legal problems render the issues even more clouded.

Arguments in the Selections

Donald Wells and **Richard L. Purtill**, in the opening two selections in this chapter, debate the merits of just war theory. Wells critically analyzes the conditions traditionally offered to justify war. As he portrays the just war theory, its purpose is to establish the circumstances under which it is permissible to perform immoral acts that in peacetime circumstances could not be justified. He takes special note of a recent revival of the just war doctrine by Joseph McKenna, who defends a list of conditions justifying war similar to the seven conditions discussed in the first section of this Introduction. Wells considers each of these conditions individually with this question in mind: "Can such criteria be made applicable to *modern* war?" His answer to this question is in the negative; he contends that even if in the past such conditions succeeded in adding a humane dimension to war, this result is no longer possible. Wells

---

* *Nuremberg and Vietnam: An American Tragedy* (Chicago: Quadrangle Books, 1971), pp. 142f.

contends that there has been such an "escalation of insensitivity" to moral considerations that present-day "unjust wars" are really little or no worse than "just wars." He concludes with a complete rejection of the just war: "If the just war ever had moral significance in the past, it is clear today that it justifies too much."

Purtill, in a brief reply to Wells, defends a set of conditions intended to justify war that differs slightly from the set considered by Wells. Purtill contends that "reasonable non-pacifists" can quite appropriately use such criteria both to justify certain wars and to criticize others as unjustified. It should not escape notice that Purtill's claim in behalf of his list of conditions is quite strong: He claims for his list that any "Nation A is justified in waging war with [any] Nation B if and only if" his set of conditions is satisfied. It is not entirely clear whether Purtill thinks simply that reasonable men *do* use these criteria (a less controversial thesis) or that reasonable men *ought to* use them, whether they do or not (see his concluding paragraph). Presumably the latter claim would involve a heavier burden of argument than the former. If Purtill is simply arguing the former thesis—that his modified list of just war criteria, properly formulated, are the criteria which "reasonable non-pacifists" do use in order to condemn or justify wars—it is not obvious that Wells would disagree, especially since Purtill leaves the issue of pacifism an open one to be justified "on its own merits." However, the thrust of Purtill's defense of the just war seems to be in the direction of determining what reasonable men ought to do; and he does go on to argue that the cause of peace is not well served by Wells's wholesale rejection of the traditional criteria of just wars.

Richard Wasserstrom, in a discussion of the laws of war, considers the widespread opinion that persons who commit war crimes—violations of the laws of war—must be held morally and legally responsible for their actions. Wasserstrom is concerned to discover the arguments allegedly supporting such a thesis and to show that the claim is a mistaken one; that is, one which is "morally unattractive." Wasserstrom sees two quite distinct but equally important arguments used to justify the thesis that the laws of war have some sort of moral significance and primacy. The first argument is one from the moral ideals of "intrinsic morality": The laws of war deserve both respect and rigorous enforcement because they "reflect, embody and give effect to fundamental moral distinctions and considerations." Against this argument Wasserstrom contends that the laws of war have an important streak of incompleteness and incoherence of the sort that would be present in a criminal code that punished, for example, only theft and not other harmful acts such as murder. Wasserstrom does not argue that morality has no place in war but only that the laws of war (as he depicts them) fail to capture this moral dimension in any significant manner. The second argument is one from beneficial consequences: General adherence to the laws of war has highly desirable effects, such as the manner in which the laws influence the behavior of participants in war. Against this argument Wasserstrom contends that it is highly doubtful that the alleged consequences actually occur. He also points out that the laws of war permit as well as prohibit, and hence they teach both soldiers and civilians that it is permissible to kill and destroy if such acts are needed for "military objectives" or for the goal of victory. This result, Wasserstrom argues, is "morally retrograde movement." However, he does not suggest that we throw out the laws of war and accept wartime anarchy; instead he appeals for a different conception of the laws of war than the one previously relied upon. In the end Wasserstrom finds existing laws of war and conventions relating to them unacceptably removed from the realm of morality, precisely because they have come into existence and are governed by non-moral, purely prudential considerations. Perhaps this overstates his case, but he seems to find the laws amoral in content and immoral by virtue of what they fail to incorporate. In any case he finds the present laws of war failures if they are intended to embody moral standards by the use of which wartime conduct can be judged.

Thomas Nagel, in the final selection in this chapter, agrees with Wasserstrom that the present laws of war do not adequately exhibit a moral basis. This basis itself is Nagel's major concern, and his article in effect attempts to give the "different conception of the laws of war" that Wasserstrom calls for. His discussion ranges over most of the issues we have just discussed, all placed in the context of the debate on whether utilitarian reasons and/or absolutist reasons provide adequate justification for an acceptable range of restrictions on the conduct of warfare. He offers what he refers to as "a somewhat qualified defense of absolutism." (To compare Nagel's and Wasserstrom's terminology: utilitarians use what Wasserstrom calls "beneficial consequence" arguments; absolutists use what he calls "intrinsic morality" arguments.) Nagel thinks utilitarianism permits deliberate killing in wartime "if enough can be gained by it." Against this view, as an absolutist, he insists that certain acts (for example deliberate killing of the harmless) cannot be justified *whatever the consequences.** He even finds the utilitarian approach positively dangerous in the context of war.

Nagel's defense of absolutism, however, is less sweeping than it might at first appear. He thinks our moral intuitions often lead to deep dilemmas in the conflict between absolutism and utilitarianism. When the refusal to follow a course of action on absolutist grounds leads to disaster, Nagel

---

* Readers may wish to compare Nagel's discussions of "whatever the consequences" with Bennett's discussion in his contribution to the chapter on abortion. Nagel's discussions throughout, and especially in Section IV, have important parallels to Bennett's claims.

thinks even the absolutist "will find it difficult to feel that a moral dilemma has been satisfactorily resolved." Because he sees no clear principles by means of which such dilemmas can be satisfactorily resolved, he thinks we may have to be content with a few "moral blind alleys."

How Much Can "the Just War" Justify? *

Donald Wells

Justification, as is well known, is not an unambiguous term. Even in the context of logical justification the criteria are debatable, but at least in this milieu justification is assumed to be a function of a set of given rules in an agreed-upon system. Within a context of a set of truth claims consistency is a necessary and almost sufficient criterion. In normative discourse, however, justification takes on an honorific and emotion-laden aura. Adequacy here entails notions of "rightness" or "goodness" in addition to putative truth claims. The problem of "The Just War" is, in this latter sense, more than a matter of the occurrence of matters of fact, more than a matter of consistency within a system of given axioms, more than a matter of demonstrating what is permissible legally, and more than an exercise in casuistry.

In a very ordinary sense of the term "justify" we may merely seek an explanation of why war is waged in the sense of showing the premises that prompted us to the conclusion to wage war. When asked, "Why did you wage this war?" we could reply, "I did it because x, y, and z had occurred," and we might now conclude that the war in question had now been justified. If, on the other hand, we justify war the way an appellant defends himself before the judge, we would then need to show that what we did was consistent with the laws under which we have agreed to operate. But suppose that the justification of war is like the famous "justification of induction" and that its resolution involves us in a metalinguistic search. In fact, the attempts to justify war, or to identify what a just war would be like, share common properties with all these interpretations. In addition, however, there is an implicit contradiction which discussants of war and justice ordinarily recognize. Since the havoc of war is nor-

---

* Published in *The Journal of Philosophy*, Vol. LXVI, No. 23 (December 4, 1969). Reprinted by permission of the author and publisher.

mally classed with immoral actions and evil consequences, what the notion of "the just war" attempts to do is to show that under some circumstances it would be "just" to perform immoral acts and to contribute to evil consequences. Some justifications of war aim to show that actions deemed normally forbidden by moral mandates are now permissible when performed under the aegis of war.

Since the history of ethical speculation has virtually no other instance of the defense of immoral acts under the extenuating circumstance of prudential risk, the "just war" concept needs special attention. It constitutes an anomalous instance in moral discourse, namely, a glaring exception to an otherwise accepted prohibition of acts of human brutality.

Traditionally the doctrine of "the just war" intended to curb excessively inhumane war practices, reduce the likelihood of war, identify who may properly declare war, ensure that the means of war bore a relation of proportion to the ends of war, and generally to promote a conscience on the practice. Incidentally, the concept functioned as a defense of national sovereignty and of the "right" of nations to defend themselves in a basically lawless world. It made national survival feasible, while making international organization unlikely.

Since the notion of "the just war" has been revived after nearly two centuries of silence on the issue, it seems appropriate to look again at the medieval claims to see whether, if they had a defense then, they have any rationale now. The entire discussion for the medievalist rested, of course, on a concession which itself needs reassessment; namely, that war has a place in the moral scheme. The traditional questions about war were prudential, and the discussion centered around such questions as the time, place, and cause for war. Wars were presumed to be neutral means which could be given moral properties under the appropriate conditions. Wars were criticized, if at all, in practice rather than in principle. In this, medieval war discussion shared a common starting point with medieval speculation on capital punishment. It wasn't the fact of killing that was the determinant; rather the reasons given for the acts of killing were decisive.

The Criteria of Saint Thomas

In order for a war to be just, three conditions had to be met: (1) an authoritative sovereign must declare the war; (2) there must be a just cause; and (3) the men who wage the war must have just intentions, so that good actually results from the war. In application of these criteria, the criticisms that did emerge of particular wars were so few as to suggest that princes were basically moral men or that the criteria were too vague to be useful. In addition, the critics were commonly persons not officially in government, so that their protests were a kind of baying at the moon. George Fox, for example, challenged the wars of Cromwell, but then Fox rejected the war method utterly. Franciscus de Victoria, a theological professor at the University of Salamanca in the sixteenth century, chastised his Spanish superiors for the wars against the Indians [1]—but the remarks of university professors, then as now, were rarely influential in the determination of foreign policy, particularly when such remarks were critical of decisions of state already made.

More recently, Joseph McKenna [2] has revived the "just war" doctrine with an expanded list of seven conditions. They are: (1) the war must be declared by the duly constituted authority; (2) the seriousness of the injury inflicted on the enemy must be proportional to the damage suffered by the virtuous; (3) the injury to the aggressor must be real and immediate; (4) there must be a reasonable chance of winning the war; (5) the use of war must be a last resort; (6) the participants must have right intentions; and (7) the means used must be moral. Our question is: "Can such criteria be made applicable to modern war?" Let us consider this in terms of some general "just war" claims.

A Just War Is One Declared by the Duly Constitututed Authority

For a theologian like Saint Augustine or Saint Thomas, who presumed some pervading and ameliorating power from Christian prelates, such a criterion could be considered to be a limitation on careless scoundrels, as well as a limitation on the number of wars that would actually be waged. By the sixteenth century, however, with the proliferation of princes and the fading away of the influence of Christian prelates, a radically new situation had emerged. By this time, the "reasons of state," as Machiavelli elaborated them, permitted every prince to wage war whenever he saw fit. Since by the eighteenth century war had become the sport of kings, it was clear that authorities were not very reliable nor sensitive.

The rise of nationalism made this first criterion undifferentiating. It became increasingly obvious that to grant to any prince the privilege of judging his neighboring prelates was an odd situation. It was this anomaly that led Grotius and Victoria to insist that, although only one side of a war could properly be considered just, in fact persons on both sides could, in good conscience, presume that they had justice on their side. In the absence of any international judge, who could determine the justice

---

[1] Franciscus de Victoria, *On the Law of War* (Washington, D.C.: The Carnegie Institute, 1917), sec. 22.

[2] "Ethics and War: A Catholic View," *American Political Science Review* (September 1960, pp. 647–58.

of the various national claims? What this criterion did do was to make clear that revolution was not to be allowed. What it could not do was to persuade or compel some prince to forego a war.

If rulers were saints and scholars there might be some reason to suppose that their judgments on war were adequate. Actually, there are no plausible reasons to suppose that secular leaders have intentions that will meet even minimal standards of humaneness. It is not necessary to have in mind Hitler, Tojo, DeGaulle, or Thieu to see that this is so. There is nothing in the nature of the process by which leaders are selected to give assurance that Johnson, Trudeau, or Wilson have moral insights that are even as good as the average, let alone sufficiently discerning to be used as the criterion for a just war. These leaders are not presumed by their loyal opposition to be especially gifted in domestic policy. Why imagine that they are so for foreign policy?

Even clerics have a rather poor reputation for moral insight or sound judgment. Witness, for example, the stand of Archbishop Groeber of Freiburg-im-Breisgau, who rejected Christian pacifism for German Catholics on the grounds that Hitler was the duly constituted authority. Pope Pius XII showed no better insight when he rejected the right of conscientious objection for German Catholics at the time of the formation of NATO. This first criterion, therefore, seems to serve no helpful purpose at all. In Vietnam, for example, it would rule out Thieu, since he is warring against his own people, while granting that L.B.J. might be right, and Ho Chi Minh just in killing American troops but not so for killing Vietnamese from the South.

A Just War Uses Means Proportional to the Ends

Franciscus de Victoria had observed (*op. cit.*, secs. 33, 37) that if to retake a piece of territory would expose a people to "intolerable ills and heavy woes" then it would not be just to retake it. We must be sure, he continued, that the evils we commit in war do not exceed the evils we claim to be averting. But how do we measure the relative ills? This is the problem of a hedonic calculus on which Mill's system foundered. Since Victoria granted princes the right to despoil innocent children if military necessity required it, it ceased to be clear what proportionality meant or whether any limit at all was being proposed.

In a recent paper on this issue Father John A. Connery [3] stated that the morality of the violence depends on the proportionality to the aggression. What is required is some calculus to make this measurement. The latitude with which conscientious persons have interpreted this

---

[3] "Morality and Nuclear Armament," in William J. Nagle, ed., *Morality and Modern Warfare* (Baltimore: Helicon, 1960), p. 92.

suggests (what was clear enough to Mill) that we possess neither the quantitative nor the qualitative yardstick for this decision. Pope Pius XII thought the annihilation of vast numbers of persons would be impermissible. John Courtney Murray [4] thought this prohibition was too restrictive. Herbert Hoover thought in 1939 that the aerial bombing of cities should be banned, although he did urge the U.S. to build bombing planes to perform this banned action. Jacques Maritain put bombing from the air in the category of an absolutely proscribed act.[5] In the early period of World War II "saturation bombing" was considered to be too inhumane for American citizens to accept. We then practiced what was euphemistically called "precision bombing." That the terms were empty became obvious when the Air Force announced, at the time of the first test shot of the Atlas missile, that a bomb that lands within fifty miles of its target is considered accurate.

Does the notion of proportionality have any discriminatory meaning? During World War II the English writer, Vera Brittain, attacked both Britain and America in her book *Massacre by Bombing*. *The Christian Century* urged in editorials that its subscribers should read the book, while taking the position that the bombing of civilians is a necessary part of a just war. The American Bar Association defeated a resolution calling for a condemnation of the bombing of civilians.[6] The *Saturday Evening Post* maintained that anyone who questioned the bombing of civilians was "unstable." [7] McKinlay Kantor said the book was "soft-hearted." The Reverend Carl McIntyre called the position of the sensitive Mrs. Brittain "un-American and pro-Fascist," and the conservative Boston clergyman, H. J. Ockenga, called the view "un-American" and said it gave aid and comfort to the enemy. Not only do Christian prelates seem a fairly callous lot, but the notion of proportionality has lost sense.

Where should we draw the line? Pope Pius XII decided that Communism was such a cosmic threat that atomic, chemical, and biological bombs could all be justifiably used. But where then is the proportion? The dilemma is not aided by the clerical dictum that "there are greater evils than the physical death and destruction wrought in war" (Nagle, 80). What civilian would be impressed by this amid the rain of bombs? Like "better dead than Red," this is a fiction, enthusiasm for which is directly proportional to the square of the distance from the potential havoc. In any case, there is simply too much horror to be subsumed under the medieval notion of proportionality. Indeed, our State Department's White Paper, which was intended to explain the ends that justified our

---

[4] "War and the Bombardment of Cities," *Commonweal* (Sept. 2, 1938).
[5] Nagle, *op. cit.*, p. 107.
[6] *New York Times* (July 15, 1939), p. 3.
[7] *Saturday Evening Post* (Nov. 21, 1942): 128.

means in Vietnam, is a monstrously casuistic document. It seems to make no proportional sense to do what we are doing against the Vietnamese if the only reward is American-style elections or freedom from the threat of creeping Communism.

The medieval thinkers rejected religion as a proper cause of a just war, and it is not egregious to point out that politics is in the same general class as religion. After all, is there really any doubt that men can live well under a variety of systems: capitalistic, communistic, monarchic, or democratic? It is equally obvious, I assume, that men may live poorly under any of these systems. Witness the blacks in Georgia, Mississippi, or Washington, D.C. Would any theologian wish to make a case for the bomb on Selma or Chicago? Surely the crimes against men are great there, and if there is any proportion in Hanoi, it would seem to follow that similar acts could be justified in Little Rock.

If there is any reasonable doubt left that the criterion calling for "just means" is simply a verbal genuflection, a brief look at what is currently called "rational nuclear armament" will banish it. A contemporary recommendation by proponents of "rationality" here is to limit bombs to the ½-megaton class. This is fifty times greater than the bomb dropped on Hiroshima. Limitation, proportion, or rationality do not seem to apply to the language of mega-kill. Once a bomb is big enough to kill every person in an area, it is not an expansion of war to use a bomb big enough to kill everyone twice, any more than it can be considered a reduction to reduce from a bomb twice as large as is needed to one the precise size that is needed to decimate the population, And, in addition, to call such a consideration "rational" may be proper to military tacticians, but alien to a concept that aimed at a moral distinction.

War May Be Justly Taken Only as a Last Resort

In conventional language the notion of "last resort" presupposes a notion of "first resorts." Thus, unless a nation could show that it indeed exhausted first resorts, it would make no sense to claim the right of last resort. Presumably, first resorts would be such alternatives as economic, social, or political boycott, negotiations either through unilateral or multilateral means, or through such an agency as the United Nations, or even the contemplation of some kind of compromise. After these had been exhausted and there appeared to be no further nonviolent alternatives, we would still need to show that the last resort ought, in this case, to be taken. It is always possible that the final resort that can be defended morally is the first resort taken. Too much of the discussion about the "justice" of war as a last resort presumes war to be proper in any case, so that the only genuine questions have to do with timing. With this kind of concession, in the first place, imagine what would happen to discussion of the War Crimes Trials after World War II. The problem facing the German Nazis was simply: "After having exhausted every resort, may we now as a last resort exterminate the Jews?"

The problem facing contemporary theorists of the "just war" is whether modern war is a means that may "justly" be granted as any resort at all. When we begin to speak of "massive retaliation" then perhaps it is time to question war itself. Is there any end at all of sufficient value that the sacrifice of persons on such a scale as is now possible could become "justified?" Something has happened to the medieval notion of last resort when our leaders destroy a city to save it. But the horror of war has never functioned as much of an intellectual deterrent to the justice of war. Thus it is antecedently unlikely that the ability to "overkill" or "megakill" makes any rational difference to the medieval concept. If war is a just resort at all, it makes no sense to deny nations its use as a last resort. Once the killing has been sanctioned in the first place, moral discussion, such as the medieval man carried out, takes on the aura of Pentagon calculations.

We find, in this vein, Paul Ramsey, a Protestant advocate of the "just war," endorsing the use of thermonuclear weapons, provided that an important *military target* could not otherwise be eliminated. While Ramsey deplored the death of so many civilians, he assured the survivors that this is not too great a price to pay for civilization. The possibility that surrender would be more moral than war is not even conceded a probability, making it clear that the discussants are speaking only for nations that win wars. The demand for "unconditional surrender" which American statesmen have regularly made, makes it clear that last resorts are the only ones they have in mind. For example, in August, 1958, the U.S. Senate voted 82 to 2 to deny government funds to any person or institution that proposes or actually conducts any study regarding the possible results of the surrender of the U.S. as an alternative to war. The sheer presence of the doctrine of "last resort" makes the compromise contingent on negotiations inadmissable.

What does our "just war" theory say to the American Indians back in the seventeenth century when they were confronted with the white man's power? Was war justified for the Indian as a last resort? It was surely a case of defense, and even white historians grant that the Indians tried many resorts short of war. Since nations with arms are loath to succumb to similar national neighbors, and more especially to do so over concern with whether war is a last resort or whether first resorts still remain, about all the theory tells us is that the "last resort" is bound to be a resort that we actually take.

A Just War Must Be Waged by Men with Right Intentions

The medieval hub of this argument was the doctrine of the "double effect." A just belligerent intended only as much death as would be proportional to the threat or the offense, and he would intend to kill only combatants. It was presumed that we ought not to kill noncombatants. In the middle ages the weapons made such concern practical. Although the archer might shoot his arrow into the air and not be too clear about where it landed, he was not in doubt about whether he was shooting it at combatant enemies. He might miss a small barn, but he hit the right city. Modern weapons make such sensitivity about the recipients of our missiles inoperable and unfeasible. Not only this, but the number of noncombatants killed in modern war usually far exceeds that of soldiers. Whereas medieval man might pardonably weep for the accidentally slain civilians, modern man intends the death of every civilian slain when he drops his bombs from the air.

In every age, however, the problem of unintended death proved a harassing one, and the pattern of resolution seems to have been to deplete the scope of the class of the noncombatant, until in the present this is a null class. Modern war is total at least in the sense that there are no innocents. We could never have dropped the bombs on Dresden, Nagasaki, Hiroshima, or Tokyo if the class of innocents had had members. But quite apart from whether one could or did intend the death of noncombatants, there would still remain the question whether the end justified the means at all. It was this sheer inapplicability of the doctrine of the "double effect" that prompted John Bennett to reject the notion completely.[8] There is, also, another procedural problem here. The doctrine of the "double effect" is one that does not trouble military or political strategists. Their interest is to win the war, and not to make theological calculations. Indeed, the only concern the military appears to have had over such niceties as intentionality is whether there would be a moral response from the public. We did not, initially, practice saturation bombing in Europe, and we were told later that the military feared a public outcry against it. Once we had practiced it on the Japanese and once military necessity demanded it, Americans lost most of their sensitivity on the problem.

No defense of the intentions of a belligerent could be satisfactorily made unless it could also be shown that the means used were also moral, and this would be so even for the combatants considered to be fair game.

---

[8] Cf. Paul Ramsey, *War and the Christian Conscience* (Durham, N.C.: Duke University Press, 1961), p. 148.

Nowhere has the ability of man to tolerate increasing doses of violence and brutality been more evident than in his history of attempts to humanize the weapons. Richard J. Krickus [9] believed that chemical bombs were moral, whereas biological bombs were not, and this because of the difficulty of control in the case of the latter. On the other hand, napalm, anti-personnel shrapnel, and thermonuclear bombs were all "just" in their intended uses. To speak of the just use of the bayonet is difficult enough for mere mortals to grasp, but to use the same approbation for mega-weapons makes the terms "just" and "moral" lose their conventional distinguishing function. Modern man has had long practice in handling these theoretically difficult problems. Since we use gas chambers in the United States for our domestic offenders, it must not have been their method that led to the War Crimes Trials against the Nazis, but simply that they gassed and cremated the wrong persons. Although there may be no way to calculate the relative horror of gas chambers in the two countries or the hedonic ratios of the death of twenty Japanese as compared with the death of twenty Americans, it is precisely this kind of question that the "just war" theorists must answer.

The discussion of "intention" in the thirteenth century, when the weapons were relatively limited in scope so that a king could implement his wish not to harm noncombatants and could practice some kind of proportionality, is something that modern men can no longer carry out. All we can consider is whether to set the projectiles in motion. From that moment on, it makes no sense to speak of proportionality, intentionality, or limitation. But here, men have attempted to think the "unthinkable." What seemed too brutal in one age becomes militarily necessary and, hence, just in the next age. As recently as twenty years ago the arms agencies deleted mention of their chemical-biological research from the public agendas for fear of a public outcry. Now there is no need for secrecy, and everyone can witness on television the operations of our nerve gas plant in Newport, Indiana, our disease-bomb research at Fort Detrick, Maryland, and the bubonic plague research of the Hartford Travellers Research Corporation to discover the most efficient means to spread the disease by airplane or on foot. The history of prudential calculation reveals that every weapon sooner or later is added to the list of morally approved ones.

There may be a credible case for claiming that the medieval discussions of the just war added to man's moral insights and implemented his humane concerns. Perhaps without such discussions, the history of war

---

[9] "On the Morality of Chemical/Biological War," *Journal of Conflict Resolution* (June 1965): 200–210.

would be even worse than it now is. Such counterfactual conditionals are, however, technically incapable of being assigned weights of probability as to truth or falsity. But what can be determined is that the use of the terms "just," "limited," "humane," "proportional," or "intention" in the context of modern war robs these terms of most of their traditional moral flavor. If it was poor military strategy to assert "thou shalt not kill," it was even worse ethics to claim, "thou mayest napalm thine enemy if thy country is threatened."

One could have hoped that as the scope of weapons increased there would have been an escalation of sensitivity as to their use. But all that happened was that there was an escalation of insensitivity, until today it is hard to imagine what an unjustly fought war would look like that is not already exhibited in the just variety. Conceivably some medieval sword thrusts might have been made justly, and some fortified cities justly sacked. The entire distinction vanishes, however, once we admit weapons that shoot farther than the eye can see. And clearly this distinction has been lost once we use mega-weapons, and even what are called "conventional" weapons like fragmentation bombs and napalm. Since we no longer admit the combatant-noncombatant distinction, what have we left to adjudicate? If the just war ever had moral significance in the past, it is clear today that it justifies too much. In the middle ages the just war was less tragic than the alternatives. Today the just war justifies Armageddon if our hearts be pure, and this is to justify too much.

Let me close with an analogy. Suppose that, instead of national war, we were discussing the battles of Aryans against Jews. Suppose we approached this subject with medieval language and modern skill. We would, of course, consistent with the position taken on war, grant to Aryans the right to wage the war of extermination of the Jews, provided of course that the pogrom be declared by the duly constituted authority, be carried out with due decorum proportional to the threat, and with a just end in view. With this much granted, citizens would then see that they must kill Jews if their prince commanded it in the name of national defense (not unlike the Aryan concern with racial defense). Citizens would then implement the State department plan of containment of Judaism (not unlike containment of Communism) and seek by every means to rid the world of the threat of creeping Judaism. With no more effort than our war leaders now exert, we would carry out essentially what the Nazis did carry out, and do it according to the laws of pogroms (not unlike the much advertised "laws of wars"). Our means would naturally be humane gas chambers and sanitary ovens. If we put it this way, then the doctrine of the "just war"—like that of the "just pogrom"—would justify too much.

On the Just War *

Richard L. Purtill

In a recent paper,[1] Donald A. Wells makes certain criticisms of one version of the "just war" theory. The criteria which Wells discusses are the following:

> (1) the war must be declared by the duly constituted authority; (2) the seriousness of the injury inflicted on the enemy must be proportional to the damage suffered by the virtuous; (3) the injury to the aggressor must be real and immediate; (4) there must be a reasonable chance of winning the war; (5) the use of war must be a last resort; (6) the participants must have right intentions; and (7) the means used must be moral.[2]

He borrows these from a paper by Joseph McKenna.[3] Wells criticizes each of these criteria, and argues that these criteria could be used to justify any war whatsoever. He concludes the paper with what he claims is an analogous case:

> Suppose that, instead of national war, we were discussing the battles of Aryans against Jews. Suppose we approached this subject with medieval language and modern skill. We would, of course, consistent with the position taken on war, grant to Aryans the right to wage the war of extermination of the Jews, provided of course that the pogrom be declared by the duly constituted authority, be carried out with due decorum proportional to the threat, and with a just end in view. With this much granted, citizens would then see that they must kill Jews if their prince commanded it in the name of national defense (not unlike the Aryan concern with racial defense). Citizens would then implement the State department plan of containment of Judaism (not unlike containment of Communism) and seek by every means

---

* From *Social Theory and Practice*, Vol. I (Spring 1971), pp. 97–102. Reprinted by permission of the author and publisher.

[1] "How Much Can 'the Just War' Justify?" *The Journal of Philosophy*, Vol. LXVI, No. 23 (Dec. 4, 1969). [Reprinted in this text.]

[2] Wells, *op. cit.*, p. 821 [p. 182 in this text].

[3] "Ethics and War: A Catholic View," *American Political Science Review* (Sept., 1960), pp. 647–58.

to rid the world of the threat of creeping Judaism. With no more effort than our war leaders now exert, we would carry out essentially what the Nazis did carry out, and do it according to the laws of pogroms (not unlike the much advertised "laws of wars"). Our means would naturally be humane gas chambers and sanitary ovens. If we put it this way, then the doctrine of the "just war"—like that of the "just pogrom"—would justify too much.[4]

And this supposed analogue gives a good general idea of his line of argument in the paper.

In this paper I defend a somewhat more sophisticated version of the "just war" theory, arguing that it not only escapes Wells' criticisms but embodies the sort of criteria which reasonable nonpacifists use in practice to criticize certain wars as unjustified, or to defend certain wars as justified. The set of criteria for a just war which I will use may be listed as follows: Nation A is justified in waging war with Nation B if and only if (A) Nation A has been attacked by Nation B or is going to the aid of Nation C, which has been attacked by Nation B. (B) The war has been legally declared by the properly constituted authorities of Nation A. (C) The intentions of Nation A in waging the war are confined to repelling the attack by Nation B and establishing a peace, fair to all. (D) Nation A has a reasonable hope of success in repelling the attack and establishing a just peace. (E) Nation A cannot secure these ends without waging war; it has considered or tried all other means and wages war only as a last resort. (F) The good done by Nation A waging war against Nation B can reasonably be expected to outweigh the evil done by waging war. (G) Nation A does not use or anticipate using any means of waging war which are themselves immoral, e.g., the avoidable killing of innocent persons.

It will be seen that there is some overlap in our lists of criteria. Of the seven conditions he borrows from McKenna, his (1) is my (B), and my (D), (E), (F) and (G) are expanded versions of his (4), (5), (6) and (7). My (C) probably embodies some of the considerations in his (2) and (3), but I reject these in the form given by Wells. The most important omission from his list is my (A), which occurs in most versions of these criteria which I am familiar with.[5]

The presence of my (A) and the expansion of some of the other criteria takes care, I think, of his final example of the hypothetical "war" waged on Jews by Aryans. Because this is an action of a government

---

[4] Wells, *op. cit.*, pp. 828–29 [p. 189 in this text].

[5] The specific list I give is taken from a radio talk by John Paul, C.S.P., but it could be duplicated from many sources. The earliest recognizable version of the theory is in Cicero, *De Re Publica* I, 43. Since Cicero is rarely original, the theory presumably derives from earlier Stoic sources.

against its own citizens, it might be foreseen that just war criteria would apply in a very strained fashion, if at all to such a situation. But applying my set of criteria, the Aryans would have to show that: (A) The Jews had attacked the Aryans, or the Aryans were going to the aid of some group attacked by the Jews. (B) The "war" has been declared by constituted authorities under the laws of the nation. (C) The intentions of the Aryans are confined to repelling the attack of the Jews and establishing a peace fair to all. (D) The Aryans have a reasonable hope of success in repelling the attack and *establishing a just peace* by the methods employed. (E) The Aryans cannot secure these ends without exterminating the Jews. (F) The good done by the extermination of the Jews will outweigh the evil done by the extermination. (G) The Aryans do not use or anticipate using any means, such as killing of innocent persons, which are themselves immoral. Obviously, neither in the historical situation obliquely referred to by Wells nor in any conceivable variation of it could these seven conditions plausibly be maintained to exist.

Similarly, in the final part of his paper Wells argues that the just war theory would justify "Armageddon." If by Armageddon he means a war resulting in the destruction of the human race, presumably no reasonable man could argue that such conditions as my (C), (D), (E), (F) and (G) could be met.

I could go on arguing with specific statements by Wells, but I think it would be more fruitful to examine the way in which reasonable men do in fact use criteria such as those which I have listed in arguing about the justification or lack thereof of particular wars. This may provide a better proof than a point by point refutation that Wells is wrong in thinking that the just war theory, although it may have had some relevance to the middle ages, is totally useless in modern circumstances. I will begin with some of the simpler and less restrictive criteria going on to the more complex and arguable cases.

Probably the least restrictive criterion is (B) the condition that war be legally declared by constituted authority. However, to see that this criterion is still used in current debates on the justifiability of particular wars we need only consider the criticism made by critics of our Vietnam involvement of President Johnson's actions in committing American forces to a war in Vietnam without a declaration of war by Congress. Here the legality of the action was in question, not Johnson's position as a duly constituted authority. Nor was the criterion itself rejected by defenders of the administration: the attempt was made to argue that the Gulf of Tonkin resolution gave authority for the commitment of troops. Again, critics of the war both in this country and abroad criticize the Thieu government as not being a duly constituted authority, and defenders of the war attempt to establish Thieu as the duly constituted authority on the basis of the recent elections. The criterion, at any rate, seems to be recognized by both parties as relevant.

Condition (A) is somewhat more complex. Obviously "they attacked first" has been widely used as a defense of the justice of a war, and is so used today. That the Confederates fired on Fort Sumter, that Hitler invaded Poland, that the Japanese attacked Pearl Harbor, that the United States invaded at the Bay of Pigs has in each case given the attacked people a firm conviction of the rightness of their cause. The Korean conflict caused nothing like the anguish created by the Vietnamese war in the minds of Americans, because there seemed to be a clear invasion across an established frontier. In Vietnam, defenders of the war argue that a similar invasion occurred and opponents of the war try to establish that American support of Diem amounted to an attack on the legitimate authority in Vietnam. Thus, seemingly both accept the principle that he who strikes first is in the wrong. The actions of Israel in the Six Days War are attacked by some as a pre-emptive strike and defended by others as a response to preparations and pressures amounting to an attack.

Condition (G) plunges us further into complexity. Those who use the recent My Lai massacre as a basis for an attack on the war (rather than merely condemning the incident itself) seem to be arguing that the government intended or permitted or at least could have reasonably foreseen the inevitability of such incidents. Defenders of the war (not of the massacre itself) argue that the government neither intended nor condoned the incident and often seem to argue that such incidents could not be foreseen or prevented by even the best-intentioned government. Again, nations which use weapons which do in fact cause the death of non-combatants frequently try to justify them on the basis that such deaths were the unintended result of actions taken against military targets. Where this justification is implausible, as in such cases as the firebombing of Dresden and Tokyo, the robot bombing of London, the atomic bomb drops in Japan, the use of anti-personnel weapons in the bombing of North Vietnam and so on, the perpetrators are widely condemned by impartial persons.

Condition (C), that the intention of a nation attempting to justify a war be restricted to repelling attack and establishing a just peace is a claim widely made, for example, by the U.S. government in the Vietnam war, by Israel in the two wars with the Arab nations, by Biafra in the recent Nigerian war. Where some doubt is cast on such claims as, for example, by Biafra's initial sally outside of Ibo territory, by Israel's colonization of the Sinai, etc., defenders of the country in question feel that the imputation of motives other than defense and just settlement is one which must be repelled.

Condition (D), reasonable hope of success, has been used by recent critics of the Vietnam war, by critics of Biafra's continued struggle in the last stages of the war and has undoubtedly influenced such events as Czechoslovakia's decision not to resist the Russian invasion militarily. Nor is the criterion denied by those against whom it is levied as an accusation: repeated claims of eventual victory are made, despite their implausibility.

For an example of Condition (E), war only as a last resort, we might turn to Wells' own example, the "war" of the Nazis against the German Jews. If the complete "freeing" of Germany from Jewish influence was the desired end, the recent example of Poland which over the past few years has caused the emigration of most of its Jewish population by social and political pressures shows that the use of violence was not the "last resort" in Germany. Despicable and horrible as the Polish tactic was, it secured the desired end without the use of violence and, ironically enough, more efficiently than Hitler's methods. Getting closer to home it is arguable that the use of violence by the students at San Francisco State and by the police in the People's Park dispute in Berkeley were far from the last resort in either case. Examples having to do with national conflicts are less easy to find, but one might cite the U.S. invasion of the Dominican Republic as an example of a case where an accusation was made that the use of a military invasion was far from the last resort to secure the end desired, an allegation resisted by Johnson's defenders. At any rate, no one seems anxious to admit that they employed war or used violence as other than a last resort.

Finally, the claim that the good done by waging a war outweighs the evil, Condition (F), is always made by those who argue that a war is justified. Where it is seriously challenged, as in the destruction of Vietnam by the current conflict, the starvation of Biafran children by the carrying on of the Biafran war and so on, then this fact in itself often leads to the condemnation of a war judged just on other grounds. Just such considerations have changed many Americans from hawks to doves, or given pause to early supporters of Biafra.

Now plainly deceitful claims are often made that such criteria are met when in fact they are not, and passion and partiality often blind participants in a conflict to gross violations of such criteria. But every one of these criteria has been used in recent times to accuse warring governments of injustice or defend their claims to have justice on their side. No one is willing to admit to violation of these criteria, everyone is anxious to show that their actions conform to them. Nor is it impossible for reasonably impartial persons to discover whether in fact these criteria are satisfied in particular instances.

Those who claim to be reasonable and well-intentioned persons but cannot accept pacifism have a special need of such criteria. The pure pacifist can condemn both sides in every war: he has no problems in this respect. But he is in practice ineffective, partly because men always have and perhaps always will make a distinction between Genghis Khan invading the peaceful village to pillage and rape, and the villagers who spring to their own defense (to choose an example safely remote).

Non-pacifists hearing of a border war between China and India, a rebellion in Biafra based on fear of genocide, an invasion in Hungary, or Cuba, or Czechoslovakia, must make up their minds about these events. No doubt it would be best if all conflicts ceased. But unless and until they do we are forced to take sides, and in taking sides are forced to use some standards.

The most frequent standard other than those listed in the traditional just war criteria is simply some version of "the righteousness of our cause." Because we are Communists (or anti-Communists), because we are white (or black), because we have the true belief which will save the world, we may make war on our opponents, using any means, disregarding any standards. It is this sort of position which is dangerous to the peace of the world. If every nation observed the traditional criteria of the just war, wars would be infrequent, short and relatively limited.

But, it may be argued, in modern nuclear warfare it is impossible in practice to observe these criteria. Just so, and a recognition of this fact on the part of the great powers may be partly responsible for keeping our uneasy peace. True, there is a "balance of terror," but there are situations in which moral considerations and fear of world reaction have played more of a part than fear of retaliation. Arguably, the position of the United States before Russia had effective atomic armaments, and the position of Russia with regard to China at the present time—are cases of this kind.

To return to Wells' criticisms of the just war theory, he points out that the just war theory has often been used to justify policies which seem to be obviously immoral, such as the saturation bombing of cities or the use of germ warfare on whole populations. But of course any theory can be twisted or distorted by partisans, and obviously such tactics are *prima facie* contrary to such principles as (F) and (G) above. It may be that casuists can attempt justifications of such actions on the basis of the just war theory, but the "righteous cause" theory can justify such actions without any acrobatics.

Another of Wells' criticisms is that just war theory is an "anomalous instance in moral discourse" in that it attempts to show that under some circumstances it would be "just" to perform immoral acts and to contribute to evil consequences.[6] But this is not the position of the just war

---

[6] Wells, *op. cit.*, p. 820 [p. 181 in this text].

theorist, nor of the ordinary non-pacifist criticizing some particular war. Neither would admit that self-defense is immoral, nor that inflicting damage on an aggressor who is attempting to destroy you is an unambiguously evil consequence. Even if certain consequences of war are taken to be clearly evil, any mature morality must make room for cases in which we must choose the lesser of two evils.

It has not been my intention in this paper to defend war as an instrument of national policy, or to justify any particular war. In fact I believe that certain modern wars have been justified, but a consistent defender of the just war theory might very well feel that modern wars inevitably violate the traditional just war criteria. But I think that the cause of peace is not well served by the rejection of the just war theory, leaving us in practice with the choice between pacifism and the "righteous cause" type of justification. As I have tried to show, the traditional criteria for just war can be regarded as an explication of the standards which are used by many people of good will to criticize actual wars. Of course, for the pure pacifist any attempt to justify or defend any war will be morally monstrous. But his is by no means an obviously true position, and it must be justified on its own merits.

The Laws of War *

Richard Wasserstrom

Many persons who consider the variety of moral and legal problems that arise in respect to war come away convinced that the firmest area for judgment is that of how persons ought to behave in time of war. Such persons feel a confidence about dealing with questions of how war ought to be conducted that is absent when other issues about war are raised. They are, for example, more comfortable with the rules relating to how soldiers ought to behave vis-a-vis enemy soldiers and enemy civilians—the laws of war—than they are with the principles relating to when war is permissible and when it is not. Thus, most commentators and critics are uneasy about the applicability to the American scene of that part of Nuremberg that deals with crimes against peace and crimes

---

* Reprinted from *The Monist,* Vol. 56, No. 1 (1972), La Salle, Illinois, with the permission of the author and publisher.

against humanity. But they have no comparable uneasiness about insisting that persons who commit war crimes, violations of the laws of war, be held responsible for their actions.

I propose to consider several features of this view—and I do think it a widely held one—which accepts the moral significance and urges the primacy of the laws of war. I am not interested in providing a genetic account of why this view gets held. I am, rather, concerned to explicate at least one version of this view and to explore the grounds upon which such a view might rest. And I want also to show why such a position is a mistaken one: mistaken in the sense that this conception of the laws of war is a morally unattractive one and one which has no special claim upon our attention or our energies.

There are two general, quite distinct arguments for this notion of the primacy of the laws of war. One is that the laws of war are important and deserving of genuine respect and rigorous enforcement because they reflect, embody and give effect to fundamental moral distinctions and considerations. The other is that, considered simply as laws and conventions, they merit this dominant role because general adherence to them has important, desirable effects. The former of these arguments emphasizes the contents of the laws of war and the connection they have with more basic moral ideals. The latter argument emphasizes the beneficial consequences that flow from their presence and acceptance.

The arguments are clearly not mutually exclusive; indeed, they are related to each other in several important respects. Nonetheless, it is useful to distinguish sharply between them for purposes of analysis and to examine the strengths and weaknesses of each in turn. Before I do so, however, it is necessary to explicate more fully the nature of the laws of war with which I shall be concerned. This is so because it is important to see that I am concerned with a particular view of the character of the laws of war and the related notion of a war crime.[1] I believe it to be the case that this account constitutes an accurate description of the existing laws of war and the dominant conception of a war crime. That is to say, I think it is what many if not most lawyers, commentators, military tribunals, and courts have in mind when they talk about the laws of war and the responsibility of individuals for the commission of war crimes. In this sense at least, the sketch I am about to give constitutes an actual, and not merely a possible, conception of the laws of war. If I am right, the criticisms that I make have substantial

---

[1] For my purpose I treat the laws of war and war crimes as identical phenomena. I recognize that for other purposes and in other contexts this would be a mistake. See, e.g., Richard Falk, Gabriel Kolko, and Robert Lifton, eds., *Crimes of War* (New York, 1971), p. 33.

practical importance. But I may of course be wrong; I may have mis-stated the actual laws of war and the rules for their applicability. To the degree that I have done so, my criticism will, perhaps, less forcefully apply to the real world, but not thereby to the conception of the laws of war I delineate below.

I

The system I am concerned to describe and discuss has the following features. There are, to begin with, a number of formal agreements, con-ventions, and treaties among countries that prescribe how countries (chiefly through their armies) are to behave in time of war. And there are, as well, generally accepted, "common law" rules and practices which also regulate behavior in warfare. Together they comprise the sub-stantive laws of war. For the most part, the laws of war deal with two sorts of things: how classes of persons are to be treated in war, e.g. prisoners of war, and what sorts of weapons and methods of attack are impermissible, e.g. the use of poison gas. Some of the laws of war—particularly those embodied in formal documents—are narrow in scope and specific in formulation. Thus, Article 4 of the Annex to the Hague Convention on Land Warfare, 1907 provided in part that all personal belongings of prisoners of war, "except arms, horses, and military papers," remain their property. Others are a good deal more general and vague. For example, Article 23(e) of the same Annex to Hague Convention prohibits resort to ". . . arms, projectiles, or material calculated to cause unnecessary suffering." Similarly, Article 3 of the Geneva Conventions on the Law of War, 1949 provides in part that "Persons taking no active part in the hostilities . . . shall in all circumstances be treated humanely. . . ." And at Nuremberg, war crimes were defined as follows:

> . . . violations of the laws or customs of war. Such violations shall include but not be limited to, murder, ill-treatment or deportation to slave-labour or for any other purpose of civilian population of or in occupied territory, murder or ill-treatment of prisoners of war or persons on the seas, killing of hostages, plunder of public property, wanton destuction of cities, towns or villages, or devastation not justi-fied by military necessity.[2]

The most important feature of this conception of the laws of war is that the laws of war are to be understood as in fact prohibiting only violence and suffering that are not connected in any direct or important way with the waging of war. As one commentator has put it, the laws of war have as their objective that ". . . the ravages of war should be

---

[2] *The Charter of the International Military Tribunal*, Article Six (b).

mitigated as far as possible by prohibiting needless cruelties, and other acts that spread death and destruction and are not reasonably related to the conduct of hostilities." [3]

This is reflected by the language of many of the laws themselves. But it is demonstrated far more forcefully by the way even relatively unambiguous and absolute prohibitions are to be interpreted. The former characteristic is illustrated by that part of the Nuremberg definition of war crimes which prohibits the ". . . *wanton* destruction of cities, towns or villages." The latter characteristic is illustrated by the following commentary upon Article 23(c) of the Hague Convention quoted above. That article, it will be recalled, prohibits the resort to arms calculated to cause unnecessary suffering. But "unnecessary suffering" means suffering that is not reasonably related to any military advantage to be derived from its infliction. "The legality of hand grenades, flamethrowers, napalm, and incendiary bombs in contemporary warfare is a vivid reminder that suffering caused by weapons with sufficiently large destructive potentialities is not 'unnecessary' in the meaning of this rule." [4]

Another way to make the same point is to indicate the way in which the doctrine of "military necessity" places a central role in this conception of the laws of war. It, too, is explicitly written into a number of the laws of war as providing a specific exception. Thus, to quote a portion of the Nuremberg definition once again, what is prohibited is ". . . devastation not justified by military necessity."

The doctrine of military necessity is, moreover, more firmly and centrally embedded in this conception of the laws of war than illustrations of the preceding type would suggest. The doctrine does not merely create an explicit exception, i.e. as in "devastation not justified by military necessity." Instead, it functions as a general justification for the violation of most, if not all, of even the specific prohibitions which constitute a portion of the laws of war. Thus, according to one exposition of the laws of war, the flat prohibition against the killing of enemy combatants who have surrendered is to be understood to permit the killing of such persons where that is required by "military necessity." There may well be times in any war when it is permissible to kill combatants who have laid down their arms and tried to surrender.

> Small detachments on special missions, or accidentally cut off from their main force, may take prisoners under such circumstances that men cannot be spared to guard them or take them to the rear, and

---

[3] Telford Taylor, *Nuremberg and Vietnam: An American Tragedy* (New York, 1970), p. 20.

[4] Georg Schwarzenberger, *The Legality of Nuclear Weapons* (London, 1958), p. 44.

that to take them along would greatly endanger the success of the mission or the safety of the unit. The prisoners will be killed by operation of the principle of military necessity, and no military or other court has been called upon, so far as I am aware, to declare such killings a war crime.[5]

Or, consider another case where, according to Taylor, the doctrine of military necessity makes ostensibly impermissible conduct permissible. In 1930, a number of nations signed the London Naval Treaty. That treaty required that no ship sink a merchant vessel "without having first placed passengers, crew, and ship's papers in a place of safety." The provisions of this treaty were regularly violated in the Second World War. Nonetheless these violations were not war crimes punished at Nuremberg. This is so, says Taylor, for two reasons. First, the doctrine of military necessity makes the treaty unworkable. If submarines are to be effective instrumentations of war, they cannot surface before they attack merchant ships, nor can they stand around waiting to pick up survivors. The answer is not that it is wrong to use submarines. Rather it is that in the interest of military necessity the prohibitions of the treaty cease to be prohibitions. And second, even if considerations of military necessity were not decisive here, violations of the London treaty would still not have been war crimes because the treaty was violated by both sides during the Second World War. And nothing is properly a war

---

[5] Taylor, p. 36. There is an ambiguity in this quotation that should be noted. Taylor may not mean that the laws of war permit an exception in this kind of case. He may mean only that the law is uncertain, that he knows of no court decision which authoritatively declares this to be either a war crime or a permitted exception. It is sufficient for my purposes if he means the weaker claim, that it is an open question.

A more serious objection to my assertion that I am accurately characterizing the existing laws of war would call attention to the following quotation from the U.S. *Army Field Manual, The Law of Land Warfare,* Chap. I, sec. I.3:

"The law of war places limits on the exercise of a belligerent's power in the interests mentioned in paragraph 2 and requires that belligerents refrain from employing any kind or degree of violence which is not actually necessary for military purposes and that they conduct hostilities with regard for the principles of humanity and chivalry.

"The prohibitory effect of the law of war is not minimized by 'military necessity' which has been defined as that principle which justifies those measures not forbidden by international law which are indispensable for securing the complete submission of the enemy as soon as possible. Military necessity has generally been rejected as a defence for acts forbidden by the customary and conventional laws of war inasmuch as the latter have been developed and framed with consideration for the concept of military necessity."

I leave it to the reader to decide exactly what this means. It seems to anticipate, on the one hand, that the laws of war and the doctrine of military necessity can conflict. It seems to suppose, on the other hand, that substantial conflicts will not arise either because the laws of war prohibit militarily unnecessary violence or because they were formulated with considerations of military necessity in mind. In substance, the view expressed in the quotation is not inconsistent with the conception I am delineating.

THE LAWS OF WAR

crime, says Taylor (at least in the absence of a genuine international tribunal) if both sides engage in the conduct in question.

> As long as enforcement of the laws of war is left to the belligerents themselves, whether during the course of hostilities or by the victors at the conclusion, the scope of their application must be limited by the extent to which they have been observed by the enforcing party. To punish the foe—especially the vanquished foe—for conduct in which the enforcing nation has engaged, would be so grossly inequitable as to discredit the laws of themselves.[6]

Finally, the question of the legality of aerial warfare is especially instructive and important. Once more I take Telford Taylor's analysis to be illustrative of the conception I have been trying to delineate. The bombing of cities was, he observes, not punished at Nuremberg and is not a war crime. Why not? For the two reasons he has already given. Since it was engaged in by the Allies—and on a much more intensive level than by the Germans or the Japanese—it would have been improper to punish the Germans and the Japanese for what we also did. But more importantly the bombing of cities with almost any kind of bomb imaginable is perfectly proper because bombing is an important instrument of the war.

There is nothing illegal about bombing population centers; there is nothing impermissible about using anti-personnel bombs. To begin with, it is not a war crime because aerial bombardments were not punished at Nuremberg. Nor, more importantly, should they be proscribed. For bombs are important weapons of war. But what about the fact that they appear to violate the general prohibition against the killing of non-combatants? They certainly do end up killing lots of civilians, Taylor concedes. But that just cannot be helped because a bomb is, unfortunately, the kind of weapon that cannot discriminate between combatants and non-combatants. What is more, bombing is an inherently inaccurate undertaking. The pilots of fast moving planes—no matter how carefully they try to annihilate only enemy soldiers—will invariably miss lots of times. And if there are civilians nearby, they will, regrettably, be wiped out instead.

The general test for the impermissibility of bombing is, says Taylor, clear enough. Bombing is a war crime if and only if there is no proportioned relationship between the military objective sought to be achieved by the bombing and the degree of destruction caused by it.

---

[6] Taylor, p. 39. Once again, there is an ambiguity here. Taylor may mean that it is procedurally unfair to punish the loser but not the victor for the same act. He may also mean, though, that there is a principle at work which legitimizes a practice which was previously proscribed on the ground that the practice has now become widespread. He does not distinguish these two positions in his book and he seems to me to hold both.

This collection of specific prohibitions, accepted conventions, and general excusing and justifying conditions is the conception of the laws of war with which I am concerned. I want now to examine the deficiencies of such a view and to indicate the respects in which I find unconvincing the two general arguments mentioned at the beginning of the paper.

II

I indicated at the outset that one argument for the importance and value of the laws of war is that they in some sense reflect, embody or give effect to fundamental moral distinctions and considerations. I can help to make clear the character of my criticism of this argument in the following fashion. There are at least three grounds upon which we might criticize any particular criminal code. We might criticize it on the ground that it contained a particular criminal law that ought not to be there because the behavior it proscribed was behavior that it was not morally wrong for people to engage in.[7]

So, we might criticize our criminal code because it punishes the use of marijuana even though there is nothing wrong with using marijuana. Or, we might criticize a criminal code because it is *incomplete*. It proscribes a number of things that ought to be proscribed and regards them with the appropriate degree of seriousness, but it omits to punish something that ought, *ceteris paribus,* to be included in the criminal law. So, we might criticize our criminal code because it fails to make criminal the commission of acts of deliberate racial discrimination.

Compare both of these cases with a criminal code that made criminal only various thefts. Such a code would be incomplete in a different way from the code that just omitted to prohibit racial discrimination. It would be systematically incomplete in the sense that it omitted to forbid many types of behavior that any decent criminal code ought to prohibit. It would, I think, be appropriate to describe such a code as a morally incoherent one and to regard this incoherence, by itself, as a very serious defect. The code would be incoherent in that it could not be rendered intelligible either in terms of the moral principles that ought to underlie any criminal code or even in terms of the moral principles that justified making theft illegal.[8] One could not, we might say, make moral sense

---

[7] I recognize that this is vague. For my purposes it does not matter. It does not matter, that is, whether the law is criticized because the behavior is not immoral, or because the behavior is immoral but not harmful, or because the behavior is harmful but not sufficiently so to justify the use of the criminal law, etc.

[8] Of course, there is still a fourth possible code. It would make illegal only those things that it is morally right and permissible to do, or that ought, on other grounds, never be made illegal. Such a code would certainly be the very worst of all. I am not claiming, it should be emphasized, that the laws of war are like this fourth possible case.

out of a scheme that regarded as most seriously wrong (and hence a fit subject for the criminal law) a variety of harmful acts against property, but which permitted, and treated as in this sense legitimate, all acts of violence against persons. It would be proper to regard such a code as odious, it should be noted, even though one thought that thefts were, on the whole, among the sorts of things that should be prohibited by the criminal law.

As I hope the following discussion makes clear, it is this last kind of criticism that I am making of the conception of the laws of war set out above. So conceived, the laws of war possess the kind of incompleteness and incoherence that would be present in a criminal code that punished only theft.

The chief defense to the accusation that the laws of war are in this sense incomplete and incoherent would, I think, rest on the claim that the laws of war are complete and coherent—the difference is that they set a lower standard for behavior than that set by the typical criminal code. Even in war, so the argument would go, morality has some place; there are some things that on moral grounds ought not be permitted even in time of war. Admittedly, the argument might continue, the place to draw the line between what is permissible and impermissible is different, is "lower," in time of war than in time of peace, but the guiding moral principles and criteria remain the same. The laws of war can quite plausibly be seen as coherently reflecting, even if imperfectly, this lower but still intelligible morality of war. Thus, the argument might conclude the laws of war are not like a criminal code that only punishes theft. Rather, they are like a criminal code that only punishes intentional homicides, rapes, and serious assaults and thefts.

Although I do not argue the point at length in this paper, I accept the idea that even in war morality has some place. What I do challenge, therefore, is the claim that the laws of war as I have sketched them can be plausibly understood as reflecting or embodying in any coherent fashion this lower, but still intelligible morality of war.

Consider first the less permissive (and hence morally more attractive) conception of the laws of war, the conception that does not always permit military necessity to be an exception or an excuse. It cannot be plausibly claimed, I submit, that this scheme of what in war is permissible and impermissible reflects a lowering of our basic moral expectations or standards. The most serious problem, I think, is that the distinction between combatants and non-combatants is not respected by the laws of war—particularly as they relate to aerial warfare and the use of weapons of mass destruction. This constitutes a deviation in kind and not merely a diminution of standards in respect to our fundamental moral notions. This is so because the failure meaningfully to distinguish between combatants and non-combatants obliterates all concern for two basic considerations: the degree of choice that persons had in getting into the position in which they now find themselves, and the likelihood that they are or are about to be in a position to inflict harm on anyone else. The distinction between combatants and non-combatants is admittedly a crude one. Some non-combatants are able in reasonably direct ways to inflict harm on others, e.g. workers in a munitions factory. And some non-combatants may very well have knowingly and freely put themselves in such a position. Concomitantly, many combatants may have been able to exercise very little choice in respect to the assumption of the role of a combatant, e.g. soldiers who are drafted into an army under circumstances where the penalties for refusing to accept induction are very severe. Difficulties such as these might make it plausible to argue that the laws of war cannot reasonably be expected to capture perfectly these distinctions. That is to say, it would, I think, be intelligible to argue that it is unreasonable to expect anyone to be able to distinguish the conscripts from the volunteers in the opponents' army. It would, perhaps, even be plausible to argue (although less convincingly, I think) that civilians who are engaged in activities that are directly connected with the prosecution of the war can reasonably be expected to understand that they will be subject to attack. If the laws of war even preserved a distinction between soldiers, munitions workers, and the like on the one hand and children, the aged, and the infirm on the other, one might maintain that the laws of war did succeed in retaining—at a low level and in an imprecise way—a distinction of fundamental moral importance. But, as we have seen, the laws of war that relate to aerial warfare and the use of weapons of mass destruction do not endeavor to preserve a distinction of even this crudity.

A similar point can be made about those laws of war that deal primarily with combatants. Here, though, there is a bit more that can be said on behalf of the rationality of some of the relevant laws of war. The strongest case is that for the special, relatively unequivocal prohibitions against the mistreatment of prisoners of war and the infliction of damage upon hospitals and medical personnel. Someone might object that these make no sense, that there is no difference between attacking a wounded soldier in a hospital and attacking an unwounded soldier with a weapon against which he is defenseless, e.g. strafing or bombing infantrymen armed with rifles. Similarly, it might be objected that there is no coherent principle that distinguishes the wrongness of killing (generally) prisoners of war and the permissibility of killing enemy soldiers who are asleep.

Such an objection would be too strong, for there does seem to be a morally relevant distinction between these two kinds of cases. It is the distinction between those who have obviously been rendered incapable of fighting back (the wounded and the prisoners of war) and those who only may be incapable of fighting back.

It would be wrong, however, to make too much of this point. In the first place, for the reasons suggested earlier, distinctions among combatants are morally less significant than the distinction between combatants and non-combatants. And in the second place, the principle justifying this distinction among combatants is a pretty crude and not wholly attractive one. In particular, it does not very convincingly, I think, establish the obvious appropriateness of using deadly force against combatants who pose no direct threat and who are defenseless against the force used.[9]

Be that as it may, this is the strongest case for these particular laws of war. There are others for which no comparable rationale can be urged. Thus, it cannot be argued successfully that the laws of war concerning combatants can be generally understood to be a reflection or embodiment of a lower, but coherent set of standards relating to how combatants ought to behave toward one another. More specifically, it cannot be maintained, as persons sometimes seek to maintain, that the laws of war relating to which weapons are permissible and which are impermissible possess a similar coherence. Someone might argue, for example, that there are some ways of killing a person that are worse, more inhumane and savage than other ways. War both permits and requires that combatants kill one another in a variety of circumstances in which, in any other context, it would be impermissible to do so. Nonetheless, so the argument might continue, the laws of war do record and give effect to this perception that some techniques of killing are so abhorrent that they ought not be employed even in war.

Once again, my response is not a direct challenge to the claim that it may be possible to distinguish on some such ground among methods of killing. Indeed, were such a distinction to be preserved by the laws of war, important and desirable alterations in the nature of war would almost surely have to take place. What I am concerned to deny is that the laws of war that deal with weapons can be plausibly viewed as reflecting distinctions of genuine moral significance. Since it is permissible to kill an enemy combatant with an anti-personnel bomb, a nuclear weapon, or even a flame-thrower, it just cannot be plausibly maintained that it is a

---

[9] It is, for example, legitimate to bomb the barracks of soldiers who are not at the front lines, to ambush unsuspecting (and possibly even unarmed) enemy soldiers, and to use all sorts of weapons against which the particular combatants may be completely defenseless. At some stage it just ceases to be very satisfactory to insist that this is unobjectionable because the combatants could defend themselves if they chose and because they chose to be combatants in the first place. For both claims about the combatants may in fact be false and known to be such.

war crime to kill a combatant with poison gas because it is morally worse to use poison gas than to invoke the former methods of human destruction.

It must be observed that so far I have been concerned with that morally more attractive view of the laws of war which does not permit a general exception to all of the laws on grounds of military necessity. Once such a general exception is permitted, whatever plausibility and coherence there is to this conception of the laws of war is diminished virtually to the vanishing point. That this is so can be shown in the following fashion.

To begin with, it is important to notice that the doctrine of "military necessity" is employed in an ambiguous and misleading fashion. "Necessity" leads us naturally to think of various sorts of extreme circumstances which excuse, if they do not justify, otherwise impermissible behavior. Thus, the exception to the rule about taking prisoners is, perhaps, a case where necessitarian language does fit: if the prisoners are taken by the patrol deep in enemy territory the captors will themselves almost surely be captured or killed. They cannot, in such circumstances, be held to the rule against killing prisoners because it is "necessary" that the prisoners be killed.

Now, one may not be convinced that necessitarian language is appropriately invoked even in this case. But what should nonetheless be apparent is the inappropriateness of describing the doctrine that justifies aerial warfare, submarine warfare, or the use of flamethrowers as one of military *necessity*. Necessity has nothing whatsoever to do with the legitimacy of the aerial bombardment of cities or the use of other weapons of mass destruction. To talk of military necessity in respect to such practices is to surround the practice with an aura of justification that is in no way deserved. The appeal to the doctrine of military necessity is in fact an appeal to a doctrine of military utility. The laws of war really prohibit (with only a few minor exceptions) some wrongful practices that also lack significant military value. The laws of war permit and treat as legitimate almost any practice, provided only that there is an important military advantage to be secured.

The more that *this* doctrine of military necessity permeates the conception of the laws of war, the less intelligible and attractive is the claim that the laws of war are a coherent, complete, or admirable code of behavior—even for the jungle of warfare. Given the pervasiveness of this doctrine of military utility, the laws of war are reducible in large measure to the principle that in war it is still wrong to kill (or maim or torture) another person for no reason at all, or for reasons wholly unrelated to the outcome of the war. But the laws of war also tell us what it is permissible and legitimate to do in time of war. Here the governing principle is that it is legitimate, appropriate (and sometimes obligatory) to do almost anything to anybody, provided only that what is done is reasonably related to an important military objective. It is, in short, to permit almost all possible moral claims to be overridden by considerations of military utility. Whatever else one may wish to claim for the preservation of such a system of the laws of war, one cannot, therefore, claim that they deserve either preservation or respect because of the connection these laws maintain with the idea of morality.

Finally, it should be noted, too, that the case is hardly improved by the condition that a practice which is otherwise prohibited ceases to be so, if the practice was engaged in by both sides. As I indicated earlier, this may not be the way to interpret the argument for not punishing the Germans for, say, engaging in unrestricted submarine warfare. But if part of the idea of a war crime is, as some of the literature surely suggests it is, that an offense ceases to be an offense once the practice becomes uniform, then this, too, must count against the possibility of making the case for this conception of the laws of war rest on moral grounds.

III

As I indicated at the outset, there is another way to approach the laws of war and to argue for their worth and significance. This route emphasizes the beneficial consequences of having and enforcing the laws of war, and is relatively unconcerned with the "intrinsic" morality of the rules. The arguments in support of such a view go something like this.

Despite some real fuzziness about the edges, (or even closer to the center) many of the laws of war are reasonably precise. A number of the laws of war are written down and embodied in rather specific conventions and agreements. It is relatively easy, therefore, to tell, at least in a good many cases, what is a war crime and what is not. It is certainly simpler to decide, for example, what constitutes a war crime than it is to determine whether a crime against peace or humanity has been committed. And the fact that the laws of war are more readily ascertainable has certain important consequences of its own.

To begin with, there is first the intellectual confidence that comes from dealing with rules that are written down and that are reasonably specific and precise. More to the point, it is this feature which makes it quite fair to hold persons responsible for violations of the laws of war. The laws of war can be ascertained in advance by the individuals concerned, they can be applied impartially by an appropriate tribunal, and they can be independently "verified" by disinterested observers. They are, in sum, more like typical criminal laws than any of the other rules or principles that relate to war.

A second argument for the primacy of the laws of war also concerns their enforcibility.

It goes like this. It is certainly not wholly unrealistic to imagine the

laws of war being enforced, even while a war is going on. More importantly it is not wholly unrealistic to imagine the laws of war being
enforced by a country against members of its own armed forces, as well
as against members of the opposing army. Such has indeed been the case
in the United States as well as in other countries. Once again, the contrast
with crimes against peace is striking. It is quite unlikely that the perpetrators of crime against peace, who will be the leaders of the enemy, will ever
be caught until the war is over. It is surely unlikely, therefore, that the
existence of rules making the waging of aggressive war a crime will ever
deter leaders from embarking on aggressive war. If they win, they have
nothing to fear. If they lose, they expect to die whether they are guilty
or not.

The case is more bleak still where the perpetrators of crimes against
peace are the leaders of one's own country. While one can in theory
imagine the courts of a country holding the leaders of the country liable
for waging aggressive war, this is a theoretical but not a practical possibility. While a war is going on the one thing that national institutions are
most unlikely to do is to subject the conduct of the leaders of the nation
to cool, critical scrutiny. The leaders of a country are hardly likely to be
deterred by the prospect that the courts of their own country will convict
them of having committed crimes against peace.

The situation in respect to crimes against war is markedly different
in both cases. Soldiers fighting on the opposing side do run a real risk of
being caught while the war is on. If they know that they may be captured,
and if they also know that they may be punished for any war crimes they
have committed, this can have a significant effect on the way they behave toward their opponents. Similarly, the knowledge that they may be
punished by their own side for misbehavior toward the enemy can influence the way soldiers in the army go about fighting the war. Hence there
is a genuine prospect that the members of both armies will behave differently just because there are laws of war than they would have were
there no such laws.

What all of this shows is that the laws of war will influence the behavior of persons in time of war. There are additional arguments, connected with those that have just been presented, to show that the
behavior will be affected in ways that are both desirable and important.

The first such argument is that, despite all of their imperfections,
the laws of war do represent the consensus that does at present exist about
how persons ought to behave in time of war. The fact that the laws of war
are embodied in conventions and treaties, most of which have been explicitly ratified by almost all the countries of the world, means that we are
dealing with conduct about whose character there can be relatively little
genuine disagreement. To be sure, the conventions may not go as far or

be as precise as we might like. The laws of war may be unambitious in scope and even incoherent in the sense described earlier. Nonetheless, they do constitute those rules and standards about which there is universal agreement concerning what may not be done, even in time of war. And the fact that all nations have consented to these laws and agreed upon them gives them an authority that is almost wholly lacking anywhere else in the area of morality and war.

Closely related to, but distinguishable from, the above is the claim that past experience provides independent evidence of the importance and efficacy of having laws of war. They have worked to save human life. If we look at wars that have been fought, we see that the laws of war have had this effect. Perhaps this was because the participants were deterred by the threat of punishment. Perhaps this was because the laws of war embody standards of behavior that men, even in time of war, thought it worth respecting. Perhaps this was because countries recognized a crude kind of self-interest in adhering to the conventions as a means of securing adherence by the other side. It does not matter very much why the laws of war were respected to the degree that they were—and they were respected to some extent in the total wars of the Twentieth Century. What matters is that they were respected. Telford Taylor has put the matter this way:

> Violated or ignored as they often are, enough of the rules are observed enough of the time so that mankind is very much better off with them than without them. The rules for the treatment of civilian populations in occupied countries are not as susceptible to technological change as rules regarding the use of weapons in combat. If it were not regarded as wrong to bomb military hospitals, they would be bombed all of the time instead of some of the time.
>
> It is only necessary to consider the rules on taking prisoners in the setting of the Second World War to realize the enormous saving of life for which they have been responsible. Millions of French, British, German and Italian soldiers captured in Western Europe and Africa were treated in general compliance with the Hague and Geneva requirements, and returned home at the end of the war. German and Russian prisoners taken in the eastern front did not fare nearly so well and died in captivity by the millions, but many survived. Today there is surely much to criticize about the handling of prisoners on both sides of the Vietnam war, but at least many of them are alive, and that is because the belligerents are reluctant to flout the laws of war too openly.[10]

The final argument for the preservation of the laws of war concerns the effect of the laws—or their absence—upon the moral sensibilities of

---

[10] Taylor, p. 40.

individuals. Were we to do away with the laws of war, were we to concede that in time of war anything and everything is permissible, the effect upon the capacity of persons generally to respond in accordance with the dictates of morality would be diminished rather than enhanced. This, too, is one of Telford Taylor's main theses. "All in all," he argues, "this has been a pretty bloody century and people do not seem to shock very easily, as much of the popular reaction to the report of Son My made depressingly plain. The kind of world in which all efforts to mitigate the horrors of war are abandoned would hardly be a world sensitive to the consequences [of total war]." [11]

The consequences for military sensibilities are at least as important, Taylor continues, as are the consequences for civilian sensibilities. The existence of the laws of war and the insistence upon their importance prevent combatants from becoming completely dehumanized and wholly vicious by their participation in war. The laws of war, Taylor asserts, are

> . . . necessary to diminish the corrosive effect of mortal combat on the participants. War does not confer a license to kill for personal reasons—to gratify perverse impulses, or to put out of the way anyone who appears obnoxious, or to whose welfare the soldier is indifferent. War is not a license at all, but an obligation to kill for reasons of state; it does not countenance the infliction of suffering for its own sake or for revenge.

> Unless troops are trained and required to draw the distinction between military and nonmilitary killings, and to retain such respect for the value of life that unnecessary death and destruction will continue to repel them, they may lose the sense for that distinction for the rest of their lives. The consequence would be that many returning soldiers would be potential murderers. [12]

It should not be difficult to foresee the sorts of objections that I believe can most tellingly be raised against these arguments. I will state them very briefly.

It is, to begin with, far less obvious than the argument would have it that the laws of war possess the kind of specificity we typically require of an ordinary criminal law. In particular, the pervasive character of the doctrine of military "necessity" comes close to leaving as unambiguously criminal only senseless or gratuitous acts of violence against the enemy.

Similarly, the fact that countries have been able to agree upon certain conventions does not seem to me to be a matter of particular significance. At the very least, it is certainly a mistake to infer from this fact of agree-

---

[11] Taylor, p. 39.
[12] Taylor, pp. 40–41.

ment that we have somehow succeeded in identifying those types of behavior that really matter the most. Indeed, it is at least as likely as not, that agreement was forthcoming just because the issues thereby regulated were not of great moment. And it is surely far more likely than not that agreement was forthcoming just because it was perceived that adherence to these laws would not affect very much the way wars got fought.

This leads me to what seem to me to be the two most significant criticisms that can be made against the assertion that beneficial consequences of various sorts flow from respecting and enforcing the laws of war. There is first the claim that adherence to the laws of war teaches important moral lessons (or prevents soldiers from becoming totally corrupt). Just what sort of things about killing do the laws of war (in theory, let alone in practice) teach soldiers; will someone who has mastered the distinctions established by the laws of war thereby be less a potential murderer? It is difficult to see that getting straight about the laws of war will permit someone to learn important moral lessons and to maintain a decent respect for the value of human life. It is difficult to be at all confident that soldiers who have mastered the distinctions established by the laws of war will be for that reason turned away from the path of murder. This is so just because the laws of war possess the kind of incompleteness and incoherence I described earlier. We can, of course, teach soldiers to obey the laws of war, whatever their content may happen to be. But we must not confuse that truth with the question of whether we will have, through that exercise, taught them to behave in morally responsible ways.[13]

The issue is made more doubtful, still, because the laws of war inescapably permit as well as prohibit; they make some conduct criminal and other conduct legitimate. The evidence is hardly all in, either from the Twentieth Century in general or Vietnam in particular. It will probably never be in. But it surely appears to be at least as likely as not that the laws of war—if they have taught anything at all—have taught soldiers and civilians alike that it is permissible and lawful to kill and maim and destroy, provided only that it will help to win the war. And I do think this constitutes morally retrograde movement.

But this still leaves unanswered what may appear to be the most important argument of all, the argument put forward by Telford Taylor and others that the laws of war are important and deserving of respect because they work. Isn't it sufficient that even somewhat irrational, incoherent and incomplete rules have the consequences of saving lives?

---

[13] Unless, of course, one holds the view that teaching persons to obey orders, or even laws, whatever they may happen to be is an important constituent of the curriculum of moral education. It is not a view I hold.

Even if it is permissible to kill women and children whenever military necessity requires it, isn't it important to save the lives of those women and children whose deaths are not necessitated by military considerations?

The argument is both sound and deceptive. Of course it is better to save some lives rather than none at all. If adhering to the laws of war as we now have them will save the lives of persons (and especially "innocent" persons) in time of war, that is a good reason (but not a decisive one) for maintaining these laws of war. If punishing soldiers (like Lieutenant Calley) for war crimes will keep other soldiers from gratuitously killing women and children, among others, in Vietnam, that is a good reason for punishing persons for the commission of these war crimes.

But to concede this is not to put an end to the matter at hand. For reasons I have tried to make plain there are costs as well as gains from concentrating our attention upon the laws of war and their enforcement. There is to put it simply a risk to human life that is quite substantial. The risk is that we inevitably and necessarily legitimate behavior that is morally indefensible, that is, truly criminal. The cost—and it is a cost in human life—is, for example, that the sanitized war in Vietnam that would result from a scrupulous adherence to the laws of war will increase still further our tolerance for and acceptance of the horror, the slaughter, and the brutality that is the essence of Twentieth Century war. There is something genuinely odious about a code of behavior that says: if there is a conflict between the attainment of an important military objective and one or more of the prohibitions of the laws of war, it is the prohibitions that quite properly are to give way. And there is something dangerous about a point of view that accepts such a system and directs us to concentrate our energies and our respect upon its enforcement. The corrosive effect of living in a world in which we embrace such a code and insist upon its value seems to me appreciably more dangerous than the effect of a refusal to accord a position of primacy to the sometimes bizarre, often morally incoherent laws of war.

The answer is not, of course, to throw out the laws of war with a view toward inculcating in us all the belief that in war anything goes. But neither is it an acceptable answer to take as given the nature of modern war and modern weapons and to conform, as best one can, the laws of war to their requirements. This, it seems to me, is the fatal flaw in the conception of the laws of war with which I have been concerned. The beginning of a morally defensible position is surely to be found in a different conception of the laws of war. A conception sufficiently ambitious that it refuses to regard as immutable the character of contemporary warfare and weaponry, and that requires instead, that war itself change so as to conform to the demands of morality.

War and Massacre *

Thomas Nagel [1]

From the apathetic reaction to atrocities committed in Vietnam by the United States and its allies, one may conclude that moral restrictions on the conduct of war command almost as little sympathy among the general public as they do among those charged with the formation of U.S. military policy. Even when restrictions on the conduct of warfare are defended, it is usually on legal grounds alone: their moral basis is often poorly understood. I wish to argue that certain restrictions are neither arbitrary nor merely conventional, and that their validity does not depend simply on their usefulness. There is, in other words, a moral basis for the rules of war, even though the conventions now officially in force are far from giving it perfect expression.

I

No elaborate moral theory is required to account for what is wrong in cases like the Mylai massacre, since it did not serve, and was not intended to serve, any strategic purpose. Moreover, if the participation of the United States in the Indo-Chinese war is entirely wrong to begin with, then that engagement is incapable of providing a justification for *any* measures taken in its pursuit—not only for the measures which are atrocities in every war, however just its aims.

But this war has revealed attitudes of a more general kind, that influenced the conduct of earlier wars as well. After it has ended, we shall still be faced with the problem of how warfare may be conducted, and the attitudes that have resulted in the specific conduct of this war will not have disappeared. Moreover, similar problems can arise in wars or rebellions fought for very different reasons, and against very different oppo-

* "War and Massacre," by Thomas Nagel, *Philosophy and Public Affairs*, Vol. I, No. 2 (copyright © 1972 by Princeton University Press). Reprinted by permission of Princeton University Press.

[1] This paper grew out of discussions at the Society for Ethical and Legal Philosophy, and I am indebted to my fellow members for their help.

nents. It is not easy to keep a firm grip on the idea of what is not permissible in warfare, because while some military actions are obvious atrocities, other cases are more difficult to assess, and the general principles underlying these judgments remain obscure. Such obscurity can lead to the abandonment of sound intuitions in favor of criteria whose rationale may be more obvious. If such a tendency is to be resisted, it will require a better understanding of the restrictions than we now have.

I propose to discuss the most general moral problem raised by the conduct of warfare: the problem of means and ends. In one view, there are limits on what may be done even in the service of an end worth pursuing—and even when adherence to the restriction may be very costly. A person who acknowledges the force of such restrictions can find himself in acute moral dilemmas. He may believe, for example, that by torturing a prisoner he can obtain information necessary to prevent a disaster, or that by obliterating one village with bombs he can halt a campaign of terrorism. If he believes that the gains from a certain measure will clearly outweigh its costs, yet still suspects that he ought not to adopt it, then he is in a dilemma produced by the conflict between two disparate categories of moral reason: categories that may be called *utilitarian* and *absolutist*.

Utilitarianism gives primacy to a concern with what will *happen*. Absolutism gives primacy to a concern with what one is *doing*. The conflict between them arises because the alternatives we face are rarely just choices between *total outcomes:* they are also choices between alternative pathways or measures to be taken. When one of the choices is to do terrible things to another person, the problem is altered fundamentally; it is no longer merely a question of which outcome would be worse.

Few of us are completely immune to either of these types of moral intuition, though in some people, either naturally or for doctrinal reasons, one type will be dominant and the other suppressed or weak. But it is perfectly possible to feel the force of both types of reason very strongly; in that case the moral dilemma in certain situations of crisis will be acute, and it may appear that every possible course of action or inaction is unacceptable for one reason or another.

II

Although it is this dilemma that I propose to explore, most of the discussion will be devoted to its absolutist component. The utilitarian component is straightforward by comparison, and has a natural appeal to anyone who is not a complete skeptic about ethics. Utilitarianism says that one should try, either individually or through institutions, to maximize good and minimize evil (the definition of these categories need not enter into the schematic formulation of the view), and that if faced with the possibility of preventing a great evil by producing a lesser, one should choose the lesser evil. There are certainly problems about the formulation of utilitarianism, and much has been written about it, but its intent is morally transparent. Nevertheless, despite the addition of various refinements, it continues to leave large portions of ethics unaccounted for. I do not suggest that some form of absolutism can account for them all, only that an examination of absolutism will lead us to see the complexity, and perhaps the incoherence, of our moral ideas.

Utilitarianism certainly justifies *some* restrictions on the conduct of warfare. There are strong utilitarian reasons for adhering to any limitation which seems natural to most people—particularly if the limitation is widely accepted already. An exceptional measure which seems to be justified by its results in a particular conflict may create a precedent with disastrous long-term effects.[2] It may even be argued that war involves violence on such a scale that it is never justified on utilitarian grounds— the consequences of refusing to go to war will never be as bad as the war itself would be, even if atrocities were not committed. Or in a more sophisticated vein it might be claimed that a uniform policy of never resorting to military force would do less harm in the long run, if followed consistently, than a policy of deciding each case on utilitarian grounds (even though on occasion particular applications of the pacifist policy might have worse results than a specific utilitarian decision). But I shall not consider these arguments, for my concern is with reasons of a different kind, which may remain when reasons of utility and interest fail.[3]

In the final analysis, I believe that the dilemma cannot always be resolved. While not every conflict between absolutism and utilitarianism creates an insoluble dilemma, and while it is certainly right to adhere to absolutist restrictions unless the utilitarian considerations favoring violation are overpoweringly weighty and extremely certain—nevertheless, when that special condition is met, it may become impossible to adhere to an absolutist position. What I shall offer, therefore, is a somewhat qualified defense of absolutism. I believe it underlies a valid and fundamental type of moral judgment—which cannot be reduced to or overridden by other principles. And while there may be other principles just as funda-

---

[2] Straightforward considerations of national interest often tend in the same direction: the inadvisability of using nuclear weapons seems to be overdetermined in this way.

[3] These reasons, moreover, have special importance in that they are available even to one who denies the appropriateness of utilitarian considerations in international matters. He may acknowledge limitations on what may be done to the soldiers and civilians of other countries in pursuit of his nation's military objectives, while denying that one country should in general consider the interests of nationals of other countries in determining its policies.

mental, it is particularly important not to lose confidence in our absolutist intuitions, for they are often the only barrier before the abyss of utilitarian apologetics for large-scale murder.

III

One absolutist position that creates no problems of interpretation is pacifism: the view that one may not kill another person under any circumstances, no matter what good would be achieved or evil averted thereby. The type of absolutist position that I am going to discuss is different. Pacifism draws the conflict with utilitarian considerations very starkly. But there are other views according to which violence may be undertaken, even on a large scale, in a clearly just cause, so long as certain absolute restrictions on the character and direction of that violence are observed. The line is drawn somewhat closer to the bone, but it exists.

The philosopher who has done most to advance contemporary philosophical discussion of such a view, and to explain it to those unfamiliar with its extensive treatment in Roman Catholic moral theology, is G. E. M. Anscombe. In 1958 Miss Anscombe published a pamphlet entitled *Mr. Truman's Degree*,[4] on the occasion of the award by Oxford University of an honorary doctorate to Harry Truman. The pamphlet explained why she had opposed the decision to award that degree, recounted the story of her unsuccessful opposition, and offered some reflections on the history of Truman's decision to drop atom bombs on Hiroshima and Nagasaki, and on the difference between murder and allowable killing in warfare. She pointed out that the policy of deliberately killing large numbers of civilians either as a means or as an end in itself did not originate with Truman, and was common practice among all parties during World War II for some time before Hiroshima. The Allied area bombings of German cities by conventional explosives included raids which killed more civilians than did the atomic attacks; the same is true of certain fire-bomb raids on Japan.

The policy of attacking the civilian population in order to induce an enemy to surrender, or to damage his morale, seems to have been

---

4 (Privately printed.) See also her essay "War and Murder," in *Nuclear Weapons and Christian Conscience,* ed. Walter Stein (London, 1963). The present paper is much indebted to these two essays throughout. These and related subjects are extensively treated by Paul Ramsey in *The Just War* (New York, 1968). Among recent writings that bear on the moral problem are Jonathan Bennett, "Whatever the Consequences," *Analysis* 26, no. 3 (1966), 83–102; and Philippa Foot, "The Problem of Abortion and the Doctrine of the Double Effect," *The Oxford Review* 5 (1967), 5–15. Miss Anscombe's replies are "A Note on Mr. Bennett," *Analysis* 26, no. 3 (1966), 208, and "Who is Wronged?" *The Oxford Review* 5 (1967), 16–17.

widely accepted in the civilized world, and seems to be accepted still, at least if the stakes are high enough. It gives evidence of a moral conviction that the deliberate killing of noncombatants—women, children, old people—is permissible if enough can be gained by it. This follows from the more general position that any means can in principle be justified if it leads to a sufficiently worthy end. Such an attitude is evident not only in the more spectacular current weapons systems but also in the day-to-day conduct of the nonglobal war in Indochina: the indiscriminate destructiveness of antipersonnel weapons, napalm, and aerial bombardment; cruelty to prisoners; massive relocation of civilians; destruction of crops; and so forth. An absolutist position opposes to this the view that certain acts cannot be justified no matter what the consequences. Among those acts is murder—the deliberate killing of the harmless: civilians, prisoners of war, and medical personnel.

In the present war such measures are sometimes said to be regrettable, but they are generally defended by reference to military necessity and the importance of the long-term consequences of success or failure in the war. I shall pass over the inadequacy of this consequentialist defense in its own terms. (That is the dominant form of moral criticism of the war, for it is part of what people mean when they ask, "Is it worth it?") I am concerned rather to account for the inappropriateness of offering any defense of that kind for such actions.

Many people feel, without being able to say much more about it, that something has gone seriously wrong when certain measures are admitted into consideration in the first place. The fundamental mistake is made there, rather than at the point where the overall benefit of some monstrous measure is judged to outweigh its disadvantages, and it is adopted. An account of absolutism might help us to understand this. If it is not allowable to *do* certain things, such as killing unarmed prisoners or civilians, then no argument about what will happen if one doesn't do them can show that doing them would be all right.

Absolutism does not, of course, require one to ignore the consequences of one's acts. It operates as a limitation on utilitarian reasoning, not as a substitute for it. An absolutist can be expected to try to maximize good and minimize evil, so long as this does not require him to transgress an absolute prohibition like that against murder. But when such a conflict occurs, the prohibition takes complete precedence over any consideration of consequences. Some of the results of this view are clear enough. It requires us to forgo certain potentially useful military measures, such as the slaughter of hostages and prisoners or indiscriminate attempts to reduce the enemy civilian population by starvation, epidemic infectious diseases like anthrax and bubonic plague, or mass incineration. It means that we cannot deliberate on whether such measures are justified by the fact that they will avert still greater evils, for as intentional measures they cannot be justified in terms of any consequences whatever.

Someone unfamiliar with the events of this century might imagine that utilitarian arguments, or arguments of national interest, would suffice to deter measures of this sort. But it has become evident that such considerations are insufficient to prevent the adoption and employment of enormous antipopulation weapons once their use is considered a serious moral possibility. The same is true of the piecemeal wiping out of rural civilian populations in airborne antiguerrilla warfare. Once the door is opened to calculations of utility and national interest, the usual speculations about the future of freedom, peace, and economic prosperity can be brought to bear to ease the consciences of those responsible for a certain number of charred babies.

For this reason alone it is important to decide what is wrong with the frame of mind which allows such arguments to begin. But it is also important to understand absolutism in the cases where it genuinely conflicts with utility. Despite its appeal, it is a paradoxical position, for it can require that one refrain from choosing the lesser of two evils when that is the only choice one has. And it is additionally paradoxical because, unlike pacifism, it permits one to do horrible things to people in some circumstances but not in others.

IV

Before going on to say what, if anything, lies behind the position, there remain a few relatively technical matters which are best discussed at this point.

First, it is important to specify as clearly as possible the kind of thing to which absolutist prohibitions can apply. We must take seriously the proviso that they concern what we deliberately do to people. There could not, for example, without incoherence, be an absolute prohibition against *bringing about* the death of an innocent person. For one may find oneself in a situation in which, no matter what one does, some innocent people will die as a result. I do not mean just that there are cases in which someone will die no matter what one does, because one is not in a position to affect the outcome one way or the other. That, it is to be hoped, is one's relation to the deaths of most innocent people. I have in mind, rather, a case in which someone is bound to die, but who it is will depend on what one does. Sometimes these situations have natural causes, as when too few resources (medicine, lifeboats) are available to rescue everyone threatened with a certain catastrophe. Sometimes the situations are man-made, as when the only way to control a campaign of terrorism is to employ terrorist tactics against the community from which it has arisen. Whatever one does in cases such as these, some innocent people will die as a result. If the absolutist prohibition forbade doing what would result in the deaths of innocent people, it would have the consequence that in such cases nothing one could do would be morally permissible.

This problem is avoided, however because what absolutism forbids is *doing* certain things to people, rather than bringing about certain *results*. Not everything that happens to others as a result of what one does is something that one has *done* to them. Catholic moral theology seeks to make this distinction precise in a doctrine known as the law of double effect, which asserts that there is a morally relevant distinction between bringing about the death of an innocent person deliberately, either as an end in itself or as a means, and bringing it about as a side effect of something else one does deliberately. In the latter case, even if the outcome is foreseen, it is not murder, and does not fall under the absolute prohibition, though of course it may still be wrong for other reasons (reasons of utility, for example). Briefly, the principle states that one is sometimes permitted knowingly to bring about as a side effect of one's actions something which it would be absolutely impermissible to bring about deliberately as an end or as a means. In application to war or revolution, the law of double effect permits a certain amount of civilian carnage as a side effect of bombing munitions plants or attacking enemy soldiers. And even this is permissible only if the cost is not too great to be justified by one's objectives.

However, despite its importance and its usefuless in accounting for certain plausible moral judgments, I do not believe that the law of double effect is a generally applicable test for the consequences of an absolutist position. Its own application is not always clear, so that it introduces uncertainty where there need not be uncertainty.

In Indochina, for example, there is a great deal of aerial bombardment, strafing, spraying of napalm, and employment of pellet- or needle-spraying antipersonnel weapons against rural villages in which guerrillas are suspected to be hiding, or from which small-arms fire has been received. The majority of those killed and wounded in these aerial attacks are reported to be women and children, even when some combatants are caught as well. However, the government regards these civilian casualties as a regrettable side effect of what is a legitimate attack against an armed enemy.

It might be thought easy to dismiss this as sophistry: if one bombs, burns, or strafes a village containing a hundred people, twenty of whom one believes to be guerrillas, so that by killing most of them one will be statistically likely to kill most of the guerrillas, then isn't one's attack on the group of one hundred a *means* of destroying the guerrillas, pure and simple? If one makes no attempt to discriminate between guerrillas and civilians, as is impossible in an aerial attack on a small village, then one cannot regard as a mere side effect the deaths of those in the group that one would not have bothered to kill if more selective means had been available.

The difficulty is that this argument depends on one particular description of the act, and the reply might be that the means used against the guerrillas is not killing everybody in the village—but rather: obliteration bombing of the *area* in which the twenty guerrillas are known to be located. If there are civilians in the area as well, they will be killed as a side effect of such action.[5]

Because of casuistical problems like this, I prefer to stay with the original, unanalyzed distinction between what one does to people and what merely happens to them as a result of what one does. The law of double effect provides an approximation to that distinction in many cases, and perhaps it can be sharpened to the point where it does better than that. Certainly the original distinction itself needs clarification, particularly since some of the things we do to people involve things happening to them as a result of other things we do. In a case like the one discussed, however, it is clear that by bombing the village one slaughters and maims the civilians in it. Whereas by giving the only available medicine to one of two sufferers from a disease, one does not kill the other, even if he dies as a result.

The second technical point to take up concerns a possible misinterpretation of this feature of the position. The absolutist focus on actions rather than outcomes does not merely introduce a new, outstanding item into the catalogue of evils. That is, it does not say that the worst thing in the world is the deliberate murder of an innocent person. For if that were all, then one could presumably justify one such murder on the ground that it would prevent several others, or ten thousand on the ground that they would prevent a hundred thousand more. That is a familiar argument. But if this is allowable, then there is no absolute prohibition against murder after all. Absolutism requires that we *avoid* murder at all costs, not that we *prevent* it at all costs.[6]

Finally, let me remark on a frequent criticism of absolutism that depends on a misunderstanding. It is sometimes suggested that such prohibitions depend on a kind of moral self-interest, a primary obligation to

---

[5] This counterargument was suggested by Rogers Albritton.

[6] Someone might of course acknowledge the *moral relevance* of the distinction between deliberate and nondeliberate killing, without being an absolutist. That is, he might believe simply that it was *worse* to bring about a death deliberately than as a secondary effect. But that would be merely a special assignment of value, and not an absolute prohibition.

preserve one's own moral purity, to keep one's hands clean no matter what happens to the rest of the world. If this were the position, it might be exposed to the charge of self-indulgence. After all, what gives one man a right to put the purity of his soul or the cleanness of his hands above the lives or welfare of large numbers of other people? It might be argued that a public servant like Truman has no right to put himself first in that way; therefore if he is convinced that the alternatives would be worse, he must give the order to drop the bombs, and take the burden of those deaths on himself, as he must do other distasteful things for the general good.

But there are two confusions behind the view that moral self-interest underlies moral absolutism. First, it is a confusion to suggest that the need to preserve one's moral purity might be the *source* of an obligation. For if by committing murder one sacrifices one's moral purity or integrity, that can only be because there is *already* something wrong with murder. The general reason against committing murder cannot therefore be merely that it makes one an immoral person. Secondly, the notion that one might sacrifice one's moral integrity justifiably, in the service of a sufficiently worthy end, is an incoherent notion. For if one were justified in making such a sacrifice (or even morally required to make it), then one would not be sacrificing one's moral integrity by adopting that course: one would be preserving it.

Moral absolutism is not unique among moral theories in requiring each person to do what will preserve his own moral purity in all circumstances. This is equally true of utilitarianism, or of any other theory which distinguishes between right and wrong. Any theory which defines the right course of action in various circumstances and asserts that one should adopt that course, ipso facto asserts that one should do what will preserve one's moral purity, simply because the right course of action *is* what will preserve one's moral purity in those circumstances. Of course utilitarianism does not assert that this is *why* one should adopt that course, but we have seen that the same is true of absolutism.

V

It is easier to dispose of false explanations of absolutism than to produce a true one. A positive account of the matter must begin with the observation that war, conflict, and aggression are relations between persons. The view that it can be wrong to consider merely the overall effect of one's actions on the general welfare comes into prominence when those actions involve relations with others. A man's acts usually affect more people than he deals with directly, and those effects must naturally be considered in his decisions. But if there are special principles governing the manner in which he should *treat* people, that will require special attention to the particular persons toward whom the act is directed, rather than just to its total effect.

Absolutist restrictions in warfare appear to be of two types: restrictions on the class of persons at whom aggression or violence may be directed and restrictions on the manner of attack, given that the object falls within that class. These can be combined, however, under the principle that hostile treatment of any person must be justified in terms of something *about that person* which makes the treatment appropriate. Hostility is a personal relation, and it must be suited to its target. One consequence of this condition will be that certain persons may not be subjected to hostile treatment in war at all, since nothing about them justifies such treatment. Others will be proper objects of hostility only in certain circumstances, or when they are engaged in certain pursuits. And the appropriate manner and extent of hostile treatment will depend on what is justified by the particular case.

A coherent view of this type will hold that extremely hostile behavior toward another is compatible with treating him as a person—even perhaps as an end in himself. This is possible only if one has not automatically stopped treating him as a person as soon as one starts to fight with him. If hostile, aggressive, or combative treatment of others always violated the condition that they be treated as human beings, it would be difficult to make further distinctions on that score *within* the class of hostile actions. That point of view, on the level of international relations, leads to the position that if complete pacifism is not accepted, no holds need be barred at all, and we may slaughter and massacre to our hearts' content, if it seems advisable. Such a position is often expressed in discussions of war crimes.

But the fact is that ordinary people do not believe this about conflicts, physical or otherwise, between individuals, and there is no more reason why it should be true of conflicts between nations. There seems to be a perfectly natural conception of the distinction between fighting clean and fighting dirty. To fight dirty is to direct one's hostility or aggression not at its proper object, but at a peripheral target which may be more vulnerable, and through which the proper object can be attacked indirectly. This applies in a fist fight, an election campaign, a duel, or a philosophical argument. If the concept is general enough to apply to all these matters, it should apply to war—both to the conduct of individual soldiers and to the conduct of nations.

Suppose that you are a candidate for public office, convinced that the election of your opponent would be a disaster, that he is an unscrupulous demagogue who will serve a narrow range of interests and seriously infringe the rights of those who disagree with him; and suppose you are convinced that you cannot defeat him by conventional means. Now imagine that various unconventional means present themselves as possibilities: you possess information about his sex life which would scandalize the electorate if made public; or you learn that his wife is an alcoholic or that in his youth he was associated for a brief period with a proscribed political party, and you believe that this information could be used to blackmail him into withdrawing his candidacy; or you can have a team of your supporters flatten the tires of a crucial subset of his supporters on election day; or you are in a position to stuff the ballot boxes; or, more simply, you can have him assassinated. What is wrong with these methods, given that they will achieve an overwhelmingly desirable result?

There are, of course, many things wrong with them: some are against the law; some infringe the procedures of an electoral process to which you are presumably committed by taking part in it; very importantly, some may backfire, and it is in the interest of all political candidates to adhere to an unspoken agreement not to allow certain personal matters to intrude into a campaign. But that is not all. We have in addition the feeling that these measures, these methods of attack are *irrelevant* to the issue between you and your opponent, that in taking them up you would not be directing yourself to that which makes him an object of your opposition. You would be directing your attack not at the true target of your hostility, but at peripheral targets that happen to be vulnerable.

The same is true of a fight or argument outside the framework of any system of regulations or law. In an altercation with a taxi driver over an excessive fare, it is inappropriate to taunt him about his accent, flatten one of his tires, or smear chewing gum on his windshied; and it remains inappropriate even if he casts aspersions on your race, politics, or religion, or dumps the contents of your suitcase into the street.[7]

The importance of such restrictions may vary with the seriousness of the case; and what is unjustifiable in one case may be justified in a more extreme one. But they all derive from a single principle: that hostility or aggression should be directed at its true object. This means both that it should be directed at the person or persons who provoke

---

[7] Why, on the other hand, does it seem appropriate, rather than irrelevant, to punch someone in the mouth if he insults you? The answer is that in our culture it is an insult to punch someone in the mouth, and not just an injury. This reveals, by the way, a perfectly unobjectionable sense in which convention may play a part in determining exactly what falls under an absolutist restriction and what does not. I am indebted to Robert Fogelin for this point.

it and that it should aim more specifically at what is provocative about them. The second condition will determine what form the hostility may appropriately take.

It is evident that some idea of the relation in which one should stand to other people underlies this principle, but the idea is difficult to state. I believe it is roughly this: whatever one does to another person intentionally must be aimed at him as a subject, with the intention that he receives it as a subject. It should manifest an attitude to *him* rather than just to the situation, and he should be able to recognize it and identify himself as its object. The procedures by which such an attitude is manifested need not be addressed to the person directly. Surgery, for example, is not a form of personal confrontation but part of a medical treatment that can be offered to a patient face to face and received by him as a response to his needs and the natural outcome of an attitude toward *him*.

Hostile treatment, unlike surgery, is already addressed *to* a person, and does not take its interpersonal meaning from a wider context. But hostile acts can serve as the expression or implementation of only a limited range of attitudes to the person who is attacked. Those attitudes in turn have as objects certain real or presumed characteristics or activities of the person which are thought to justify them. When this background is absent, hostile or aggressive behavior can no longer be intended for the reception of the victim as a subject. Instead it takes on the character of a purely bureaucratic operation. This occurs when one attacks someone who is not the true object of one's hostility—the true object may be someone else, who can be attacked through the victim; or one may not be manifesting a hostile attitude toward anyone, but merely using the easiest available path to some desired goal. One finds oneself not facing or addressing the victim at all, but operating on him—without the larger context of personal interaction that surrounds a surgical operation.

If absolutism is to defend its claim to priority over considerations of utility, it must hold that the maintenance of a direct interpersonal response to the people one deals with is a requirement which no advantages can justify one in abandoning. The requirement is absolute only if it rules out any calculation of what would justify its violation. I have said earlier that there may be circumstances so extreme that they render an absolutist position untenable. One may find then that one has no choice but to do something terrible. Nevertheless, even in such cases absolutism retains its force in that one cannot claim *justification* for the violation. It does not become *all right*.

As a tentative effort to explain this, let me try to connect absolutist limitations with the possibility of justifying *to the victim* what is being done to him. If one abandons a person in the course of rescuing several others from a fire or a sinking ship, one *could* say to him, "You understand, I have to leave you to save the others." Similarly, if one subjects an unwilling child to a painful surgical procedure, one can say to him, "If you could understand, you would realize that I am doing this to help you." One could *even* say, as one bayonets an enemy soldier, "It's either you or me." But one cannot really say while torturing a prisoner, "You understand, I have to pull out your fingernails because it is absolutely essential that we have the names of your confederates" nor can one say to the victims of Hiroshima, "You understand, we have to incinerate you to provide the Japanese government with an incentive to surrender."

This does not take us very far, of course, since a utilitarian would presumably be willing to offer justifications of the latter sort to his victims, in cases where he thought they were sufficient. They are really justifications to the world at large, which the victim, as a reasonable man, would be expected to appreciate. However, there seems to me something wrong with this view, for it ignores the possibility that to treat someone else horribly puts you in a special relation to him, which may have to be defended in terms of other features of your relation to him. The suggestion needs much more development; but it may help us to understand how there may be requirements which are absolute in the sense that there can be no justification for violating them. If the justification for what one did to another person had to be such that it could be offered to him specifically, rather than just to the world at large, that would be a significant source of restraint.

If the account is to be deepened, I would hope for some results along the following lines. Absolutism is associated with a view of oneself as a small being interacting with others in a large world. The justifications it requires are primarily interpersonal. Utilitarianism is associated with a view of oneself as a benevolent bureaucrat distributing such benefits as one can control to countless other beings, with whom one may have various relations or none. The justifications it requires are primarily administrative. The argument between the two moral attitudes may depend on the relative priority of these two conceptions.[8]

VI

Some of the restrictions on methods of warfare which have been adhered to from time to time are to be explained by the mutual interests of the involved parties: restrictions on weaponry, treatment of prisoners,

---

[8] Finally, I should mention a different possibility, suggested by Robert Nozick: that there is a strong general presumption against benefiting from the calamity of another, whether or not it has been deliberately inflicted for that or any other reason. This broader principle may well lend its force to the absolutist position.

etc. But that is not all there is to it. The conditions of directness and relevance which I have argued apply to relations of conflict and aggression apply to war as well. I have said that there are two types of absolutist restrictions on the conduct of war: those that limit the legitimate targets of hostility and those that limit its character, even when the target is acceptable. I shall say something about each of these. As will become clear, the principle I have sketched does not yield an unambiguous answer in every case.

First let us see how it implies that attacks on some people are allowed, but not attacks on others. It may seem paradoxical to assert that to fire a machine gun at someone who is throwing hand grenades at your emplacement is to treat him as a human being. Yet the relation with him is direct and straightforward.[9] The attack is aimed specifically against the threat presented by a dangerous adversary, and not against a peripheral target through which he happens to be vulnerable but which has nothing to do with that threat. For example, you might stop him by machine-gunning his wife and children, who are standing nearby, thus distracting him from his aim of blowing you up and enabling you to capture him. But if his wife and children are not threatening your life, that would be to treat them as means with a vengeance.

This, however, is just Hiroshima on a smaller scale. One objection to weapons of mass annihilation—nuclear, thermonuclear, biological, or chemical—is that their indiscriminateness disqualifies them as direct instruments for the expression of hostile relations. In attacking the civilian population, one treats neither the military enemy nor the civilians with that minimal respect which is owed to them as human beings. This is clearly true of the direct attack on people who present no threat at all. But it is also true of the character of the attack on those who *are* threatening you, viz., the government and military forces of the enemy. Your aggression is directed against an area of vulnerability quite distinct from any threat presented by them which you may be justified in meeting. You are taking aim at them through the mundane life and survival of their countrymen, instead of aiming at the destruction of their military capacity. And of course it does not require hydrogen bombs to commit such crimes.

This way of looking at the matter also helps us to understand the importance of the distinction between combatants and noncombatants, and the irrelevance of much of the criticism offered against its intelligibility and moral significance. According to an absolutist position, deliberate killing of the innocent is murder, and in warfare the role of the innocent is filled by noncombatants. This has been thought to raise

---

[9] It has been remarked that according to my view, shooting at someone establishes an I-thou relationship.

two sorts of problems: first, the widely imagined difficulty of making a division, in modern warfare, between combatants and noncombatants; second, problems deriving from the connotation of the word "innocence."

Let me take up the latter question first.[10] In the absolutist position, the operative notion of innocence is not moral innocence, and it is not opposed to moral guilt. If it were, then we would be justified in killing a wicked but noncombatant hairdresser in an enemy city who supported the evil policies of his government, and unjustified in killing a morally pure conscript who was driving a tank toward us with the profoundest regrets and nothing but love in his heart. But moral innocence has very little to do with it, for in the definition of murder "innocent" means "currently harmless," and it is opposed not to "guilty" but to "doing harm." It should be noted that such an analysis has the consequence that in war we may often be justified in killing people who do not deserve to die, and unjustified in killing people who do deserve to die, if anyone does.

So we must distinguish combatants from noncombatants on the basis of their immediate threat or harmfulness. I do not claim that the line is a sharp one, but it is not so difficult as is often supposed to place individuals on one side of it or the other. Children are not combatants even though they may join the armed forces if they are allowed to grow up. Women are not combatants just because they bear children or offer comfort to the soldiers. More problematic are the supporting personnel, whether in or out of uniform, from drivers of munitions trucks and army cooks to civilian munitions workers and farmers. I believe they can be plausibly classified by applying the condition that the prosecution of conflict must direct itself to the cause of danger, and not to what is peripheral. The threat presented by an army and its members does not consist merely in the fact that they are men, but in the fact that they are armed and are using their arms in the pursuit of certain objectives. Contributions to their arms and logistics are contributions to this threat; contributions to their mere existence as men are not. It is therefore wrong to direct an attack against those who merely serve the combatants' needs as human beings, such as farmers and food suppliers, even though survival as a human being is a necessary condition of efficient functioning as a soldier.

This brings us to the second group of restrictions: those that limit what may be done even to combatants. These limits are harder to explain clearly. Some of them may be arbitrary or conventional, and some may have to be derived from other sources; but I believe that the condition of directness and relevance in hostile relations accounts for them to a considerable extent.

Consider first a case which involves both a protected class of non-

---

10 What I say on this subject derives from Anscombe.

combatants and a restriction on the measures that may be used against combatants. One provision of the rules of war which is universally recognized, though it seems to be turning into a dead letter in Vietnam, is the special status of medical personnel and the wounded in warfare. It might be more efficient to shoot medical officers on sight and to let the enemy wounded die rather than be patched up to fight another day. But someone with medical insignia is supposed to be left alone and permitted to tend and retrieve the wounded. I believe this is because medical attention is a species of attention to completely general human needs, not specifically the needs of a combat soldier, and our conflict with the soldier is not with his existence as a human being.

By extending the application of this idea, one can justify prohibitions against certain particularly cruel weapons: starvation, poisoning, infectious diseases (supposing they could be inflicted on combatants only), weapons designed to maim or disfigure or torture the opponent rather than merely to stop him. It is not, I think, mere casuistry to claim that such weapons attack the men, not the soldiers. The effect of dum-dum bullets, for example, is much more extended than necessary to cope with the combat situation in which they are used. They abandon any attempt to discriminate in their effects between the combatant and the human being. For this reason the use of flamethrowers and napalm is an atrocity in all circumstances that I can imagine, whoever the target may be. Burns are both extremely painful and extremely disfiguring—far more than any other category of wound. That this well-known fact plays no (inhibiting) part in the determination of U. S. weapons policy suggests that moral sensitivity among public officials has not increased markedly since the Spanish Inquisition.[11]

---

[11] Beyond this I feel uncertain. Ordinary bullets, after all, can cause death, and nothing is more permanent than that. I am not at all sure why we are justified in trying to kill those who are trying to kill us (rather than merely in trying to stop them with force which may also result in their deaths). It is often argued that incapacitating gases are a relatively humane weapon (when not used, as in Vietnam, merely to make people easier to shoot). Perhaps the legitimacy of restrictions against them must depend on the dangers of escalation, and the great utility of maintaining *any* conventional category of restriction so long as nations are willing to adhere to it.

Let me make clear that I do not regard my argument as a defense of the moral immutability of the Hague and Geneva Conventions. Rather, I believe that they rest partly on a moral foundation, and that modifications of them should also be assessed on moral grounds.

But even this connection with the actual laws of war is not essential to my claims about what is permissible and what is not. Since completing this paper I have read an essay by Richard Wasserstrom entitled "The Laws of War" [reprinted in this text] which argues that the existing laws and conventions do not even attempt to embody a decent moral position: that their provisions have been determined by other interests, that they are in fact immoral in substance, and that it is a grave mistake to refer to them as standards in forming moral judgments about warfare. This possibility deserves serious consideration, and I am not sure what to say about it, but it does not affect my view of the moral issues.

Finally, the same condition of appropriateness to the true object of hostility should limit the scope of attacks on an enemy country: its economy, agriculture, transportation system, and so forth. Even if the parties to a military conflict are considered to be not armies or governments but entire nations (which is usually a grave error), that does not justify one nation in warring against every aspect or element of another nation. That is not justified in a conflict between individuals, and nations are even more complex than individuals, so the same reasons apply. Like a human being, a nation is engaged in countless other pursuits while waging war, and it is not in those respects that it is an enemy.

The burden of the argument has been that absolutism about murder has a foundation in principles governing all one's relations to other persons, whether aggressive or amiable, and that these principles, and that absolutism, apply to warfare as well, with the result that certain measures are impermissible no matter what the consequences.[12] I do not mean to romanticize war. It is sufficiently utopian to suggest that when nations conflict they might rise to the level of limited barbarity that typically characterizes violent conflict between individuals, rather than wallowing in the moral pit where they appear to have settled, surrounded by enormous arsenals.

VII

Having described the elements of the absolutist position, we must now return to the conflict between it and utilitarianism. Even if certain types of dirty tactics become acceptable when the stakes are high enough, the most serious of the prohibited acts, like murder and torture, are not just supposed to require unusually strong justification. They are supposed *never* to be done, because no quantity of resulting benefit is thought capable of *justifying* such treatment of a person.

The fact remains that when an absolutist knows or believes that the utilitarian cost of refusing to adopt a prohibited course will be very high, he may hold to his refusal to adopt it, but he will find it difficult to feel that a moral dilemma has been satisfactorily resolved. The same may be true of someone who rejects an absolutist requirement and adopts instead the course yielding the most acceptable consequences. In either case, it is possible to feel that one has acted for reasons insufficient to justify

---

12 It is possible to draw a more radical conclusion, which I shall not pursue here. Perhaps the technology and organization of modern war are such as to make it impossible to wage as an acceptable form of interpersonal or even international hostility. Perhaps it is too impersonal and large-scale for that. If so, then absolutism would in practice imply pacifism, given the present state of things. On the other hand, I am, skeptical about the unstated assumption that a technology dictates its own use.

violation of the opposing principle. In situations of deadly conflict, particularly where a weaker party is threatened with annihilation or enslavement by a stronger one, the argument for resorting to atrocities can be powerful, and the dilemma acute.

There may exist principles, not yet codified, which would enable us to resolve such dilemmas. But then again there may not. We must face the pessimistic alternative that these two forms of moral intuition are not capable of being brought together into a single, coherent moral system, and that the world can present us with situations in which there is no honorable or moral course for a man to take, no course free of guilt and responsibility for evil.

The idea of a moral blind alley is a perfectly intelligible one. It is possible to get into such a situation by one's own fault, and people do it all the time. If, for example, one makes two incompatible promises or commitments—becomes engaged to two people, for example—then there is no course one can take which is not wrong, for one must break one's promise to at least one of them. Making a clean breast of the whole thing will not be enough to remove one's reprehensibility. The existence of such cases is not morally disturbing, however, because we feel that the situation was not unavoidable: one had to do something wrong in the first place to get into it. But what if the world itself, or someone else's actions, could face a previously innocent person with a choice between morally abominable courses of action, and leave him no way to escape with his honor? Our intuitions rebel at the idea, for we feel that the constructibility of such a case must show a contradiction in our moral views. But it is not in itself a contradiction to say that someone can do X or not do X, and that for him to take either course would be wrong. It merely contradicts the supposition that *ought* implies *can*—since presumably one ought to refrain from what is wrong, and in such a case it is impossible to do so.[13] Given the limitations on human action, it is naïve to suppose that there is a solution to every moral problem with which the world can face us. We have always known that the world is a bad place. It appears that it may be an evil place as well.

SELECTED SUPPLEMENTARY READING

ANSCOMBE, G. E. M., "War and Murder," in *Nuclear Weapons: A Catholic Response,* ed. Walter Stein. New York: Sheed and Ward, 1961.
BAIER, KURT, "Guilt and Responsibility," in *Individual and Collective Responsi-*

---

[13] This was first pointed out to me by Christopher Boorse.

bility: The Massacre at My Lai, ed. P. French. Cambridge, Mass.: Schenkman Publishing Company, 1972.

BATES, S., "My Lai and Vietnam: The Issues of Responsibility," in *Individual and Collective Responsibility: The Massacre at My Lai,* ed. P. French. Cambridge, Mass.: Schenkman Publishing Company, 1972.

BEDAU, HUGO ADAM, "Military Service and Moral Obligation," *Inquiry,* 14 (1971). With a "Comment" by S. R. Doss.

BRANDT, R. B., "Utilitarianism and the Rules of War," *Philosophy and Public Affairs,* 1 (1972), 145–65.

CHRISTENSEN, WILLIAM N., and JOHN KING-FARLOW, "Aquinas and the Justification of War," *Thomist,* 35 (1971). (Reply to Wells)

COHEN, CARL, "A Case for Selective Pacifism," *The Nation* (July 8, 1968).

———, "Conscientious Objection," *Ethics,* 78 (1968).

COOPER, DAVID, "Responsibility and the 'System,' " in *Individual and Collective Responsibility: The Massacre at My Lai,* ed. P. French. Cambridge, Mass.: Schenkman Publishing Company, 1972.

DOWNIE, R. S., "Responsibility and Social Roles," in *Individual and Collective Responsibility: The Massacre at My Lai,* ed. P. French. Cambridge, Mass.: Schenkman Publishing Company, 1972.

FAIN, HASKELL, "Some Moral Infirmities of Justice," in *Individual and Collective Responsibility: The Massacre at My Lai,* ed. P. French. Cambridge, Mass.: Schenkman Publishing Company, 1972.

FALK, RICHARD A., *Law, Morality, and War in the Contemporary World.* New York: Praeger, 1963.

GINSBERG, ROBERT, ed., *The Critique of War.* Chicago: Henry Regnery, 1969.

GOTTLIEB, GIDON, "The New International Law, Toward the Legitimation of War," *Ethics,* 78 (1968).

HARE, R. M., "Peace," in *Applications of Moral Philosophy.* Berkeley, Calif.: University of California Press, 1972.

———, "Rules of War and Moral Reasoning," *Philosophy and Public Affairs,* 1 (1972).

HELD, VIRGINIA, "Moral Responsibility and Collective Action," in *Individual and Collective Responsibility: The Massacre at My Lai,* ed. P. French. Cambridge, Mass.: Schenkman Publishing Company, 1972.

HOLMES, ROBERT L., "On Pacifism," *The Monist,* 57 (1973).

LEVINSON, SANFORD, "Responsibility for Crimes of War," *Philosophy and Public Affairs,* 2 (1973), 244–73.

LEWIS, H. D., "The Non-moral Notion of Collective Responsibility," in *Individual and Collective Responsibility: The Massacre at My Lai,* ed. P. French. Cambridge, Mass.: Schenkman Publishing Company, 1972.

LEWY, G., "Superior Orders, Nuclear Warfare, and the Dictates of Conscience," *The American Political Science Review,* 55 (1961). Reprinted in Wasserstrom.

O'CONNOR, D. T., "A Reappraisal of the Just-War Tradition," *Ethics,* 84 (1974).

"Philosophy of War," *The Monist,* 57 (October 1973). (Entire issue)

RAMSEY, PAUL, *The Just War.* New York: Scribner's, 1968.

RAWLS, JOHN, *A Theory of Justice*. Cambridge, Mass.: Harvard University Press, 1972, esp. pp. 368–82.

SCHILLER, MARVIN, "Military Service and Moral Obligation," *Canadian Journal of Philosophy*, 1 (1972).

SINGER, PETER, "Conscientious Objection," in *Democracy and Disobedience*. Oxford: Clarendon Press, 1973.

STRUCKMEYER, FREDERICK R., "The 'Just War' and the Right of Self-Defense," *Ethics*, 82 (1971), 48–55.

TAYLOR, TELFORD, *Nuremberg and Vietnam: An American Tragedy*. Chicago: Quadrangle Books, 1971.

WALZER, MICHAEL, "Moral Judgment in War," *Dissent*, 14, No. 3 (1967).

———, *Obligations: Essays on Disobedience, War, and Citizenship*, Part II. Cambridge, Mass.: Harvard University Press, 1970.

———, "World War II: Why Was This War Different?" *Philosophy and Public Affairs*, 1 (1971).

WASSERSTROM, RICHARD, "On the Morality of War: A Preliminary Inquiry," *Stanford Law Review*, 21 (1969), 1626–56. Abridged in R. Wasserstrom, ed., *War and Morality*. Belmont, Calif.: Wadsworth Publishing Company, Inc., 1970.

———, "The Relevance of Nuremberg," *Philosophy and Public Affairs*, 1 (1971).

———, "Review of Taylor's *Nuremberg and Vietnam: An American Tragedy*," *The New York Review of Books*, 3 (1971).

———, "Three Arguments Concerning the Morality of War," *Journal of Philosophy*, 65 (1968).

———, ed., *War and Morality*. Belmont, Calif.: Wadsworth Publishing Company, Inc., 1970.

WELLS, DONALD A., *The War Myth*. New York: Pegasus, 1967.

———, "What Does the Conviction of Calley Imply?" *Journal of Social Philosophy*, 2 (1971).

Chapter **5**

MORAL ENFORCEMENT

INTRODUCTION

The successful functioning of a heterogeneous mass of people collected together in a single state depends upon some systematic ordering of human affairs. That ordering process, when formalized and codified, becomes a system of laws. Ideally laws exist to protect people and society, most obviously from physical abuse, but from psychic and emotional abuse as well. Presumably, then, laws function to safeguard individual and societal rights and liberties. But the law has two sides. By ensuring liberty to one set of persons, the law may restrict the liberty of others. A law by its very function places a limit on what was formerly a free exercise or action. The acceptability of such limitation depends upon its justifiability, and when an adequate justification is not forthcoming, the law can easily become an instrument of oppression. Despite this danger, no one, save perhaps an anarchist, would deny that *some* laws should exist which restrict certain types of behavior. But which sorts of activities and which types of behavior are appropriate for legal restriction? In what instances does insurance of the rights of individuals require that restrictions be placed on the freedoms of others?

In this chapter we address the specific question whether, and if so, to what extent, the law should be designed as a safeguard against the destruction of a society's cherished moral beliefs, especially its sexual codes. The question is whether in a pluralistic society deviant moral conduct of any sort, however serious and controversial, is sufficient justification for limiting freedom by making such behavior illegal. This issue is especially troublesome when the sexual acts involved are widely regarded in the society as sexual perversions, and yet are also purely private affairs involving only consenting adults. Homosexuality is the most frequently mentioned example, but the ethical problems involving sanctions on sexual activity extend far beyond this one case.

Crimes Without Victims

In considering how laws should function with reference to moral questions, especially those focused on sexual conduct, it is useful to distinguish between (1) crimes in which there is no victim because no person is directly harmed and everyone involved voluntarily consents, and (2) crimes in which there is a victim. Prostitution, homosexuality, gambling, smoking marijuana, and sexual stimulation in "massage parlors" are now familiar examples of crimes without victims. Rape—whether heterosexual or homosexual—is clearly a crime that does have a victim. The ethical issue is whether crimes without victims should be considered crimes at all.* Perhaps legal restrictions on homosexuality, for example, constitute unwarranted restrictions of liberty. It may be that even if the citizens of a state consider homosexual acts perverse, society should nonetheless allow individuals the personal freedom to engage in homosexual relations (and perhaps even marriage) between consenting adults, in the same way it allows such relations between heterosexual partners.

It is not because they are thought to harm citizens that crimes without victims are usually made illegal, but rather because they are thought to be inherently degrading, evil, or perverse. For this reason, states that legislate against such acts seem to become straightforwardly involved in the enforcement of morals—that is, in ensuring the maintenance of a community's moral standards. If such restriction of individual freedom is to be allowed, it clearly should be limited to those situations involving extremely serious matters. Though it has never been made clear what is to count as such a serious matter, questions of the advisability and ethical

---

* There may, of course, be *indirect* victims of crimes that themselves do not have victims. If gambling houses force families below the poverty level and to a shortage of nourishing food, the children are indirect victims. It is also arguable that some participants—e.g., prostitutes—*are* direct victims in an ethically significant sense.

permissibility of legal enforcement have arisen over a wide range of sensitive issues. All activities involving the following actions—which are not limited to matters of sexual morality—have been considered candidates for legislation:

1. Private use of pornographic films
2. Private use of drugs
3. Voluntary euthanasia
4. Voluntary psychosurgery
5. Gambling
6. Suicide
7. Cruelty to and experimentation on animals

It is imperative in a society which espouses the fair and nonoppressive rule of law that anyone seeking prohibitions on free moral choices provide adequate justification for substantial restrictions of individual freedoms. One must be able to advance some justification for legislating against certain private acts and not against other private acts that are similarly private, even if not identical in nature.

Historical Landmarks: Mill and the Wolfenden Committee

Although many ethical philosophers have been concerned with questions about the legal enforcement of morals, John Stuart Mill's monograph *On Liberty* (1859) has occupied and continues to occupy an especially prominent position. Mill inquired after the nature and limits of social control over the individual. The following passage is Mill's own summary of his central theses:

> The object of this Essay is to assert one very simple principle. . . . That principle is, that the sole end for which mankind are warranted, individually or collectively, in interfering with the liberty of action of any of their number, is self-protection. That the only purpose for which power can be rightfully exercised over any member of a civilized community, against his will, is to prevent harm to others. His own good, either physical or moral, is not a sufficient warrant. He cannot rightfully be compelled to do or forbear because it will be better for him to do so, because it will make him happier, because in the opinion of others, to do so would be wise, or even right. These are good reasons for remonstrating with him, or reasoning with him or persuading him, or entreating him, but not for compelling him, or visiting him with any evil in case he do otherwise. To justify that, the conduct from which it is desired to deter him must be calculated to produce evil to someone else. The only part of the conduct of anyone, for which he is amenable to society, is that which

concerns others. In the part which merely concerns himself, his independence is, of right, absolute.

Mill supposed he had articulated a general ethical principle which properly restricted social control over private morality, regardless of whether such control is legal, religious, economic, or of some other type. Mill defended his views with the utilitarian argument that such a principle, however dangerous to prevailing social beliefs, would produce the best possible conditions both for social progress and for the development of individual talents. Though widely disputed his views have been enormously influential.

Since Mill, many attempts either to enforce morals or to eliminate existing enforcements have been made, but one attempt has become the classic case. In 1957 a report was produced in England by the Wolfenden Committee. This committee had been established in 1954 in response to complaints that aspects of English law dealing with homosexuality and prostitution were ineffective and unjust. The committee recommended both that English criminal law be amended so that homosexuality not be a crime, if engaged in by consenting adults, and that there be no change in existing laws which did not hold acts of prostitution intrinsically illegal. Their recommendations at several points read as if they were an application of Mill's general political-social theory. The committee first argued that firm distinctions should be drawn between crime and sin and between public decency and private morality. They then maintained that while the law must govern matters of public decency, private morality is not a matter to be legislated since "the function of the criminal law" is "to preserve public order and decency, to protect the citizen from what is offensive or injurious, and to provide sufficient safeguards against exploitation and corruption of others." They further maintained that it should not be considered the purpose of the law "to intervene in the private lives of citizens, or to seek to enforce any pattern of behavior" unless the purposes of the law outlined above were shown relevant.

The clear intent of the committee was to say that unless it could be shown that public indecency or personal exploitation were involved, the law should not prohibit activities such as homosexuality and prostitution. Their justification for this recommendation, which is both legal and ethical in character, was simply that the state does not and should not have the right to restrict any private moral actions which affect only the consenting adults involved. The state should not have this right, they argued, because of the supreme importance both social ethics and the law place on "individual freedom of choice and action in matters of private morality . . . which is, in brief and crude terms, not the law's business."

As we shall see in some detail, Lord Patrick Devlin is the most prominent spokesman in opposition to both Mill and the Wolfenden Report. His article, reprinted here, is in many respects another historical landmark.

Major and Minor Issues Concerning Moral Enforcement

In their struggle to provide rationally acceptable justifications for regulating or not regulating certain areas of moral conduct, ethicists have taken different positions on several fundamental issues. There is one major issue and several important minor issues. The major issue, as by now should be evident, is whether the immorality of any human action ever can, solely because *immoral*, provide a sufficient justification for making that type of action illegal. More briefly, is it justifiable for the law to be used as a means for enforcing moral beliefs? Three positions have typically been defended on this issue, the first unfavorable to enforcement, the other two favorable.

1. *Arguments from the Principle of Individual Liberty.* The first argument springs from Mill's principle that state coercion is never permissible unless an individual's actions produce harm to others (the principle of individual liberty). This principle requires tolerance of all ethical perspectives, it is argued, and is not in the slightest in conflict with principles that require legal protection from harmful acts. Although there are several forms of this argument, the thrust of the contentions may be represented as follows: Any attempt to make immoral conduct illegal (criminal), when the conduct is not harmful to others, is unacceptable because it directly violates the principle of individual liberty. But suppose the conduct is harmful. If one is to be justifiably punished under law it must be because one's action harms someone else, not because a particular moral practice is involved. That any particular moral belief or practice is involved should be an irrelevant factor, so far as the law is concerned. One should not be punished, in other words, because one engages in an immoral act A, though one may be punishable because he harmed someone in an illegal way by engaging in A. According to this argument, the law should never be based on the view that a certain moral perspective is intolerable, but rather should be based on the view that harmful treatment is always intolerable. Though he never quite phrases his point this way, Mill seems generally to support this line of thought. This also seems to be one argument used in the Wolfenden Report, where it is said that "there must remain a realm of private morality and immorality" which is outside the province of law.

2. *Arguments from the Principle of Democratic Rule.* Here the argument is made that if some practice is regarded as an outrageously immoral action by the vast majority of citizens in a community, this in

itself is sufficient to justify making the behavior illegal. It is maintained that both the principle of democratic rule and the institution of morality must be protected even at the expense of a risk to individual liberties. In democracies it is the weight of community sentiment that makes the law, and laws provide the standards of justice. Any majority-sanctioned law is valid and appropriate, unless unconstitutional. There is no tradition in Western democracies, ethical or legal, which stipulates that morality cannot be legislated against. For these reasons the supporters of this view conclude that a society is perfectly justified in protecting itself by legislating against at least some immoral actions. Lord Devlin pays tribute, if not full allegiance, to this view when he concludes that: (1) a society is partially constituted by a "community of ideas," including moral ideas "about the way its members *should* behave and govern their lives"; and (2) if homosexuality is "a vice so abominable that its mere presence is an offense. . . . I do not see how society can be denied the right to eradicate it."

3. *Arguments from the Social Necessity of Morality.* Some authors have argued that the legal enforcement of morals is justified whenever threats to moral rules challenge the very order of society itself. The argument is that just as law and order through government are necessary to a stable society, so moral conformity is essential to a society's very continuation. Sometimes the justification seems to be purely pragmatic ("If you want to survive as a society, then you must preserve your moral canons"), while at other times it seems to be an argument from society's inherent right to protect its existence. In either view, individual liberties are said to be protected when, but only when, they do *not* erode those standards essential to the life of society. All supporters of this view agree that we ought to be cautious in declaring a practice intolerably immoral. But the point remains, they insist, that we have the *right* to pass criminal laws enforcing morality if they be required. Lord Devlin again pays allegiance to this view when he argues that "society may use the law to preserve morality in the same way as it uses it to safeguard *anything* else that is essential to its existence."

Supplementing this major issue are several minor but fundamental questions. Philosophers have given a wide variety of answers to these questions, and these answers have in turn contributed to the development of positions on the major issue. Among the important minor questions are the following: (1) How are we to explicate the notion of an action that is *harmful to others*? This key expression is often used to delineate the types of conduct that have public impact, yet its analysis is notoriously difficult. (2) What is meant by the expressions "sexual morality" and "sexual perversion"? If one assumes that, by the very meaning of the term "perversion," all perversions are to be condemned, one is more likely to seek their eradication than if one takes the word to be purely descriptive and classificatory, and hence without negative moral connotations. (3) How are we to distinguish, if it be possible, between the realm of private morality (or private affairs) and the realm of public morality (or public affairs)? (4) Are practices such as homosexuality and prostitution fairly categorized as crimes *without* victims? (5) Since any human community is constituted by a diverse group of individuals, how are we to decide what the prevailing ethical standards of the community are? One possible answer to this question is that there is no such thing as a community standard which is ethical; the *only* community standards are legal. (6) Can a society's sexual code be properly considered part of its morality, or are the two significantly different? (7) What is morality? This surprisingly complex question has provoked several answers which substantively affect treatment of the major issue.

Arguments in the Selections

Lord Patrick Devlin, in the opening essay in this chapter, opposes the report of the Wolfenden Committee. Long the most prominent spokesman for the enforcement of morals, Devlin argues that society has the right to enforce "public morality" because society cannot exist, or at least remain secure, without preserving a basic community of moral ideas which determine how citizens are to control their lives. The community's common moral convictions concerning behavior constitute, for Devlin, its "moral structure." He allows that society must tolerate "the maximum individual freedom that is consistent with the integrity of society." But he also maintains that society is justified, as a matter of principle, in legislating against privately conducted immoral conduct *if* that conduct is of the sort likely to be injurious to society by endangering the moral order necessary for its preservation. Adultery, for example, cannot be tolerated because it would undermine the institution of marriage, which Devlin takes to be indispensable for the stability of society. He also contends that homosexuality and prostitution undermine the moral fabric of society. Each can quite properly be legislated against, he argues, because the integrity and very existence of society is threatened if such laws do not exist.

H. L. A. Hart has been Devlin's leading critic, as well as a selective defender of both Mill and the Wolfenden Report. He argues that a heavy burden of justification, including empirical evidence of likely social disintegration, is required for legislation against acts such as homosexuality. Hart regards Devlin's conclusion that the fabric of society is endangered as insufficiently argued. He thinks that—like some conclusions reached by recent sociologists—Devlin's contention is merely a disguised conservative defense of the conventional moral order. Hart further contends that it attempts to sweep all legal restrictions against allegedly immoral practices (for example, bigamy, killings, and dishonesty) under the same rug, as if there were no morally relevant difference between them and as if morality were a single, indivisible whole without separate justifications for its separate principles. Although Hart is willing to agree with Devlin that the loss of certain shared moral principles might well threaten the very existence of society, he argues that there is no empirical evidence to indicate that the practices of sexual deviants lead to a disintegration of common morality. Hart concludes that any defense of moral enforcement would do better to rely on a candid conservatism (an evaluative position) than on a disintegration thesis (an empirical position).

Ernest Nagel, in a discussion of the main issues in the Devlin-Hart debate, tries both to clarify the issues and to show several deficiencies in the individual arguments presented by Mill, by Devlin, and by Hart. He then discusses whether there is a realm of conduct which, irrespective of its relation to morality, falls outside the legitimate boundaries of the law. In a cautious statement he argues that there can be no satisfactory *general* answer to this question, because the principles involved (for example, "the domain of personal freedom should be diminished as little as possible") are too vague to be shown explicitly applicable in all cases, and because the compromises which must be effected are subject to all too many diverse interests and shifting conditions. He concludes that each case, including changes in laws regulating sexual activity, must be considered on its own merits.

Joel Feinberg places these discussions in a somewhat wider framework in the final selection. He begins by considering two typical charges against Mill: (1) that his justification of coercion allows *too much* interference in individual affairs; and (2) that it allows *too little* interference and is only one among other proper justifications. Feinberg attempts to arbitrate these disputes and suggests a flexible form of moral reasoning that is similar to "the reasonings that are prevalent in law courts." He then draws an important distinction between immoral conduct that is socially harmful and immoral conduct that is not socially harmful. He sees "the problem of the enforcement of morality" as applying only to the latter, since the former could properly be legislated against simply on the grounds that it is harmful. He contends that the central problem cases rest with so-called offenses against morality and decency ranging from sexual offenses to cruelty to animals. These cases are difficult because of their nonpublic character—that is, because there is a lack of any clear connection between them and social harm.

Feinberg first treats morals offenses as essentially private. He discusses certain hard cases for this principle, including an animal cruelty case intended to challenge our intuition that private behavior should not be legislated against. He then turns to morals offenses that are not essentially private—or at least not clearly so—such as obscene literature and pornographic displays which are deliberately published for "the eyes of others." Feinberg argues that even the most dedicated and reluctant liberal will be tempted in a limited range of cases to legislate against freedom of expression not simply on the basis of *harm* to others but on the basis of *offensiveness*. (The "Offense Principle," then, will be used to supplement the "Harm Principle.") However, Feinberg concludes that he sees no convincing reasons, on this basis, for the suppression of obscene literature.

Morals and the Criminal Law *

Patrick Devlin

I think it is clear that the criminal law as we know it is based upon moral principle. In a number of crimes its function is simply to enforce a moral principle and nothing else. The law, both criminal and civil, claims to be able to speak about morality and immorality generally. Where does it get its authority to do this and how does it settle the moral principles which it enforces? Undoubtedly, as a matter of history, it derived both from Christian teaching. But I think that the strict logician is right when he says that the law can no longer rely on doctrines in which citizens are entitled to disbelieve. It is necessary therefore to look for some other source.

In jurisprudence . . . everything is thrown open to discussion and, in the belief that they cover the whole field, I have framed three interrogatories addressed to myself to answer:

1. Has society the right to pass judgement at all on matters of morals? Ought there, in other words, to be a public morality, or are morals always a matter for private judgement?
2. If society has the right to pass judgement, has it also the right to use the weapon of the law to enforce it?

---

* From *The Enforcement of Morals* by Lord Devlin. © Oxford University Press 1965. Reprinted by permission of the publishers.

3. If so, ought it to use that weapon in all cases or only in some; and if only in some, on what principles should it distinguish?

[1]* I shall begin with the first interrogatory and consider what is meant by the right of society to pass a moral judgement, that is, a judgement about what is good and what is evil. The fact that a majority of people may disapprove of a practice does not of itself make it a matter for society as a whole. Nine men out of ten may disapprove of what the tenth man is doing and still say that it is not their business. There is a case for a collective judgement (as distinct from a large number of individual opinions which sensible people may even refrain from pronouncing at all if it is upon somebody else's private affairs) only if society is affected. Without a collective judgement there can be no case at all for intervention. Let me take as an illustration the Englishman's attitude to religion as it is now and as it has been in the past. His attitude now is that a man's religion is his private affair; he may think of another man's religion that it is right or wrong, true or untrue, but not that it is good or bad. In earlier times that was not so; a man was denied the right to practise what was thought of as heresy, and heresy was thought of as destructive of society.

The language [in] . . . the Wolfenden Report suggests the view that there ought not to be a collective judgement about immorality *per se*. Is this what is meant by 'private morality' and 'individual freedom of choice and action'? Some people sincerely believe that homosexuality is neither immoral nor unnatural. Is the 'freedom of choice and action' that is offered to the individual, freedom to decide for himself what is moral or immoral, society remaining neutral; or is it freedom to be immoral if he wants to be? The language of the Report may be open to question, but the conclusions at which the Committee arrive answer this question unambiguously. If society is not prepared to say that homosexuality is morally wrong, there would be no basis for a law protecting youth from 'corruption' or punishing a man for living on the 'immoral' earnings of a homosexual prostitute, as the Report recommends.[1] This attitude the Committee make even clearer when they come to deal with prostitution. In truth, the Report takes it for granted that there is in existence a public morality which condemns homosexuality and prostitution. What the Report seems to mean by private morality might perhaps be better described as private behaviour in matters of morals.

This view—that there is such a thing as public morality—can also be justified by *a priori* argument. What makes a society of any sort is community of ideas, not only political ideas but also ideas about the way its

---

* Insertions in brackets are additions to the original text. Ed.
[1] Para. 76.

members should behave and govern their lives; these latter ideas are its morals. Every society has a moral structure as well as a political one: or rather, since that might suggest two independent systems, I should say that the structure of every society is made up both of politics and morals. Take, for example, the institution of marriage. Whether a man should be allowed to take more than one wife is something about which every society has to make up its mind one way or the other. In England we believe in the Christian idea of marriage and therefore adopt monogamy as a moral principle. Consequently the Christian institution of marriage has become the basis of family life and so part of the structure of our society. It is there not because it is Christian. It has got there because it is Christian, but it remains there because it is built into the house in which we live and could not be removed without bringing it down. The great majority of those who live in this country accept it because it is the Christian idea of marriage and for them the only true one. But a non-Christian is bound by it, not because it is part of Christianity but because, rightly or wrongly, it has been adopted by the society in which he lives. It would be useless for him to stage a debate designed to prove that polygamy was theologically more correct and socially preferable; if he wants to live in the house, he must accept it as built in the way in which it is.

We see this more clearly if we think of ideas or institutions that are purely political. Society cannot tolerate rebellion; it will not allow argument about the rightness of the cause. Historians a century later may say that the rebels were right and the Government was wrong and a percipient and conscientious subject of the State may think so at the time. But it is not a matter which can be left to individual judgement.

The institution of marriage is a good example for my purpose because it bridges the division, if there is one, between politics and morals. Marriage is part of the structure of our society and it is also the basis of a moral code which condemns fornication and adultery. The institution of marriage would be gravely threatened if individual judgements were permitted about the morality of adultery; on these points there must be a public morality. But public morality is not to be confined to those moral principles which support institutions such as marriage. People do not think of monogamy as something which has to be supported because our society has chosen to organize itself upon it; they think of it as something that is good in itself and offering a good way of life and that it is for that reason that our society has adopted it. I return to the statement that I have already made, that society means a community of ideas; without shared ideas on politics, morals, and ethics no society can exist. Each one of us has ideas about what is good and what is evil; they cannot be kept private from the society in which we live. If men and women try to create a society in which there is no fundamental agreement about good and evil they will fail; if, having based it on common agreement, the agreement goes, the society will disintegrate. For society is not something that is kept together physically; it is held by the invisible bonds of common thought. If the bonds were too far relaxed the members would drift apart. A common morality is part of the bondage. The bondage is part of the price of society; and mankind, which needs society, must pay its price.

Common lawyers used to say that Christianity was part of the law of the land. That was never more than a piece of rhetoric as Lord Sumner said in *Bowman* v. *The Secular Society*.[2] What lay behind it was the notion which I have been seeking to expound, namely that morals—and up till a century or so ago no one thought it worth distinguishing between religion and morals—were necessary to the temporal order. In 1675 Chief Justice Hale said: 'To say that religion is a cheat is to dissolve all those obligations whereby civil society is preserved.'[3] In 1797 Mr. Justice Ashurst said of blasphemy that it was 'not only an offence against God but against all law and government from its tendency to dissolve all the bonds and obligations of civil society.'[4] By 1908 Mr. Justice Phillimore was able to say: 'A man is free to think, to speak and to teach what he pleases as to religious matters, but not as to morals.'[5]

[2] You may think that I have taken far too long in contending that there is such a thing as public morality, a proposition which most people would readily accept, and may have left myself too little time to discuss the next question which to many minds may cause greater difficulty: to what extent should society use the law to enforce its moral judgements? But I believe that the answer to the first question determines the way in which the second should be approached and may indeed very nearly dictate the answer to the second question. If society has no right to make judgements on morals, the law must find some special justification for entering the field of morality: if homosexuality and prostitution are not in themselves wrong, then the onus is very clearly on the lawgiver who wants to frame a law against certain aspects of them to justify the exceptional treatment. But if society has the right to make a judgement and has it on the basis that a recognized morality is as necessary to society as, say, a recognized government, then society may use the law to preserve morality in the same way as it uses it to safeguard anything else that is essential to its existence. If therefore the first proposition is securely established with all its implications, society has a prima facie right to legislate against immorality as such.

---

[2] (1917), A.C. 406, at 457.
[3] *Taylor's Case*, 1 Vent. 293.
[4] *R.* v. *Williams*, 26 St. Tr. 653, at 715.
[5] *R.* v. *Boulter*, 72 J.P. 188.

The Wolfenden Report, notwithstanding that it seems to admit the right of society to condemn homosexuality and prostitution as immoral, requires special circumstances to be shown to justify the intervention of the law. I think that this is wrong in principle and that any attempt to approach my second interrogatory on these lines is bound to break down. I think that the attempt by the Committee does break down and that this is shown by the fact that it has to define or describe its special circumstances so widely that they can be supported only if it is accepted that the law is concerned with immorality as such.

The widest of the special circumstances are described as the provision of 'sufficient safeguards against exploitation and corruption of others, particularly those who are specially vulnerable because they are young, weak in body or mind, inexperienced, or in a state of special physical, official or economic dependence.' [6] The corruption of youth is a well-recognized ground for intervention by the State and for the purpose of any legislation the young can easily be defined. But if similar protection were to be extended to every other citizen, there would be no limit to the reach of the law. The 'corruption and exploitation of others' is so wide that it could be used to cover any sort of immorality which involves, as most do, the co-operation of another person. Even if the phrase is taken as limited to the categories that are particularized as 'specially vulnerable,' it is so elastic as to be practically no restriction. This is not merely a matter of words. For if the words used are stretched almost beyond breaking-point, they still are not wide enough to cover the recommendations which the Committee make about prostitution.

Prostitution is not in itself illegal and the Committee do not think that it ought to be made so.[7] If prostitution is private immorality and not the law's business, what concern has the law with the ponce or the brothel-keeper or the householder who permits habitual prostitution? The Report recommends that the laws which make these activities criminal offences should be maintained or strengthened and brings them (so far as it goes into principle; with regard to brothels it says simply that the law rightly frowns on them) under the head of exploitation.[8] There may be cases of exploitation in this trade, as there are or used to be in many others, but in general a ponce exploits a prostitute no more than an impresario exploits an actress. The Report finds that 'the great majority of prostitutes are women whose psychological makeup is such that they choose this life because they find in it a style of living which is to them easier, freer and more profitable than would be provided by any other occupation. . . .

---

[6] Para. 13.
[7] Paras. 224, 285, and 318.
[8] Paras. 302 and 320.

In the main the association between prostitute and ponce is voluntary and operates to mutual advantage.' [9] The Committee would agree that this could not be called exploitation in the ordinary sense. They say: 'It is in our view an oversimplification to think that those who live on the earnings of prostitution are exploiting the prostitute as such. What they are really exploiting is the whole complex of the relationship between prostitute and customer; they are, in effect, exploiting the human weaknesses which cause the customer to seek the prostitute and the prostitute to meet the demand.' [10]

All sexual immorality involves the exploitation of human weaknesses. The prostitute exploits the lust of her customers and the customer the moral weakness of the prostitute. If the exploitation of human weaknesses is considered to create a special circumstance, there is virtually no field of morality which can be defined in such a way as to exclude the law.

I think, therefore, that it is not possible to set theoretical limits to the power of the State to legislate against immorality. It is not possible to settle in advance exceptions to the general rule or to define inflexibly areas of morality into which the law is in no circumstances to be allowed to enter. Society is entitled by means of its laws to protect itself from dangers, whether from within or without. Here again I think that the political parallel is legitimate. The law of treason is directed against aiding the king's enemies and against sedition from within. The justification for this is that established government is necessary for the existence of society and therefore its safety against violent overthrow must be secured. But an established morality is as necessary as good government to the welfare of society. Societies disintegrate from within more frequently than they are broken up by external pressures. There is disintegration when no common morality is observed and history shows that the loosening of moral bonds is often the first stage of disintegration, so that society is justified in taking the same steps to preserve its moral code as it does to preserve its government and other essential institutions.[11] The suppression

---

[9] Para. 223.

[10] Para. 306.

[11] It is somewhere about this point in the argument that Professor Hart in *Law, Liberty and Morality* discerns a proposition which he describes as central to my thought. He states the proposition and his objection to it as follows (p. 51). 'He appears to move from the acceptable proposition that *some* shared morality is essential to the existence of any society [this I take to be the proposition on p. 12] to the unacceptable proposition that a society is identical with its morality as that is at any given moment of its history, so that a change in its morality is tantamount to the destruction of a society. The former proposition might be even accepted as a necessary rather than an empirical truth depending on a quite plausible definition of society as a body of men who hold certain moral views in common. But the latter proposition is absurd. Taken strictly, it would prevent us saying that the morality of a given society had changed, and would compel us instead to say that one society had dis-

of vice is as much the law's business as the suppression of subversive activities; it is no more possible to define a sphere of private morality than it is to define one of private subversive activity. It is wrong to talk of private morality or of the law not being concerned with immorality as such or to try to set rigid bounds to the part which the law may play in the suppression of vice. There are no theoretical limits to the power of the State to legislate against treason and sedition, and likewise I think there can be no theoretical limits to legislation against immorality. You may argue that if a man's sins affect only himself it cannot be the concern of society. If he chooses to get drunk every night in the privacy of his own home, is any one except himself the worse for it? But suppose a quarter or a half of the population got drunk every night, what sort of society would it be? You cannot set a theoretical limit to the number of people who can get drunk before society is entitled to legislate against drunkenness. The same may be said of gambling. The Royal Commission on Betting, Lotteries, and Gaming took as their test the character of the citizen

---

appeared and another one taken its place. But it is only on this absurd criterion of what it is for the same society to continue to exist that it could be asserted without evidence that any deviation from a society's shared morality threatens its existence.' In conclusion (p. 82) Professor Hart condemns the whole thesis in the lecture as based on 'a confused definition of what a society is'.

I do not assert that *any* deviation from a society's shared morality threatens its existence any more than I assert that *any* subversive activity threatens its existence. I assert that they are both activities which are capable in their nature of threatening the existence of society so that neither can be put beyond the law.

For the rest, the objection appears to me to be all a matter of words. I would venture to assert, for example, that you cannot have a game without rules and that if there were no rules there would be no game. If I am asked whether that means that the game is 'identical' with the rules, I would be willing for the question to be answered either way in the belief that the answer would lead to nowhere. If I am asked whether a change in the rules means that one game has disappeared and another has taken its place, I would reply probably not, but that it would depend on the extent of the change.

Likewise I should venture to assert that there cannot be a contract without terms. Does this mean that an 'amended' contract is a 'new' contract in the eyes of the law? I once listened to an argument by an ingenious counsel that a contract, because of the substitution of one clause for another, had 'ceased to have effect' within the meaning of a statutory provision. The judge did not accept the argument; but if most of the fundamental terms had been changed, I daresay he would have done.

The proposition that I make in the text is that if (as I understand Professor Hart to agree, at any rate for the purposes of the argument) you cannot have a society without morality, the law can be used to enforce morality as something that is essential to a society. I cannot see why this proposition (whether it is right or wrong) should mean that morality can never be changed without the destruction of society. If morality is changed, the law can be changed. Professor Hart refers (p. 72) to the proposition as 'the use of legal punishment to freeze into immobility the morality dominant at a particular time in a society's existence'. One might as well say that the inclusion of a penal section into a statute prohibiting certain acts freezes the whole statute into immobility and prevents the prohibitions from ever being modified.

These points are elaborated in the sixth lecture at pp. 115–16.

as a member of society. They said: 'Our concern with the ethical significance of gambling is confined to the effect which it may have on the
character of the gambler as a member of society. If we were convinced
that whatever the degree of gambling this effect must be harmful we
should be inclined to think that it was the duty of the state to restrict
gambling to the greatest extent practicable.' [12]

[3] In what circumstances the State should exercise its power is the
third of the interrogatories I have framed. But before I get to it I must
raise a point which might have been brought up in any one of the three.
How are the moral judgements of society to be ascertained? By leaving
it until now, I can ask it in the more limited form that is now sufficient
for my purpose. How is the law-maker to ascertain the moral judgements of society? It is surely not enough that they should be reached by
the opinion of the majority; it would be too much to require the individual assent of every citizen. English law has evolved and regularly
uses a standard which does not depend on the counting of heads. It is
that of the reasonable man. He is not to be confused with the rational
man. He is not expected to reason about anything and his judgment may
be largely a matter of feeling. It is the viewpoint of the man in the street
—or to use an archaism familiar to all lawyers—the man in the Clapham
omnibus. He might also be called the right-minded man. For my purpose I should like to call him the man in the jury box, for the moral
judgement of society must be something about which any twelve men or
women drawn at random might after discussion be expected to be unanimous. This was the standard the judges applied in the days before Parliament was as active as it is now and when they laid down rules of public
policy. They did not think of themselves as making law but simply as
stating principles which every right-minded person would accept as
valid. It is what Pollock called 'practical morality', which is based not on
theological or philosophical foundations but 'in the mass of continuous
experience half-consciously or unconsciously accumulated and embodied
in the morality of common sense'. He called it also 'a certain way of
thinking on questions of morality which we expect to find in a reasonable
civilized man or a reasonable Englishman, taken at random.' [13]

Immorality then, for the purpose of the law, is what every right-
minded person is presumed to consider to be immoral. Any immorality
is capable of affecting society injuriously and in effect to a greater or
lesser extent it usually does; this is what gives the law its *locus standi*.
It cannot be shut out. But—and this brings me to the third question—
the individual has a *locus standi* too; he cannot be expected to surrender

---

[12] (1951) Cmd. 8190, para. 159.
[13] *Essays in Jurisprudence and Ethics* (1882), Macmillan, pp. 278 and 353.

to the judgement of society the whole conduct of his life. It is the old and familiar question of striking a balance between the rights and interests of society and those of the individual. This is something which the law is constantly doing in matters large and small. To take a very down-to-earth example, let me consider the right of the individual whose house adjoins the highway to have access to it; that means in these days the right to have vehicles stationary in the highway, sometimes for a considerable time if there is a lot of loading or unloading. There are many cases in which the courts have had to balance the private right of access against the public right to use the highway without obstruction. It cannot be done by carving up the highway into public and private areas. It is done by recognizing that each have rights over the whole; that if each were to exercise their rights to the full, they would come into conflict; and therefore that the rights of each must be curtailed so as to ensure as far as possible that the essential needs of each are safeguarded.

I do not think that one can talk sensibly of a public and private morality any more than one can of a public or private highway. Morality is a sphere in which there is a public interest and a private interest, often in conflict, and the problem is to reconcile the two. This does not mean that it is impossible to put forward any general statements about how in our society the balance ought to be struck. Such statements cannot of their nature be rigid or precise; they would not be designed to circumscribe the operation of the law-making power but to guide those who have to apply it. While every decision which a court of law makes when it balances the public against the private interest is an *ad hoc* decision, the cases contain statements of principle to which the court should have regard when it reaches its decision. In the same way it is possible to make general statements of principle which it may be thought the legislature should bear in mind when it is considering the enactment of laws enforcing morals.

I believe that most people would agree upon the chief of these elastic principles. There must be toleration of the maximum individual freedom that is consistent with the integrity of society. It cannot be said that this is a principle that runs all through the criminal law. Much of the criminal law that is regulatory in character—the part of it that deals with *malum prohibitum* rather than *malum in se*—is based upon the opposite principle, that is, that the choice of the individual must give way to the convenience of the many. But in all matters of conscience the principle I have stated is generally held to prevail. It is not confined to thought and speech; it extends to action, as is shown by the recognition of the right to conscientious objection in war-time; this example shows also that conscience will be respected even in times of national danger. The principle appears to me to be peculiarly appropriate to all questions of morals.

Nothing should be punished by the law that does not lie beyond the limits of tolerance. It is not nearly enough to say that a majority dislike a practice; there must be a real feeling of reprobation. Those who are dissatisfied with the present law on homosexuality often say that the opponents of reform are swayed simply by disgust. If that were so it would be wrong, but I do not think one can ignore disgust if it is deeply felt and not manufactured. Its presence is a good indication that the bounds of toleration are being reached. Not everything is to be tolerated. No society can do without intolerance, indignation, and disgust;[14] they are the forces behind the moral law, and indeed it can be argued that if they or something like them are not present, the feelings of society cannot be weighty enough to deprive the individuals of freedom of choice. I suppose that there is hardly anyone nowadays who would not be disgusted by the thought of deliberate cruelty to animals. No one proposes to relegate that or any other form of sadism to the realm of private morality or to allow it to be practised in public or in private. It would be possible no doubt to point out that until a comparatively short while ago nobody thought very much of cruelty to animals and also that pity and kindliness and the unwillingness to inflict pain are virtues more generally esteemed now than they have ever been in the past. But matters of this sort are not determined by rational argument. Every moral judgement, unless it claims a divine source, is simply a feeling that no right-minded man could behave in any other way without admitting that he was doing wrong. It is the power of a common sense and not the power of reason that is behind the judgements of society. But before a society can put a practice beyond the limits of tolerance there must be a deliberate judgement that the practice is injurious to society. There is, for example, a general abhorrence of homosexuality. We should ask ourselves in the first instance whether, looking at it calmly and dispassionately, we regard it as a vice so abominable that its mere presence is an offence. If that is the genuine feeling of the society in which we live, I do not see how society can be denied the right to eradicate it. Our feeling may not be so intense as that. We may feel about it that, if confined, it is tolerable, but that if it spread it might be gravely injurious; it is in this way that most societies look upon fornication, seeing it as a natural weakness which must be kept within bounds but which cannot be rooted out. It becomes then a question of balance, the danger to society in one scale and the extent of the restriction in the other. On this sort of point the value of an investigation by such a body as the Wolfenden Committee and of its conclusions is manifest.

The limits of tolerance shift. This is supplementary to what I have

---

[14] These words which have been much criticized, are considered again in the Preface at p. viii.

been saying but of sufficient importance in itself to deserve statement as a separate principle which law-makers have to bear in mind. I suppose that moral standards do not shift; so far as they come from divine revelation they do not, and I am willing to assume that the moral judgements made by a society always remain good for that society. But the extent to which society will tolerate—I mean tolerate, not approve—departures from moral standards varies from generation to generation. It may be that over-all tolerance is always increasing. The pressure of the human mind, always seeking greater freedom of thought, is outwards against the bonds of society forcing their gradual relaxation. It may be that history is a tale of contraction and expansion and that all developed societies are on their way to dissolution. I must not speak of things I do not know; and anyway as a practical matter no society is willing to make provision for its own decay. I return therefore to the simple and observable fact that in matters of morals the limits of tolerance shift. Laws, especially those which are based on morals, are less easily moved. It follows as another good working principle that in any new matter of morals the law should be slow to act. By the next generation the swell of indignation may have abated and the law be left without the strong backing which it needs. But it is then difficult to alter the law without giving the impression that moral judgement is being weakened. This is now one of the factors that is strongly militating against any alteration to the law on homosexuality.

A third elastic principle must be advanced more tentatively. It is that as far as possible privacy should be respected. This is not an idea that has ever been made explicit in the criminal law. Acts or words done or said in public or in private are all brought within its scope without distinction in principle. But there goes with this a strong reluctance on the part of judges and legislators to sanction invasions of privacy in the detection of crime. The police have no more right to trespass than the ordinary citizen has; there is no general right of search; to this extent an Englishman's home is still his castle. The Government is extremely careful in the exercise even of those powers which it claims to be undisputed. Telephone tapping and interference with the mails afford a good illustration of this. A Committee of three Privy Councillors who recently inquired [15] into these activities found that the Home Secretary and his predecessors had already formulated strict rules governing the exercise of these powers and the Committee were able to recommend that they should be continued to be exercised substantially on the same terms. But they reported that the power was 'regarded with general disfavour'.

This indicates a general sentiment that the right to privacy is some-

---

[15] (1957) Cmd. 283.

thing to be put in the balance against the enforcement of the law. Ought the same sort of consideration to play any part in the formation of the law? Clearly only in a very limited number of cases. When the help of the law is invoked by an injured citizen, privacy must be irrelevant; the individual cannot ask that his right to privacy should be measured against injury criminally done to another. But when all who are involved in the deed are consenting parties and the injury is done to morals, the public interest in the moral order can be balanced against the claims of privacy. The restriction on police powers of investigation goes further than the affording of a parallel; it means that the detection of crime committed in private and when there is no complaint is bound to be rather haphazard and this is an additional reason for moderation. These considerations do not justify the exclusion of all private immorality from the scope of the law. I think that, as I have already suggested, the test of 'private behaviour' should be substituted for 'private morality' and the influence of the factor should be reduced from that of a definite limitation to that of a matter to be taken into account. Since the gravity of the crime is also a proper consideration, a distinction might well be made in the case of homosexuality between the lesser acts of indecency and the full offence, which on the principles of the Wolfenden Report it would be illogical to do.

Social Solidarity and the Enforcement of Morality *

H. L. A. Hart

It is possible to extract from Plato's *Republic* and *Laws*, and perhaps from Aristotle's *Ethics* and *Politics*, the following thesis about the role of law in relation to the enforcement of morality: the law of the city-state exists not merely to secure that men have the opportunity to lead a morally good life, but to see that they do. According to this thesis not only may the law be used to punish men for doing what morally it is wrong for them to do, but it should be so used; for the promotion of

* Reprinted by permission of the author and publisher, from 35 *U. Chi. L. Rev.* 1 (1967). Footnotes included.

moral virtue by these means and by others is one of the Ends or Purposes of a society complex enough to have developed a legal system. This theory is strongly associated with a specific conception of morality as a uniquely true or correct set of principles—not man-made, but either awaiting man's discovery by the use of his reason or (in a theological setting) awaiting its disclosure by revelation. I shall call this theory "the classical thesis" and not discuss it further.

From the classical thesis there is to be distinguished what I shall call "the disintegration thesis." This inverts the order of instrumentality between society on the one hand and morality on the other as it appears in the classical thesis; for in this thesis society is not the instrument of the moral life; rather morality is valued as the cement of society, the bond, or one of the bonds, without which men would not cohere in society. This thesis is associated strongly with a relativist conception of morality: according to it, morality may vary from society to society, and to merit enforcement by the criminal law, morality need have no rational or other specific content. It is not the quality of the morality but its cohesive power which matters. "What is important is not the quality of the creed but the strength of the belief in it. The enemy of society is not error but indifference." [1] The case for the enforcement of morality on this view is that its maintenance is necessary to prevent the disintegration of society.

The disintegration thesis, under pressure of the request for empirical evidence to substantiate the claim that the maintenance of morality is in fact necessary for the existence of society, often collapses into another thesis which I shall call "the conservative thesis." This is the claim that society has a right to enforce its morality by law because the majority have the right to follow their own moral convictions that their moral environment is a thing of value to be defended from change.[2]

The topic of this article is the disintegration thesis, but I shall discharge in relation to it only a very limited set of tasks. What I shall mainly do is attempt to discover what, when the ambiguities are stripped away, is the empirical claim which the thesis makes and in what directions is it conceivable that a search for evidence to substantiate this claim would be rewarding. But even these tasks I shall discharge only partially.

---

[1] P. Devlin, *The Enforcement of Morals* 114 (1965) [hereinafter cited as Devlin]. *Cf. id.* at 94: "Unfortunately bad societies can live on bad morals just as well as good societies on good ones."

[2] This characterization of the conservative thesis is taken from Dworkin, "Lord Devlin and the Enforcement of Morals," 75 *Yale L.J.* 986 (1966). Professor Dworkin distinguishes the parts played in Lord Devlin's work by the disintegration thesis and the conservative thesis, and his essay is mainly concerned with the critical examination of Lord Devlin's version of the latter. The present essay, by contrast, is mainly concerned to determine what sort of evidence is required if the disintegration thesis is not to collapse into or to be abandoned for the conservative thesis.

I

The disintegration thesis is a central part of the case presented by Lord Devlin [3] justifying the legal enforcement of morality at points where followers of John Stuart Mill and other latter day liberals would consider this an unjustifiable extension of the scope of the criminal law. The morality, the enforcement of which is justified according to Lord Devlin, is variously described as "the moral structure" of society, "a public morality," "a common morality," "shared ideas on politics, morals, and ethics," "fundamental agreement about good and evil," and "a recognised morality." [4] This is said to be part of the "invisible bonds of common thought" which hold society together; and "if the bonds were too far relaxed the members would drift apart." [5] It is part of "the bondage . . . of society" and is "as necessary to society as, say, a recognised government." [6] The justification for the enforcement of this recognised morality is simply that the law may be used to preserve anything essential to society's existence. "There is disintegration when no common morality is observed and history shows that the loosening of moral bonds is often the first stage of disintegration." [7] If we consider these formulations they seem to constitute a highly ambitious empirical generalisation about a necessary condition for the existence or continued existence of a society and so give us a sufficient condition for the disintegration of society. Apart from the one general statement that "history shows that the loosening of moral bonds is often the first stage of disintegration," no evidence is given in support of the argument and no indication is given of the kind of evidence that would support it, nor is any sensitivity betrayed to the need for evidence.

In disputing with Lord Devlin,[8] I offered him the alternative of supplementing his contentions with evidence, or accepting that his statements about the necessity of a common morality for the existence of society were not empirical statements at all but were disguised tautologies or necessary truths depending entirely on the meaning given to the expressions "society," "existence," or "continued existence" of society. If the continued existence of a society meant living according to some specific

---

[3] See principally the lecture by Lord Devlin entitled "The Enforcement of Morals" which he delivered as the Second Maccabaean Lecture in Jurisprudence of the British Academy and which is reproduced in Devlin, Chap. I, as "Morals and the Criminal Law."

[4] Devlin, 9–11.

[5] Devlin, 10.

[6] Devlin, 10–11.

[7] Devlin, 13.

[8] See H. L. A. Hart, *Law, Liberty and Morality* (1963).

shared moral code, then the preservation of a moral code is logically and not causally or contingently necessary to the continued existence of society and this seems too unexciting a theme to be worth ventilating. Yet at points Lord Devlin adopts a definition of society ("a society *means* a community of ideas" [9]) which seems to suggest that he intended his statements about the necessity of a morality to society's existence as a definitional truth. Of course, very often the expressions "society," "existence of society," and "the same society" are used in this way: that is, they refer to a form or type of social life individuated by a certain morality or moral code or by distinctive legal, political, or economic institutions. A society in the sense of a form or type of social life can change, disappear, or be succeeded by different forms of society without any phenomenon describable as "disintegration" or "members drifting apart." In this sense of "society," post-feudal England was a different society from feudal England. But if we express this simple fact by saying that *the same English society* was at one time a feudal society and at another time not, we make use of another sense of society with different criteria of individuation and continued identity. It is plain that if the threat of disintegration or "members drifting apart" is to have any reality, or if the claim that a common morality is "as necessary to society as, say, a recognised government" is taken to be part of an argument for the enforcement of morality, definitional truths dependent upon the identification of society with its shared morality are quite irrelevant. Just as it would be no reply to an anarchist who wished to preserve society to tell him that government is necessary to an organised society, if it turned out that by "organised society" we merely meant a society with a government, so it is empty to argue against one who considers that the preservation of society's code of morality is not the law's business, that the maintenance of the moral code is necessary to the existence of society, if it turns out that by society is meant a society living according to this moral code.

The short point is that if we *mean* by "society ceasing to exist" not "disintegration" nor "the drifting apart" of its members but a radical change in its common morality, then the case for using the law to preserve morality must rest not on any disintegration thesis but on some variant of the claim that when groups of men have developed a common form of life rich enough to include a common morality, this is something which ought to be preserved. One very obvious form of this claim is the conservative thesis that the majority have a right in these circumstances to defend their existing moral environment from change. But this is no longer an empirical claim.

---

[9] Devlin, 10 (emphasis added). But *cf. id.* at 9: "What makes a society of any sort is community of ideas. . . ."

II

Views not dissimilar from Lord Devlin's, and in some cases hovering in a similar way between the disintegration thesis and the conservative thesis, can be found in much contemporary sociological theory of the structural and functional prerequisites of society. It would, for example, be profitable, indeed necessary for a full appreciation of Talcott Parson's work, to take formulations of what is apparently the disintegration thesis which can be found in almost every chapter of his book *The Social System*, and enquire (i) what precisely they amount to; (ii) whether they are put forward as empirical claims; and (iii) if so, by what evidence they are or could be supported. Consider, for example, such formulations as the following: "The sharing of such common value patterns . . . creates a solidarity among those mutually oriented to the common values. . . . [W]ithout attachment to the constitutive common values the collectivity tends to dissolve." [10] "This integration of a set of common value patterns with the internalised need-disposition structure of the constituent personalities is the core phenomenon of the dynamics of social systems. That the stability of any social system is dependent on a degree of such integration may be said to be the fundamental dynamic theorem of sociology." [11] The determination of the precise status and the role of these propositions in Parson's complex works would be a task of some magnitude, so I shall select from the literature of sociology Durkheim's elaboration of a form of the disintegration theory, because his variant of the theory as expounded in his book, *The Division of Labour in Society*, is relatively clear and briefly expressed, and is also specifically connected with the topic of the enforcement of morality by the criminal law.

Durkheim distinguishes two forms of what he calls "solidarity" or factors tending to unify men or lead them to cohere in discriminable and enduring societies. The minimum meaning attached to society here is that of a group of men which we can distinguish from other similar groups and can recognise as being the same group persisting through a period of time though its constituent members have been replaced during that time by others. One of the forms of solidarity, "mechanical solidarity," springs from men's resemblances and the other, "organic solidarity," from their differences. Mechanical solidarity depends on, or perhaps indeed consists in, sharing of common beliefs about matters of fact and common standards of behaviour among which is a common morality. This blend of common belief and common standards constitutes the *"conscience collective,"* which draws upon all the ambiguities of the French word *con-*

---

[10] T. Parsons, *The Social System* 41 (1951).
[11] *Id.* at 42.

science as between consciousness or knowledge and conscience. The point of the use of this terminology of *conscience* is largely that the beliefs and subscription to the common standards become internalised as part of the personality or character of the members of society.

Organic solidarity by contrast depends on the dissimilarities of human beings and their mutual need to be complemented by association in various forms with others who are unlike themselves. The most prominent aspect of this interdependence of dissimilars is the division of labour, but Durkheim warns us that we must not think of the importance of this as a unifying element of society as residing simply in its economic payoff. "[T]he economic services that it [the division of labour] can render are picayune compared to the moral effect that it produces, and its true function is to create in two or more persons a feeling of solidarity." [12] Generally, mechanical solidarity is the dominant form of solidarity in simple societies and diminishes in importance, though apparently it is never eliminated altogether as a unifying factor, as organic solidarity develops in more complex societies. According to Durkheim the law presents a faithful mirror of both forms of solidarity, and can be used as a gauge of the relative importance at any time of the two forms. The criminal law, with its repressive sanctions, reflects mechanical solidarity; the civil law reflects organic solidarity, since it upholds the typical instruments of interdependence, *e.g.*, the institution of contract, and generally provides not for repressive sanctions, but for restitution and compensation.

Somewhat fantastically Durkheim thinks that the law can be used as a measuring instrument. We have merely to count the number of rules which at any time constitute the criminal law and the number of rules which constitute the civil law expressing the division of labour, and then we know what fraction to assign to the relative importance of the two forms of solidarity.[13] This fantasy opens formidable problems concerning the individuation and countability of legal rules which occupied Bentham a good deal [14] but perhaps need not detain us here. What is of great interest, however, is Durkheim's view of the role of the criminal law in relation to a shared morality. Durkheim is much concerned to show the hollowness of rationalistic and utilitarian accounts of the institution of criminal punishment. For him, as for his English judicial counterpart, utilitarian theory fails as an explanatory theory

---

[12] E. Durkheim, *The Division of Labour in Society* 56 (3d ed. Simpson transl. 1964).

[13] *Id.* at 68.

[14] Bentham devoted a whole book to the questions: What is one law? What is part of a law? What is a complete law? See J. Bentham, *The Limits of Jurisprudence Defined* (C. Everett ed. 1945).

for it distorts the character of crime and punishment and considered as a normative theory would lead to disturbing results. Durkheim therefore provides fresh definitions of both crime and punishment. For him a crime is essentially (though in developed societies there are secondary senses of crime to which this definition does not apply directly) a serious offence against the collective conscience—the common morality which holds men together at points where its sentiments are both strong and precise. Such an act is not condemned by that morality because it is independently a crime or wrong, it is a crime or wrong because it is so condemned. Above all, to be wrong or a crime an act need not be, nor even be believed to be, harmful to anyone or to society in any sense other than that it runs counter to the common morality at points where its sentiments are strong and precise. These features of Durkheim's theory are striking analogues of Lord Devlin's observation that it is not the quality of the morality that matters but the strength of the belief in it and its consequent cohesive power and his stipulation that the morality to be enforced must be up to what may be called concert pitch: it must be marked by "intolerance, indignation, and disgust." [15]

What, then, on this view, is punishment? Why punish? And how severely? Punishment for Durkheim is essentially the hostility excited by violations of the common morality which may be either diffused throughout society or administered by official action when it will usually have the form of specifically graduated measures. His definition, therefore, is that punishment is "a passionate reaction of graduated intensity" to offences against the collective conscience. [16] The hollowness of utilitarian theory as an explanation of criminal punishment is evident if we look at the way that, even in contemporary society, criminal punishments are graduated. They are adapted not to the utilitarian aim of preventing what would be ordinarily described as harmful conduct, but to the appropriate expression of the degree of feeling excited by the offence, on the footing that such appropriate expression of feeling is a means of sustaining the belief in the collective morality. [17] Many legal phenomena bear this out. We punish a robber, even if he is likely to offend again, less severely than a murderer whom we have every reason to think will not offend again. We adopt the principle that ignorance of the law is no excuse in criminal matters and, he might have added, we punish attempts less severely than completed offences thereby reflecting a dif-

---

[15] Devlin, viii-ix, 17.
[16] E. Durkheim, *The Division of Labour in Society* 90 (3d ed. Simpson transl. 1964).
[17] *Cf.* Devlin, 114: "When considering intangible injury to society it is moral belief that matters; immoral activity is relevant only insofar as it promotes disbelief."

ference in the resentment generated for the completed as compared with the uncompleted crime.

Hence, to the question "Why punish?" Durkheim's answer is that we do so primarily as a symbolic expression of the outraged common morality the maintenence of which is the condition of cohesion resulting from men's likenesses. Punishing the offender is required to maintain social cohesion because the common conscience, violated by the offence, "would necessarily lose its energy if an emotional reaction of the community [in the form of punishment] did not come to compensate its loss, and it would result in a breakdown of social solidarity." [18]

This thumbnail sketch of Durkheim's theory presents its essentials, but there are two complexities of importance, as there are also in Lord Devlin's case. Both have to do with the possibilities of change in the common morality. Both theorists seem to envisage a spontaneous or natural change and warn us in different ways that the enforcement of morality must allow for this. Thus Lord Devlin issues prudential warnings to the legislator that "[t]he limits of tolerance shift" [19] and that we should not make criminal offences out of moral opinion which is likely soon to change and leave the law high, and, so to speak, morally dry. Durkheim similarly says that his theory does not mean that it is necessary to conserve a penal rule because it once corresponded to the collective sentiments, but only if the sentiment is still "living and energetic." If it has disappeared or enfeebled, nothing is worse than trying to keep it alive artificially by the law.[20] This means that we must distinguish a natural or nonmalignant change in the social morality or a natural "shift in its limits of tolerance" from a malignant form of change against which society is to be protected and which is the result of individual deviation from its morality. It is, however, a further complexity in these theories that the function of punishment, or rather the mechanism by which punishment operates in preserving a social morality from malignant change, differs as between Durkheim and Lord Devlin. For Lord Devlin punishment protects the existing morality by repressing or diminishing the number of immoral actions which in themselves are considered "to threaten" or weaken the common morality. For Durkheim, however, punishment sustains the common morality, not mainly by repressing the immoral conduct, but principally by giving satisfactory vent

---

[18] E. Durkheim, *The Division of Labour in Society* 108 (3d ed. Simpson transl. 1964).

[19] Devlin, 18. *Cf. id.* at 114: "[T]here is nothing inherently objectionable about the change of an old morality for a new one. . . . [I]t is the interregnum of disbelief that is perilous."

[20] E. Durkheim, *The Division of Labour in Society* 107, n. 45 (3d ed. Simpson transl. 1964).

to a sense of outrage because if the vent were closed the common conscience would "lose its energy" and the cohesive morality would weaken.

III

If we ask in relation to theories such as Lord Devlin's and Durkheim's precisely what empirical claim they make concerning the connection between the maintenance of a common morality and the
existence of society, some further disentangling of knots has to be done.

It seems a very natural objection to such theories that if they are
to be taken seriously as variants of the disintegration thesis, the justification which they attempt to give for the enforcement of social morality
is far too general. It is surely both possible and good sense to discriminate
between those parts of a society's moral code (assuming it has a single
moral code) which are essential for the existence of a society and those
which are not. Prima facie, at least, the need for such a discrimination
seems obvious even if we assume that the moral code is only to be enforced where it is supported by "sentiments which are strong and precise" (Durkheim) or by "intolerance, indignation and disgust" (Devlin).
For the decay of all moral restraint or the free use of violence or deception would not only cause individual harm but would jeopardise
the existence of a society since it would remove the main conditions which
make it possible and worthwhile for men to live together in close prox-
imity to each other. On the other hand the decay of moral restraint on,
say, extramarital intercourse, or a general change of sexual morality
in a permissive direction seems to be quite another matter and not
obviously to entail any such consequences as "distintegration" or "men
drifting apart." [21]

---

[21] Lord Devlin in a footnote concedes that not every *breach* of a society's moral
code threatens its existence. His words are: "I do not assert that *any* deviation from
a society's shared morality threatens its existence any more than I assert that *any*
subversive activity threatens its existence. I assert that they are both activities which
are capable in their nature of threatening the existence of society so that neither can
be put beyond the law." Devlin, 13, n. 1. (emphasis in original). This passage does
not mean or imply that there are any parts of a social morality which though supported
by indignation, intolerance, and disgust can be regarded as not essential for society's
existence: on this point Lord Devlin plainly inclines towards the conception of a
social morality as a seamless web. Devlin, 115. But Professor Dworkin argues, convincingly in my opinion, that Lord Devlin uses the same criterion (in effect "passionate
public disapproval") to determine both that a deviation from public morality *may*
conceivably threaten its existence and that it in fact *does* so, so as to justify actual
punishment. Dworkin, "Lord Devlin and the Enforcement of Morals," 75 *Yale L.J.*
986, 990–92 (1966). This leaves his version of the disintegration thesis without
empirical support. Thus, according to Lord Devlin: "We should ask ourselves in the
first instance whether, looking at homosexuality calmly and dispassionately, we regard it as a vice so abominable that its mere presence is an offence. If that is the
genuine feeling of the society in which we live, I do not see how society can be

It seems, therefore, worthwhile pausing to consider two possible ways of discriminating within a social morality the parts which are to be considered essential.

i. The first possibility is that the common morality which is essential to society, and which is to be preserved by legal enforcement, is that part of its social morality which contains only those restraints and prohibitions that are essential to the existence of any society of human beings whatever. Hobbes and Hume have supplied us with general characterisations of this moral minimum essential for social life: they include rules restraining the free use of violence and minimal forms of rules regarding honesty, promise keeping, fair dealing, and property. It is, however, quite clear that neither Devlin nor Durkheim means that only these elements, which are to be found in common morality, are to be enforced by law, since any utilitarian or supporter of the Wolfenden Report would agree to that. Quite clearly the argument of both Lord Devlin and Durkheim concerns moral rules which may differ from society to society. Durkheim actually insists that the common morality, violations of which are to be punished by the criminal law, may have no relation to utility: "It was not at all useful for them [these prohibitions] to be born, but once they have endured, it becomes necessary that they persist in spite of their irrationality." [22] The morality to be punished includes much that relates "neither to vital interests of society nor to a minimum of justice." [23]

ii. The second possibility is this: the morality to be enforced, while not coextensive with every jot and tittle of an existent moral code, includes not only the restraints and prohibitions such as those relating to the use of violence or deception which are necessary to any society whatever, but also what is essential for a particular society. The guiding thought here is that for any society there is to be found, among the provisions of its code of morality, a central core of rules or principles which constitutes its pervasive and distinctive style of life. Lord Devlin frequently speaks in this way of what he calls monogamy adopted "as a moral principle," [24] and of course this does deeply pervade our society in two principal ways. First, marriage is a *legal* institution and the recog-

---

denied the right to eradicate it." Devlin, 17. But he offers no evidence that in these circumstances the legal toleration of homosexuality would in fact endanger society's existence. Contrast the foregoing with the principles applied by Lord Devlin to fornication in relation to which "feeling may not be so intense." In *that* case: "It becomes *then* a question of balance, the danger to society in one scale and the extent of the restriction in the other." Devlin, 17–18 (emphasis added).

[22] E. Durkheim, *The Division of Labour in Society* 107 (3d ed. Simpson transl. 1964).

[23] *Id.* at 81.

[24] Devlin, 9.

nition of monogamy as the sole legal form of marriage carries implications for the law related to wide areas of conduct: the custody and education of children, the rules relating to inheritance and distribution of property, etc. Second, the principle of monogamy is also morally pervasive: monogamous marriage is at the heart of our conception of family life, and with the aid of the law has become part of the structure of society. Its disappearance would carry with it vast changes throughout society so that without exaggeration we might say that it had changed its character.

On this view the morality which is necessary to the existence of society is neither the moral minimum required in all societies (Lord Devlin himself says that the polygamous marriage in a polygamous society may be an equally cohesive force as monogamy is in ours),[25] nor is it every jot and tittle of a society's moral code. What is essential and is to be preserved is the central core. On this footing it would be an open and empirical question whether any particular moral rule or veto, e.g., on homosexuality, adultery, or fornication, is so organically connected with the central core that its maintenance and preservation is required as a vital outwork or bastion. There are perhaps traces of some of these ideas in Lord Devlin but not in Durkheim. But even if we take this to be the position, we are still not really confronted with an empirical claim concerning the connection of the maintenance of a common morality and the prevention of disintegration or "drifting apart." Apart from the point about whether a particular rule is a vital outwork or bastion of the central core, we may still be confronted only with the unexciting tautology depending now on the identification of society, not with the whole of its morality but only with its central core or "character" and this is not the disintegration thesis.

IV

What is required to convert the last mentioned position into the disintegration thesis? It must be the theory that the maintenance of the core elements in a particular society's moral life is in fact necessary to prevent disintegration, because the withering or malignant decay of the central morality is a disintegrating factor. But even if we have got thus far in identifying an empirical claim, there would of course be very many questions to be settled before anything empirically testable could be formulated. What are the criteria in a complex society for determining the existence of a single recognised morality or its central core? What is "disintegration" and "drifting apart" under modern conditions? I shall not

---

[25] Devlin, 114.

investigate these difficulties but I shall attempt to describe in outline the types of evidence that might conceivably be relevant to the issue if and when these difficulties are settled. They seem to be the following:

a. Crude historical evidence in which societies—not individuals—are the units. The suggestion is that we should examine societies which have disintegrated and inquire whether their disintegration was preceded by a malignant change in their common morality. This done, we should then have to address ourselves to the possibility of a causal connection between decay of a common morality and disintegration. But of course all the familiar difficulties involved in macroscopic generalisations about society would meet us at this point, and anyone who has attempted to extract generalisations from what is called the decline and fall of the Roman Empire would know that they are formidable. To take only one such difficulty: suppose that all our evidence was drawn from simple tribal societies or closely knit agrarian societies (which would seem to be the most favorable application of Durkheim's theory of mechanical solidarity). We should not, I take it, have much confidence in applying any conclusions drawn from these to modern industrial societies. Or, if we had, it would be because we had some well developed and well evidenced theory to show us that the differences between simple societies and our own were irrelevant to these issues as the differences in the size of a laboratory can safely be ignored as irrelevant to the scope of the generalisations tested by laboratory experiments. Durkheim, it may be said, is peculiarly obscure on just this point, since it is not really clear from his book whether he means that in advanced societies characterised by extensive division of labour the mechanical solidarity which would still be reflected in its criminal law would be disregarded or not.

b. The alternative type of evidence must be drawn presumably from social psychology and must break down into at least two subforms according to the way in which we conceive the alternatives to the maintenance of a common morality. One alternative is general uniform *permissiveness* in the area of conduct previously covered by the common morality. The lapse, for example, of the conception that the choices between two wives or one, heterosexuality or homosexuality, are more than matters of personal taste. This (the alternative of permissiveness) is what Lord Devlin seems to envisage or to fear when he says: "The enemy of society is not error but indifference," and "Whether the new belief is better or worse than the old, it is the interregnum of disbelief that is perilous." [26] On the other hand the alternative may be not permissiveness but *moral pluralism* involving divergent submoralities in relation to the same area of conduct.

---

[26] *Id.*

To get off the ground with the investigation of the questions that either of these two alternatives opens up, it would be reasonable to abandon any general criteria for the disintegration of society in favor of something sufficiently close to satisfy the general spirit of the disintegration thesis. It would be no doubt sufficient if our evidence were to show that malignant change in a common morality led to a general increase in such forms of antisocial behaviour as would infringe what seem the minimum essentials: the prohibitions and restraints of violence, disrespect for property, and dishonesty. We should then require some account of the conceivable psychological mechanisms supposed to connect the malignant decay of a social morality with the increase in such forms of behaviour. Here there would no doubt be signal differences between the alternatives of permissiveness and moral pluralism. On the permissiveness alternative, the theory to be tested would presumably be that in the "interregnum conditions," without the discipline involved in the submission of one area of life, e.g., the sexual, to the requirements of a common morality, there would necessarily be a weakening of the general capacity of individuals for self-control. So, with permissiveness in the area formally covered by restrictive sexual morality, there would come increases in violence and dishonesty and a general lapse of those restraints which are essential for any form of social life. This is the view that the morality of the individual constitutes a seamless web. There is a hint that this, in the last resort, is Lord Devlin's view of the way in which the "interregnum" constitutes a danger to the existence of society: for he replied to my charge that he had assumed without evidence that morality was a seamless web by saying that though "[s]eamlessness presses the simile rather hard," "most men take their morality as a whole." [27] But surely this assumption cannot be regarded as obviously true. The contrary view seems at least equally plausible: permissiveness in certain areas of life (even if it has come about through the disregard of a previously firmly established social morality) might make it easier for men to submit to restraints on violence which are essential for social life.

If we conceive the successor to the "common morality" to be not permissiveness but moral pluralism in some area of conduct once covered by a sexual morality which has decayed through the flouting of its restrictions, the thesis to be tested would presumably be that where moral pluralism develops in this way quarrels over the differences generated by divergent moralities must eventually destroy the minimal forms of restraints necessary for social cohesion. The counter-thesis would be that plural moralities in the conditions of modern large scale societies might perfectly well be mutually tolerant. To many indeed it might seem that

---

[27] Devlin, 115.

the counter-thesis is the more cogent of the two, and that over wide areas of modern life, sometimes hiding behind lip service to an older common morality, there actually are divergent moralities living in peace.

I have done no more than to sketch in outline the type of evidence required to substantiate the disintegration thesis. Till psychologists and sociologists provide such evidence, supporters of the enforcement of morality would do better to rest their case candidly on the conservative rather than on the disintegration thesis.

The Enforcement of Morals *

Ernest Nagel

I

An adequate account of the different ways in which moral principles enter into the development, the operation, and the evaluation of legal systems would require an examination of a broad spectrum of difficult issues. Such an account is certainly not a task to which a relatively short paper can do justice, and the present paper is not an attempt to do the impossible. I am therefore restricting myself in it almost entirely to but one issue that arises in considering the relation of law to morality—to the question whether there is a sharply delimited domain of human conduct that is by its very nature excluded from justifiable legal control, and in particular whether a society is ever warranted in using the law to enforce what are held to be widely accepted moral rules. The question has a long ancestry in discussions of moral and political theory, and is closely related to issues raised in historical doctrines of natural law and inalienable rights. However, the question can be examined without reference to natural law theory, and in any case it is not simply of antiquarian interest, but is of vital interest to humanist writers. It is also directly relevant to a number of currently debated social problems, among others to problems created by changing attitudes toward euthanasia, obscenity, and deviant sexual practices; and it received considerable attention in

* This article first appeared in *The Humanist*, XXVIII, No. 3 (May/June 1968 issue), 20–27. Reprinted by permission of *The Humanist*.

recent years from legislators, judges, sociologists, and psychologists, as well as from philosophers and writers on jurisprudence.

Many current philosophical and jurisprudential discussions of the question I want to consider take as their point of departure a challenging essay by Lord Patrick Devlin—a distinguished British judge, who was for many years a Justice of the High Court, Queen's Bench, and subsequently a Lord of Appeal in Ordinary. Devlin's essay, entitled "The Enforcement of Morals" and published in 1959, tried to show that a fundamental principle to which many moral theorists subscribe and which had been recently invoked in support of certain recommendations for amending the English criminal law, is untenable—for reasons I will presently mention. Devlin's views have found some defenders, but have also been the subject of much severe criticism. Since my paper is for the most part a commentary on the main points in dispute between Devlin and his critics—especially H. L. A. Hart in the latter's *Law, Liberty, and Morality* (1963)—I must describe briefly the problem to which Devlin's essay was addressed, and the context in which the debate over his views has its locus.

In 1954, in response to widespread criticism of the provisions of the English criminal law dealing with prostitution and homosexual practices, a committee was appointed, headed by Sir John Wolfenden, to look into the matter and to recommend needed changes in the law. The Report of the Committee was issued in 1957, and proposed a number of modifications in the existing law relating to various kinds of sexual offenses. The factual findings and the detailed proposals of the Committee are not pertinent here. What is of interest is that the Wolfenden Committee based its recommendations on the view that

> . . . the function of the criminal law . . . is to preserve public order and decency, to protect the citizen from what is offensive or injurious, and to provide sufficient safeguards against exploitation and corruption of others, particularly those who are specially vulnerable because they are young, weak in body or mind, inexperienced, or in a state of special physical, offical or economic dependence.
>
> It is not the function of the law [the report went on] to intervene in the private lives of citizens, or to seek to enforce any pattern of behavior, further than is necessary to carry out the purposes we have outlined.

Moreover, in recommending that solicitation of the young should continue to be punishable by law, but that "homosexual behavior between consenting adults should no longer be a criminal offence," the Wolfenden Report offered what it called a "decisive" reason, namely:

> . . . the importance which society and the law ought to give to indi-

vidual freedom of choice and action in matters of private morality. Unless a deliberate attempt is to be made by society, acting through the agency of the law, to equate the sphere of crime with that of sin, *there must remain a realm of private morality and immorality which is, in brief and crude terms, not the law's business.* To say this is not to condone or encourage private immorality.[1]

Some of the Report's proposals were eventually adopted by Parliament. However, it is not my aim to examine either the merits of these recommendations or the recent history of English legislation. The question I do want to discuss is the adequacy of the general principle underlying the specific proposals of the Wolfenden Committee—that there is a realm of conduct which, irrespective of its morality or immorality, is not the law's business and by its very nature falls outside the legitimate concerns of the law. It is this principle that Devlin challenged on grounds that I will presently describe, even though he eventually expressed himself as being in agreement with some of the Report's specific recommendations; and it is largely to a critique of Devlin's stand on this principle that Hart's own book previously mentioned is devoted.

However, as the Wolfenden Report explicitly notes, the principle is stated by it only in brief and crude terms, without any attempt to articulate it clearly or to give supporting reasons for it. But there is little doubt that in its statement of the principle the Report was invoking the far more inclusive political doctrine which John Stuart Mill expounded at some length in his classic essay *On Liberty* (1859), and was simply applying that doctrine to the particular problem of the legal regulation of sexual practices. Accordingly, since both Devlin and Hart make constant reference to Mill's views on individual liberty, and since I want to discuss the principle espoused by the Wolfenden Committee when it is stated in its most general and influential form, it is desirable to quote the passage in which Mill expressed the central idea of his political philosophy. Mill declared that

> . . . The sole end for which mankind is warranted, individually or collectively, in interfering with the liberty of action of any of their number is self-protection. That the only purpose for which power can be rightfully exercised over any member of a civilized community, against his will, is to prevent harm to others. His own good, whether physical or moral, is not a sufficient warrant. He cannot rightfully be compelled to do or forbear because it will be better for him to do so, because it will make him happier, because, in the opinion of others, to do so would be wise, or even right. These are

---

[1] Patrick Devlin, *The Enforcement of Morals* (New York: Oxford University Press, 1965), pp. 2–3 [my italics]. All references to Devlin are to this book.

good reasons for remonstrating with him, or reasoning with him or
persuading him, or entreating him, but not for compelling him, or
visiting him with any evil in case he do otherwise. To justify that,
the conduct from which it is desired to deter him must be calculated
to produce evil to someone else. The only part of the conduct of anyone, for which he is amenable to society, is that which concerns
others. In the part which merely concerns himself, his independence
is, of right, absolute.[2]

Mill thus advanced a comprehensive rule for determining the limits
of warranted interference with men's conduct through the use of *any*
agency of social control and compulsion—not only through the operation
of the law, whether civil or criminal, but also through other institutions,
such as religious organizations, economic associations, or more temporary
groups that may be formed to achieve particular ends. But in any event,
the rule appears to provide a firm support for the recommendations of
the Wolfenden Report, for on the face of it the general principle Mill
enunciates excludes the use of the machinery of the law to enforce what
the Report calls "private morality."

Nevertheless, the principle is not as determinate as it is often alleged
to be; and it is debatable whether, in view of the complications involved
in attempts to apply it to concrete cases, it suffices to define categorically
a realm of conduct that is inherently outside the scope of the law. I propose to enter into this debate, by reviewing some of the problems con-
fronting a doctrine such as Mill's that seeks to circumscribe the area of
conduct into which no measure of social control can be justifiably introduced. I am afraid that little if anything I have to say will be unfamiliar, for the problems have been repeatedly canvassed; nor do I have
a neat resolution for the controversy over the legal enforcement of morals,
for if I am right there can be no wholesale answer to the question. But
I hope that by distinguishing several issues that are often confounded,
I will succeed in placing the controversy in clearer light.

II

Mill offers two formulations—a broader and a narrower one—for his
principle to distinguish between conduct that does and conduct that does
not fall within the scope of permissible social control. (1) According to
the broad formulation, a person's actions are matters for legitimate social
scrutiny only if they are of "concern" to others, but not if they "merely
concern himself." On this criterion for deciding on the justifiability of
social control, the relevant question to ask is not whether an action is

---

[2] J. S. Mill, *Utilitarianism, Liberty, and Representative Government* (New York:
Dutton, 1950, Everyman's Library edition), p. 73.

performed in private (e.g., within the walls of a man's home) or in public, but whether it has *consequences* that in some way may affect other men. However, as has often been noted, there are few if any actions, even when done in private, which can be guaranteed to have no effects whatsoever on others than the actors themselves, so that on this formulation of the principle the domain of conduct that is reserved for the exercise of individual liberty is at best extremely narrow.

(2) In point of fact, it is not upon this broad formulation of his principle that Mill relies, but on the narrower one according to which no adult member of a civilized community can be rightfully compelled to perform or to desist from performing an act, unless the action or the failure to perform it is likely to produce *harm* or *evil* to others. But it takes little to see that even on this narrower injunction relatively few human actions are in principle excluded from social regulation. For example, a successful courtship may bring joy to a lover but acute anguish to his rival; the acclaim won by a musician or a scientist may produce self-destructive feelings of inferiority in those who do not achieve such distinction; and the vigorous expression of heterodox opinions may cause severe distress in those hearing them. Mill himself was fully aware of this, and qualified his principle by excluding from the class of actions he regarded as "harmful to others" (in the sense that they are subject to social control) many actions which, though they may affect others adversely by causing them physical or mental pain, he designated as merely "inconveniences"; and he maintained that society should tolerate such inconveniences, without attempting to control the actions that are their source, on the ground that this is the price men must be prepared to pay for the enjoyment of individual liberty.

However, the actions mentioned by Mill as productive of inconveniences only, rather than of serious evils that warrant social intervention, are in some instances highly idiosyncratic; but they frequently also reflect attitudes and standards of conduct that were held by many other men of Mill's time and station in life. Thus, he saw in the prohibition of the sale of alcoholic beverages an infringement of personal liberty, despite the social evils that excessive consumption of alcohol may produce; and he maintained that though a person attempting to cross an unsafe bridge should be warned of the risk he is incurring, no public official would be warranted in forcibly preventing the person from exposing himself to danger. But Mill also believed that society is justified in compelling parents to educate their young; that society is warranted in forbidding marriages between individuals who cannot prove that they have the means to support a family; and that contracts between persons should be prohibited, even if no one else is affected by the agreements, when the parties bind themselves to abide by some arrangement for an indefinite number of years, if not in perpetuity, without the power to revoke the agreement. On the other hand, though Mill had no doubt that society must tolerate fornication and gambling, he evaded answering the question whether a person should be free to be a pimp or a gambling-house keeper.

I do not believe it is possible to state a firm rule underlying Mill's selection of conduct for inclusion in the category of actions whose consequences for others are merely annoying inconveniences, rather than serious evils that justify the adoption of some form of social regulation. Indeed, it is obvious that his principle for demarcating a realm of behavior which is exempt from social control excludes virtually *nothing* from the scope of justifiable legal enactment—*unless* some agreement is first reached on what to count as "harm or evil to others." But two points are no less clear: (1) an explication of what is to be understood as harmful to others (in the sense of warranting some type of social control), cannot escape reference to some more or less explicit and comprehensive system of moral and social assumptions—more fully articulated than Mill's, whether or not the moral theory involved in the explication is one about which reasonable men may differ; and (2) even when agreement on general moral principles can be taken for granted, it may be difficult to decide whether a given type of conduct is indeed harmful to others, especially if the circumstances under which the actions take place may vary considerably, or if the number of individuals who engage in them should increase. Each point merits brief comment.

1. There are various categories of behavior whose harmful character (as distinct from its mere inconvenience to others) is in general not disputed in our society—for example, actions resulting in physical injury to others, or in depriving them of their possessions (as in theft); and no elaborate moral theory is usually invoked in justifying legal measures designed to prevent such actions. Nevertheless, the point needs stressing that though in a given society certain kinds of conduct seem unquestionably harmful, the classification of such conduct as harmful may, and frequently does, involve far-reaching assumptions about the public weal—assumptions which may be modified for a variety of reasons, and which may not be operative in other societies. This is evident when we reflect that even in our own society not all actions resulting in physical injury to others, or in depriving others of their possessions, are held to be harmful in the sense here relevant. Thus the infliction of physical injury on others in duels or feuds currently counts as action that is harmful, but the infliction of such injury is not so regarded when it occurs in boxing contests, in acts of self-defense, or in many though not in all surgical operations. Moral assumptions and considerations of social policy surely control this classification of such conduct; and there have been societies in which those actions have been classified differently.

Again, it is pertinent to ask in the case of alleged theft, whether the article taken from a person "really" belonged to him. But the question is not settled by ascertaining whether the article had been in the person's actual possession—even when we limit ourselves to those relatively simple cases in which it makes sense to suppose that the articles under consideration can literally be in someone's physical possession. For in the context in which the question is being asked, the relevant answer to it is that the article is (or is not) his *property*. However, as is now widely recognized, the notion of property is a *legal* category, whose meaning and content are defined by some system of laws, and generally vary with different societies. Thus, a piece of land or a painting is a man's property, and not simply something in his possession, if he acquired the item in ways prescribed by the laws of the land. Similarly, a song composed by a musician is his property, only if there are copyright laws which grant him certain rights in it; it is his property only during the period of copyright, but not after it has run its course; and if the copyright laws are changed, the status of the song as property is also altered. Accordingly, whether an action is a case of theft, and hence liable to legal sanctions, depends on whether the article taken from a man or used without his consent is indeed his property. In consequence, to justify the use of any form of social duress for compelling a man to abstain from theft, one must in the end justify the social policy, and therefore the moral commitments, underlying the laws that determine what is to count as property.

Let me cite one further example. Suppose that one individual promises another to perform an action in return for some favor, and assume that if the promise is breached the person to whom it was given suffers a loss, but leaving it open whether or not anybody else does so. Is such a breach of promise a harmful action, or only an inconvenience? There are many promises whose breach is ignored by the laws of our society, even when the breach is the source of great inconvenience to others than the parties to the agreement—for example, in return for the use of a colleague's car, a promise to coach his son for an important examination. But there are also many promises whose breaking society does not ignore, and the legal institution of contract is a social technique for the enforcement of promissory agreements. On the other hand, complete freedom of contract is not an unmixed blessing, as Mill recognized; and there are a variety of contractual arrangements that are forbidden in many societies—for example, in our society no one is permitted to sell himself into slavery. Accordingly, society does not intervene into a large class of promises, even when their consequences affect others than those making them, but regulates other kinds of promises even when their results do not appear to impinge directly on those not party to them. Moreover, in placing restrictions on the freedom to contract, society seeks through the in-

strumentalities of the law to achieve what is assumed to be a greater
social good, often in the form of establishing more equitable conditions
for the exercise of individual liberty than could be achieved without the
regulation of what at first blush seem to be purely "private transactions."
As Morris R. Cohen observed, contract law has a function not entirely
dissimilar from that of criminal law—for both seek to standardize conduct
by penalizing departures from certain norms whose validation involves
moral considerations.

In short, attempts such as Mill's to delimit *a priori* a realm of conduct
that is exempt from social regulation presuppose a fairly detailed moral
philosophy that articulates what actions are to count as harmful to others.
But the discussion thus far has also suggested that unless individual
freedom (as the maximum non-interference with individual conduct) is
taken as an inalienable and *absolute* right, which must never be com-
promised or curtailed for the sake of satisfying other human needs (such
as security from physical want or the development of human excellence),
there appear to be no determinate and fixed limits to the scope of
justifiable legal regulation of conduct.

2. I will return to this observation, but will now comment on the
second point mentioned earlier. Given some explication of the notion of
"harm (or evil) to others," the question whether a certain form of
conduct is indeed harmful can be settled only by an empirical study of
its consequences—it cannot be resolved by appeal to uncriticized custom
or by considering that conduct in isolation from the enormously complex
field of human relations in which it may actually be embedded. Now it
may in principle be always possible to find reliable answers to such
questions, and frequently such answers are undoubtedly available; but
it is also the case that in a large number of instances adequate answers
are difficult to obtain. Thus, to mention a trivial example, it appears
quite certain in the light of current physical and biological knowledge
that the kind of clothing a man wears, especially in the privacy of his
home, has no "harmful" consequences for others—although in this connection some geneticists have raised (but as far I know not resolved)
the question whether the kind of clothing men wear affects the mutation
rate of genes, and therefore the character of the gene stock in inbreeding
human populations. On the other hand, while there are reasons to believe that were artificial insemination practiced with the full consent of
both parties to a marriage, no undesirable consequences would ensue
either for those directly involved or for anyone else, no one can say
today with any surety what effects the practice might have on the institution of the family or on current systems of property relations, if the
practice were to become widespread. More generally, one should not
ignore the truism that men's actions have unintended consequences; and

Hegel was at least partly correct in his claim that the owl of Minerva spreads its wings only when the dusk begins to fall.

These comments must not be construed to mean that no deliberate changes in policies of social control in respect to some type of conduct should ever be made, until thoroughly competent knowledge becomes available concerning the likely consequences for others of the proposed policy change. For the desired knowledge can often be acquired only if the change is instituted; and refusal to make a change in the absence of fully adequate knowledge of its consequences is itself a policy decision, whose own likely effects may also be unknown to us. The conclusion that does emerge from these observations is that the distinction between conduct which is merely of concern to the actors (and hence, according to Mill, should be excluded from the scope of the law), and conduct that affects others adversely (and hence may be a proper subject for social regulation), cannot be drawn precisely or once for all, and may require repeated revision as conditions change and our funded knowledge grows.

III

In the light of these reflections, I want now to examine the grounds on which Lord Devlin defends the thesis that under certain conditions the enforcement of morals through the agency of criminal law is justifiable. Devlin bases his argument on the premise that a society is constituted not only by individuals with certain more or less concordant habits of behavior which they exhibit despite differences in personal aims, but also by a "community of ideas"—and in particular moral ideas "about the way its members *should* behave and govern their lives." [3] The shared convictions of a community concerning what is the "right" mode of conduct in such matters as marriage or the protection of life and property make up what he calls the "public morality" or the "moral structure" of a society. And according to him, every threat to the moral order of a society is a threat to the continued existence of the society itself. But since on this view "society has the right to make a judgment [on morals], and has it on the basis that a recognized morality is as necessary to society as . . . a recognized government," Devlin concludes that "society may use the law to preserve morality in the same way as it uses it to safeguard anything else that is essential to its existence" (p. 11). To be sure, he believes that "there must be toleration of the maximum individual freedom that is consistent with the integrity of society" (p. 16), and also recognizes that "the extent to which society will tolerate . . . departures from moral standards varies from generation to

---

[3] Devlin, *op. cit.*, p. 9 [my italics].

generation" (p. 18). He nevertheless maintains that if in the collective but deliberate judgment of society some practice, even though it is carried on in private, would be gravely injurious to the moral order were it to become widespread, then society may well be justified *as a matter of general principle* in outlawing that "immoral" conduct—just as it is justified in taking steps to preserve its government by enacting laws against treason (p. 13).

In my opinion, Devlin makes out a strong case for the impossibility of constructing a firm and enduring boundary between conduct that is a matter for individual conscience or private morality, and conduct that properly belongs to the domain of public concern. On the other hand, although I also think that his argument for the conclusion that under certain conditions the state may be justified in using the criminal law to enforce rules of public morality is *formally* sound, the conclusion rests on premises whose content is unclear and whose merits appear to me doubtful. Let me mention some of my difficulties.

1. In the first place, while Devlin seems to me to be on firm ground in claiming that every social system involves a community of certain ideas among its members, he does not explain what is to be understood by the "preservation" or "destruction" of a social order (as distinct from the persistence or collapse of its form of government), or just how one is to distinguish between the supposition that a social order has been *destroyed* and the supposition that there has been only a *change* in some pervasive pattern of institutionalized behavior. Much talk about societies continues to be based on the model which compares them to living organisms, and there is a point to the analogy. But the analogy is misleading if it leads us to assume that a society can die or flourish in the same sense that a biological organism does. Thus, an organism is usually defined to be a living one, if its so-called "vital functions"—such as respiration or assimilation of food—are being maintained, and to be dead when these processes no longer continue. In the case of societies, there are also processes (such as the maintenance of the food supply or the education of the young) that are sometimes compared with biological vital functions; and a society could therefore be said to have perished when these processes have ceased or, in the extreme instance, when its members have been permanently dispersed or have died without leaving any progeny. But with the possible exception of this extreme case, there appears to be no general agreement on the activities that *define* what it is for a society to be destroyed, rather than to be undergoing some alteration in its modes of organizing human conduct. It is therefore difficult to know what Devlin is asserting when he says that a given society fails or succeeds in preserving itself.

2. But secondly, Devlin does not establish his claim that any *specific*

tenet of public morality—that is, any concrete moral conviction most members of a community ostensibly share about how men should behave and govern their lives in connection with some determinate activity, such as the conviction that marriages should be monogamous or that animals should not be mistreated—is *actually included* in the community of ideas whose maintenance he thinks is *indispensable* for the preservation of a social order. There is considerable evidence for believing that members of a given community do have in common a variety of more or less *general* ideas and attitudes as to what are the proper ways in which men should conduct themselves—for example, in many societies if not in all, most men expect others to have some regard for the sanctity of the lives of fellow members in their society, to comply with current laws or customs and the rules for changing them, or to make allowances for differences in the conduct of others because of differences in age and capacity. Moreover, it is quite plausible to hold that human societies would be impossible without the existence of a community of such general moral ideas. Indeed, given the biological makeup of men, their common desire to live and to procreate, and their dependence on the services rendered by others, it would be surprising if this were not so. But however this may be, and assuming that the notion of what it is for a society to be destroyed has been clarified, neither logic nor history appears to support the supposition that the violation of any *specific* moral standards prescribed by public morality may threaten the life of a social order.

An example may help to make the point clearer. Assume for the sake of the argument that no society can exist if it does not have *some* form of private property and if its members do not in the main believe that *some* ways of acquiring private property are morally justifiable. On this assumption, the preservation of a given society therefore requires the preservation of the conviction among its members that private ownership is morally warranted. But suppose further that in a particular society slavery is legal during a certain period, that during this period most of its members think it is entirely moral to own human beings as articles of private property, but that because of widespread protests against the institution of slavery the conviction that the institution is moral becomes seriously weakened. However, it does not follow from the basic premise of the argument that a weakening of *this* particular conviction is a threat to the social order—for on that premise, a necessary condition for the preservation of society is not the continued commitment to the morality of *human slavery*, but rather the continued commitment to the justifiability of *private property* in some form; and it is evident that this latter commitment is entirely compatible with the rejection of the former one.

Moreover, it is difficult to find in the historical record unquestionable instances in which a society collapsed because some one specific tenet of public morality had been extensively violated in actual practice, or because widely held beliefs in such a tenet had been seriously weakened. Human societies do not appear to be such fragile systems that they cannot survive a successful challenge to some established norm of conduct, nor are they such rigid structures that they are unable to accommodate their institutions to deviations from customary patterns of behavior and approved moral standards. Thus, since the end of the eighteenth century there have been radical transformations in the U.S. not only in commonly held ideas about the morality of numerous forms of private property but also in ideas about the morality of various kinds of individual conduct—including sexual practices, the treatment of children by parents, and personal attitudes toward members of minority groups. On the face of it, at any rate, the society (or societies) occupying the territory of the U.S. during this period has adjusted itself to these changes in public morality. Or ought one to say that because of these changes in what were at various times deeply felt moral beliefs, American society has failed to preserve itself? In the absence of an unambiguous characterization of what constitutes the American social order and what is essential for its continuing existence, the question can be answered to suit one's preference. But if this is so, Devlin's major premise is either unproven (so that it cannot serve as a reason for accepting his conclusion), or the premise is so indeterminate in its content that a conclusion different from the one he reaches can also be drawn from it. There is therefore only a farfetched analogy at best between violations of public morality and treasonable actions—for there is no clear sense in which a social order is alleged to be capable of destruction by the former, while the downfall of established political authority can sometimes be correctly attributed to the latter. Accordingly, to build a case for the enforcement of morals on this analogy, as Devlin in effect does, is to build it on insubstantial foundations.

3. There are two other related assumptions in Devlin's argument that require brief notice. (a) Although he recognizes that public morality is subject to change, he appears to have no doubt that there is a quite definite community of moral ideas among members of a society during a given period. Moreover, he believes that the content of this morality can be ascertained without inordinate difficulty; and he suggests that for the purposes of the law, immorality is what any so-called "right-minded person" or "man in the Clapham omnibus," any jury of twelve men or women selected at random, is presumed to consider to be immoral.

However, neither assumption seems to me plausible. There have been communities in the past, and there are still some in the present, which were exposed to but a single intellectual and moral tradition, and were unaccustomed to the exchange and criticism of ideas on diverse subjects; and for such communities, the notion of a public morality which directs the energies of men into definite channels makes good sense. But in large urban societies such as our own, in which divergent ideals of life (often based on new scientific discoveries) are widely discussed, and technological advances in medicine as well as industry create opportunities for developing novel patterns of behavior, men differ widely in what they take to be moral conduct, and are in some measure tolerant of moral ideals which they do not themselves espouse. It is by no means evident whether in such pluralistic societies the notion of a public morality as Devlin conceives it is strictly applicable. For example, he declares that "The Institution of marriage would be gravely threatened if individual judgments were permitted about the morality of adultery; on [this matter] there must be a public morality" (p. 10). But there is reason to believe that Devlin overestimates the extent of current agreement on the immorality of extramarital relations and, as recent discussions of proposed reforms of divorce laws suggest, it is by no means certain that there is a real consensus on the immorality of adultery upon which the persistence of the institution of marriage is alleged to be contingent. Moreover, the educative and transformation function of the law must not be ignored. For while the effectiveness of a legal system undoubtedly depends on the support it receives from the prevailing moral convictions of a community, the law does not simply *reflect* those convictions, but is in turn frequently an agency for *modifying* accepted moral standards. The supposition that even during a relatively brief period there is a determinate and clearly identifiable public morality is not a realistic picture of modern societies.

(b) Devlin's recommendation on how to ascertain the content of public morality is certainly simple. But is it also sound? If the moral convictions of members of contemporary societies are as diverse and divergent as I have suggested they are, what reason is there to suppose that the unanimous judgment of a dozen individuals drawn at random to serve on a jury is representative of the moral standards (for what may be to them an unfamiliar type of conduct) that are entertained throughout the society? Moreover, since on Devlin's view actions judged to be criminal because they are held to be immoral are actions which threaten the safety of the social order, why should we assume that twelve "right-minded persons" in a jury box—who presumably have no specialzed training for evaluating the effects on others of some form of deviant behavior, nor the opportunity to undertake a careful study of what is already known about them—are more qualified to make competent judgments on what may be complex moral issues, than they are to pass on the significance of a scientific idea or on the merits of a surgical technique? To be sure, Devlin does not intend, as some commentators accuse him of doing, that the snap decisions of unreflective morality based on mere feelings of dislike and indignation are to be the ground on which a practice is to be made criminal. Thus he declares that "before a society can put a practice beyond the limits of tolerance [and hence make it a criminal offense], there must be a *deliberate* judgment that the practice is injurious to society" (p. 17, my italics). Nor does he maintain, as some critics have suggested, that "the arm of the law" should always be used to enforce society's judgment as to what is immoral—on the contrary, he presents a number of important prudential considerations which severely restrict the use of the criminal law to eradicate such immoral behavior. But except for the suggestion that a reliable symptom of practices that could destroy a social order is whether they generate in all members of a jury (and inferentially, in a majority of "right-minded persons" in the community) strong feelings of reprobation and intolerance (p. 17), he gives no reasons for supposing that the "deliberate judgments" he has emphasized as essential can be obtained by the procedure he recommends for ascertaining whether some conduct is detrimental to the social order; and he does not even discuss obvious alternatives to his proposal, such as the use of special commissions like the Wolfenden Committee itself to determine whether a practice does indeed have adverse consequences for society.

In short, while Mill's attempt to delimit a category of conduct which is permanently immune to legal as well as other forms of social control seems to me unsuccessful, I also think the difficulties I have been surveying make inconclusive Devlin's argument that the use of the criminal law to enforce moral standards for so-called "private conduct" is justifiable, if it is essential for preserving the integrity of society.

IV

However, Devlin has been criticized by Professor Hart and others for disavowing Mill's doctrine on the justifiable limits of interference with an individual's freedom, and especially for dissenting from Mill's view that it is never warranted to compel a person to do or refrain from doing an action merely for the sake of his own welfare. I want therefore to examine briefly the main line of Hart's defense of Mill.

There are a variety of practices which are illegal in many countries, though on the face of it only the parties directly involved in their performance are affected by them. I have already noted that Mill himself approved a number of such laws; but despite the doubtful consistency of his doing so, he offered no clear rationale for them. On the other hand, Devlin maintains that the existence of such laws can be explained only on the assumption that they illustrate society's efforts "to enforce a moral principle and nothing else."[4] But Hart rejects this interpretation, and in

---

[4] H. L. A. Hart, *Law, Liberty, and Morality* (Stanford, Cal.: Stanford University Press, 1963), p. 7.

his discussion of several examples of such laws, he proposes what he claims to be a different one. I will comment on his views as he presents them in the context of two examples.

1. Bigamy is a crime in many countries. Why should it be made a criminal offense, especially since in most jurisdictions a married man is doing nothing illegal if, while his legal spouse is alive, he lives with another woman and appears in public with her as husband and wife—*unless* he also goes through a marriage ceremony with her? Hart denies that the law is justified as an attempt "to enforce private morality as such"; and after expressing some sympathy for the view that the law might be "accepted as an attempt to protect religious feelings from offence by a public act desecrating the ceremony" of marriage, he declares that on this view "the bigamist is punished neither as irreligious nor as immoral but as a *nuisance*. For the law is then concerned with the *offensiveness to others* of his *public conduct*, not with the immorality of his private conduct." [5] However, as Devlin has been quick to note, a marriage ceremony can be performed in the privacy of some civil servant's office, with no one but the celebrants and their intimate friends any the wiser; and it is therefore difficult to make sense of Hart's suggestion that the bigamist is being punished for the offense created by a public act, if there was no such offense because the bigamous marriage ceremony was in fact performed in private. But however this may be, there is a more fundamental point to be made. Hart is begging the question if he assumes that to judge an action to be a nuisance (or offensive) to others, is always independent of any judgment of its morality. If bigamous marriages and other kinds of public conduct are crimes in the U.S. because they are offensive to others in America, they are in fact not offensive to members of other cultures in which Puritanical conceptions of moral behavior are not widespread; and such examples make it difficult to deny that some conduct is regarded as a nuisance to others, just because those others regard the conduct as immoral. Accordingly, if bigamy is a crime because it is a nuisance to others, it does not follow without further argument that the bigamist is not punished because he is judged by society to be immoral, but for some other reason. This further argument Hart does not supply; but without it, he has not presented a clear alternative to the claim that in the case of bigamy at any rate the law is being used to enforce morals.

2. Hart's second example is as follows. With some exceptions such as rape, the criminal law does not permit, and has never permitted, the consent of the victim in a case involving physical injury to be used as an argument for the defense. But if one person makes a pact with a second

---

[5] *Ibid.*, p. 41 [my italics].

to be beaten or even killed, and the second one does as he promised, why should he be liable to punishment by society, if the parties to the agreement were of sane mind when they made it, both entered into it voluntarily, and no one else was injured by the transaction? (Incidentally, the example is not as grotesque as it may seem—it states the situation covered by current laws forbidding voluntary euthanasia.) To punish the defendant in this case is in direct conflict with Mill's explicit injunction that the law must never be used to interfere with an individual's freedom to make his "private" arrangements as he thinks best, even though as others see the matter his best interests are not served by his actions. Can this rule of law be justified? Devlin thinks it can, but only in one way; and he offers the justification that will by now be familiar, namely, that "there are certain standards of behavior or moral principles which society requires to be observed; and the breach of them is an offence not merely against the person who is injured but against society as a whole." [6] On the other hand, Hart denies this claim. How then does he justify this rule of law? He maintains that "The rules excluding the victim's consent as a defence to charges of murder or assault may perfectly well be explained as a piece of *paternalism,* designed to protect individuals against themselves." [7] In consequence, he finds fault with Devlin for failing to distinguish between what Hart calls "legal moralism" (the doctrine he attributes to Devlin and which justifies the use of the law to enforce positive morality), and "legal paternalism" (the doctrine which justifies using the law to protect people against themselves). According to Hart, Mill's principle of liberty excludes legal moralism. But while in general he aligns himself with Mill's principle, he believes that if it is to accommodate such rules of law as the one under discussion, the principle must be amended; and although he does not present a formulation of the revised principle, he suggests that the amended form must be consonant with legal paternalism.

However, Hart does little to make clear just how legal moralism differs from legal paternalism, and that it is not a distinction without difference. He suggests that while a legal moralist justifies a law regulating actions that are allegedly not harmful to others, on the ground that its aim is to enforce morality "as such"—whatever the phrase "as such" may signify—a legal paternalist who endorses the law will justify it on the ground that it seeks to protect people against themselves. But is there a substantive difference here? Can there be a rule of law that is compatible with legal moralism, but which is necessarily excluded by legal paternalism? Could not any law that is said to be simply an attempt to enforce

---

[6] Devlin, *op. cit.,* pp. 6–7.
[7] Hart, *op. cit.,* p. 31 [my italics].

morality be also construed as an attempt to protect men against themselves? Thus, Hart argues that the English law making the sale of narcotics a criminal offense is not concerned with punishing the seller for his immorality, as legal moralists claim, but with protecting the would-be purchaser.[8] But could not a legal paternalist offer an analogous support for *any* law endorsed by a legal moralist? And conversely, in endorsing the narcotics law on the ground that it punishes the seller for his immorality, the legal moralist can maintain that the seller is immoral *because* he makes available to others an article that is harmful to its users.

Hart also defends the distinction between legal paternalism and legal moralism by claiming that the former is a sounder moral policy than the latter. For according to him, the conceptions of men's best interests that legal paternalism seeks to enforce are the products of what he calls "critical morality," while the conceptions legal moralism would enforce are the creatures of blind custom and unexamined tradition. If there is this difference, it is undoubtedly an important one. But even if there is, Hart's claim presupposes that the distinction between legal moralism and legal paternalism has already been established; and it assumes without argument that there is a unique system of critical morality which underlies the proposals of legal paternalism, and that this system is a sound one. It is plain, however, that many systems of critical morality have been developed, and that their conceptions of what is to men's best interests do not always agree. There is certainly no consensus even among deeply reflective men as to which system of critical morality is the most adequate one, so that legal paternalists are likely to differ among themselves as well as with legal moralists as to the rules that should guide men's conduct. It surely does not follow that because legal paternalism is based on a critical morality, its proposals for regulating men's actions are necessarily sounder than the proposals of legal moralists.

But however this may be, if legal paternalism is a justifiable policy in the law—as Hart appears to hold—its adoption as a principle of legislation destroys the possibility of establishing a permanent division between conduct that is only of private concern and conduct that is of legitimate public interest. Adoption of the policy certainly permits the introduction of legal controls at which Mill would have been aghast.

V

I have taken much time to belabor the simple point that Mill's principle is not an adequate guide to legal and other forms of social control of men's behavior. My excuse for doing so is that the principle is still very

---

[8] *Ibid.*, p. 32.

much alive in current discussions of legal and social philosophy, as the controversy between Devlin and his critics makes evident. Moreover, though the limitations of Mill's views on liberty have been often noted, they stress an important component in a reasonable ideal of human life— a component that needs to be stressed, if it is not to be swept aside by more insistent demands directed to realizing other human aspirations. But while I think Mill overdid the stress, how the ideal of individual freedom can be adjusted to competing aspirations is to me a question of perennial interest.

Like Tocqueville, Mill feared some of the leveling tendencies in modern democracies, and was apprehensive of the intolerance that custom-bound and unenlightened majorities can exhibit toward new ideas, fresh sensibilities, and intellectual as well as artistic excellence. He prized these achievements above all else, and believed they are indissolubly linked with the possession of maximum individual freedom that is compatible with life in society as he knew it. He therefore sought to secure the continuance of these achievements; and his principle of liberty was not only an expression of his conception of the human good, but also a protective wall to safeguard its pursuit.

As in the case of other political philosophers who saw in the pursuit of a multiplicity of objectives a danger to the realization of what they prized highly, Mill thus made individual freedom an absolute good to which he formally subordinated all other objectives—though his actual evaluations of social practices and his recommendations of changes in them are not always consonant with his formal principle. However, the elevation of individual liberty to the rank of the supreme good is clearly arbitrary. Most men do not cherish personal freedom above all else, even after prolonged and careful reflection; and in any case, they prize other things as well—indeed, sometimes as indispensable to a satisfactory and well-ordered life—such as health, some measure of worldly success and security, friendship and family, achievement and recognition by one's peers, or influence in the affairs of men. Moreover, maximum personal freedom is in general neither a necessary condition for the realization of all other legitimate objectives, nor is it compatible with some of them.

Accordingly, since many different interests, some of which may be conflicting ones, must be recognized in dealings with social problems, and since no one interest dominates the others permanently and in all contexts, it does not seem possible to set fixed limits to justifiable legal control of men's conduct. On the other hand, though it is frequently claimed that a compromise must be effected between the interests involved in a given problem, how the compromise should be made and in conformity with what rules, are questions to which I know no satisfactory answer. To be sure, broad rules have been proposed for dealing with this issue—for example, that the domain of personal freedom should be diminished as little as possible, or that the compromise should be so made as to maximize the expected social utility. But the proposed rules are vague and do not carry us very far. For in the absence of effective techniques for assessing the relative importance (or the utilities) of the various interests involved in the problem, it is not clear how the rules are to be applied, and despite the development of modern decision theory, there is no prospect that the needed techniques will soon be available.

There is then no general answer to the question whether certain categories of actions should be legally controlled and whether certain standards of conduct should be legally enforced. The question can be resolved only case by case, and though the proposed answers cannot be guaranteed to be the best ones possible, they are often the best ones available. And I cannot do better by way of a conclusion to this reflection than to quote a brief passage from Learned Hand:

> We shall never get along in matters of large public interest, if we proceed by generalization, indeed, if you insist, by principles, put forward as applicable in all circumstances. . . . The only way that public affairs can be succesfully managed is by treating each case by itself; even so, the trouble is far from ended. We must ask what a proposed measure will do in fact, how all the people whom it touches react and respond to it? . . . Then—and this the more difficult part—one must make a choice between the values that will be affected, for there are substantially always conflicts of group interest.[9]

---

[9] Learned Hand, *The Spirit of Liberty* (New York: Alfred A. Knopf, Inc., 1960), pp. 172–73.

Moral Enforcement and the Harm Principle *

Joel Feinberg

Lines of Attack on Mill

Arguments against Mill's unsupplemented harm principle (his claim that the private and public harm principles state the *only* grounds for justified interference with liberty) have been mainly of two different

---

kinds.[1] Many have argued that the harm principle justifies too much social and political interference in the affairs of individuals. Others allow that the prevention of individual and social harm is always a ground for interference but insist that it is by no means the only ground.

"No Man Is an Island"

Mill maintained in *On Liberty* that social interference is never justified in those of a man's affairs that concern himself only. But no man's affairs have effects on himself alone. There are a thousand subtle and indirect ways in which every individual act, no matter how private and solitary, affects others. It would therefore seem that society has a right, on Mill's own principles, to interfere in every department of human life. Mill anticipated this objection and took certain steps to disarm it. Let it be allowed that no human conduct is entirely, exclusively, and to the last degree self-regarding. Still, Mill insisted, we can distinguish between actions that are plainly other-regarding and those that are "directly," "chiefly," or "primarily" self-regarding. There will be a twilight area of cases difficult to classify, but that is true of many other workable distinctions, including that between night and day.

It is essential to Mill's theory that we make a distinction between two different kinds of consequences of human actions: the consequences *directly* affecting the interests of others, and those of primarily self-regarding behavior which only *indirectly* or *remotely* affect the interests of others. "No person ought to be punished simply for being drunk," Mill wrote, "but a soldier or policeman should be punished for being drunk on duty." [2] A drunk policeman directly harms the interests of others. His conduct gives opportunities to criminals and thus creates grave risk of harm to other citizens. It brings the police into disrepute, and makes the work of his colleagues more dangerous. Finally, it may lead to loss of the policeman's job, with serious consequences for his wife and children.

Consider, on the other hand, a hard working bachelor who habitually spends his evening hours drinking himself into a stupor, which he then sleeps off, rising fresh in the morning to put in another hard day's work. His drinking does not *directly* affect others in any of the ways of the drunk policeman's conduct. He has no family; he drinks alone and sets no direct example; he is not prevented from discharging any of his public duties; he creates no substantial risk of harm to the interests of other

---

[1] Cf. H. L. A. Hart, *Law, Liberty, and Morality* (Stanford: Stanford University Press, 1963), p. 5.

[2] John Stuart Mill, *On Liberty* (New York: Liberal Arts Press, 1956), pp. 99–100.

individuals. Although even his private conduct will have some effects on the interests of others, these are precisely the sorts of effects Mill would call "indirect" and "remote." First, in spending his evenings the way he does, our solitary tippler is *not* doing any number of other things that might be of greater utility to others. In not earning and spending more money, he is failing to stimulate the economy (except for the liquor industry) as much as he might. Second, he fails to spend his evening time improving his talents and making himself a better person. Perhaps he has a considerable native talent for painting or poetry, and his wastefulness is depriving the world of some valuable art. Third, he may make those of his colleagues who like him sad on his behalf. Finally, to those who know of his habits, he is a "bad example." [3] All of these "indirect harms" together, Mill maintained, do not outweigh the direct and serious harm that would result from social or legal coercion.

Mill's critics have never been entirely satisfied by this. Many have pointed out that Mill is concerned not only with political coercion and legal punishment but also with purely social coercion—moral pressure, social avoidance, ostracism. No responsible critic would wish the state to punish the solitary tippler, but social coercion is another matter. We can't prevent people from disapproving of an individual for his self-regarding faults or from expressing that disapproval to others, without undue restriction on *their* freedom. Such expressions, in Mill's view, are inevitably coercive, constituting a "milder form of punishment." Hence "social punishment" of individuals for conduct that directly concerns only themselves—the argument concludes—is both inevitable and, according to Mill's own principles, proper.

Mill anticipated this objection, too, and tried to cope with it by making a distinction between types of social responses. We cannot help but lower in our estimation a person with serious self-regarding faults. We will think ill of him, judge him to be at fault, and make him the inevitable and proper object of our disapproval, distaste, even contempt. We may warn others about him, avoid his company, and withhold gratuitous benefits from him—"not to the oppression of his individuality but in the exercise of ours." [4] Mill concedes that all of these social responses can function as "penalties"—but they are suffered "only in so far as they are the natural and, as it were, the spontaneous consequences of the faults themselves, not because they are purposely inflicted on him for the sake of punishment." [5] Other responses, on the other hand,

---

[3] Mill has a ready rejoinder to this last point: If the conduct in question is supposed to be greatly harmful to the actor himself, "the example, on the whole must be more salutory" than harmful socially, since it is a warning lesson, rather than an alluring model, to others. See Mill, *On Liberty*, p. 101.

[4] Mill, *On Liberty*, p. 94.

[5] Mill, *On Liberty*, p. 95.

add something to the "natural penalties"—pointed snubbing, economic reprisals, gossip campaigns, and so on. The added penalties, according to Mill, are precisely the ones that are never justified as responses to merely self-regarding flaws—"if he displeases us, we may express our distaste; and we may stand aloof from a person as well as from a thing that displeases us, but we shall not therefore feel called on to make his life uncomfortable." [6]

Other Proposed Grounds for Coercion

The distinction between self-regarding and other-regarding behavior, as Mill intended it to be understood, does seem at least roughly service-able, and unlikely to invite massive social interference in private affairs. I think most critics of Mills would grant that, but reject the harm principle on the opposite ground that it doesn't permit enough interference. These writers would allow at least one, and as many as five or more, additional valid grounds for coercion. Each of these proposed grounds is stated in a principle listed below. One might hold that restriction of one person's liberty can be justified:

1. To prevent harm to others, either
   a. injury to individual persons (*The Private Harm Principle*), or
   b. impairment of institutional practices that are in the public interest (*The Public Harm Principle*);
2. To prevent offense to others (*The Offense Principle*);
3. To prevent harm to self (*Legal Paternalism*);
4. To prevent or punish sin, i.e., to "enforce morality as such" (*Legal Moralism*);
5. To benefit the self (*Extreme Paternalism*);
6. To benefit others (*The Welfare Principle*).

The liberty-limiting principles on this list are best understood as stating neither necessary nor sufficient conditions for justified coercion, but rather specifications of the *kinds* of reasons that are always relevant or acceptable in support of proposed coercion, even though in a given case they may not be conclusive. [7] Each principle states that interference might be permissible *if* (but not *only if*) a certain condition is satisfied. Hence the principles are not mutually exclusive; it is possible to hold two or more of them at once, even all of them together, and it is possible

---

[6] Mill, *On Liberty*, p. 96.

[7] I owe this point to Professor Michael Bayles. See his contribution to *Issues in Law and Morality*, ed. Norman Care and Thomas Trelogan (Cleveland: The Press of Case Western Reserve University, 1973).

to deny all of them. Moreover, the principles cannot be construed as stating sufficient conditions for legitimate interference with liberty, for even though the principle is satisfied in a given case, the general presumption against coercion might not be outweighed. The harm principle, for example, does not justify state interference to prevent a tiny bit of inconsequential harm. Prevention of minor harm always counts in favor of proposals (as in a legislature) to restrict liberty, but in a given instance it might not count *enough* to outweigh the general presumption against interference, or it might be outweighed by the prospect of practical difficulties in enforcing the law, excessive costs, and forfeitures of privacy. A liberty-limiting principle states considerations that are always good reasons for coercion, though neither exclusively nor, in every case, decisively good reasons.

It will not be possible to examine each principle in detail here, and offer "proofs" and "refutations." The best way to defend one's selection of principles is to show to which positions they commit one on such issues as censorship of literature, "morals offenses," and compulsory social security programs. General principles arise in the course of deliberations over particular problems, especially in the efforts to defend one's judgments by showing that they are consistent with what has gone before. If a principle commits one to an antecedently unacceptable judgment, then one has to modify or supplement the principle in a way that does the least damage to the harmony of one's particular and general opinions taken as a group. On the other hand, when a solid, well-entrenched principle entails a change in a particular judgment, the overriding claims of consistency may require that the judgment be adjusted. This sort of dialectic is similar to the reasonings that are prevalent in law courts. When similar cases are decided in opposite ways, it is incumbent on the court to distinguish them in some respect that will reconcile the separate decisions with each other and with the common rule applied to each. Every effort is made to render current decisions consistent with past ones unless the precedents seem so disruptive of the overall internal harmony of the law that they must, reluctantly, be revised or abandoned. In social and political philosophy every person is on his own, and the counterparts to "past decisions" are the most confident judgments one makes in ordinary normative discourse. The philosophical task is to extract from these "given" judgments the principles that render them consistent, adjusting and modifying where necessary in order to convert the whole body of opinions into an intelligble, coherent system. There is no a priori way of refuting another's political opinions, but if our opponents are rational men committed to the ideal of consistency, we can always hope to show them that a given judgment is inconsistent with one of their own acknowledged principles. Then something will have to give.

Morals Offenses and Legal Moralism

Immoral conduct is no trivial thing, and we should hardly expect societies to tolerate it; yet if men are *forced* to refrain from immorality, their own choices will play very little role in what they do, so that they can hardly develop critical judgment and moral traits of a genuinely praiseworthy kind. Thus legal enforcement of morality seems to pose a dilemma. The problem does not arise if we assume that all immoral conduct is socially harmful, for immoral conduct will then be prohibited by law not just to punish sin or to "force men to be moral," but rather to prevent harm to others. If, however, there are forms of immorality that do not necessarily cause harm, "the problem of the enforcement of morality" becomes especially acute.

The central problem cases are those criminal actions generally called "morals offenses." Offenses against morality and decency have long constituted a category of crimes (as distinct from offenses against the person, offenses against property, and so on). These have included mainly sex offenses, such as adultery, fornication, sodomy, incest, and prostitution, but also a miscellany of nonsexual offenses, including cruelty to animals, desecration of the flag or other venerated symbols, and mistreatment of corpses. In a useful article,[8] Louis B. Schwartz maintains that what sets these crimes off as a class is not their special relation to morality (murder is also an offense against morality, but it is not a "morals offense") but the lack of an essential connection between them and social harm. In particular, their suppression is not required by the public security. Some morals offenses may harm the perpetrators themselves, but the risk of harm of this sort has usually been consented to in advance by the actors. Offense to other parties, when it occurs, is usually a consequence of perpetration of the offenses *in public*, and can be prevented by statutes against "open lewdness," or "solicitation" in public places. That still leaves "morals offenses" committed by consenting adults in private. Should they really be crimes?

In addition to the general presumption against coercion, other arguments against legislation prohibiting private and harmless sexual practices are drawn from the harm principle itself; laws governing private affairs are extremely awkward and expensive to enforce, and have side effects that are invariably harmful. Laws against homosexuality, for example, can only be occasionally and randomly enforced, and this leads to the inequities of selective enforcement and opportunities for blackmail and private vengeance. Moreover, "the pursuit of homosexuals involves

---

[8] Louis B. Schwartz, "Morals Offenses and the Model Penal Code," *Columbia Law Review*, LXIII (1963), 669 ff.

policemen in degrading entrapment practices, and diverts attention and effort" [9] from more serious (harmful) crimes of aggression, fraud, and corruption.

These considerations have led some to argue against statutes that prohibit private immorality, but, not surprisingly, it has encouraged others to abandon their exclusive reliance on the harm and/or offense principles, at least in the case of morals offenses. The alternative principle of "legal moralism" has several forms. In its more moderate version it is commonly associated with the views of Patrick Devlin,[10] whose theory, as I understand it, is really an application of the public harm principle. The proper aim of criminal law, he agrees, is the prevention of harm, not merely to individuals, but also (and primarily) to society itself. A shared moral code, Devlin argues, is a necessary condition for the very existence of a community. Shared moral convictions function as "invisible bonds" tying individuals together into an orderly society. Moreover, the fundamental unifying morality (to switch the metaphor) is a kind of "seamless web"; [11] to damage it at one point is to weaken it throughout. Hence, society has as much right to protect its moral code by legal coercion as it does to protect its equally indispensable political institutions. The law cannot tolerate politically revolutionary activity, nor can it accept activity that rips asunder its moral fabric. "The suppression of vice is as much the law's business as the suppression of subversive activities; it is no more possible to define a sphere of private morality than it is to define one of private subversive activity." [12]

H. L. A. Hart finds it plausible that some shared morality is necessary to the existence of a community, but criticizes Devlin's further contention "that a society is identical with its morality as that is at any given moment of its history, so that a change in its morality is tantamount to the destruction of a society." [13] Indeed, a moral critic might admit that we can't exist as a society without some morality, while insisting that we can perfectly well exist without *this* morality (if we put a better one in its place). Devlin seems to reply that the shared morality *can* be changed even though protected by law, and, when it does change, the emergent

---

9 Schwartz, "Morals Offenses and the Model Penal Code," 671.

10 Patrick Devlin, *The Enforcement of Morals* (London: Oxford University Press, 1965).

11 The phrase is not Devlin's but that of his critic, H. L. A. Hart, in *Law, Liberty, and Morality* (Stanford: Stanford University Press, 1963), p. 51. In his rejoinder to Hart, Devlin writes: "Seamlessness presses the simile rather hard but apart from that, I should say that for most people morality is a web of beliefs rather than a number of unconnected ones." Devlin. *The Enforcement of Morals*, p. 115

12 Devlin, *The Enforcement of Morality*, pp. 13–14.

13 Hart, *Law, Liberty, and Morality*, p. 51.

reformed morality in turn deserves *its* legal protection.[14] The law then functions to make moral reform difficult, but there is no preventing change where reforming zeal is fierce enough. How does one bring about a change in prevailing moral beliefs when they are enshrined in law? Presumably by advocating conduct which is in fact illegal, by putting into public practice what one preaches, and by demonstrating one's sincerity by marching proudly off to jail for one's convictions:

> there is . . . a natural respect for opinions that are sincerely held. When such opinions accumulate enough weight, the law must either yield or it is broken. In a democratic society . . . there will be a strong tendency for it to yield—not to abandon all defenses so as to let in the horde, but to give ground to those who are prepared to fight for something that they prize. To fight may be to suffer. A willingness to suffer is the most convincing proof of sincerity. Without the law there would be no proof. The law is the anvil on which the hammer strikes.[15]

In this remarkable passage, Devlin has discovered another argument for enforcing "morality as such," and incidentally for principled civil disobedience as the main technique for initiating and regulating moral change. A similar argument, deriving from Samuel Johnson and applying mainly to changes in religious doctrine, was well known to Mill. According to this theory, religious innovators deserve to be persecuted, for persecution allows them to prove their mettle and demonstrate their disinterested good faith, while their teachings, insofar as they are true, cannot be hurt, since truth will always triumph in the end. Mill held this method of testing truth, whether in science, religion, or morality, to be both uneconomical and ungenerous.[16] But if self-sacrificing civil disobedience is *not* the most efficient and humane remedy for the moral reformer, what instruments of moral change are available to him? This question is not only difficult to answer in its own right, it is also the rock that sinks Devlin's favorite analogy between "harmless" immorality and political subversion.

Consider the nature of subversion. Most modern law-governed countries have a constitution, a set of duly constituted authorities, and a body of statutes created and enforced by these authorities. The ways of changing these things will be well known, orderly, and permitted by the constitution. For example, constitutions are amended, legislators are elected, and new legislation is introduced. On the other hand, it is easy to conceive of various sorts of unpermitted and disorderly change—through assassina-

---

[14] Devlin, *The Enforcement of Morality*, pp. 115 ff.
[15] Devlin, *The Enforcement of Morality*, p. 116.
[16] John Stuart Mill, *On Liberty*, pp. 33–34.

tion and violent revolution, or bribery and subornation, or the use of legitimately won power to extort and intimidate. Only these illegitimate methods of change can be called "subversion." But here the analogy between positive law and positive morality begins to break down. There is no "moral constitution," no well-known and orderly way of introducing moral legislation to duly constituted moral legislators, no clear convention of majority rule. Moral subversion, if there is such a thing, must consist in the employment of disallowed techniques of change instead of the officially permitted "constitutional" ones. It consists not simply of change as such, but of illegitimate change. Insofar as the notion of legitimately induced moral change remains obscure, illegitimate moral change is no better. Still, there is enough content to both notions to preserve some analogy to the political case. A citizen works *legitimately* to change public moral beliefs when he openly and forthrightly expresses his own dissent, when he attempts to argue, persuade, and offer reasons, and when he lives according to his own convictions with persuasive quiet and dignity, neither harming others nor offering counterpersuasive offense to tender sensibilities. A citizen attempts to change mores by *illegitimate* means when he abandons argument and example for force and fraud. If this is the basis of the distinction between legitimate and illegitimate techniques of moral change, then the use of state power to affect moral belief *one way or the other*, when harmfulness is not involved, is a clear ex-example of illegitimacy. Government enforcement of the conventional code is not to be called "moral subversion," of course, because it is used on behalf of the status quo; but whether conservative or innovative, it is equally in defiance of our "moral constitution" (if anything is).

The second version of legal moralism is the pure version, not some other principle in disguise. Enforcement of morality as such and the attendant punishment of sin are not justified as means to some further social aim (such as preservation of social cohesiveness) but are ends in themselves. Perhaps J. F. Stephen was expressing this pure moralism when he wrote that "there are acts of wickedness so gross and outrageous that . . . [protection of others apart], they must be prevented at any cost to the offender and punished if they occur with exemplary severity." [17] From his examples it is clear that Stephen had in mind the very acts that are called "morals offenses" in the law.

It is sometimes said in support of pure legal moralism that the world as a whole would be a better place without morally ugly, even "harmlessly immoral," conduct, and that our actual universe is intrinsically worse for having such conduct in it. The threat of punishment, the argument con-

---

[17] James Fitzjames Stephen, *Liberty, Equality, Fraternity* (London: 1873), p. 163.

tinues, deters such conduct. Actual instances of punishment not only back up the threat, and thus help keep future moral weeds out of the universe's garden, they also erase past evils from the universe's temporal record by "nullifying" them, or making it as if they never were. Thus punishment, it is said, contributes to the intrinsic value of the universe in two ways: by canceling out past sins and preventing future ones.[18]

There is some plausibility in this view when it is applied to ordinary harmful crimes, especially those involving duplicity or cruelty, which really do seem to "set the universe out of joint." It is natural enough to think of repentance, apology, or forgiveness as "setting things straight," and of punishment as a kind of "payment" or a wiping clean of the moral slate. But in cases where it is natural to resort to such analogies, there is not only a rule infraction, there is also a *victim*—some person or society of persons who have been harmed. Where there is no victim—and especially where there is no profit at the expense of another—"setting things straight" has no clear intuitive content.

Punishment may yet play its role in discouraging harmless private immoralities for the sake of "the universe's moral record." But if fear of punishment is to keep people from illicit intercourse (or from desecrating flags, or mistreating corpses) in the privacy of their own rooms, then morality shall have to be enforced with a fearsome efficiency that shows no respect for individual privacy. If private immoralities are to be deterred by threat of punishment, the detecting authorities must be able to look into the hidden chambers and locked rooms of anyone's private domicile. When we put this massive forfeiture of privacy into the balance along with the usual costs of coercion—loss of spontaneity, stunting of rational powers, anxiety, hypocrisy, and the rest—the price of securing mere outward conformity to the community's moral standards (for that is all that can be achieved by the penal law) is exorbitant.

Perhaps the most interesting of the nonsexual morals offenses, and the most challenging case for application of liberty-limiting principles, is cruelty to animals. Suppose that John Doe is an intelligent, sensitive person with one very severe neurotic trait—he loves to see living things suffer pain. Fortunately, he never has occasion to torture human beings (he would genuinely regret that), for he can always find an animal for the purpose. For a period he locks himself in his room every night, draws the blind, and then beats and tortures a dog to death. The sounds of shrieks and moans, which are music to his ears, are nuisances to his neighbors, and when his landlady discovers what he has been doing she

---

[18] Cf. C. D. Broad, "Certain Features in Moore's Ethical Doctrines," in P. A. Schilpp, *The Philosophy of G. E. Moore* (Evanston, Ill.: Northwestern University Press, 1942), pp. 48 ff.

is so shocked she has to be hospitalized. Distressed that he has caused harm to human beings, Doe leaves the rooming house, buys a five hundred acre ranch, and moves into a house in the remote, unpopulated center of his own property. There, in the perfect privacy of his own home, he spends every evening maiming, torturing, and beating to death his own animals.

What are we to say of Doe's bizarre behavior? We have three alternatives. First we can say that it is perfectly permissible since it consists simply in a man's destruction of his own property. How a man disposes in private of his own property is no concern of anyone else providing he causes no nuisance such as loud noises and evil smells. Second, we can say that this behavior is patently immoral even though it causes no harm to the interests of anyone other than the actor; further, since it obviously should *not* be permitted by the law, this is a case where the harm principle is inadequate and must be supplemented by legal moralism. Third, we can extend the harm principle to animals, and argue that the law can interfere with the private enjoyment of property not to enforce "morality as such," but rather to prevent harm to the animals. The third alternative is the most inviting, but not without its difficulties. We *must* control animal movements, exploit animal labor, and, in many cases, deliberately slaughter animals. All these forms of treatment would be "harm" if inflicted on human beings, but cannot be allowed to count as harm to animals if the harm principle is to be extended to them in a realistic way. The best compromise is to recognize one supreme interest of animals, namely the interest in freedom from cruelly or wantonly inflicted pain, and to count as "harm" all and only invasions of *that* interest.

Obscenity and the Offense Principle

Up to this point we have considered the harm and offense principles together in order to determine whether between them they are sufficient to regulate conventional immoralities, or whether they need help from a further independent principle, legal moralism. Morals offenses were treated as essentially private so that the offense principle could not be stretched to apply to them. Obscene literature and pornographic displays would appear to be quite different in this respect. Both are materials deliberately published for the eyes of others, and their existence can bring partisans of the unsupplemented harm principle into direct conflict with those who endorse *both* the harm and offense principles.

In its untechnical, prelegal sense, the word "obscenity" refers to material dealing with nudity, sex, or excretion in an offensive manner. Such material becomes obscene in the legal sense when, because of its offensiveness or for some other reason [this question had best be left open in the definition], it is or ought to be without legal protection. The legal definition then incorporates the everyday sense, and essential to both is the requirement that the material be *offensive*. An item may offend one person and not another. "Obscenity," if it is to avoid this subjective relativity, must involve an interpersonal objective sense of "offensive." Material must be offensive by prevailing community standards that are public and well known, or be such that it is apt to offend virtually everyone.

Not all material that is generally offensive need also be harmful in any sense recognized by the harm principle. It is partly an empirical question whether reading or witnessing obscene material causes social harm; reliable evidence, even of a statistical kind, of causal connections between obscenity and antisocial behavior is extremely hard to find.[19] In the absence of clear and decisive evidence of harmfulness, the American Civil Liberties Union insists that the offensiveness of obscene material cannot be a sufficient ground for its repression:

> . . . the question in a case involving obscenity, just as in every case involving an attempted restriction upon free speech, is whether the words or pictures are used in such circumstances and are of such a nature as to create a clear and present danger that they will bring about a substantial evil that the state has a right to prevent. . . . We believe that under the current state of knowledge, there is grossly insufficient evidence to show that obscenity brings about *any* substantive evil.[20]

The A.C.L.U. argument employs *only* the harm principle among liberty-limiting principles, and treats literature, drama, and painting as forms of expression subject to the same rules as expressions of opinion. In respect to both types of expression, "every act of deciding what should be barred carries with it a danger to the community." [21] The suppression itself is an evil to the author who is squelched. The power to censor and punish involves risks that socially valuable material will be repressed along with the "filth." The overall effect of suppression, the A.C.L.U. concludes, is almost certainly to discourage nonconformist and eccentric expression generally. In order to override these serious risks, there must be in a given case an even more clear and present danger that the obscene material, if not squelched, will cause even greater harm; such countervailing evidence

---

[19] There have been some studies made, but the results have been inconclusive. See the *Report of the Federal Commission on Obscenity and Pornography* (New York: Bantam Books, 1970), pp. 169–308.

[20] *Obscenity and Censorship* (Pamphlet published by the American Civil Liberties Union, New York, March, 1963), p. 7.

[21] *Obscenity and Censorship*, p. 4.

is never forthcoming. (If such evidence were to accumulate, the A.C.L.U. would be perfectly willing to change its position on obscenity.)

The A.C.L.U. stand on obscenity seems clearly to be the position dictated by the unsupplemented harm principle and its corollary, the clear and present danger test. Is there any reason at this point to introduce the offense principle into the discussion? Unhappily, we may be forced to if we are to do justice to all of our particular intuitions in the most harmonious way. Consider an example suggested by Professor Schwartz. By the provisions of the new Model Penal Code, he writes, "a rich homosexual may not use a billboard on Times Square to promulgate to the general populace the techniques and pleasures of sodomy." [22] If the notion of "harm" is restricted to its narrow sense, that is, contrasted with "offense," it will be hard to reconstruct a rationale for this prohibition based on the harm principle. There is unlikely to be evidence that a lurid and obscene public poster in Times Square would create a clear and present danger of injury to those who fail to avert their eyes in time as they come blinking out of the subway stations. Yet it will be surpassingly difficult for even the most dedicated liberal to advocate freedom of expression in a case of this kind. Hence, if we are to justify coercion in this case, we will likely be driven, however reluctantly, to the offense principle.

There is good reason to be "reluctant" to embrace the offense principle until driven to it by an example like the above. People take perfectly genuine offense at many socially useful or harmless activities, from commercial advertisements to inane chatter. Moreover, widespread irrational prejudices can lead people to be disgusted, shocked, even morally repelled by perfectly innocent activities, and we should be loath to permit their groundless repugnance to override the innocence. The offense principle, therefore, must be formulated very precisely and applied in accordance with carefully formulated standards so as not to open the door to wholesale and intuitively unwarranted repression. At the very least we should require that the prohibited conduct or material be of the sort apt to offend almost everybody, and not just some shifting majority or special interest group.

It is instructive to note that a strictly drawn offense principle would not only justify prohibition of conduct and pictured conduct that is in its inherent character repellent, but also conduct and pictured conduct that is inoffensive in itself but offensive in inappropriate circumstances. I have in mind so-called indecencies such as public nudity. One can imagine an advocate of the unsupplemented harm principle arguing against the public nudity prohibition on the grounds that the sight of a naked body does no one any harm, and the state has no right to impose standards of dress

---

[22] Schwartz, "Morals Offenses and the Penal Code," 680.

or undress on private citizens. How one chooses to dress, after all, is a form of self-expression. If we do not permit the state to bar clashing colors or bizarre hair styles, by what right does it prohibit total undress? Perhaps the sight of naked people could at first lead to riots or other forms of antisocial behavior, but that is precisely the sort of contingency for which we have police. If we don't take away a person's right of free speech for the reason that its exercise may lead others to misbehave, we cannot in consistency deny his right to dress or undress as he chooses for the same reason.

There may be no answering this challenge on its own ground, but the offense principle provides a ready rationale for the nudity prohibition. The sight of nude bodies in public places is for almost everyone acutely *embarrassing*. Part of the explanation no doubt rests on the fact that nudity has an irresistible power to draw the eye and focus the thoughts on matters that are normally repressed. The conflict between these attracting and repressing forces is exciting, upsetting, and anxiety-producing. In some persons it will create at best a kind of painful turmoil, and at worst that experience of exposure to oneself of "peculiarly sensitive, intimate, vulnerable aspects of the self" [23] which is called *shame*. "One's feeling is involuntarily exposed openly in one's face; one is uncovered . . . taken by surprise . . . made a fool of." [24] The result is not mere "offense," but a kind of psychic jolt that in many normal people can be a painful wound. Even those of us who are better able to control our feelings might well resent the *nuisance* of having to do so.

If we are to accept the offense principle as a supplement to the harm principle, we must accept two corollaries which stand in relation to it similarly to the way in which the clear and present danger test stands to the harm principle. The first, the *standard of universality*, has already been touched upon. For the offensiveness (disgust, embarrassment, outraged sensibilities, or shame) to be sufficient to warrant coercion, it should be the reaction that could be expected from almost any person chosen at random from the nation as a whole, regardless of sect, faction, race, age, or sex. The second is the *standard of reasonable avoidability*. No one has a right to protection from the state against offensive experiences if he can effectively avoid those experiences with no unreasonable effort or inconvenience. If a nude person enters a public bus and takes a seat near the front, there may be no effective way for other patrons to avoid intensely shameful embarrassment (or other insupportable feelings) short of leaving the bus, which would be an unreasonable inconvenience.

---

[23] Helen Merrill Lynd, *On Shame and the Search for Identity* (New York: Science Editions, Inc., 1961), p. 33.

[24] Lynd, *On Shame and the Search for Identity*, p. 32.

Similarly, obscene remarks over a loudspeaker, homosexual billboards in Times Square, and pornographic handbills thrust into the hands of passing pedestrians all fail to be reasonably avoidable.

On the other hand, the offense principle, properly qualified, can give no warrant to the suppression of *books* on the grounds of obscenity. When printed words hide decorously behind covers of books sitting passively on bookstore shelves, their offensiveness is easily avoided. The contrary view is no doubt encouraged by the common comparison of obscenity with "smut," "filth," or "dirt." This in turn suggests an analogy to nuisance law, which governs cases where certain activities create loud noises or terrible odors offensive to neighbors, and "the courts must weigh the gravity of the nuisance [substitute "offense"] to the neighbors against the social utility [substitute "redeeming social value"] of the defendant's conduct." [25] There is, however, one vitiating disanalogy in this comparison. In the case of "dirty books" the offense is easily avoidable. There is nothing like the evil smell of rancid garbage oozing right out through the covers of a book. When an "obscene" book sits on a shelf, who is there to be offended? Those who want to read it for the sake of erotic stimulation presumably will not be offended (or else they wouldn't read it), and those who choose not to read it will have no experience by which to be offended. If its covers are too decorous, some innocents may browse through it by mistake and be offended by what they find, but they need only close the book to escape the offense. Even this offense, minimal as it is, could be completely avoided by prior consultation of trusted book reviewers. I conclude that there are no sufficient grounds derived either from the harm or offense principles for suppressing obscene literature, unless that ground be the protection of children; but I can think of no reason why restrictions on sales to children cannot work as well for printed materials as they do for cigarettes and whiskey.

SELECTED SUPPLEMENTARY READING

BAYLES, MICHAEL, "Comments on Feinberg: Offensive Conduct and the Law," in *Issues in Law and Morality*, eds. N. S. Care and T. K. Trelogan. Cleveland: Case Western Reserve Press, 1973.

DEVLIN, LORD PATRICK, *The Enforcement of Morals*. Oxford: Oxford University Press, 1964.

———, "Law, Democracy, and Morality," *University of Pennsylvania Law Review*, 110 (1962).

---

[25] William L. Prosser, *Handbook of the Law of Torts* (St. Paul: West Publishing Co., 1955), p. 411.

DWORKIN, RONALD, "Lord Devlin and the Enforcement of Morals," *Yale Law Journal*, 75 (May 1966).

FEINBERG, JOEL, "Harmless Immoralities and Offensive Nuisances," in *Issues in Law and Morality*, eds. N. S. Case and T. K. Trelogan. Cleveland: Case Western Reserve Press, 1973. With a Reply to Bayles.

GUSSFIELD, J., "On Legislating Morals," *California Law Review*, 56 (1968).

HART, H. L. A., "Immorality and Treason," *The Listener* (July 1959). Reprinted in *The Law as Literature*, ed. L. J. Blom-Cooper. Bodley Head, 1961.

————, *Law, Liberty and Morality*. Stanford, Calif.: Stanford University Press, 1963.

————, "The Use and Abuse of the Criminal Law," *Oxford Lawyer*, 4 (1961).

HENKIN, LOUIS, "Morals and the Constitution: The Sin of Obscenity," *Columbia Law Review*, 63 (1963).

HUGHES, GRAHAM, "Morals and the Criminal Law," *Yale Law Journal*, 71 (1962).

GILBY, THOMAS, O. P., "The Crimination of Sin," *Blackfriars*, 41 (1960).

GINSBERG, MORRIS, "Law and Morals," *The British Journal of Criminology* (January 1964).

MACPHERSON, C. B., "The Maximization of Democracy," in *Philosophy, Politics and Society* (Third Series), ed. Peter Laslett and W. G. Runciman. Oxford: Basil Blackwell, 1967.

MEWETT, ALAN W., "Morality and the Criminal Law," *University of Toronto Law Journal*, 14 (1962).

MILL, JOHN STUART, *On Liberty*. London, 1859.

MITCHELL, B., *Law, Morality and Religion in a Secular Society*. London: Oxford University Press, 1967.

NAGEL, THOMAS, "Sexual Perversion," *The Journal of Philosophy*, 66 (1969).

"Private Consensual Adult Behavior: The Requirement of Harm to Others in the Enforcement of Morality," *U.C.L.A. Law Review*, 14 (1967).

RADCLIFF, PETER, ed., *Limits of Liberty*. Belmont, Calif.: Wadsworth Publishing Company, Inc., 1966.

ROSTOW, EUGENE, "The Enforcement of Morals," *Cambridge Law Journal* (1960). Reprinted in E. Rostow, *The Sovereign Prerogative*. New Haven, Conn.: Yale University Press, 1962.

SCHUR, EDWIN M., *Crimes Without Victims*. Englewood Cliffs, N.J.: Prentice-Hall, Inc., 1965.

SKOLNICK, J., "Coercion to Virtue," *Southern California Law Review*, 41 (1968).

WASSERSTROM, RICHARD, ed., *Morality and the Law*. Belmont, Calif.: Wadsworth Publishing Company, Inc., 1971.

WHITELEY, C. H., and W. M. WHITELEY, *Sex and Morals*. New York: Basic Books, 1967.

WILLIAMS, GLANVILLE, *The Sanctity of Life and the Criminal Law*. New York: Alfred A. Knopf, 1957.

————, "Sex and Morals in the Criminal Law," *Criminal Law Review* (1964).

"Wolfenden Report." Report of the Committee on Homosexual Offences and Prostitution, 1957, Cmd. 247.

WOLLHEIM, RICHARD, "Crime, Sin and Mr. Justice Devlin," *Encounter* (November 1959).

WOOTTON, BARBARA, *Crime and the Criminal Law*. London: Stevens and Sons, 1963.

Chapter **6**

ABORTION

INTRODUCTION

It is generally taken as a measure of our superiority over the lower creatures that we have cultivated and adopted a belief in the sanctity of human life. As civilized people we insist that it is wrong to take a human life. Accordingly, the answer to the question of whether abortions should or should not be performed is often considered ethically clear: the fetus is a human life and its intentional destruction is therefore morally wrong. Yet personal, social, and professional crises that make it difficult for some to accept this principle can, and regularly do, occur. For example: (1) A working woman with four children becomes pregnant, despite precautions; she and her husband realize that they cannot continue to provide for their family if she stops working and cannot, in any case, support a fifth child. (2) An entire nation is vastly overpopulated, disease-ridden, and impossibly short of food; but its citizens are totally ignorant of birth control measures. (3) A doctor about to deliver a child is faced with an emergency and a dilemma: If he allows labor to progress naturally, the fetus will die simply because labor is taking too long; but if he intervenes surgically to deliver the child, the mother will die from the complications of surgery.

In each of these situations difficult ethical decisions must be made involving whether or not to allow the abortion of a human fetus—or its death. The fact that the decision to be made may be social, as in the overpopulation case, or professional, as in the case of the doctor, or purely personal as in the case of the married couple, does not minimize its ethical character. In each circumstance the superficially simple question of whether there is ever justification for intentionally sacrificing a human life arises in the most difficult and real dimensions, and presents us with a moral dilemma.

Two Fundamental Issues

There are, of course, readily understandable reasons, in addition to those just surveyed, why people seek abortions. Among these are cardiac complications, a suicidal condition of mind, psychological trauma, pregnancy caused by rape, and the use of fetus-deforming drugs. Such reasons certainly *explain* why abortions are often viewed as attractive means to extricate a woman from difficult circumstances. But the primary ethical issue remains: Are any such reasons sufficient to justify the act of aborting a human fetus? A philosopher concerned with abortion seeks a principled justification where ethical reasons are advanced for one's conclusions and even in defense of one's set of fundamental principles. One might, of course, decide that in only some of the above circumstances would an abortion be warranted, whereas in others it would not be justified. Even so, such a decision presupposes some set of general criteria that enable one to discriminate ethically justified abortions from ethically unjustified ones. Finding these criteria is the heart of the ethicist's concern with abortion.

Unfortunately, an adequate set of criteria is difficult to procure. It remains unclear precisely what counts as human life and what, if anything, counts as an exceptional circumstance allowing us to destroy forms of life. It is this dual confusion that has inspired philosophical reflection on abortion. Consequently, the following two issues—which are often difficult to separate in writings on abortion—have come to be thought the main problems requiring attention in discussions of the ethical justifiability of abortion:

1. The issue of the moral status of the unborn
2. The issue of which ethical reasons (in the form of rights, claims, and duties) have priority in abortion situations when a conflict between ethical reasons arises

Positions taken on (1) will naturally have a direct bearing on positions pertaining to (2). Hence both positions are likely to vary in accordance with different estimates of the nature of a fetus, including its nature in different stages of development.

Some ethicists regard a fetus, at any stage of development, as a human being whose life must be taken no more lightly than that of any other human being. If this view is judged correct, then the personal, social, and professional crises mentioned above probably either would be judged ethically irrelevant or would be judged to be circumstances in which homicide is justifiable. Other ethicists, however, believe that a fetus, at some stage of development, is less than fully human. They do not believe that all abortions, if any, violate principles against the taking of human life. If this view is accepted, the question of homicide never arises (if the abortion is performed during a "legitimate" stage of fetal development). But because our criteria of human life are so systematically unclear in regard to the status of a fetus, ethicists continue to debate under what circumstances, if any, abortions are morally justified.

Continuity and Discontinuity Theories

Quite diverse positions have been taken on these questions of justification. Many theories center on the attempt to draw a nonarbitrary line between human and nonhuman existence (in the hope that a nonarbitrary line can derivatively be drawn between the rights of the mother and the at least postulated rights of the fetus). For convenience' sake, these theories can be divided into the following polarities (though it is clear that many further gradations exist between the four categories): *

1. Strong continuity theories
2. Weak continuity theories
3. Weak discontinuity theories
4. Strong discontinuity theories

Strong continuity theories maintain that human life is the direct result of fertilization of human ova by human sperm. From this moment there is only a process of functional maturation, not increasing humanness. Accordingly, the fetus is regarded as a human lacking only certain functional capacities, a lack that also exists among certain diseased members of the adult community. The fetus, in this theory, is fully, not

---

* The classification system I have adopted is sometimes explained in terms of differences between "liberal" and "conservative" views. I have avoided this terminology because such political labels can be both distracting and inaccurate. Whether or not one considers the fetus to be human, for example, is a separate issue not at all clearly linked to liberalism or conservatism, whether political or legal in character. I am indebted to Professor Daniel Robinson for some features in this classification scheme.

merely potentially, a human life; its intentional destruction is therefore immoral because it is an act of murder. Roman Catholics have traditionally been among the leading exponents of the strong continuity theory, but they are by no means its only advocates.

Weak continuity theories maintain that the fetus has a quite special status but insist that the fetus is not a human being until some point later in pregnancy, rather than at conception. For this reason they hold that abortions after a specifiable stage of development (for example, first trimester of pregnancy, quickening, or viability) are destructions of human life and are morally permissible only if some paramount evil such as the death of the mother is to be averted by doing so. The principle of averting greater evil by doing a lesser evil is explicitly appealed to in this form of justification. Though legal rather than ethical in character, some arguments in the 1973 United States Supreme Court decision on abortion written by Justice Blackmun resemble this weak continuity posture.

Weak discontinuity theories agree partially with this latter position in that they take the fetus to have a special status which precludes the mother from adopting any treatment she wishes. But exponents of this theory also maintain that removal of the fetus is not at any specific stage tantamount to a destruction of human life and that many reasons for abortion override objections to it. For example, they contend that cases of rape, the possible death of the mother, and drug-deformed fetuses are serious ethical reasons which outweigh other ethical reasons against abortion. This stance has been favored by civil libertarians who place strong emphasis on the rights of individual citizens and who seek to minimize the authority of church and state in the realm of personal decisions.

Finally, *strong discontinuity theories* hold that a fetus does not have an ethically significant, special status but rather is analogous to a bit of tissue or to something a person possesses in the body, such as an appendix. When the fetus is unwanted, the person has a right to remove it, and this abortion operation is no more reprehensible than an appendectomy. This position has frequently been advocated by those adherents of women's liberation who emphasize the right of a woman to her own body; but the position is by no means restricted to such groups, and advocates of women's liberation have probably just as frequently endorsed some form of the weak discontinuity theory.

The Problem of Conflicting Rights

If either of the two *strong* positions is adopted, the problem of morally justifying abortion may appear to admit of rather easy resolution. If one endorses the strong *discontinuity* theory—that a fetus does not enjoy an ethically significant claim to treatment as a human being—the problem quickly disappears: abortions are not morally reprehensible and are prudentially justified much as other medical operations are. On the other hand, if one endorses the strong *continuity* theory—that a fetus at any stage of development is fully a human life, possibly a person— one may find the saying "abortion is murder" irresistible. By this reasoning abortion is never under any conditions justified, or at least could be permitted only if it were an instance of "justified homicide." Many strong continuity theorists would not accept this last qualification. Killing of the innocent, they would argue, is never permitted. Since abortion is a case of the deliberate destruction of innocent human life, it must under no circumstances be permitted and cannot ever be correctly classified as justifiable homicide.

A strong continuity theory, however, is not committed by its account of the nature of the fetus (as a human life) to take precisely this latter ethical position. A strong continuity theorist may argue that there are cases of justified homicide involving the unborn. For example, it might be argued that a pregnant woman may legitimately "kill" the fetus in "self-defense" if only one of the two may survive or if both will die unless the life of the fetus is terminated. In order to claim that abortion is *always* wrong, strong continuity advocates must justify maintaining the position that the fetus's "right to life" *always* overrides all the pregnant woman's rights, including *her* "right to life."

Most strong continuity theorists may have in fact maintained that a woman's rights are always overridden; but this is an accidental matter of historical fact. Even if the strong continuity theory is construed so that it entails that the unborn have rights because of their moral status, nothing in the theory requires that these moral rights always override all moral rights. Here a defender of the strong continuity theory confronts the problem of the morality of abortion on the level of conflicting rights: the unborn possess some rights (including a right to life) and pregnant women also possess rights (including a right to life). Each of these rights carries at least a prima facie moral claim to be treated in accordance with the right. But what is to be done when these rights conflict?

This problem is in some respects even greater for those who hold either of the two *weak* theories of the status of the fetus. Since both weak continuity and weak discontinuity theories provide moral grounds against arbitrary termination of fetal life (the fetus has some claim to protection against the actions of others) yet do not grant to the unborn (at least in some stages) the same right to life possessed by those already born, advocates of these theories are faced with the problem of specifying which rights or claims are sufficiently weighty that they take precedence over other rights or claims. More precisely, one must decide which rights or claims justify or fail to justify abortions or possibly even make abortions a matter of duty. Is the woman's right to decide what happens to her body sufficient to justify abortion? Is pregnancy as a result of rape sufficient? Is the likely death of the mother sufficient? Is psychological damage (sometimes used to justify "therapeutic abortion") sufficient? Is knowledge of a grossly deformed fetus, which produces severe mental suffering to the pregnant woman, sufficient? Also, both weak discontinuity and weak continuity theorists must decide at what stage of development there is a morally relevant difference in the fetus which allows abortion at an earlier stage and prohibits it at a later stage. Clearly this decision also must be a principled and not a merely arbitrary one.

It is not at all clear that one can resolve the problem of conflicting rights if one begins merely with rights or claims to which the unborn or the born have a strong presumption. It seems likely that a deeper resolution must be sought by development of a comprehensive normative ethical theory. One obviously crucial question in normative ethics bearing on the abortion issue is whether there are any *absolute,* as distinguished from merely *prima facie,* obligations: Are there duties pertaining to the rights of others that are never outweighed by other duties and moral claims with which they might come into conflict? It may be that no theory of abortion that confronts the problem of conflicting rights can provide a satisfactory resolution of the problem until this issue of the nature and kinds of obligations has been worked out.

Finally, it should not go unmentioned that one could claim that neither the moral status nor the rights of the fetus is the central issue in the abortion dispute. Instead, one could take the consequentialist position that abortion is a practice whose justification is a *social* issue. From this perspective the permissibility of abortion must be judged in terms of the consequences it has for society as a whole: If the consequences are generally better than the consequences of not allowing abortion, then it should be permitted, either as a rule or in particular cases, depending on the kind of argument from consequences being advanced.

Arguments in the Selections

Judith Thomson and *Baruch Brody* assume, for the sake of the issues they are debating, that a fetus is from conception a human life, with at least some rights. They then discuss whether, even under such conditions, abortion can sometimes be justified. Thomson rejects the claim that one can argue from the premise that a fetus is a person to the conclusion that abortion is impermissible. She argues that a woman has a right to defend her own life against a threat posed by her unborn child, even though the fetus has some justifiable claim to life. She takes seriously, and attempts to defend, the feminist slogan, "This body is *my* body!" She argues that even if a lesser reason than the mother's life is employed, and even if human beings do generally have a right to life, still "having a right to life does not guarantee having either a right to be given the use of or a right to be allowed continued use of another person's body—even if one needs it for life itself." Using this wedge Thomson contends that in some cases, such as rape, abortion is not *unjust* killing. She is quick to add, however, that she does not think abortion *always* morally permissible.

But even with this final qualification, Brody finds Thomson's arguments unconvincing. He first attempts to show that since a fetus is not attempting to take the mother's life, it is doubful that abortion can sometimes be justified on general grounds of self-defense. To Thomson's "the woman's body is hers, not the fetus's" argument, Brody replies that Thomson's argument is irrelevant. At stake is the right of a woman to *kill* the fetus in order to get back the sole use of her body. Here Brody distinguishes between one's duty to *save* life and one's duty *not to take* life. In abortion cases in which the woman's life is at stake, one must choose between saving the woman and taking the life of the fetus. In such circumstances, Brody contends, a woman's normal rights to her body have no relevance.

Brody's views have long been supported, in an extended form, by strong continuity theories that uphold the "doctrine of double effect." According to this doctrine it is absolutely wrong to kill an innocent person *intentionally*, though it is not absolutely wrong to adopt a course of action that one knows will *result in* the death of an innocent person. Applied to abortion situations in which one must choose between the life of the mother and that of the child, this doctrine requires that it is wrong to save a mother's life by intentionally causing the death of her fetus, but it is not wrong to allow the mother to die by (intentionally) not operating. Presumably a doctor would be intending the death of the child but only allowing, not intending, the death of the mother.

Jonathan Bennett vigorously attacks this doctrine of double effect. Bennett thinks the doctrine confused because "the action/consequence distinction" on which it rests does not clearly apply to obstetrical cases. Bennett attacks the doctrine's relevance as a general criterion of the moral rightness of actions. He finds the difference between "X killed Y" and "X let Y die" morally negligible—that is, not a morally relevant distinction to which we can appeal either in abortion cases or elsewhere. He concludes that only moral fanatics accept principles of the form "It would always be wrong to kill an innocent human, *whatever the consequences* of not doing so."

John Casey, however, maintains in a brief reply that Bennett is attacking an argument no intelligent absolutist would defend. Casey thinks the obstetrician faced with killing a child or letting the mother die is in fact faced with an insoluble moral dilemma, for any act he performs seems to be wrong on general moral grounds. Casey thinks the absolutist can thus free himself from Bennett's charges.

Daniel Dinello, in a second reply to Bennett, provides counter-examples to show that Bennett's construal of the "killing/letting die" distinction is irrelevant. Dinello then attempts to delineate correct conditions for making the distinction between killing and letting die. After this reconstruction Dinello argues that the distinction certainly can be morally significant and that Bennett certainly has not refuted "the conservative position." However, Dinello questions how widely the distinction can be correctly used as a moral criterion. Presumably he does not disagree with Bennett that it may well be irrelevant to many abortion decisions.

A Defense of Abortion *

Judith Jarvis Thomson [1]

Most opposition to abortion relies on the premise that the fetus is a human being, a person, from the moment of conception. The premise is argued for, but, as I think, not well. Take, for example, the most common argument. We are asked to notice that the development of a human being from conception through birth into childhood is continuous; then it is said that to draw a line, to choose a point in this development and say "before this point the thing is not a person, after this point it is a person" is to make an arbitrary choice, a choice for which in the nature of things no good reason can be given. It is concluded that the fetus is, or anyway that we had better say it is, a person from the moment of conception. But this conclusion does not follow. Similar things might be

---

* "A Defense of Abortion," by Judith Jarvis Thomson, *Philosophy and Public Affairs,* Vol. I, No. 1 (copyright © 1971 by Princeton University Press), pp. 47–66. Reprinted by permission of the author and Princeton University Press.

[1] I am very much indebted to James Thomson for discussion, criticism, and many helpful suggestions.

said about the development of an acorn into an oak tree, and it does not follow that acorns are oak trees, or that we had better say they are. Arguments of this form are sometimes called "slippery slope arguments" —the phrase is perhaps self-explanatory—and it is dismaying that opponents of abortion rely on them so heavily and uncritically.

I am inclined to agree, however, that the prospects for "drawing a line" in the development of the fetus look dim. I am inclined to think also that we shall probably have to agree that the fetus has already become a human person well before birth. Indeed, it comes as a surprise when one first learns how early in its life it begins to acquire human characteristics. By the tenth week, for example, it already has a face, arms and legs, fingers and toes; it has internal organs, and brain activity is detectable.[2] On the other hand, I think that the premise is false, that the fetus is not a person from the moment of conception. A newly fertilized ovum, a newly implanted clump of cells, is no more a person than an acorn is an oak tree. But I shall not discuss any of this. For it seems to me to be of great interest to ask what happens if, for the sake of argument, we allow the premise. How, precisely, are we supposed to get from there to the conclusion that abortion is morally impermissible? Opponents of abortion commonly spend most of their time establishing that the fetus is a person, and hardly any time explaining the step from there to the impermissibility of abortion. Perhaps they think the step too simple and obvious to require much comment. Or perhaps instead they are simply being economical in argument. Many of those who defend abortion rely on the premise that the fetus is not a person, but only a bit of tissue that will become a person at birth; and why pay out more arguments than you have to? Whatever the explanation, I suggest that the step they take is neither easy nor obvious, that it calls for closer examination than it is commonly given, and that when we do give it this closer examination we shall feel inclined to reject it.

I propose, then, that we grant the fetus is a person from the moment of conception. How does the argument go from here? Something like this, I take it. Every person has a right to life. So the fetus has a right to life. No doubt the mother has a right to decide what shall happen in and to her body; everyone would grant that. But surely a person's right to life is stronger and more stringent than the mother's right to decide what happens in and to her body, and so outweighs it. So the fetus may not be killed; an abortion may not be performed.

---

[2] Daniel Callahan, *Abortion: Law, Choice and Morality* (New York, 1970), p. 373. This book gives a fascinating survey of the available information on abortion. The Jewish tradition is surveyed in David M. Feldman, *Birth Control in Jewish Law* (New York, 1968), Part 5, the Catholic tradition in John T. Noonan, Jr., "An Almost Absolute Value in History," in *The Morality of Abortion,* ed. John T. Noonan, Jr. (Cambridge, Mass., 1970).

It sounds plausible. But now let me ask you to imagine this. You wake up in the morning and find yourself back to back in bed with an unconscious violinist. A famous unconscious violinist. He has been found to have a fatal kidney ailment, and the Society of Music Lovers has canvassed all the available medical records and found that you alone have the right blood type to help. They have therefore kidnapped you, and last night the violinist's circulatory system was plugged into yours, so that your kidneys can be used to extract poisons from his blood as well as your own. The director of the hospital now tells you, "Look, we're sorry the Society of Music Lovers did this to you—we would never have permitted it if we had known. But still, they did it, and the violinist now is plugged into you. To unplug you would be to kill him. But never mind, it's only for nine months. By then he will have recovered from his ailment, and can safely be unplugged from you." Is it morally incumbent on you to accede to this situation? No doubt it would be very nice of you if you did, a great kindness. But do you *have* to accede to it? What if it were not nine months, but nine years? Or longer still? What if the director of the hospital says, "Tough luck, I agree, but you've now got to stay in bed, with the violinist plugged into you, for the rest of your life. Because remember this. All persons have a right to life, and violinists are persons. Granted you have a right to decide what happens in and to your body, but a person's right to life outweighs your right to decide what happens in and to your body. So you cannot ever be unplugged from him." I imagine you would regard this as outrageous, which suggests that something really is wrong with that plausible-sounding argument I mentioned a moment ago.

In this case, of course, you were kidnapped; you didn't volunteer for the operation that plugged the violinist into your kidneys. Can those who oppose abortion on the ground I mentioned make an exception for a pregnancy due to rape? Certainly. They can say that persons have a right to life only if they didn't come into existence because of rape; or they can say that all persons have a right to life, but that some have less of a right to life than others, in particular, that those who came into existence because of rape have less. But these statements have a rather unpleasant sound. Surely the question of whether you have a right to life at all, or how much of it you have, shouldn't turn on the question of whether or not you are the product of a rape. And in fact the people who oppose abortion on the ground I mentioned do not make this distinction, and hence do not make an exception in case of rape.

Nor do they make an exception for a case in which the mother has to spend the nine months of her pregnancy in bed. They would agree that would be a great pity, and hard on the mother; but all the same, all persons have a right to life, the fetus is a person, and so on. I suspect, in fact, that they would not make an exception for a case in which, miraculously enough, the pregnancy went on for nine years, or even the rest of the mother's life.

Some won't even make an exception for a case in which continuation of the pregnancy is likely to shorten the mother's life; they regard abortion as impermissible even to save the mother's life. Such cases are nowadays very rare, and many opponents of abortion do not accept this extreme view. All the same, it is a good place to begin: a number of points of interest come out in respect to it.

1. Let us call the view that abortion is impermissible even to save the mother's life "the extreme view." I want to suggest first that it does not issue from the argument I mentioned earlier without the addition of some fairly powerful premises. Suppose a woman has become pregnant, and now learns that she has a cardiac condition such that she will die if she carries the baby to term. What may be done for her? The fetus, being a person, has a right to life, but as the mother is a person too, so has she a right to life. Presumably they have an equal right to life. How is it supposed to come out that an abortion may not be performed? If mother and child have an equal right to life, shouldn't we perhaps flip a coin? Or should we add to the mother's right to life her right to decide what happens in and to her body, which everybody seems to be ready to grant—the sum of her rights now outweighing the fetus' right to life?

The most familiar argument here is the following. We are told that performing the abortion would be directly killing [3] the child, whereas doing nothing would not be killing the mother, but only letting her die. Moreover, in killing the child, one would be killing an innocent person, for the child has committed no crime, and is not aiming at his mother's death. And then there are a variety of ways in which this might be continued. (1) But as directly killing an innocent person is always and absolutely impermissible, an abortion may not be performed. Or, (2) as directly killing an innocent person is murder, and murder is always and absolutely impermissible, an abortion may not be performed.[4] Or, (3) as one's duty to refrain from directly killing an innocent person is more

---

[3] The term "direct" in the arguments I refer to is a technical one. Roughly, what is meant by "direct killing" is either killing as an end in itself, or killing as a means to some end, for example, the end of saving someone else's life. See footnote 6 for an example of its use.

[4] Cf. *Encyclical Letter of Pope Pius XI on Christian Marriage*, St. Paul Editions (Boston, n.d.), p. 32: "however much we may pity the mother whose health and even life is gravely imperiled in the performance of the duty allotted to her by nature, nevertheless what could ever be a sufficient reason for excusing in any way the direct murder of the innocent? This is precisely what we are dealing with here." Noonan (*The Morality of Abortion,* p. 43) reads this as follows: "What cause can ever avail to excuse in any way the direct killing of the innocent? For it is a question of that."

stringent than one's duty to keep a person from dying, an abortion may not be performed. Or, (4) if one's only options are directly killing an innocent person or letting a person die, one must prefer letting the person die, and thus an abortion may not be performed.[5]

Some people seem to have thought that these are not further premises which must be added if the conclusion is to be reached, but that they follow from the very fact that an innocent person has a right to life.[6] But this seems to me to be a mistake, and perhaps the simplest way to show this is to bring out that while we must certainly grant that innocent persons have a right to life, the theses in (1) through (4) are all false. Take (2), for example. If directly killing an innocent person is murder, and thus is impermissible, then the mother's directly killing the innocent person inside her is murder, and thus is impermissible. But it cannot seriously be thought to be murder if the mother performs an abortion on herself to save her life. It cannot seriously be said that she *must* refrain, that she *must* sit passively by and wait for her death. Let us look again at the case of you and the violinist. There you are, in bed with the violinist, and the director of the hospital says to you, "It's all most distressing, and I deeply sympathize, but you see this is putting an additional strain on your kidneys, and you'll be dead within the month. But you *have* to stay where you are all the same. Because unplugging you would be directly killing an innocent violinist, and that's murder, and that's impermissible." If anything in the world is true, it is that you do not commit murder, you do not do what is impermissible, if you reach around to your back and unplug yourself from that violinist to save your life.

The main focus of attention in writings on abortion has been on what a third party may or may not do in answer to a request from a woman for an abortion. This is in a way understandable. Things being as they are, there isn't much a woman can safely do to abort herself. So the question asked is what a third party may do, and what the mother may do, if it is mentioned at all, is deduced, almost as an afterthought,

---

[5] The thesis in (4) is in an interesting way weaker than those in (1), (2), and (3): they rule out abortion even in cases in which both mother *and* child will die if the abortion is not performed. By contrast, one who held the view expressed in (4) could consistently say that one needn't prefer letting two persons die to killing one.

[6] Cf. the following passage from Pius XII, *Address to the Italian Catholic Society of Midwives:* "The baby in the maternal breast has the right to life immediately from God.—Hence there is no man, no human authority, no science, no medical, eugenic, social, economic or moral 'indication' which can establish or grant a valid juridical ground for a direct deliberate disposition of an innocent human life, that is a disposition which looks to its destruction either as an end or as a means to another end perhaps in itself not illicit.—The baby, still not born, is a man in the same degree and for the same reason as the mother" (quoted in Noonan, *The Morality of Abortion*, p. 45).

from what it is concluded that third parties may do. But it seems to me that to treat the matter in this way is to refuse to grant to the mother that very status of person which is so firmly insisted on for the fetus. For we cannot simply read off what a person may do from what a third party may do. Suppose you find yourself trapped in a tiny house with a growing child. I mean a very tiny house, and a rapidly growing child—you are already up against the wall of the house and in a few minutes you'll be crushed to death. The child on the other hand won't be crushed to death; if nothing is done to stop him from growing he'll be hurt, but in the end he'll simply burst open the house and walk out a free man. Now I could well understand it if a bystander were to say, "There's nothing we can do for you. We cannot choose between your life and his, we cannot be the ones to decide who is to live, we cannot intervene." But it cannot be concluded that you too can do nothing, that you cannot attack it to save your life. However innocent the child may be, you do not have to wait passively while it crushes you to death. Perhaps a pregnant woman is vaguely felt to have the status of house, to which we don't allow the right of self-defense. But if the woman houses the child, it should be remembered that she is a person who houses it.

I should perhaps stop to say explicitly that I am not claiming that people have a right to do anything whatever to save their lives. I think, rather, that there are drastic limits to the right of self-defense. If someone threatens you with death unless you torture someone else to death, I think you have not the right, even to save your life, to do so. But the case under consideration here is very different. In our case there are only two people involved, one whose life is threatened, and one who threatens it. Both are innocent: the one who is threatened is not threatened because of any fault, the one who threatens does not threaten because of any fault. For this reason we may feel that we bystanders cannot intervene. But the person threatened can.

In sum, a woman surely can defend her life against the threat to it posed by the unborn child, even if doing so involves its death. And this shows not merely that the theses in (1) through (4) are false; it shows also that the extreme view of abortion is false, and so we need not canvass any other possible ways of arriving at it from the argument I mentioned at the outset.

2. The extreme view could of course be weakened to say that while abortion is permissible to save the mother's life, it may not be performed by a third party, but only by the mother herself. But this cannot be right either. For what we have to keep in mind is that the mother and the unborn child are not like two tenants in a small house which has, by an unfortunate mistake, been rented to both: the mother *owns* the house. The fact that she does adds to the offensiveness of deducing that the

mother can do nothing from the supposition that third parties can do nothing. But it does more than this: it casts a bright light on the supposition that third parties can do nothing. Certainly it lets us see that a third party who says "I cannot choose between you" is fooling himself if he thinks this is impartiality. If Jones has found and fastened on a certain coat, which he needs to keep him from freezing, but which Smith also needs to keep him from freezing, then it is not impartiality that says "I cannot choose between you" when Smith owns the coat. Women have said again and again "This body is *my* body!" and they have reason to feel angry, reason to feel that it has been like shouting into the wind. Smith, after all, is hardly likely to bless us if we say to him, "Of course it's your coat, anybody would grant that it is. But no one may choose between you and Jones who is to have it."

We should really ask what it is that says "no one may choose" in the face of the fact that the body that houses the child is the mother's body. It may be simply a failure to appreciate this fact. But it may be something more interesting, namely the sense that one has a right to refuse to lay hands on people, even where it would be just and fair to do so. This justice might call for somebody to get Smith's coat back from Jones, and yet you have a right to refuse to be the one to lay hands on Jones, a right to refuse to do physical violence to him. This, I think, must be granted. But then what should be said is not "no one may choose," but only "I cannot choose," and indeed not even this, but "*I* will not *act*," leaving it open that somebody else can or should, and in particular that anyone in a position of authority, with the job of securing people's rights, both can and should. So this is no difficulty. I have not been arguing that any given third party must accede to the mother's request that he perform an abortion to save her life, but only that he may.

I suppose that in some views of human life the mother's body is only on loan to her, the loan not being one which gives her any prior claim to it. One who held this view might well think it impartiality to say "I cannot choose." But I shall simply ignore this possibility. My own view is that if a human being has any just, prior claim to anything at all, he has a just, prior claim to his own body. And perhaps this needn't be argued for here anyway, since, as I mentioned, the arguments against abortion we are looking at do grant that the woman has a right to decide what happens in and to her body.

But although they do grant it, I have tried to show that they do not take seriously what is done in granting it. I suggest the same thing will reappear even more clearly when we turn away from cases in which the mother's life is at stake, and attend, as I propose we now do, to the vastly more common cases in which a woman wants an abortion for some less weighty reason than preserving her own life.

3. Where the mother's life is not at stake, the argument I mentioned at the outset seems to have a much stronger pull. "Everyone has a right to life, so the unborn person has a right to life." And isn't the child's right to life weightier than anything other than the mother's own right to life, which she might put forward as ground for an abortion?

This argument treats the right to life as if it were unproblematic. It is not, and this seems to me to be precisely the source of the mistake.

For we should now, at long last, ask what it comes to, to have a right to life. In some views having a right to life includes having a right to be given at least the bare minimum one needs for continued life. But suppose that what in fact *is* the bare minimum a man needs for continued life is something he has no right at all to be given? If I am sick unto death, and the only thing that will save my life is the touch of Henry Fonda's cool hand on my fevered brow, then all the same, I have no right to be given the touch of Henry Fonda's cool hand on my fevered brow. It would be frightfully nice of him to fly in from the West Coast to provide it. It would be less nice, though no doubt well meant, if my friends flew out to the West Coast and carried Henry Fonda back with them. But I have no right at all against anybody that he should do this for me. Or again, to return to the story I told earlier, the fact that for continued life that violinist needs the continued use of your kidneys does not establish that he has a right to be given the continued use of your kidneys. He certainly has no right against you that *you* should give him continued use of your kidneys. For nobody has any right to use of your kidneys unless you give him such a right; and nobody has the right against you that you shall give him this right—if you do allow him to go on using your kidneys, this is a kindness on your part, and not something he can claim from you as his due. Nor has he any right against anybody else that *they* should give him continued use of your kidneys. Certainly he had no right against the Society of Music Lovers that they should plug him into you in the first place. And if you now start to unplug yourself, having learned that you will otherwise have to spend nine years in bed with him, there is nobody in the world who must try to prevent you, in order to see to it that he is given something he has a right to be given.

Some people are rather stricter about the right to life. In their view, it does not include the right to be given anything, but amounts to, and only to, the right not to be killed by anybody. But here a related difficulty arises. If everybody is to refrain from killing that violinist, then everybody must refrain from doing a great many different sorts of things. Everybody must refrain from slitting his throat, everybody must refrain from shooting him—and everybody must refrain from unplugging you from him. But does he have a right against everybody that they shall refrain from unplugging you from him? To refrain from doing this is to allow him to continue to use your kidneys. It could be argued that he has a right against us that *we* should allow him to continue to use your kidneys. That is, while he had no right against us that we should give him the use of your kidneys, it might be argued that he anyway has a right against us that we shall not now intervene and deprive him of the use of your kidneys. I shall come back to third-party interventions later. But certainly the violinist has no right against you that *you* shall allow him to continue to use your kidneys. As I said, if you do allow him to use them, it is a kindness on your part, and not something you owe him.

The difficulty I point to here is not peculiar to the right to life. It reappears in connection with all the other natural rights; and it is something which an adequate account of rights must deal with. For present purposes it is enough just to draw attention to it. But I would stress that I am not arguing that people do not have a right to life—quite to the contrary, it seems to me that the primary control we must place on the acceptability of an account of rights is that it should turn out in that account to be a truth that all persons have a right to life. I am arguing only that having a right to life does not guarantee having either a right to be given the use of or a right to be allowed continued use of another person's body—even if one needs it for life itself. So the right to life will not serve the opponents of abortion in the very simple and clear way in which they seem to have thought it would.

4. There is another way to bring out the difficulty. In the most ordinary sort of case, to deprive someone of what he has a right to is to treat him unjustly. Suppose a boy and his small brother are jointly given a box of chocolates for Christmas. If the older boy takes the box and refuses to give his brother any of the chocolates, he is unjust to him, for the brother has been given a right to half of them. But suppose that, having learned that otherwise it means nine years in bed with that violinist, you unplug yourself from him. You surely are not being unjust to him, for you gave him no right to use your kidneys, and no one else can have given him any such right. But we have to notice that in unplugging yourself, you are killing him; and violinists, like everybody else, have a right to life, and thus in the view we were considering just now, the right not to be killed. So here you do what he supposedly has a right you shall not do, but you do not act unjustly to him in doing it.

The emendation which may be made at this point is this: the right to life consists not in the right not to be killed, but rather in the right not to be killed unjustly. This runs a risk of circularity, but never mind: it would enable us to square the fact that the violinist has a right to life with the fact that you do not act unjustly toward him in unplugging yourself, thereby killing him. For if you do not kill him unjustly, you do not violate his right to life, and so it is no wonder you do him no injustice.

But if this emendation is accepted, the gap in the argument against abortion stares us plainly in the face: it is by no means enough to show that the fetus is a person, and to remind us that all persons have a right to life—we need to be shown also that killing the fetus violates its right to life, i.e., that abortion is unjust killing. And is it?

I suppose we may take it as a datum that in a case of pregnancy due to rape the mother has not given the unborn person a right to the use of her body for food and shelter. Indeed, in what pregnancy could it be supposed that the mother has given the unborn person such a right? It is not as if there were unborn persons drifting about the world, to whom a woman who wants a child says "I invite you in."

But it might be argued that there are other ways one can have acquired a right to the use of another person's body than by having been invited to use it by that person. Suppose a woman voluntarily indulges in intercourse, knowing of the chance it will issue in pregnancy, and then she does become pregnant; is she not in part responsible for the presence, in fact the very existence, of the unborn person inside her? No doubt she did not invite it in. But doesn't her partial responsibility for its being there itself give it a right to the use of her body? [7] If so, then her aborting it would be more like the boy's taking away the chocolates, and less like your unplugging yourself from the violinist—doing so would be depriving it of what it does have a right to, and thus would be doing it an injustice.

And then, too, it might be asked whether or not she can kill it even to save her own life: If she voluntarily called it into existence, how can she now kill it, even in self-defense?

The first thing to be said about this is that it is something new. Opponents of abortion have been so concerned to make out the independence of the fetus, in order to establish that it has a right to life, just as its mother does, that they have tended to overlook the possible support they might gain from making out that the fetus is *dependent* on the mother, in order to establish that she has a special kind of responsibility for it, a responsibility that gives it rights against her which are not possessed by any independent person—such as an ailing violinist who is a stranger to her.

On the other hand, this argument would give the unborn person a right to its mother's body only if her pregnancy resulted from a voluntary act, undertaken in full knowledge of the chance a pregnancy might result from it. It would leave out entirely the unborn person whose exist-

---

[7] The need for a discussion of this argument was brought home to me by members of the Society for Ethical and Legal Philosophy, to whom this paper was originally presented.

ence is due to rape. Pending the availability of some further argument, then, we would be left with the conclusion that unborn persons whose existence is due to rape have no right to the use of their mothers' bodies, and thus that aborting them is not depriving them of anything they have a right to and hence is not unjust killing.

And we should also notice that it is not at all plain that this argument really does go even as far as it purports to. For there are cases and cases, and the details make a difference. If the room is stuffy, and I therefore open a window to air it, and a burglar climbs in, it would be absurd to say, "Ah, now he can stay, she's given him a right to the use of her house—for she is partially responsible for his presence there, having voluntarily done what enabled him to get in, in full knowledge that there are such things as burglars, and that burglars burgle." It would be still more absurd to say this if I had had bars installed outside my windows, precisely to prevent burglars from getting in, and a burglar got in only because of a defect in the bars. It remains equally absurd if we imagine it is not a burglar who climbs in, but an innocent person who blunders or falls in. Again, suppose it were like this: people-seeds drift about in the air like pollen, and if you open your windows, one may drift in and take root in your carpets or upholstery. You don't want children, so you fix up your windows with fine mesh screens, the very best you can buy. As can happen, however, and on very, very rare occasions does happen, one of the screens is defective; and a seed drifts in and takes root. Does the person-plant who now develops have a right to the use of your house? Surely not—despite the fact that you voluntarily opened your windows, you knowingly kept carpets and upholstered furniture, and you knew that screens were sometimes defective. Someone may argue that you are responsible for its rooting, that it does have a right to your house, because after all you *could* have lived out your life with bare floors and furniture, or with sealed windows and doors. But this won't do—for by the same token anyone can avoid a pregnancy due to rape by having a hysterectomy, or anyway by never leaving home without a (reliable!) army.

It seems to me that the argument we are looking at can establish at most that there are *some* cases in which the unborn person has a right to the use of its mother's body, and therefore *some* cases in which abortion is unjust killing. There is room for much discussion and argument as to precisely which, if any. But I think we should sidestep this issue and leave it open, for at any rate the argument certainly does not establish that all abortion is unjust killing.

5. There is room for yet another argument here, however. We surely must all grant that there may be cases in which it would be morally indecent to detach a person from your body at the cost of his life. Suppose

you learn that what the violinist needs is not nine years of your life, but only one hour: all you need do to save his life is to spend one hour in that bed with him. Suppose also that letting him use your kidneys for that one hour would not affect your health in the slightest. Admittedly you were kidnapped. Admittedly you did not give anyone permission to plug him into you. Nevertheless it seems to me plain you *ought* to allow him to use your kidneys for that hour—it would be indecent to refuse.

Again, suppose pregnancy lasted only an hour, and constituted no threat to life or health. And suppose that a woman becomes pregnant as a result of rape. Admittedly she did not voluntarily do anything to bring about the existence of a child. Admittedly she did nothing at all which would give the unborn person a right to the use of her body. All the same it might well be said, as in the newly emended violinist story, that she *ought* to allow it to remain for that hour—that it would be indecent in her to refuse.

Now some people are inclined to use the term "right" in such a way that it follows from the fact that you ought to allow a person to use your body for the hour he needs, that he has a right to use your body for the hour he needs, even though he has not been given that right by any person or act. They may say that it follows also that if you refuse, you act unjustly toward him. This use of the term is perhaps so common that it cannot be called wrong; nevertheless it seems to me to be an unfortunate loosening of what we would do better to keep a tight rein on. Suppose that box of chocolates I mentioned earlier had not been given to both boys jointly, but was given only to the older boy. There he sits, stolidly eating his way through the box, his small brother watching enviously. Here we are likely to say "You ought not to be so mean. You ought to give your brother some of those chocolates." My own view is that it just does not follow from the truth of this that the brother has any right to any of the chocolates. If the boy refuses to give his brother any, he is greedy, stingy, callous—but not unjust. I suppose that the people I have in mind will say it does follow that the brother has a right to some of the chocolates, and thus that the boy does act unjustly if he refuses to give his brother any. But the effect of saying this is to obscure what we should keep distinct, namely the difference between the boy's refusal in this case and the boy's refusal in the earlier case, in which the box was given to both boys jointly, and in which the small brother thus had what was from any point of view clear title to half.

A further objection to so using the term "right" that from the fact that A ought to do a thing for B, it follows that B has a right against A that A do it for him, is that it is going to make the question of whether or not a man has a right to a thing turn on how easy it is to provide him with it; and this seems not merely unfortunate, but morally unacceptable. Take the case of Henry Fonda again. I said earlier that I had no right to the touch of his cool hand on my fevered brow, even though I needed it to save my life. I said it would be frightfully nice of him to fly in from the West Coast to provide me with it, but that I had no right against him that he should do so. But suppose he isn't on the West Coast. Suppose he has only to walk across the room, place a hand briefly on my brow—and lo, my life is saved. Then surely he ought to do it, it would be indecent to refuse. Is it to be said "Ah, well, it follows that in this case she has a right to the touch of his hand on her brow, and so it would be an injustice in him to refuse"? So that I have a right to it when it is easy for him to provide it, though no right when it's hard? It's rather a shocking idea that anyone's rights should fade away and disappear as it gets harder and harder to accord them to him.

So my own view is that even though you ought to let the violinist use your kidneys for the one hour he needs, we should not conclude that he has a right to do so—we should say that if you refuse, you are, like the boy who owns all the chocolates and will give none away, self-centered and callous, indecent in fact, but not unjust. And similarly, that even supposing a case in which a woman pregnant due to rape ought to allow the unborn person to use her body for the hour he needs, we should not conclude that he has a right to do so; we should conclude that she is self-centered, callous, indecent, but not unjust, if she refuses. The complaints are no less grave; they are just different. However, there is no need to insist on this point. If anyone does wish to deduce "he has a right" from "you ought," then all the same he must surely grant that there are cases in which it is not morally required of you that you allow that violinist to use your kidneys, and in which he does not have a right to use them, and in which you do not do him an injustice if you refuse. And so also for mother and unborn child. Except in such cases as the unborn person has a right to demand it—and we were leaving open the possibility that there may be such cases—nobody is morally *required* to make large sacrifices, of health, of all other interests and concerns, of all other duties and commitments, for nine years, or even for nine months, in order to keep another person alive.

6. We have in fact to distinguish between two kinds of Samaritan: the Good Samaritan and what we might call the Minimally Decent Samaritan. The story of the Good Samaritan, you will remember, goes like this:

> A certain man went down from Jerusalem to Jericho, and fell among thieves, which stripped him of his raiment, and wounded him, and departed, leaving him half dead.
> And by chance there came down a certain priest that way; and when he saw him, he passed by on the other side.

And likewise a Levite, when he was at the place, came and looked on him, and passed by on the other side.

But a certain Samaritan, as he journeyed, came where he was; and when he saw him he had compassion on him.

And went to him, and bound up his wounds, pouring in oil and wine, and set him on his own beast, and brought him to an inn, and took care of him.

And on the morrow, when he departed, he took out two pence, and gave them to the host, and said unto him, "Take care of him; and whatsoever thou spendest more, when I come again, I will repay thee."   (Luke 10:30–35)

The Good Samaritan went out of his way, at some cost to himself, to help one in need of it. We are not told what the options were, that is, whether or not the priest and the Levite could have helped by doing less than the Good Samaritan did, but assuming they could have, then the fact they did nothing at all shows they were not even Minimally Decent Samaritans, not because they were not Samaritans, but because they were not even minimally decent.

These things are a matter of degree, of course, but there is a difference, and it comes out perhaps most clearly in the story of Kitty Genovese, who, as you will remember, was murdered while thirty-eight people watched or listened, and did nothing at all to help her. A Good Samaritan would have rushed out to give direct assistance against the murderer. Or perhaps we had better allow that it would have been a Splendid Samaritan who did this, on the ground that it would have involved a risk of death for himself. But the thirty-eight not only did not do this, they did not even trouble to pick up a phone to call the police. Minimally Decent Samaritanism would call for doing at least that, and their not having done it was monstrous.

After telling the story of the Good Samaritan, Jesus said "Go, and do thou likewise." Perhaps he meant that we are morally required to act as the Good Samaritan did. Perhaps he was urging people to do more than is morally required of them. At all events it seems plain that it was not morally required of any of the thirty-eight that he rush out to give direct assistance at the risk of his own life, and that it is not morally required of anyone that he give long stretches of his life—nine years or nine months—to sustaining the life of a person who has no special right (we were leaving open the possibility of this) to demand it.

Indeed, with one rather striking class of exceptions, no one in any country in the world is *legally* required to do anywhere near as much as this for anyone else. The class of exceptions is obvious. My main concern here is not the state of the law in respect to abortion, but it is worth drawing attention to the fact that in no state in this country is any man compelled by law to be even a Minimally Decent Samaritan to any person; there is no law under which charges could be brought against the thirty-eight who stood by while Kitty Genovese died. By contrast, in most states in this country women are compelled by law to be not merely Minimally Decent Samaritans, but Good Samaritans to unborn persons inside them. This doesn't by itself settle anything one way or the other, because it may well be argued that there should be laws in this country—as there are in many European countries—compelling at least Minimally Decent Samaritanism.[8] But it does show that there is a gross injustice in the existing state of the law. And it shows also that the groups currently working against liberalization of abortion laws, in fact working toward having it declared unconstitutional for a state to permit abortion, had better start working for the adoption of Good Samaritan laws generally, or earn the charge that they are acting in bad faith.

I should think, myself, that Minimally Decent Samaritan laws would be one thing, Good Samaritan laws quite another, and in fact highly improper. But we are not here concerned with the law. What we should ask is not whether anybody should be compelled by law to be a Good Samaritan, but whether we must accede to a situation in which somebody is being compelled—by nature, perhaps—to be a Good Samaritan. We have, in other words, to look now at third-party interventions. I have been arguing that no person is morally required to make large sacrifices to sustain the life of another who has no right to demand them, and this even where the sacrifices do not include life itself; we are not morally required to be Good Samaritans or anyway Very Good Samaritans to one another. But what if a man cannot extricate himself from such a situation? What if he appeals to us to extricate him? It seems to me plain that there are cases in which we can, cases in which a Good Samaritan would extricate him. There you are, you were kidnapped, and nine years in bed with that violinist lie ahead of you. You have your own life to lead. You are sorry, but you simply cannot see giving up so much of your life to the sustaining of his. You cannot extricate yourself, and ask us to do so. I should have thought that—in light of his having no right to the use of your body—it was obvious that we do not have to accede to your being forced to give up so much. We can do what you ask. There is no injustice to the violinist in our doing so.

7. Following the lead of the opponents of abortion, I have throughout been speaking of the fetus merely as a person, and what I have been asking is whether or not the argument we began with, which proceeds only from the fetus' being a person, really does establish its conclusion. I have argued that it does not.

---

[8] For a discussion of the difficulties involved, and a survey of the European experience with such laws, see *The Good Samaritan and the Law*, ed. James M. Ratcliffe (New York, 1966).

But of course there are arguments and arguments, and it may be said that I have simply fastened on the wrong one. It may be said that what is important is not merely the fact that the fetus is a person, but that it is a person for whom the woman has a special kind of responsibility issuing from the fact that she is its mother. And it might be argued that all my analogies are therefore irrelevant—for you do not have that special kind of responsibility for that violinist, Henry Fonda does not have that special kind of responsibility for me. And our attention might be drawn to the fact that men and women both *are* compelled by law to provide support for their children.

I have in effect dealt (briefly) with this argument in section 4 above; but a (still briefer) recapitulation now may be in order. Surely we do not have any such "special responsibility" for a person unless we have assumed it, explicitly or implicitly. If a set of parents do not try to prevent pregnancy, do not obtain an abortion, and then at the time of birth of the child do not put it out for adoption, but rather take it home with them, then they have assumed responsibility for it, they have given it rights, and they cannot *now* withdraw support from it at the cost of its life because they now find it difficult to go on providing for it. But if they have taken all reasonable precautions against having a child, they do not simply by virtue of their biological relationship to the child who comes into existence have a special responsibility for it. They may wish to assume responsibility for it, or they may not wish to. And I am suggesting that if assuming responsibility for it would require large sacrifices, then they may refuse. A Good Samaritan would not refuse—or anyway, a Splendid Samaritan, if the sacrifices that had to be made were enormous. But then so would a Good Samaritan assume responsibility for that violinist; so would Henry Fonda, if he is a Good Samaritan, fly in from the West Coast and assume responsibility for me.

8. My argument will be found unsatisfactory on two counts by many of those who want to regard abortion as morally permissible. First, while I do argue that abortion is not impermissible, I do not argue that it is always permissible. There may well be cases in which carrying the child to term requires only Minimally Decent Samaritanism of the mother, and this is a standard we must not fall below. I am inclined to think it a merit of my account precisely that it does *not* give a general yes or a general no. It allows for and supports our sense that, for example, a sick and desperately frightened fourteen-year-old schoolgirl, pregnant due to rape, may *of course* choose abortion, and that any law which rules this out is an insane law. And it also allows for and supports our sense that in other cases resort to abortion is even positively indecent. It would be indecent in the woman to request an abortion, and indecent in a doctor to perform it, if she is in her seventh month, and wants the abortion just to avoid the nuisance of postponing a trip abroad. The very fact that the

arguments I have been drawing attention to treat all cases of abortion, or even all cases of abortion in which the mother's life is not at stake, as morally on a par ought to have made them suspect at the outset.

Second, while I am arguing for the permissibility of abortion in some cases, I am not arguing for the right to secure the death of the unborn child. It is easy to confuse these two things in that up to a certain point in the life of the fetus it is not able to survive outside the mother's body; hence removing it from her body guarantees its death. But they are importantly different. I have argued that you are not morally required to spend nine months in bed, sustaining the life of that violinist; but to say this is by no means to say that if, when you unplug yourself, there is a miracle and he survives, you then have a right to turn round and slit his throat. You may detach yourself even if this costs him his life; you have no right to be guaranteed his death, by some other means, if unplugging yourself does not kill him. There are some people who will feel dissatisfied by this feature of my argument. A woman may be utterly devastated by the thought of a child, a bit of herself, put out for adoption and never seen or heard of again. She may therefore want not merely that the child be detached from her, but more, that it die. Some opponents of abortion are inclined to regard this as beneath contempt—thereby showing insensitivity to what is surely a powerful source of despair. All the same, I agree that the desire for the child's death is not one which anybody may gratify, should it turn out to be possible to detach the child alive.

At this place, however, it should be remembered that we have only been pretending throughout that the fetus is a human being from the moment of conception. A very early abortion is surely not the killing of a person, and so is not dealt with by anything I have said here.

Thomson on Abortion *

Baruch Brody

There is a familiar argument that purports to show that it is always wrong for an expectant woman to have an abortion. It runs as follows: (1) from the moment of conception, a foetus is a human being with the

* "Thomson on Abortion," by Baruch Brody, *Philosophy and Public Affairs*, Vol. I, No. 3 (copyright © 1972 by Princeton University Press), pp. 335–40. Reprinted by permission of the author and Princeton University Press.

same rights to life as any other human being; (2) it is always wrong to take (directly) the life of an innocent human being; (3) therefore, it is always wrong to have an abortion. Judith Jarvis Thomson, in her recent article,[1] criticized the above argument by challenging (2). More importantly, she argued that (at least in most cases) a woman has the right to secure an abortion even if (1) is true, although there are cases in which it would be positively indecent to exercise this right. It seems to me, however, that her discussions of these points, as interesting as they are, are not entirely convincing. I would like in this note to explain why.

I

Professor Thomson unfortunately offers as her counterexample to (2) her very problematic account of the violinist, a case to which we will return below. There are, however, far more straightforward cases that show that (2) is false. One such case—another will be discussed briefly at the end of this note—is the one in which Y is about to shoot X and X can save his life only by taking Y's life. We would certainly want to say that, as part of his right of self-defense, X has the right to take Y's life, and he has that right even if Y is a perfectly innocent child. So the right of self-defense includes in some cases the taking of innocent lives, (2) is false, and the above argument against abortion collapses.

This point raises important theoretical issues and it is therefore worth elaborating upon. In a normal case of self-defense, the following three factors seem to be involved: (a) the continued existence of Y poses a threat to the life of X, a threat that can be met only by the taking of Y's life; (b) Y is unjustly attempting to take X's life; (c) Y is responsible for his attempt to take X's life and is therefore guilty of attempting to take X's life. There is, moreover, a very plausible argument that would seem to suggest that all three of these factors must be involved if X is to be justified in taking Y's life in self-defense. It runs as follows: Why is X justified in killing Y? Isn't it Y's guilt for his attempt to take X's life together with the threat that Y's continued existence poses for X's life that justifies X's killing Y? Or, to put it another way, Y's guilt makes X's life take precedence over Y's. But if this is the justification for taking a life in self-defense, then conditions (a), (b), and (c) must be satisfied. If (a) is not satisfied, then Y's living is no threat to X, and if (b) and (c) are not satisfied, then there is no relevant guilt on Y's part that makes X's life take precedence over his.

What our example of the child shows is that this plausible argument

---

[1] "A Defense of Abortion," *Philosophy & Public Affairs* I, no. 1 (Fall 1971): 47–66. (Page numbers in the text refer to this source; page numbers in brackets refer to the article as reprinted in this text.)

will not do. Even if conditions (a) and (b), but not (c), are satisfied, X has the right to take Y's life in self-defense. This means that the above justification is not the justification for acts of self-defense. And this raises two fundamental and interrelated questions: What is the justification for taking a life in self-defense, and what conditions are required for an act of self-defense to be justified? The answers to these questions are not clear.[2] One thing is, however, certain. X is not justified in taking Y's life merely because condition (a) is satisfied, and the justification for acts of self-defense is not simply that one has the right to do anything one has to in order to save one's life. After all, if Z threatens to, and will, kill X unless X kills Y, then Y's continued existence poses a threat to the life of X that can only be met by the taking of Y's life. Nevertheless, X is not therefore justified in killing Y. We would understand X's killing Y, and we might even excuse the action, but he would certainly have killed Y unjustly.

All of this has great relevance to the problem of abortion. While our discussion has shown that Professor Thomson is right in claiming that step (2) of the standard argument against abortion is mistaken, it also casts considerable doubt upon a standard argument for abortion. It is often argued that, no matter what status we ascribe to the foetus, the woman has, as part of her right of self-defense, the right to abort the foetus if the continuation of the pregnancy threatens her life. Now the foetus certainly does not satisfy condition (c), but that, as we have seen, is not required for the woman's being able to destroy it in self-defense. However, the foetus is not even attempting to take her life, and it therefore doesn't even satisfy condition (b). This must therefore cast doubt upon the claim that, no matter what the status of the foetus, abortions can sometimes be justified on grounds of self-defense.

II

Assuming that the foetus is human and that one should look at an abortion as a standard case of self-defense, we have seen that even when the foetus' continued existence poses a threat to the life of the woman, she probably has no right, as an act of self-defense, to an abortion. How then does Professor Thomson defend her claim that even if (1) is true the woman (at least in most cases) has the right to have an abortion, whether or not her life is threatened and whether or not she has consented to the act of intercourse in which the foetus is conceived? At one point, she makes the following strange suggestion: "In our case there are

---

[2] I have offered partial answers to these questions, and have related them to the problem of abortion, in my "Abortion and the Sanctity of Human Life," *American Philosophical Quarterly*, 10 (April 1973) and reprinted in J. Feinberg, ed., *The Problem of Abortion* (Belmont, Calif.: Wadsworth Publishing Co., Inc., 1973).

only two people involved, one whose life is threatened and one who threatens it. Both are innocent: the one who is threatened is not threatened because of any fault, the one who threatens does not threaten because of any fault. For this reason we may feel that we bystanders cannot intervene. But the person threatened can" (p. 53 [p. 312]). But surely this description is equally applicable to the following case. X and Y are adrift in a lifeboat. Y has a disease which he can survive but which will kill X if he contracts it, and the only way X can avoid that is by killing Y and pushing him overboard. Surely, X has no right to do this. So there must be some other reason why the woman has, if she does, the right to abort the foetus.

There is, however, an important difference between our lifeboat case and an abortion, one that leads us to the heart of Professor Thomson's argument. In the case we envisaged, both X and Y had equal right to be in the lifeboat; but the woman's body is hers, not the foetus', and she has first rights to its use. This is why the woman has a right to an abortion if her life is threatened (and even if it is not). Professor Thomson summarizes this argument, which she illustrates by her violinist example, as follows: "I am arguing only that having a right to life does not guarantee having either a right to be given the use of or a right to be allowed continued use of another person's body—even if one needs it for life itself" (p. 56 [p. 315]).

One part of this claim is clearly correct. I have no duty to X to save X's life by giving him the use of my body (or my life savings, my wife, etc.) and X has no right, even to save his life, to any of those things. Thus, if a foetus were conceived in a test tube and would die unless it were implanted in a woman's body, that foetus has no right to any woman's body. But all of this is irrelevant to the abortion issue, for what is at stake there is something else, the right of the woman to kill X to get back the sole use of her body, and that is an entirely different matter.

This point can also be put as follows: we must distinguish the taking of X's life from the saving of X's life, even if we assume that one has a duty not to do the former and to do the latter. Now that second duty, if it exists at all, is much weaker than the first duty; many things will relieve us of it which will not relieve us of the first one. Thus, I am certainly relieved of my duty to save X's life by the fact that fulfilling it means a loss of my life savings. It may be noble for me to save X's life at the cost of everything I have, but I certainly have no duty to do that. And the same thing is true in cases in which I can save X's life by giving him use of my body for an extended period of time. However, I am not relieved of my duty not to take X's life by the fact that fulfilling it means the loss of everything I have and not even by the mere fact that fulfilling it means the loss of my life. As the original example of Y threatening X shows, something more is required before rights like self-defense become applicable. A fortiori, it would seem that I am not relieved of my duty not to take X's life by the fact that its fulfillment means that some other person, who is innocently occupying it, continues to use my body. I cannot see, then, how the woman's right to her body gives her a right to take the life of the foetus.

Perhaps we are missing the point of Professor Thomson's argument. Could we perhaps view her argument as follows: consider the case (and only the case) in which the foetus threatens the life of the woman. Then don't we have a choice between saving the woman and saving the foetus, and doesn't the woman come first because it is her body? I think, once more, that there is a point to such a claim. When one has a choice between using all or part of a woman's body to save her or the foetus, the fact that it is her body gives her precedence. But that is not the choice in the case of an abortion. There one chooses between saving the woman by taking the life of the foetus and not taking the life of the foetus, thereby failing to save the woman. Given that choice, as we have seen, her rights to her body have no relevance.

I conclude, therefore, that Professor Thomson has not established the truth of her claims about abortion, primarily because she has not attended to the distinction between our duty to save X's life and our duty not to take it. Once one attends to that distinction, it would seem that if (1) is true, it is wrong to perform an abortion even to save the life of the woman.

III

What has been said above might seem to suggest that if (1) is true, then it is always wrong for a woman to secure an abortion. I think that this suggestion is a mistake, and I should like, in this final section, to propose [3] that there is at least one case in which, even if (1) is true, the woman has the right to secure an abortion.

The general principle about the taking of human lives that lies behind this case is rather complicated. It can best be stated as follows: it is permissible for X to take Y's life in order to save his own life if Y is going to die anyway in a relatively short time, taking Y's life is the only way to save X's life, and either (i) taking X's life (or doing anything else) will not save Y's life or (ii) there is a way to save Y's life but it has been determined by a fair random method that X's life should be saved rather than Y's. The rationale for this principle is that, in such a case, there is everything to gain by X's taking Y's life and nothing to lose. After all, both

---

[3] This proposal is developed more fully in my "Abortion and the Sanctity of Human Life."

X and Y will die soon anyway if nothing is done, so Y loses nothing by X's killing him. Moreover, there is a reason why X should be saved rather than Y; either Y's life cannot be saved or X won over Y in a fair random choice.

It should be noted that this is not a principle of self-defense, for in some of the cases that it covers Y is in no way attempting to take X's life and is doing no action that leads to X's death. It should also be noted that this principle has nothing to do with the objectionable principles that would allow one to save several lives by taking a single innocent life. All such maximization-of-lives-saved principles, but not our principle, fall prey to the same objection that destroys all standard maximization-of-happiness principles, viz., that they fail to insure that no one will be treated unjustly when we maximize the quantity in question.

If we apply this principle to the question of abortion, we see that an abortion would be justified if, were the abortion not performed, both the woman and foetus would die soon, and if we either cannot save the foetus or have determined by a fair random procedure that it is the woman that should be saved.

One important point should be noted about this argument. It makes no appeal to any special fact about the foetus, the woman, or their relation. It depends solely upon a general principle about the taking of some human lives to save others. It is for just this reason that there can be no doubt about its conclusion being perfectly compatible with the claim that the foetus is just another human being.

Whatever the Consequences *

Jonathan Bennett

The following kind of thing can occur.[1] A woman in labour will certainly die unless an operation is performed in which the head of her unborn child is crushed or dissected; while if it is not performed the child

---

* Whatever the Consequences" (*Analysis*, Vol. 26, 1966). Reprinted by permission of the author and Basil Blackwell Publisher.

[1] J. K. Feeney and A. P. Barry in *Journal of Obstetrics and Gynaecology of the British Empire* (1954), p. 61; R. L. Cecil and H. F. Conn (eds.), *The Specialties in General Practice* (Philadelphia, 1957), p. 410.

can be delivered, alive, by post-mortem Caesarian section. This presents a straight choice between the woman's life and the child's.

In a particular instance of this kind, some people would argue for securing the woman's survival on the basis of the special facts of the case: the woman's terror, or her place in an established network of affections and dependences, or the child's physical defects, and so on. For them, the argument could go the other way in another instance, even if only in a very special one—e.g., where the child is well formed and the woman has cancer which will kill her within a month anyway.

Others would favour the woman's survival in any instance of the kind presented in my opening paragraph, on the grounds that women are human while unborn children are not. This dubious argument does not need to be attacked here, and I shall ignore it.

Others again would say, just on the facts as stated in my first paragraph, that the *child* must be allowed to survive. Their objection to any operation in which an unborn child's head is crushed, whatever the special features of the case, goes like this:

> To do the operation would be to kill the child, while to refrain from doing it would not be to kill the woman but merely to conduct oneself in such a way that—as a foreseen but unwanted consequence —the woman died. The question we should ask is not: "The woman's life or the child's? " but rather: "To kill, or not to kill, an innocent human?" The answer to *that* is that it is always absolutely wrong to kill an innocent human, even in such dismal circumstances as these.

This line of thought needs to be attacked. Some able people find it acceptable; it is presupposed by the Principle of Double Effect [2] which permeates Roman Catholic writing on morals; and I cannot find any published statement of the extremely strong philosophical case for its rejection.

I shall state that case as best I can. My presentation of it owes much to certain allies and opponents who have commented on earlier drafts. I gratefully acknowledge my debt to Miss G. E. M. Anscombe, A. G. N. Flew, A. Kenny and T. J. Smiley; and especially to the late Douglas F. Wallace.

The Plan of Attack

There is no way of disproving the principle: "It would always be wrong to kill an innocent human, whatever the consequences of not doing

---

[2] See G. Kelly, *Medico-Moral Problems* (Dublin, 1955), p. 20; C. J. McFadden, *Medical Ethics* (London, 1962), pp. 27–33; T. J. O'Donnell, *Morals in Medicine* (London, 1959), pp. 39–44; N. St. John-Stevas, *The Right to Life* (London, 1963), p. 71.

so." The principle is consistent and reasonably clear; it can be fed into moral syllogisms to yield practical conclusions; and although its application to borderline cases may raise disturbing problems, this is true of any moral principle. Someone who thinks that the principle is laid down by a moral authority whose deliverances are to be accepted without question, without *any* testing against the dictates of the individual conscience, is vulnerable only to arguments about the credentials of his alleged authority; and these are not my present concern. So I have no reply to make to anyone who is prepared to say: "I shall obey God's command never to kill an innocent human. I shall make no independent moral assessment of this command—whether to test the reasonableness of obeying it, or to test my belief that it *is* God's command, or for any other purpose." My concern is solely with those who accept the principle: "It would always be wrong to kill an innocent human, whatever the consequences of not doing so," not just because it occurs in some received list of moral principles but also because they think that it can in some degree be recommended to the normal conscience. Against this, I shall argue that a normal person who accepts the principle must either have failed to see what it involves or be passively and unquestioningly obedient to an authority.

I do not equate "the normal conscience" with "the 'liberal' conscience." Of course, the principle *is* rejected by the "liberal" majority; but I shall argue for the stronger and less obvious thesis that the principle is in the last resort on a par with "It would always be wrong to shout, whatever the consequences of not doing so," or "It would always be wrong to leave a bucket in a hallway, whatever, etc." It is sometimes said that we "should not understand" someone who claimed to accept such wild eccentricities as these as fundamental moral truths—that he would be making a logical mistake, perhaps about what it is for something to be a "moral" principle. I need not claim so much. It is enough to say that such a person, if he was sincere and in his right mind, could safely be assumed to have delivered himself over to a moral authority and to have opted out of moral thinking altogether. The same could be said of anyone who accepted *and really understood* the principle: "It would always be wrong to kill an innocent human, whatever the consequences of not doing so." This principle is accepted by reasonable people who, though many of them give weight to some moral authority, have not abdicated from independent moral thinking. Clearly, they regard the principle as one which others might be led to accept, or at least to take seriously, on grounds other than subservience to an authority. From this fact, together with the thesis for which I shall argue, it follows that those who accept the principle (like others who at least treat it with respect) have not thought it through, have not seen what it comes to in concrete cases where it yields a different practical conclusion from that yielded by "It is wrong to kill an innocent human unless there are very powerful reasons for doing so." I aim to show what the principle comes to in these cases, and so to expose it for what it is.

My arguments will tell equally against any principle of the form "It would always be wrong to . . . , whatever the consequences of not doing so"; but I shall concentrate on the one principle about killing, and indeed on its application to the kind of obstetrical situation described in my opening paragraph.

I need a label for someone who accepts principles of the form: "It would always be wrong to . . . , whatever the consequences of not doing so." "Roman Catholic" is at once too wide, and too narrow; "intrinsicalist" is nasty; "absolutist" is misleading; "deontologist" means too many other things as well. Reluctantly, I settle for "conservative." This use has precedents, but I offer it as a stipulative definition—an expository convenience and not a claim about "conservatism" in any ordinary sense.

Well then: When the conservative condemns the operation described in my opening paragraph, he does so *partly* because the operation involves the death of an innocent human. So does its non-performance; but for the conservative the dilemma is asymmetrical because the two alternatives involve human deaths in different ways: in one case the death is part of a killing, in the other there is no killing and a death occurs only as a consequence of what is done. From the premiss that operating would be killing an innocent human, together with the principle: "It would always be wrong to kill an innocent human, whatever, etc.," it does follow that it would be wrong to operate. But the usual conservative—the one I plan to attack—thinks that his principle has *some* measure of acceptability on grounds other than unquestioning obedience to an authority. He must therefore think that the premiss: "In this case, operating would be killing an innocent human while not-operating would involve the death of an innocent human only as a consequence" gives *some* reason for the conclusion: "In this case, operating would be wrong." I shall argue that it gives no reason at all: once the muddles have been cleared away, it is just not humanly possible to see the premiss as supporting the conclusion, however weakly, except by accepting the principle "It would always be wrong, etc." as an unquestionable *donnée*.

The Action/Consequence Distinction

When James killed Henry, what happened was this: James contracted his fingers round the handle of a knife, and moved his hand in such a way that the knife penetrated Henry's body and severed an artery; blood escaped from the wound, the rate of oxygen-transfer to Henry's body-cells fell drastically, and Henry died. In general, someone's performing a physical action includes his moving some part or parts of his body. (The difference between "He moved his hand" and "His hand moved" is not in question here: I am referring to movements which he *makes*.) He does this in a physical environment, and other things happen in consequence. A description of what he *did* will ordinarily entail something not only about his movements but also, *inter alia*, about some of their upshots. Other upshots will not ordinarily be covered by any description of "what he did," but will be counted amongst "the consequences of what he did." There are various criteria for drawing the line between what someone did and the consequences of what he did; and there can be several proper ways of drawing it in a given case.

This last point notwithstanding, there are wrong ways of dividing a set of happenings into action and consequences. Even where it is not positively wrong to give a very parsimonious account of "what he did," it may be preferable to be more inclusive. If in my chosen example the obstetrician does the operation, it is true that he crushes the child's head with the consequence that the child dies, but a better account, perhaps, would say that he *kills* the child by crushing its head. There can certainly be outright wrongness at the other end of the scale: we cannot be as inclusive as we like in our account of "what he did." If at the last time when the operation could save the woman's life the obstetrician is resignedly writing up his notes, it is just not true that, as he sits at his desk, he is killing the woman; nor, indeed, is he killing her at any other time.

The use of the action/consequence distinction in the conservative premiss is, therefore, perfectly correct. Operating *is* killing; not-operating is not. What are we saying when we say this? By what criteria is the action/consequence distinction drawn in the present case? I shall try, by answering this, to show that in this case one cannot attach moral significance to the fact that the line drawn by the distinction falls where it does. Briefly, the criteria for the action/consequence distinction fall into two groups: those which could support a moral conclusion but which do not apply to every instance of the obstetrical example; and those which do apply to the example but which it would be wildly eccentric to think relevant to the moral assessment of courses of action. There is no overlap between the two groups.

Aspects of the Distinction: First Group

Some differences which tend to go with the action/consequence distinction, and are perhaps to be counted amongst the criteria for it, clearly do have moral significance. None of them, however, is generally present in the obstetrical example.

Given a question about whether some particular upshot of a movement I made is to be covered by the description of what I *did:*

a. The answer may depend in part upon whether in making the movement I was entirely confident that that upshot would ensue; and this could reasonably be thought relevant to the moral assessment of my conduct. This aspect of the action/consequence distinction, however, is absent from most instances of the obstetrical example. The classification of not-operating as something other than killing does not imply that the obstetrician rates the woman's chance of survival (if the operation is not performed) higher than the child's chance of survival (if it is performed). If it did imply this then, by contraposition, not-operating would in many such cases have to be classified as killing after all.

b. The answer may depend in part upon how certain or inevitable it was that that upshot would ensue from my movement, or upon how confidently I ought to have expected it to ensue; and that too may have a strong bearing on the moral assessment of my conduct. But it gets no grip on the obstetrical example, for in many cases of that kind there is moral certainty on both sides of the dilemma. If the conservative says that the action/consequence distinction, when correctly drawn, is always associated with morally significant differences in the inevitability of upshots of movements, then he is vulnerable to an argument by contraposition like the one in (a). He is vulnerable in other ways as well, which I shall discuss in my next section.

c. The answer may depend in part upon whether I made the movement partly or wholly for the sake of achieving that upshot; and this is a morally significant matter. But the obstetrical example is symmetrical in that respect also: if the obstetrician crushes the child's head he does so not because this will lead to the child's death or because it constitutes killing the child, but because that is his only way of removing the child's body from the woman's.

To summarize: moral conclusions may be supported by facts (a) about what is expected, but in the example each upshot is confidently expected; (b) about what is inevitable, but in the example each upshot is inevitable; or (c) about what is ultimately aimed at, but in the example neither upshot is aimed at.

I have suggested that a conservative might say: "The action/consequence distinction is always associated with a morally significant difference in the degree to which upshots are certain or inevitable." This is false; but let us grant it in order to see whether it can help the conservative on the obstetrical example. I concede, for purposes of argument, that if the operation is not performed the woman will pretty certainly die, while if it is performed the child will even more certainly die.

What use can the conservative make of this concession? Will he say that the practical decision is to be based on a weighing of the comparative desirability of upshots against the comparative certainty of their achievement? If so, then he must allow that there *could* be a case in which it was right to kill the child—perhaps a case where a healthy young widow with four children is bearing a hydrocephalic child, and where her chance of survival if the operation is not performed is *nearly* as bad as the child's chance of survival if it is performed. If a professed "conservative" allows that there could, however improbably, be such a case, then he is not a conservative but a consequentialist; he does after all base his final judgment on the special features of the case; and he has misrepresented his position by using the language of action and consequence to express his implausible views about the comparative inevitability of upshots. On the other hand, if the conservative still absolutely rules out the killing of the child, whatever the details of the particular case, then what could be his point in claiming that there is a difference in degree of inevitability? The moral significance of this supposed difference would, at best, have to be conceded to be an obscure one which threw no light on why anyone should adopt the conservative view.

A certain conservative tactic is at issue here. Miss G. E. M. Anscombe has said:

> If someone really thinks, *in advance*, that it is open to question whether such an action as procuring the judicial execution of the innocent should be quite excluded from consideration—I do not want to argue with him; he shows a corrupt mind.[3]

The phrase "quite excluded from consideration" clearly places Miss Anscombe as what I am calling a "conservative." (The phrase "a corrupt mind," incidentally, tends to confirm my view that conservatives think their position can stand the light of day, i.e., that they do not see it as tenable only by those who passively obey some moral authority.) Now, in the course of a footnote to this passage Miss Anscombe remarks:

> In discussion when this paper was read, as was perhaps to be expected, this case was produced: a government is required to have an innocent man tried, sentenced and executed under threat of a "hydrogen bomb war." It would seem strange to me to have much hope of averting a war threatened by such men as made this demand. But the most important thing about the way in which cases like this are invented in discussions, is the assumption that only two courses are open: here, compliance and open defiance. No one can say in advance of such a situation what the possibilities are going to be—

---

[3] G. E. M. Anscombe, "Modern Moral Philosophy," *Philosophy*, Vol. 33 (1958), p. 17.

e.g., that there is none of stalling by a feigned willingness to comply, accompanied by a skilfully arranged "escape" of the victim.

This makes two points about the case as described: there might be nothing we could do which would have a good chance of averting a war; and if there were one such thing we could do there might be several. The consequentialist might meet this by trying yet again to describe a case in which judicially executing an innocent man *is* the only thing we could do which would have a good chance of averting a war. When he had added the details which block off the other alternatives, his invented case may well be far removed from present political likelihood; it may even be quite fantastic. Still, what does the conservative say about it?

Here is Miss Anscombe, at her most gamesome, on the subject of "fantastic" examples:

> A point of method I would recommend to the corrupter of the youth would be this: concentrate on examples which are either banal: you have promised to return a book, but . . . and so on, or fantastic: what you ought to do if you have to move forward, and stepping with your right foot meant killing twenty-five young men, while stepping with your left foot would kill fifty drooling old ones. (Obviously the right thing to do would be to jump and polish off the lot.) [4]

The cards are now well stacked; but this is a game in which a conservative should not be taking a hand at all. Someone may say (i): "In no situation could it be right to procure the judicial execution of the innocent: political probability aside, the judicial execution of the innocent is absolutely impermissible in any possible circumstances." Or some may say (ii): "It is never right to procure the judicial execution of the innocent: a situation in which this would be right has never arisen, isn't going to arise, and cannot even be described without entering into the realm of political fantasy." These are different. The former is conservatism, according to which "the judicial execution of the innocent should be quite excluded from consideration." The latter is not conservatism: according to it, the judicial execution of the innocent is taken into consideration, assessed in the light of the political probabilities of the world we live in, and excluded on that basis. The former is Miss Anscombe's large type; the latter, apparently, is her footnote. The difference between (i) "In no situation could it be right . . ." and (ii) "No situation is even remotely likely to occur in which it would be right . . ." can be masked by dis-

---

[4] G. E. M. Anscombe, "Does Oxford Moral Philosophy Corrupt the Youth?" *The Listener,* February 14, 1957, p. 267. See also the correspondence in ensuing numbers, and Michael Tanner, "Examples in Moral Philosophy," *Proceedings of the Aristotelian Society,* Vol. 65 (1964–65).

missing what is relevant but unlikely as "fantastic" and therefore negligible. But the difference between the two positions is crucial even if in the first instance it can be brought out only by considering "fantastic" possibilities. The two may yield the same real-life practical conclusions, but (ii) can be understood and argued with in a way in which (i) cannot. If someone accepts (ii), and is not afraid to discuss a "fantastic" but possible situation in which he would approve the judicial execution of an innocent man, he can be challenged to square this with his contrary judgment in regard to some less fantastic situation. Whether he could meet the challenge would depend on the details of his moral position and of the situations in question. The point is that we should know where we stood with him: for example, we should know that it was *relevant* to adduce evidence about how good the chances would be of averting war in this way in this situation, or in that way in that. It is just this sort of thing which the unwavering conservative must regard as irrelevant; and that is what is wrong with his position. Miss Anscombe says: "No one can say in advance of such a situation what the possibilities are going to be"; but the central objection to conservatism is, precisely, that it says in advance that for the judging of the proposed course of action *it does not matter* what the possibilities are going to be. Why, then, go on about them—if not to disguise conservatism as something else when the going gets tough?

I have based this paper on the obstetrical example in the hope that, without being jeered at for having "invented" an example which is "fantastic," I could present a kind of case in which a conservative principle would yield a practical conclusion different from any likely to be arrived at by consequentialist arguments. The claim that in these cases there would always be a morally significant difference between the woman's chance of survival and the child's could only be another attempt to get the spotlight off conservatism altogether—to get the consequentialist to accept the conservative's conclusion and forget about his principle. In the obstetrical example, the attempt is pretty desperate (though, with the aid of judiciously selected statistics, it is made often enough); with other kinds of examples, used to examine this or other conservative principles, it might be easier for the conservative to make a show of insisting on the addition of details which render the examples "fantastic." But this does not mean that the case against conservatism is stronger here than elsewhere. It means only that the obstetrical example gives less scope than most for the "there-might-be-another-way-out" move, or protective-coloration gambit, which some conservatives sometimes use when they shelter their position by giving the impression that it does not really exist.

A conservative might invoke inevitability, without comparing degrees of it in the consequentialist manner, by saying that if the operation is not performed the woman still has *some* chance of survival while if it is performed the child has *none*. Barring miracles, this is wrong about the woman; not barring miracles, it is wrong about the child. It could seem plausible only to someone who did not bar miracles but took a peculiar view of how they operate. Some people do attach importance in this regard to the fact that if the operation is not performed the woman may take some time to die: they seem to think—perhaps encouraged by an eccentric view of God as powerful but *slow*—that the longer an upshot is delayed the more room there is for a miraculous intervention. This belief, whatever the assumptions which underlie it, gives no help to the conservative position. For suppose the obstetrician decides to try, after operating and delivering the child, to repair its head by microsurgery. The woman's supposed "some chance" of survival if the child's head is not crushed is of the same kind as the obstetrician's "some chance" of saving the child after crushing its head: in each case there is what the well-informed plain man would call "no chance," but in each case it will take a little time for the matter to be finally settled by the events themselves—for the woman to die or the obstetrician to admit failure. Would the conservative say that the obstetrician's intention to try to save the child in this way, though hopeless, completely alters the shape of the problem and perhaps makes it all right for the obstetrician to crush the child's head? If so, then what we have here is a morality of gestures and poses.

Aspects of the Distinction: Second Group

I return to the main thread of my argument. Of the remaining three aspects of the action/consequence distinction, it was not quite true to say that all are present in (every instance of) the obstetrical example; for the first of them has not even that merit. The main point, however, is that even if it were always present it would not help the conservative— though it might help us to diagnose his trouble.

d. Someone's decision whether an upshot of a movement of mine is to be covered by his description of what I *did* may depend partly on his moral assessment of my role in the total situation. Your condemnation of me, or perhaps your approval, may be reflected in your putting on the "action" side of the line an upshot which an indifferent onlooker would count as merely a "consequence." This aspect of the action/consequence distinction—if indeed it is one independently of those already discussed— cannot help the conservative who believes that a premiss using the distinction tends to *support* a moral conclusion. That belief demands a relevance relation which slopes the other way.

There seem to be just two remaining aspects to the action/consequence distinction. Certainly, there are only two which do appear in all instances of the obstetrical example. These two must be the sole justification for saying that operating would be killing while not-operating would not be killing; and so they must bear the whole weight of any conservative but non-authoritarian case against killing the child.

e. Operating is killing-the-child because if the obstetrician operates there is a high degree of *immediacy* between what he does with his hands and the child's dying. This immediacy consists in the brevity or absence of time-lag, spatial nearness, simplicity of causal connexions, and paucity of intervening physical objects. The relations amongst these are complex; but they are severally relevant to the action/consequence distinction, and in the obstetrical example they all pull together, creating an overwhelming case for calling the performance of the operation the *killing* of the child.

f. Not-operating is not killing-the-woman because it is not *doing* anything at all but is merely *refraining* from doing something.

Since (e) and (f) are so central to the action/consequence distinction generally, it is appropriate that they should sometimes bear its whole weight, as they do in the conservative's (correct) application of the distinction to the obstetrical example. But if (e) and (f) are all there is to the premiss: "In this case, operating would be killing an innocent human while not-operating would involve the death of an innocent human only as a consequence," then this premiss offers no support at all to the conclusion: "In this case, operating would be wrong."

The matters which I group under "immediacy" in (e) may borrow moral significance from their loose association with facts about whether and in what degree upshots are (a) expected, (b) inevitable or (c) aimed at. In none of these respects, however, is there a relevant asymmetry in the obstetrical example. The question is: why should a difference in degree of immediacy, unaccompanied by other relevant differences, be taken to support a moral discrimination? I cannot think of a remotely plausible answer which does not consist solely in an appeal to an authority.[5]

Suggestions come to mind about "not getting one's hands dirty"; and the notion of what I call "immediacy" does help to show how the literal and the metaphorical are mingled in some uses of that phrase. In so doing, however, it exposes the desire to "keep one's hands clean," in cases like the obstetrical example, as a symptom of muddle or primness or, worst of all, a moral egoism like Pilate's. (To be fair: I do not think that many

---

[5] Conservatives use words like "direct" to cover a jumble of factors of which immediacy is the most prominent. Pius XII has said that a pain-killing, life-shortening drug may be used "if there exists no direct causal link, either through the will of interested parties or by the nature of things, between the induced consciousness [*sic*] and the shortening of life . . ." (Quoted in St. John-Stevas, *op. cit.*, p. 61.)

conservatives would answer in this way. If they used similar words it would probably not be to express the nasty sentiment I have mentioned but rather to say something like: "I must obey God's law; and the rest is up to God." Because this suggests a purely authoritarian basis, and because it certainly has nothing to do with immediacy, it lies beyond my present scope.)

Similarly with the acting/refraining distinction in (f). I shall argue in my next section that our criteria for this distinction do not invest it with any moral significance whatever—except when the distinction is drawn on the basis of independently formed moral judgments, and then it cannot help the conservative case for the reason given in (d). And if neither (e) immediacy nor (f) acting/refraining separately has moral significance, then clearly they cannot acquire any by being taken together.

Acting and Refraining

Suppose the obstetrician does not operate, and the woman dies. He does not kill her, but he *lets her die*. The approach suggested by these words is just an unavoidable nuisance, and I shall not argue from it. When I say "he lets her die," I mean only that he knowingly refrains from preventing her death which he alone could prevent, and he cannot say that her survival is in a general way "none of my business" or "not [even *prima facie*] my concern." If my arguments so far are correct, then this one fact—the fact that the non-operating obstetrician *lets the woman die* but does not *kill her*—is the only remaining feature of the situation which the conservative can hope to adduce as supporting his judgment about what ought to be done in every instance of the obstetrical example.[6] Let us examine the difference between "X killed Y" and "X let Y die."

Some cases of letting-die are also cases of killing. If on a dark night X knows that Y's next step will take him over the edge of a high cliff, and he refrains from uttering a simple word of warning because he doesn't care or because he wants Y dead, then it is natural to say not only that X lets Y die but also that he kills him—even if it was not X who suggested the route, removed the fence from the cliff-top, etc. Cases like this, where a failure-to-prevent is described as a doing partly *because* it is judged to be wicked or indefensible, are beside my present point; for I want to see what difference there is between killing and letting-die which might be a *basis for* a moral judgment. Anyway, the letting-die which is also killing must involve malice or wanton indifference, and there is nothing like that in the obstetrical example. In short, to count these cases as relevant to the

---

[6] In a case where the child cannot survive anyway: "It is a question of the *direct taking* of one innocent life or merely *permitting* two deaths. In other words, there is question of one *murder* against two deaths . . ." Kelly, *op. cit.*, p. 181.

obstetrical example would be to suggest that not-operating would after all be killing the woman—a plainly false suggestion which I have disavowed. I wish to criticise the conservative's argument, not to deny his premiss. So from now on I shall ignore cases of letting-die which are also cases of killing; and it will make for brevity to pretend that they do not exist. For example, I shall say that killing involves moving one's body—which is false of some of these cases, but true of all others.

One more preliminary point: the purposes of the present enquiry do not demand that a full analysis be given either of "X killed Y" or of "X let Y die." We can ignore any implications either may have about what X (a) expected, (b) should have expected, or (c) was aiming at; for the obstetrical example is symmetrical in all those respects. We can also ignore the fact that "X killed Y" loosely implies something about (e) immediacy which is not implied by "X let Y die," for immediacy in itself has no moral significance.

Consider the statement that *Joe killed the calf*. A certain aspect of the analysis of this will help us to see how it relates to *Joe let the calf die*. To say that Joe killed the calf is to say that

(1) Joe moved his body

and

(2) the calf died;

but it is also to say something about how Joe's moving was connected with the calf's dying—something to the effect that

(3) if Joe had not moved as he did, the calf would not have died.

How is (3) to be interpreted? We might take it, rather strictly, as saying

(3') If Joe had moved in *any* other way, the calf would not have died.

This, however, is too strong to be a necessary condition of Joe's having killed the calf. Joe may have killed the calf even if he could have moved in other ways which would equally have involved the calf's dying. Suppose that Joe cut the calf's throat, but could have shot it instead: in that case he clearly killed it; but (3') denies that he killed it, because the calf might still have died even if Joe had moved in just the way he did.

We might adopt a weaker reading of (3), namely as saying

(3") Joe could have moved in *some* other way without the calf's dying.

But where (3') was too strong to be necessary, (3") is too weak to express a sufficient connexion between Joe's moving and the calf's dying. It counts Joe as having killed the calf not only in cases where we should ordinarily say that he killed it but also in cases where the most we should say is that he let it die.

The truth lies somewhere between (3'), which is appropriate to "Joe killed the calf in the only way open to him," and (3"), which is appropriate to "Joe killed the calf or let it die." Specifically, the connexion between Joe's moving and the calf's dying which is appropriate to "Joe killed the calf" but not to "Joe let the calf die" is expressed by

(3''') Of all the other ways in which Joe might have moved, *relatively few* satisfy the condition: if Joe had moved like that, the calf would have died.

And the connexion which is appropriate to "Joe let the calf die" but not to "Joe killed the calf" is expressed by

(4) Of all the other ways in which Joe might have moved, *almost all* satisfy the condition: if Joe had moved like that, the calf would have died.

This brings me to the main thesis of the present section: apart from the factors I have excluded as already dealt with, the difference between "X killed Y" and "X let Y die" *is* the difference between (3''') and (4). When the killing/letting-die distinction is stripped of its implications regarding immediacy, intention, etc.—which lack moral significance or don't apply to the example—all that remains is a distinction having to do with where a set of movements lies on the scale which has "the only set of movements which would have produced that upshot" at one end and "movements other than the only set which would have produced that upshot" at the other.

This, then, is the conservative's residual basis for a moral discrimination between operating and not-operating. Operating would be killing: if the obstetrician makes movements which constitute operating, then the child will die; and there are very few other movements he could make which would also involve the child's dying. Not-operating would only be letting-die: if throughout the time when he could be operating the obstetrician makes movements which constitute not-operating, then the woman will die; but a vast majority of alternative movements he could make during that time would equally involve the woman's dying. I do not see how anyone doing his own moral thinking about the matter could find the least shred of moral significance in *this* difference between operating and not-operating.

Suppose you are told X killed Y in the only way possible in the circumstances; and this, perhaps together with certain other details of the case, leads you to judge X's conduct adversely. Then you are told: "You have been misled: there is another way in which X could have killed Y." Then a third informant says: "That is wrong too: there are two other ways . . . , etc." Then a fourth: "No there are three other ways . . . , etc." Clearly, these successive corrections put no pressure at all on your original judgment: you will not think it relevant to your judgment on X's killing of Y that it could have been carried out in any one of n different ways. But the move from "X killed Y in the only possible way" to "X killed Y in one of the only five possible ways" is of the same *kind* as the move from "X killed Y" to "X let Y die" (except for the latter's implications about immediacy); and the moral insignificance of the former move is evidence for the moral insignificance of the latter move also.

The difference between "X killed Y" and "X let Y die" is the sumtotal of a vast number of differences such as that between "X killed Y in one of the only n possible ways" and "X killed Y in one of the only $n + 1$ possible ways." If the difference between ". . . n . . ." and " . . . $n + 1$ . . ." were morally insignificant only because it was *too small* for any moral discrimination to be based upon it, then the sumtotal of millions of such differences might still have moral significance. But in fact the differences in question, whatever their size, are of the *wrong kind* for any moral discrimination to be based upon them. Suppose you have judged X adversely, on the basis of the misinformation: "X killed Y in the only way possible in the circumstances"; and this is then replaced, in one swoop, by the true report: "X did not kill Y at all, though he did knowingly let Y die." Other things being equal, would this give you the slightest reason to retract your adverse judgment? Not a bit of it! It would be perfectly reasonable for you to reply: "The fact remains that X chose to conduct himself in a way which he knew would involve Y's death. At first I thought his choice could encompass Y's death only by being the choice of some rather specific course of conduct whereas the revised report shows me that X's choice could have encompassed Y's death while committing X to very little. At first I thought it had to be a choice to act; I now realize that it could have been a choice to refrain. What of it?"

There are several things a conservative is likely to say at this point—all equivalent. "When we know that the crucial choice could have been a choice to refrain from something, we can begin to allow for the possibility that it may have been a choice to refrain from doing something wrong, such as killing an innocent human." Or: "You say 'other things being equal,' but in the obstetrical example they aren't equal. By representing letting-die as a kind of wide-optioned killing you suppress the fact that the alternative to letting the woman die is killing the child."

Replies like these are available to the conservative only if he does not need them and can break through at some other point; for they assume the very point which is at issue, namely that in every instance of the obstetrical example it would be wrong to kill the child. I think that in some cases it would indeed be wrong—(I do not press for a blanket judgment on all instances of the example—quite the contrary); and in such a case the obstetrician, if he rightly let the woman die, could defend his doing so on the basis of the details of the particular case. Furthermore, he might wish to begin his defence by explaining: "I let the woman die, but I did not kill her"; for letting-die is in general likely to be more defensible than killing. My analysis incidentally shows one reason why: the alternatives to killing are always very numerous, and the odds are that at least one of them provides an acceptable way out of the impasse; whereas the alternative to letting-die is always some fairly specific course of conduct, and if there are conclusive objections to *that* then there's an end of the matter. All this, though, is a matter of likelihoods. It is no help in the rare case where the alternatives to killing, numerous as they are, arguably do *not* include an acceptable way out of the impasse because they all involve something of the same order of gravity as a killing, namely a letting-die. The conservative may say: "Where innocent humans are in question, letting-die is not of the same order of gravity as killing: for one of them is not, and the other is, absolutely wrong in all possible circumstances." But this, like the re- joinders out of which this paragraph grew, assumes the very point which is at issue. All these conservative moves come down to just one thing: "At this point your argument fails; for the wrongness of killing the child, in any instance of the obstetrical example, *can* be defended on the basis of your own analysis of the acting/refraining distinction—plus the extra premiss that it would always be wrong to kill the child."

The Stress on the Specific

My argument is finished; but its strategy might be thought to be open to a certain criticism which I want to discuss.

The obstetrical example is a *kind* of situation, on every instance of which the conservative makes a certain judgment. I have argued that this judgment, as applied to many instances of the example, cannot be defended except by the unquestioning invocation of authority. This would have been damaging to the conservative position even if I had appealed only to "fantastic" kinds of instances such as seldom or never occur; but in fact my claims have been true of many real-life instances of the obstetrical example. Still, a conservative might resist my drive towards the relatively specific, my insistence upon asking: "What is there about *this* kind of instance which justifies your judgment upon it?" He might claim that even my opening paragraph presents so special a kind of situation that he cannot fairly be asked to find in *it* something which supports his judgment other than by a blanket appeal to his general principle that it would always be wrong to kill an innocent human. There are two ways in which he might defend this stand: they look alike, but their fatal defects are very different.

The first is by the use of a sub-Wittgensteinian argument from the nature of language. Although I have never encountered it, it is a possible and plausible objection to my strategy of argument. The conservative might say: "Granted that facts (a) expectation, (b) inevitability and (c) intention are irrelevant to the way the action/consequence distinction applies to the obstetrical example; it does not follow that when we apply the distinction to the example *all* we are doing—apart from (d) reflecting our already-formed moral judgments—is to report facts about (e) immediacy and (f) acting/refraining. Language and thought don't work like this. When we say: 'Operating would be killing; not-operating would not be killing though it would have death as a consequence,' we are not *just* talking about immediacy and specificity of options. We are using words which, *qua* words in the language, are laden with associations having to do with (a)–(d); and these associations of the words cannot simply be ignored or forgotten in a particular case. Language is not atomic in that way, and it would be at best a clumsy instrument if it were."

I agree that we often do, and perhaps must sometimes, decide our conduct in one situation partly through verbal carry-overs from others in which similar conduct could be justified more directly. But I think that everyone will agree that the more serious a practical problem is, the greater is our obligation to resist such verbal carry-overs and scrutinize the particular problem in order to see what there is about *it* which would justify this or that solution to it. A practical problem in which human lives are at stake is a deeply serious one, and it would be an abdication from all moral seriousness to settle it by verbal carry-overs. I am not saying: "Take pity on the poor woman, and never mind what the correct description of the situation is." I am opposing someone who says: "This is the correct description of the situation—never mind what its force is in this particular case."

The second objection to my stress on the particular case, or the specific kind of case, is one which conservatives do sometimes use; and it connects with a muddle which is not special to conservatives. It goes like this: "We must have rules. If every practical problem had to be solved on the spot, on the basis of the fine details of the particular case, the results would be disastrous. Take a situation which falls under some rule which I know to be justified in most situations. There may not be time or means for me to learn much more about the present situation than just that it does fall under the rule; the details of the case, even if I can discover them, may be too complex for me to handle; my handling of them, even if intellectually efficient, may without my knowing it be self-interested or corrupt; by deciding, however uncorruptly, not to follow the rule on this occasion, I may weaken its hold on me in other situations where it clearly ought to be followed; and even if I could be sure that I was in no such danger, I might help others into it by publicly breaking the rule." [7]

This is all true, but it does not help the conservative. Notice first that it tells against undue attention to individual cases rather than against undue attention to limited kinds of cases: its target is not the specific but the particular. Still, it could be developed into an attack on over-stressing very specifically detailed kinds of cases: its opening words would then have to be replaced by: "We must have rather general rules." This is true too, but it is still no help to the conservative.

This argument for our bringing practical problems under rather general rules is based on the consequences of our not doing so: it points to the dangers attendant on suspending a general rule and considering whether one's practical problem might be better resolved by applying a less general one. But sometimes these dangers will be far too slight to justify doing what a given general rule enjoins in a particular situation. If the thesis under discussion is to have any practical upshot which is not ludicrous ("Never break any general rule which would enjoin the right action in more cases than not"), or vague to the point of vacuity ("Always apply some fairly general rule"), or merely question-begging ("Never break a rule forbidding an action which really is absolutely impermissible"), then it must allow us to raise questions of the form: "Need we be deterred by the dangers attendant on suspending *this* rule in favour of *this* more specific rule in this kind of situation?" The answer will depend upon what the challenged general rule is, what the proposed substitute for it is, the intelligence and character of the agent, and the likelihood that his breaking the rule (if it comes to that) would become generally known and, if known, demoralizing to others. These matters need not be so complex as to defeat finite intelligence, or so primrose-strewn that fallen man dare not venture among them. Furthermore, they can themselves be embodied in rules carefully formulated in advance—meta-rules about the kinds of situations in which this or that ground-level general rule may be suspended in favour of this or that more specific one.

Here is a possible case. A certain obstetrician accepts the rule, "Do not kill innocent humans," as applicable in every kind of situation he has thought of except the kind described in my opening paragraph. He wants a rule for this kind too, as a shield against the confusions, temptations and pressures of the concrete situation; and after reflection he

---

[7] For a gesture in this direction, see St. John-Stevas, *op. cit.*, pp. 14–16. See also McFadden, *op. cit.*, p. 133.

adopts the following: "If the child is not hydrocephalic it is not to be killed. If it is hydrocephalic it is to be killed unless either (a) the woman is bound to die within a month anyway, or (b) the woman has no other children under eighteen and she is known to be a chronic acute depressive. If (a) or (b) or both are true, the child is not to be killed."

By preferring this rule to the more general one for instances of the obstetrical example, the obstetrician is not rendering it likely that in some situation he will flounder around not knowing what rule about killing to apply. For he has a clear enough meta-rule: "If the only way to save a woman's life is to kill the child she is bearing, apply this rule: . . . ; otherwise apply the rule: Do not kill innocent humans."

The obstetrician is not satisfied with his ground-level rule for instances of the obstetrical example, and he hopes to be able to improve it. Still, he is resigned to his rule's ignoring various matters which, though they are relevant to what the ideally right action would be, would involve him in the dangers of over-specificity mentioned above. "Is the woman a potential murderess or the child a mongol?"—the answers are probably unobtainable. "In what ways would the woman's death represent a real loss to others?"—the answer, even if discoverable, could be so complex as to elude any manageable rule. "Would either course of action bring the medical profession into undeserved but seriously damaging disrepute?" —it would be too easy for that to be unconsciously conflated with the question of which course would best further the obstetrician's own career. "Would the child, if delivered alive, be especially helpful to students of hydrocephalus?"—asking that could be the first step on a downward path: by allowing one woman to die partly because her child will be medically interesting if alive, even an uncorrupt man may ease the way towards allowing some other woman to die partly because *she* will be medically interesting when dead.

Although he pays heed—neurotically pays far too much heed—to the conservative's warnings against over-specificity, this obstetrician arrives at a conclusion quite different from the conservative's. That is the crux. The conservative who warns against the dangers of overspecifying is trying to find a consequentialist basis for his whole position. Unlike the "protective-coloration gambit" discussed earlier, this is legitimate enough in itself; but it simply does not yield the conservative position on the matter under discussion. For it to do so, the conservative would have to show that our obstetrician's more specific rule is *too* dangerous in the ways mentioned above; and he would have to do this without applying danger-inflating standards which would commit him also to condemning as too dangerous the suspension of the general rule: "Never leave a bucket in a hall-way." He may object: "Buckets in hallways are not important enough to provide a fair analogy. Where something as grave as killing is in question, we should be especially sensitive to the dangers of suspending a general rule." But then when something as grave as letting someone die is involved in applying the rule, we should be especially reluctant to accept, without good empirical evidence, popular clichés about the dangers of suspending general rules. The two points cancel out.

Of course, there are these dangers, and we should guard against them. To assess them at all precisely, though, would require more than we know of sociology, psychology and the philosophy of mind; and so our guarding against them can consist only in our keeping the urge towards specificity under some restraint, our remembering that in this matter it is not always true that the sky is the limit. The conservative who hopes to secure his position by pointing out these dangers must claim that he *can* assess them, and can discover in them a simple, sweeping pattern which picks out a certain list of general rules as the ones which ought never to be suspended by anyone in any circumstances. No one would explicitly make so preposterous a claim.

"So you do at any rate retreat from act- to rule-utilitarianism?" No. Rule-utilitarianism can be presented (1) as a quasi-mystical doctrine about the importance of rule following "per se," or (2) as a doctrine about the importance of rule-following because of what rule-following empirically *is,* because of what happens when people follow rules and what happens when they don't. In version (1), rule-utilitarianism is a distinct doctrine which has nothing to recommend it. In version (2), it is just part of a thorough act-utilitarianism. (In most actual presentations, there is a cloudy attempt to combine (2)'s reasonableness with (1)'s rejection of act-utilitarianism.) In this section I have been discussing what the consequences might be, for myself or others, of my suspending or breaking a given general rule. These are among, not additional to, the consequential factors whose relevance I have been urging all through the paper. There has been no retreat.

Conclusion

Principles of the form: "It would always be wrong to . . . , whatever the consequences of not doing so" seem defensible because the action/consequence distinction does often have a certain kind of moral significance. But in proportion as a situation gives real work to the rider ". . . whatever the consequences of not doing so," in proportion as it puts pressure on this rider, in proportion as the "consequences of not doing so" give some moral reason for "doing so"—to that extent the action/consequence distinction lacks moral significance in that situation. The obstetrical example is just an extreme case: there the rider serves to dismiss the entire moral case against applying the principle; and, proportionately, the action/consequence distinction carries no moral weight at all.

The phenomenon of conservatism, then, can be explained as follows. The conservative naturally thinks that the action/consequence distinction has great moral significance because of its frequent connexion with differences concerning (a) expectation, (b) inevitability, (c) intention and (d) independently formed moral judgments. He then encounters cases like the obstetrical example, where (a)–(d) are irrelevant but where the distinction can still be applied because of facts about (e) immediacy and (f) acting/refraining. Failing to see that in these cases the distinction has lost absolutely all its moral bite, and perhaps encouraged by a mistake about "rule-following per se," he still applies his principle in the usual way. Those who do not follow him in this he finds lax or opportunist or corrupt; and many of them half agree, by conceding to his position a certain hard and unfeeling uprightness. Both are wrong. Conservatism, when it is not mere obedience, is mere muddle.

Killing and Letting Die:

A Reply to Bennett *

John Casey

In an article entitled 'Whatever the consequences' [1] Jonathan Bennett sets out to show that *no* moral principle of the form 'It is always wrong to do X whatever the consequences of not doing so' can possibly commend itself to a normal person unless (a) he is merely confused about its implications, or (b) he is 'passively and unquestioningly obedient to an authority'. These categories are intended to be exhaustive: 'Conservatism, when it is not mere obedience, is mere muddle.' [2] Now Bennett does

---

* From *Morality and Moral Reasoning*, edited by J. Casey. Reprinted by permission of Methuen & Co., Ltd.

[1] *Analysis*, vol. 26, No. 3 (January 1966). Page references in brackets are to this article as reprinted above.

[2] *Ibid.*, p. 102 [p. 348]. 'Conservative' is the term which Mr. Bennett has coined, in preference to the terms 'absolutist' or 'deontologist,' for one who adheres to principles of the form 'It is always wrong to do X whatever the consequences of not

not advance a *general* argument against the rationality of absolutist principles, but he analyses a particular case in which, he suggests, such a principle could only be defended by a false moral weight being given to the distinction between *acting* and *refraining from action*. Bennett's argument, if successful, would certainly be conclusive. We cannot take a moral principle seriously if it necessarily places moral weight upon trivial differences between actions or states of affairs. If it can be shown that any absolutist principle must do this, then it could be shown either that it is not a genuinely *moral* principle, or that it is irrational. I shall accept the stronger claim that it would be irrational, and I shall assume that if this were so then it could not be taken seriously as a moral principle. Moral principles of the form 'It is always wrong to do X whatever the consequences of not doing so' are of the kind I have called 'absolutist'. Moral schemes in which such principles are central will characteristically claim that if there is a moral difference between two courses of action, then this will be because they do not both fall under the same moral principle. Since on this view moral differences in particular cases result from the application of principles, it will be crucial for the rationality of the principles that they do not treat insignificant differences between actions as morally crucial. If it can really be shown that *any* absolutist principle must inevitably claim that there is a moral difference between two courses of action where the normal conscience simply could not see any such difference, then it will have been demonstrated that no absolutist principle is rationally defensible. It seems likely that we *can* settle the question whether there is always a decisive moral difference between doing something and refraining from doing something (for instance, refraining from preventing something). So if Bennett's arguments are right, he will have shown how the dispute is to be resolved; and he will actually have resolved it by disposing of a whole tradition of moral philosophy, including the central tradition of Catholic moral thought.

The case Bennett takes is that of a woman in labour who will certainly die unless an operation is performed to kill the unborn child, while if the operation is not performed the child can be delivered alive by post-mortem Caesarian section. In this case, according to Bennett, the obstetrician is presented with a 'a straight choice between the woman's life and the child's'. [3] The moral absolutist who holds to the principle 'it is always wrong to kill the innocent, whatever the consequences of not doing so' would condemn the operation on the obvious grounds that it involves killing an innocent child. Of course the non-performance of

---

doing so'. I prefer the more traditional term 'absolutist' which, for present purposes, I do not wish to distinguish from 'deontologist'. I realize that these terms are apt to be misleading, but so, I think, is 'conservative'.

[3] *Ibid.*, p. 83 [pp. 328–29].

the operation would also involve the death of an innocent—the mother—
but for the absolutist the dilemma is asymmetrical

> because the two alternatives involve human deaths in different ways:
> in one case the death is part of a killing, in the other there is no kill-
> ing and a death occurs only as a consequence of what is done.[4]

Assuming that the absolutist does not subscribe to the principle 'It is
always wrong to kill the innocent, whatever the consequences of not
doing so' simply out of obedience to a moral authority, then, in Bennett's
view, he must think that the premise, 'In this case, operating would be
killing an innocent human being while not operating would involve the
death of an innocent human being only as a consequence of what is done',
gives *some* reason for the conclusion 'In this case operating would be
wrong'.[5] Bennett's contention is that it gives no reason whatsoever.

Bennett advances an account of the distinction between killing and
letting die. He envisages a scale with 'the only set of movements which
would have produced (the death)' at one end, and 'movements other
than the only set which would have produced (the death)' at the other:[6]

> This, then, is the conservative's residual basis for a moral discrimina-
> tion between operating and not-operating. Operating would be kill-
> ing: if the obstetrician makes movements which constitute operating,
> then the child will die; and there are very few other movements he
> could make which would also involve the child's dying. Not-operating
> would only be letting-die: if throughout the time when he could be
> operating the obstetrician makes movements which constitute not-
> operating, then the woman will die; but the vast majority of alterna-
> tive movements he could make during that time would equally involve
> the woman's dying. I do not see how anyone doing his own moral
> thinking could find the least shred of moral significance in *this* differ-
> ence between operating and not-operating.[7]

If no moral weight can be put upon the distinction between killing
and letting die, then the fact that not-operating would only be letting
the mother die, whereas operating would be killing the child, gives no
reason for the conclusion 'In this case operating would be wrong'. Bennett
thinks that, in its application to the obstetrical case, the moral principle
'It is always wrong to kill the innocent, whatever the consequences of
not doing so' can *only* be commended to the normal conscience if the
distinction between killing and letting die always does mark a decisive

---

[4] *Ibid.*, p. 85 [p. 331]
[5] *Ibid.*, p. 85 [p. 331].
[6] *Ibid.*, p. 95 [p. 341].
[7] *Ibid.*, p. 96 [p. 341].

moral difference. Since there is no such difference, the absolutist who wishes to base his moral principle on reason rather than authority has failed to do so.

Later I shall try to show that the distinction between killing and letting die has been formulated in such a way as to beg the question against the absolutist. Certain considerations of agency and responsibility which any moral principle must take into account if it is to be rational seem to have been overlooked (Parts II and III of the present paper). First, however, I shall argue that there is another way in which Bennett has overlooked considerations of agency and responsibility, and has thus produced what looks like a general argument against absolutism, when really he is criticizing a principle which no intelligent absolutist should wish to defend. An absolutist who pays due attention to notions of agency will *admit* that there is no moral difference (at least in some cases) between killing and letting die; and this is because killing and letting die are both ways of being responsible for a death. The same state of affairs—a death—is necessarily the result both of killing and letting die. The concept of killing and the concept of letting die are connected in such a way that they must necessarily fall under the same moral principle whatever moral scheme one has. So a moral principle which forbids the killing of the innocent must, if it is to be rational, be construed as forbidding both killing and letting die.

Nor does this apply only to killing and letting die. It would, for instance, obviously be odd to condemn killing and yet not to condemn being an accessory to a killing. This is recognized by criminal law, which attaches a degree of guilt to being an accessory to murder which is sometimes as great as that which attaches to actually carrying out the killing. We *could* describe the criminal law as employing two quite independent principles, one covering murder, the other covering cases of being an accessory to murder. But a criminal code which punished murder but did not also punish being an accessory to murder, would be irrational (and unjust). It would also be irrational not to regard certain cases of being an accessory to murder as being as bad as murder, as involving a guilt as great as that of actually carrying out the killing. This is because to hand a murderer the gun which he is to use to carry out his crime may, in certain circumstances, be to participate in what he does to such an extent that two persons are equally involved as agents, and share equal responsibility.

Such locutions as 'He let X happen' and 'He failed to prevent Y' normally involve a man in the production of a state of affairs by ascribing responsibility to him for it. They may involve him in the state of affairs as surely as if it had been the result of his direct agency. It is for this reason that any moral scheme must include both doing something and being responsible for the same state of affairs under the same moral principle.

Let us take, for example, the case of slander. Strawson[8] has given an analysis of moral attitudes which connects them with such feelings as resentment and remorse. Resentment at being slandered, and remorse at having slandered someone else seem to be necessary conditions for genuinely believing slander to be morally wrong. A man who resented being slandered, but who never felt remorse at having slandered someone else could scarcely be said to believe that slander was morally wrong. He would be evincing hostility to certain cases of slander, but not moral *disapproval*. And even if he does feel remorse at having slandered someone, this would not be sufficient for saying that he holds, as a genuine moral principle, that it is wrong to slander. If he is ready to feel remorse at having slandered, then he ought also to be ready to feel indignation at hearing someone slandered. This 'vicarious analogue of resentment' (as Strawson calls it) is, as much as remorse, part of what it is for a man to hold as a genuine moral principle that it is wrong to slander. But if a readiness to feel indignation is an important criterion of a man's sincerely holding such a moral principle, then we seem to be moving towards saying that a person in a position to prevent the promulgation of a slander who feels no disposition whatever to do so—experiences no desire to contradict it, for instance—can only doubtfully be said to hold that slander is wrong. The doubt would be much stronger if he never felt any regret at having failed to prevent or contradict the slander. Such a man, we might say, cannot see what is wrong with slander, what is the harm of it. But if it is a criterion of a man's sincerely holding that it is morally wrong to slander that he should feel remorse at having slandered, indignation at hearing someone else slandered or regret at having let someone be slandered, then it must be a sign of his sincerity in holding the principle that he should feel remorse or regret at being *responsible* for a slander—either through conniving at it, or through remaining silent. One could have no proper grasp of a principle forbidding slander without seeing that it also covered cases of being responsible for a slander. Nor, without seeing how it covered cases of being responsible for a slander, could one really understand how, as a moral principle, it applied to cases of actually slandering.

However, a definition of slander such as 'the malicious misrepresentation of a man's actions so as to defame him' contains, among other things, a reference to the state of affairs necessarily produced by a successful slander; if the slander is believed, the man is defamed. It is hard to

[8] Cf. 'Freedom and resentment,' in P. F. Strawson (Ed.), *Studies in the Philosophy of Thought and Action* (Oxford, 1968).

imagine how someone could feel indignation or remorse at a slander unless he considered the situation which results from a successful slander was bad. The wrongness of slander must at least be connected with the wrongness of a man's being defamed. It is only if one deplores a man's being defamed—only if one sees that as an evil—that one can feel indignation or remorse at slander. So if one thinks that it is morally wrong to slander, one must also think it wrong for a man to be defamed; and one must also think it wrong to be responsible for a man's being defamed—for instance, by letting him be slandered.

Similarly, any moral principle which forbids the killing of the innocent must involve the condemnation of some state of affairs—such as someone's deliberately depriving an innocent person of life. So given such a principle, any act of commission or omission which falls under the generic description 'being responsible for the death of an innocent' will define an action covered by the principle. This will include having someone killed, aiding and abetting a murder, and all courses of action covered by the quasi-legal fiction of an 'act'—such as an 'act of omission'. One may let someone die, neglect someone such that he dies, or refrain from preventing a death. These are all ways of being responsible for a death. This analysis applies to a principle which holds that it is *always* wrong deliberately to deprive an innocent person of life, just as much as to any other.

Thus the obstetrical example can be faced by the absolutist. To say that there is no decisive moral difference between killing and letting die is to say that there is *one* moral principle which covers both. To say that there *is* a moral difference is to say that there are two principles. Now the irrationality of assuming a sharp moral distinction between killing and letting die is connected with the oddity, in certain cases, of denying that doing X and letting X happen involve a man in the same degree of agency,[9] or of failing to see the close conceptual connection between murder and being an accessory to murder. Therefore in saying that a person who holds that it is always wrong to kill the innocent should also, if he is not to be arbitrary or irrational, hold that it is wrong *in the same way and to the same degree* (in certain cases) to let the innocent die, one is surely saying that in a moral scheme in which the first principle were asserted, but in which all cases of letting die were always regarded and judged quite differently, it would actually be difficult to be sure that notions of agency were fully connected with moral principles—in

---

[9] I find it useful to use the term 'agency' to cover cases of responsibility. If a man directly kills, he is guilty in respect of the death as agent; if he lets die, he is guilty in respect of the death as being responsible. Furthermore, as we shall see, the nature of a man's agency—what sort of agent he is—may determine the degree and nature of his responsibility.

which case it would be impossible to see how, in such a scheme, morality connected with responsibility. There could not be a moral scheme which made such arbitrary distinctions without involving itself in radical confusions about agency and responsibility. Now to deny, in certain cases, that there is a decisive moral difference between doing X and letting it happen is to point out that there is a conceptual connection between doing something and allowing it to happen which is revealed in the notion of responsibility (this explains the logical difference between the claim that 'Do not kill' includes 'Do not let die' and a claim that 'Do not kill' includes 'Do not drink beer'). The same applies, for instance, to telling an untruth, allowing an untruth to be believed, not correcting a falsehood and so on. Those cases, coming under the second and third descriptions, which are 'as bad as' telling a lie are also cases which are as good as telling a lie—which are the moral equivalent of lying. There are not three, logically independent principles covering the three types of case. To relate the second and third to the first is to engage in casuistry, not in the production of new moral principles.

Returning then to the obstetrician, we see that he is involved in a *dilemma*: The premise 'In this case operating would be killing the child . . . not operating would be letting the mother die' gives *some* reason for the conclusion 'In this case operating would be wrong' (indeed, taken with the relevant principle, it entails it). But similarly this premise gives an equal reason for the conclusion 'In this case, not operating would be wrong'. Thus there is a dilemma irresoluble by the principle. From the fact that the premise counts towards the conclusion 'In this case operating would be wrong' it does not follow that it must count against the conclusion 'In this case not operating would be wrong', or for the conclusion 'In this case, not operating would be right'. Whether or not the production of an irresoluble dilemma is to the discredit of the principle is scarcely to be settled in the abstract. That a principle give rise to irresoluble moral conflict does not *ipso facto* refute it; certainly nothing has yet been said against the possibility of such dilemmas. There might well be reason for adhering to a principle other than a belief that it is unlikely to give rise to tragic dilemmas, and the fact that in this particular case it is (perhaps) impossible to act in obedience to the principle, whichever course of action is decided upon, does not of itself refute it. A moral principle is not *ipso facto* better the fewer dilemmas it produces.

Now if the killing/letting die distinction did mark a moral difference, it would show that in this case adherence to the general principle does not produce a dilemma. The dilemma is avoided because it becomes clear that the obstetrician should save the child and let the mother die. But this result can only be counted as giving support to the principle itself if, first, the less a principle can be convicted of producing a dilemma the better it is, or secondly, we have some other grounds for holding that it is better that the mother should die than that the child should. What is clear is that this particular absolutist principle understood in the way I have suggested—the only way which does not involve radical confusions about action concepts—ceases to be vulnerable to Bennett's argument.

On Killing and Letting Die *

Daniel Dinello

Jonathan Bennett in his paper 'Whatever the Consequences' (*Analysis*, 26. 3) attempts to refute what he refers to as the conservative position on the following problem:

> A woman in labour will certainly die unless an operation is performed in which the head of her unborn child is crushed or dissected; while if it is not performed the child can be delivered, alive, by postmortem Caesarian section. This presents a straight choice between the woman's life and the child's (p. 83). [pp. 328–29 above]

The conservative position is as follows: The child's death is part of a killing; but, in the case of the mother, there is no killing and death occurs only as a consequence of what is done. Therefore, the principle, 'It would always be wrong to kill an innocent human being whatever the consequences', when added to the premise, 'operating involves the killing of an innocent human being', yields the conclusion: 'it would be wrong to operate'.

Part I of this paper is a brief exposition of Bennett's attempt to refute the conservative position; Part II consists of two counter-examples to Bennett's position; and, Part III is my analysis of the issue.

I

Bennett states correctly that, without an appeal to authority as ground for the principle, the conservative must argue that the premise: 'In this case, operating would be killing an innocent human while not-

---

* "On Killing and Letting Die" (*Analysis* Vol. 31, 1971). Reprinted by permission of Basil Blackwell Publishers.

operating would involve the death of an innocent human only as a consequence' gives some reason for the conclusion. The conservatives have drawn the action/consequence distinction correctly, namely, operating is killing while not-operating is not. The questions are: By what criteria is the distinction drawn and are the criteria morally significant in this case?

Bennett argues correctly that a number of criteria could support a moral conclusion, but are irrelevant in this case. One criterion remains, namely, not-operating is not killing-the-woman because it is not doing anything at all, but is merely refraining from doing something. This is the conservative's final support. The question now is: Is there any moral significance in the acting/refraining (*i.e.*, killing/letting die) distinction?

Bennett suggests that the conditions for distinguishing between 'x killed y' and 'x let y die' are the following:

(1) x kills y if (a) x moved his body
               (b) y died
               (c) there are relatively few other ways x could have moved which satisfy the condition: if x moved like that, y would have died.

(2) x lets y die if (a) x moved his body
                 (b) y died
                 (c) almost all the ways x could have moved satisfy the condition: if x moved like that, y would have died.

Bennett concludes that since the conservative position rests on there being a morally significant difference between killing and letting die, and since there is no moral significance in the distinction based on the number of moves the agent can make, the conservative position has absolutely no moral bite.

II

The following two counter-examples show that Bennett's conditions for drawing the 'killing/letting die' distinction are incorrect.

Case I: Jones and Smith are watching television. Jones intentionally swallows a quantity of poison sufficient to kill himself. Smith, who knows the antidote, pulls out a pistol, shoots, and *kills* Smith. But, according to Bennett's criteria, this would be a case of 'letting die' since almost all the moves Jones could make (*i.e.*, moves other than, *e.g.*, forcing the antidote down Smith's throat) would satisfy the condition 'if Jones moved like that, y would have died'.

Case II: Jones and Smith are spies who have been captured by the enemy. They have been wired to each other such that a movement by one would electrocute the other. Jones moves and kills Smith. But, according to Bennett's criteria, this too would be a case of 'letting die' since almost all the moves Jones could make, *etc.*

Bennett's conditions for drawing the distinction are clearly wrong, but it remains to be seen whether his conclusion ('the conservative position has no moral bite') is correct.

III

The following are what I take to be the conditions which distinguish 'x killed y' from 'x let y die':

(A) x killed y if x caused y's death by performing movements which affect y's body such that y dies as a result of these movements.

(B) x let y die if (a) there are conditions affecting y, such that if they are not altered, y will die.

    (b) x has reason to believe that the performance of certain movements will alter conditions affecting y, such that y will not die.

    (c) x is in a position to perform such movements.

    (d) x fails to perform these movements.

The following are clarification and justification of these conditions:

(1) Part (b) is necessary, in that we would not want to say that a person who knew no way of altering conditions that are affecting y had let y die. For example, suppose y is dying of an incurable disease and a doctor, x, has no choice, but to watch y die. It would not be true that x let y die.

(2) (c) is necessary because the other conditions could be fulfilled, and if y were incapable of performing the movements, we would not say that he had let y die. For example: y is dying. X knows what movements would alter the conditions affecting y, but he has been securely tied to a chair.   •

The 'killing/letting die' distinction drawn in terms of the number of moves the agent could make clearly can have no moral significance. It is not obvious, though, that the distinction as I have now drawn it could have no moral significance. Consider the following example: Jones and Smith are in a hospital. Jones cannot live longer than two hours unless he gets a heart transplant. Smith, who had had one kidney removed, is dying of an infection in the other kidney. If he does not get a kidney transplant, he will die in about four hours. When Jones dies, his one good kidney can be transplanted to Smith, or Smith could be killed and his heart transplanted to Jones. Circumstances are such that there are no other hearts or kidneys available within the time necessary to save either one. Further, the consequences of either alternative are approximately equivalent, that is, heart transplants have been perfected, both have a wife and no children, *etc.* On Bennett's analysis, there is no morally significant difference between letting Jones die and killing Smith: the consequences of either alternative are equivalent and there is no moral distinction between killing and letting die. But, it seems clear that it would, in fact, be wrong to kill Smith and save Jones, rather than letting Jones die and saving Smith.

Further, suppose that Jones and Smith are in the same situation, but there is one difference between them: Jones has a wife and Smith does not. Bennett would have to say that since killing and letting die are morally distinguishable only by reference to the consequences of each alternative, the doctor ought to kill Smith and save Jones (Jones' death would sadden his wife, but Smith has no wife and other things are equal). But, this also seems to be wrong.

Bennett argued that the conservative has absolutely no morally relevant factor to which he could appeal, i.e., the 'killing/letting die' distinction is not morally significant. The preceding two examples show this conclusion to be false: There are cases where consequences are equivalent and cases where the consequences of killing are preferable, yet still wrong to kill. The distinction as I have drawn it has some moral bite: it seems intuitively clear that causing a death is morally somewhat more reprehensible than knowingly refraining from altering conditions which are causing a death. Bennett has not refuted the conservative position because the question of whether an act is one of killing or letting die *is* relevant in determining the morality of the act. The conservative, though, gives this factor absolute status. In order to refute this position it must be shown that in many cases other factors outweigh this one. In other words, the question is not whether the conservative position has moral bite, but rather how much moral bite it has.*

SELECTED SUPPLEMENTARY READING

BENN, S. I., "Abortion, Infanticide, and Respect for Persons," in *The Problem of Abortion*, ed. J. Feinberg. Belmont, Calif.: Wadsworth Publishing Company, Inc., 1973.

BRANDT, R. B., "The Morality of Abortion," *The Monist*, 36 (1972).

BRODY, BARUCH A., "Abortion and the Law," *Journal of Philosophy*, 68 (1971).

———, "Abortion and the Sanctity of Human Life," *American Philosophical Quarterly*, 10 (April 1973).

CALLAHAN, DANIEL, *Abortion: Law, Choice and Morality*. New York: Macmillan, 1970.

---

* I am indebted to David Blumenfeld (University of Illinois, Chicago Circle) for criticisms of earlier versions of this paper.

COOKE, ROBERT E. et al., *The Terrible Choice: The Abortion Dilemma*. New York: Bantam, 1968.

DRINAN, ROBERT F., "The Morality of Abortion Laws," *The Catholic Lawyer*, 14 (1968).

ENGLEHARDT, H. TRISTRAM, JR., "The Ontology of Abortion," *Ethics*, 84 (1974).

FEINBERG, JOEL, ed., *The Problem of Abortion*. Belmont, Calif.: Wadsworth Publishing Company, Inc., 1973.

FINNIS, JOHN, "The Rights and Wrongs of Abortion: A Reply to Judith Thomson," *Philosophy and Public Affairs*, 2 (Winter 1973).

FOOT, PHILLIPPA, "The Problem of Abortion and the Doctrine of Double Effect," *The Oxford Review*, 5 (1967).

GERBER, D., "Abortion: The Uptake Argument," *Ethics*, 83 (1972).

GERBER, R. J., "Abortion: Parameters for Decision," *Ethics*, 82 (1972).

GOODRICH, T., "The Morality of Killing," *Philosophy*, 44 (1969).

GRANFIELD, DAVID, *The Abortion Decision*. Garden City, N. Y.: Doubleday Image Books, 1971.

Grisez, Germain G., *Abortion: The Myths, The Realities, and the Arguments*. New York: Corpus Books, 1970.

GUTTMACHER, ALAN F., ed., *The Case for Legalized Abortion Now*. Berkeley, Calif.: Diablo Press, 1967.

HALL, ROBERT E., *Abortion in a Changing World* (Vols. I and II). New York: Columbia University Press, 1970.

KOHL, MARVIN, "Abortion and the Argument from Innocence," *Inquiry*, 14 (1971).

MARGOLIS, JOSEPH, "Abortion," *Ethics*, 84 (1973).

McCORMICK, RICHARD A., "Past Church Teaching on Abortion," *Proceedings of the Catholic Theological Society of America*, 23 (1968).

MURRAY, JOHN COURTNEY, *We Hold These Truths*. New York: Sheed and Ward, 1960.

NOONAN, JOHN T., JR., ed., *The Morality of Abortion: Legal and Historical Perspectives*. Cambridge, Mass.: Harvard University Press, 1970.

PERKINS, ROBERT, ed., *Abortion*. Cambridge, Mass.: Schenkman Publishing Company, 1974.

RAMSEY, PAUL, "Abortion: A Review Article," *The Thomist*, 37 (1973).

————, "The Morality of Abortion," in *Life or Death: Ethics and Options*, ed. Daniel H. Labby. Seattle, Wash.: University of Washington Press, 1968.

RUDINOW, JOEL, "On 'the slippery slope,'" *Analysis*, 34 (1974).

SCHUR, EDWIN M., *Crimes without Victims*. Englewood Cliffs, N.J.: Prentice-Hall, Inc., 1965.

SMITH, D. T., ed., *Abortion and the Law*. Cleveland, O.: The Press of Case Western Reserve University, 1967.

THOMSON, JUDITH JARVIS, "Rights and Deaths," *Philosophy and Public Affairs*, 2 (Winter 1972).

TOOLEY, MICHAEL, "Abortion and Infanticide," *Philosophy and Public Affairs*, 2 (1972).

WARREN, MARY ANNE, "On the Moral and Legal Status of Abortion," *The Monist*, 56 (January 1973).

WERTHEIMER, ROGER, "Understanding the Abortion Argument," *Philosophy and Public Affairs*, 1 (1971).

WILLIAMS, GLANVILLE, "Euthanasia and Abortion," *University of Colorado Law Review*, 38 (1966).

————, *The Sanctity of Life and the Criminal Law*. London: Faber and Faber, 1958.

Chapter 7

BIOMEDICAL TECHNOLOGY

INTRODUCTION

Recent technology in biological and medical fields has shown that we are now capable of intentionally prolonging life and intervening in the course of human development in ways previously unavailable. Our capacity for control is likely to increase at a stunning pace. These unprecedented circumstances have captured the public's attention not only because of their intrinsic interest and practical medical importance, but because nothing short of the future development of mankind seems at stake. The species itself can be genetically engineered; the death of its members can be indefinitely prolonged. The results of biological and medical research bearing on these matters have been enthusiastically supported by some, while others have been alarmed at the possibilities for manipulation and even destruction which have surfaced. It is possible that these biomedical results are neither as miraculous nor as dangerous as they have sometimes been proclaimed to be, but certainly they are of sufficient importance that ethicists are warranted in serious reflection on the permissibility and impermissibility of certain practices these technological developments make possible.

When we talk of "biomedical control" what technological capacities does this term cover? In his essay Leon Kass organizes biomedical technologies into three groups, according to the following three major purposes:

1. Control of death and life
2. Control of human potentialities
3. Control of human achievement

He suggests the following three biomedical technologies corresponding to these three major purposes:

1. Medicine (insofar as it prolongs life and controls reproduction)
2. Genetic engineering
3. Neurological and psychological manipulation

Even if somewhat oversimplified (and the categories not mutually exclusive), this piece of mapping is a useful way of organizing the fields of control. We might also relate these fields to other areas of human engineering such as behavior control and environmental control, but Kass is probably correct in restricting biomedical technology to the above fields.

We cannot hope in the short span of this chapter to survey even most of the ethical issues in biomedicine, a field often referred to as "bioethics." This field covers ethical questions as diverse as the nature of death, restrictions on population growth, sterilization without consent, pharmacological alteration of personality, psychosurgery, health care delivery, experimentation with human subjects, and the allocation of scarce medical resources. We shall, however, study three problems that have aroused as much interest as any others: biological engineering, euthanasia, and the allocation of scarce medical resources. All involve ethical questions about the permissibility of certain kinds of individual, social, and legal control. In the case of biological engineering we want to know when, if ever, we are morally justified in controlling human potentialities by biological means. In the case of euthanasia, we want to know what moral grounds, if any, would justify either the active taking of one's own or another's life for reasons of incurable illness and/or senility. In the case of scarce resource allocation, we seek an answer to the question, "On what moral grounds shall some be permitted to live when not all can live?"

Biological Engineering

What actual or potential ethical problems motivate us to be concerned about the possibilities for engineering people by biological means? Some problems have long been obvious: As we lower infant mortality rates and devise means of increasing fecundity, while also extending life spans, we dangerously increase population. Biological birth control devices provide one possible means to control the increase. But which devices, if any, should be utilized? And, even more important, should we under any circumstances allow the state to *require* citizens to take certain steps toward population control, including perhaps a requirement of sterilization for retarded people or for carriers of deleterious genes that may be passed on to future generations?

Although these more familiar ethical problems are certainly important, they are only the beginning. Once the so-called genetic code was broken and we began to learn the genetic processes that control human development, an area rife with possibilities for human engineering emerged. For example, inheritable alterations in human cells (developing in tissue culture) have been produced by means such as the initiation of viral infection. This produces the possibility that both "favorable" and "unfavorable" alterations may be required by the state, or at least introduced on a massive scale by doctors. Further, medical diagnostic procedures now allow not only prenatal determination of the sex of infants, but also limited detection of crucial genetic deficiencies. This capacity will in all likelihood enormously increase. We will be thus enabled to control both the sex and genetic character of the population (assuming, of course, a widespread use of abortion).

All these *biological* possibilities motivate ethical concerns. But it is on the *engineering* side of biological engineering that the specter of control emerges. Potentially we can engineer the production of children, "improve" as a whole the human stock we breed, and in general plan the kind of society we want in a hitherto undreamed-of manner. There is widespread agreement that the greatest fears concerning social control are generated by genetic engineering and psychological manipulation (especially psychosurgery). Unlike medicine, which is commonly understood as an attempt simply to restore patients to a normal state of affairs (as governed by criteria of "health"), genetic engineering renders possible alterations and new capacities for future generations, and psychosurgery could conveniently be used not so much for restoration to a normal state of affairs as for the creation of a new state of affairs. Hence, while medical control is largely confined by present understandings of health and fitness, genetic and psychosurgical control invite *reconstructions* of the concepts of health and fitness in the image of those who sanction the envisioned alterations. (This is not to say, of course, that genetic and psychosurgical techniques are not and cannot be used strictly as medical means to the restoration of health. Presumably they can be so used.)

In order to discuss ethical problems of biological control, an important distinction between negative and positive eugenics has been introduced. Eugenics is the technological science that deals with the improvement of hereditary qualities. The distinction centers around what sort of "improvement" is to be made. *Negative* eugenics supposedly has only medical objectives of eliminating or otherwise treating inherited genetic diseases. Since genetic diseases are both prevalent and flourishing and since they are universally regarded as worthy of elimination, negative eugenics is generally praised as an advance in biomedical technology; it raises only a few important ethical issues.

Positive eugenics, however, raises a cluster of issues, since its purported objective is the positive betterment of the human hereditary condition. Hermann Muller is famous for the following sketch of the objectives he thought could be and ought to be eugenically produced: "on the physical side, more robust health; on the intellectual side, keener, deeper, and more creative intelligence; on the moral side, more genuine warmth of fellow feeling and cooperative disposition; on the apperceptive side, richer appreciation and its more adequate expression." * However well intentioned, comments such as these have quite naturally raised fears of gross abuse: Political tyranny, loss of free social pursuit, loss of human adaptability, and an attendant deterioration in the human gene pool because of a loss of genetic variety have all been cited as potential dangers.

In addition to these objections to a program of positive eugenics, other objections to various forms of biological engineering have been advanced. Perhaps the most prominent are the following two interconnected objections: (1) There seems no acceptable method either for acquiring *knowledge* concerning which traits should be produced or for deciding who shall decide on these traits; and it is highly unlikely that there will be general agreement on the desirability of traits. (2) Given objection 1 (or even without it) some dictatorial exercise of power—or at least serious incursion into freedom—at some point seems inevitable. Once instituted, such tyrannical power is likely to expand.

Some writers, most notably Paul Ramsey,† have not so much stated objections to programs of eugenics as they have argued that we must resolve a serious ethical dilemma: On the one hand, if we refuse to employ the means of biological control at our disposal, overcrowding, starvation, gene deterioration, and inheritable disease will result. On the other hand, if we employ these controls, we may inadvertently produce equally undesirable genetic consequences or later come to think our intervention

---

* As quoted in Charles Frankel, "The Specter of Eugenics," *Commentary,* 57 (March 1974), 30.

† See his *Fabricated Man* (New Haven, Conn.: Yale University Press, 1970), pp. 2–11.

a subversion of worthy human values, especially human freedom and dignity. Readers familiar with objections to other forms of control, such as behavior control, political control, environmental control—and even moral enforcement and punishment—will immediately recognize that these objections are broad ones by no means restricted to biological engineering. They are objections frequently voiced against, for example, B. F. Skinner's vision of social engineering. But the enormous promise of biological control has brought them home with new force in recent years—and rightly so, for there is but a thin line between the positive promise of negative eugenics and the negative promise of positive eugenics.

Euthanasia

In the early 1960s suicide was legalized in England. This legislation has been hailed by some and disparaged by others because it seems to manifest a new social attitude toward the intentional taking of life. To its proponents this attitude favors human dignity and responsibility over the coercive strictures of law. To its antagonists it represents an increasing moral permissiveness and an indifference toward the taking of human life—one so serious that it threatens our belief in the sanctity of life. Euthanasia, insofar as it is voluntarily consented to, is reasonably construable as a form of suicide that for reasons mentioned below has not met with the same legislative success as suicide in general. But recent advances in biomedicine have introduced an array of methods for the prolongation of life that make the issue of euthanasia more and more pressing. The literature on euthanasia reveals three pervasive arguments for euthanasia and four against. Arguments favoring its moral legitimacy and/or legalization include the following:

1. *An argument from individual liberty.* Many people argue that a primary moral principle, which ought to be incorporated into law wherever possible, is the right of free pursuit. They argue that state coercion is never permissible unless an individual's actions produce harm to others. Since the sufferer's choosing to accelerate death does not harm others, it is a permissible exercise of individual liberty and ought not to be subject to the compulsion of law. (This seems to be what is often meant by the phrase "the right to die.")

2. *An argument from loss of human dignity.* The prolongation of life made possible by medical technology has actually increased, and will continue to increase, our capacity to keep people alive only to see themselves gradually stripped of their former character and of all the activities they formerly enjoyed. Such patients are not only subjected to intense and abiding pain; they are often aware of their own deterioration, as well as of the burden they have become to others. To some it seems uncivilized and incompassionate, under these conditions, not to allow them to choose their own death.

3. *An argument from the reduction of suffering.* Some kinds of suffer-

ing are so intense and others so protracted as to be unendurable. This suffering can be borne by patient and family alike. As in (2) it seems to some immoral under such circumstances not to allow patients (*not* their family) to choose their own death. Euthanasia is said to be justified on grounds of prevention of cruelty.

Arguments against euthanasia include the following:

1. *An argument from the sanctity of human life.* Anti-euthanasiasts often appeal to the principle that human life is inviolable, and for this reason ought not to be taken under any circumstances. The reasons for this appeal to the sacredness of human life vary. Some are religiously based; others are rooted in the conviction that this principle is the pillar of social order; and still others spring from reflection on various ancient and modern periods in human history when human lives were disposed of at the whim of the state or family.

2. *An argument from deteriorating standards.* Some appeal to the so-called "wedge argument": If we once permit the taking of human life by consent of patients as a permissible practice, this will erode other strictures against the taking of life. Such enthanasia proposals are the "thin end of a wedge" leading to euthanasia without as well as with consent, infanticide, and so on. Euthanasia proposals must be resisted in the beginning, it is argued, or we will ultimately be unable to draw the line ending practices which take human life; for it is not so distant a move from the incurably ill to the unorthodox political thinker.

3. *Arguments from probable abuse.* This argument appeals to the likelihood of abuse by doctors, family, and other interested parties. The claim is that provision of wide discretion to medical practitioners concerning the methods of terminating life introduces a risk of abuse so serious that it outweighs any possible benefits of euthanasia. There are serious problems concerning whether the conditions under which a patient gives his consent are appropriate, especially when one considers possible family and financial pressures.

4. *Arguments from wrong diagnoses and new treatments.* This argument is encapsulated in the saying "Where there is life there is hope." It is well known that doctors often misdiagnose maladies. This is less serious when the diagnoses are correctable, but in cases of euthanasia if the information given is wrong, or if a new treatment appears shortly after death, the case is incorrectable. And there are many cases on record of "hopelessly incurable" patients who completely recovered.

These arguments generally presuppose a distinction between *voluntary* and *involuntary* euthanasia.* All parties to the arguments agree that involuntary or compulsory euthanasia requires a different and perhaps

---

* Another relevant, but different distinction is that between killing and letting-die, as discussed in the chapter on abortion. It is used to distinguish *active* from *passive* euthanasia. Allowing defective newborns to die, for example, is often sharply distinguished from putting them to death.

more difficult battery of arguments. Supporters of voluntary euthanasia are generally quick to qualify their arguments by proposing that euthanasia should not be permitted unless a rational and mature patient expressly requests it. They also insist that the "right to die" does not entail the "right to kill." Accordingly, they oppose the linking of *mercy-killing* (including the killing of deformed infants, the senile, and so on) with *euthanasia*. Although some arguments in favor of involuntary euthanasia are arguments in support of some forms of mercy-killing, proponents of voluntary euthanasia usually insist (whether justifiably or not) that death by request is not a form of killing at all.

Problems of euthanasia and mercy-killing are likely to become both more agonizing and more pressing, especially if doctors are felt to be obliged in every situation to use every means available to save patients. One crucial issue on which such discussions will turn is the so-called problem of the allocation of scarce medical resources, which we will now consider.

The Allocation of Scarce Resources

As medicine has expanded, an economic problem has accompanied the expansion: scarce resources have become even scarcer. And this scarcity is not just of expensive equipment and medicine; highly specialized practitioners, artificial organs, and donors for organ transplant operations are all in scarce supply. Hemodialysis and both kidney and heart transplantation have vividly brought this fact to public consciousness. This outstripping of supply by demand has raised an acute problem for both ethicists and hospital administrators: Who shall receive medical benefits, and who shall be denied them? In the case of certain diseases/ equipment, the problems are especially acute, for here the question is, "Who shall live when not everyone can live?" Unlike voluntary euthanasia, this question is not decided *by* the patient but *for* the patient by others. And there is direct competition between individuals for life itself, just as there is in the proverbial case of a lifeboat where some must go overboard in order that the others stay afloat. Here ethicists are called upon to construct acceptable criteria for choosing the set of patients who will live at the expense of those who will die unless treatment is provided.

To almost all who have written on this subject of scarce resources, it has seemed that reliance purely on the moral intuitions of attending physicians is insufficient, though this was the original system for hemodialysis (in Seattle, where such treatment originated) and is perhaps still the most widespread practice. In the hope of finding a more satisfactory ethical basis for making such decisions, three prominent positions have been advanced.

1. *Complex criteria systems.* Some authors have argued that a cluster of criteria should determine allocation decisions. Generally the argument has not so much been that satisfaction of one or more of these criteria is necessary in order to justify receiving treatment, but that, depending upon available resources, those who satisfy the most criteria (a quantitative consideration), especially the most important criteria (a qualitative consideration), ought to receive treatment. Possible criteria for selecting include (a) medical acceptability (capacity to benefit, without complicating ailments), (b) ability to contribute either financially or experimentally as a subject of research, (c) age and life expectancy, and (d) past and potential future contributions of the patient to society. Naturally there is widespread disagreement concerning the appropriateness and relative importance, if any, of these criteria.

2. *Random selection systems.* Other authors have argued either that complex criteria systems are inherently unworkable and in all likelihood discriminatory or that such judgments reduce persons to their social roles, violate human dignity, and jeopardize the doctor-patient relationship. They have opted instead for a natural random selection system ("first come, first served") or for a formal random selection system, such as a lottery. They generally argue for such systems on the grounds that they preserve human dignity as well as best implement principles of justice and equality of opportunity.

3. *No-treatment systems.* A minority, but nonetheless important view, has been that since the ethical context is one in which some must be selected to die and in which no one can save himself except by allowing another to die, we ought not to select at all. Instead, treatment should be given to none, because none should live when not all can. This answer, which seems highly implausible, makes better sense when thought of as analogous to the sinking lifeboat circumstance. One might challenge, of course, whether it is sufficiently analogous to the lifeboat case.

Arguments in the Selections

Leon Kass discusses the different forms of "social engineering" that have emerged and relates them to several ethical isues. He systematically treats problems of justly distributing scarce resources, of the easy abuse of power in areas such as positive eugenics, and of self-degradation and dehumanization where medical technology has placed patients in the situation of "only a less-than-human, vegetating existence." After specifying what he takes to be the greatest dangers inherent in each problem, Kass argues that our well-intentioned efforts to eradicate human suffering sometimes present more problems than they resolve, especially where different aims of scientific research come into conflict. He counsels considerable caution and even delay in the appropriation of the achievements of biomedical technology. This leads him to the controversial conclusion that the researchers' maxim "no restrictions on scientific research" is disingenuous. He argues that each new proposed area of research requires justification on its own merits. Kass is here balancing the dangers of regulation against the dangers inherent in the new biomedicine. He clearly thinks the burden of proof is on the proponents of new biomedical technologies.

Martin P. Golding writes about problems of delineating and justifying goals in biological engineering. He argues that the aims of *positive* eugenics suffer from a lack of clarity concerning (a) the traits that are to be enhanced, (b) the actual advantageousness to the community of enhancing these traits, and (c) the institutional framework of the social program. He points out that strong elitist and ideological overtones, as well as questionable inferences from genetic studies, are present in the arguments of some proponents of positive eugenics. He notes that this fact is one reason why strong disagreement will remain over the "ideal" traits to be produced. Golding finds *negative* eugenics more difficult to assess. He discusses conflicting opinions among professional medical practitioners, a lack of evidence on whether such practices are unharmful to valuable hereditary qualities, and a lack of proof that the benefits outweigh the risks. Golding also mentions the problem of who shall control the agencies of biological control. Like Kass, he thinks it is almost inevitable that some "policing" will be necessary, and he hopes it will be initially exercised by scientists themselves. In conclusion, Golding urges considerable restraint in proceeding with any large-scale program of eugenics, especially in the light of our factual ignorance and normative unclarities.

Antony Flew stakes out the moral grounds for legalization of voluntary euthanasia. Flew contends that for moral reasons we should all be given a legal right to voluntary euthansia, even if it would sometimes be morally wrong to exercise that right. Flew contends that there are two decisive reasons favoring "the principle of euthanasia": (1) Forced cruelty—laws preventing those afflicted with incurable and painful diseases from choosing death are cruel laws; (2) forced degradation—laws which prohibit voluntary termination of life when one's personality is eroding and one's existence is that of constant demoralization are degrading laws. After briefly arguing, on these grounds, for voluntary euthanasia, Flew presents objections to his own position. These objections are, in effect, the case against euthanasia outlined above.

Nicholas Rescher proposes a system for the allocation of scarce medical lifesaving therapy. He conceives the problem as one of constructing criteria to govern the selection of those who are to be given a chance of survival at the expense of those who will be condemned to die. Rescher argues for a two-level, cluster-of-criteria system. Criteria on the first level determine those who will be admitted into consideration for treatment.

The main criterion here seems to be the "prospect-of-success" factor, which is a medical determination of which patients have a substantial promise of success and which do not. Criteria on the second level provide a plausible list of both biomedical and social considerations that would enable one to make final selections. Rescher does not make strong claims in behalf of his list, conceding that it works only as well as one can expect any single system to work. He makes appeals to the claims of both utility and justice to support his contentions, but, as he notes at one point, his argument is in the final analysis based on pragmatic grounds. This helps explain why Rescher opts partially for a random selection system: "If there are no really major disparities within [the final group of candidates]—then the final selection is made by *random* selection."

The New Biology: What Price Relieving Man's Estate? *

Leon R. Kass

Recent advances in biology and medicine suggest that we may be rapidly acquiring the power to modify and control the capacities and activities of men by direct intervention and manipulation of their bodies and minds. Certain means are already in use or at hand, others await the solution of relatively minor technical problems, while yet others, those offering perhaps the most precise kind of control, depend upon further basic research. Biologists who have considered these matters disagree on the question of how much how soon, but all agree that the power for "human engineering," to borrow from the jargon, is coming and that it will probably have profound social consequences.

These developments have been viewed both with enthusiasm and with alarm; they are only just beginning to receive serious attention. Several biologists have undertaken to inform the public about the technical possibilities, present and future. Practitioners of social science

———————
* "The New Biology: What Price Relieving Man's Estate?" Kass, L. R., *Science*, Vol. 174, pp. 779–88. Copyright November 19, 1971 by the American Association for the Advancement of Science. Reprinted by permission of the author and publisher.

"futurology" are attempting to predict and describe the likely social consequences of and public responses to the new technologies. Lawyers and legislators are exploring institutional innovations for assessing new technologies. All of these activities are based upon the hope that we can harness the new technology of man for the betterment of mankind.

Yet this commendable aspiration points to another set of questions, which are, in my view, sorely neglected—questions that inquire into the meaning of phrases such as the "betterment of mankind." A *full* understanding of the new technology of man requires an exploration of ends, values, standards. What ends will or should the new techniques serve? What values should guide society's adjustments? By what standards should the assessment agencies assess? Behind these questions lie others: what is a good man, what is a good life for man, what is a good community? This article is an attempt to provoke discussion of these neglected and important questions.

While these questions about ends and ultimate ends are never unimportant or irrelevant, they have rarely been more important or more relevant. That this is so can be seen once we recognize that we are dealing here with a group of technologies that are in a decisive respect unique: the object upon which they operate is man himself. The technologies of energy or food production, of communication, of manufacture, and of motion greatly alter the implements available to man and the conditions in which he uses them. In contrast, the biomedical technology works to change the user himself. To be sure, the printing press, the automobile, the television, and the jet airplane have greatly altered the conditions under which and the way in which men live; but men as biological beings have remained largely unchanged. They have been, and remain, able to accept or reject, to use and abuse the technologies; they choose, whether wisely or foolishly, the ends to which these technologies are means. Biomedical technology may make it possible to change the inherent capacity for choice itself. Indeed, both those who welcome and those who fear the advent of "human engineering" ground their hopes and fears in the same prospect: *that man can for the first time recreate himself.*

Engineering the engineer seems to differ in kind from engineering his engine. Some have argued, however, that biomedical engineering does not differ qualitatively from toilet training, education, and moral teachings—all of which are forms of so-called "social engineering," which has man as its object, and is used by one generation to mold the next. In reply, it must at least be said that the techniques which have hitherto been employed are feeble and inefficient when compared to those on the horizon. This quantitative difference rests in part on a qualitative difference in the means of intervention. The traditional influences operate by speech or by symbolic deeds. They pay tribute to man as the animal who lives by speech and who understands the meanings of actions. Also, their effects are, in general, reversible, or at least subject to attempts at reversal. Each person has greater or lesser power to accept or reject or abandon them. In contrast, biomedical engineering circumvents the human context of speech and meaning, bypasses choice, and goes directly to work to modify the human material itself. Moreover, the changes wrought may be irreversible.

In addition, there is an important practical reason for considering the biomedical technology apart from other technologies. The advances we shall examine are fruits of a large, humane project dedicated to the conquest of disease and the relief of human suffering. The biologist and physician, regardless of their private motives, are seen, with justification, to be the well-wishers and benefactors of mankind. Thus, in a time in which technological advance is more carefully scrutinized and increasingly criticized, biomedical developments are still viewed by most people as benefits largely without qualification. The price we pay for these developments is thus more likely to go unrecognized. For this reason, I shall consider only the dangers and costs of biomedical advance. As the benefits are well known, there is no need to dwell upon them here. My discussion is deliberately partial.

I begin with a survey of the pertinent technologies. Next, I will consider some of the basic ethical and social problems in the use of these technologies. Then, I will briefly raise some fundamental questions to which these problems point. Finally, I shall offer some very general reflections on what is to be done.

The Biomedical Technologies

The biomedical technologies can be usefully organized into three groups, according to their major purpose: (i) control of death and life, (ii) control of human potentialities, and (iii) control of human achievement. The corresponding technologies are (i) medicine, especially the arts of prolonging life and of controlling reproduction, (ii) genetic engineering, and (iii) neurological and psychological manipulation. I shall briefly summarize each group of techniques.

1. *Control of death and life.* Previous medical triumphs have greatly increased average life expectancy. Yet other developments, such as organ transplantation or replacement and research into aging, hold forth the promise of increasing not just the average, but also the maximum life expectancy. Indeed, medicine seems to be sharpening its tools to do battle with death itself, as if death were just one more disease.

More immediately and concretely, available techniques of prolonging life—respirators, cardiac pacemakers, artificial kidneys—are already in the lists against death. Ironically, the success of these devices in forestalling death has introduced confusion in determining that death has, in fact, occurred. The traditional signs of life—heartbeat and respiration—can now be maintained entirely by machines. Some physicians are now busily trying to devise so-called "new definitions of death," while others maintain that the technical advances show that death is not a concrete event at all, but rather a gradual process, like twilight, incapable of precise temporal localization.

The real challenge to death will come from research into aging and senescence, a field just entering puberty. Recent studies suggest that aging is a genetically controlled process, distinct from disease, but one that can be manipulated and altered by diet or drugs. Extrapolating from animal studies, some scientists have suggested that a decrease in the rate of aging might also be achieved simply by effecting a very small decrease in human body temperature. According to some estimates, by the year 2000 it may be technically possible to add from 20 to 40 useful years to the period of middle life.

Medicine's success in extending life is already a major cause of excessive population growth: death control points to birth control. Although we are already technically competent, new techniques for lowering fertility and chemical agents for inducing abortion will greatly enhance our powers over conception and gestation. Problems of definition have been raised here as well. The need to determine when individuals acquire enforceable legal rights gives society an interest in the definition of human life and of the time when it begins. These matters are too familiar to need elaboration.

Technologies to conquer infertility proceed alongside those to promote it. The first successful laboratory fertilization of human egg by human sperm was reported in 1969.[1] In 1970, British scientists learned how to grow human embryos in the laboratory up to at least the blastocyst stage [that is, to the age of 1 week].[2] We may soon hear about the next stage, the successful reimplantation of such an embryo into a woman previously infertile because of oviduct disease. The development of an artificial placenta, now under investigation, will make possible full laboratory control of fertilization and gestation. In addition, sophisticated biochemical and cytological techniques of monitoring the "quality" of the fetus have been and are being developed and used. These develop-

---

[1] R. G. Edwards, B. D. Bavister, P. C. Steptoe, *Nature* 221, 632 (1969).
[2] R. G. Edwards, P. C. Steptoe, J. M. Purdy, *ibid.* 227, 1307 (1970).

ments not only give us more power over the generation of human life, but make it possible to manipulate and to modify the quality of the human material.

2. *Control of human potentialities.* Genetic engineering, when fully developed, will wield two powers not shared by ordinary medical practice. Medicine treats existing individuals and seeks to correct deviations from a norm of health. Genetic engineering, in contrast, will be able to make changes that can be transmitted to succeeding generations and will be able to create new capacities, and hence to establish new norms of health and fitness.

Nevertheless, one of the major interests in genetic manipulation is strictly medical: to develop treatments for individuals with inherited diseases. Genetic disease is prevalent and increasing, thanks partly to medical advances that enable those affected to survive and perpetuate their mutant genes. The hope is that normal copies of the appropriate gene, obtained biologically or synthesized chemically, can be introduced into defective individuals to correct their deficiencies. This *therapeutic* use of genetic technology appears to be far in the future. Moreover, there is some doubt that it will ever be practical, since the same end could be more easily achieved by transplanting cells or organs that could compensate for the missing or defective gene product.

Far less remote are technologies that could serve *eugenic* ends. Their development has been endorsed by those concerned about a general deterioration of the human gene pool and by others who believe that even an undeteriorated human gene pool needs upgrading. Artificial insemination with selected donors, the eugenic proposal of Herman Muller,[3] has been possible for several years because of the perfection of methods for long-term storage of human spermatozoa. The successful maturation of human oocytes in the laboratory and their subsequent fertilization now make it possible to select donors of ova as well. But a far more suitable technique for eugenic purposes will soon be upon us—namely, nuclear transplantation, or cloning. Bypassing the lottery of sexual recombination, nuclear transplantation permits the asexual reproduction or copying of an already developed individual. The nucleus of a mature but unfertilized egg is replaced by a nucleus obtained from a specialized cell of an adult organism or embryo (for example, a cell from the intestines or the skin). The egg with its transplanted nucleus develops as if it had been fertilized and, barring complications, will give rise to a normal adult organism. Since almost all the hereditary material (DNA) of a cell is contained within its nucleus, the renucleated egg and the individual into which it

---

[3] H. J. Muller, *Science* 134, 643 (1961).

develops are genetically identical to the adult organism that was the source of the donor nucleus. Cloning could be used to produce sets of unlimited numbers of genetically identical individuals, each set derived from a single parent. Cloning has been successful in amphibians and is now being tried in mice; its extension to man merely requires the solution of certain technical problems.

Production of man-animal chimeras by the introduction of selected nonhuman material into developing human embryos is also expected. Fusion of human and nonhuman cells in tissue culture has already been achieved.

Other, less direct means for influencing the gene pool are already available, thanks to our increasing ability to identify and diagnose genetic diseases. Genetic counselors can now detect biochemically and cytologically a variety of severe genetic defects (for example, Mongolism, Tay-Sachs disease) while the fetus is still in utero. Since treatments are at present largely unavailable, diagnosis is often followed by abortion of the affected fetus. In the future, more sensitive tests will also permit the detection of heterozygote carriers, the unaffected individuals who carry but a single dose of a given deleterious gene. The eradication of a given genetic disease might then be attempted by aborting all such carriers. In fact, it was recently suggested that the fairly common disease cystic fibrosis could be completely eliminated over the next 40 years by screening all pregnancies and aborting the 17,000,000 unaffected fetuses that will carry a single gene for this disease. Such zealots need to be reminded of the consequences should each geneticist be allowed an equal assault on his favorite genetic disorder, given that each human being is a carrier for some four to eight such recessive, lethal genetic diseases.

3. *Control of human achievement.* Although human achievement depends at least in part upon genetic endowment, heredity determines only the material upon which experience and education impose the form. The limits of many capacities and powers of an individual are indeed genetically determined, but the nurturing and perfection of these capacities depend upon other influences. Neurological and psychological manipulation hold forth the promise of controlling the development of human capacities, particularly those long considered most distinctively human: speech, thought, choice, emotion, memory, and imagination.

These techniques are now in a rather primitive state because we understand so little about the brain and mind. Nevertheless, we have already seen the use of electrical stimulation of the human brain to produce sensations of intense pleasure and to control rage, the use of brain surgery (for example, frontal lobotomy) for the relief of severe anxiety, and the use of aversive conditioning with electric shock to treat sexual perversion. Operant-conditioning techniques are widely used, apparently with success, in schools and mental hospitals. The use of so-called consciousness-expanding and hallucinogenic drugs is widespread, to say nothing of tranquilizers and stimulants. We are promised drugs to modify memory, intelligence, libido, and aggressiveness.

The following passages from a recent book by Yale neurophysiologist José Delgado— a book instructively entitled *Physical Control of the Mind: Toward a Psychocivilized Society*—should serve to make this discussion more concrete. In the early 1950's, it was discovered that, with electrodes placed in certain discrete regions of their brains, animals would repeatedly and indefatigably press levers to stimulate their own brains, with obvious resultant enjoyment. Even starving animals preferred stimulating these so-called pleasure centers to eating. Delgado comments on the electrical stimulation of a similar center in a human subject.[4]

> [T]he patient reported a pleasant tingling sensation in the left side of her body 'from my face down to the bottom of my legs.' She started giggling and making funny comments, stating that she enjoyed the sensation 'very much.' Repetition of these stimulations made the patient more communicative and flirtatious, and she ended by openly expressing her desire to marry the therapist. (p. 185)

And one further quotation from Delgado.

> Leaving wires inside of a thinking brain may appear unpleasant or dangerous, but actually the many patients who have undergone this experience have not been concerned about the fact of being wired, nor have they felt any discomfort due to the presence of conductors in their heads. Some women have shown their feminine adaptability to circumstances by wearing attractive hats or wigs to conceal their electrical headgear, and many people have been able to enjoy a normal life as out-patients, returning to the clinic periodically for examination and stimulation. In a few cases in which contacts were located in pleasurable areas, patients have had the opportunity to stimulate their own brains by pressing the button of a portable instrument, and this procedure is reported to have therapeutic benefits. (p. 188)

It bears repeating that the sciences of neurophysiology and psychopharmacology are in their infancy. The techniques that are now available are crude, imprecise, weak, and unpredictable, compared to those that may flow from a more mature neurobiology.

---

[4] J. M. R. Delgado, *Physical Control of the Mind: Toward a Psychocivilized Society* (Harper & Row, New York, 1969).

Basic Ethical and Social Problems
in the Use of Biomedical Technology

After this cursory review of the powers now and soon to be at our disposal, I turn to the questions concerning the use of these powers. First, we must recognize that questions of use of science and technology are always moral and political questions, never simply technical ones. All private or public decisions to develop or to use biomedical technology —and decisions *not* to do so—inevitably contain judgments about value. This is true even if the values guiding those decisions are not articulated or made clear, as indeed they often are not. Secondly, the value judgments cannot be derived from biomedical science. This is true even if scientists themselves make the decisions.

These important points are often overlooked for at least three reasons.

1. They are obscured by those who like to speak of "the control of nature by science." It is men who control, not that abstraction "science." Science may provide the means, but men choose the ends; the choice of ends comes from beyond science.

2. Introduction of new technologies often appears to be the result of no decision whatsoever, or of the culmination of decisions too small or unconscious to be recognized as such. What can be done is done. However, someone is deciding on the basis of some notions of desirability, no matter how self-serving or altruistic.

3. Desires to gain or keep money and power no doubt influence much of what happens, but these desires can also be formulated as reasons and then discussed and debated.

Insofar as our society has tried to deliberate about questions of use, how has it done so? Pragmatists that we are, we prefer a utilitarian calculus: we weigh "benefits" against "risks," and we weigh them for both the individual and "society." We often ignore the fact that the very definitions of a "a benefit" and "a risk" are themselves based upon judgments about value. In the biomedical areas just reviewed, the benefits are considered to be self-evident: prolongation of life, control of fertility and of population size, treatment and prevention of genetic disease, the reduction of anxiety and aggressiveness, and the enhancement of memory, intelligence, and pleasure. The assessment of risk is, in general, simply pragmatic—will the technique work effectively and reliably, how much will it cost, will it do detectable bodily harm, and who will complain if we proceed with development? As these questions are familiar and congenial, there is no need to belabor them.

The very pragmatism that makes us sensitive to considerations of economic cost often blinds us to the larger social costs exacted by biomedical advances. For one thing, we seem to be unaware that we may not be able to maximize all the benefits, that several of the goals we are promoting conflict with each other. On the one hand, we seek to control population growth by lowering fertility; on the other hand, we develop techniques to enable every infertile woman to bear a child. On the one hand, we try to extend the lives of individuals with genetic disease; on the other, we wish to eliminate deleterious genes from the human population. I am not urging that we resolve these conflicts in favor of one side or the other, but simply that we recognize that such conflicts exist. Once we do, we are more likely to appreciate that most "progress" is heavily paid for in terms not generally included in the simple utilitarian calculus.

To become sensitive to the larger costs of biomedical progress, we must attend to several serious ethical and social questions. I will briefly discuss three of them: (i) questions of distributive justice, (ii) questions of the use and abuse of power, and (iii) questions of self-degradation and dehumanization.

Distributive Justice

The introduction of any biomedical technology presents a new instance of an old problem—how to distribute scarce resources justly. We should assume that demand will usually exceed supply. Which people should receive a kidney transplant or an artificial heart? Who should get the benefits of genetic therapy or of brain stimulation? Is "first-come, first-served" the fairest principle? Or are certain people "more worthy," and if so, on what grounds?

It is unlikely that we will arrive at answers to these questions in the form of deliberate decisions. More likely, the problem of distribution will continue to be decided ad hoc and locally. If so, the consequence will probably be a sharp increase in the already far too great inequality of medical care. The extreme case will be longevity, which will probably be, at first, obtainable only at great expense. Who is likely to be able to buy it? Do conscience and prudence permit us to enlarge the gap between rich and poor, especially with respect to something as fundamental as life itself?

Questions of distributive justice also arise in the earlier decisions to acquire new knowledge and to develop new techniques. Personnel and facilities for medical research and treatment are scarce resources. Is the development of a new technology the best use of the limited resources, given current circumstances? How should we balance efforts aimed at prevention against those aimed at cure, or either of these against efforts to redesign the species? How should we balance the delivery of available levels of care against further basic research? More fundamentally, how should we balance efforts in biology and medicine against efforts to eliminate poverty, pollution, urban decay, discrimination, and poor education? This last question about distribution is perhaps the most profound. We should reflect upon the social consequences of seducing many of our brightest young people to spend their lives locating the biochemical defects in rare genetic diseases, while our more serious problems go begging. The current squeeze on money for research provides us with an opportunity to rethink and reorder our priorities.

Problems of distributive justice are frequently mentioned and discussed, but they are hard to resolve in a rational manner. We find them especially difficult because of the enormous range of conflicting values and interests that characterizes our pluralistic society. We cannot agree—unfortunately, we often do not even try to agree—on standards for just distribution. Rather, decisions tend to be made largely out of a clash of competing interests. Thus, regrettably, the question of how to distribute justly often gets reduced to who shall decide how to distribute. The question about justice has led us to the question about power.

Use and Abuse of Power

We have difficulty recognizing the problems of the exercise of power in the biomedical enterprise because of our delight with the wondrous fruits it has yielded. This is ironic because the notion of power is absolutely central to the modern conception of science. The ancients conceived of science as the *understanding* of nature, pursued for its own sake. We moderns view science as power, as *control* over nature; the conquest of nature "for the relief of man's estate" was the charge issued by Francis Bacon, one of the leading architects of the modern scientific project.[5]

Another source of difficulty is our fondness for speaking of the abstraction "Man." I suspect that we prefer to speak figuratively about "Man's power over Nature" because it obscures an unpleasant reality about human affairs. It is in fact particular men who wield power, not Man. What we really mean by "Man's power over Nature" is a power exercised by some men over other men, with a knowledge of nature as their instrument.

While applicable to technology in general, these reflections are especially pertinent to the technologies of human engineering, with which men deliberately exercise power over future generations. An excellent discussion of this question is found in *The Abolition of Man*, by C. S. Lewis.[6]

---

[5] F. Bacon, *The Advancement of Learning, Book I*, H. G. Dick, Ed. (Random House, New York, 1955), p. 193.

[6] C. S. Lewis, *The Abolition of Man* (Macmillan, New York, 1965), pp. 69–71.

It is, of course, a commonplace to complain that men have hitherto used badly, and against their fellows, the powers that science has given them. But that is not the point I am trying to make. I am not speaking of particular corruptions and abuses which an increase of moral virtue would cure: I am considering what the thing called "Man's power over Nature" must always and essentially be. . . .

In reality, of course, if any one age really attains, by eugenics and scientific education, the power to make its descendants what it pleases, all men who live after it are the patients of that power. They are weaker, not stronger: for though we may have put wonderful machines in their hands, we have pre-ordained how they are to use them. . . . The real picture is that of one dominant age . . . which resists all previous ages most successfully and dominates all subsequent ages most irresistibly, and thus is the real master of the human species. But even within this master generation (itself an infinitesimal minority of the species) the power will be exercised by a minority smaller still. Man's conquest of Nature, if the dreams of some scientific planners are realized, means the rule of a few hundreds of men over billions upon billions of men. There neither is nor can be any simple increase of power on Man's side. Each new power won *by* man is a power *over* man as well. Each advance leaves him weaker as well as stronger. In every victory, besides being the general who triumphs, he is also the prisoner who follows the triumphal car.

Please note that I am not yet speaking about the problem of the misuse or abuse of power. The point is rather that the power which grows is unavoidably the power of only some men, and that the number of powerful men decreases as power increases.

Specific problems of abuse and misuse of specific powers must not, however, be overlooked. Some have voiced the fear that the technologies of genetic engineering and behavior control, though developed for good purposes, will be put to evil uses. These fears are perhaps somewhat exaggerated, if only because biomedical technologies would add very little to our highly developed arsenal for mischief, destruction, and stultification. Nevertheless, any proposal for large-scale human engineering should make us wary. Consider a program of positive eugenics based upon the widespread practice of asexual reproduction. Who shall decide what constitutes a superior individual worthy of replication? Who shall decide which individuals may or must reproduce, and by which method? These are questions easily answered only for a tyrannical regime.

Concern about the use of power is equally necessary in the selection of means for desirable or agreed-upon ends. Consider the desired end of limiting population growth. An effective program of fertility control is likely to be coercive. Who should decide the choice of means? Will the program penalize "conscientious objectors"?

Serious problems arise simply from obtaining and disseminating information, as in the mass screening programs now being proposed for detection of genetic disease. For what kinds of disorders is compulsory screening justified? Who shall have access to the data obtained, and for what purposes? To whom does information about a person's genotype belong? In ordinary medical practice, the patient's privacy is protected by the doctor's adherence to the principle of confidentiality. What will protect his privacy under conditions of mass screening?

More than privacy is at stake if screening is undertaken to detect psychological or behavioral abnormalities. A recent proposal, tendered and supported high in government, called for the psychological testing of all 6-year-olds to detect future criminals and misfits. The proposal was rejected; current tests lack the requisite predictive powers. But will such a proposal be rejected if reliable tests become available? What if certain genetic disorders, diagnosable in childhood, can be shown to correlate with subsequent antisocial behavior? For what degree of correlation and for what kinds of behavior can mandatory screening be justified? What use should be made of the data? Might not the dissemination of the information itself undermine the individual's chance for a worthy life and contribute to his so-called antisocial tendencies?

Consider the seemingly harmless effort to redefine clinical death. If the need for organs for transplantation is the stimulus for redefining death, might not this concern influence the definition at the expense of the dying? One physician, in fact, refers in writing to the revised criteria for declaring a patient dead as a "new definition of heart donor eligibility." [7]

Problems of abuse of power arise even in the acquisition of basic knowledge. The securing of a voluntary and informed consent is an abiding problem in the use of human subjects in experimentation. Gross coercion and deception are now rarely a problem; the pressures are generally subtle, often related to an intrinsic power imbalance in favor of the experimentalist.

A special problem arises in experiments on or manipulations of the unborn. Here it is impossible to obtain the consent of the human subject. If the purpose of the intervention is therapeutic—to correct a known genetic abnormality, for example—consent can reasonably be implied. But can anyone ethically consent to nontherapeutic interventions in which parents or scientists work their wills or their eugenic visions on the child-to-be? Would not such manipulation represent in itself an abuse of power, independent of consequences?

There are many clinical situations which already permit, if not invite,

_____

[7] D. D. Rutstein, *Daedalus* (Spring 1969), p. 526.

the manipulative or arbitrary use of powers provided by biomedical technology: obtaining organs for transplantation, refusing to let a person die with dignity, giving genetic counselling to a frightened couple, recommending eugenic sterilization for a mental retardate, ordering electric shock for a homosexual. In each situation, there is an opportunity to violate the will of the patient or subject. Such opportunities have generally existed in medical practice, but the dangers are becoming increasingly serious. With the growing complexity of the technologies, the technician gains in authority, since he alone can understand what he is doing. The patient's lack of knowledge makes him deferential and often inhibits him from speaking up when he feels threatened. Physicians *are* sometimes troubled by their increasing power, yet they feel they cannot avoid its exercise. "Reluctantly," one commented to me, "we shall have to play God." With what guidance and to what ends I shall consider later. For the moment, I merely ask: "By whose authority?"

While these questions about power are pertinent and important, they are in one sense misleading. They imply an inherent conflict of purpose between physician and patient, between scientist and citizen. The discussion conjures up images of master and slave, of oppressor and oppressed. Yet it must be remembered that conflict of purpose is largely absent, especially with regard to general goals. To be sure, the purposes of medical scientists are not always the same as those of the subjects experimented on. Nevertheless, basic sponsors and partisans of biomedical technology are precisely those upon whom the technology will operate. The will of the scientist and physician is happily married to (rather, is the offspring of) the desire of all of us for better health, longer life, and peace of mind.

Most future biomedical technologies will probably be welcomed, as have those of the past. Their use will require little or no coercion. Some developments, such as pills to improve memory, control mood, or induce pleasure, are likely to need no promotion. Thus, even if we should escape from the dangers of coercive manipulation, we shall still face large problems posed by the voluntary use of biomedical technology, problems to which I now turn.

Voluntary Self-degradation
and Dehumanization

Modern opinion is sensitive to problems of restriction of freedom and abuse of power. Indeed, many hold that a man can be injured only by violating his will. But this view is much too narrow. It fails to recognize the great dangers we shall face in the use of biomedical technology, dangers that stem from an excess of freedom, from the uninhibited exercises of will. In my view, our greatest problem will increasingly be one of voluntary self-degradation, or willing dehumanization.

Certain desired and perfected medical technologies have already had some dehumanizing consequences. Improved methods of resuscitation have made possible heroic efforts to "save" the severely ill and injured. Yet these efforts are sometimes only partly successful; they may succeed in salvaging individuals with severe brain damage, capable of only a less-than-human, vegetating existence. Such patients, increasingly found in the intensive care units of university hospitals, have been denied a death with dignity. Families are forced to suffer seeing their loved ones so reduced, and are made to bear the burdens of a protracted death watch.

Even the ordinary methods of treating disease and prolonging life have impoverished the context in which men die. Fewer and fewer people die in the familiar surroundings of home or in the company of family and friends. At that time of life when there is perhaps the greatest need for human warmth and comfort, the dying patient is kept company by cardiac pacemakers and defibrillators, respirators, aspirators, oxygenators, catheters, and his intravenous drip.

But the loneliness is not confined to the dying patient in the hospital bed. Consider the increasing number of old people who are still alive, thanks to medical progress. As a group, the elderly are the most alienated members of our society. Not yet ready for the world of the dead, not deemed fit for the world of the living, they are shunted aside. More and more of them spend the extra years medicine has given them in "homes for senior citizens," in chronic hospitals, in nursing homes—waiting for the end. We have learned how to increase their years, but we have not learned how to help them enjoy their days. And yet, we bravely and relentlessly push back the frontiers against death.

Paradoxically, even the young and vigorous may be suffering because of medicine's success in removing death from their personal experience. Those born since penicillin represent the first generation ever to grow up without the experience or fear of probable unexpected death at an early age. They look around and see that virtually all of their friends are alive. A thoughtful physician, Eric Cassell, has remarked on this in "Death and the physician" [8]

> [W]hile the gift of time must surely be marked as a great blessing, the *perception* of time, as stretching out endlessly before us, is somewhat threatening. Many of us function best under deadlines, and tend to procrastinate when time limits are not set. . . . Thus, this unquestioned boon, the extension of life, and the removal of the

---

[8] E. J. Cassell, *Commentary* (June 1969), p. 73.

threat of premature death, carries with it an unexpected anxiety: the anxiety of an unlimited future.

In the young, the sense of limitless time has apparently imparted not a feeling of limitless opportunity, but increased stress and anxiety, in addition to the anxiety which results from other modern freedoms: personal mobility, a wide range of occupational choice, and independence from the limitations of class and familial patterns of work. . . . A certain aimlessness (often ringed around with great social consciousness) characterizes discussions about their own aspirations. The future is endless, and their inner demands seem minimal. Although it may appear uncharitable to say so, they seem to be acting in a way best described as "childish"—particularly in their lack of a time sense. They behave as though there were no tomorrow, or as though the time limits imposed by the biological facts of life had become so vague for them as to be nonexistent.

Consider next the coming power over reproduction and genotype. We endorse the project that will enable us to control numbers and to treat individuals with genetic disease. But our desires outrun these defensible goals. Many would welcome the chance to become parents without the inconvenience of pregnancy; others would wish to know in advance the characteristics of their offspring (sex, height, eye color, intelligence); still others would wish to design these characteristics to suit their tastes. Some scientists have called for the use of the new technologies to assure the "quality" of all new babies.[9] As one obstetrician put it: "The business of obstetrics is to produce *optimum* babies." But the price to be paid for the "optimum baby" is the transfer of procreation from the home to the laboratory and its coincident transformation into manufacture. Increasing control over the product is purchased by the increasing depersonalization of the process. The complete depersonalization of procreation (possible with the development of an artificial placenta) shall be, in itself, seriously dehumanizing, no matter how optimum the product. It should not be forgotten that human procreation not only issues new human beings, but is itself a human activity.

Procreation is not simply an activity of the rational will. It is a more complete human activity precisely because it engages us bodily and spiritually, as well as rationally. Is there perhaps some wisdom in that mystery of nature which joins the pleasure of sex, the communication of love, and the desire for children in the very activity by which we continue the chain of human existence? Is not biological parenthood a built-in "mechanism," selected because it fosters and supports in parents an adequate concern for and commitment to their children? Would not the lab-

---

[9] B. Glass, *Science* 171, 23 (1971).

oratory production of human beings no longer be *human* procreation? Could it keep human parenthood human?

The dehumanizing consequences of programmed reproduction extend beyond the mere acts and processes of life-giving. Transfer of procreation to the laboratory will no doubt weaken what is presently for many people the best remaining justification and support for the existence of marriage and the family. Sex is now comfortably at home outside of marriage; child-rearing is progressively being given over to the state, the schools, the mass media, and the child-care centers. Some have argued that the family, long the nursery of humanity, has outlived its usefulness. To be sure, laboratory and governmental alternatives might be designed for procreation and child-rearing, but at what cost?

This is not the place to conduct a full evaluation of the biological family. Nevertheless, some of its important virtues are, nowadays, too often overlooked. The family is rapidly becoming the only institution in an increasingly impersonal world where each person is loved not for what he does or makes, but simply because he is. The family is also the institution where most of us, both as children and as parents, acquire a sense of continuity with the past and a sense of commitment to the future. Without the family, we would have little incentive to take an interest in anything after our own deaths. These observations suggest that the elimination of the family would weaken ties to past and future, and would throw us, even more than we are now, to the mercy of an impersonal, lonely present.

Neurobiology and psychobiology probe most directly into the distinctively human. The technological fruit of these sciences is likely to be both more tempting than Eve's apple and more "catastrophic" in its result.[10] One need only consider contemporary drug use to see what people are willing to risk or sacrifice for novel experiences, heightened perceptions,

---

[10] It is, of course, a long-debated question as to whether the fall of Adam and Eve ought to be considered "catastrophic," or more precisely, whether the Hebrew tradition considered it so. I do not mean here to be taking sides in this quarrel by my use of the term "catastrophic," and, in fact, tend to line up on the negative side of the questions, as put above. Curiously, as Aldous Huxley's *Brave New World* [(Harper & Row, New York, 1969)] suggests, the implicit goal of the biomedical technology could well be said to be the reversal of the Fall and a return of man to the hedonic and immortal existence of the Garden of Eden. Yet I can point to at least two problems. First, the new Garden of Eden will probably have no gardens; the received, splendid world of nature will be buried beneath asphalt, concrete, and other human fabrications, a transformation that is already far along. (Recall that in *Brave New World* elaborate consumption-oriented, mechanical amusement parks—featuring, for example, centrifugal bumble-puppy—had supplanted wilderness and even ordinary gardens.) Second, the new inhabitant of the new "Garden" will have to be a creature for whom we have no precedent, a creature as difficult to imagine as to bring into existence. He will have to be simultaneously an innocent like Adam and a technological wizard who keeps the "Garden" running. (I am indebted to Dean Robert Goldwin, St. John's College, for this last insight.)

or just "kicks." The possibility of drug-induced, instant, and effortless gratification will be welcomed. Recall the possibilities of voluntary self-stimulation of the brain to reduce anxiety, to heighten pleasure, or to create visual and auditory sensations unavailable through the peripheral sense organs. Once these techniques are perfected and safe, is there much doubt that they will be desired, demanded, and used?

What ends will these techniques serve? Most likely, only the most elemental, those most tied to the bodily pleasures. What will happen to thought, to love, to friendship, to art, to judgment, to public-spiritedness in a society with a perfected technology of pleasure? What kinds of creatures will we become if we obtain our pleasure by drug or electrical stimulation without the usual kind of human efforts and frustrations? What kind of society will we have?

We need only consult Aldous Huxley's prophetic novel *Brave New World* for a likely answer to these questions. There we encounter a society dedicated to homogeneity and stability, administered by means of instant gratifications and peopled by creatures of human shape but of stunted humanity. They consume, fornicate, take "soma," and operate the machinery that makes it all possible. They do not read, write, think, love, or govern themselves. Creativity and curiosity, reason and passion, exist only in a rudimentary and multilated form. In short, they are not men at all.

True, our techniques, like theirs, may in fact enable us to treat schizophrenia, to alleviate anxiety, to curb aggressiveness. We, like they, may indeed be able to save mankind from itself, but probably only at the cost of its humanness. In the end, the price of relieving man's estate might well be the abolition of man.[11]

There are, of course, many other routes leading to the abolition of man. There are many other and better known causes of dehumanization. Disease, starvation, mental retardation, slavery, and brutality—to name just a few—have long prevented many, if not most, people from living a fully human life. We should work to reduce and eventually to eliminate these evils. But the existence of these evils should not prevent us from appreciating that the use of the technology of man, uninformed by wisdom concerning proper human ends, and untempered by an appro-

---

[11] Some scientists naively believe that an engineered increase in human intelligence will steer us in the right direction. Surely we have learned by now that intelligence, whatever it is and however measured, is not synonymous with wisdom and that, if harnessed to the wrong ends, it can cleverly perpetrate great folly and evil. Given the activities in which many, if not most, of our best minds are now engaged, we should not simply rejoice in the prospect of enhancing IQ. On what would this increased intelligence operate? At best, the programming of further increases in IQ. It would design and operate techniques for prolonging life, for engineering reproduction, for delivering gratifications. With no gain in wisdom, our gain in intelligence can only enhance the rate of our dehumanization.

priate humility and awe, can unwittingly render us all irreversibly less than human. For, unlike the man reduced by disease or slavery, the people dehumanized à la *Brave New World* are not miserable, do not know that they are dehumanized, and, what is worse, would not care if they knew. They are, indeed, happy slaves, with a slavish happiness.

Some Fundamental Questions

The practical problems of distributing scarce resources, of curbing the abuses of power, and of preventing voluntary dehumanization point beyond themselves to some large, enduring, and most difficult questions: the nature of justice and the good community, the nature of man and the good for man. My appreciation of the profundity of these questions and my own ignorance before them makes me hesitant to say any more about them. Nevertheless, previous failures to find a shortcut around them have led me to believe that these questions must be faced if we are to have any hope of understanding where biology is taking us. Therefore, I shall try to show in outline how I think some of the larger questions arise from my discussion of dehumanization and self-degradation.

My remarks on dehumanization can hardly fail to arouse argument. It might be said, correctly, that to speak about dehumanization presupposes a concept of "the distinctively human." It might also be said, correctly, that to speak about wisdom concerning proper human ends presupposes that such ends do in fact exist and that they may be more or less accessible to human understanding, or at least to rational inquiry. It is true that neither presupposition is at home in modern thought.

The notion of the "distinctively human" has been seriously challenged by modern scientists. Darwinists hold that man is, at least in origin, tied to the subhuman; his seeming distinctiveness is an illusion or, at most, not very important. Biochemists and molecular biologists extend the challenge by blurring the distinction between the living and the non-living. The laws of physics and chemistry are found to be valid and are held to be sufficient for explaining biological systems. Man is a collection of molecules, an accident on the stage of evolution, endowed by chance with the power to change himself, but only along determined lines.

Psychoanalysts have also debunked the "distinctly human." The essence of man is seen to be located in those drives he shares with other animals—pursuit of pleasure and avoidance of pain. The so-called "higher functions" are understood to be servants of the more elementary, the more base. Any distinctiveness or "dignity" that man has consists of his superior capacity for gratifying his animal needs.

The idea of "human good" fares no better. In the social sciences, historicists and existentialists have helped drive this question underground. The former hold all notions of human good to be culturally and historically bound, and hence mutable. The latter hold that values are subjective: each man makes his own, and ethics becomes simply the cataloging of personal tastes.

Such appear to be the prevailing opinions. Yet there is nothing novel about reductionism, hedonism, and relativism; these are doctrines with which Socrates contended. What is new is that these doctrines seem to be vindicated by scientific advance. Not only do the scientific notions of nature and of man flower into verifiable predictions, but they yield marvelous fruit. The technological triumphs are held to validate their scientific foundations. Here, perhaps, is the most pernicious result of technological progress—more dehumanizing than any actual manipulation or technique, present or future. We are witnessing the erosion, perhaps the final erosion, of the idea of man as something splendid or divine, and its replacement with a view that sees man, no less than nature, as simply more raw material for manipulation and homogenization. Hence, our peculiar moral crises. We are in turbulent seas without a landmark precisely because we adhere more and more to a view of nature and of man which both gives us enormous power and, at the same time, denies all possibility of standards to guide its use. Though well-equipped, we know not who we are nor where we are going. We are left to the accidents of our hasty, biased, and ephemeral judgments.

Let us not fail to note a painful irony: our conquest of nature has made us the slaves of blind chance. We triumph over nature's unpredictabilities only to subject ourselves to the still greater unpredictability of our capricious wills and our fickle opinions. That we have a method is no proof against our madness. Thus, engineering the engineer as well as the engine, we race our train we know not where.[12]

---

[12] The philosopher Hans Jonas has made the identical point: "Thus the slow-working accidents of nature, which by the very patience of their small increments, large numbers, and gradual decisions, may well cease to be "accident" in outcome, are to be replaced by the fast-working accidents of man's hasty and biased decisions, not exposed to the long test of the ages. His uncertain ideas are to set the goals of generations, with a certainty borrowed from the presumptive certainty of the means. The latter presumption is doubtful enough, but this doubtfulness becomes secondary to the prime question that arises when man indeed undertakes to 'make himself': in what image of his own devising shall he do so, even granted that he can be sure of the means? In fact, of course, he can be sure of neither, not of the end, nor of the means, once he enters the realm where he plays with the roots of life. Of one thing only can he be sure: of his power to move the foundations and to cause incalculable and irreversible consequences. Never was so much power coupled with so little guidance for its use." [*J. Cent. Conf. Amer. Rabbis* (January 1968), p. 27.] These remarks demonstrate that, contrary to popular belief, we are not even on the right road toward a rational understanding of and rational control over human nature and human life. It is indeed the height of irrationality triumphantly to pursue rationalized technique, while at the same time insisting that questions of ends, values, and purposes lie beyond rational discourse.

While the disastrous consequences of ethical nihilism are insufficient to refute it, they invite and make urgent a reinvestigation of the ancient and enduring questions of what is a proper life for a human being, what is a good community, and how are they achieved.[13] We must not be deterred from these questions simply because the best minds in human history have failed to settle them. Should we not rather be encouraged by the fact that they considered them to be the most important questions?

As I have hinted before, our ethical dilemma is caused by the victory of modern natural science with its nonteleological view of man. We ought therefore to reexamine with great care the modern notions of nature and of man, which undermine those earlier notions that provide a basis for ethics. If we consult our common experience, we are likely to discover some grounds for believing that the questions about man and human good are far from closed. Our common experience suggests many difficulties for the modern "scientific view of man." For example, this view fails to account for the concern for justice and freedom that appears to be characteristic of all human societies.[14] It also fails to account for or to explain the fact that men have speech and not merely voice, that men can choose and act and not merely move or react. It fails to explain why men engage in moral discourse, or, for that matter, why they speak at all. Finally, the "scientific view of man" cannot account for scientific inquiry itself, for why men seek to know. Might there not be something the matter with a knowledge of man that does not explain or take account of his most distinctive activities, aspirations, and concerns? [15]

---

[13] It is encouraging to note that these questions are seriously being raised in other quarters—for example, by persons concerned with the decay of cities or the pollution of nature. There is a growing dissatisfaction with ethical nihilism. In fact, its tenets are unwittingly abandoned, by even its staunchest adherents, in any discussion of "what to do." For example, in the biomedical area, everyone, including the most unreconstructed and technocratic reductionist, finds himself speaking about the use of powers for "human betterment." He has wandered unawares onto ethical ground. One cannot speak of "human betterment" without considering what is meant by *the human* and by the related notion of *the good for man*. These questions can be avoided only by asserting that practical matters reduce to tastes and power, and by confessing that the use of the phrase "human betterment" is a deception to cloak one's own will to power. In other words, these questions can be avoided only by ceasing to discuss.

[14] Consider, for example, the widespread acceptance, in the legal systems of very different societies and cultures, of the principle and the practice of third-party adjudication of disputes. And consider why, although many societies have practiced slavery, no slaveholder has preferred his own enslavement to his own freedom. It would seem that some notions of justice and freedom, as well as right and truthfulness, are constitutive for any society, and that a concern for these values may be a fundamental characteristic of "human nature."

[15] Scientists may, of course, continue to believe in righteousness or justice or truth, but these beliefs are not grounded in their "scientific knowledge" of man. They rest instead upon the receding wisdom of an earlier age.

Having gone this far, let me offer one suggestion as to where the difficulty might lie: in the modern understanding of knowledge. Since Bacon, as I have mentioned earlier, technology has increasingly come to be the basic justification for scientific inquiry. The end is power, not knowledge for its own sake. But power is not only the end. It is also an important *validation* of knowledge. One definitely knows that one knows only if one can make. Synthesis is held to be the ultimate proof of understanding.[16] A more radical formulation holds that one knows only what one makes: knowing *equals* making.

Yet therein lies a difficulty. If truth be the power to change or to make the object studied, then of what do we have knowledge? If there are no fixed realities, but only material upon which we may work our wills, will not "science" be merely the "knowledge" of the transient and the manipulatable? We might indeed have knowledge of the laws by which things change and the rules for their manipulation, but no knowledge of the things themselves. Can such a view of "science" yield any knowledge about the nature of man, or indeed, about the nature of anything? Our questions appear to lead back to the most basic of questions: What does it mean to know? What is it that is knowable? [17]

---

[16] This belief, silently shared by many contemporary biologists, has recently been given the following clear expression: "One of the acid tests of understanding an object is the ability to put it together from its component parts. Ultimately, molecular biologists will attempt to subject their understanding of all structure and function to this sort of test by trying to synthesize a cell. It is of some interest to see how close we are to this goal." [P. Handler, Ed., *Biology and the Future of Man* (Oxford Univ. Press, New York, 1970), p. 55.]

[17] When an earlier version of this article was presented publicly, it was criticized by one questioner as being "antiscientific." He suggested that my remarks "were the kind that gave science a bad name." He went on to argue that, far from being the enemy of morality, the pursuit of truth was itself a highly moral activity, perhaps the highest. The relation of science and morals is a long and difficult question with an illustrious history, and it deserves a more extensive discussion than space permits. However, because some reader may share the questioner's response, I offer a brief reply. First, on the matter of reputation, we should recall that the pursuit of truth may be in tension with keeping a good name (witness Oedipus, Socrates, Galileo, Spinoza, Solzhenitsyn). For most of human history, the pursuit of truth (including "science") was not a reputable activity among the many, and was, in fact, highly suspect. Even today, it is doubtful whether more than a few appreciate knowledge as an end in itself. Science has acquired a "good name" in recent times largely because of its technological fruit; it is therefore to be expected that a disenchantment with technology will reflect badly upon science. Second, my own attack has not been directed against science, but against the use of *some* technologies and, even more, against the unexamined belief—indeed, I would say, superstition—that all biomedical technology is an unmixed blessing. I share the questioner's belief that the pursuit of truth is a highly moral activity. In fact, I am inviting him and others to join in a pursuit of the truth about whether all these new technologies are really good for us. This is a question that merits and is susceptible of serious intellectual inquiry. Finally, we must ask whether what we call "science" has a monopoly on the pursuit of truth. What is "truth"? What is knowable, and what does it mean to

We have seen that the practical problems point toward and make urgent certain enduring, fundamental questions. Yet while pursuing these questions, we cannot afford to neglect the practical problems as such. Let us not forget Delgado and the "psychocivilized society." The philosophical inquiry could be rendered moot by our blind, confident efforts to dissect and redesign ourselves. While awaiting a reconstruction of theory, we must act as best we can.

What Is to Be Done?

First, we sorely need to recover some humility in the face of our awesome powers. The arguments I have presented should make apparent the folly of arrogance, of the presumption that we are wise enough to remake ourselves. Because we lack wisdom, caution is our urgent need. Or to put it another way, in the absence of that "ultimate wisdom," we can be wise enough to know that we are not wise enough. When we lack sufficient wisdom to do, wisdom consists in not doing. Caution, restraint, delay, abstention are what this second-best (and, perhaps, only) wisdom dictates with respect to the technology for human engineering.

If we can recognize that biomedical advances carry significant social costs, we may be willing to adopt a less permissive, more critical stance toward new developments. We need to reexamine our prejudice not only that all biomedical innovation is progress, but also that it is inevitable. Precedent certainly favors the view that what can be done will be done, but is this necessarily so? Ought we not to be suspicious when technologists speak of coming developments as automatic, not subject to human control? Is there not something contradictory in the notion that we have the power to control all the untoward consequences of a technology, but lack the power to determine whether it should be developed in the first place?

What will be the likely consequences of the perpetuation of our permissive and fatalistic attitude toward human engineering? How will the large decisions be made? Technocratically and self-servingly, if our experience with previous technologies is any guide. Under conditions of laissez-faire, most technologists will pursue techniques, and most private industries will pursue profits. We are fortunate that, apart from the drug manufacturers, there are at present in the biomedical area few large industries that influence public policy. Once these appear, the voice of "the public interest" will have to shout very loudly to be heard above

---

know? Surely, these are also questions that can be examined. Unless we do so, we shall remain ignorant about what "science" is and about what it discovers. Yet "science"—that is, modern natural science—cannot begin to answer them; they are philosophical questions, the very ones I am trying to raise at this point in the text.

their whisperings in the halls of Congress. These reflections point to the need for institutional controls.

Scientists understandably balk at the notion of the regulation of science and technology. Censorship is ugly and often based upon ignorant fear; bureaucratic regulation is often stupid and inefficient. Yet there is something disingenuous about a scientist who professes concern about the social consequences of science, but who responds to every suggestion of regulation with one or both of the following: "No restrictions on scientific research," and "Technological progress should not be curtailed." Surely, to suggest that *certain* technologies ought to be regulated or forestalled is not to call for the halt of *all* technological progress (and says nothing at all about basic research). Each development should be considered on its own merits. Although the dangers of regulation cannot be dismissed, who for example, would still object to efforts to obtain an effective, complete, global prohibition on the development, testing, and use of biological and nuclear weapons?

The proponents of laissez-faire ignore two fundamental points. They ignore the fact that not to regulate is as much a policy decision as the opposite, and that it merely postpones the time of regulation. Controls will eventually be called for—as they are now being demanded to end environmental pollution. If attempts are not made early to detect and diminish the social costs of biomedical advances by intelligent institutional regulation, the society is likely to react later with more sweeping, immoderate, and throttling controls.

The proponents of laissez-faire also ignore the fact that much of technology is already regulated. The federal government is already deep in research and development (for example, space, electronics, and weapons) and is the principal sponsor of biomedical research. One may well question the wisdom of the direction given, but one would be wrong in arguing that technology cannot survive social control. Clearly, the question is not control versus no control, but rather what kind of control, when, by whom, and for what purpose.

Means for achieving international regulation and control need to be devised. Biomedical technology can be no nation's monopoly. The need for international agreements and supervision can readily be understood if we consider the likely American response to the successful asexual reproduction of 10,000 Mao Tse-tungs.

To repeat, the basic short-term need is caution. Practically, this means that we should shift the burden of proof to the *proponents* of a new biomedical technology. Concepts of "risk" and "cost" need to be broadened to include some of the social and ethical consequences discussed earlier. The probable or possible harmful effects of the widespread use of a new technique should be anticipated and introduced as "costs" to be weighed in deciding about the *first* use. The regulatory institutions should be encouraged to exercise restraint and to formulate the grounds for saying "no." We must all get used to the idea that biomedical technology makes possible many things we should never do.

But caution is not enough. Nor are clever institutional arrangements. Institutions can be little better than the people who make them work. However worthy our intentions, we are deficient in understanding. In the *long* run, our hope can only lie in education: in a public educated about the meanings and limits of science and enlightened in its use of technology; in scientists better educated to understand the relationships between science and technology on the one hand, and ethics and politics on the other; in human beings who are as wise in the latter as they are clever in the former.

Ethical Issues in Biological Engineering *

Martin P. Golding

Positive Eugenics

. . . I shall consider aspects of some possible programs of biological engineering. My discussion is confined, in the main, to their goal-component. Except for a few instances I pass no judgment on their desirability. I am concerned, rather, to bring to light issues that have to be settled in order for such judgments to be made. It goes without saying that I approach the topic with trepidation, as any layman must.

I begin with positive eugenics[1] because I find it simpler for me to handle. This type of biological engineering, according to Julian Huxley who is one of its leading exponents, "has a far larger scope and importance than negative [eugenics]. It is not concerned merely to prevent genetic deterioration, but aims to raise human capacity and performance to a new level." Moreover, according to Huxley, "negative eugenics is of

---

*From 15 *UCLA Law Review*, 463–79 (1968). Reprinted by permission of the Regents of the University of California.

[1] See "Symposium: Reflections on the New Biology," 15 *UCLA Law Review* (February 1968): Batt, p. 529; Gorney, p. 294 and Grad, pp. 486, 491.

minor evolutionary importance and the need for it will gradually be superseded by efficient measures of positive eugenics." [2]

Except for *Rassenhygiene*, I am not aware of any attempt to carry out a program of positive eugenics on a wide scale excluding animal stock-breeding. One of the reasons for this is the lack of clearly defined aims.[3] The clarification of these aims would necessarily have two facets. One involves specification of the traits that are to be enhanced, and the other would be a showing that their enhancement would truly be advantageous for the community for which they are to be enhanced. As far as I can tell, there is paltry attention given to the second. There is a tendency readily to assume that characteristics which we all take to be desirable, and whose absence we deplore, would not only be valuable under all conditions but also would be universally more valuable if they could be improved on. This may be true, but it needs to be supported by argument. Mere reference to the fact that culture can survive only if human beings possess the genetic equipment which is favorable for culture is not sufficient. To know only that culture has a genetic basis is not much more useful than knowing it has a solar basis. Perhaps it is asking for what no one could possibly supply, but it seems to me that what is required is the establishment of connections between genetic constitution and specifically characterized features of culture. However, it is generally accepted that "genes determine the possibility of culture but not its content." [4]

The first of the facets mentioned above has been more widely discussed. It is interesting to take note of the shift from the talk of races or strains, found in earlier eugenic literature, to talk of mental or social characteristics. Thus, Francis Galton, the coiner of the term "eugenics," states that the aim of eugenics is "to give to the more suitable races or strains of blood a better chance of prevailing speedily over the less suitable than they otherwise would have had." [5] Behind this way of speaking were, first, Galton's conviction "that the English propertied and governing classes were a repository of virtually all that is biologically precious in the English nation and possibly in mankind," [6] and, second, an incorrect theory of heredity (blending inheritance). Even such a liberal-minded follower of Galton as the English philosopher F. C. S. Schiller lapses into this way of speaking. Consider, for example, his statement that "the reason why the symptoms of racial decay are not more pro-

---

[2] Huxley, "Eugenics in Evolutionary Perspective," 54 *Eugenics Rev.* 123, 135 (1962).

[3] See C. Auerbach, *The Science of Genetics* 97–99 (1961).

[4] Dobzhansky, "Evolution at Work," 127 *Science* 1091, 1097 (1958).

[5] Quoted in L. Dunn & T. Dobzhansky, *Heredity, Race and Society* 9 (1946).

[6] *Id.* at 8.

nounced is probably that European civilization is still living on its biological capital, on the qualities bred into the Nordic stock by the severest natural selection, while it was still barbarian, only 1500 years ago." [7]

With the rise and development of genetics such talk tends to disappear and is replaced with the notion of the production of the "ideal genotype." A strong elitist tone remains, however, with ideological overtones. This is illustrated in Hermann J. Muller's removing of Marx and Sun Yat Sen from his 1935 list of eminent men and his adding of Einstein and Lincoln.[8] If Muller is now sanguine about the prospects of positive eugenics, it seems that in 1932 he was prepared to jettison the whole affair. In a speech given before the Eugenics Society in New York, he said:

> Only the impending revolution in our economic system will bring us into a position where we can properly judge, from a truly social point of view, what characteristics are most worthy of a man. . . .
>
> Thus [he concluded] it is up to us, if we want eugenics that functions, to work for it in the only way now practicable, by first turning our hand to help throw over the incubus of the old, outworn society.[9]

The ideological overtone is also to be found in a 1962 article by Julian Huxley, who would stress:

> . . . the need for planning the environment in such a way as will promote our eugenic aims. By 1936, it was already clear that the net effect of present-day social policies could not be eugenic, and was in all probability dysgenic. But, as Muller has demonstrated, this was not always so. In that long period of human history during which our evolving and expanding hominid ancestors lived in small and tightly knit groups competing for territorial and technological success, the social organization promoted selection for intelligent exploration of possibilities, devotion and co-operative altruism: the cultural and genetic systems reinforced each other. It was only much later, with the growth of bigger social units of highly organized civilization based on status and class differentials, that the two became antagonistic. . . .[10]

I do not wish to suggest that ideological perspectives are irrelevant to the choice of an ideal genotype; obviously they are not. But this is one reason

---

[7] F. Schiller, *Eugenics and Politics* 92 (1926).

[8] See Muller, "The Guidance of Human Evolution," in *Evolution after Darwin*, ed. S. Tax (1960), note 5, at 230; noted by Dunn, note 11 below, at 75.

[9] Quoted in G. Hardin, note 14, at 230; 15 *UCLA Law Review*.

[10] Huxley, *supra* note 2, at 133.

why there is likely to be much disagreement over the choice. Furthermore, the moral to be drawn from Muller's changing of his list is that—assuming we could produce our ideal genotype of today—we might regret our choice in 25 years. And we still need assurance that the kind of culture we regard as desirable could in fact be maintained by our ideal genotype.[11]

In any case, if I correctly understand the exponents of positive eugenics, it is not an ideal genotype that they wish to produce, but an ideal phenotype. This would be in line with their insistence on planning the proper environment for the development of certain human capacities. Huxley explicitly maintains that eugenics needs a phenotypic approach, and goes so far as to criticize the "geneticism" of Medawar and Penrose in their purely scientific work.[12] While the phenotypic approach makes more sense to me, it is clear that it poses serious difficulties for biological engineering. It seems that there are few normal human characters that are governed by allelomorphs of a single gene (e.g., ability or inability to taste PTC). Most characteristics are brought about through the interplay of many different genes. Matters are complicated by the fact that so-called graded characters (e.g., stature), and certainly mental and social traits, depend on many genes and on *environmental* influences. Therefore, "any simple genetical analysis is ruled out."[13] I have the distinct impression that although many of the more enthusiastic exponents of biological engineering always say that a sharp heredity-environment dichotomy must be rejected, this amounts to lip-service.[14] The production of definite phenotypes by means of genic selection seems impossible. "Few of us would have advocated preferential multiplication of Hitler's genes through germinal selection. Yet who can say that in a different cul-

---

[11] See L. C. Dunn, "Cross Currents in the History of Human Genetics," 54 *Eugenics Rev.* 69 (1962), at 75.

[12] Huxley, *supra* note 2, at 132, 137.

[13] C. Auerbach, *supra* note 3, at 60.

[14] I shall not list examples. The following comment is of interest: "Statements such as the 'Jukes-Kallikaks, "bad heredity" concept may have been too enthusiastically rejected by perfectionists,' and meaningless pronouncements such as 'Heredity controls intelligence more than twice as much as does environment in families that adopt one of a pair of white identical twins' add nothing but noise to our available information.

"These statements, derived from a paper presented by an American Nobel laureate, William Shockley, must be disturbing to any serious scientist, not because they reflect an uncongenial set of social attitudes, but because they revive an outmoded but ever recurring dichotomy between nature and nurture. Any contemporary mode of thought concerning behavior and genetics which continuously fails to appreciate the functional inseparability of gene complex and environment in the development of phenotype is scientifically worthless." Birch, "Bright Rats and Dull Rats," 10 *Colum. U.F.* 30 (1967).

tural context Hitler might not have been one of the truly great leaders of men, or that Einstein might not have been a diabolical villain." [15]

It would be very misleading and unfair to Huxley and Muller, at least, to imply that they propose as a goal the production of an ideal phenotype. Judging from the criticisms frequently made of them, they do give this impression. But they are now quite explicit that there is no single type that they have in mind. What they seek is an increase in the relative number of individuals who possess such human excellences as altruism, a spirit of cooperativeness, fellow-feeling, imagination, a sense of discipline and duty, and intelligence.[16] Whether they intend that these should be produced only in combination, and not singly, is unclear to me; but if I am not mistaken they would support a relative increase in the number of persons who have any of these traits. Moreover, they would support an increase in the strength of any of these traits. The method they propose is artificial insemination by deliberately preferred donors. Muller goes on to add that the sperm of the chosen ones be stored for later use.[17]

This program raises a number of questions. (1) Are these characteristics hereditary? (2) If they are, and if it were technologically feasible to produce them, would it be desirable to do so? (3) What should be the institutional framework of such a program? I shall briefly take up each.

A detailed discussion of the first question would take me way out of my competence, so I shall only raise a few issues that seem to me to call for attention. With respect to all of the traits except intelligence, I know of no experimental studies that are designed to establish whether or not they are inherited. (It would be fascinating to have an experiment for testing the inheritability of vanity, to take something out of the scope of the above list). Of course, one is always in a position to say that there *must* be a genetic basis for them. This would be to make the term "genetic basis" a panchreston that explains everything in general, but nothing in particular. In any case, it is not easy to see how such experiments are to be designed. One of the problems is conceptual. Consider altruism. What does the term refer to: a feeling? a motive? or a set of behavior patterns? Is it not the case that the social meaning of altruism (as well as the other "social virtues") depends on the kinds of context that elicit altruistic feelings, motives, and behavior? The problem here is very much like one that besets those who argued that criminal tendencies are heritable. What constitutes a crime may vary from society to society and

---

[15] Beadle, "Genes, Culture, and Man," 8 *Colum. U.F.* 12, 15–16 (1965).

[16] See Huxley, *supra* note 2, at 133; Muller, *supra* note 8, at 440–45.

[17] "Moreover, those who repeatedly proved their worth would surely be called upon to reappear age after age until the population in general had caught up with them." Muller, *supra* note 8, at 454.

from legal system to legal system. Whatever it is that the altruistic donor might transmit to his progeny, it is hardly necessary that it should be exhibited as anything that would be recognized as altruism (or any of the other social virtues that would be involved).[18] The following remark hits the nail on the head:

> Our distinguished geneticist [Muller] has suggested that fellowship, co-operation, moral courage and integrity, appreciation of nature and art, and aptness of expression and communication are desirable human traits. One must agree. But, since each of these qualities has meanings peculiar to its particular evolutionary stage and social type, he surely cannot mean they are genetically determined.[19]

The heritability of intelligence is a complicated topic. There have been numerous studies on it. Identical and non-identical twins have been researched, and there have been longitudinal family studies on mental retardation. Generations of school children have been I.Q.'d. I am quite prepared to admit that intelligence has a genetic basis: I take my own children as evidence. In a more serious vein, however, what seems to be established is that certain tendencies that fall within a wide range are inherited.[20] Studies of long-lasting eminent families do not permit the strengthening of this conclusion, for the unsuccessful branches are lost to history.[21] On the question of I.Q., the following seem to me to be words of wisdom:

> [T]here are two questions the geneticist may be asked. The first is: if for example individuals with higher I.Q.s breed more than those with lower (or vice versa) will the I.Q. of the population change, and at what rate? The second question is, if we were effectively to encourage such differential reproduction in favor of I.Q., what would be the consequent changes in characteristics other than I.Q.? The first of these is of course difficult enough to answer, witness the problem of interpreting the facts concerning correlations of I.Q. and family size. The second is at present impossible to answer for even if we

---

[18] I am unsure as to what generalizations are permissible from the study of animal ethology. (Lorenz, Tinbergen, etc.) Neither side of the dispute over the heritability of aggression convinces me, anyway. And when these arguments are extended to deal with the question whether "war is in our genes," I am even less convinced. One of the problems, as above, is the social meaning of aggression. If a layman may be allowed to express agreement with an expert, I would also endorse the following statement: "Perhaps the most ubiquitous difficulty in interpreting the data of behavioral genetics is that the genetics is sometimes sound but almost always the behavioral analysis is terribly poor." Birch, *supra* note 14, at 31.

[19] Steward, in 3 *Evolution after Darwin* 241.

[20] Cf. Burt, "The Inheritance of Mental Ability," 13 *Am. Psychologist* 1 (1958), who seems both properly cautious and over-enthusiastic in generalizing from his data.

[21] See, *e.g.*, A. Wagner, *English Ancestry* (1961).

were to suspect negative correlations between other attributes we deem desirable and I.Q., establishment of the facts concerning the degree to which the correlations had genetic causes would be a difficult task indeed.[22]

It is sometimes suggested that mankind as a whole or at least a considerable segment of it may be evolving in the direction of less intelligence.[23] If true, this would be a reason for undertaking a particular kind of program of biological engineering. Although it may readily be conceded that heredity is a strong factor in intelligence (as is shown by studies on twins and foster children), a comparison of results of intelligence tests given to Scottish school children in 1932 and 1947 seems to indicate that this is not true.[24] In conclusion we may say that considerably more research needs to be done on the genetic basis of intelligence before we give the go-ahead to Professors Muller and Huxley. (It is not necessary for me to compound the problem by here taking up the questions of the definition of "intelligence" and the role of environmental influences.)

But suppose the heritability of the various mental and social characters could be established. Would it be desirable to enhance their occurrence if it could be accomplished? I need not repeat my previous points that turn upon the issue of whether this would be desirable *for* the community of the future. Here I wish to bring out other issues. Consider, for example, the sense of discipline and duty to which Huxley refers. Now, I would not go so far as David Hume who maintains that the various social virtues are approved of solely on grounds of their tendency to maximize utility (happiness).[25] Nevertheless, I strongly doubt that anyone would endorse the enhancement of a sense of discipline and duty under what he regards as an evil social system and in the presence of immoral values. Admittedly, we may have a kind of morbid admiration for the Nazi's sense of discipline and duty, but we would have gladly preferred its *dis*-enhancement. A similar line of argument applies to other of the social virtues. It would seem that their promotion would

---

[22] Thoday, "Causes and Functions of Genetic Variety," 54 *Eugenics Rev.* 195 (1963).

[23] See G. Simpson, *This View of Life* 277 (1964). I do not present the considerations that support this suggestion. Simpson implies that they are not conclusive, and the matter is in need of study. I fully agree that we should approach it with an unbiased mind.

[24] See C. Auerbach, *supra* note 3, at 149–52. Perhaps I am only betraying my own ignorance, but if intelligence *is* declining, we may ask when this decline began. It seems to me ludicrous that there should be a significantly higher proportion of stupid individuals in the world today than there was in the time of Caesar.

[25] *An Inquiry Concerning the Principles of Morals* §§ II–III (Hendel ed. 1957).

be undesirable unless we could also determine the conditions of life of the community of the future, including also its values. Secondly, it is doubtful that we would welcome an increase in the relative numbers of intelligent men unless altruists could be increased in the same proportions, otherwise the result may be a disadvantageously large number of clever and crafty mean men. But what guarantee is there that selective eugenic insemination—if that is the method adopted—would work itself out in the desired manner? Finally, I submit that no one knows what would be the effects of an enhancement of the social virtues, although we all imagine that the world would be a happier place. It is quite conceivable, however, that the survival of culture is dependent upon a certain blend of altruism and self-interest for example, and that this would be upset by the program of biological engineering.

Assuming that these matters could be laid to rest, we still have the institutional framework of the social program to consider. This is an important matter, for institutional frameworks are not morally neutral. The construction of such frameworks is, as indicated previously, a complicated task; moreover frameworks must be adjusted to the techniques that are to be employed. Therefore, only a brief general discussion of a few points is possible here. One of these techniques, A.I.D. with preferred donors, has already been mentioned. Others include controlled mating and controlled breeding (by devices other than A.I.D.). It may some day be possible chemically to modify the phenotype by improving the genetic material, as is suggested by discoveries about the structure of D.N.A. Other possibilities that cannot now be foreseen may be in the offing.

The ethical issues relative to the institutional framework turn on: (a) the degree to which the use of these techniques would be dependent on voluntary adoption or coercive measures; and (b) the degree to which their utilization would be subject to democratic control, with safeguards against abuse. Obviously, no ethical assessment of any social program of biological engineering can be made until these points are straightened out.

Two of the leading exponents of the A.I.D. method of positive eugenics, Huxley and Muller, insist that adoption should be completely voluntary. In answering the objection that effective selection needs authoritarian methods, Huxley writes:

> For one thing, dogmatic tyranny in the modern world is becoming increasingly self-defeating: partly because it is dogmatic and therefore essentially unscientific, partly because it is tyrannical and therefore in the long run intolerable. But the chief point is that human improvement never works solely or even mainly by such methods and is

doing so less and less as man commits himself more thoroughly to the process of general self-education.[26]

This, I think, misses the point. The objector could perfectly well agree with everything just said. And he would stress that human improvement would not result from a program of positive eugenics because it needs authoritarian methods: rather than making better men, it would make men worse. It is no reply for Huxley to say that authoritarian methods wouldn't work.

Muller, if I understand him rightly, adds another point in support of voluntary adoption:

> If we are to preserve that self-determination which is an essential feature of human intelligence, success and happiness, our individual actions in the realm of genetics must be steps based upon our own personal judgments and inclinations. Although these decisions are all conditioned by the mores about us, these mores can be specifically shaped and channelized by our own distinctive personalities.[27]

This I interpret to imply that authoritarian methods would counteract the goal of the program, namely, the maximization of intelligence and the social virtues. If true, this is tantamount to the admission of the *environmental* factor in these characters, and raises again the question as to the degree to which they are genetically transmitted, if at all.

In the last analysis, the question of whether positive eugenics can be effective without authoritarian methods remains open. It is a straightforward question of fact, once the standard of effectiveness is specified. My personal opinion—for what it is worth—is that authoritarian methods would be required. Plato and the Spartans, who respectively supported controlled mating and breeding, were more realistic than their modern counterparts. (Plato supposed that married couples could be made to believe that their unions were based on voluntary choice.) I am not convinced by the instancing of the spread of voluntary birth control. But if authoritarian methods are required it is doubtful that the game is worth the candle. The argument that since assortive mating occurs anyway there can be nothing wrong with the complete coercive control of mating is hardly deserving of a reply.

In the absence of a detailed proposal for an institutional framework it is difficult to discuss the question of democratic control and safeguards against abuse. Suffice it to say that the benevolence of Professors Huxley

---

[26] Huxley, *supra* note 2, at 138.
[27] Muller, *supra* note 8, at 460.

and Muller is no guarantee against abuse by a state subject to changing ideals and tastes.[28]

In closing this section it is appropriate to call attention to the profound social consequences that programs of positive eugenics (by a currently contemplated technique) would have. It would be bound, for example, to alter the institution of the family. Now this institution is already undergoing change, but it is hardly clear what these changes are or whether they are changes for the better. Plainly, selection by "delegated parenthood runs counter to a deep-rooted sense of proprietary parenthood." [29] The adoption of this method is certain to have a profound impact on the conditions of life in the community of the future. I do not share Huxley's confidence that these changes are bound to be beneficent.[30]

I should add that my strong doubts about the desirability of a social program of positive eugenics do not necessarily bear upon the use of A.I.D. in individual cases. My general outlook is that we should maintain strict principles (against its use), but be flexible in practice. However, this is another matter.

Negative Eugenics [31]

Negative eugenics is a subject that the layman approaches with even greater trepidation. In addition to lacking a proper grounding in the technicalities of genetics, he faces the problem of "what to do when doctors disagree." For we do not find complete unanimity among experts on the necessity for certain types of social programs of negative eugenics or their effectiveness. The following discussion is guided by what seem to me the most persuasive arguments. I refer the reader to my remarks in the opening section on the advantage of the layman's speaking out. Most of the topics I shall discuss in this section are not in themselves ethical issues, but nevertheless bear upon the question of whether we ought to engage in programs of biological engineering that aim at the reduction of genetically caused defects. A number of the points that I have tried to make in the preceding sections are relevant here. But I shall not review them. They should be fairly obvious to the reader who has made it this far.

It is well known that various defects (both psychic and physical) are heritable. Indeed, for certain defects, the probability that a child born

---

[28] See Dunn, *supra* note 11, at 75.

[29] Huxley, *supra* note 2, at 139.

[30] Cf. Matthews, "Eugenics and the Family," 53 *Eugenics Rev.* 193 (1962). Matthews is a moderate proponent of eugenics.

[31] See note 1: Gorney, p. 293; Grad, p. 487.

of a "defective" parent will also have such a defect can be calculated. The genetics of abnormality, in fact, is better known than the genetics of normality. The agents of transmission of these heritable defects are the genes. Some harmful genes are, of course, eliminated in each generation before their carriers have a chance to reproduce. War, famine, disease, etc., make a contribution in this regard, although they also eliminate "good" genes. In addition, a deleterious gene may be eliminated by virtue of its killing off its carrier. New defective genes, however, enter the gene pool by a process of mutation. Some of these are transmitted to future generations. The maintenance of biological efficiency for a species is dependent upon the operation of selective survival, the winnowing out of a large number of carriers of harmful genes before they have a chance to reproduce. The natural processes of selection are no longer operating with the degree that is required for the human species to maintain its efficiency in the long run (Huxley's 5,000 to 10,000 years). Medical technology, by prolonging the lives of defect carriers, enables the transmission of harmful genes; it has a "dysgenic" effect. The "load of mutations" thus increases in every generation. Some type of artificial selection for survival is needed, lest man commit biological suicide.[32]

The above paragraph is a condensed statement of the justification for a social program of biological engineering aimed at reducing the "unfit." I do not find it convincing, nor do many experts in the field. First, it is not clear that medicine *is* dysgenic in its effects. Secondly, it is not clear that any program of negative eugenics would be much help in dealing with the problem in any way that would be significant for the species. And thirdly, it is not clear that any such a program wouldn't do more harm than good. I shall present a condensed statement of the counter-considerations.

Whether medicine has dysgenic effects is a normative question, though not necessarily an ethical one. It is true that medicine protects certain genes from natural selection. But the harmfulness of a gene (or of any trait) is partially dependent, at the very least, on its environment.[33] We do not have the genetic capacity to synthesize certain vitamins. This cannot be thought of as a defect so long as we can get an adequate supply of vitamins in our food or in chemical compounds. Some genes which are "bad" in one environment are "good" in another (as is the case with certain genes that determine susceptibility to malaria and sickle-cell anemia). Moreover, and especially, if the harmful effects of a gene can be overcome by medical technology it is not clear that the situation can be

---

[32] See Gorney, *supra*, note 1, p. 306.
[33] See Thoday, *supra* note 22, at 198.

described as dysgenic. "If, for instance, diabetes mellitus (known to involve a strong genetic predisposition) can be fully controlled by simple and universally available medication, then the predisposing genes do no harm and their spread in a population would do no harm." [34] We can expect further advances in medicine that not only will protect deleterious genes from natural selection, but also provide an environmental adjustment to the genetic system. Medical science might not be able to handle completely the effects of the harmful gene, but then neither would negative eugenics.

For many hereditary defects there are no known treatments. The negative eugenist proposes that these be reduced by eliminating as far as possible the harmful genes. The methods suggested are, usually, sterilization or controlled mating. No one seems prepared to opt for Spartanism, for reasons discussed by Golding in *UCLA Law Review* 15, Section IV. Of the other two, sterilization would be the more efficient, and I shall confine myself to its prospects.

Even if a thoroughgoing program of sterilization of carriers of defective genes were adopted (and one of the difficulties here is that all of us probably carry a few harmful genes), its success would depend upon the type of gene involved. Dominant genes with complete penetration show up in every carrier, so that even if new ones arose by mutation, a program of sterilization would readily eliminate them. Huntington's chorea (a highly debilitating nervous disease) is due to such a gene. However, it usually appears too late for action to take place before reproduction. In any case such genes are rare. Moreover, for many of the most harmful dominant genes sterilization is not necessary, as they are self-eliminating. They kill or sterilize their carriers. Most new occurrences of such genes are due to mutation rather than inheritance, so that the complete elimination of such genes is impossible.

In the case of deleterious recessive genes, the prospects of sterilization are decidedly poor. The rarer the gene the more slowly does the elimination take place. It has been calculated that it would take sterilization about two hundred generations to reduce the proportion of albinos in the population to half the present frequency.[35] Most recessive harmful genes are rare, and they are carried more often in heterozygotes than in homozygotes. The elimination of these genes by sterilizing the visibly affected rare homozygotes would have a low rate of success.[36] Here we are supposing that sterilization would be employed against all persons visibly

[34] G. Simpson, *supra* note 23, at 279. See also C. Auerbach, *supra* note 3, at 95.
[35] L. Dunn & T. Dobzhansky, *supra* note 5, at 87–92.
[36] See C. Auerbach, *supra* note 3, at 86–91.

affected by a harmful gene. The success rate would be even lower if many such persons escape sterilization. I need not go into the ethical issues that a program of coercive sterilization occasions.[37]

Nothing that I have said above negates the desirability of a program of genetic counselling. Such a program is designed to aid the individual family in reducing the risks of personal tragedy. Nor does anything I have said necessarily rule out sterilization when these risks are high and the defect serious (*e.g.*, in the case of amaurotic idiocy). Undoubtedly, as genetics learns how to identify harmful genes in phenotypically normal persons, genetic counselling and education should be expanded. We do desire a full and satisfactory life for our children, and ought to avail ourselves of all the resources of biological science to realize it. But, as I have argued, this is quite different from programs that aim at promoting a desirable life for the community of the remote future. "It is, perhaps, not too selfish to say that posterity should be allowed to tackle its own problems and to hope that it may have better means for doing so than we have." [38]

Finally, it is not clear that a social program of negative eugenics wouldn't do more harm than good. This, of course, might depend upon the kind of defects that it would aim to eliminate. Nevertheless it is plain that "good" genes would be reduced in the process. A conflict could arise between the aims of positive and negative eugenics. Sweden has had a ban on the marriage of endogenous epileptics since 1757. This has been attacked by a Swedish geneticist not only on the grounds that the chances for an epileptic to have epileptic children are not very high, but also on the grounds "that many epileptics are highly intelligent and socially valuable members of their community, well fitted to bring up children, and that they may carry valuable genes whose transmission will be prevented by the existing law." [39]

I do not suppose that anyone will go so far as to maintain that society should insure itself a supply of defectives so as to provide occasions for altruism and self-sacrifice, which are classified among the highest virtues. Nevertheless, eugenics is certain to find itself in a dilemma in the cases of "a blind poet, a deaf musician, a consumptive novelist, and a hunchback physicist [who] have contributed so much to our intellectual

---

[37] Huxley, if I understand him correctly, supports a program of *voluntary* sterilization. See Huxley, *supra* note 2, at 135. I think it utopian to suppose that such a program would be very effective.

[38] L. Dunn & T. Dobzhansky, *supra* note 5, at 93–94.

[39] C. Auerbach, *supra* note 3, at 94; see Gorney, p. 308 and Grad, p. 492, *supra*, note 1.

heritage as to be classified as geniuses." [40] Secondly, and here I repeat myself, we do not know what the conditions of life in the remote future will be. It is difficult to imagine that certain severe defects will ever have a good side to them, yet we may be doing a great favor for the future if we preserve genetic diversity even on pain of allowing various defectives to transmit their genes to the future. There is something to be said for "genetic waste." [41]

The Control of Biological Control [42]

In this section I wish to stress the need for mutual confidence between layman and biological scientist. A breakdown in confidence can only be detrimental to both parties. To secure this trust the layman, on his part, must keep himself informed as far as possible on scientific advance thereby to acquire an intelligent appreciation of the requirements of the developing discipline; and the scientist, on his part, must act with a sense of responsibility towards the community. Our technological civilization is dependent upon science, and this is a fact which the layman knows. He can never hope to master the specialized sciences; he can get a "feel" for them, at best. Inevitably, the layman, if he wishes to preserve this civilization, must have some measure of faith in the moral integrity of the scientist. And this faith will be impaired whenever the scientist fails to act responsibly in the layman's judgment. Plainly, this judgment ought to be grounded upon the intelligent appreciation of the science, and not on ignorance or caprice. The scientist on his side must both act and appear to act in a manner that justifies the layman's faith. He must therefore not only show a concern for the advancement of his discipline, but also for its bearing upon the communal good. Among other things this means that the scientist must allow for the possibility that the communal good might at times over-ride scientific advance. In order to act responsibly towards the community, the scientist must be conscientious. That is to say, he must attempt to judge his prospective conduct from an impartial perspective, and not merely as a scientist interested in advancing his discipline. He must pass moral judgments upon himself, and be willing to let such judgments influence his conduct as a scientist. In this way the layman's trust in the scientist can be maintained.

It is in the field of biological engineering that we are likely to have a crisis of confidence. Control over the direction of mutation, which is

---

[40] Steward, "Evolutionary Principles and Social Types," in 2 *Evolution after Darwin* 169.

[41] See G. Hardin, *Nature and Man's Fate* (1961), Ch. 13. See also Thoday, *supra* note 22, at 199.

[42] See generally Burger, p. 436, 15 *UCLA Law Review*.

possible now in a limited area, is bound to be extended. If it has not already been done, babies will be grown in test-tubes. The imagination is staggered by the possibilities—for evil as well as good. Both positive and negative eugenics, which are the products of benevolent if often misguided men (in my opinion), will be overtaken by *atypogenics*, the creation of the abnormal, the weird, and the bizarre. It is generally true that any new technique which is discovered is put to use. The strange world of the science fiction writer will become a reality.

There is much concern today over moral problems raised by experimental medicine.[43] These problems are occasioned by a shift in the traditional orientation of medicine, which is therapeutic and patient-centered. Rather than aiming at doing good for the patient, curing not merely the disease but the whole man, there is a trend towards viewing the patient as a subject or specimen for study and research. These problems, however, are likely to pale in the light of atypogenics, which *ab novo* will be able to create its subjects for research.

At this point a crisis in confidence could become real. There is a certain casuistry of the mind whereby men convince themselves that everything is permitted. This is a special danger when one has in view an apparently good end, such as the expansion of human knowledge. But even knowledge doesn't justify any and every act. If we should ever come to believe this we shall be in the death-throes of the struggle between man's creations and himself. This is the moral of the story of Dr. Frankenstein, a piece of fiction that will soon become fact.

Perhaps I am exaggerating. Nevertheless it does seem to me that some recent statements by a leading geneticist are hardly calculated to inspire the layman's confidence in the biological engineer. Professor Joshua Lederberg can "see nothing fundamentally different between vaccinating with a live virus and introducing new genetic information into an individual." Now presumably this need not frighten us so long as we understand that this might be old-fashioned negative eugenics using new techniques. But Professor Lederberg is also reported as saying that "an overzealous policing to keep people from doing seemingly bizarre genetic experiments would be as dangerous as forcing their use on society." [44] These remarks sound like a threat, a threat which is not likely to be well-taken by the layman. It is important, to say the least, that Professor Leder-

---

[43] See Beecher, "Ethics and Clinical Research," 274 *N. Eng. J. Med.* 1354 (1966); Freund, "Ethical Problems in Human Experimentation," 273 *N. Eng. J. Med.* 687 (1965); Stumpf, "Some Moral Dimensions of Medicine, 64 *Annals Internal Med.* 460 (1966); "Informed Consent in Drug Research," *Columbia Journal of Law and Social Problems*, Oct. 24, 1966, at 4–8.

[44] Report of a symposium on genetics and development held at Columbia University. *N.Y. Times*, Oct. 22, 1967, at 67, col. 1.

berg should clarify his position. Furthermore, it is important that geneticists at large should make their views explicit.

With all due respect for Professor Lederberg, I suggest that we are heading towards the day when policing of atypogenics will become necessary. Naturally, we should wish to avoid "overzealous" policing, and it can be avoided only if the geneticist maintains the confidence of the lay public. This he can do by showing his conscientiousness.

I would propose that control of atypogenics, and of genetic experimentation in general, be initially exercised by the discipline itself. Geneticists at large must become the conscience that passes judgment on the conduct of the individual researcher. This requires full *publicity* regarding prospective experiments and their results. Discussion should then take place over whether or how the work should proceed, a judgment on its permissibility should be rendered. *Primum non nocere*—first, do no harm—may serve as a guiding principle. Individuals who violate either the requirement of publicity or the sense of the discipline on permissibility, should be censured, and perhaps be subject to some kind of penalty. I do not know how to construct the institutional framework for the control of biological control, but I think we are approaching the day when its construction will become necessary. It is possible that the discipline of genetics will be unable to police itself and that legal sanctions will be necessary to deter what the public (in its ignorance, perhaps) regards as abuses. This, of course, is not a happy prospect. The legal control of biological engineering is itself liable to abuse in ways that are easily imagined, especially after our imagination has been stretched by the thought of atypogenics.

Concluding Remarks

As control is extended over the direction of mutation, the subjects of positive and negative eugenics will need re-thinking. In this paper, I have argued, on the whole, against lending our assent to programs of these types. It may turn out, however, that we shall not have to make a choice between positive or negative eugenics, on the one hand, and the amelioration of failings and ills by more standard methods, on the other. The choice may be between eugenics and atypogenics. In any case, it would be sad if we had no choice in the matter at all. Many experts in the field assure us that atypogenics lies far in the future. Let us hope so. Meanwhile, we would do well to bear in mind the words of Benjamin Jowett, one of the Victorian commentators on Plato: "We know how human nature may be degraded; we do not know how by artificial means any improvement in the breed can be effected." [45]

[45] I *Works of Plato* 246 (B. Jowett transl. 1937).

The Principle of Euthanasia *

Antony Flew

I

My particular concern here is to deploy a general moral case for the establishment of a legal right to voluntary euthanasia. The first point to emphasize is that the argument is about *voluntary* euthanasia. Neither I nor any other contributor to the present volume advocates the euthanasia of either the incurably sick or the miserably senile except in so far as this is the strong, constant, and unequivocally expressed wish of the afflicted candidates themselves. Anyone, therefore, who dismisses what is in fact being contended on the gratuitously irrelevant grounds that he could not tolerate compulsory euthanasia, may very reasonably be construed as thereby tacitly admitting inability to meet and to overcome the case actually presented.

Second, my argument is an argument for the establishment of a legal right. What I am urging is that any patient whose condition is hopeless and painful, who secures that it is duly and professionally certified as such, and who himself clearly and continuously desires to die should be enabled to do so: and that he should be enabled to do so without his incurring, or his family incurring, or those who provide or administer the means of death incurring, any legal penalty or stigma whatsoever. To advocate the establishment of such a legal right is not thereby to be committed even to saying that it would always be morally justifiable, much less that it would always be morally obligatory, for any patient to exercise this right if he found himself in a position so to do. For a legal right is not as such necessarily and always a moral right; and hence, *a fortiori*, it is not necessarily and always a moral duty to exercise whatever legal rights you may happen to possess.

This is a vital point. It was—to refer first to an issue now at last happily resolved—crucial to the question of the relegalization in Great Britain of homosexual relations between consenting male adults. Only when it was at last widely grasped, and grasped in its relation to this

---

* "The Principle of Euthanasia" by Antony Flew from *Euthanasia and the Right to Death*, ed. A. B. Downing, published by Peter Owen, London, and Humanities Press, New York. Reprinted by permission.

particular question, could we find the large majorities in both Houses of Parliament by which a liberalizing bill was passed into law. For presumably most members of those majorities not only found the idea of homosexual relations repugnant—as most of us do—but also believed such relations to be morally wrong—as I for one do not. Yet they brought themselves to recognize that neither the repugnance generally felt towards some practice, nor even its actual wrongness if it actually is wrong, by itself constitutes sufficient reason for making or keeping that practice illegal. By the same token it can in the present instance be entirely consistent to urge, both that there ought to be a legal right to voluntary euthanasia, and that it would sometimes or always be morally wrong to exercise that legal right.

Third, the case presented here is offered as a moral one. In developing and defending such a case I shall, of course, have to consider certain peculiarly religious claims. Such claims, however, become relevant here only in so far as they either constitute, or may be thought to constitute, or in so far as they warrant, or may be thought to warrant, conclusions incompatible with those which it is my primary and positive purpose to urge.

Fourth, and finally, this essay is concerned primarily with general principles, not with particular practicalities. I shall not here discuss or —except perhaps quite incidentally—touch upon any questions of comparative detail: questions, for instance, of how a Euthanasia Act ought to be drafted; [1] of what safeguards would need to be incorporated to prevent abuse of the new legal possibilities by those with disreputable reasons for wanting someone else dead; of exactly what and how much should be taken as constituting an unequivocal expression of a clear and constant wish; of the circumstances, if any, in which we ought to take earlier calculated expressions of a patient's desires as constituting still adequate grounds for action when at some later time the patient has become himself unable any longer to provide sufficiently sober, balanced, constant and unequivocal expressions of his wishes; and so on.

I propose here as a matter of policy largely to ignore such particular and practical questions. This is not because I foolishly regard them as unimportant, or irresponsibly dismiss them as dull. Obviously they could become of the most urgent interest. Nor yet is it because I believe that my philosophical cloth disqualifies me from contributing helpfully to any down-to-earth discussions. On the contrary, I happen to be one of those numerous academics who are convinced, some of them correctly, that they are practical and businesslike men! The decisive reason for neglecting these vital questions of detail here in, and in favour of, a

---

[1] See Appendix in *Euthanasia and the Right to Death*, edited by A. B. Downing.

THE PRINCIPLE OF EUTHANASIA

consideration of the general principle of the legalization of voluntary euthanasia is that they are all secondary to that primary issue. For no such subordinate question can properly arise as relevantly practical until and unless the general principle is conceded. Some of these practical considerations are in any event dealt with by other contributors to this volume.

II

So what can be said in favour of the principle? There are two main, and to my mind decisive, moral reasons. But before deploying these it is worth pausing for a moment to indicate why the onus of proof does not properly rest upon us. It may seem as if it does, because we are proposing a change in the present order of things; and it is up to the man who wants a change to produce the reasons for making whatever change he is proposing. This most rational principle of conservatism is in general sound. But here it comes into conflict with the overriding and fundamental liberal principle. It is up to any person and any institution wanting to prevent anyone from doing anything he wishes to do, or to compel anyone to do anything he does not wish to do, to provide positive good reason to justify interference. The question should therefore be: *not* 'Why should people be given this new legal right?'; *but* 'Why should people in this matter be restrained by law from doing what they want?'

Yet even if this liberal perspective is accepted, as it too often is not, and even if we are able to dispose of any reasons offered in defence of the present legal prohibitions, still the question would arise, whether the present state of the law represents a merely tiresome departure from sound liberal principles of legislation, or whether it constitutes a really substantial evil. It is here that we have to offer our two main positive arguments.

1. First, there are, and for the foreseeable future will be, people afflicted with incurable and painful diseases who urgently and fixedly want to die quickly. The first argument is that a law which tries to prevent such sufferers from achieving this quick death, and usually thereby forces other people who care for them to watch their pointless pain helplessly, is a very cruel law. It is because of this legal cruelty that advocates of euthanasia sometimes speak of euthanasia as 'mercy-killing'. In such cases the sufferer may be reduced to an obscene parody of a human being, a lump of suffering flesh eased only by intervals of drugged stupor. This, as things now stand, must persist until at last every device of medical skill fails to prolong the horror.

2. Second, a law which insists that there must be no end to this process—terminated only by the overdue relief of 'death by natural causes'

—is a very degrading law. In the present context the full force of this second reason may not be appreciated immediately, if at all. We are so used to meeting appeals to 'the absolute value of human personality', offered as the would-be knock-down objection to any proposal to legalize voluntary euthanasia, that it has become hard to realize that, in so far as we can attach some tolerably precise meaning to the key phrase, this consideration would seem to bear in the direction precisely opposite to that in which it is usually mistaken to point. For the agonies of prolonged terminal illness can be so terrible and so demoralizing that the person is blotted out in ungovernable nerve reactions. In such cases as this, to meet the patient's longing for death is a means of showing for human personality that respect which cannot tolerate any ghastly travesty of it. So our second main positive argument, attacking the present state of the law as degrading, derives from a respect for the wishes of the individual person, a concern for human dignity, an unwillingness to let the animal pain disintegrate the man.

Our first main positive argument opposes the present state of the law, and of the public opinion which tolerates it, as cruel. Often and appositely this argument is supported by contrasting the tenderness which rightly insists that on occasion dogs and horses must be put out of their misery, with the stubborn refusal in any circumstances to permit one person to assist another in cutting short his suffering. The cry is raised, 'But people are not animals!' Indeed they are not. Yet this is precisely not a ground for treating people worse than brute animals. Animals are like people, in that they too can suffer. It is for this reason that both can have a claim on our pity and our mercy.[2]

But people are also more than brute animals. They can talk and think and wish and plan. It is this that makes it possible to insist, as we do, that there must be no euthanasia unless it is the firm considered wish of the person concerned. People also can, and should, have dignity as human beings. That is precisely why we are urging that they should be helped and not hindered when they wish to avoid or cut short the often degrading miseries of incurable disease or, I would myself add, of advanced senile decay.

III

In the first section I explained the scope and limitations of the present chapter. In the second I offered—although only after suggesting that the onus of proof in this case does not really rest on the proposition

---

[2] Thus Jeremy Bentham, urging that the legislator must not neglect animal sufferings, insists that the 'question is not "Can they *reason?*" nor "Can they *talk?*" but "Can they *suffer?*"' (*Principles of Morals and Legislation*, Chap. XVII, *n.*)

—my two main positive reasons in favour of euthanasia. It is time now to begin to face, and to try to dispose of, objections. This is the most important phase in the whole exercise. For to anyone with any width of experience and any capacity for compassion the positive reasons must be both perfectly obvious and strongly felt. The crucial issue is whether or not there are decisive, overriding objections to these most pressing reasons of the heart.

1. Many of the objections commonly advanced, which are often mistaken to be fundamental, are really objections only to a possible specific manner of implementing the principle of voluntary euthanasia. Thus it is suggested that if the law permitted doctors on occasion to provide their patients with means of death, or where necessary to do the actual killing, and they did so, then the doctors who did either of these things would be violating the Hippocratic Oath, and the prestige of and public confidence in the medical profession would be undermined.

As to the Hippocratic Oath, this makes two demands which in the special circumstances we have in mind may become mutually contradictory. They then cannot both be met at the same time. The relevant section reads: 'I will use treatments to help the sick according to my ability and judgment, but never with a view to injury and wrong-doing. I will not give anyone a lethal dose if asked to do so, nor will I suggest such a course.' [3] The fundamental undertaking 'to help the sick according to my ability and judgment' may flatly conflict with the further promise not to 'give anyone a lethal dose if asked to do so'. To observe the basic undertaking a doctor may have to break the further promise. The moral would, therefore, appear to be: not that the Hippocratic Oath categorically and unambiguously demands that doctors must have no dealings with voluntary euthanasia; but rather that the possible incompatibility in such cases of the different directives generated by two of its logically independent clauses constitutes a reason for revising that Oath.

As to the supposed threat to the prestige of and to our confidence in the medical profession, I am myself inclined to think that the fears expressed are—in more than one dimension—disproportionate to the realities. But whatever the truth about this the whole objection would bear only against proposals which permitted or required doctors to do, or directly to assist in, the actual killing. This is not something which is essential to the whole idea of voluntary euthanasia, and the British Euthanasia Society's present draft bill is so formulated as altogether to avoid this objection. It is precisely such inessential objections as this which I

---

[3] The Greek text is most easily found in *Hippocrates and the Fragments of Heracleitus,* ed. W. H. S. Jones and E. T. Withington for the Loeb series (Harvard Univ. Pr. and Heinemann), Vol. I, p. 298. The translation in the present essay is mine.

have undertaken to eschew in this essay, in order to consider simply the general principle.

2. The first two objections which do really bear on this form a pair. One consists in the contention that there is no need to be concerned about the issue, since in fact there are not any, or not many, patients who when it comes to the point want to die quickly. The other bases the same complacent conclusion on the claim that in fact, in the appropriate cases, doctors already mercifully take the law into their own hands. These two comfortable doctrines are, like many other similarly reassuring bromides, both entirely wrong and rather shabby.

a. To the first the full reply would probably have to be made by a doctor, for a medical layman can scarcely be in a position to make an estimate of the number of patients who would apply and could qualify for euthanasia.[4] But it is quite sufficient for our immediate purposes to say two things. First, there can be few who have reached middle life, and who have not chosen to shield their sensibilities with some impenetrable carapace of dogma, who cannot recall at least one case of an eager candidate for euthanasia from their own experience—even from their own peacetime experience only. If this statement is correct, as my own inquiries suggest that it is, then the total number of such eager candidates must be substantial. Second, though the need for enabling legalization becomes progressively more urgent the greater the numbers of people personally concerned, I wish for myself to insist that it still matters very much indeed if but one person who would have decided for a quick death is forced to undergo a protracted one.

b. To the second objection, which admits that there are many cases where euthanasia is indicated, but is content to leave it to the doctors to defy the law, the answer is equally simple. First, it is manifestly not true that all doctors are willing on the appropriate occasions either to provide the means of death or to do the killing. Many, as they are Roman Catholics, are on religious grounds absolutely opposed to doing so. Many others are similarly opposed for other reasons, or by force of training and habit. And there is no reason to believe that among the rest the proportion of potential martyrs is greater than it is in any other secular occupational group. Second, it is entirely wrong to expect the members of one profession as a regular matter of course to jeopardize their whole careers by breaking the criminal law in order to save the rest of us the labour and embarrassment of changing that law.

Here I repeat two points made to me more than once by doctor friends. First, if a doctor were convinced he ought to provide euthanasia

---

[4] See Downing, pp. 20–1; also pp. 23–4 for his reference to Professor Hinton's work, *Dying* (Pelican, 1967).

in spite of the law, it would often be far harder for him to do so un-detected than many laymen think, especially in our hospitals. Second, the present attitude of the medical establishment is such that if a doctor did take the chance, was caught and brought to trial, and even if the jury, as they well might, refused to convict, still he must expect to face complete professional disaster.

3. The next two objections, which in effect bear on the principle, again form a pair. The first pair had in common the claim that the facts were such that the question of legislative action need not arise. The second pair are alike in that whereas both might appear to be making contentions of fact, in reality we may have in each a piece of exhortation or of metaphysics masquerading as an empirical proposition.

a. Of this second relevant pair the first suggests that there is no such thing as an incurable disease. This implausible thesis becomes more intelligible, though no more true, when we recall how medical ideologues sometimes make proclamations: 'Modern medicine cannot recognize any such thing as a disease which is incurable'; and the like. Such pronouncements may sound like reports on the present state of the art. It is from this resemblance that they derive their peculiar idiomatic point. But the advance of medicine has not reached a stage where all diseases are cur-able. And no one seriously thinks that it has. At most this continuing advance has suggested that we need never despair of finding cures *some day*. But this is not at all the same thing as saying, what is simply not true, that *even now* there is no condition which is at any stage incurable. This medical ideologue's slogan has to be construed as a piece of ex-hortation disguised for greater effect as a paradoxical statement of pur-ported fact. It may as such be instructively compared with certain favourite educationalists' paradoxes: 'We do not teach subjects, we teach children!'; or 'There are no bad children, only bad teachers!'

b. The second objection of this pair is that no one can ever be cer-tain that the condition of any particular patient is indeed hopeless. This is more tricky. For an objection of this form might be given two radically different sorts of content. Yet it would be easy and is common to slide from one interpretation to the other, and back again, entirely unwittingly.

Simply and straightforwardly, such an objection might be made by someone whose point was that judgments of incurability are, as a matter of purely contingent fact, so unreliable that no one has any business to be certain, or to claim to know, that anyone is suffering from an incurable affliction. This contention would relevantly be backed by appealing to the alleged fact that judgments that 'this case is hopeless, *period*' are far more frequently proven to have been mistaken than judgments that, for instance, 'this patient will recover fully, *provided that* he undergoes the appropriate operation'. This naïve objector's point could be made out, or decisively refuted, only by reference to quantitative studies of the actual relative reliabilities and unreliabilities of different sorts of medical judgments. So unless and until such quantitative empirical studies are actually made, and unless and until their results are shown to bear upon the question of euthanasia in the way suggested, there is no grounded and categorical objection here to be met.

But besides this first and straightforwardly empirical interpretation there is a second interpretation of another quite different sort. Suppose someone points to an instance, as they certainly could and well might, where some patient whom all the doctors had pronounced to be beyond hope nevertheless recovers, either as the result of the application of new treatment derived from some swift and unforeseen advance in medical science, or just through nature taking its unexpected course. This happy but chastening outcome would certainly demonstrate that the doctors concerned had on this occasion been mistaken; and hence that, though they had sincerely claimed to know the patient's condition to have been incurable, they had not really known this. The temptation is to mistake it that such errors show that no one ever really knows. It is this perfectly general contention, applied to the particular present case of judgments of incurability, which constitutes the second objection in its second interpretation. The objector seizes upon the point that even the best medical opinion turns out sometimes to have been wrong (as here). He then urges, simply because doctors thus prove occasionally to have been mistaken (as here) and because it is always—theoretically if not practically— possible that they may be mistaken again the next time, that therefore none of them ever really knows (at least in such cases). Hence, he concludes, there is after all no purchase for the idea of voluntary euthanasia. For this notion presupposes that there are patients recognizably suffering from conditions known to be incurable.

The crux to grasp about this contention is that, notwithstanding that it may be presented and pressed as if it were somehow especially relevant to one particular class of judgments, in truth it applies—if it applies at all— absolutely generally. The issue is thus revealed as not medical but metaphysical. If it follows that if someone is ever mistaken then he never really knows, and still more if it follows that if it is even logically possible that he may be mistaken then he never really knows, then, surely, the consequence must be that none of us ever does know—not *really*. (When a metaphysician says that something is never really such and such, what he really means is that it very often is, *really*.) For it is of the very essence of our cognitive predicament that we do all sometimes make mistakes; while always it is at least theoretically possible that we may. Hence the argument, if it holds at all, must show that knowledge, *real* knowledge, is for all us mortal men for ever unattainable.

What makes the second of the present pair of objections tricky to handle is that it is so easy to pass unwittingly from an empirical to a metaphysical interpretation. We may fail to notice, or noticing may fail convincingly to explain, how an empirical thesis has degenerated into metaphysics, or how metaphysical misconceptions have corrupted the medical judgment. Yet, once these utterly different interpretations have been adequately distinguished, two summary comments should be sufficient.

First, in so far as the objection is purely metaphysical, to the idea that *real* knowledge is possible, it applies absolutely generally; or not at all. It is arbitrary and irrational to restrict it to the examination of the principle of voluntary euthanasia. If doctors never really know, we presumably have no business to rely much upon any of their judgments. And if, for the same metaphysical reasons, there is no knowledge to be had anywhere, then we are all of us in the same case about everything. This may be as it may be, but it is nothing in particular to the practical business in hand.

Second, when the objection takes the form of a pretended refusal to take any decision in matters of life and death on the basis of a judgment which theoretically might turn out to have been mistaken, it is equally unrealistic and arbitrary. It is one thing to claim that judgments of incurability are peculiarly fallible: if that suggestion were to be proved to be correct. It is quite another to claim that it is improper to take vital decisions on the basis of sorts of judgment which either are in principle fallible, or even prove occasionally in fact to have been wrong. It is an inescapable feature of the human condition that no one is infallible about anything, and there is no sphere of life in which mistakes do not occur. Nevertheless we cannot as agents avoid, even in matters of life and death and more than life and death, making decisions to act or to abstain. It is only necessary and it is only possible to insist on ordinarily strict standards of warranted assertability, and on ordinarily exacting rather than obsessional criteria of what is beyond reasonable doubt.

Of course this means that mistakes will sometimes be made. This is in practice a corollary of the uncontested fact that infallibility is not an option. To try to ignore our fallibility is unrealistic, while to insist on remembering it only in the context of the question of voluntary euthanasia is arbitrary. Nor is it either realistic or honourable to attempt to offload the inescapable burdens of practical responsibility, by first claiming that we never really *know*, and then pretending that a decision not to act is somehow a decision which relieves us of all proper responsibility for the outcome.

4. The two pairs of relevant objections so far considered have both been attempts in different ways to show that the issue does not, or at any

rate need not, arise as a practical question. The next concedes that the question does arise and is important, but attempts to dispose of it with the argument that what we propose amounts to the legalization, in certain circumstances, of murder, or suicide, or both; and that this cannot be right because murder and suicide are both gravely wrong always. Now even if we were to concede all the rest it would still not follow, because something is gravely wrong in morals, that there ought to be a law against it; and that we are wrong to try to change the law as it now subsists. We have already urged that the onus of proof must always rest on the defenders of any restriction.

a. In fact the rest will not do. In the first place, if the law were to be changed as we want, the present legal definition of 'murder' would at the same time have to be so changed that it no longer covered the provision of euthanasia for a patient who had established that it was his legal right. 'Does this mean,' someone may indignantly protest, 'that right and wrong are created by Acts of Parliament?' Emphatically, yes: and equally emphatically, no. Yes indeed, if what is intended is *legal* right and *legal* offence. What is meant by the qualification 'legal' if it is not that these rights are the rights established and sanctioned by the law? Certainly not, if what is intended is *moral* right and *moral* wrong. Some moral rights happen to be at the same time legal rights, and some moral wrongs similarly also constitute offences against the law. But, notoriously, legislatures may persist in denying moral rights; while, as I insisted earlier, not every moral wrong either is or ought to be forbidden and penalized by law.

Well then, if the legal definition of 'murder' can be changed by Act of Parliament, would euthanasia nevertheless be murder, morally speaking? This amounts to asking whether administering euthanasia legally to someone who is incurably ill, and who has continually wanted it, is in all relevant respects similar to, so to speak, a standard case of murder; and whether therefore it is to be regarded morally as murder. Once the structure of the question is in this way clearly displayed it becomes obvious that the cases are different in at least three important respects. First, whereas the murder victim is (typically) killed against his will, a patient would be given or assisted in obtaining euthanasia only if he steadily and strongly desired to die. Second, whereas the murderer kills his victim, treating him usually as a mere object for disposal, in euthanasia the object of the exercise would be to save someone, at his own request, from needless suffering, to prevent the degradation of a human person. Third, whereas the murderer by his action defies the law, the man performing euthanasia would be acting according to law, helping another man to secure what the law allowed him.

It may sound as if that third clause goes back on the earlier repudiation of the idea that moral right and wrong are created by Act of Parliament. That is not so. For we are not saying that this action would now be justifiable, or at least not murder morally, simply because it was now permitted by the law; but rather that the change in the law would remove one of possible reasons for moral objection. The point is this: that although the fact that something is enjoined, permitted, or forbidden by law does not necessarily make it right, justifiable, or wrong morally, nevertheless the fact that something is enjoined or forbidden by a law laid down by established authority does constitute one moral reason for obedience. So a doctor who is convinced that the objects of the Euthanasia Society are absolutely right should at least hesitate to take the law into his own hands, not only for prudential but also for moral reasons. For to defy the law is, as it were, to cast your vote against constitutional procedures and the rule of law, and these are the foundations and framework of any tolerable civilized society. (Consider here the injunction posted by some enlightened municipal authorities upon their public litter bins: 'Cast your vote here for a tidy New York!'—or wherever it may be.)

Returning to the main point, the three differences which we have just noticed are surely sufficient to require us to refuse to assimilate legalized voluntary euthanasia to the immoral category of murder. But to insist on making a distinction between legalized voluntary euthanasia and murder is not the same thing as, nor does it by itself warrant, a refusal to accept that both are equally immoral. What an appreciation of these three differences, but crucially of the first, should do is to suggest that we ought to think of such euthanasia as a special case not of murder but of suicide. Let us therefore examine the second member of our third pair of relevant objections.

b. This objection was that to legalize voluntary euthanasia would be to legalize, in certain conditions, the act of assisting suicide. The question therefore arises: 'Is suicide always morally wrong?'

The purely secular considerations usually advanced and accepted are not very impressive. First, it is still sometimes urged that suicide is unnatural, in conflict with instinct, a breach of the putative law of self-preservation. All arguments of this sort, which attempt directly to deduce conclusions about what *ought* to be from premises stating, or mis-stating, only what *is* are—surely—unsound: they involve what philosophers label, appropriately, the 'Naturalistic Fallacy'. There is also a peculiar viciousness about appealing to what is supposed to be a descriptive law of nature to provide some justification for the prescription to obey that supposed law. For if the law really obtained as a description of what always and unavoidably happens, then there would be no point in prescribing that it should; whereas if the descriptive law does not in fact hold, then the basis of the supposed justification does not exist.[5] Furthermore, even if an argument of this first sort could show that suicide is always immoral, it could scarcely provide a reason for insisting that it ought also to be illegal.

Second, it is urged that the suicide by his act deprives other people of the services which he might have rendered them had he lived longer. This can be a strong argument, especially where the suicide has a clear, positive family or public obligations. It is also an argument which, even in a liberal perspective, can provide a basis for legislation. But it is irrelevant to the circumstances which advocates of the legalization of voluntary euthanasia have in mind. In such circumstances as these, there is no longer any chance of being any use to anyone, and if there is any family or social obligation it must be all the other way—to end your life when it has become a hopeless burden both to yourself and to others.

Third, it is still sometimes maintained that suicide is in effect murder—'self murder'. To this, offered in a purely secular context, the appropriate and apparently decisive reply would seem to be that by parity of reasoning marriage is really adultery—'own-wife-adultery'. For, surely, the gravamen of both distinctions lies in the differences which such paradoxical assimilations override. It is precisely because suicide is the destruction of oneself (by one's own choice), while murder is the destruction of somebody else (against his wishes), that the former can be, and is, distinguished from the latter.

Yet there is a counter to this own-wife-adultery-move. It begins by insisting, rightly, that sexual relations—which are what is common to both marriage and adultery—are not in themselves wrong: the crucial question is, 'Who with?' It then proceeds to claim that what is common to both murder and suicide is the killing of a human being; and here the questions of 'Which one?' or 'By whom?' are not, morally, similiarly decisive. Finally appeal may be made, if the spokesman is a little old-fashioned, to the Sixth Commandment, or if he is in the contemporary swim, to the Principle of the Absolute Sanctity of Human Life.

The fundamental difficulty which confronts anyone making this counter move is that of finding a formulation for his chosen principle about the wrongness of all killing, which is both sufficiently general not to appear merely question-begging in its application to the cases in dispute, and which yet carries no consequences that the spokesman himself is not prepared to accept. Thus, suppose he tries to read the Sixth Commandment as constituting a veto on any killing of human beings. Let us waive here the immediate scholarly objections: that such a reading in-

---

[5] I have argued this kind of point more fully in *Evolutionary Ethics* (London: Macmillan, 1967). See Chap. IV, 'From *Is* to *Ought*'.

volves accepting the mistranslation 'Thou shalt not kill' rather than the more faithful 'Thou shalt do no murder'; and that neither the children of Israel nor even their religious leaders construed this as a law forbidding all war and all capital punishment.[6] The question remains whether our spokesman himself is really prepared to say that all killing, without any exception, is morally wrong.

It is a question which has to be pressed, and which can only be answered by each man for himself. Since I cannot give your answer, I can only say that I know few if any people who would sincerely say 'Yes'. But as soon as any exceptions or qualifications are admitted, it becomes excessively difficult to find any presentable principle upon which these can be admitted while still excluding suicide and assistance to suicide in a case of euthanasia. This is not just because, generally, once any exceptions or qualifications have been admitted to any rule it becomes hard or impossible not to allow others. It is because, particularly, the case for excluding suicide and assisting suicide from the scope of any embargo on killing people is so strong that only some absolutely universal rule admitting no exceptions of any sort whatever could have the force convincingly to override it.

Much the same applies to the appeal to the Principle of the Absolute Sanctity of Human Life. Such appeals were continually made by conservatives—many of them politically not Conservative but Socialist—in opposition to the recent efforts to liberalize the British abortion laws. Such conservatives should be, and repeatedly were, asked whether they are also opponents of all capital punishment and whether they think that it is always wrong to kill in a 'just war'. (In fact none of those in Parliament could honestly have answered 'Yes' to both questions.) In the case of abortion their position could still be saved by inserting the qualification 'innocent', a qualification traditionally made by cautious moralists who intend to rest on this sort of principle. But any such qualification, however necessary, must make it almost impossible to employ the principle thus duly qualified to proscribe all suicide. It would be extraordinarily awkward and far-fetched to condemn suicide or assisting suicide as 'taking an innocent life'.

Earlier in the present subsection I described the three arguments I have been examining as secular. This was perhaps misleading. For all three are regularly used by religious people: indeed versions of all three are to be found in St Thomas Aquinas's *Summa Theologica*, the third being there explicitly linked with St Augustine's laboured interpretation

---

[6] See, f.i., Joseph Fletcher, *Morals and Medicine* (1954; Gollancz, 1955), pp. 195–6. I recommend this excellent treatment by a liberal Protestant of a range of questions in moral theology too often left too far from liberal Roman Catholics.

of the Sixth Commandment to cover suicide.[7] And perhaps the incongruity of trying to make the amended Principle of the Absolute Sanctity of Innocent Human Life yield a ban on suicide is partly to be understood as a result of attempting to derive from secularized premises conclusions which really depend upon a religious foundation. But the next two arguments are frankly and distinctively religious.

The first insists that human beings are God's property: 'It is our duty to take care of God's property entrusted to our charge—our souls and bodies. They belong not to us but to God'; [8] 'Whoever takes his own life sins against God, even as he who kills another's slave sins against that slave's master'; [9] and 'Suicide is the destruction of the temple of God and a violation of the property rights of Jesus Christ.' [10]

About this I restrict myself to three comments here. First, as it stands, unsupplemented by appeal to some other principle or principles, it must apply, if it applies at all, equally to *all* artificial and intentional shortening *or* lengthening of any human life, one's own *or* that of anyone else. Alone and unsupplemented it would commit one to complete quietism in all matters of life and death; for all interference would be interference with someone else's property. Otherwise one must find further particular moral revelations by which to justify capital punishment, war, medicine, and many other such as first flush impious practices. Second, it seems to presuppose that a correct model of the relation between man and God is that of slave and slavemaster, and that respect for God's property ought to be the fundamental principle of morals. It is perhaps significant that it is to this image that St Thomas and the pagan Plato, in attacking suicide, both appeal. This attempt to derive not only theological but all obligations from the putative theological fact of Creation is a commonplace of at least one tradition of moral theology. In this derivation the implicit moral premise is usually that unconditional obedience to a Creator, often considered as a very special sort of owner, is the primary elemental obligation.[11] Once this is made explicit it does not appear to be self-evidently true; nor is it easy to see how a creature in absolute ontological dependence could be the genuinely responsible subject of

---

[7] Part II: Q. 64, A5. The Augustine reference is to *The City of God*, 1, 20. It is worth comparing, for ancient Judaic attitudes, E. Westermarck's *Origin and Development of the Moral Ideas*, Vol. 1, pp. 246–7.

[8] See the Rev. G. J. MacGillivray, 'Suicide and Euthanasia', p. 10, a widely distributed Catholic Truth Society pamphlet.

[9] Aquinas, *loc. cit.*

[10] Koch-Preuss, *Handbook of Moral Theology*, Vol. II, p. 76. This quotation has been taken from Fletcher, *op. cit.*, p. 192.

[11] Cf., for convenience, MacGillivray, *loc. cit.*; and for a Protestant analogue the Bishop of Exeter quoted by P. Nowell-Smith in *Ethics* (Penguin, 1954), pp. 37–8 n.

obligations to his infinite Creator.[12] Third, this objection calls to mind one of the sounder sayings of the sinister Tiberius: 'If the gods are insulted let them see to it themselves.' This remark is obviously relevant only to the question of legalization, not to that of the morality or the prudence of the action itself.

The second distinctively religious argument springs from the conviction that God does indeed see to it Himself, with a penalty of infinite severity. If you help someone to secure euthanasia, 'You are sending him from the temporary and comparatively light suffering of this world to the eternal suffering of hell.' Now if this appalling suggestion could be shown to be true it would provide the most powerful moral reason against helping euthanasia in any way, and for using any legislative means which might save people from suffering a penalty so inconceivably cruel. It would also be the strongest possible prudential reason against 'suiciding onself'.[13] (Though surely anyone who knowingly incurred such a penalty would by that very action prove himself to be genuinely of unsound mind; and hence not *justly* punishable at all. Not that a Being contemplating such unspeakable horrors could be expected to be concerned with justice!)

About this second, peculiarly religious, argument there is, it would seem, little to be done except: either simply to concede that for anyone holding this belief it indeed is reasonable to oppose euthanasia, and to leave it at that; or, still surely conceding this, to attempt to mount a general offensive against the whole system of which it forms a part.

5. The final objection is one raised, with appropriate modifications, by the opponents of every reform everywhere. It is that even granting that the principle of the reform is excellent it would, if adopted, lead inevitably to something worse; and so we had much better not make any change at all. Thus G. K. Chesterton pronounced that the proponents of euthanasia now seek only the death of those who are a nuisance to themselves, but soon it will be broadened to include those who are a nuisance to others.[14] Such cosy arguments depend on two assumptions: that the

---

[12] I have developed this contention in *God and Philosophy* (Hutchinson, 1966), §§ 2.34 ff.

[13] This rather affected-sounding gallicism is adopted deliberately: if you believe, as I do, that suicide is not always and as such wrong, it is inappropriate to speak of 'committing suicide'; just as correspondingly if you believe, as I do not, that (private) profit is wrong, it becomes apt to talk of those who 'commit a profit'.

[14] I take this quotation, too, from Fletcher, *op. cit.*, p. 201: it originally appeared in *The Digest* (Dec. 23, 1937). Another, much more recent specimen of this sort of obscurantist flim-flam may be found in Lord Longford's speech to the House of Lords against Mr. David Steel's Abortion Bill as originally passed by the Commons. Lord Longford (formerly Pakenham) urged that if that bill were passed, we might see the day when senile members of their lordships' House were put down willy-nilly.

supposedly inevitable consequences are indeed evil and substantially worse than the evils the reform would remove; and that the supposedly inevitable consequences really are inevitable consequences.

In the present case we certainly can grant the first assumption, if the consequence supposed is taken to be large-scale legalized homicide in the Nazi manner. But whatever reason is there for saying that this would, much less inevitably must, follow? For there are the best of reasons for insisting that there is a world of difference between legalized voluntary euthanasia and such legalized mass-murder. Only if public opinion comes to appreciate their force will there be any chance of getting the reform we want. Then we should have no difficulty, in alliance doubtless with all our present opponents, in blocking any move to legalize murder which might conceivably arise from a misunderstanding of the case for voluntary euthanasia. Furthermore, it is to the point to remind such objectors that the Nazi atrocities they probably have in mind were in fact not the result of any such reform, but were the work of people who consciously repudiated the whole approach to ethics represented in the argument of the present essay. For this approach is at once human and humanitarian. It is concerned above all with the reduction of suffering; but concerned at the same time with other values too, such as human dignity and respect for the wishes of the individual person. And always it is insistent that morality should not be 'left in the dominion of vague feeling or inexplicable internal conviction, but should be . . . made a matter of reason and calculation'.[15]

---

[15] J. S. Mill's essay on Bentham quoted in F. R. Leavis, *Mill on Bentham and Coleridge* (Chatto & Windus, 1950), p. 92.

The Allocation of Exotic Medical Lifesaving Therapy *

Nicholas Rescher

I. The Problem

Technological progress has in recent years transformed the limits of the possible in medical therapy. However, the elevated state of sophistication of modern medical technology has brought the economists' classic problem of scarcity in its wake as an unfortunate side product. The enormously sophisticated and complex equipment and the highly trained teams of experts requisite for its utilization are scarce resources in relation to potential demand. The administrators of the great medical institutions that preside over these scarce resources thus come to be faced increasingly with the awesome choice: *Whose life to save?*

A (somewhat hypothetical) paradigm example of this problem may be sketched within the following set of definitive assumptions: We suppose that persons in some particular medically morbid condition are "mortally afflicted": It is virtually certain that they will die within a short time period (say ninety days). We assume that some very complex course of treatment (e.g., a heart transplant) represents a substantial probability of life prolongation for persons in this mortally afflicted condition. We assume that the facilities available in terms of human resources, mechanical instrumentalities, and requisite materials (e.g., hearts in the case of a heart transplant) make it possible to give a certain treatment—this "exotic (medical) lifesaving therapy," or ELT for short— to a certain, relatively small number of people. And finally we assume that a substantially greater pool of people in the mortally afflicted condition is at hand. The problem then may be formulated as follows: How is one to select within the pool of afflicted patients the ones to be given the ELT treatment in question; how to select those "whose lives are to be saved"? Faced with many candidates for an ELT process that can be

* Nicholas Rescher, "The Allocation of Exotic Medical Lifesaving Therapy," *Ethics*, April 1969, pp. 173–87. Reprinted by permission of the author and the University of Chicago Press.

made available to only a few, doctors and medical administrators confront the decision of who is to be given a chance at survival and who is, in effect, to be condemned to die.

As has already been implied, the "heroic" variety of spare-part surgery can pretty well be assimilated to this paradigm. One can foresee the time when heart transplantation, for example, will have become pretty much a routine medical procedure, albeit on a very limited basis, since a cardiac surgeon with the technical competence to transplant hearts can operate at best a rather small number of times each week and the elaborate facilities for such operations will most probably exist on a modest scale. Moreover, in "spare-part" surgery there is always the problem of availability of the "spare parts" themselves. A report in one British newspaper gives the following picture: "Of the 150,000 who die of heart disease each year [in the U.K.], Mr. Donald Longmore, research surgeon at the National Heart Hospital [in London] estimates that 22,000 might be eligible for heart surgery. Another 30,000 would need heart and lung transplants. But there are probably only between 7,000 and 14,000 potential donors a year." [1] Envisaging this situation in which at the very most something like one in four heart-malfunction victims can be saved, we clearly confront a problem in ELT allocation.

A perhaps even more drastic case in point is afforded by long-term haemodialysis, an ongoing process by which a complex device—an "artificial kidney machine"—is used periodically in cases of chronic renal failure to substitute for a non-functional kidney in "cleaning" potential poisons from the blood. Only a few major institutions have chronic haemodialysis units, whose complex operation is an extremely expensive proposition. For the present and the foreseeable future the situation is that "the number of places available for chronic haemodialysis is hopelessly inadequate." [2]

---

[1] Christine Doyle, "Spare-Part Heart Surgeons Worried by Their Success," *Observer*, May 12, 1968.

[2] J. D. N. Nabarro, "Selection of Patients for Haemodialysis," *British Medical Journal* (March 11, 1967), p. 623. Although several thousand patients die in the U.K. each year from renal failure—there are about thirty new cases per million of population—only 10 per cent of these can for the foreseeable future be accommodated with chronic haemodialysis. Kidney transplantation—itself a very tricky procedure—cannot make a more than minor contribution here. As this article goes to press, I learn that patients can be maintained in home dialysis at an operating cost about half that of maintaining them in a hospital dialysis unit (roughly an $8,000 minimum). In the United States, around 7,000 patients with terminal uremia who could benefit from haemodialysis evolve yearly. As of mid-1968, some 1,000 of these can be accommodated in existing hospital units. By June 1967, a world-wide total of some 120 patients were in treatment by home dialysis. (Data from a forthcoming paper, "Home Dialysis," by C. M. Conty and H. V. Murdaugh. See also R. A. Baillod *et al.*, "Overnight Haemodialysis in the Home," *Proceedings of the European Dialysis and Transplant Association*, VI [1965], 99 ff.).

The traditional medical ethos has insulated the physician against facing the very existence of this problem. When swearing the Hippocratic Oath, he commits himself to work for the benefit of the sick in "whatsover house I enter." [3] In taking this stance, the physician substantially renounces the explicit choice of saving certain lives rather than others. Of course, doctors have always in fact had to face such choices on the battlefield or in times of disaster, but there the issue had to be resolved hurriedly, under pressure, and in circumstances in which the very nature of the case effectively precluded calm deliberation by the decision maker as well as criticism by others. In sharp contrast, however, cases of the type we have postulated in the present discussion arise predictably, and represent choices to be made deliberately and "in cold blood."

It is, to begin with, appropriate to remark that this problem is not fundamentally a medical problem. For when there are sufficiently many afflicted candidates for ELT then—so we may assume—there will also be more than enough for whom the purely medical grounds for ELT allocation are decisively strong in any individual case, and just about equally strong throughout the group. But in this circumstance a selection of some afflicted patients over and against others cannot *ex hypothesi* be made on the basis of purely medical considerations.

The selection problem, as we have said, is in substantial measure not a medical one. It is a problem *for* medical men, which must somehow be solved by them, but that does not make it a medical issue—any more than the problem of hospital building is a medical issue. As a problem it belongs to the category of philosophical problems—specifically a problem of moral philosophy or ethics. Structurally, it bears a substantial kinship with those issues in this field that revolve about the notorious whom-to-save-on-the-lifeboat and whom-to-throw-to-the-wolves-pursuing-the-sled questions. But whereas questions of this just-indicated sort are artificial, hypothetical, and far-fetched, the ELT issue poses a *genuine* policy question for the responsible administrators in medical institutions, indeed a question that threatens to become commonplace in the foreseeable future.

Now what the medical administrator needs to have, and what the philosopher is presumably *ex officio* in a position to help in providing, is a body of *rational guidelines* for making choices in these literally life-or-death situations. This is an issue in which many interested parties have a substantial stake, including the responsible decision maker who wants to satisfy his conscience that he is acting in a reasonable way. Moreover, the family and associates of the man who is turned away—to say nothing

---

[3] For the Hippocratic Oath see *Hippocrates: Works* (Loeb ed.; London, 1959), I, p. 298.

of the man himself—have the right to an acceptable explanation. And indeed even the general public wants to know that what is being done is fitting and proper. All of these interested parties are entitled to insist that a reasonable code of operating principles provides a defensible rationale for making the life-and-death choices involved in ELT.

II. The Two Types of Criteria

Two distinguishable types of criteria are bound up in the issue of making ELT choices. We shall call these *Criteria of Inclusion* and *Criteria of Comparison*, respectively. The distinction at issue here requires some explanation. We can think of the selection as being made by a two-stage process: (1) the selection from among all possible candidates (by a suitable screening process) of a group to be taken under serious consideration as candidates for therapy, and then (2) the actual singling out, within this group, of the particular individuals to whom therapy is to be given. Thus the first process narrows down the range of comparative choice by eliminating *en bloc* whole categories of potential candidates. The second process calls for a more refined, case-by-case comparison of those candidates that remain. By means of the first set of criteria one forms a selection group; by means of the second set, an actual selection is made within this group.

Thus what we shall call a "selection system" for the choice of patients to receive therapy of the ELT type will consist of criteria of these two kinds. Such a system will be acceptable only when the reasonableness of its component criteria can be established.

III. Essential Features of an Acceptable ELT Selection System

To qualify as reasonable, an ELT selection must meet two important "regulative" requirements: it must be *simple* enough to be readily intelligible, and it must be *plausible*, that is, patently reasonable in a way that can be apprehended easily and without involving ramified subtleties. Those medical administrators responsible for ELT choices must follow a modus operandi that virtually all the people involved can readily understand to be acceptable (at a reasonable level of generality, at any rate). Appearances are critically important here. It is not enough that the choice be made in a *justifiable* way; it must be possible for people—*plain* people—to "see" (i.e., understand without elaborate teaching or indoctrination) that *it is justified,* insofar as any mode of procedure can be justified in cases of this sort.

One "constitutive" requirement is obviously an essential feature of a reasonable selection system: all of its component criteria—those of inclusion and those of comparison alike—must be reasonable in the sense of being *rationally defensible*. The ramifications of this requirement call for detailed consideration. But one of its aspects should be noted without further ado: it must be *fair*—it must treat relevantly like cases alike, leaving no room for "influence" or favoritism, etc.

IV. The Basic Screening Stage: Criteria of Inclusion (and Exclusion)

Three sorts of considerations are prominent among the plausible criteria of inclusion/exclusion at the basic screening stage: the constituency factor, the progress-of-science factor, and the prospect-of-success factor.

A. The Constituency Factor

It is a "fact of life" that ELT can be available only in the institutional setting of a hospital or medical institute or the like. Such institutions generally have normal clientele boundaries. A veterans' hospital will not concern itself primarily with treating nonveterans, a children's hospital cannot be expected to accommodate the "senior citizen," an army hospital can regard college professors as outside its sphere. Sometimes the boundaries are geographic—a state hospital may admit only residents of a certain state. (There are, of course, indefensible constituency principles—say race or religion, party membership, or ability to pay; and there are cases of borderline legitimacy, e.g., sex.[4]) A medical institution is justified in considering for ELT only persons within its own constituency, provided this constituency is constituted upon a defensible basis. Thus the haemodialysis selection committee in Seattle "agreed to consider only those applications who were residents of the state of Washington. . . . They justified this stand on the grounds that since the basic research . . . had been done at . . . a state-supported institution—the people whose taxes had paid for the research should be its first beneficiaries."[5]

While thus insisting that constituency considerations represent a valid and legitimate factor in ELT selection, I do feel there is much to be said for minimizing their role in life-or-death cases. Indeed a refusal to recognize them at all is a significant part of medical tradition, going back to the very oath of Hippocrates. They represent a departure from

---

[4] Another example of borderline legitimacy is posed by an endowment "with strings attached," e.g., "In accepting this legacy the hospital agrees to admit and provide all needed treatment for any direct descendant of myself, its founder."

[5] Shana Alexander, "They Decide Who Lives, Who Dies," *Life*, LIII (November 9, 1962), 102–25 (see p. 107).

the ideal arising with the institutionalization of medicine, moving it away from its original status as an art practiced by an individual practitioner.

B. The Progress-of-Science Factor

The needs of medical research can provide a second valid principle of inclusion. The research interests of the medical staff in relation to the specific nature of the cases at issue is a significant consideration. It may be important for the progress of medical science—and thus of potential benefit to many persons in the future—to determine how effective the ELT at issue is with diabetics or persons over sixty or with a negative RH factor. Considerations of this sort represent another type of legitimate factor in ELT selection.

A very definitely *borderline* case under this head would revolve around the question of a patient's willingness to pay, not in monetary terms, but in offering himself as an experimental subject, say by contracting to return at designated times for a series of tests substantially unrelated to his own health, but yielding data of importance to medical knowledge in general.

C. The Prospect-of-Success Factor

It may be that while the ELT at issue is not without *some* effectiveness in general, it has been established to be highly effective only with patients in certain specific categories (e.g., females under forty of a specific blood type). This difference in effectiveness—in the absolute or in the probability of success—is (we assume) so marked as to constitute virtually a difference in kind rather than in degree. In this case, it would be perfectly legitimate to adopt the general rule of making the ELT at issue available only or primarily to persons in this substantial-promise-of-success category. (It is on grounds of this sort that young children and persons over fifty are generally ruled out as candidates for haemodialysis.)

We have maintained that the three factors of constituency, progress of science, and prospect of success represent legitimate criteria of inclusion for ELT selection. But it remains to examine the considerations which legitimate them. The legitimating factors are in the final analysis practical or pragmatic in nature. From the practical angle it is advantageous—indeed to some extent necessary—that the arrangements governing medical institutions should embody certain constituency principles. It makes good pragmatic and utilitarian sense that progress-of-science considerations should be operative here. And, finally, the practical aspect is reinforced by a whole host of other considerations—including moral ones—in supporting the prospect-of-success criterion. The workings of each of these factors are of course conditioned by the ever-present element of limited availability. They are operative only in this context, that is, prospect of success is a legitimate consideration at all only because we are dealing with a situation of scarcity.

V. The Final Selection Stage: Criteria of Selection

Five sorts of elements must, as we see it, figure primarily among the plausible criteria of selection that are to be brought to bear in further screening the group constituted after application of the criteria of inclusion: the relative-likelihood-of-success factor, the life-expectancy factor, the family role factor, the potential-contributions factor, and the services-rendered factor. The first two represent the *biomedical* aspect, the second three the *social* aspect.

A. The Relative-Likelihood-of-Success Factor

It is clear that the relative likelihood of success is a legitimate and appropriate factor in making a selection within the group of qualified patients that are to receive ELT. This is obviously one of the considerations that must count very significantly in a reasonable selection procedure.

The present criterion is of course closely related to item *C* of the preceding section. There we were concerned with prospect-of-success considerations categorically and *en bloc*. Here at present they come into play in a particularized case-by-case comparison among individuals. If the therapy at issue is not a once-and-for-all proposition and requires ongoing treatment, cognate considerations must be brought in. Thus, for example, in the case of a chronic ELT procedure such as haemodialysis it would clearly make sense to give priority to patients with a potentially reversible condition (who would thus need treatment for only a fraction of their remaining lives).

B. The Life-Expectancy Factor

Even if the ELT is "successful" in the patient's case he may, considering his age and/or other aspects of his general medical condition, look forward to only a very short probable future life. This is obviously another factor that must be taken into account.

C. The Family Role Factor

A person's life is a thing of importance not only to himself but to others—friends, associates, neighbors, colleagues, etc. But his (or her) relationship to his immediate family is a thing of unique intimacy and significance. The nature of his relationship to his wife, children, and parents, and the issue of their financial and psychological dependence upon him, are obviously matters that deserve to be given weight in the ELT selection process. Other things being anything like equal, the mother of minor children must take priority over the middle-aged bachelor.

D. The Potential Future-Contributions Factor (Prospective Service)

In "choosing to save" one life rather than another, "the society," through the mediation of the particular medical institution in question—which should certainly look upon itself as a trustee for the social interest—is clearly warranted in considering the likely pattern of future *services to be rendered* by the patient (adequate recovery assumed), considering his age, talent, training, and past record of performance. In its allocations of ELT, society "invests" a scarce resource in one person as against another and is thus entitled to look to the probable prospective "return" on its investment.

It may well be that a thoroughly egalitarian society is reluctant to put someone's social contribution into the scale in situations of the sort at issue. One popular article states that "the most difficult standard would be the candidate's value to society," and goes on to quote someone who said: "You can't just pick a brilliant painter over a laborer. The average citizen would be quickly eliminated." [6] But what if it were not a brilliant painter but a brilliant surgeon or medical researcher that was at issue? One wonders if the author of the *obiter dictum* that one "can't just pick" would still feel equally sure of his ground. In any case, the fact that the standard is difficult to apply is certainly no reason for not attempting to apply it. The problem of ELT selection is inevitably burdened with difficult standards.

Some might feel that in assessing a patient's value to society one should ask not only who if permitted to continue living can make the greatest contribution to society in some creative or constructive way, but also who by dying would leave behind the greatest burden on society in assuming the discharge of their residual responsibilities. [7] Certainly the philosophical utilitarian would give equal weight to both these considerations. Just here is where I would part ways with orthodox utilitarianism. For—though this is not the place to do so—I should be prepared to argue that a civilized society has an obligation to promote the furtherance of

---

[6] Lawrence Lader, "Who Has the Right To Live?" *Good Housekeeping* (January 1968), p. 144.

[7] This approach could thus be continued to embrace the previous factor, that of family role, the preceding item (C).

positive achievements in cultural and related areas even if this means the assumption of certain added burdens.[8]

E. The Past Services-Rendered Factor (Retrospective Service)

A person's services to another person or group have always been taken to constitute a valid basis for a claim upon this person or group— of course a moral and not necessarily a legal claim. Society's obligation for the recognition and reward of services rendered—an obligation whose discharge is also very possibly conducive to self-interest in the long run —is thus another factor to be taken into account. This should be viewed as a morally necessary correlative of the previously considered factor of *prospective* service. It would be morally indefensible of society in effect to say: "Never mind about services you rendered yesterday—it is only the services to be rendered tomorrow that will count with us today." We live in very future-oriented times, constantly preoccupied in a distinctly utilitarian way with future satisfactions. And this disinclines us to give much recognition to past services. But parity considerations of the sort just adduced indicate that such recognition should be given *on grounds of equity*. No doubt a justification for giving weight to services rendered can also be attempted along utilitarian lines. ("The reward of past services rendered spurs people on to greater future efforts and is thus socially advantageous in the long-run future.") In saying that past services should be counted "on grounds of equity"—rather than "on grounds of utility"—I take the view that even if this utilitarian defense could somehow be shown to be fallacious, I should still be prepared to maintain the propriety of taking services rendered into account. The position does not rest on a utilitarian basis and so would not collapse with the removal of such a basis.[9]

As we have said, these five factors fall into three groups: the bio-medical factors A and B, the familial factor C, and the social factors D and E. With items A and B the need for a detailed analysis of the medical considerations comes to the fore. The age of the patient, his

---

[8] Moreover a doctrinaire utilitarian would presumably be willing to withdraw a continuing mode of ELT such as haemodialysis from a patient to make room for a more promising candidate who came to view at a later stage and who could not otherwise be accommodated. I should be unwilling to adopt this course, partly on grounds of utility (with a view to the demoralization of insecurity), partly on the non-utilitarian ground that a "moral commitment" has been made and must be honored.

[9] Of course the difficult question remains of the relative weight that should be given to prospective and retrospective service in cases where these factors conflict. There is a good reason to treat them on a par.

medical history, his physical and psychological condition, his specific disease, etc., will all need to be taken into exact account. These biomedical factors represent technical issues: they call for the physicians' expert judgment and the medical statisticians' hard data. And they are ethically uncontroversial factors—their legitimacy and appropriateness are evident from the very nature of the case.

Greater problems arise with the familial and social factors. They involve intangibles that are difficult to judge. How is one to develop subcriteria for weighing the relative social contributions of (say) an architect or a librarian or a mother of young children? And they involve highly problematic issues. (For example, should good moral character be rated a plus and bad a minus in judging services rendered?) And there is something strikingly unpleasant in grappling with issues of this sort for people brought up in times greatly inclined towards maxims of the type "Judge not!" and "Live and let live!" All the same, in the situation that concerns us here such distasteful problems must be faced, since a failure to choose to save some is tantamount to sentencing all. Unpleasant choices are intrinsic to the problem of ELT selection; they are of the very essence of the matter.[10]

But is reference to all these factors indeed inevitable? The justification for taking account of the medical factors is pretty obvious. But why should the social aspect of services rendered and to be rendered be taken into account at all? The answer is that they must be taken into account not from the *medical* but from the *ethical* point of view. Despite disagreement on many fundamental issues, moral philosophers of the present day are pretty well in consensus that the justification of human actions is to be sought largely and primarily—if not exclusively—in the principles of utility and of justice.[11] But utility requires reference of services to be rendered and justice calls for a recognition of services that have been rendered. Moral considerations would thus demand recognition

---

[10] This in the symposium on "Selection of Patients for Haemodialysis," *British Medical Journal* (March 11, 1967), pp. 622–24. F. M. Parsons writes: "But other forms of selecting patients [distinct from first come, first served] are suspect in my view if they imply evaluation of man by man. What criteria could be used? Who could justify a claim that the life of a mayor would be more valuable than that of the humblest citizen of his borough? Whatever we may think as individuals none of us is indispensable." But having just set out this hard-line view he immediately backs away from it: "On the other hand, to assume that there was little to choose between Alexander Fleming and Adolf Hitler . . . would be nonsense, and we should be naive if we were to pretend that we could not be influenced by their achievements and characters if we had to choose between the two of them. Whether we like it or not we cannot escape the fact that this kind of selection for long-term haemodialysis will be required until very large sums of money become available for equipment and services [so that *everyone* who needs treatment can be accommodated]."

[11] The relative fundamentality of these principles is, however, a substantially disputed issue.

of these two factors. (This, of course, still leaves open the question of whether the point of view provides a valid basis of action: Why base one's actions upon moral principles?—or, to put it bluntly—Why be moral? The present paper is, however, hardly the place to grapple with so fundamental an issue, which has been canvassed in the literature of philosophical ethics since Plato.)

VI. More Than Medical Issues Are Involved

An active controversy has of late sprung up in medical circles over the question of whether non-physician laymen should be given a role in ELT selection (in the specific context of chronic haemodialysis). One physician writes: "I think that the assessment of the candidates should be made by a senior doctor on the [dialysis] unit, but I am sure that it would be helpful to him—both in sharing responsibility and in avoiding personal pressure—if a small unnamed group of people [presumably including laymen] officially made the final decision. I visualize the doctor bringing the data to the group, explaining the points in relation to each case, and obtaining their approval of his order of priority.[12]

Essentially this procedure of a selection committee of laymen has for some years been in use in one of the most publicized chronic dialysis units, that of the Swedish Hospital of Seattle, Washington.[13] Many physicians are apparently reluctant to see the choice of allocation of medical therapy pass out of strictly medical hands. Thus in a recent symposium on the "Selection of Patients for Haemodialysis,"[14] Dr. Ralph Shakman writes: "Who is to implement the selection? In my opinion it must ultimately be the responsibility of the consultants in charge of the renal units . . . I can see no reason for delegating this responsibility to lay persons. Surely the latter would be better employed if they could be persuaded to devote their time and energy to raise more and more money for us to spend on our patients."[15] Other contributors to this symposium strike much the same note. Dr. F. M. Parsons writes: "In an attempt to overcome . . . difficulties in selection some have advocated introducing certain specified lay people into the discussions. Is it wise? I doubt whether a committee of this type can adjudicate as satisfactorily as two medical colleagues, particularly as successful therapy involves close co-

---

12 J. D. N. Nabarro, *op. cit.*, p. 622.

13 See Shana Alexander, *op. cit.*

14 *British Medical Journal* (March 11, 1967), pp. 622–24.

15 *Ibid.*, p. 624. Another contributor writes in the same symposium, "The selection of the few [to receive haemodialysis] is proving very difficult—a true 'Doctor's Dilemma'—for almost everybody would agree that this must be a medical decision, preferably reached by consultation among colleagues" (Dr. F. M. Parsons, *ibid.*, p. 623).

operation between doctor and patient." [16] And Dr. M. A. Wilson writes in the same symposium: "The suggestion has been made that lay panels should select individuals for dialysis from among a group who are medically suitable. Though this would relieve the doctor-in-charge of a heavy load of responsibility, it would place the burden on those who have no personal knowledge and have to base their judgments on medical or social reports. I do not believe this would result in better decisions for the group or improve the doctor-patient relationship in individual cases." [17]

But no amount of flag waving about the doctor's facing up to his responsibility—or prostrations before the idol of the doctor-patient relationship and reluctance to admit laymen into the sacred precincts of the conference chambers of medical consultations—can obscure the essential fact that ELT selection is not a wholly medical problem. When there are more than enough places in an ELT program to accommodate all who need it, then it will clearly be a medical question to decide who does have the need and which among these would successfully respond. But when an admitted gross insufficiency of places exists, when there are ten or fifty or one hundred highly eligible candidates for each place in the program, then it is unrealistic to take the view that purely medical criteria can furnish a sufficient basis for selection. The question of ELT selection becomes serious as a phenomenon of scale—because, as more candidates present themselves, strictly medical factors are increasingly less adequate as a selection criterion precisely because by numerical category-crowding there will be more and more cases whose "status is much the same" so far as purely medical considerations go.

The ELT selection problem clearly poses issues that transcend the medical sphere because—in the nature of the case—many residual issues remain to be dealt with once *all* of the medical questions have been faced. Because of this there is good reason why laymen as well as physicians should be involved in the selection process. Once the medical considerations have been brought to bear, fundamental social issues remain to be resolved. The instrumentalities of ELT have been created through the social investment of scarce resources, and the interests of the society deserve to play a role in their utilization. As representatives of their social interests, lay opinions should function to complement and supplement

---

[16] "The Selection of Patients for Haemodialysis," *op. cit.* (n. 10 above), p. 623.

[17] Dr. Wilson's article concludes with the perplexing suggestion—wildly beside the point given the structure of the situation at issue—that "the final decision will be made by the patient." But this contention is only marginally more ludicrous than Parson's contention that in selecting patients for haemodialysis "gainful employment in a well chosen occupation is necessary to achieve the best results" since "only the minority wish to live on charity" (*ibid.*).

medical views once the proper arena of medical considerations is left behind.[18] Those physicians who have urged the presence of lay members on selection panels can, from this point of view, be recognized as having seen the issue in proper perspective.

One physician has argued against lay representation on selection panels for haemodialysis as follows: "If the doctor advises dialysis and the lay panel refuses, the patient will regard this as a death sentence passed by an anonymous court from which he has no right of appeal." [19] But this drawback is not specific to the use of a lay panel. Rather, it is a feature inherent in every selection procedure, regardless of whether the selection is done by the head doctor of the unit, by a panel of physicians, etc. No matter who does the selecting among patients recommended for dialysis, the feelings of the patient who has been rejected (and knows it) can be expected to be much the same, provided that he recognizes the actual nature of the choice (and is not deceived by the possibly convenient but ultimately poisonous fiction that because the selection was made by physicians it was made entirely on medical grounds).

In summary, then, the question of ELT selection would appear to be one that is in its very nature heavily laden with issues of medical research, practice, and administration. But it will not be a question that can be resolved on solely medical grounds. Strictly social issues of justice and utility will invariably arise in this area—questions going outside the medical area in whose resolution medical laymen can and should play a substantial role.

VII. The Inherent Imperfection (Non-optimality) of Any Selection System

Our discussion to this point of the design of a selection system for ELT has left a gap that is a very fundamental and serious omission. We have argued that five factors must be taken into substantial and explicit account:

A. *Relative likelihood of success.*—Is the chance of the treatment's being "successful" to be rated as high, good, average, etc.? [20]

---

[18] To say this is of course not to deny that such questions of applied medical ethics will invariably involve a host of medical considerations—it is only to insist that extramedical considerations will also invariably be at issue.

[19] M. A. Wilson, "Selection of Patients for Haemodialysis," *op. cit.*, p. 624.

[20] In the case of an ongoing treatment involving complex procedure and dietary and other mode-of-life restrictions—and chronic haemodialysis definitely falls into this category—the patient's psychological makeup, his willpower to "stick with it" in the face of substantial discouragements—will obviously also be a substantial factor here. The man who gives up, takes not his life alone, but (figuratively speaking) also that of the person he replaced in the treatment schedule.

B. *Expectancy of future life.*—Assuming the "success" of the treatment, how much longer does the patient stand a good chance (75 per cent or better) of living—considering his age and general condition?

C. *Family role.*—To what extent does the patient have responsibilities to others in his immediate family?

D. *Social contributions rendered.*—Are the patient's past services to his society outstanding, substantial, average, etc.?

E. *Social contributions to be rendered.*—Considering his age, talents, training, and past record of performance, is there a substantial probability that the patient will—*adequate recovery being assumed*—render in the future services to his society that can be characterized as outstanding, substantial, average, etc.?

This list is clearly insufficient for the construction of a reasonable selection system, since that would require not only *that these factors be taken into account* (somehow or other), but—going beyond this—would specify *a specific set of procedures for taking account of them.* The specific procedures that would constitute such a system would have to take account of the interrelationship of these factors (e.g., *B* and *E*), and to set out exact guidelines as to the relevant weight that is to be given to each of them. This is something our discussion has not as yet considered.

In fact, I should want to maintain that there is no such thing here as a single rationally superior selection system. The position of affairs seems to me to be something like this: (1) It is necessary (for reasons already canvassed) to *have* a system, and to have a system that is rationally defensible, and (2) to be rationally defensible, this system must take the factors *A–E* into substantial and explicit account. But (3) the exact manner in which a rationally defensible system takes account of these factors cannot be fixed in any one specific way on the basis of general considerations. Any of the variety of ways that give *A–E* "their due" will be acceptable and viable. One cannot hope to find within this range of workable systems some one that is *optimal* in relation to the alternatives. There is no one system that does "the (uniquely) best"—only a variety of systems that do "as well as one can expect to do" in cases of this sort.

The situation is structurally very much akin to that of rules of partition of an estate among the relations of a decedent. It is important *that there be* such rules. And it is reasonable that spouse, children, parents, siblings, etc., be taken account of in these rules. But the question of the exact method of division—say that when the decedent has neither living spouse nor living children then his estate is to be divided, dividing 60 per cent between parents, 40 per cent between siblings versus dividing 90 per cent between parents, 10 per cent between siblings—cannot be settled on the basis of any general abstract considerations of reasonableness. Within broad limits, a *variety* of resolutions are all perfectly acceptable—so that no one procedure can justifiably be regarded as "the (uniquely) best" because it is superior to all others.[21]

VIII. A Possible Basis for a Reasonable Selection System

Having said that there is no such thing as the *optimal* selection system for ELT, I want now to sketch out the broad features of what I would regard as *one acceptable* system.

The basis for the system would be a point rating. The scoring here at issue would give roughly equal weight to the medical considerations (*A* and *B*) in comparison with the extramedical considerations (*C* = family role, *D* = services rendered, and *E* = services to be rendered), also giving roughly equal weight to the three items involved here (*C*, *D*, and *E*). The result of such a scoring procedure would provide the essential *starting point* of our ELT selection mechanism. I deliberately say "starting point" because it seems to me that one should not follow the results of this scoring in an *automatic* way. I would propose that the actual selection should only be guided but not actually be dictated by this scoring procedure, along lines now to be explained.

IX. The Desirability of Introducing an Element of Chance

The detailed procedure I would propose—not of course as optimal (for reasons we have seen), but as eminently acceptable—would combine the scoring procedure just discussed with an element of chance. The resulting selection system would function as follows:

1. First the criteria of inclusion of Section IV above would be applied to constitute a *first phase selection group*—which (we shall suppose) is substantially larger than the number *n* of persons who can actually be accommodated with ELT.

2. Next the criteria of selection of Section V are brought to bear via a scoring procedure of the type described in Section VIII. On this basis a *second phase selection group* is constituted which is only *somewhat* larger—say by a third or a half—than the critical number *n* at issue.

3. If this second phase selection group is relatively homogeneous as regards rating by the scoring procedure—that is, if there are no really

---

[21] To say that acceptable solutions can range over broad limits is *not* to say that there are no limits at all. It is an obviously intriguing and fundamental problem to raise the question of the factors that set these limits. This complex issue cannot be dealt with adequately here. Suffice it to say that considerations regarding precedent and people's expectations, factors of social utility, and matters of fairness and sense of justice all come into play.

major disparities within this group (as would be likely if the initial group was significantly larger than n)—then the final selection is made by *random* selection of n persons from within this group.

This introduction of the element of chance—in what could be dramatized as a "lottery of life and death"—must be justified. The fact is that such a procedure would bring with it three substantial advantages.

First, as we have argued above (in Section VII), any acceptable selection system is inherently non-optimal. The introduction of the element of chance prevents the results that life-and-death choices are made by the automatic application of an admittedly imperfect selection method.

Second, a recourse to chance would doubtless make matters easier for the rejected patient and those who have a specific interest in him. It would surely be quite hard for them to accept his exclusion by relatively mechanical application of objective criteria in whose implementation subjective judgment is involved. But the circumstances of life have conditioned us to accept the workings of chance and to tolerate the element of luck (good or bad): human life is an inherently contingent process. Nobody, after all, has an absolute right to ELT—but most of us would feel that we have "every bit as much right" to it as anyone else in significantly similar circumstances. The introduction of the element of chance assures a like handling of like cases over the widest possible area that seems reasonable in the circumstances.

Third (and perhaps least), such a recourse to random selection does much to relieve the administrators of the selection system of the awesome burden of ultimate and absolute responsibility.

These three considerations would seem to build up a substantial case for introducing the element of chance into the mechanism of the system for ELT selection in a way limited and circumscribed by other weightier considerations, along some such lines as those set forth above.[22]

It should be recognized that this injection of *man-made* chance supplements the element of *natural* chance that is present inevitably and in any case (apart from the role of chance in singling out certain persons as victims for the affliction at issue). As F. M. Parsons has observed: "any vacancies [in an ELT program—specifically haemodialysis] will be filled

---

[22] One writer has mooted the suggestion that: "Perhaps the right thing to do, difficult as it may be to accept, is to select [for haemodialysis] from among the medical and psychologically qualified patients on a strictly random basis" (S. Gorovitz, "Ethics and the Allocation of Medical Resources," *Medical Research Engineering*, V [1966], p. 7). Outright random selection would, however, seem indefensible because of its refusal to give weight to considerations which, under the circumstances, *deserve* to be given weight. The proposed procedure of superimposing a certain degree of randomness upon the rational-choice criteria would seem to combine the advantages of the two without importing the worst defects of either.

immediately by the first suitable patients, even though their claims for therapy may subsequently prove less than those of other patients refused later." [23] Life is a chancy business and even the most rational of human arrangements can cover this over to a very limited extent at best.[24]

SELECTED SUPPLEMENTARY READING

AIKEN, HENRY D., "Life and the Right to Life," in *Ethical Issues in Human Genetics,* ed. D. Callahan, et al. New York: Plenum Publishing Corporation, 1973.

BAIER, KURT, and NICHOLAS RESCHER, eds. *Values and the Future: The Impact of Technological Change on American Values.* New York: Free Press, 1969.

CAMPBELL, A. V., *Moral Dilemmas in Medicine.* Baltimore: Williams and Wilkins, 1972.

CHILDRESS, JAMES F., "Who Shall Live When Not All Can Live?" *Soundings,* LIII (Winter 1970). Reprinted in Wertz (below).

COHEN, CARL. "Have I a Right to a Voice in Decisions That Affect My Own Life?" *Nous,* V (1971).

DAVIS, BERNARD D., "Prospects for Genetic Intervention in Man," *Science,* 170 (1970–71).

DOBZHANSKY, THEODOSIUS, *Genetic Diversity and Human Equality.* New York: Basic Books, 1973.

————, *Mankind Evolving.* New Haven, Conn.: Yale University Press, 1962.

DOWNING, A. B., ed., *Euthanasia and the Right to Death.* Los Angeles: Nash Publishing Co., 1969.

FLETCHER, JOSEPH, *The Ethics of Genetic Control.* Garden City, N.Y.: Doubleday Anchor, 1974.

————, *Morals and Medicine.* Boston: Beacon Press, 1964.

FRANKEL, CHARLES, "The Specter of Eugenics," *Commentary,* 57 (March 1974).

GAYLIN, WILLARD, "Genetic Screening: The Ethics of Knowing," *New England Journal of Medicine,* 286 (June 1972).

---

[23] "Selection of Patients for Haemodialysis," *op. cit.,* p. 623. The question of whether a patient for chronic treatment should ever be terminated from the program (say if he contracts cancer) poses a variety of difficult ethical problems with which we need not at present concern ourselves. But it does seem plausible to take the (somewhat anti-utilitarian) view that a patient should not be terminated simply because a "better qualified" patient comes along later on. It would seem that a quasi-contractual relationship has been created through established expectations and reciprocal understandings, and that the situation is in this regard akin to that of the man who, having undertaken to sell his house to one buyer, cannot afterward unilaterally undo this arrangement to sell it to a higher bidder who "needs it worse" (thus maximizing the over-all utility).

[24] I acknowledge with thanks the help of Miss Hazel Johnson, Reference Librarian at the University of Pittsburgh Library, in connection with the works cited.

GOLDING, MARTIN P., "Obligations to Future Generations," *The Monist*, 56 (1972).

GOODFIELD, JUNE, "Reflections on the Hippocratic Oaths," *Hastings Center Studies*, 1 (1973).

GOROVITZ, SAMUEL, "Teaching Medical Ethics: A Report on One Approach," Monograph. Cleveland: Case-Western Reserve Press, 1973.

GUSTAFSON, JAMES, "Basic Ethical Issues in the Bio-medical Fields, *Soundings*, 53 (1970).

JONAS, HANS, *Philosophical Essays: From Ancient Creed to Technological Man*. Englewood Cliffs, N.J.: Prentice-Hall, Inc., 1974.

KAMISAR, YALE, "Euthanasia Legislation: Some Non-religious Objections," in *Euthanasia and the Right to Death*, ed. A. B. Downing. Los Angeles: Nash Publishing Co., 1969.

KASS, LEON R., "Babies by Means of In Vitro Fertilization: Unethical Experiments on the Unborn?" *New England Journal of Medicine*, 285 (November 1971).

———, "Making Babies: The New Biology and the Old Morality," *Public Interest*, 26 (1972).

KOHL, M., "The Sanctity-of-Life Principle: A Philosophic Background for the Consideration of Euthanasia," in *Humanistic Perspectives in Medical Ethics*, ed. M. B. Visscher. Buffalo: Prometheus Books, 1972.

KOHL, M., *The Morality of Killing*. New York: Humanities Press (1974).

LONDON, PERRY, *Behavior Control*. New York: Harper and Row, 1971.

NAGEL, THOMAS, "Death," *Nous*, IV (1970).

NARVESON, JAN, "Utilitarianism and New Generations," *Mind*, 76 (1967).

NOZICK, ROBERT, "Distributive Justice," *Philosophy and Public Affairs*, 3 (1973).

RAMSEY, PAUL, *Fabricated Man: The Ethics of Genetic Control*. New Haven, Conn.: Yale University Press, 1970.

———, *The Patient as Person*. New Haven, Conn.: Yale University Press, 1970.

"Symposium: Reflections on the New Biology," *UCLA Law Review* 15 (February 1968).

SZASZ, THOMAS, "The Right to Health," *Georgetown Law Journal*, 57 (1969).

TORREY, E. FULLER, ed., *Ethical Issues in Medicine*. Boston: Little, Brown, & Co., 1968.

VAN EVRA, JAMES, "On Death as a Limit," *Analysis*, 31 (1971).

WERTZ, R. W., ed., *Readings on Ethical and Social Issues in Biomedicine*. Englewood Cliffs, N.J.: Prentice-Hall, Inc., 1973.

WILLIAMS, GLANVILLE, "Euthanasia Legislation: A Rejoinder to Non-religious Objections," in *Euthanasia and the Right to Live*, ed. A. B. Downing. Los Angeles: Nash Publishing Co., 1969.

———, *The Sanctity of Life and the Criminal Law*. New York: Alfred A. Knopf, 1957.